## Helpful Lists and Charts

# The Rinehart Handbook for Writers

## ABOUT THE TITLE OF THIS BOOK

**Stanley M. Rinehart, Jr.** (1897–1969), was a distinguished book publisher. In 1929, he, his brother Frederick, and editor John Farrar founded the publishing house of Farrar & Rinehart, which later became (in 1946) Rinehart & Company, and then (in 1960) Holt, Rinehart and Winston. As president of Rinehart & Company, Stanley Rinehart published such works as Norman Mailer's *The Naked and the Dead,* the "Nero Wolfe" detective novels of Rex Stout, and Rinehart Editions, a series of quality paperback editions of classic literature. The firm began its college department in 1934 and soon became a major publisher in the field, specializing in the humanities and social sciences. Today, Harcourt Brace Jovanovich College Publishers carries on this same tradition of publishing excellence through such noteworthy volumes as *The Rinehart Handbook for Writers, The Rinehart Guide to Grammar and Usage,* and *The Rinehart Reader.*

# The Rinehart Handbook for Writers

Third Edition

Bonnie Carter
Craig Skates
University of Southern Mississippi

**Harcourt Brace College Publishers**
Fort Worth Philadelphia San Diego
New York Orlando Austin San Antonio
Toronto Montreal London Sydney Tokyo

*Editor-in-Chief* Ted Buchholz
*Acquisitions Editor* Michael Rosenberg
*Developmental Editors* Christine Caperton, Fritz Schanz
*Senior Project Editor* Cliff Crouch
*Production Manager* Mandy Van Dusen
*Book Designer* Diana Jean Parks

Book design adapted from original text design by Caliber Design Planning and cover design by Albert D'Agostino.

**Library of Congress Catalog Card Number:** 92-52935
**ISBN:** 0-15-500269-4



*Address editorial correspondence to:* 301 Commerce Street, Suite 3700
Fort Worth, Texas 76102
*Address orders to:* 6277 Sea Harbor Drive
Orlando, Florida 32887
1-800-782-4479, or 1-800-433-0001 (in Florida)

Printed in the United States of America
3 4 5 6 7 8 9 0 1 2 039 9 8 7 6 5 4 3

# Preface: To the Instructor

Each composition class is unique. The abilities and attitudes of students vary from class to class, and the teaching styles of instructors change as their experience, priorities, and students change. Because of this special environment, *The Rinehart Handbook for Writers,* Third Edition, is comprehensive and flexible. It suits a variety of teaching methods and a broad spectrum of course content. For a given class, you can choose either a single strategy or a combination of strategies from the following options.

## Language Study

Instructors who wish to focus on language can begin with Part I ("Review of the Basics"), which describes the traditional system of word classes, and can then move to Parts II ("Structural and Grammatical Problems") and III ("Punctuation and Mechanics"), which emphasize clarity and correctness. Part IV ("Style") concentrates on techniques for manipulating material and appealing to audiences through word choice and sentence structure. Language is also the focus of Section 39e ("Evaluation of Evidence"), which treats such subjective topics as emotional appeals and diversions, imprecision, equivocation, and logical fallacies. Appendices A and B contain information on spelling, dictionary use, and vocabulary development, as well as history of the language and etymology. The Glossary of Usage demonstrates that preferred usage depends sometimes on clarity and logic and other times on fashion and the choices made by influential writers.

## Traditional Composition

Instructors who prefer to teach a traditional course in composition will find that Part V ("The Writing Process") explains how to develop a paper—from choosing a subject through revising the final draft. "Argument and Critical Thinking" (Chapter 39), new to this edition, leads students through the stages of an argumentative paper—developing the subject and the conflict, framing a thesis, gathering evidence, examining logic, and choosing a structure. This chapter also emphasizes the critical thinking required in any writing project.

## Research Paper Writing

Instructors who wish to teach the research paper will find a complete guide in Chapters 40 and 41. In fact, there is ample material for an entire course on research writing. "Research Paper in Progress" and "Research Papers and Documentation" make up a comprehensive and practical manual for researching, writing, incorporating sources, documenting, and typing. These chapters explain three styles of documentation (MLA, APA, and the number system from *Science*) and include three student models (one on Mark Twain's desertion from the military, one on discrimination in Japanese business, and one on scientific research into the sense of taste). In addition, Chapter 39 ("Argument and Critical Thinking"), Chapter 43 ("Critical Reviews"), and the material on investigation papers in Chapter 45 ("Reports") stress gathering and evaluating evidence.

## Writing across the Curriculum

This handbook provides many, varied writing projects appropriate for students taking courses in the liberal arts, science, business, and many other disciplines. In Part V ("The Writing Process"), sample subjects and paragraphs illustrate prose from disciplines such as archaeology, sociology, film, history, sports, language, biology, zoology, law, literature, ecology, aviation, chemistry, computer science, recreation, and technology. This mix, which extends throughout the handbook, stresses the importance of writing outside the composition classroom. Also, model papers in various chapters include material from many disciplines—for example, community-supported agriculture, mandatory public service, prelaw education, waste management, animal behavior, premedical education, real estate, computer laboratories, water purity, weight-loss clinics, campsites, entrance examinations, and employment.

## Technical Writing

Increasingly, instructors are teaching technical writing skills in both freshman and upper-level courses. This handbook provides wide experience in the kinds of papers frequently written in science, technology, and business. Many examples and models throughout the book have technical subjects—for example, engineering, science, ecology, computer technology, and business. In addition, one of the student research papers is a literature review of taste research, and one of the styles of documentation is based on that used in *Science,* the publication of the American Association for the Advancement of Science. Chapter 46 ("Reports") is especially relevant, covering progress reports, proposals, investigation reports, and instructions, and emphasizing their purposes, components, and formats.

## Word Processing

Material on word processing appears throughout the text wherever it is pertinent to the tasks that students are undertaking. The "Introduction: To the Student" includes advice on getting started and on choosing software. Highlighted boxes labelled *The Computer Connection,* which appear frequently throughout Part V ("The Writing Process"), help students use computers to find a subject, organize the paper, draft the paragraphs, revise, and edit the final work. These *Computer Connection* boxes also provide detailed information explaining how to use computerized spell checkers, thesauruses, library references, and indexes. In addition, an entry on computer terms (comprising over a score of subentry terms) appears in the Glossary of Terms and contains a handy reference list for students just beginning to use a word processor.

Whatever your focus, students will benefit from developing their skills and transforming their prose into a satisfactory product. They will, we hope, learn to view this handbook as a reference tool for use inside and outside the composition classroom.

## The Teaching and Learning Package

### For the Instructor

*Resources Manual.* This ancillary provides instructors with new, alternative, and additional suggestions for using the *Handbook* to its full potential. Included are sample syllabi; explanations of teaching strategies; further assignments and examples; ideas for integrating critical thinking, collaborative projects, and computer instruction into the curriculum; and advice for meeting the needs of an ESL or cross-curricular environment. This manual is especially helpful for teaching assistants.

*Printed Diagnostic Tests.* The package offers pre- and post-tests in both essay and objective forms. It also includes models for the specific state tests given in Florida, Tennessee, and Texas. With charts that match questions and sections in the *Handbook,* these tests will help instructors target the troublesome areas unique to their classes.

*Overhead Transparencies.* Drawing from key concepts, outlines, charts, and instructions, these 80 transparencies highlight important topics in the *Handbook* for instructors to emphasize in lecture.

### For the Student

*Manual for Collaborative Learning.* This manual discusses collaborative learning techniques and provides sample essays with revision examples to guide collaborative activity.

*The HBJ Composition Workbook* provides additional exercises for students to practice and perfect grammar, writing, and research skills covered in the *Handbook.* An alternate table of contents cross-references the workbook with appropriate sections of the *Handbook.*

*Writing in the Disciplines.* With comprehensive coverage of the MLA, APA, and CBE documentation styles, this guide helps students write research papers in the humanities, social sciences, sciences, and business. Several sample papers these disciplines are also included.

*Supplementary Exercises.* These exercises, cross-referenced to corresponding chapters in the *Handbook,* give students additional grammar and writing practice.

## Software

### For the Instructor

*ExaMaster.* A computerized test bank available for the IBM and Mac, *ExaMaster* includes 800 questions for skill testing, diagnostic evaluation, and for practice of the Florida, Texas, and Tennessee state tests. These questions will include chapter references to the *Handbook,* allowing instructors to direct students to particular sections for clarification and further study. Questions appear in six different formats: fill-in, multiple choice, true/false, matching, essay, and short answer. Instructors can utilize this versatility by choosing questions by type, by chapter, or at random; they can even write their own. *ExaMaster* is available with a Scantron interface.

*Scantron Interface.* This new program interfaces *ExaMaster* and Scantron tests. It collects and analyzes the objective right/wrong answers provided by the Scantron tests then presents them in a variety of ways: tabular and statistical reports for individual and class performance, number and percent of incorrect/correct answers, *Handbook* reference, frequency of items missed, etc.

*Exam Record.* This gradebook program calculates grades, converts letter grades to numeric, prints grades for posting, and determines distributions and curves. It complements *ExaMaster,* both IBM and Mac versions, but can be used in any testing situation.

### For the Student

*Writing Tutor III.* This individualized software tutorial program provides additional instruction and practice on topics that range from commas to paragraph development. The program offers a variety of exercise formats (highlighting, completion, sentence and paragraph writing) and encourages students to make several attempts at incorrect questions. Also, the program maintains students' scores and prints sentence and paragraph work. It is available for the IBM, Apple, and Mac.

*Rinehart On-Line.* As an on-line handbook, *Rinehart On-Line* works with any word processing program to give students ready access to handbook references while composing. It is a must-have ancillary for any English department that includes a computer writing lab equipped with either IBM or Mac PCs.

*PC Type II.* This word processing program for the IBM features document formatting, a spell-check function, mail-merge, and on-line help screens.

*Research Helper.* Composed of two programs, the *Research Helper* assists students in organizing and documenting a formal research paper. NOTEFILER stores and sorts information, organizing it by either its source or a keyword. These "notecards" can be rearranged when planning a paper. DOCUMENTER formats bibliographic information in MLA or APA styles when students enter publication information into appropriate fields. *Research Helper* is available for IBM, Mac, and Apple systems.

For complimentary copies of these teaching and learning aids, please contact your local sales representative, or write to: English Acquisitions Editor, Harcourt Brace Jovanovich College Publishers, 301 Commerce, Suite 3700, Fort Worth, Texas 76102.

## Acknowledgments

We thank the following colleagues for the comments and advice on previous editions: Steve Adams, Northeast Louisiana University; Joy Allameh, Eastern Kentucky University; Kristine Anderson, Southern Technical Institute; Bruce Appleby, Southern Illinois University; Tracey Baker, University of Alabama—Birmingham; Conrad Bayley, Glendale Community College; Jane Bouterse, Texarkana College;

Henry Brown, Midwestern State University; Alma Bryant, Fort Valley State College; Rebecca Butler, Dalton College; James Bynum, Georgia Tech; Joe Christopher, Tarleton State University; Peggy Cole, Arapahoe Community College; Deborah Core, Eastern Kentucky University; James Creel, Alvin Community College; Joseph Davis, Memphis State University; Ralph Dille, University of Southern Colorado; Charles Dodson, University of North Carolina; Linda Doran, Volunteer State Community College; Joseph Dunne, St. Louis Community College at Meremac; Elizabeth Fifer, Lehigh College; Eleanor Garner, George Washington University; Jan Goodrich, Embry-Riddle Aeronautical University; George Haich, University of North Carolina—Wilmington; Charles Hall, Memphis State University; June Hankins, Southwest Texas State University; Stephen Hathway, Wichita State University; David Higgins, Cameron University; Gertrude Hopkins, Harford Community College; Peggy Jolly, University of Alabama—Birmingham; Edwina Jordan, Illinois Central College; Edward Kline, University of Notre Dame; Cheryl Koski, Louisiana State University; Ruth Laux, Arkansas Technical University; Jane E. Lewis, University of Southern Mississippi; Russell Long, Tarleton State University; Andrea Lunsford, University of British Columbia; Robert Lynch, New Jersey Institute of Technology; Lisa McClure, Southern Illinois University—Carbondale; Beverly McKay, Lenoir Community College; Louis Molina, Miami-Dade Community College South; Sam Phillips, Gaston College; Kenneth Rainey, Memphis State University; Sally Reagan, University of Missouri—St. Louis; Edward Reilly, St. Joseph's College; John Reuter, Florida Southern College; Michael Rossi, Merimack College; Cheryl Ruggiero, Virginia Polytechnic Institute and State University; Gary Simmers, Dalton College; Mike Slaughter, Illinois Central College; Joyce Smoot, Virginia Polytechnic Institute and State University; Charles Sphar, Delmar College; Jo Tarvers, University of North Carolina—Chapel Hill; John Taylor, South Dakota State University; Elizabeth Thomas, University of New Orleans—Lake Front; George Trail, University of Houston; Daryl Troyer, El Paso Community College; Gloria Tubb, Jones County Junior College; Richard Vandeweghe, University of Colorado at Denver; Harold Veeser, Wichita State University; Art Wagner, Macomb Community College; Laura Weaver, University of Evansville; Betty Wells, Central Virginia Community College; Jack White, Mississippi State University; Marie Wolf, Bergen Community College; and Peter Zoller, Wichita State University.

We thank the following colleagues for their comments and advice on the third edition: Carolyn Drakeford, Benedict College; Chick White, West Texas State University; Noel Mawer, Edward Waters College; Patricia Phillips, Detroit College of Business; Donald Anderson, Marist College; David Rosenwasser, Muhlenberg College; Virginia Polanski, Stonehill College; Richard Kleinman, Cumberland College; Charlotte Perlin, University of Miami; Chris Baker, Lamar University; and Albert Wilhelm, Tennessee Technical University.

We thank the staff at Harcourt Brace Jovanovich who made *The Rinehart Handbook for Writers* possible. In particular, we are indebted to DeVilla Williams, who introduced us to the company and got the original project started; to Michael Rosenberg, our acquisitions editor; to Christine Caperton and Fritz Schanz, our developmental editors, who made sure we responded to our audience and our reviews; to Mandy Van Dusen and Diana Jean Parks, who contributed much to this edition's production and design; and to Clifford Crouch, who patiently transformed the previous edition into this new work. Our greatest debt is to Charlyce Jones Owen, who not only gave us the chance to write this book but also, as its original publisher, guided and encouraged us through every step. Finally, we thank our former professor, Marice C. Brown, who taught us that grammar is worthy of study. To all, in Shakespeare's words, "thanks, and thanks, and ever thanks."

*B.C.*
*C.S.*

# Introduction: To the Student

A handbook should be handy. In other words, you should have no difficulty finding in it the material you need. If you are using *The Rinehart Handbook for Writers,* Third Edition, in a composition class, your instructor can help you learn how to locate information. Remember, however, that you will not always have an instructor to guide you. Therefore, you should become familiar with the organization so that you can find information quickly and easily.

Look carefully at the table of contents to determine what material is available and where it appears. Learn to use the index and glossaries. Make sure you understand the correction symbols and the numbering system of the book. Pay close attention to cross-references; they direct you to related sections of the text. Also, if you use a word processor for writing, consult the highlighted boxes labelled *The Computer Connection.* These boxes appear throughout the text to offer advice for using a word processor creatively and efficiently.

*The Rinehart Handbook for Writers* contains all the information you need for writing in the classroom and most of what you need for writing in a professional setting. If you use the book effectively, you may be surprised at how much your writing skills improve—and with them your confidence in yourself and your future.

## The Computer Connection

Throughout this handbook, you will find highlighted boxes that are labelled *The Computer Connection.* Each box contains advice on how to use word processing for specific writing tasks; each relates directly to the material immediately preceding the box. In addition, words and phrases common to word processing appear in the Glossary of Terms.

If you have decided to write with a computer for the first time, investigate the process and a few programs before you spend any money. Once you understand the fundamentals, you can more easily choose software appropriate for your needs. You do not want to pay for capabilities that you will never use or that will frustrate you. Look for a program that relieves the physical labor of writing without increasing the mental labor.

## Suggestions for Choosing Software

- Visit the writing laboratory on your campus. Most writing labs use software that can be mastered very quickly; and because the staff is accustomed to novices, you need not be embarrassed to ask for help.
- Get help from a friend who uses a word processing program. In less than an hour, he or she can teach you the fundamentals, such as how to start up the program; type in a passage; add, rearrange, and delete text; save the work; and print it.
- Visit computer stores, and ask for demonstrations of programs. Beware, however, of salespeople who can make an expensive and complicated program seem like a bargain and a breeze. Insist on trying out programs yourself.
- Do not pay for special features like graphics and footnoting unless you plan to use them. Few papers require graphics, and few disciplines currently use footnotes.
- Consider a program with instructions primarily on-screen, so that you do not have to rely heavily on a printed manual.
- Ask whether a program saves text automatically. This feature lessens the possibility that you will lose text produced after considerable time and effort.
- Be wary of grammar checkers and style checkers. The quality of these features varies widely, and only an experienced writer can judge their effectiveness. They may lead you astray more often than they help.
- If you are not yet comfortable with word processing, choose a simple and inexpensive program. You can always upgrade as you become more expert.

# Contents

# PART I

# A Review of the Basics

The grammar of a language is a system of predictable patterns: words fit together to form phrases; phrases join to form clauses; clauses create sentences. If you can recognize the system's components, you can understand descriptions of acceptable or effective constructions, and you can look up information in an index or glossary. In short, recognition underlies improvement of your writing skills.

# 1

# Nouns

**Nouns** are commonly defined as "words that name persons, places, or things." Although this definition is rather limited, it does contain a key word—*name.* Anything in the physical and mental worlds can be named with a noun.

| | |
|---|---|
| PEOPLE: | Susan, doctor, singer, family |
| PLACES: | ocean, Canada, home, campus |
| THINGS: | popsicle, shoe, fingernail, crater |
| QUANTITIES: | pound, quart, inch, dollar |
| SENSES: | sound, smell, taste, feel |
| FEELINGS: | hope, disappointment, anxiety, peace |
| OCCURRENCES: | earthquake, wedding, party, contest |
| ACTIONS: | handshake, smile, leap, wink |

You can usually recognize a noun by its function, that is, the position it fills in a phrase or a sentence.

- Nouns follow the articles *a, an,* and *the.*

  a field　　the light
  an apple　　the car

- Nouns appear in phrases after descriptive words called modifiers.

  a muddy field　　the bright light
  a red apple　　the new car

- Nouns join with prepositions to form prepositional phrases.

  through a field    behind the light
  in an apple    under the car

- Nouns join with other nouns to form compounds and phrases.

  field house    light bulb
  apple pie    car wreck

- Nouns join with verbs to form sentences.

  A field lay between the house and the lake.
  Pat gave the teacher an apple.
  The light was brilliant.
  My most pressing problem was my car.

## 1a Proper and Common Nouns

**Proper nouns** are official names, such as names of people, organizations, geographical locations, holidays, languages, and historical events. You can easily recognize proper nouns in prose because they begin with capital letters. **Common nouns,** all other nouns, are usually not capitalized unless they appear as the first word in a sentence. (See 31a, 31b, 31h.)

| Proper Nouns | Common Nouns |
|---|---|
| Muhammad Ali | athlete |
| United Kingdom | country |
| Saks | store |
| Okefenokee | swamp |
| English | language |

### ❑ EXERCISE 1

For each common noun listed, give a corresponding proper noun.

Example: building Pentagon

1. political party
2. religion
3. family member
4. governmental body
5. historical figure
6. holiday
7. city
8. river
9. club
10. war

## 1b Singular and Plural Nouns

Nouns have **number**—that is, they are either **singular** or **plural.** Singular nouns refer to one person, place, or thing; plural nouns to more than one. Disregarding number can lead to errors in agreement of subject and verb. (See Chapter 10.)

### (1) Simple nouns

Most nouns form plurals with the addition of *-s* or *-es*, sometimes with a slight adjustment in spelling, such as changing *y* to *i* or doubling a consonant.

| SINGULAR | PLURAL |
|---|---|
| week | weeks |
| box | boxes |
| quiz | quizzes |
| destiny | destinies |
| hero | heroes |

Some nouns form plurals in unpredictable ways.

| SINGULAR | PLURAL |
|---|---|
| leaf | leaves |
| foot | feet |
| mouse | mice |
| child | children |
| salmon | salmon |
| criterion | criteria |

### (2) Compound nouns

A compound noun is made up of two or more words functioning as a single noun. The forms of compounds are somewhat unpredictable. In some, the words are separated (*half dollar*); in others, hyphenated (*man-of-war*); and in others, written together (*holdup*). Furthermore, plurals of compounds are formed in different ways. Sometimes, the first word is plural (*sisters-in-law*); sometimes, the last word (*pocket knives*); and sometimes, either the first or last word (*attorney generals* or *attorneys general*). When you are not sure of the correct singular or plural form of a compound, consult a dictionary.

### ❑ EXERCISE 2

Find the nouns, both common and proper, in the following sentences. Identify each as singular or plural.

1. The traditional gift for a sixtieth wedding anniversary is a diamond.
2. The Mohave Desert has unusual varieties of cacti.
3. Vitamin D, important for bone development, is derived from sunlight.
4. Bristlecone pines, which grow in the White Mountains of California, are thought to be the oldest trees in the world.
5. The ecology of the lake has been upset.
6. Reindeer are capable of running thirty miles an hour.

### ❑ EXERCISE 3

Give the plural form (or forms) for each singular noun listed. If you have any doubt about a correct form, you should consult a dictionary.

1. shrimp
2. passerby
3. wolf
4. day
5. candy
6. bypass
7. crisis
8. index
9. antenna
10. box
11. ox
12. poet laureate

## 1c Possessive Nouns

Nouns have **possessive forms,** which indicate a variety of meanings, such as

Ownership: my sister's house (house belonging to my sister)
Authorship: Ibsen's plays (plays by Ibsen)
Source: the mayor's permission (permission from the mayor)
Measurement: a year's leave (leave of a year)
Description: men's dormitory (dormitory for men)

You can recognize possessive nouns in prose because they contain apostrophes. Some possessive nouns are formed by the addition of an apostrophe and an *s*; others, by just an apostrophe after a final *s*: *institution's, James's, doctors', Raiders'*.

For a more detailed discussion of the formation and use of possessive nouns, see 26a.

## ❑ EXERCISE 4

Form a possessive from each of the following phrases.

1. the constitution of Texas
2. the wishes of the alumni
3. absence of five months
4. food for the three cats
5. the plot of the novel

# 2

# Pronouns

The word **pronoun** means literally "for a noun," and pronouns do, in fact, occur in most of the same positions as nouns and noun phrases.

| | |
|---|---|
| NOUN: | Students can have identification cards made at the sports arena. |
| PRONOUN: | You can have identification cards made at the sports arena. |
| NOUN PHRASE: | I left your coat with the attendant at the door. |
| PRONOUN: | I left your coat with someone at the door. |
| NOUN PHRASE: | The collie ate the whole turkey. |
| PRONOUN: | The collie ate what? |

Often, pronouns substitute for previously stated nouns or noun phrases, called **antecedents.**

Voters did not turn out today. They were deterred by the weather.

The curry was so hot that few people could eat it.

A taxpayer whose returns are audited should hire an accountant.

Although they make up a relatively small class of words, pronouns are in constant use. Notice that of the two passages that follow, the one without pronouns sounds unnatural.

WITHOUT PRONOUNS

Emily Dickinson is regarded as a great American poet. Even though Emily Dickinson lived in seclusion, Dickinson's poems have universal significance: Dickinson's poems concern the relationship between the inner self and the outer world. Dickinson regarded the relationship between the inner self and the outer world as tragic. Dickinson examined the relationship between the inner self and the outer world with irony and wit.

WITH PRONOUNS

Emily Dickinson is regarded as a great American poet. Even though she lived in seclusion, her poems have universal significance: they concern the relationship between the inner self and the outer world. She examined this relationship, which she regarded as tragic, with irony and wit.

## 2a Personal Pronouns

The seven **personal pronouns** have different forms for different functions.

I, me, my, mine

you, your, yours

he, him, his

she, her, hers

it, its

we, us, our, ours

they, them, their, theirs

These personal pronouns are classified by person, number, gender, and case.

- *First person singular (I)* refers to the speaker; *first person plural* (*we*), to the speaker and another person or group. *Second person* (*you*) refers to the person(s) spoken to, and *third person* (*he, she, it,* and *they*), to the person(s) or thing(s) spoken about.
- *Number* refers to whether the pronoun is singular (*I*) or plural (*we*).
- *Gender* is the sex represented by third-person singular pronouns: masculine (*he*), feminine (*she*), neuter (*it*).
- *Case* involves the various forms a pronoun takes according to

its use in a sentence. For example, *they* is a subject form (*they* are my friends). *Them* is an object form (don't call *them*). *Their* is a possessive form (*their* house is on Main Street). Case forms and their uses are discussed in Chapter 14.

### The *-self/-selves* personal pronouns

In addition to case forms, personal pronouns also have compound forms, made by adding the suffixes (endings) *-self* or *-selves: myself, yourself, himself* (not *hisself*), *herself, itself, ourselves, yourselves, themselves* (not *theirselves*). These forms are used in two ways.

- *As reflexives, the* -self/-selves pronouns function as objects that rename the subjects of sentences: We enjoyed *ourselves.*
- *As emphatics, the* -self/-selves pronouns repeat, for emphasis, the words and phrases they refer to: She races the boat *herself.*

### ❑ EXERCISE 1

**Identify the personal pronouns in the following passage.**

Guy Fawkes felt that his Catholic countrymen were being oppressed in seventeenth-century England. He said, "We are being treated as though we were dogs—verminous dogs." A group of Catholics wanted to act on Fawkes's recommendation: "Let us strike at the source where they make the laws." The conspirators decided to blow up the House of Lords by digging a tunnel and filling it with gunpowder. Before the fuse could be lit, the plot was discovered, and Fawkes himself was seized and executed. Strangely enough, he has been immortalized in a Mother Goose rhyme:

Please to remember
The fifth of November,
    Gunpowder treason and plot.
I see no reason
Why gunpowder treason
    Should ever be forgot.

## 2b Demonstrative Pronouns

The only **demonstrative pronouns** are *this* and *that*, along with their corresponding plurals, *these* and *those.* A demonstrative can be used alone to point out that something is relatively near to or far from the speaker.

This certainly has been a better year than that. [*This* year is the present year; *that* is past.]

I prefer these to those. [*These* are closer to the speaker than *those*.]

A demonstrative pronoun usually precedes a noun and functions like the determiner *the* to indicate that something has been previously mentioned.

Dieters should avoid beef, pork, and lamb when dining out, since these meats are high in both calories and fat. [*These meats* refers to beef, pork, and lamb.]

In the last game of the season, the coach threw a chair at the referee; that tantrum cost him his job. [*That tantrum* refers to the coach's behavior.]

## ❑ EXERCISE 2

**Identify the demonstrative pronouns in the following passage.**

**In 1938, the citizens of Grovers Mill, New Jersey, thought they were being invaded by Martians. This was the year of the radio broadcast of "The War of the Worlds." Those who heard the program panicked. They ran into the streets and tied up traffic. Those who have never heard the show cannot imagine the impact of the dramatization with its realistic "news flashes." That dramatization brought to life the Martians with "saliva dripping from . . . rimless lips" invading Grovers Mill. Details like these even caused one farmer to shoot at the water tower, mistaking it for the aliens' spacecraft.**

# 2c Relative Pronouns

The **relative pronouns** are as follows.

who,* whom* (referring to people)

which, what (referring to things)

that, whose* (referring to either people or things)

Since their function is to introduce adjective clauses (7c.2) and noun clauses (7c.3), you can use relative pronouns to combine sentences and eliminate choppy prose.

*These forms represent different cases: subjective *(who)*, objective *(whom)*, and possessive *(whose)*. See Chapter 14.

CHOPPY: I voted for the candidate. He promised the least.

IMPROVED: I voted for the candidate who promised the least.

CHOPPY: Julian arrived in a limousine. He had rented it at great expense.

IMPROVED: Julian arrived in a limousine, which he had rented at great expense.

CHOPPY: Only one creature recognized Ulysses. It was his dog.

IMPROVED: The only creature that recognized Ulysses was his dog.

The relatives *who, which,* and *what* sometimes appear with the suffix *-ever* in noun clauses.

Whoever raises the most money wins the trip.

Discuss first whichever question seems easiest to you.

He said whatever came to his mind.

## ❑ EXERCISE 3

Identify the relative pronouns in the following passage.

An enjoyable hobby that does not involve any talent or expense is collecting what I call "sign bloopers." The term refers to any sign that is misleading or unintentionally humorous. For example, here are two from my own collection:

Sign on door of high school: "Please use other door. This door is broke."

Sign in lounge: "We reserve the right to refuse service to everyone."

Anyone who has a notebook and pencil can start a collection. Furthermore, anyone whose mind is alert to the written word can accumulate quite a few prized items in a short while. Most bloopers appear in hand-lettered signs, which are common in family-owned businesses and places where employees want to give temporary instructions. Two more bloopers that I have collected can illustrate.

Sign in diner: "No chicks please."

Sign in tax collector's office: "Motor vehicles use other line."

# 2d Interrogative Pronouns

The **interrogative pronouns** (*who, whom, whose, which,* and *what*) introduce questions that ask for information, rather than a yes or no answer. (For the distinction between *who* and *whom*, see 14c.)

Who painted the ceiling of the Sistine Chapel?

Whose idea was it to tell stories on the way to Canterbury?

Which house was Liberace's?

What did Arthur call his sword?

## 2e Indefinite Pronouns

Most **indefinite pronouns** need not refer to specific people or things and can be completely general, such as those in the following two sentences.

Anyone can raise tropical fish.

To an adolescent, everything seems a crisis.

However, indefinites can also refer to something definite—a noun or noun phrase already named or about to be named.

Numerous needleleaf trees grow in the Southeast, but few are as graceful as the loblolly pine.

Many of the North American totems depict birds and fish.

Many indefinite pronouns can serve as determiners, modifying nouns. (See 6c.)

Neither apartment had enough closet space.

We expected some support from the local media.

**Indefinite Pronouns**

| | | |
|---|---|---|
| all | everyone | no one |
| another | everything | nothing |
| any | few | one |
| anybody | many | other |
| anyone | more | others |
| anything | most | several |
| both | much | some |
| each | neither | somebody |
| either | nobody | someone |
| everybody | none | something |

Two indefinites, called **reciprocal pronouns,** require antecedents. *Each other* refers to two persons or things; *one another,* to more than two.

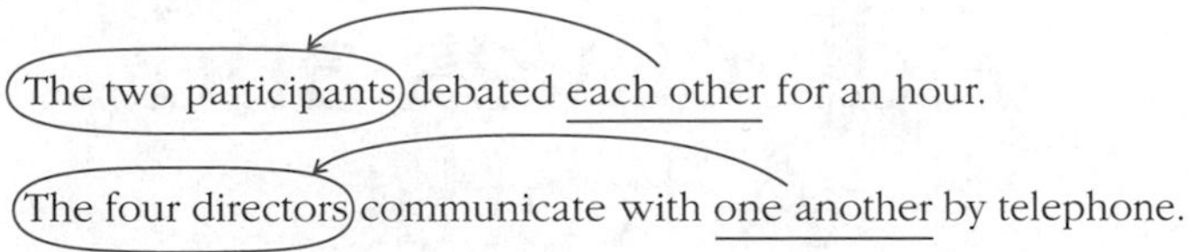

The two participants debated each other for an hour.
The four directors communicate with one another by telephone.


## ☐ EXERCISE 4

**Identify the indefinite and interrogative pronouns in the following passage.**

Horse-racing records aren't often broken; in fact, few have been broken in fifteen years. Who knows why? Some think that the trainers want to win races, not break records. Others think that the best horses now go into breeding before they reach their full speed. Still others believe that horses cannot run faster than they run now. What is the reason? In the opinion of many, the training methods are outdated. Until someone comes up with effective new methods, everything around the racetrack will probably stay the same.

## ☐ EXERCISE 5

**Locate the pronouns in the following passage and identify their types.**

Who gives us the best advice about nutrition? The advice we get is often contradictory and leaves us thoroughly confused. For example, some advisors condone vitamin supplements; others advise against them. According to some authorities, meat is nutritionally indispensable. However, many studies suggest that it contributes to coronary problems and cancer. Nutritional controversies also rage over salt, sugar, fiber, and fat. These substances are usually recommended for our diets, but in different quantities—sometimes liberal, sometimes limited. When the authorities don't agree, what are we to do? We can only await new studies that may provide answers.

# 3

# Adjectives and Adverbs

**Adjectives** and **adverbs** are modifiers—that is, they describe, limit, or qualify some other word or words. Sometimes modifiers are not part of the basic sentence structure; they flesh out the skeletal structure but do not change it. For example, if the underlined modifiers were deleted, the structure of the following sentence would be unaltered.

> Suddenly I came over a steep rise and saw a panoramic sweep of brilliantly blue water and alabaster sand.

Other times modifiers are not merely descriptive additions but part of the basic sentence structure. For example, if the underlined words in the following sentences were deleted, the structures would be unfinished.

> The water is cold.
>
> Grady seemed angry.
>
> The court declared the law unconstitutional.
>
> The auditor is here.

## 3a Adjectives

**Adjectives** modify nouns and a few pronouns to express attributes such as quality, quantity, or type. You can usually identify adjectives by their characteristic positions, or functions.

- Before nouns (and occasionally pronouns)

  rusty scissors

  flexible plastic

  new one

- After *very*

  very rusty

  very flexible

  very new

- After forms of the verb *be*

  The scissors are rusty.

  This plastic is flexible.

  That one is new.

### EXERCISE 1

**Insert adjectives to modify the nouns in the following sentences.**

1. Around the house were hills, forests, and meadows.
2. We entered the lobby from a stairway.
3. The waiter served tea from a pot.
4. The job led her to consider a change.
5. A bonfire shed a light on the beach.
6. The announcer spoke with a dialect.
7. His library was filled with maps.
8. The interviewer's attitude grated on my nerves.
9. Moss covered the worms in the can.
10. The boat had a sail made of a shirt.

## 3b Adverbs

**Adverbs** modify adjectives, other adverbs, verbs, and whole clauses. Consequently, you will find adverbs in a variety of forms and positions.

- Most adverbs are made by the addition of *–ly* to adjectives: *boldly, smoothly, actively, gracefully, suddenly.* These adverbs can usually be moved about in sentences.

Suddenly, all the lights went out.

All the lights suddenly went out.

All the lights went out suddenly.

- A small but widely used group of adverbs includes *now, then, soon, still, last, here, there, always, never, once*—expressions of time, place, distance, and frequency. These adverbs, too, can often be moved about in sentences.

Now we hope to buy a condominium.

We now hope to buy a condominium.

We hope to buy a condominium now.

- Also movable are the conjunctive adverbs: *furthermore, however, therefore, also, thus, instead, consequently,* and so forth. Sometimes called transitional expressions, the conjunctive adverbs modify whole clauses and provide transition between sentences and paragraphs. (See the chart of transitional expressions on page 412.)

The commercial is extremely annoying; also, it is insulting to women.

The commercial is extremely annoying; it is also insulting to women.

- Another type of movable adverb is produced by the combination of *some, any, every,* and *no* with words like *how, place, where,* and *why: somehow, someplace, anyway, anywhere, everywhere, nowhere.*

Somehow we managed to get the canoe righted.

We somehow managed to get the canoe righted.

We managed somehow to get the canoe righted.

We managed to get the canoe righted somehow.

- The suffixes *–ward* and *–wise* produce adverbs like *backward, southward, lengthwise,* and *clockwise.* These adverbs usually occur after a verb or its object.

The man was walking backward.

Cut the board lengthwise.

- Some adverbs, the qualifiers, restrict or intensify adjectives and other adverbs: *very, quite, really, rather, hardly, somewhat,* and so forth. The qualifiers appear immediately before the words they modify.

The boat was hardly visible from shore.

He turned down my request very cheerfully.

- Some prepositions can also function as adverbs: *in, out, up, down, over, under, inside, outside,* and so forth. These adverbs usually express place or direction and appear with verbs.

We were locked inside.

Don't look down.

- Adverbs that function as interrogatives—*when, where, why,* and *how*—normally appear at the beginning of a clause or before an infinitive.

Where is the next meeting?

We don't know when the funds will be available.

The first chapter explains how to string a guitar.

## ❑ EXERCISE 2

**Write sentences containing the following types of adverbs.**

1. an adverb made by adding *-ly* to an adjective
2. an adverb made with the suffix *-ward*
3. a qualifier modifying an adverb
4. a qualifier modifying an adjective
5. an adverb that can also be a preposition

## ❑ EXERCISE 3

**Identify the modifiers in the following sentences as adjectives or adverbs.**

1. The value of the new stock jumped dramatically.
2. The old town had a rather efficient sawmill; nevertheless, the economy was distressed.
3. The company now reluctantly accepts full responsibility.
4. Abruptly, the local newspaper quit printing the controversial cartoon.
5. The white Persian kittens were extremely fat.
6. The painting graphically portrayed the cruel war.
7. Sometimes anti-inflammatory drugs can permanently damage an athlete.
8. The obviously professional thieves carried out a lucrative theft.
9. The pedantic professors discussed their views on genetic engineering.
10. The contributions of Edward R. Murrow are very important to contemporary journalism.

## 3c Adjective and Adverb Forms

Most adjectives and adverbs have three forms, sometimes called **degrees.** The **positive** form is the simple form of a modifier *(a new building)*. The **comparative** form makes a comparison between two people or things *(the newer of the two buildings)* and between a person or thing and other individual members of a group *(a building newer than any other in town)*. The **superlative** form compares three or more people or things *(the newest of the three buildings)* and describes the position of a person or thing within its group *(the newest building in town)*.

Most one-syllable and some two-syllable adjectives and adverbs show degree with *–er/–est* forms *(short, shorter, shortest; funny, funnier, funniest; near, nearer, nearest)*.

**Adjective**

POSITIVE: The lake is large.

COMPARATIVE: Sardis is the larger of the two lakes.

SUPERLATIVE: Superior is the largest of the Great Lakes.

**Adverb**

POSITIVE: I arrived early for the dinner party.

COMPARATIVE: I arrived earlier than anyone else.

SUPERLATIVE: Of all the guests, I arrived earliest.

Some adjectives and adverbs have irregular comparative and superlative forms, for example, *good, better, best; many, more, most; badly, worse, worst*.

POSITIVE: In light years, Mercury is not far from the sun.

COMPARATIVE: Saturn is farther from the sun than Jupiter.

SUPERLATIVE: Pluto is farthest from the sun.

Adjectives and adverbs without *–er/–est* forms show degree with *more* and *most* or *less* and *least*. These adjectives and adverbs have at least two but usually three or more syllables *(careful, more careful, most careful; important, less important, least important; fully, more fully, most fully; suddenly, less suddenly, least suddenly)*.

**Adjective**

POSITIVE: The kitchen was spacious.

COMPARATIVE: The kitchen was more spacious than the den.

SUPERLATIVE: The kitchen was the most spacious room in the house.

**Adverb**

POSITIVE: The campaign was carefully planned.

COMPARATIVE: This year's campaign was less carefully planned than last year's.

SUPERLATIVE: This year's campaign was the least carefully planned of the three.

You can be sure that any word with degree is either an adjective or an adverb. For a discussion of the appropriate use of comparatives and superlatives, see 15b.

## ❏ EXERCISE 4

In each sentence, use the appropriate form of the adjective or adverb shown in parentheses.

1. Electric cars ran (fast) than steam cars.
2. Of all those who spoke, the first candidate gave the (weak) speech.
3. The Egyptian exhibit was (fascinating) than any other.
4. Shaw's play *Pygmalion* was transformed into *My Fair Lady*, one of the (popular) musicals of all time.
5. The (small) species of shark grows to no longer than six inches.
6. Her backhand was (good) than anyone else's on the team.
7. Last night we saw the (bad) movie of the year.
8. My partner played her cards (expertly) than I.
9. The language with the (large) vocabulary is English.
10. Your apartment is (near) campus than mine.

# 4 Verbs and Verb Phrases

**Verbs** and **verb phrases** are often defined as parts of speech that state action, occurrence, or existence. This definition, however, does not adequately convey the importance of verbs in communication; they make up the most versatile and intricate word class in the language. Their characteristic forms, positions, and functions combine to provide an enormous range of meaning and a variety of subtle distinctions. Therefore, the effective use of language requires mastering the verb system.

## 4a Basic Forms

All verbs and verb phrases include one of the basic forms. Three of these forms—base, past, and past participle—are often called the three **principal parts.** As the charts illustrate, regular verbs make their past forms and past participles by adding –*d* or –*ed* to the base; irregular verbs do not follow this predictable pattern.

In addition to the three principal parts, two other forms exist for all verbs, both regular and irregular: the –*s* form, made by adding *–s* or *–es* to the base, and the present participle, made by adding *–ing* to the base. Thus, all verbs (except *be*, which is treated separately) can be said to have a total of five possible forms.

**Examples of Regular Verbs**

| *Base* | *–s Form* | *Past* | *Past Participle* | *Present Participle* |
|---|---|---|---|---|
| assume | assumes | assumed | assumed | assuming |
| drag | drags | dragged | dragged | dragging |
| dry | dries | dried | dried | drying |
| enjoy | enjoys | enjoyed | enjoyed | enjoying |
| fix | fixes | fixed | fixed | fixing |

**Examples of Irregular Verbs**

| *Base* | *–s Form* | *Past* | *Past Participle* | *Present Participle* |
|---|---|---|---|---|
| begin | begins | began | begun | beginning |
| cut | cuts | cut | cut | cutting |
| draw | draws | drew | drawn | drawing |
| eat | eats | ate | eaten | eating |
| leave | leaves | left | left | leaving |
| think | thinks | thought | thought | thinking |

You will find a complete list of irregular verbs and their principal parts under *irregular verb* in the Glossary of Terms. Also, for information about correct use of verb forms, see Chapter 11.

The verb *be* does not follow the patterns of other verbs; it has eight forms, including three for the -s form and two for the past form.

**Forms of *Be***

| *Base* | *–s Form* | *Past* | *Past Participle* | *Present Participle* |
|---|---|---|---|---|
| be | am<br>is<br>are | was<br>were | been | being |

## ❑ EXERCISE 1

Fill in the following chart.

| *Base* | *– s Form* | *Past Form* | *Past Participle* | *Present Participle* |
|---|---|---|---|---|
| EX. lift | lifts | lifted | lifted | lifting |
| 1. forbid | | | | |
| 2. spin | | | | |
| 3. shred | | | | |
| 4. burn | | | | |
| 5. lead | | | | |
| 6. beat | | | | |
| 7. burst | | | | |
| 8. creep | | | | |

## ❑ EXERCISE 2

Supply the verbs called for in the parentheses.

1. The sea gull (past of *dive*) into the water.
2. Fate has (past participle of *deal*) him a cruel blow.
3. The camper (past of *lie*) on the cold ground all night.
4. The consumer ( – *s* form of *pay*) the price for advertisements.
5. The stations are (present participle of *get*) interference.
6. The stock has (past participle of *be*) listed in the exchange for the past year.
7. The troops (past of *flee*) the battlefield.
8. He ( – *s* form of *try*) to play halfback.
9. The project has (past participle of *have*) a number of setbacks.
10. The map will (base form of *show*) you the shortest route.

# 4b Auxiliaries and Verb Phrases

Frequently, the verb in a sentence is not a single word but a phrase. In the phrase, the last verb is the **main verb,** and all preceding verbs are **auxiliaries.**

> Intense heat <u>does</u> not <u>affect</u> the paint.
>
> The orchestra <u>has been rehearsing</u>.
>
> The wallet <u>might have been stolen</u>.

There are four categories of auxiliaries that combine with one another and with main verbs to create a variety of structures and subtle shades of meaning.

## (1) *Be* auxiliary

The *be* auxiliary appears in one of eight forms (*am, is, are, was, were, be, being, been*) and is always followed by the present or past participle.

| | |
|---|---|
| AUXILIARY + PRESENT PARTICIPLE OF *LEAVE*: | He is leaving. |
| AUXILIARY + PAST PARTICIPLE OF *FIRE*: | I was fired today. |

## (2) *Have* auxiliary

The *have* auxiliary appears in one of four forms (*have, has, had, having*) and is always followed by a past participle.

| | |
|---|---|
| AUXILIARY + PAST PARTICIPLE OF *FORGET*: | I have forgotten the combination. |
| AUXILIARY + PAST PARTICIPLE OF *BREAK*: | The quarterback had broken his ankle. |

## (3) Modal auxiliaries

The **modal** auxiliaries influence the "mood" of verbs by expressing ideas such as ability, advisability, necessity, and possibility. For example, the verb *complete* takes on slightly different meanings when accompanied by different modal auxiliaries.

| | |
|---|---|
| ABILITY: | The crew can complete the job in one week. |
| OBLIGATION: | You should complete the investigation before you begin the report. |
| NECESSITY: | We must complete the remodeling by June. |
| POSSIBILITY: | I may complete the course in time for graduation. |

The common modal auxiliaries are *will, would, can, could, shall, should, may, might,* and *must.* These auxiliaries are followed by the base form of either the main verb, the *be* auxiliary, or the *have* auxiliary.

| | |
|---|---|
| AUXILIARY + BASE FORM OF *ARRANGE*: | The director will arrange a meeting. |

AUXILIARY + BASE FORM OF *BE* AUXILIARY: She might be living in Paris.

AUXILIARY + BASE FORM OF *HAVE* AUXILIARY: I could have taken three courses this summer.

### (4) *Do* auxiliary

The *do* auxiliary appears in one of three forms (*do, does, did*) and is always followed by the base form of the main verb. This auxiliary is unique in that it cannot combine with other auxiliaries.

AUXILIARY + BASE FORM OF *REVEAL*: The studies do reveal current trends.

AUXILIARY + BASE FORM OF *BLOOM*: The tree did not bloom this year.

## ❏ EXERCISE 3

**Rewrite the following sentences, changing the verbs in order to add the auxiliaries indicated.**

EXAMPLE: We finished the work before dark. (must) → We must finish the work before dark.

1. Their shop sells homemade quilts. (will)
2. The general led a successful coup. (can)
3. The chefs prepare an excellent chocolate mousse. (have)
4. The museum has sold the painting. (may)
5. The newspaper reported the murder. (did)
6. He played the stock market. (should)
7. The hotel made a profit. (has)
8. A conference on pollution takes place in August. (is)
9. We will leave by Friday. (have)
10. A library staff has assembled the collection. (been)

## ❏ EXERCISE 4

**Write sentences containing verb phrases in the combinations of auxiliaries and main verbs listed.**

EXAMPLE: modal auxiliary + *have* auxiliary + past participle of *see* → You should have seen the game last night.

1. modal auxiliary + base form of *sell*
2. *have* auxiliary + past participle of *go*
3. *be* auxiliary + present participle of *live*
4. modal auxiliary + *be* auxiliary + present participle of *sleep*
5. modal auxiliary + *have* auxiliary + past participle of *know*
6. *do* auxiliary + base form of *deny*
7. *have* auxiliary + *be* auxiliary + present participle of *read*
8. modal auxiliary + *have* auxiliary + *be* auxiliary + past participle of *see*

## 4c Tense

**Tense** suggests the verb's time frame. For example, present tense usually states constant or repetitive actions. Past tense shows that an action was completed in the past. Future tense can express future events. Present perfect can suggest that an action begun in the past is not yet complete. Nevertheless, you should remember that tense may not be equivalent to time and that the meanings expressed by the tenses can overlap. Some ideas, for instance, can be expressed in either the present or the future tense.

PRESENT TENSE: **Intense heat causes the surface to crack.**

FUTURE TENSE: **Intense heat will cause the surface to crack.**

The following charts show the range of meanings that can be expressed by the three simple tenses (present, past, and future) and the three perfect tenses (present perfect, past perfect, and future perfect).

**Simple Tenses**

| *Formation* | *Uses* | *Examples* |
|---|---|---|
| **Present**<br>–*s* form in third person singular; base form everywhere else | present time with certain verbs, especially referring to senses | I hear a car in the driveway. |
| | statements of fact | The Amazon empties into the Atlantic. |
| | repetitive action | She walks to school. |
| | references to works of art and literature | In the *Mona Lisa,* the woman smiles enigmatically. |
| | future time | The races start tomorrow. |
| **Past**<br>past form | past occurrences | The Rams won the game. |
| **Future**<br>*will* + base form and sometimes *shall* + base form* | future time | The store will open in May. |
| | results of conditions | If suddenly heated, air will expand violently. |

*In current usage, *shall* and *will* often suggest different meanings. *Shall we go?* is an invitation—"Would you like to go?" *Will we go?* asks "Are we going?" *Shall* also occurs in set expressions (*we shall overcome*), in laws and resolutions (*the court shall set the fine*), and in heightened prose (*we shall never surrender*).

**Perfect Tenses**

| *Formation* | *Uses* | *Examples* |
|---|---|---|
| **Present Perfect** | | |
| *have/has* + past participle | occurrences completed at an unspecified time in the past | He has sung at the Met. |
| | action begun in the past and continuing to the present | We have always gone to Vermont in June. |
| **Past Perfect** | | |
| *had* + past participle | past action occurring before some other past action | The troops had reached the river when the message arrived |
| **Future Perfect** | | |
| *will* + *have* + past participle | action that will occur before or by the time of another future action | We will have left by the time he arrives |

## ❑ EXERCISE 5

Identify the tense of each verb and verb phrase in the following sentences.

1. They have planned the museum's textile exhibit carefully.
2. He collected all Glenn Gould's recordings of Bach.
3. The freighter travels down the Mississippi to New Orleans every spring.
4. Trisodium phosphate will remove grease and heavy stains.
5. He had hoped for one victory on the PGA tour.
6. The veterinarian now does dental work on dogs.
7. The erosion will have caused an irreversible problem by next year.
8. In Goethe's drama, Faust sold his soul to Mephistopheles.
9. He had not applied for the job before the deadline.
10. The dancers have practiced pirouettes for two hours.

## ❑ EXERCISE 6

Write a sentence using each verb in the tense indicated. Include enough detail in each sentence so that the tense seems appropriate.

In other words, avoid writing sentences such as *I see, I ran, I will tell you,* and the like.

EXAMPLE: Past perfect tense of *leave*

The train had left a half hour before I reached the station.

1. present tense of *clean*
2. past tense of *ride*
3. future tense of *type*
4. present perfect tense of *select*
5. past perfect tense of *hope*
6. future perfect tense of *complete*

## 4d Progressive Forms

The six tenses have **progressive forms** that indicate actions in progress. A progressive verb is made with a form of the verb *be* followed by a present participle (an – *ing* form of the verb). The following chart explains the progressive forms and their uses.

| **Simple Progressive Forms** | | |
|---|---|---|
| *Formation* | *Uses* | *Examples* |
| **Present Progressive** | | |
| *am/is/are* + present participle | action currently in progress | Crowds are lining the streets. |
| | future time | He is sailing Monday |
| **Past Progressive** | | |
| *was/were* + present participle | past action in progress | I was sleeping when he called. |
| **Future Progressive** | | |
| *will be* + present participle | future action in progress | James will be traveling next month. |
| | future action that is not continuous | She will be arriving at noon. |

| Perfect Progressive Forms | | |
|---|---|---|
| *Formation* | *Uses* | *Examples* |
| **Present Perfect Progressive** *have/has + been* + present participle | continuous past actions still occurring or occurring until recently | The committee has been considering the issue all week. |
| **Past Perfect Progressive** *had + been* + present participle | past action in progress until another past action occurred | He had been lifting weights daily before his doctor advised restraint. |
| **Future Perfect Progressive** *will + have + been* + present participle | continuous future action that will be complete at some other future time | He will have been pitching for fifteen years by the time the season ends. |

## ❑ EXERCISE 7

In the following sentences, identify the tense of each progressive verb form.

1. The agency is now considering candidates for director.
2. Red wines from France's Rhone region were selling well.
3. After the new guidelines are established, the commission will be rating movies on a scale of one to four.
4. Before the recession, the company had been growing rapidly.
5. In May the factory will have been using robots for six months.
6. Psychics have been predicting earthquakes in Tennessee.
7. Experts are restoring the building to its original state.
8. The hurricane had been moving toward Texas when it suddenly reversed its course.
9. At sunrise the barges were crossing the river.
10. The city has been issuing bonds for school construction for the past ten years.

## ❑ EXERCISE 8

Write sentences using each of the following verb forms. Include enough detail so that readers can see why each verb is appropriate to its sentence.

EXAMPLE: had given
I had given the painting away before I found out how valuable it was.

1. catch
2. burns
3. is fighting
4. rode
5. had hurt
6. was drawing
7. has been selling
8. were sleeping
9. had been drinking
10. will learn

# 4e Voice

Some verbs can be expressed in either active or passive voice. In **active voice,** the subject acts or in some way controls the action of the verb, and the object receives the action. Active-voice sentences have this pattern:

| ACTOR | VERB | RECEIVER |
|---|---|---|
| An auditor | has checked | the figures. |
| Snow | covers | the mountains. |
| My dog | ate | my lunch. |
| Disney | is filming | the movie. |

In **passive voice,** the subject receives the action. The actor or agent, if named, appears in a prepositional phrase beginning with *by* or *with*. It is easy to recognize passive-voice verbs: they always contain a form of *be* plus the past participle. Sentences with passive-voice verbs have this pattern:

| RECEIVER | FORM OF BE | PAST PARTICIPLE | BY OR WITH | ACTOR |
|---|---|---|---|---|
| The figures | have been | checked | by | an auditor. |
| The mountains | are | covered | with | snow. |
| My lunch | was | eaten | by | my dog. |
| The movie | is being | filmed | by | Disney. |

Often in passive voice, the agent is not named: the *by* or *with* phrase is omitted.

ACTIVE: The horse threw the rider over the fence.

PASSIVE: The rider was thrown over the fence by the horse.

PASSIVE: The rider was thrown over the fence.

ACTIVE: Trash littered the streets.

PASSIVE: The streets were littered with trash.

PASSIVE: The streets were littered.

For a discussion of when to avoid and when to use the passive voice, see 33c.2.

## ❑ EXERCISE 9

Identify the verbs in the following sentences as active or passive.

1. The tour leader was lecturing the group in the Library of Congress.
2. The proposition was explained to the marketing representatives.
3. The radio advertisement is not attracting buyers.
4. Airlines offer reduced fares to people over sixty-five.
5. The bank has notified the company by telephone.
6. The essays in the collection are all written by scientists.
7. Clam chowder is always served on Friday.
8. The courier must deliver the package by five o'clock.

## ❑ EXERCISE 10

Change the following passive-voice sentences to active.

EXAMPLE: The dents in the car were made by hailstones.→Hailstones made the dents in the car.

1. Nutritional problems are sometimes overlooked by doctors.
2. Few memberships have been accepted by the club.
3. In *The Pride of the Yankees,* Lou Gehrig was played by Gary Cooper.
4. Gas production has been hampered by control laws.
5. The hillsides were blanketed with wild flowers.

## ❑ EXERCISE 11

Change the following active voice sentences to passive and delete the resulting *by* phrase.

EXAMPLE: The citizens elect a president every four years.→A president is elected every four years.

1. Witnesses saw the suspect driving a red convertible.
2. The school named her Outstanding Teacher of the Year.
3. You can purchase tickets two weeks in advance.
4. The company publishes the book only in paperback.
5. People expect doctors to be infallible.

# 4f Mood

The **mood** of a verb indicates whether the idea expressed is a fact (indicative mood), a command (imperative mood), or a matter of desire or possibility (subjunctive). The three moods are expressed through special verb forms.

## (1) Indicative mood

The **indicative mood** is used to make statements and ask questions.

She paints murals.

Squirrels ate the birdseed.

Who is your senator?

Has the mail arrived?

This mood has six tenses, explained by the charts in 4c and 4d.

## (2) Imperative mood

The **imperative mood** is used to give commands. The omitted but understood subject of all imperative verbs is the singular or plural *you*. In addition, for all verbs except *be,* the imperative is the form used with *you* in the present tense.

| POSITIVE | NEGATIVE |
|---|---|
| Answer the memo. | Do not/Don't answer the memo. |
| Order the sirloin. | Do not/Don't order the sirloin. |

The imperative of the verb *be* is always *be* for positive commands and *do not/don't be* for negative commands.

| POSITIVE | NEGATIVE |
|---|---|
| Be serious. | Do not/Don't be serious. |
| Be an observer. | Do not/Don't be an observer. |

## (3) Subjunctive mood

The forms of **subjunctive** verbs (other than *be*) are the same as the forms of the indicative except in one respect: the −*s* is not added in the third-person singular present tense.

SUBJUNCTIVE: Heaven forbid.
INDICATIVE: Heaven forbids.

With *be*, the present tense subjunctive is always *be;* the past tense subjunctive is always *were*.

SUBJUNCTIVE: We demand that the accused be tried in a court of law.
INDICATIVE: The accused is tried in a court of law.

SUBJUNCTIVE: Even if the movie were free, I would not see it.
INDICATIVE: The movie was free, but I did not see it.

In current English, the *subjunctive mood* has limited use, appearing only in three special contexts.

- The subjunctive is present in a few traditional expressions, such as farewells and blessings.

SUBJUNCTIVE: Peace be with you.
INDICATIVE: Peace is with you.

SUBJUNCTIVE: Long live the queen.
INDICATIVE: The queen lives long.

- The subjunctive is used in clauses introduced by conjunctions such as *if, as if,* and *as though* to express hypothetical situations or conditions contrary to fact.

SUBJUNCTIVE: If a left turn signal were installed, traffic flow would improve.
INDICATIVE: When a left turn signal was installed, traffic flow improved.
SUBJUNCTIVE: If I were you, I would not smoke.
INDICATIVE: I am not you, but I don't think you should smoke.

- The subjunctive occurs in *that* clauses naming demands, recommendations, wishes, and needs.

SUBJUNCTIVE: We demand that the terms of the contract be met.
INDICATIVE: The demands of the contract are met.

SUBJUNCTIVE: The committee recommended that he submit a proposal.
INDICATIVE: He submits a proposal.

SUBJUNCTIVE: I wish I were good at math. [*That* is understood after *wish*.]

INDICATIVE: I am good at math.

SUBJUNCTIVE: It is urgent that the police department enforce zoning regulations.
INDICATIVE: The police department enforces zoning regulations.

## ❑ EXERCISE 12

Determine whether the mood of each underlined verb is indicative, imperative, or subjunctive.

1. Stalin planned to liquidate some of his political associates.
2. The constitution requires that a majority be present to vote.
3. To keep your terrarium from souring, add broken charcoal.
4. The dreadful extravaganza will cost about ten million.
5. Two free throws were made in the final minute.
6. Describe what you see in the ink blots.
7. Most Asian countries insist that a visitor receive cholera injections before entry.
8. If I were in Italy during August, I would avoid Venice.
9. The sprinklers have been running all weekend.
10. It is imperative that she have privacy.

# 5

# Verbals and Verbal Phrases

A **verbal** is a present participle (*winning*), a past participle (*won*), or an infinitive (*to win*) functioning in a sentence as something other than a verb. A verbal may function as a noun, an adjective, or an adverb.

> Winning was all that mattered to him.
>
> Teams are rated by the number of games won.
>
> We were surprised to win.

A **verbal phrase** is a verbal plus any words that complete its meaning.

> Winning the game was all that mattered to him.
>
> Teams are rated by the number of games won within the conference.
>
> We were surprised to win so easily.

## 5a Infinitives and Infinitive Phrases

**Infinitives** begin with *to,* followed by a verb (*to go, to think, to seem*). These verbals appear alone or in phrases and can function as adverbs, adjectives, and nouns.

As Adverbs

> The audience rose to cheer the performance. [modifying *rose*]
>
> This exercise machine is difficult to use. [modifying *difficult*]

The river flows too slowly to do much damage. [modifying *slowly*]

To return to my question, is the government interfering in another country's affairs? [modifying the rest of the sentence]

AS ADJECTIVES

Many writers have a tendency to use too many commas. [modifying *tendency*]

A poison to kill fire ants is now available. [modifying *poison*]

AS NOUNS

To invest successfully in oil requires the instincts of a good gambler. [subject of *requires*]

Darwin believed natural selection to be important in the origin of plants and animals. [object of *believed*]

The delegates argued about how to cast the votes. [object of *about*]

The "sign" of the infinitive, *to,* is omitted after certain verbs like *let, make, hear, see,* and *feel.*

Let the record show that only four people were present.

We saw her steal the necklace.

## ❑ EXERCISE 1

**Combine the following pairs of sentences by changing the second sentence in each pair to an infinitive phrase.**

EXAMPLE: **Listen to your voice on a tape recording. You can find out how you sound to other people. → To find out how you sound to other people, listen to your voice on a tape recording.**

1. **The plant must install equipment. The equipment must limit the pollutants emitted.**
2. **The jockey uses a crop. The crop gives a horse special signals.**
3. **Galileo designed the sector. The sector aids draftsmen.**
4. **At night the hippopotamus leaves the water. At night the hippopotamus feeds on land.**
5. **Packwood and Brinson Inc. has been hired. Packwood and Brinson Inc. will design the museum.**
6. **The United States uses artificial satellites. The satellites obtain weather information.**
7. **The tourists visited Argentina. The tourists will see Buenos Aires.**
8. **Hannibal's military genius helped him. Hannibal defeated armies much larger than his.**

9. The Argonauts sailed with Jason. The Argonauts searched for the Golden Fleece.
10. The scientists use a particle accelerator. The scientists study atomic particles such as neutrinos.

## 5b Participles and Participial Phrases

**Participles** exist in two forms: the present participle and the past participle. You can always identify a present participle by its *–ing* ending—for example, *walking, thinking, singing*. The past participle is the form that can follow *have* in a verb phrase—for example, *walked, thought, sung*. Participles, alone or in phrases, can act as adjectives to modify nouns or pronouns.

> The missing passengers apparently drowned after the ferry capsized. [present participle modifying *passengers*]
>
> The passengers, missing after the ferry capsized, apparently drowned. [present participial phrase modifying *passengers*]
>
> The frightened people panicked and fled the hostile "Martians." [past participle modifying *people*]
>
> Frightened by the broadcast, people panicked and fled the hostile "Martians." [past participial phrase modifying *people*]

### ☐ EXERCISE 2

**Combine each pair of sentences by changing the second to a participial phrase. Position the participle carefully so that it clearly refers to the word it modifies.**

EXAMPLE: **Vivaldi's works included instrumental compositions and operas. Vivaldi's works were admired by Bach.→Admired by Bach, Vivaldi's works included instrumental compositions and operas.**

1. **The book describes current medical discoveries. The discoveries are revolutionizing cancer treatment.**
2. **The people filled the street in front of the Capitol. The people were protesting the law.**
3. **The tour goes to forty destinations. The destinations include ten stops in China.**

4. We purchased a charcoal grill. The charcoal grill was designed for a commercial restaurant.
5. The first European explorers found that many Indian tribes farmed the land. European explorers arrived in South America.
6. Authorities continued searching for three members of a family. The family was missing after a twister ripped apart their house.
7. At one time Thebes was the most powerful city-state in all Greece. Thebes supposedly was founded by Cadmus.
8. Tutankhamen's tomb contained a coffin of solid gold. The coffin is now located in the Cairo Museum.

## 5c Gerunds and Gerund Phrases

**Gerunds** are present participles (*walking, believing, feeling*) functioning as nouns. Like other verbals, gerunds can appear alone or in phrases.

> Selling beer without a license is illegal. [subject of *is*]
>
> The patient had lost his hearing because of a childhood illness. [object of *had lost*]
>
> Mendel devoted his time to studying genetics. [object of *to*]

### ❑ EXERCISE 3

Identify the gerunds and gerund phrases in the following sentences.

1. By marrying a Persian princess, Alexander the Great encouraged intermarriage.
2. Looking too far into the future can be frightening.
3. A typewriter's bell prevents typing past the right margin.
4. *All the King's Men* describes the making of a powerful Southern politician.
5. Amoebas reproduce by fission, or splitting apart.
6. Many experts consider jogging the best aerobic exercise.
7. A current fad among amateur photographers is developing film.
8. Fred Astaire gave dancing an athletic grace.
9. Balancing a job and school can take careful planning.
10. Sunlight, temperature, precipitation, soil condition, plants, and animals—all these elements go into forming a "natural community."

# 5d Absolute Verbal Phrases

An **absolute phrase** does not modify any one element in a sentence but instead modifies the rest of the sentence. Thus, the absolute phrase seems rather loosely connected. There are two types of absolute verbal phrases.

- The first is a familiar expression containing a participle or an infinitive.

  Speaking of friends, Susan let me use her credit card when I was broke.

  To tell the truth, my vacation was more work than my job.

- The second is the nominative absolute—a phrase beginning with a noun or pronoun that acts as the subject of the verbal. The nominative absolute is somewhat formal and usually explains causes or adds details to sentences.

  His fortune squandered on cards and horses, he went to work as a valet.

  The seas being rough, we put into harbor.

  The estate will be liquidated, everything to be sold at auction.

  The gunfighter of Hollywood westerns was casually sinister—guns slung low on his hips, hat cocked rakishly over one eye, steps measured and slow.

## ❑ EXERCISE 4

**Which of the following sentences contain absolute phrases?**

1. **Attaching itself to a shark, the remora gets both transportation and protection.**
2. **The weather being cool and dry, they suggested an old-fashioned hayride.**
3. **To make a long story short, the only fish we caught swam into the boat when it capsized.**
4. **Strictly speaking, the tomato is not a vegetable.**
5. **Suddenly we saw the dog, his hackles raised and his teeth bared for attack.**
6. **To escape the noise of the dormitory, I began studying in the library.**
7. **Soaring through the clouds, the little plane looked much like a graceful seagull.**

8. We searched for the location of the town, the map spread out before us.
9. I awoke slowly, my head pounding, my eyes burning with fever.
10. To conclude, the program cannot survive without federal funds.

## ❑ EXERCISE 5

Identify each verbal phrase in the following sentences. Then classify the phrase as an infinitive, gerund, participial, or absolute phrase.

1. The athlete has our gratitude for representing our country so well in the Olympics.
2. A peninsula jutting out from the northwest corner of France, Brittany was once an independent state.
3. Use the expression "Very truly yours" to close a particularly formal letter.
4. My head nodding and eyelids drooping, I struggled in vain to pay attention to the speaker.
5. To praise the computer as the answer to all financial problems is ridiculous.
6. Sometimes crying about a problem is the first step toward facing it.
7. Soaring in ascending circles, the eagle rose higher and higher.
8. The publication contains all the maps relating to the Lewis and Clark expedition.
9. When cheating on taxes becomes excessive, more money must be put into enforcement.
10. The three-barred cross, also known as the Russian cross, is a symbol of the Russian Orthodox Church.
11. This combination of chemicals has the potential to explode.
12. It is important for members of our diplomatic corps to know foreign languages.
13. Cargo fits in containers shaped to conform to the airplane's interior.
14. Some reporters, going beyond the boundary of reasonable questions, threaten an individual's privacy.
15. Completed last year, the excavation uncovered a Roman street.

# 6

# Function Words

Nouns, verbs, adjectives, and adverbs make up the greater part of our vocabulary and convey most of the semantic meaning of sentences. However, meaning also depends on **function words:** prepositions, conjunctions, determiners, and expletives. These words create structure. If the function words are removed from a sentence, all that remains is a list of unrelated vocabulary items.

| | |
|---|---|
| WITH FUNCTION WORDS: | Under the canopy sat a man and a woman waiting for the bus. |
| WITHOUT FUNCTION WORDS: | canopy sat man woman waiting bus |

You might think of the vocabulary items as bricks and of the function words as the mortar that holds them together: both are necessary to build meaning.

## 6a Prepositions and Prepositional Phrases

A **prepositional phrase** contains a preposition and its object, usually a noun, noun phrase, or pronoun. The following list includes some of the most common prepositions. Although most are one word, some (called *phrasal prepositions*) are two and even three words.

| | | |
|---|---|---|
| above | during | onto |
| across | except | out |
| after | except for | outside of |
| against | for | over |
| around | from | past |
| as | in | since |
| at | in front of | through |
| away from | in spite of | toward |
| because of | into | under |
| before | like | until |
| beneath | near | up |
| between | of | with |
| by | off | within |
| by means of | on | without |
| down | | |

A prepositional phrase can modify a noun *(boats in the harbor),* a noun phrase *(a rusty bicycle without wheels),* or a pronoun *(everything on the back porch).* A prepositional phrase can also modify a verb *(ran through the alley),* a verbal *(performing at Christmas),* or an adjective *(optimistic about the future).*

In addition to their use as modifiers, prepositional phrases can also function like nouns. Occasionally, a prepositional phrase appears as the subject of a sentence: *After Thursday will be too late.* More often, a prepositional phrase with a noun function appears as an object: *The creature emerged from behind the snowbank.*

## ❑ EXERCISE 1

**Identify the prepositional phrases in the following sentences.**

1. Because of the music, this advertisement about soft drinks appeals to young people.
2. In the nineteenth century, American literature broke away from British tradition.
3. We were happy about their arrival and ecstatic over their departure.
4. For thousands of years, monks have used chant as a part of their sacred liturgy.
5. In the mornings before ten will be convenient.

func
6b

## 6b Conjunctions

**Conjunctions** are grammatical connectors that link sentence elements and express relationships between ideas. For instance, conjunctions attribute causes and effects; signal time sequences; indicate alternatives, parallels, or contrasts. As you can see from reading the following passage, prose without conjunctions can be disjointed.

WITHOUT CONJUNCTIONS

We rarely think in terms of meters/liters. We are accustomed to inches/pounds. There has been an effort to change to the metric system. The changeover has met strong opposition. We are familiar with a foot. We can estimate length fairly accurately in feet. We can easily stride off a distance to measure it in yards.

The addition of conjunctions makes clear the relationships of the ideas.

WITH CONJUNCTIONS

We rarely think in terms of meters <u>and</u> liters <u>because</u> we are accustomed to inches <u>and</u> pounds. <u>Although</u> there has been an effort to change to the metric system, the changeover has met strong opposition. We are <u>so</u> familiar with a foot <u>that</u> we can estimate length in feet fairly accurately, <u>and</u> we can easily stride off a distance to measure it in yards.

### (1) Coordinating conjunctions

**Coordinating conjunctions** connect words, phrases, and clauses to grammatically coordinate, or equal, structures. Five coordinators—*and, but, or, nor,* and *yet*—can join any structures that are grammatically equal.

| | |
|---|---|
| NOUNS: | I always order fish <u>or</u> chicken. |
| VERBS: | We did not eat <u>nor</u> sleep for five days. |
| ADJECTIVES: | The singer was loud <u>but</u> off-key. |
| PREPOSITIONAL PHRASES: | The road runs through the valley <u>and</u> up the mountains. |
| CLAUSES: | He was a stern man, <u>yet</u> he was patient. |

Two coordinators—*for* and *so*—connect only independent clauses.

INDEPENDENT CLAUSES: The conductor stopped, for the cellist had begun to snore.

INDEPENDENT CLAUSES: English has only a few inflections, so it does not have a very flexible word order.

## EXERCISE 2

**Use coordinating conjunctions to combine the pairs of sentences. Join either words, phrases, or clauses.**

1. You can work out on the Nautilus machines. On the other hand, you can work out on the free weights.
2. Politicians came to the meeting in Chicago. Financiers came to the meeting in Chicago.
3. There are nearly fifty legal grounds for divorce. The majority of American suits are filed for cruelty.
4. Alec Guinness appeared in *The Bridge on the River Kwai.* He appeared in *Lawrence of Arabia.*
5. The sky is crystal clear. The moon is almost full.

### (2) Correlative conjunctions

A special type of coordinating conjunction, the **correlative,** has two parts that connect elements of equal grammatical structure—two nouns, two verbs, two adjectives, two dependent clauses, two independent clauses, and so forth. The correlatives *both . . . and* and *not . . . but* connect elements within clauses.

ADJECTIVES: The program includes both isometric and aerobic exercise.

NOUNS: The problem is not the hardware but the software.

Three sets of correlatives—*not only . . . but also, either . . . or, neither . . . nor*—can connect two independent clauses as well as elements within independent clauses.

ADJECTIVES: The stove is not only compact but also fuel efficient.

PREPOSITIONAL PHRASES: Paper is made either by a mechanical process or by a chemical process.

NOUNS: Neither Melville nor Hawthorne is as popular with students as Poe is.

CLAUSES: Not only did the Egyptians distinguish between planets and stars, but also they devised a 365-day calendar.

### (3) Subordinating conjunctions

**Subordinating conjunctions** introduce dependent clauses (7c) and express relationships such as cause, contrast, condition, manner, place, and time. Some commonly used subordinators are listed here.

| | | |
|---|---|---|
| after | except that | than |
| although | if | that |
| as | in case | unless |
| as if | in that | until |
| as though | now that | when |
| because | once | whenever |
| before | since | where |
| even though | so that | while |

The following examples suggest the versatility of subordinate clauses, but for a more complete discussion, see 7c.1.

MODIFYING A VERB: You should act as though you are accustomed to such elegance.

MODIFYING AN ADJECTIVE: I am sure that he has forgotten the appointment.

MODIFYING A CLAUSE: When the movie began, the theater was empty.

## ❑ EXERCISE 3

**Combine the pairs of sentences by using subordinating conjunctions.**

EXAMPLE: I did not pay my bill for two months. So the phone company disconnected my telephone.→ The phone company disconnected my telephone because I did not pay my bill for two months.

1. The plane descended. We saw the Washington Monument.
2. Prehistoric humans did no cultivating. They were forced into nomadic life.
3. Father grew older. He became less and less able to farm without help.
4. I was only twelve. But I could fly a P51 Mustang.
5. Their favorite restaurant was an outdoor cafe. They had both worked there ten years before.

### (4) Comparative conjunctions

A special type of subordinating conjunction has two parts—for example, *so . . . that* and *as . . . as.* These conjunctions usually introduce clauses of measurement or degree; that is, they introduce ideas that express how much or to what extent. The following are the most common **comparatives.**

- as . . . as

  She is not as clever as I thought she was.

- so . . . that

  Paul was so scared that he was shaking.

- such . . . that

  He is such a nice man that people take advantage of him.

- A comparative form of an adjective or adverb . . . *than*

  The river is cleaner than it was last year.

  This pump works more efficiently than the old one did.

- A superlative form of an adjective . . . *that*

  His Thunderbird was the fanciest car that I had ever seen.

  The game is the most complicated that the company has designed.

## ❑ EXERCISE 4

**Use a comparative conjunction and a clause to specify degree in each of the following sentences.**

EXAMPLE

ORIGINAL: The area is subject to flooding. (How subject is it to flooding?)

REVISED: The area is so subject to flooding that no one should build a house there.

1. **The drink was bitter. (How bitter was it?)**
2. **They are close friends. (How close are they?)**
3. **The picnic was enjoyable. The dance was enjoyable. (Which one was more enjoyable?)**
4. **The skater performed poorly. (How poorly did she perform?)**
5. **This racetrack is fast. (How fast is it?)**

## ☐ EXERCISE 5

**Use conjunctions to combine the sets of sentences. You can choose coordinating, correlative, subordinating, or comparative conjunctions—whichever is appropriate. Identify each you choose.**

EXAMPLE

ORIGINAL: The computer program is efficient. It makes editing simpler. It eliminates retyping.

COMBINED: The computer program is efficient because it makes editing simpler and eliminates retyping.

1. **The presidential seal shows the American eagle clutching arrows in one talon. The eagle is clutching an olive branch in the other.**
2. **Nuclear plants produce electricity without air pollution. Nuclear fission has several disadvantages.**
3. **Bob Marley died in 1981. He is considered the creator of the best Jamaican reggae music.**
4. **The moon's revolution is irregular. The irregular revolution is due to the fact that its orbit is elliptical.**
5. **The camera is versatile. The camera comes with a telephoto lens. It also comes with a wide-angle lens.**
6. **The little fishing village becomes populated in the summer. It is populated like a bustling city.**
7. ***Tropic of Cancer* was published. Then Henry Miller became a famous figure. He also became a controversial figure.**
8. **This organism flourishes in fresh water. It also flourishes in brackish water.**
9. **The street was hot. It burned my feet through my shoes.**
10. **Plants do not live alone. Animals do not live alone.**

# 6c Determiners

**Determiners** signal that a noun will follow, if not immediately, then shortly. Some words are always determiners.

- The articles—*a, an, the*

  A new theory about dinosaurs has been proposed.

  Where did you hide the chocolate chip cookies?

- Some possessive pronouns—*my, her, its, our, your, their, whose*

Her German accent sounds authentic.

Whose music did they play?

- An indefinite pronoun—*every*

  Every item was marked down 50 percent.

In addition, some nouns and pronouns frequently function as determiners.

- Possessives: *his, everyone's, Kathy's, today's,* and so on

  DETERMINER: Leading the discussion is his responsibility.
  PRONOUN: The responsibility is his.

- Demonstrative pronouns: *this, that, these, those*

  DETERMINER: You must pack these provisions for the trip.
  PRONOUN: The necessary provisions are these: food, water, and first-aid equipment.

- Indefinite pronouns: *each, either, neither, all, some, many, much, any, few, more, less,* and so on

  DETERMINER: Few inventors achieve success.
  PRONOUN: Of the thousands of inventors, few achieve success.

- Interrogative pronouns: *which, what*

  DETERMINER: We could not determine which virus was present.
  PRONOUN: A virus was present, but we could not determine which.

- Cardinal numbers—*one, two, three,* and so on

  DETERMINER: The terrorists showed pictures of four hostages.
  NOUN: There were six hostages, but the terrorists showed pictures of only four.

## ❑ EXERCISE 6

**Identify the determiners in the following sentences.**

1. Our instructor sent his first story to *Harper's.*
2. December's weather has ruined the fruit crops.
3. Every spring, a heavy rain causes floods in that section of town.
4. Which kinds of cars will people buy this year?
5. The three projects helped eliminate the downtown traffic snarl.
6. Only an inadequate bank account kept him from a life of luxury.

# 6d Expletives

The two **expletives,** *it* and *there,* are "filler words" that introduce clauses and allow the real subjects to be delayed until after the verbs or verb auxiliaries. *There* usually introduces a clause with a noun or noun phrase as the subject.

SUBJECT FIRST: A phone is ringing.
SUBJECT DELAYED: There is a phone ringing.

SUBJECT FIRST: A notice from the bank is on your desk.
SUBJECT DELAYED: There is a notice from the bank on your desk.

When the real subject of a clause is an infinitive or a *that* clause, beginning with the expletive *it* sounds more natural than beginning with the subject.

SUBJECT FIRST: To call is important.
SUBJECT DELAYED: It is important to call.

SUBJECT FIRST: That the dam will break is unlikely.
SUBJECT DELAYED: It is unlikely that the dam will break.

The expletive *it* has an additional function—to introduce constructions that have no real subject.

It is raining.

It is noisy in here.

CAUTION: The words *it* and *there* are not always expletives. *There* can function as an adverb; *it* is frequently a pronoun. Compare the following pairs of sentences:

EXPLETIVE: There are three horses in the paddock.
ADVERB: Three horses are there in the paddock.

EXPLETIVE: It is dangerous to jog after eating.
PRONOUN: Jogging after meals is dangerous. It should be avoided.

## ❑ EXERCISE 7

In the following passage, indicate whether each *there* is used as an expletive or an adverb. Also, indicate whether each *it* is used as an expletive or a pronoun.

There are two effective aids to kicking the cigarette habit. First, it helps to motivate yourself by thinking of all the bad effects of smoking—such as wrinkles, coughs, expense, and diseases. You can even tape the list to your bathroom mirror. There you will see it every morning when shaving or putting on makeup. Second, it is advisable to avoid environments like bars and coffeehouses, environments that tempt people to smoke.

# 7

# Clauses and Sentences

A **clause** is a grammatical construction with both a subject and a predicate. The simple subject consists of at least one noun (or noun equivalent); the complete subject consists of the noun and its modifiers. The predicate consists of at least one verb and its modifiers. In addition, the predicate may include one or more complements, that is, words necessary to complete the meaning of the verb. As the following examples show, the predicate makes an assertion about its subject.

| Subject | Predicate |
|---|---|
| Travis | defended the Alamo. |
| Everyone in the elevator | panicked. |
| The convention | will be in Des Moines next year. |

An independent, or main, clause expresses a complete idea and can occur by itself as a **sentence** (see 7b). A dependent, or subordinate, clause must occur as part of a sentence. Both independent and dependent clauses have the same structural patterns.

## 7a Clause Patterns

In all clause patterns, the subject is a noun (or noun equivalent) and any modifiers. What distinguishes the patterns from one another is the predicate structure, which is determined by the type of verb it contains—intransitive, transitive, or linking.

### (1) Intransitive verb pattern

Technically, an **intransitive verb** is complete by itself and is the only element needed in the predicate structure.

| SUBJECT | + | INTRANSITIVE VERB |
|---|---|---|
| The doctor | | smiled. |
| The prisoner | | has escaped. |
| They | | were leaving. |

Frequently, however, the pattern is fleshed out by an adverbial modifier following the verb.

The doctor smiled sheepishly.

The prisoner has escaped through a tunnel.

They were leaving before the party was over.

### (2) Transitive verb patterns

A **transitive verb** in the active voice requires a direct object, a complement that receives the action. Notice that without the direct objects, the verbs in the following sentences do not seem complete. In addition, some transitive verbs allow indirect objects, and some allow object complements. As a result, there are three transitive verb patterns.

- In one pattern, the subject performs the verb's action, and the direct object receives or is affected by the verb's action.

| SUBJECT | + | TRANSITIVE VERB | + | DIRECT OBJECT |
|---|---|---|---|---|
| The FBI | | investigated | | him. |
| A local press | | has published | | her memoirs. |
| Energy shortages | | would change | | our lifestyles. |

One way that you can test this pattern is to convert it to the passive voice (see 4e). In this conversion, you move the direct object to the subject position, where it still receives the verb's action.

He was investigated by the FBI.

Her memoirs have been published by a local press.

Our lifestyles would be changed by energy shortages.

- Another kind of complement, the indirect object, is common with a few transitive verbs—including *give, make, tell, show, bring, send, sell,* and *offer.* This object appears between the verb and the direct object; like the direct object, it completes the verb's meaning.

| Subject | Transitive Verb | Indirect Object | Direct Object |
|---|---|---|---|
| Our courts | cannot deny | a felon | due process. |
| My uncle | knitted | me | a wool sweater. |
| The professor | asked | us | only one question. |

You can identify an indirect object by converting it to a prepositional phrase (with *to, for,* or occasionally *of*) and shifting it to follow the direct object.

Our courts cannot deny due process to a felon.

My uncle knitted a wool sweater for me.

The professor asked only one question of us.

- Still another kind of complement, the object complement, can occur with a few transitive verbs—including *make, consider, call, elect, appoint, declare, name,* and *choose.* In this pattern, the complement is an adjective or a noun that follows the direct object and refers to it. Without the complement, the verb often means something a bit different or makes no sense. For instance, try reading the following examples with and then without the object complement.

| Subject | Transitive Verb | Direct Object | Object Complement |
|---|---|---|---|
| The fog | will make | travel | dangerous. |
| The reporter | called | the senator | devious. |
| I | kept | the letter | a secret. |
| Most people | consider | the tomato | a vegetable. |

You can identify an object complement by making a kind of equation between it and the direct object: *Travel is dangerous. The senator is devious. The letter is a secret. The tomato is a vegetable.*

## ❑ EXERCISE 1

In the following sentences, determine which verbs are intransitive and which are transitive. If you have trouble, use the passive-voice conversion to identify direct objects.

1. The mayor favors higher taxes.
2. Classes begin on September 1.
3. As usual, bad news traveled fast.
4. The Coast Guard rescued the couple after a three-day search.
5. Lightning flashed ominously in the western sky.
6. The author typed her entire 700-page manuscript on a manual typewriter.
7. I bathe and groom both dogs once a week.
8. The disagreement progressed quickly to a shouting match.

## ❑ EXERCISE 2

Determine which of the following sentences contain indirect objects and which contain object complements. You can identify an indirect object by using the prepositional phrase conversion; you can identify the object complements by using the equation test.

1. Our company awarded the investors a dividend.
2. The city council declared the water unsafe.
3. Bad weather makes my dog nervous.
4. Critics called the play "a sleazy joke."
5. Sing me the lyrics one more time.
6. The old man built the children a carousel.
7. She considered Elizabeth I her role model.
8. After much delay, they offered me the position.

### (3) Linking verb patterns

A **linking verb** requires a subject complement, which completes the meaning of the verb and refers to the subject.

- An adjective can fill the position of subject complement with almost all linking verbs—*be;* verbs with meanings similar to *be* (including *seem, appear, become, grow, remain*); and verbs that refer to the senses (*look, taste, smell, sound,* and *feel*).

| SUBJECT | + | LINKING VERB | + | ADJECTIVE SUBJECT COMPLEMENT |
|---|---|---|---|---|
| Most of the guests | | were | | obnoxious. |
| The surface | | feels | | rough. |
| The crowd | | grew | | restless. |
| The witness | | seemed | | hostile. |

Notice that you can test the pattern by making a noun phrase with the subject and subject complement: *obnoxious guests, rough surface, restless crowd, hostile witness.*

- Sometimes the subject complement is a *predicate nominative*—a noun or pronoun that names or refers to the subject. The most common verbs in this pattern are *be, become, remain, seem,* and *appear.*

| SUBJECT | + | LINKING VERB | + | NOUN OR PRONOUN SUBJECT COMPLEMENT |
|---|---|---|---|---|
| The main problem | | is | | you. |
| Stacy | | became | | a jockey. |
| All the cousins | | remained | | friends. |

You can test the pattern by making an equation of the subject and the subject complement: *problem = you; Stacy = jockey; cousins = friends.*

- With *be* and *become,* the subject complement can be a possessive:

| SUBJECT | + | LINKING VERB | + | POSSESSIVE SUBJECT COMPLEMENT |
|---|---|---|---|---|
| That Jaguar | | is | | Karen's. |
| The responsibility | | became | | mine. |
| The loss | | would be | | everyone's. |

Notice that the subject and complement make a noun phrase: *Karen's Jaguar; my responsibility; everyone's loss.*

- Finally, with *be* only, the complement can be an adverb or an adverb phrase that locates the subject in time or space.

| SUBJECT | + | LINKING VERB | + | ADVERB SUBJECT COMPLEMENT |
|---|---|---|---|---|
| A police officer | | is | | outside. |
| The meeting | | will be | | tomorrow. |
| The game | | was | | at 7:30. |

As elsewhere, the subject and subject complement can combine to form a noun phrase. In this pattern, however, the complement follows the subject: *police officer outside; meeting tomorrow; game at 7:30.*

## ❑ EXERCISE 3

**All the following sentences contain linking verbs and subject complements. Identify each verb and determine whether its complement is an adjective, a noun, a possessive, or an adverb.**

1. Gradually, I grew weary of his jealousy.
2. The stew tastes bitter.
3. This project has been a disaster.
4. Your umbrella was in the hall closet.
5. For most of us, medical school seemed an endurance test.
6. He remained optimistic in spite of any setbacks.
7. At her father's death, the estate became hers.
8. The best time for the reunion would be July 4th.
9. That pen on your desk is mine.
10. Without my cats, I felt very lonely.

## ❑ EXERCISE 4

**Each of the following sentences conforms to one of the five clause patterns listed here. Match each sentence with the pattern of its structure.**

(a) SUBJECT + INTRANSITIVE VERB
(b) SUBJECT + TRANSITIVE VERB + DIRECT OBJECT
(c) SUBJECT + TRANSITIVE VERB + INDIRECT OBJECT + DIRECT OBJECT
(d) SUBJECT + TRANSITIVE VERB + DIRECT OBJECT + OBJECT COMPLEMENT
(e) SUBJECT + LINKING VERB + SUBJECT COMPLEMENT

1. In 1846, Thoreau spent one night in jail.
2. Leaf-cutter ants can strip a tree bare in a day.
3. The Internal Revenue office is downstairs.
4. The Islamic religion is strictly monotheistic.
5. Gerald Ford was the first nonelected vice president.
6. Freshly grated nutmeg tastes superior to the commercially ground variety.
7. For America's national symbol, Benjamin Franklin proposed the turkey.
8. Three ounces of lean beef give an individual 169 calories.

9. The Interior Department has declared the peregrine falcon an endangered species.
10. Chess became an obsession to Rex.
11. The asparagus seems unsuited for gardens in south Florida.
12. During the winter, the South Pole is dark twenty-four hours a day.
13. My houseguest has been here since last month.
14. Copyrights now last for the life of an author plus fifty years.
15. Every year the Academy of Television Arts and Sciences awards the best dramatic series an Emmy.
16. Many connoisseurs consider the prepared mustards of Dijon or Dusseldorf best.
17. The refrigerator is one of the biggest users of energy in the home all year round.
18. Vanilla seems the most popular ice-cream flavor in this area.
19. American industry can learn from the success of Japanese industry.
20. Edison called his research laboratory at Menlo Park an "invention factory."

## 7b Independent Clauses

**Independent clauses** (sometimes called *main clauses*) may stand by themselves as sentences.

| SUBJECT | PREDICATE |
|---|---|
| The book | examines human cruelty. |
| The ideas | are not pessimistic. |
| A hostile crowd | had gathered. |
| Serbian assassins | waited. |

In addition, independent clauses can be joined to produce compound sentences.

> The book examines human cruelty, but the ideas are not pessimistic.
>
> A hostile crowd had gathered; the Serbian assassins waited.

## 7c Dependent Clauses

Like independent clauses, **dependent clauses** (also called *subordinate clauses*) have subjects and predicates. Unlike independent clauses, they cannot stand alone as sentences, and they usually begin with an introductory word that signals dependence.

| INTRODUCTORY WORD | SUBJECT | PREDICATE |
|---|---|---|
| because | it | causes tarnishing |
| that | we | call Baalbeck |
| if | their tires | are underinflated |

Because they are not complete in themselves, dependent clauses must be attached to independent clauses:

> Pewter articles no longer contain lead because it causes tarnishing.
>
> The town that we call Baalbeck was known to the Greeks as Heliopolis.
>
> Drivers waste gasoline if their tires are underinflated.

Dependent clauses function in sentences as modifiers or as nouns and are generally classified as adverb clauses, adjective clauses, and noun clauses.

### (1) Adverb clauses

The most versatile of dependent clauses is the **adverb clause,** which can modify verbs, adjectives, adverbs, and whole clauses. In fact, any dependent clause that does not act as a noun or modify a noun can safely be called an adverb clause.

Adverb clauses are introduced by subordinating conjunctions to express relationships such as time, cause, purpose, condition, contrast, comparison, place, and manner. Most of the subordinating conjunctions can be grouped according to these relationships.

Time

*when, whenever, while, after, before, as, just as, as soon as, until, since, ever since, once, as long as*

> The British blockaded Germany when World War II broke out.
>
> As soon as a dolphin is born, the mother pushes it to the water's surface for its first breath of air.

Cause

*because, since, now that, once, as, in case*

Because some years produce better wines, experts often judge quality by the vintage year.

In Nebraska, most farmers must install irrigation systems in case rainfall is under 10 inches a year.

### Purpose

*so that, in order that*

So that his arrival would be noticed, the star hired teenagers to mob the airport.

Place bluebird houses facing south in order that the birds can avoid the north wind.

### Condition

*if, unless, once, provided that, whatever, whoever, whichever, whether or not, no matter how (which, what, when, who, where), assuming that*

Please check the color-coded map if you do not know the correct subway line.

No matter how much he eats, he never gains weight.

### Contrast

*although, even though, even if, though, except (that), whereas*

Even though the superhighways have made travel faster, they have also made it less scenic.

The Aztec capital was as large as a European city, although the Indians neither domesticated animals nor used wheels.

### Comparison

*as . . . as, so . . . as, so . . . that, more . . . than, most . . . that, than*

The Royal Canadian Mounted Police are as effective in reality as they are in legend.

The Imperial Hotel in Tokyo was so well built that it survived the destructive 1923 earthquake.

### Place

*where, wherever*

We saw nothing but litter where the fair had been.

The migrant workers went wherever jobs were available.

Manner

*as, as if, as though, just as, just as if*

She walked with her shoulders squared and head erect as though life were her adversary.

The Celtics played as if the championship were at stake.

## ❑ EXERCISE 5

**Combine the following pairs of sentences by making the second one an adverb clause that shows the meaning indicated in the parentheses.**

EXAMPLE: The students at Lincoln High School were in seventh-period classes. The fire alarm went off. (time) → The students at Lincoln High were in seventh-period classes when the fire alarm went off.

1. This state judges criminals insane. They cannot distinguish right from wrong. (condition)
2. Wegener formally proposed the theory of continental drift in 1912. Others had suggested the idea as early as 1629. (contrast)
3. Dante's poetry helped establish the common language of Italy. Chaucer's writings helped establish English. (manner)
4. The Allies kept the plans for the invasion of Normandy a secret. They could deceive the Germans about the true landing site. (purpose)
5. The archer was accurate. Every arrow hit the gold center. (comparison)
6. In the familiar version, Little Red Riding Hood escapes the wolf. In the original version, she does not. (contrast)
7. I used to catch colds every winter. Then I began taking massive doses of vitamin C. (time)
8. Snakes weren't a real worry at the campsite. Snakes are fairly sluggish in the dry season. (cause)

### (2) Adjective clauses

**Adjective clauses** modify nouns and pronouns. These clauses are often called *relative clauses* because they are introduced by relative pronouns *(who/whom/whose, which, that)* or relative adverbs *(when, where, why)*. Unlike a subordinating conjunction, which merely connects an adverb clause to a main clause, a relative introducer functions within an adjective clause as a noun or an adverb. Also, the relative introducer follows and refers to the word or phrase being modified.

> One fifth of the water that runs off the earth's surface is carried by the Amazon.
>
> Afghanistan is a land-locked country whose strategic location has affected its history.
>
> Ellen Terry, who played all of Shakespeare's heroines, was a celebrated actress for almost fifty years.
>
> A tax on tea brought about the Boston Tea Party, which triggered the Revolutionary War.
>
> In Connecticut, November is the month when the wild animals and insects retreat to shelter.

Sometimes an adjective clause appears without a relative introducer. In such cases, the introducer is understood to be *that.*

> The playwright [that] he emulates is Tennessee Williams.
>
> The robots [that] they manufacture are installed in chemical plants.

The adjective clause is sometimes set off with commas and sometimes not, depending on its relationship to the noun it modifies. For a discussion of how to punctuate adjective clauses, see 21c. For a discussion of when to use *who/whom* and *whoever/whomever,* see 14c.

## ❑ EXERCISE 6

**Combine each pair of sentences by converting the second sentence of the pair to an adjective clause.**

EXAMPLE: **Destructive waves are caused by undersea earthquakes or hurricanes. The waves sweep in from the ocean. →Destructive waves that sweep in from the ocean are caused by undersea earthquakes or hurricanes.**

1. **The hotel was designed for the very rich. The very rich can afford unlimited luxuries.**
2. **During a thunderstorm, you should avoid dangerous locations. Dangerous locations are significantly higher than their surroundings.**
3. **The trilogy by Tolkien tells of a ring. The ring's wearer can control the world.**

4. The computer has a graphics index. The graphics index will file and retrieve pictures.
5. Goya's "black paintings" are painted directly on the walls of his house. Goya's "black paintings" depict scenes nightmarish and grotesque.
6. On September 2, 1945, World War II ended. On September 2, 1945, the Japanese signed the "instrument of surrender."
7. A Frisbee is named for the Frisbie Bakery. At the Frisbie Bakery, pie tins resembling the plastic disk were used.
8. Orthodox physicians drove Dr. Mesmer from practice in Vienna. Dr. Mesmer developed hypnotism.

## (3) Noun clauses

**Noun clauses** function in the same ways that all nouns do—as subjects, objects, and complements. These clauses are introduced with a variety of words, most of which begin with *wh-*.

> that, who, whom, whose, which, what
>
> whoever, whomever, whatever, whichever, however
>
> whether, where, when, how, if

### Noun Clauses As Subjects

A noun clause can occur as a subject at the beginning of a sentence, but that position is not very common.

> What parents believe is usually what children reject.
>
> Whatever you decide is acceptable to me.

A more natural position for a noun clause used as a subject is at the end of the sentence. In the following examples, *it* is an expletive and the noun clause is a delayed subject. (See 6d.)

> It is unlikely that a waste-management policy will be adopted this year.
>
> It doesn't matter what you study.

### Noun Clauses As Direct Objects

Noun clauses probably appear most frequently as direct objects after verbs like *say, believe, think, decide, propose, hope,* and *prove*—usually verbs that name some sort of mental activity.

> The scientist calculated that a million black holes exist in our galaxy.
>
> The group proposed that San Francisco ban the building of more skyscrapers downtown.

Sometimes the subordinator *that* is left out, although it is understood by a reader.

Ecologists hope [that] the whooping crane can be saved.

Buddhists believe [that] monks should live a life of poverty.

### Noun Clauses As Objects of Prepositions

When the noun clause appears as the object of a preposition, the clause usually begins with *whether, how, what, whatever, whoever,* or some other interrogative word.

After improving the telephone, Edison turned his attention to how one might permanently record sound.

When he received his "visions," Edgar Cayce was totally unconscious of what went on around him.

### Noun Clauses As Subject Complements

Sometimes, after the verb *be,* noun clauses function as subject complements (predicate nominatives) to rename the subject.

The problem was that Edward the Confessor died without an heir.

The candidate will be whoever can afford to run.

## ❑ EXERCISE 7

**In the following sentences, identify each noun clause and its function.**

1. **What made *The Bridge on the River Kwai* an interesting film was its complex characters with both good and bad traits.**
2. **Scientists believe there may be millions of insects not yet classified.**
3. **It is not clear when the composer will finish the music for the new ballet.**
4. **The new supervisor will be whoever has the best sales record.**
5. **What interested me most was the exhibition on the history of flight.**
6. **A part of the legend of Hercules is that under Hera's jealous influence, Hercules killed his wife and children.**
7. **The British scientists discovered that Piltdown man's skull had the jawbone of a modern ape.**
8. **From the information in the book, we can draw conclusions about what the early settlers thought.**

# 7d Elliptical Clauses

In an **elliptical clause,** one or more words that can be readily understood by the reader are dropped from the complete structure. The most common omissions in elliptical clauses are a relative pronoun *(that* or *whom),* the subject and a form of *be,* or a previously stated verb or predicate.

> Most economists believe [that] the bond market is improving.
>
> Dylan Thomas died at age thirty-nine while [he was] on an American tour.
>
> The Appalachian National Scenic Trail is longer than any other hiking trail in the country [is long].
>
> As a rule, private colleges charge more tuition than public colleges [charge].
>
> Bats of some species roost in colonies of millions; others [roost], in solitude.

## ❑ EXERCISE 8

Identify the elliptical clauses in the following sentences, and supply the missing words in each.

EXAMPLE: I bought the camera while visiting Japan.
I bought the camera while [I was] visiting Japan.

1. Perseus was given a brass shield as bright as a mirror.
2. Fluorescent lights give more light at a lower energy cost than incandescent bulbs with the same wattage.
3. Some stars burn their hydrogen fuel so fast they explode as supernovas.
4. While analyzing the data on the printout, the astronomers discovered the existence of background radiation.
5. Courtney played with seven different baseball leagues; Chiti, with four.

## ❑ EXERCISE 9

In the following sentences, underline the independent clauses once and the dependent clauses twice. Indicate whether the dependent clauses are functioning as nouns, adjectives, or adverbs.

1. The principal river in the United States is the Mississippi, whose chief literary interpreter was Mark Twain.

2. Robots are now being installed in the factory, where they can make almost any manufactured product.
3. They argued over whether they should go to the beach or to the mountains.
4. One study estimated that illiteracy costs the United States approximately $500 billion a year.
5. Woodrow Wilson suffered a stroke just as he was striving to popularize his ideas for a League of Nations.
6. Once people are in a hypnotic trance, they can focus their attention on one thing and ignore distractions.
7. Some abbreviations that are acceptable in technical reports may not be appropriate in formal essays.
8. In order that his son could win bicycle races, Dunlop developed the pneumatic tire.
9. The fight ended as abruptly as it had begun.
10. Although Dracula died with a stake through his heart in the first film, the monster has reappeared in many sequels.
11. *The New Yorker,* which was founded in 1925, was first edited by Harold Ross.
12. It is likely that a raccoon raided the kitchen.

## 7e Kinds of Sentences

Independent clauses appear alone or in combinations—with other independent clauses or with dependent clauses. One method of classifying sentences is based on the number and kinds of clauses in a single construction. According to this classification system, there are four categories of sentences: simple, compound, complex, and compound-complex.

### (1) Simple sentence

A **simple sentence** is made up of only one independent clause. The sentence may contain modifiers and compound elements (for example, compound subjects and verbs); but it may not contain more than one subject-predicate structure.

> Cigarette smoke contains carbon monoxide.
>
> For most college students, computers and calculators have become essential.

The Rhone flows south through France and then empties into the Mediterranean.

## (2) Compound sentence

A **compound sentence** is made up of two or more independent clauses. The primary ways to coordinate independent clauses are with commas and coordinating conjunctions *(and, but, or, for, nor, so, yet)* and with semicolons.

For centuries, Brittany was an independent state, but now the area is part of France.

The restaurant was dark, the air was filled with smoke, and the music was deafening.

Socrates wrote nothing; his thoughts are known only through the works of Plato and Xenophon.

## (3) Complex sentence

A **complex sentence** is made up of one independent clause and one or more dependent clauses—adverb, adjective, or noun.

Although most rifle experts have 20/20 vision, pistol experts are often very nearsighted.

The game involves three contestants who spin a roulette wheel.

Whoever could solve the riddle of the Sphinx would be spared her wrath.

## (4) Compound-complex sentence

A **compound-complex sentence** is made up of two or more independent clauses and one or more dependent clauses.

London's Great Exhibition, which opened in 1851, was designed to show human progress; it brought together in the "Crystal Palace" industrial displays remarkable for their day.

Alchemists believed that they could change lesser metals into gold, and although they failed, they helped establish the science of chemistry.

The fathom once was the distance that a Viking could encompass in a hug; a gauge was the distance that lay between the wheels of a Roman chariot; an acre was an area that could be plowed in one day by a team of two oxen.

## EXERCISE 10

Identify each clause in the following sentences as independent or dependent. Then determine whether each sentence is simple, compound, complex, or compound-complex.

1. Some fishermen locate schools of fish by devices similar to those used for detecting enemy submarines.
2. Plastic machine parts run silently, yet they need little or no oiling.
3. Although the fans booed and threw lemons, Babe Ruth hit one of the longest homers that has ever been recorded
4. We arrived in Germany on June 27, and one of the first things that we did was head for the Mosel to taste wines and eat fresh trout.
5. To prevent piracy, manufacturers of computer programs have spent much time developing systems that have "copy protection."
6. Giddons, who wrote his first novel at age twenty, had made his reputation by age thirty; but he accomplished nothing after he turned forty.

## EXERCISE 11

Combine each of the following sets of sentences to create the kind of sentence indicated. If you have trouble punctuating the combined sentences, see Chapter 21 and Chapter 22.

EXAMPLE: She grew tired of the incessant gossip. She slipped quietly off from the group. (simple) → She grew tired of the incessant gossip and slipped quietly off from the group.

1. The programmers worked for twenty-one hours without a break. They managed to complete the project on time. (complex)
2. Helium appears in natural gas deposits. Helium appears in the atmosphere. (simple)
3. Hieroglyphics sometimes read from left to right. Usually, they read from right to left or top to bottom. (compound)
4. Pterodactyls could fly. They were not birds. They were reptiles. (compound-complex)
5. Speed reading is practical for easy material. Slower reading is more effective for complex, challenging works. (compound)
6. Ms. Bloom reported the missing funds. Ms. Bloom had stolen the money herself. (complex)
7. My great-grandfather was one of ten children. My great-grandmother was one of seven. (compound)
8. John Culhane was an aggressive skater. In one game he met his match. A burly defenseman bumped him to the ice five times. (compound-complex)

## ❑ EXERCISE 12

The prose in the following passages is choppy, and the relationship between ideas is not always clear. Vary the sentence types to include simple, compound, complex, and compound-complex sentences.

1. Readers often have trouble understanding supernatural stories. The action may truly take place. The action may take place only in the narrator's mind. For example, the narrator of Poe's "The Fall of the House of Usher" verges on insanity. Readers do not know the truth about the strange events. The events take place in a gloomy mansion. The events take place in a decayed mansion. In Henry James' "The Jolly Corner," Brydon sees a ghost. Brydon pursues the ghost. Brydon thinks the ghost is physically real. But the reader wonders. Is the ghost real? Is the ghost a symbol of Brydon's inner being?

2. I have always loved Thanksgiving. I love turkey and dressing. I love family dinners. At family dinners, relatives get together. They eat, drink, and laugh. After dinner, they relax. They watch football games. They swap stories. I also love Thanksgiving for another reason. It is not commercialized. For instance, salesclerks don't dress up like Pilgrims. People don't feel obligated to buy presents. Parents aren't frantically looking for the last Pocahontas doll in town. Thanksgiving is the ideal holiday. It brings families together. It doesn't cost much money.

# Review Exercise

1. Match the underlined words in the passage with their grammatical descriptions listed here.

    1. singular common noun
    2. plural common noun
    3. possessive noun
    4. personal pronoun in the subjective case
    5. personal pronoun in the objective case
    6. personal pronoun in the possessive case
    7. relative pronoun
    8. indefinite pronoun
    9. positive adjective
    10. comparative adjective
    11. conjunctive adverb
    12. adverb qualifier
    13. *-ly* adverb
    14. auxiliary verb
    15. modal auxiliary verb
    16. verb in the subjunctive mood
    17. verb in the simple past tense
    18. infinitive
    19. participle used as an adjective
    20. preposition
    21. coordinating conjunction
    22. correlative conjunctions
    23. subordinating conjunction
    24. determiner
    25. expletive

There is an increasing disregard in this country for good manners. This problem is obvious in very glaring ways. For example, drivers display rude and obscene bumper stickers without regard for the sensibilities of other people. Talk-show hosts verbally attack their guests. Parents allow their children not only to misbehave in public but also to ignore rights and property of others. People use parking lots as garbage dumps—tossing away food wrappers, beer cans, and even disposable diapers.

Rudeness is also obvious in the demise of small courtesies. For example, in the past when I stopped to let a motorist out into a moving line of traffic, I always received a wave of thanks. Now, when I stop, motorists simply pull out in front of me with no acknowledgment of my gesture. When I hold a door open for people behind me, they seldom say "thank you" or even give me a nod. Recently, in a large discount store, I was in the checkout line behind a customer who had among his purchases a picture frame with cracked glass. When I called his attention to the damaged frame, he asked the clerk whether he could exchange it. Then after walking all the way across the store and getting another frame, he checked out—never thanking me or even looking at me. Furthermore, the clerk who checked him out acted as if this behavior were normal.

It did not occur to me that the problem might be the result of ignorance until one day in a college classroom. While returning papers, my instructor accidentally bumped a student's desk and said, "Excuse me." The student simply sat and said nothing. My instructor said, "Now, we're going to do this again. I bump into your desk and say, "Excuse me.' You say, "Certainly.'" Then she bumped into the desk again, apologized again, and the flabbergasted student said, "Certainly." The instructor said, "Very good. That's how it works."

That experience suggested to me that perhaps we need a television program to encourage better manners. Actors could demonstrate polite behavior, and then members of the audience could ask questions and make comments—but only if they said "please" and "thank you."

2. Match the underlined phrases and clauses in the passages below with their grammatical descriptions listed here.

1. infinitive phrase
2. gerund phrase
3. participial phrase
4. prepositional phrase
5. independent clause with an intransitive verb
6. independent clause with a transitive verb
7. independent clause with a linking verb
8. dependent adverb clause
9. dependent adjective clause
10. dependent noun clause

11. elliptical clause
12. compound sentence
13. complex sentence
14. compound-complex sentence

Advertising constantly bombards us with the message that pain is unnatural, and, as a result, we immediately tackle any ache with some kind of painkiller. Unfortunately, painkillers can be very dangerous. By deadening pain, they can conceal illness; thus, they may allow a serious problem to go undetected.

Actually, most pain is very normal; it results from everyday living—for example, from tension, lack of sleep and exercise, tight clothes, fatigue, and poor diet. Thus, we can relieve most of our pain with simple common sense. For instance, if the headache sufferer lies down and relaxes, the headache will usually go away, without pills that irritate the stomach's lining. A stuffy nose can often be relieved by a hot shower instead of an antihistamine, and the sufferer will be not only less groggy but also cleaner. Feet aching from a long day of abuse will feel better after a soak in warm water. The stomach is a very sensitive organ, which vibrates to surrounding noises, such as loud, pulsating music. A stomach problem, therefore, frequently responds favorably to a good dose of silence. Backaches are often the result of poor posture or strain. Thus, someone with recurring back pain may need to stand and sit up straighter—or at the very least stop lying face down to work algebra problems and watch television at the same time.

When these common-sense remedies work, we save ourselves money as well as wear and tear on the body. When they do not work, the pain continues. Then we know that it is time to see a doctor. Therefore, we really should not fear pain so intensely. In fact, when acting as an alarm system, pain is a very good friend.

# PART II

# Structural and Grammatical Problems

When you write, you must concentrate on matters such as content, organization, purpose, and audience. Naturally, incorrect constructions are likely to appear in early drafts of a composition. Therefore, before you complete a final draft, you must read your work carefully and revise any sentences that contain structural or grammatical problems. Careful revision will help ensure clear and logical prose.

# 8

# Sentence Fragments

A **sentence fragment** is an incomplete structure punctuated as a complete sentence but lacking the necessary independent clause. The following passage shows how confusing sentence fragments can be.

> Humans accept death as their certain destiny. In nature, however, everything does not die. The hydra, a freshwater, tube-shaped creature. The hydra's body cells regenerate every two weeks. Giving it an unlimited life expectancy. Except for predators and diseases, some fish might never die. Because they never stop growing. In a sense, the amoeba doesn't die. It simply divides. And thus not only survives but also multiplies.

The six complete sentences in the passage express complete thoughts, even out of context.

> Humans accept death as their certain destiny.
>
> In nature, however, everything does not die.
>
> The hydra's body cells regenerate every two weeks.
>
> Except for predators and disease, some fish might never die.
>
> In a sense, the amoeba doesn't die.
>
> It simply divides.

In contrast, the four fragments seem meaningless.

> The hydra, a freshwater, tube-shaped creature.
>
> And thus not only survives but also multiplies.

Giving it an unlimited life expectancy.

Because they never stop growing.

In a few special instances, fragments do not handicap communication.

- Dialogue: "Now," thought William. "Now."
- Deliberate stylistic effects: The play catches everyone and everything in its swirl. Rather like a tornado.
- Questions and answers: When? Only ten years from now.
- Interjections: Oh! Well.
- Advertising: The best hardware for your best software.
- Idioms: The sooner the better. So much for that.

As a general rule, however, you should avoid fragments. If you do find a fragment while revising your prose, you can either attach it to a complete sentence or convert it to a complete sentence.

## 8a Dependent Clause Fragments

A dependent clause contains a subject and a predicate and begins with a subordinating word such as *since, if, because, although, who, which, that* (see 7c). When punctuated as a complete sentence, a dependent clause is considered a fragment.

FRAGMENT: Registration was a nightmare. Although I did get the courses I wanted.

REVISED: Registration was a nightmare, although I did get the courses I wanted.

REVISED: Registration was a nightmare. I did, however, get the courses I wanted.

FRAGMENT: At age twenty-six, Jefferson began Monticello. Which he did not complete until he was sixty-eight.

REVISED: At age twenty-six, Jefferson began Monticello, which he did not complete until he was sixty-eight.

REVISED: At age twenty-six, Jefferson began Monticello, but he did not finish it until he was sixty-eight.

### ❑ EXERCISE 1

**Rewrite to eliminate the fragment in each group of words.**

1. Mel Tillis, the country music star, has no trouble singing. Although he stutters when he speaks.
2. While arthritis rarely threatens life. It can be a frustrating, painful experience.
3. As we were strolling casually along a tree-lined boulevard. We were approached by a man begging for money.
4. The company was plagued with both personnel and equipment problems. Which finally resulted in bankruptcy.
5. Noise places strain on the mind. Because it interferes with speech and hearing.

## 8b Phrase Fragments

A phrase is a construction without a subject and a predicate. Ordinarily, a phrase should not appear alone, punctuated as though it were a complete sentence.

FRAGMENT: Manufacturers will hold a trade fair in St. Louis next month. The fair to promote new sports equipment.

REVISED: Manufacturers will hold a trade fair in St. Louis next month to promote new sports equipment.

REVISED: Manufacturers will hold a trade fair in St. Louis next month. The event will promote new sports equipment.

FRAGMENT: The department's bloodhound has trailed 165 missing people. And has found 85 percent of them.

REVISED: The department's bloodhound has trailed 165 missing people and has found 85 percent of them.

REVISED: The department's bloodhound has trailed 165 missing people; she has found 85 percent of them.

FRAGMENT: Spider-Man's strength and climbing ability came from a remarkable source. The bite of a radioactive spider.

REVISED: Spider-Man's strength and climbing ability came from a remarkable source: the bite of a radioactive spider.

REVISED: Spider-Man's strength and climbing ability came from a remarkable source. He was bitten by a radioactive spider.

FRAGMENT: I quit smoking last Christmas. Because of a chronic cough.

REVISED: I quit smoking last Christmas because of a chronic cough.

REVISED: I quit smoking last Christmas. At that time, my cough had become chronic.

## ❑ EXERCISE 2

Revise the structures to eliminate fragments.

1. He lost a million dollars in just a few months. His cocaine habit ruining his financial judgment.
2. The car is a network of computer controls. Controls for improving performance and maintenance.
3. They bought color-coordinated exercise suits. With the intention of getting into shape.
4. Our agency has promoted the development of synthetic fuels. Fuels to eliminate a dependence on oil.
5. The slogan is often worn on a button. Or displayed on a bumper sticker.
6. The professor was trying to explain computer speeds. Speeds such as milliseconds, microseconds, and nanoseconds.
7. Pedestrians had to dash through the spray of the lawn sprinkler. Or walk around it, out into the road.
8. I swung at the third pitch. Grazing the ball as it hurtled past.
9. Athletes should drink water frequently. Before, during, and after sports activities.
10. The record for completed passes was held by Rupert Gonzales. The first college quarterback to be drafted this year.

## ❑ EXERCISE 3

Revise the following passage to eliminate fragments.

The bicycle has been used in wars since 1870, but rarely by the United States. The French first trying bicycles for scouting expeditions in the Franco-Prussian War. In 1875 when Italians tried maneuvers on bicycles. Because of the pneumatic tire, reduced weight, and the ability to be folded up. By World War I, European troops used bikes extensively on the front lines. When World War II broke out, soldiers on bicycles frequently seen in Europe and Asia. Yet American troops traveled by ships, planes, trucks, and trains. In Europe, soldiers used bicycles to destroy railroads and bridges behind German lines. And to move supplies when the motors of trucks and jeeps broke down. Bicycles, which helped the Japanese move through thick jungles to take over Malaya and Singapore. During the Vietnam War, the Viet Cong used bicycles to carry supplies. Because bicycles made little noise and seldom broke down. Perhaps American troops with their dependence on modern technology overlooked an effective vehicle—the bicycle.

cs/fs
9a

# 9 Comma Splices and Fused Sentences

Two independent clauses joined with only a comma create a **comma splice,** so called because the clauses are "spliced" together. Two clauses run together without a conjunction or proper punctuation create a **fused sentence,** also called a run-on or run-together sentence.

COMMA SPLICE: Pickpockets have become a serious problem, tourists should be especially alert in crowded areas.

FUSED SENTENCE: Pickpockets have become a serious problem tourists should be especially alert in crowded areas.

Neither of these constructions is acceptable in standard written English. If you find a comma splice or a fused sentence in your rough drafts, you can revise it in one of five ways.

- Use a comma and a coordinating conjunction.
- Use a semicolon.
- Use a colon.
- Create two sentences.
- Create a dependent structure.

## 9a Revision with a Comma and a Coordinating Conjunction

Comma splices and fused sentences can often be revised by connecting the clauses with both a comma and a coordinating conjunction (*and, but, or, nor, for, so, yet*). This option works well when the sentence does not contain much internal punctuation and one of the conjunctions expresses the proper relationship between the two clauses.

COMMA SPLICE: Winter lasts six months in Wyoming, life gets hard at 20 to 40 degrees below zero.

FUSED SENTENCE: Winter lasts six months in Wyoming life gets hard at 20 to 40 degrees below zero.

REVISED: Winter lasts six months in Wyoming, and life gets hard at 20 to 40 degrees below zero.

COMMA SPLICE: My dormitory room is supposed to house two people comfortably, actually it has only enough space for a six-year-old child.

FUSED SENTENCE: My dormitory room is supposed to house two people comfortably actually it has only enough space for a six-year-old child.

REVISED: My dormitory room is supposed to house two people comfortably, but actually it has only enough space for a six-year-old child.

## 9b Revision with a Semicolon

A semicolon works well when the clauses in a comma splice or fused sentence do not have a relationship easily expressed by one of the coordinating conjunctions.

COMMA SPLICE: The novel is remarkable, Mr. Wright has written over 50,000 words without once using the letter *e*.

FUSED SENTENCE: The novel is remarkable Mr. Wright has written over 50,000 words without once using the letter *e*.

REVISED: The novel is remarkable; Mr. Wright has written over 50,000 words without once using the letter *e*.

The semicolon can also be used in addition to a coordinating conjunction when the first clause has internal punctuation.

COMMA SPLICE: Standing on the pier, her blond hair blowing in the breeze, she looked frail, innocent, and vulnerable, she was actually planning a robbery.

REVISED: Standing on the pier, her blond hair blowing in the breeze, she looked frail, innocent, and vulnerable; yet she was actually planning a robbery.

The semicolon is especially appropriate when the second independent clause begins with a transitional expression (or conjunctive adverb) such as *therefore, consequently, finally, for example, nevertheless, however, then*. (For a more complete list of these expressions, see the chart of transitional expressions on page 412.)

Be careful not to confuse coordinating conjunctions and transitional expressions. A conjunction actually links clauses grammatically and cannot move from its position between the two.

POSSIBLE: They discovered that the library ceiling contained asbestos, but the school could not afford to have the material removed.

IMPOSSIBLE: They discovered that the library ceiling contained asbestos; the school could not, but, afford to have the material removed.

A transitional expression, on the other hand, is not a conjunction but an adverb and can move about in its clause.

POSSIBLE: They discovered that the library ceiling contained asbestos; however, the school could not afford to have the material removed.

POSSIBLE: They discovered that the library ceiling contained asbestos; the school could not, however, afford to have the material removed.

An easy way to distinguish between the two types of words is to remember that all the coordinating conjunctions have only two or three letters, whereas all the transitional expressions have four or more.

## 9c Revision with a Colon

Occasionally, one independent clause is followed by another that explains or amplifies it. In this very special case, you can join the two clauses with a colon.

COMMA SPLICE: The economics of the country caused the 1848 revolution, harvests and commerce were at a low.

REVISED: The economics of the country caused the 1848 revolution: harvests and commerce were at a low.

## 9d Revision by Creating Two Sentences

You can effectively revise many comma splices and fused sentences by creating two separate sentences—particularly when you want a major break between the clauses. This revision is especially useful when the two clauses are long or when you want to emphasize each clause.

COMMA SPLICE: Unlike most of my friends, I cannot abide watching those silly, mindless situation comedies, for one thing, I resent having the laugh track tell me when to be entertained.

REVISED: Unlike most of my friends, I cannot abide watching those silly, mindless situation comedies. For one thing, I resent having the laugh track tell me when to be entertained.

## 9e Revision with a Dependent Clause or Phrase

Often you can correct a comma splice or fused sentence by changing one of the independent clauses to a dependent clause or phrase. This correction is a good solution when you want to indicate a special relationship—a relationship such as time, place, condition/result, cause/effect, contrast, and so forth.

FUSED SENTENCE: Sometimes I craved fried foods floating in grease then I ate in the school cafeteria.

REVISED WITH A DEPENDENT CLAUSE: When I craved fried foods floating in grease, I ate in the school cafeteria.

REVISED WITH A PHRASE: Craving fried foods floating in grease, I ate in the school cafeteria.

This correction also works well when the two independent clauses have a noun or noun phrase in common.

COMMA SPLICE: We desperately need zoning laws, the construction of unsightly commercial buildings could be prevented by zoning laws.

REVISED WITH A DEPENDENT CLAUSE: We desperately need zoning laws, which could prevent the construction of unsightly commercial buildings.

REVISED WITH A PHRASE: We desperately need zoning laws to prevent the construction of unsightly commercial buildings.

## ❑ EXERCISE 1

Revise each comma splice or fused sentence by using the option indicated in brackets.

1. A weekend guest should send a house gift to the hosts it should be neither expensive nor comic. [comma and coordinate conjunction]
2. Columbus mistook a group of manatees for mermaids, in fact, a blubbery manatee looks like Grover Cleveland with a moustache. [semicolon]
3. What the people want is clear, they want maximum government services and minimum taxes. [colon]
4. The pizza parlor refused to take our order, we had requested a pizza with one-third pepperoni, one-fourth ground beef, and five-twelfths ham. [dependent clause]
5. Struggling with the English language, he was frustrated by the pronunciation of *though, bough,* and *through,* no logic seemed to help. [two sentences]

## ❑ EXERCISE 2

Revise each comma splice and fused sentence by one of the options described in 9a through 9e. Choose an option that produces an effective sentence.

1. Sweat is extremely important, it is the primary way the body cools itself.
2. In Paris, the first week of fashion shows is "closed," admittance is limited to professional buyers, the invited press, and privileged clients.
3. Bibliographies are arranged topically, chronologically, or alphabetically, however, the alphabetical arrangement is the most common.
4. My friend has little time to study the stock market consequently, he has invested in a mutual fund.

5. Compulsive gambling is a psychiatric disorder, few treatment centers exist.
6. Sometimes the operations manuals are too technical for students, then the lab assistants must interpret the instructions.
7. Some areas of Texas got two inches of rain, most of the state got only a trace.
8. Fiercely competing for audiences, the soap operas are shooting on location in exotic settings, in addition, the shows are featuring unrealistic plots involving international crime, natural disasters, and travel in outer space.



## ❑ EXERCISE 3

Revise the following passages to eliminate comma splices and fused sentences.

1. In Paris, travel by taxi is easy. Taxis are plentiful, there are numerous stands. You can go to the "Tête de Station," obviously, you should take the first taxi in line. Some private cars serve as taxis, however, before taking them, you should settle the price. The easiest way to get a taxi is through your hotel concierge or porter whoever summons the taxi should get a one franc tip.

2. Studying for most objective tests is very different from studying for essay tests. Objective tests usually require only a knowledge of facts, however, essay tests also require the ability to interpret.

To study for objective tests, I put each fact to be learned on a 3 × 5 card then I arrange the cards in logical order. When I learn a fact, I put that card into a separate stack. Gradually, the "learned stack" becomes larger and larger, finally, it contains all the cards, and I am ready for my test.

My method for essay tests is very different. I go through my textbook taking notes, then I combine them with my class notes. From this composite set of notes, I make an outline. Next, I try to predict possible test questions and group appropriate headings from my outline under the questions, therefore, I am able to assemble information into meaningful units. Also, I can practice analyzing the information I must use on the test.

In short, studying for an objective test is like getting ready for a trivia match, however, studying for an essay test is like preparing for a debate.

s/v agr 10

# 10

# Subject-Verb Agreement

Standard English requires **subject-verb agreement**—that is, a verb form appropriate for the subject. In general, agreement depends on three factors: person, number, and tense.

- *Person* refers to whether the subject is speaking, spoken to, or spoken about.

| | |
|---|---|
| First Person: | The subject is *I* or *we.* |
| Second Person: | The subject is *you.* |
| Third Person: | The subject is any noun or pronoun except *I, we*, or *you.* |

- *Number* refers to singular (one) and plural (more than one).
- *Tense* is the verb feature that indicates time. (See 4c.) All verbs require agreement in the third person of the present tense and the present perfect tense. Notice the *–s* form of the verb (4a) appears in the singular of these tenses but not in the plural.

**Present Tense**

| Person | Singular | Plural |
|---|---|---|
| First: | I upset him. | We upset him. |
| Second: | You upset him. | You upset him. |
| Third: | Anything upsets him. | All things upset him. |

**Present Perfect Tense**

| Person | Singular | Plural |
|---|---|---|
| First: | I have upset him. | We have upset him. |
| Second: | You have upset him. | You have upset him. |
| Third: | Something has upset him. | Several things have upset him. |

The verb *be* requires agreement in more instances than other verbs. Notice in the following examples that the singular and plural forms differ in the first and third persons of the present tense, in the first and third persons of the past tense, and in the third person of the present perfect tense.

**Present Tense**

| PERSON | SINGULAR | PLURAL |
|---|---|---|
| FIRST: | I am a student. | We are students. |
| SECOND: | You are a student. | You are students. |
| THIRD: | She is a student. | They are students. |

**Past Tense**

| PERSON | SINGULAR | PLURAL |
|---|---|---|
| FIRST: | I was a student. | We were students. |
| SECOND: | You were a student. | You were students. |
| THIRD: | Amy was a student. | Amy and Jake were students. |

**Present Perfect Tense**

| PERSON | SINGULAR | PLURAL |
|---|---|---|
| FIRST: | I have been a student. | We have been students. |
| SECOND: | You have been a student. | You have been students. |
| THIRD: | The professor has been a student. | Professors have been students. |

When the subject of a sentence is simple and appears next to its verb, subject-verb agreement usually presents no problems. But some subjects are tricky. As you edit your writing, watch for constructions such as the following that can cause agreement problems.

## 10a Intervening Words between Subject and Verb

Often the subject of a sentence is followed by a phrase or clause that contains a noun. Be sure that the verb agrees with the true subject and not with a noun that follows the subject.

> Emission that pours from the smoke stacks has polluted the area.
>
> The instructions outlined in the manual were not clear.
>
> A collection of glass animals was arranged on the table.
>
> The development of new techniques leads to increasingly accurate test results.

## 10b Subjects Joined by *And*

In general, when a sentence has two or more subjects joined by *and,* use a plural verb.

The governor and the attorney general drive limousines.

Sun and wind cause skin burn.

McDonald's, Wendy's, and Burger King have been waging commercial warfare.

CAUTION: This convention does not apply to subjects joined by phrases such as *as well as, together with, in addition to.*

The governor, as well as the attorney general, drives a limousine.

Hot sun, together with strong wind, causes severe skin burn.

McDonald's, in addition to Wendy's and Burger King, has been waging commercial warfare.

EXCEPTIONS: Use a singular verb in two instances.

- When *each* or *every* precedes subjects joined by *and*

  Each governor and each attorney general was assigned a limousine.

  Every hamburger chain and every fried chicken franchise has been engaged in commercial warfare.

- When the subjects joined by *and* refer to a single person, thing, or idea

  Red beans and rice is a popular Cajun dish.

  My best friend and confidant has betrayed me.

## 10c Subjects Joined by *Or/Nor*

When the subjects of a sentence are joined by *or* or *nor* (or *either . . . or, neither . . . nor*), make the verb agree with the subject closer to it. If the closer subject is singular, the verb is singular; if the closer subject is plural, the verb is plural.

Neither the boxwood nor the roses have survived the ice storm.

Neither the roses nor the boxwood has survived the ice storm.

CAUTION: This practice can cause awkward constructions, particularly with the verb *be* when the subjects are in different persons: *Either Steve or I am in charge.* Although this sentence is technically correct, you may want to avoid awkwardness by using two clauses instead of one: *Either Steve is in charge, or I am.*

### ❑ EXERCISE 1

**Choose the correct verb for each sentence, making sure that it agrees with its subject. The problems involve compound subjects and words intervening between subjects and verbs.**

1. Either the bonds or the real estate (is/are) sufficient collateral for the loan.
2. An assortment of diamonds, emeralds, and sapphires (gleams/gleam) from the pendant.
3. Her coach and mentor (was/were) the only person she consulted.
4. On a tool bit, the clearance and relief angles, which are ground on the bit, (determines/determine) the quality of the work.
5. France, along with Germany and Italy, (produces/produce) most European wines.
6. The second major section of the balance sheet, the liabilities, (lists/list) the debts that the company must pay.
7. Organization and planning (is/are) the key requirements for a successful recording session.
8. Clouds of red clay dust (has/have) settled on the fields.
9. The students or the professor (has/have) confused the examination date.
10. My roommate, together with three friends, (is/are) giving me a birthday dinner.

## 10d Indefinite Pronouns As Subjects

Singular verbs are required with most indefinite pronouns used as subjects.

| | | |
|---|---|---|
| another | everybody | nothing |
| anybody | everyone | one |
| anyone | everything | other |
| anything | neither | somebody |
| each | nobody | someone |
| either | no one | something |

s/v agr 10d

Neither is acceptable.

Each was published in 1989.

Everyone comments on the vivid colors.

When phrases and clauses follow these indefinite pronouns, be careful not to mistake an intervening noun for the subject of the verb.

Neither of these essays is acceptable.

Each of the studies was published in 1989.

Everyone who sees the paintings comments on the vivid colors.

Some indefinite pronouns can be singular or plural.

| all | more | none |
|---|---|---|
| any | most | some |

If the indefinite pronoun refers to a noncountable noun *(confusion, laughter, art),* use a singular verb. If the indefinite pronoun refers to a plural, countable noun *(residents, pages, machines),* use a plural verb.

| | |
|---|---|
| NONCOUNT/SINGULAR: | Most of the confusion was over. |
| COUNT/PLURAL: | Most of the residents were elderly. |
| NONCOUNT/SINGULAR: | Some of the laughter was dying. |
| COUNT/PLURAL: | Some of the pages were missing. |

Some writers always use a singular verb with *none,* even when it refers to a plural, countable noun.

None of the players was fined.

Nevertheless, most contemporary writers prefer a plural verb when the reference is plural.

None of the players were fined.

Plural verbs are required with a few indefinite pronouns.

| both | few | several |
|---|---|---|
| many | others | |

Both have graduated with honors.

Many claim to have seen UFOs.

## 10e Relative Pronouns As Subjects



When a relative pronoun *(that, which, who)* is the subject of a clause, make the verb agree with the pronoun's antecedent—the word or phrase that the pronoun stands for.

> The Phantom is powered by engines that deliver 17,900 pounds of thrust. [engines deliver]
>
> Her celebrated collection of photographs, which documents Christmas in rural America, is on display during December. [collection documents]

When the relative pronoun is preceded by *one of those* . . . or *one of the* . . . make the verb plural.

> He is one of those students who always study early. [students study]

When the relative pronoun is preceded by *the only one of*. . . , make the verb singular.

> He is the only one of the students who always studies early. [one studies]

### ☐ EXERCISE 2

**Choose the correct verb for each sentence, making sure it agrees with its subject—an indefinite or a relative pronoun.**

1. Neither of the labor leaders (was/were) willing to negotiate further.
2. Winston Brown is one of those journalists who (satirizes/satirize) politics.
3. None of the instruction manuals fully (explains/explain) the procedure.
4. Each of the techniques reviewed in this report (requires/require) further research.
5. Pair ice-skating is the only one of the Olympic events that (suggests/suggest) romantic love.

## 10f Subjects of Linking Verbs

Very often a linking verb connects a singular subject with a plural complement or a plural subject with a singular complement. (See

7a.3.) Regardless of the number of the complement, the verb agrees with its subject.

My chief entertainment was the old movies on television.

The old movies on television were my chief entertainment.

## 10g Subjects That Follow Verbs

Verbs agree with their subjects even when normal sentence order is inverted and the subjects are delayed.

There are three reasons for the mistake.

There is a good reason for the mistake.

Covering the wall were dozens of ancestral portraits.

Covering the wall was a medieval tapestry.

### ❑ EXERCISE 3

**Choose the correct verb for each sentence, making sure it agrees with its subject. The problems involve linking verbs and subjects that follow verbs.**

1. The main expense (was/were) supplies, such as balsam, droppers, and Bunsen burners.
2. In the 1940s, all along the highway (was/were) sequences of Burma-Shave signs.
3. There (has/have) been six accidents at this intersection in three months.
4. My parents' main concern (is/are) my grades.
5. Hanging in her closet (was/were) three fur-lined coats.

## 10h Collective Nouns and Amounts As Subjects

A collective noun refers to a group that forms some sort of unit, for example, *team, class, audience, enemy, orchestra, panel, crew, family, club.* When these nouns refer to the group as a whole, use a singular verb; when they refer to the individual members of the group, use a plural verb.

Parliament sits in majestic houses along the Thames. [*Parliament* refers to the governing body as a unit.]

Parliament disagree on the tax issue. [*Parliament* refers to the individuals within the group since a unit cannot disagree with itself.]

The team is on the court. [*Team* refers to the group as a unit.]

The team are taking their practice shots. [*Team* refers to the individuals within the group since each team member must take practice shots by himself or herself.]

A plural verb with a collective noun (*team are*) sounds peculiar to most people and is therefore uncommon. Instead, writers usually prefer to pair a plural verb with a subject that is obviously plural.

The members of Parliament disagree on the tax issue.

The players are taking their practice shots.

When the subject refers to a unit amount, a kind of lump sum, use a singular verb. When the subject refers to several units, use a plural verb.

Four days seems a reasonable time.

Four days were marked off on the calendar.

With some amounts, either a singular or a plural verb is appropriate.

Three truckloads of gravel was (or were) needed to fill the hole.

When the word *number* is the subject and is preceded by *the,* use a singular verb. When *number* is preceded by *a,* use a plural verb.

The number of students taking workshops has increased.

A number of students have signed up for the workshop.

## ❑ EXERCISE 4

**Choose the correct verb for each sentence, making sure the verb agrees with its subject—a collective noun or an amount.**

1. The jury (disagrees/disagree) with public opinion.
2. The number of accidents (has/have) decreased since the new drunk-driving laws have been in effect.
3. Nine weeks (is/are) a sufficient time to complete the exit ramps.
4. The crew (is/are) wearing their new uniforms.
5. Six tons of crushed shells (was/were) used in the project to prevent erosion.

## 10i Titles As Subjects

Titles are considered singular, regardless of whether the words in them are singular or plural.

> *African Kingdoms* is assigned reading.
>
> *Gulliver's Travels* satirizes human nature.

## 10j Foreign Nouns As Subjects

Some nouns borrowed from foreign languages have retained their foreign plurals and do not "look" plural to an English speaker. If you are not sure about the number of a foreign noun, consult an up-to-date, standard dictionary. There you will find, for example, that *genera* is the plural form of *genus; alumni,* the plural of *alumnus;* and *media,* the plural of *medium.*

*Data* is probably the most commonly used of these foreign nouns because it occurs frequently in technical literature. Traditionally, *datum* is the singular form and *data* is the plural.

> The data were gathered over a six-month period.

Increasingly, however, *data* is treated as a noncountable noun (such as *information*) and is used with a singular verb.

> The data was gathered over a period of six months.

## 10k Subjects Ending in *-ics*

A number of words in English end in *-ics: linguistics, physics, mathematics, economics, ceramics, statistics, ballistics, athletics, aerobics, gymnastics, calisthenics, acoustics, politics, ethics,* and so on. When referring to a body of knowledge or a field of study, a noun ending in *-ics* requires a singular verb. When referring to activities or characteristics, the same noun requires a plural verb.

> Politics is one of the major industries in this country.
>
> His politics make me nervous.

> Calisthenics is required in the qualification trials.
>
> Calisthenics are simple gymnastic exercises.

# 10 l "Words" As Subjects



A word cited as the word itself is marked in one of two ways: either enclosed in quotation marks or underlined (counterpart of italic type). Whether singular or plural, the word cited requires a singular verb.

> "Fiddlesticks" was my grandmother's favorite expression.
>
> In law, *person* means either a human being or an organization with legal rights.
>
> *People* is a plural noun.

## ❑ EXERCISE 5

**Choose the correct verb for each sentence, making sure it agrees with its subject—a title, a proper name, a foreign noun, a noun ending in *-ics,* or a word used as a word.**

1. *Six Years with Cecil* (is/are) a new novel by Sarah Hughes.
2. "Politics (make/makes) strange bedfellows."
3. Sometimes, the media (seem/seems) to revel in tragedy.
4. The acoustics in the new auditorium (is/are) not good.
5. *Cattle* (has/have) no singular form.
6. Ballistics, which (is/are) the study of projectiles, has become a highly intricate discipline.
7. The bases of the argument (seems/seem) to be rather petty.
8. Niagara Falls (is/are) a breathtaking sight.
9. When I was a child, "The Three Little Pigs" (was/were) my favorite story.
10. In most of the junk mail I receive, "free gifts" (appears/appear) at least ten times.

## ❑ EXERCISE 6

**Correct any errors in subject-verb agreement in the following passage.**

The only one of life's rules that have no exceptions is this: the other lane or line always move faster than the one you are in. Let's take, for example, my drive into town every morning. There are studies in "lane theory" that suggests that the left lane is preferable because people usually keep right. When I leave my house in the mornings, I pull into the closer lane: the left. For a few minutes I cruise along at a rapid pace. Suddenly in front of my car is about fifty drivers moving at 20 miles per hour. At this point cars in the right lane begins zipping past me like jackrabbits. I move quickly into the right lane, which slow immediately to a near halt. And so on it goes until I arrive at my destination, exhausted and frustrated.

Or take my weekly visit to the grocery store. After I've collected my groceries, I start evaluating the check-out lines. There is three things I consider: Does the check-out person move fast? How full is the baskets of the customers? How many people are in the line? Then I make a choice. Sometimes all the factors is in my favor: the person at the register is hustling, and three people with only a few purchases are ahead of me. But does my deliberations pay off? No. The first person in line has an item that is not priced, so someone working in the store walk down eight aisles, find the item price, and return to report. The second of the three customers want to write a check for $3.20 on a bank in another country, and the manager must be called to stare at the check and the customer for five minutes. The third customer has a large envelope full of coupons to sort through. As it turns out, six people with seventy-five dollars worth of groceries apiece gets through the line next to me while I have been standing in mine.

And let's take banks. At the drive-in window, I always get behind one of those people who is doing the daily deposits of businesses. Inside the bank, I get behind a crowd who is obtaining travelers' checks, wrapping coins into paper cylinders, or wiring money to Canada.

Since I cannot escape my fate, I am going to change my habits. I will leave home in the morning a half hour early and put books in my purse to read while standing in lines.

# 11

# Nonstandard Verb Forms



**Nonstandard verb forms** occur most commonly for three reasons.

1. Because a writer does not know the correct principal parts of irregular verbs and thus writes a verb such as *had went* for *had gone*
2. Because a writer transfers the sounds of speech to writing and drops a letter, producing a verb such as *use to* for *used to*
3. Because a writer confuses a verb with a word that closely resembles it, using *loose,* for example, instead of *lose*

The wrong verb form may not always obscure meaning. If you make the errors just described, a reader will possibly understand what you mean but will judge you uneducated—or at the very least, careless. Therefore, when revising your prose, make sure you have used verbs and their forms correctly.

## 11a Nonstandard Principal Parts

The principal parts of verbs include three forms—the base, or infinitive form; the past tense form; and the past participle. (See 4a.) Ordinarily, problems do not arise with regular verbs because the past form and the past participle are identical *(cure, cured, cured; look, looked, looked).* Irregular verbs, however, have unpredictable forms for the past tense and the past participle *(do, did, done; break, broke, broken).* Furthermore, the forms have different uses. The past form expresses a past occurrence and is used alone—without auxiliaries. The past participle is used after forms of *have* to express the perfect tenses and after forms of *be* to express the passive voice.

PAST: The axle broke for the third time.
PRESENT PERFECT: The axle has broken for the third time.
PASSIVE VOICE: The axle was broken by the impact.

The wrong form of an irregular verb is considered nonstandard English. If you are ever unsure of the principal parts of a verb, check the forms in a dictionary or in the Glossary of Terms under the heading *irregular verbs*.

NONSTANDARD: The letter come yesterday.
STANDARD: The letter came yesterday.
NONSTANDARD: The child busted the balloon.
STANDARD: The child burst the balloon.
NONSTANDARD: Someone had stole my tennis racquet.
STANDARD: Someone had stolen my tennis racquet.

### ❑ EXERCISE 1

**Correct any errors in the forms of verbs.**

1. **The man had dove off the bridge before he could be stopped.**
2. **The committee give the award to an Egyptian writer.**
3. **The earthquakes have shook the hotel on five different occasions.**
4. **We seen the movie that was nominated for an Academy Award.**
5. **Their boat is sank a mile from shore.**
6. **All the silver and jewelry had been took in the robbery.**
7. **The whole turkey was ate at dinner.**
8. **Have you chose your tennis partner?**

## 11b Dropped *-s/-es* and *-d/-ed* Verb Endings

Two important verb endings are *-s/-es* and *-d/-ed*. The *-s/-es* occurs with all verbs in the present tense singular, except those whose subjects are *I, we,* and *you*. The *-d/-ed* occurs with regular verbs to form the past tense and past participle. In conversation, speakers sometimes drop these endings, producing verb forms such as the ones in the following sentences.

| | |
|---|---|
| *-s* DROPPED: | He exist on potato chips and sodas. |
| *-d* DROPPED: | We use to go to New Orleans every year. |
| *-ed* DROPPED: | They box the equipment yesterday. |

In writing, however, you must retain the *-s*/*-es* and *-d*/*-ed*, regardless of whether you would pronounce them. Dropping these important endings will result in nonstandard verb forms:

NONSTANDARD: That reporter always ask personal questions.
STANDARD: That reporter always asks personal questions.

NONSTANDARD: The players are suppose to practice every day.
STANDARD: The players are supposed to practice every day.

NONSTANDARD: You cannot successfully reheat bake potatoes.
STANDARD: You cannot successfully reheat baked potatoes.

## ❑ EXERCISE 2

**In the following passage, add *-s/-es* and *-d/-ed* endings on verbs and verb forms where necessary.**

**I have a friend who insist that she never sleeps over three hours a night and thinks she is suppose to sleep about eight hours. Since I use to have the same problem, I suggested a few steps she might take before she waste money on a sleep-therapy course that cost $300.**

**First, anyone rest better when completely relax. Therefore, an insomniac should stop worrying about sleep because worry increase tension. Second, if a sleepless person resist eating spicy foods (such as barbecue potato chips and pizza), sleep will be more peaceful. Also, going to bed at a fix time helps develop a rhythm and makes it easier to fall asleep. In case everything else fail, there are always sheep to count.**

# 11c Verbs Confused with Similar Words

Writers sometimes confuse verbs with words that are similar in spelling, pronunciation, or meaning—for example, *affect/effect, lie/lay, imply/infer.* Regardless of the source of confusion, you can solve the problem by looking up a troublesome verb in a dictionary. There you will find the principal parts, the meaning, and sometimes notes on usage. Furthermore, the following pairs of words are discussed in the "Glossary of Usage."

| | |
|---|---|
| accept, except | ensure, insure |
| advice, advise | hanged, hung |
| affect, effect | imply, infer |
| aggravate, irritate | lay, lie |
| bring, take | lend, loan |
| burst, bust | lose, loose |
| censor, censure | orient, orientate |
| complement, compliment | precede, proceed |
| comprise, compose | prosecute, persecute |
| convince, persuade | raise, rise |
| device, devise | set, sit |
| emigrate, immigrate | use, utilize |

## ❑ EXERCISE 3

Look up the following pairs of words in the "Glossary of Usage" at the end of this textbook. For each word, write a sentence that illustrates its meaning.

1. advise/advice
2. censor/censure
3. device/devise
4. ensure/insure
5. lie/lay
6. sit/set

## ❑ EXERCISE 4

Choose the correct word for each sentence.

1. The Vietnam War had a profound (affect/effect) on the generation of the 1960s.
2. The weak connection caused the transmitter to (lose/loose) power.
3. The "Delta" refers to the region that (lays/lies) between the Mississippi and the Yazoo rivers.
4. (Lie/Lay) this quilt across the foot of the bed.
5. By her facial expression, she (implied/inferred) more than she actually said.

## ❑ EXERCISE 5

In the following passage, insert the correct past and past participle forms of the verbs called for. Pay particular attention to irregular verbs and verbs easily confused with other words. Also, be sure to retain the *-d/-ed* ending on verbs like *used (to)*.

Last Saturday, a crowd of several hundred gathered to watch the demolition of the old Edgewater Beach Hotel, a structure that had (stand) for more than a hundred years. In the nineteenth century, the Edgewater had (be) a gathering place for the idle rich. In the twentieth, it had (see) elderly couples reliving their youth, teenagers attending basketball tournaments, and even the wrath of Hurricane Camille. Last Saturday, the demolition crew was (suppose) to destroy it so that a new Sears store could be (build) in its place.

On Friday the crew had (set) the charges. And on Saturday the crowd gathered to cheer for the Edgewater, expecting in some vague way that she might defy this onslaught as she (use) to defy tourists, teenagers, and hurricanes for decades.

The crew (put) on their hard hats, (wave) the crowd back to a safe distance, and (detonate) the charges. Nothing (happen). The Edgewater (stand) fast. The crowd (cheer) madly.

For three hours, the crew (reset) the charges. A strange hush (lie) over the crowd. No one (leave). Finally, the crew (signal) again. The levers (go) down. The Edgewater (shudder), then (shake), but (stand). A great roar (burst) from the crowd. Then people (begin) to sing "We Shall Overcome." But they had (forget) the deadly certainty of technology.

The crew (dive) in again. And after hours of labor, they (blow) down the Edgewater. She (sink) into a pile of rubble.

ref
12a

# 12

# Pronoun Reference

A pronoun's antecedent is the person, thing, or idea to which the pronoun refers. Normally, a pronoun takes its meaning from its antecedent.

> The French flag is called the "Tricolor" because it has three vertical bands of different colors. [The pronoun *it* stands for the antecedent *the French flag*.]
>
> Nathaniel Currier issued his first two prints in 1835. [The pronoun *his* stands for the antecedent *Nathaniel Currier*.]

When you revise, make sure that the antecedent of each pronoun is absolutely clear. The following discussion covers the common problems of **pronoun reference.**

## 12a Implied Reference

A pronoun's antecedent must be stated, not merely implied. In the following sentence, the appropriate antecedent of *one* is *horse,* but *horse* does not appear.

> IMPLIED REFERENCE: At first, horseback riding scared me because I had never been on one.

To avoid implied reference, you can provide a clear antecedent or remove the pronoun.

| | |
|---|---|
| CLEAR ANTECEDENT: | At first, I was scared to ride a horse because I had never been on one. |
| REMOVAL OF PRONOUN: | At first, horseback riding scared me because I had never ridden before. |

In the next sentence, the possessive *Homer's* is functioning as a modifier, not as a noun, and therefore cannot serve as the antecedent of *he.*

| | |
|---|---|
| IMPLIED REFERENCE: | In Homer's poems, he recounts the events of the Trojan War. |

An antecedent *Homer* can be provided, or *he* can be eliminated.

| | |
|---|---|
| CLEAR ANTECEDENT: | In his poems, Homer recounts the events of the Trojan War. |
| REMOVAL OF PRONOUN: | Homer's poems recount the events of the Trojan War. |

## 12b Broad Reference

In broad reference, a pronoun has no antecedent and stands instead for an idea or ideas expressed in the preceding discussion. Although readers can sometimes understand broad reference, it is usually not clear and should be avoided. For example, in the following passage, a reader cannot be sure what the writer means by the pronoun *this.*

BROAD: The space above the spout of a boiling kettle of water is filled with an invisible gas called "water vapor," or "steam." The visible cloud above this space is not steam but droplets of water formed when the gas cools. This is called "condensation."

To avoid this kind of broad reference, you can supply a noun or noun phrase that describes the idea referred to.

REVISED: The space above the spout of a boiling kettle of water is filled with an invisible gas called "water vapor," or "steam." The visible cloud above this space is not steam but droplets of water formed when the gas cools. This droplet formation is called "condensation."

Another kind of broad reference involves a dependent clause that begins with *which.*

BROAD: Next semester, personal computers can be connected to the university system, which will reduce the amount of equipment students will need to work at home.

The pronoun *which* seems to refer to *university system* but, in fact, refers to the entire idea expressed by the preceding clause: "Next semester, personal computers can be connected to the university system." The sentence should be revised to provide a clear antecedent for *which* or to remove the pronoun.

CLEAR ANTECEDENT: Next semester, personal computers can be connected to the university system—an arrangement which will reduce the amount of equipment students will need to work at home.

REMOVAL OF PRONOUN: Next semester, personal computers can be connected to the university system, reducing the amount of equipment students will need to work at home.

## 12c Indefinite *You, They,* and *It*

In conversation, speakers frequently use *you, they,* and *it* indefinitely—that is, to refer to people or things in general. This kind of reference, however, is not acceptable in formal writing.

INDEFINITE *YOU:* You can inherit certain diseases.

REVISED: People can inherit certain diseases.

INDEFINITE *THEY:* In Houston they have thousands of acres of parks.

REVISED: Houston has thousands of acres of parks.

INDEFINITE *IT:* It states in the Declaration of Independence that everyone is created equal.

REVISED: The Declaration of Independence states that everyone is created equal.

### ❑ EXERCISE 1

**Revise the following sentences to correct any errors in implied, broad, or indefinite pronoun reference.**

1. **The fabric can be cleaned, but it must be done by a professional.**
2. **Keep the steps short, and do not combine them. This simplifies the job of converting the steps into a chart.**

3. In many states, they do not require a test for the renewal of a driver's license.
4. It says in the article that the number of "reentry" students is increasing rapidly.
5. You can give pills to a dog by hiding them in hot dogs, which is called the "hollow-weenie" method.
6. Although society attempts to educate and reform the criminal, this is largely unsuccessful.
7. The Keeshond has been a guard dog for centuries, unlike other breeds that have recently been trained for it.
8. The information was not available, which forced the researcher to make an educated guess.
9. Vary the size of the letters. That will break the monotony.
10. Consumers like microwave ovens; this is evident from the sales figures.



## 12d Ambiguous Reference

A pronoun should refer unmistakably to one antecedent. If a pronoun seems to refer to more than one, the meaning is ambiguous. Consequently, readers cannot immediately identify which possible antecedent is meant. For example, in the following sentence, *they* can refer to *fire fighters,* to *city council members,* or to both.

AMBIGUOUS REFERENCE: When the fire fighters met with the city council members, they outlined the problems.

The sentence must be revised to eliminate the ambiguity.

REVISED: The fire fighters, who outlined the problems, met with the city council members.

REVISED: The fire fighters met with the city council members, who outlined the problems.

REVISED: At the meeting, the fire fighters and the council members outlined the problems.

## 12e Mixed Uses of *It*

The word *it* is used in several ways.

- As a personal pronoun referring to a noun or noun phrase previously mentioned

As soon as I saw that Corvette, I knew I wanted it. [*It* refers to *that Corvette.*]

ref 12e

- As an expletive—a function word that begins a sentence and delays the subject

  It is dangerous to sleep in the sun. [*It* is an expletive; *to sleep in the sun* is the subject.]

- With *do,* as a predicate substitute

  If you really want to go to law school, you should do it. [*Do it* stands for part of the predicate, *go to law school.*]

When the uses are mixed in the same sentence or in sequential sentences, the result is awkward.

Awkward Mixed Use

Our financial adviser suggests that we sell our house since it [personal pronoun] has become a drain on our budget. It [expletive] is hard, however, to let go of a place with beautiful memories; and we really don't want to do it [predicate substitute].

For clarity's sake, the passage should be rewritten to eliminate mixed use of *it.* In the following revised version, *it* is used twice as a personal pronoun, referring to *house.*

Revised

Our financial adviser suggests that we sell our house since it has become a drain on our budget. The house is so full of beautiful memories, however, that we don't want to give it up.

## ❑ EXERCISE 2

**In the following sentences, correct any errors in ambiguous pronoun reference and in the mixed uses of *it.***

1. My job at Jiffy Car Wash was to take the hubcaps off the wheels and wash them.
2. When Max received the award for outstanding athlete, it was obvious that he expected to win it.
3. I threw my radio against the window and shattered it.
4. The chef told the headwaiter that his job was not to flatter customers.
5. He wrote the song "Take My Love or Take a Bus." It said in the interview that it was for a country-and-western band that he wrote it.
6. Insert the ear attachments of the stethoscope in your ears so that they tilt slightly forward.

7. Some parents resort to extreme punishments because they work.
8. Because of the poor sales of the soft drink, the company said that it was important to withdraw it from the market.



## 12f Remote Reference

A pronoun must be close enough to its antecedent to make the reference instantly clear. For example, in the following passage, a sentence intervenes between the pronoun *they* and its antecedent *fairies*.

REMOTE ANTECEDENT

Fairies—small, magical creatures—appear in most of the folklore of the Middle Ages. During that time, belief in magic exerted a strong influence on human behavior. They might be mischievous, helpful, or fearsome; but always they interfered in the daily lives of the folk.

The pronouns are so remote from their antecedent that the reference is unclear. Repeating the noun antecedent solves the problem.

REVISED

Fairies—small, magical creatures—appear in most of the folklore of the Middle Ages. During that time, belief in magic exerted a strong influence on human behavior. Fairies might be mischievous, helpful, or fearsome; but always they interfered in the daily lives of the folk.

## 12g Titles and Headings As Antecedents

Titles of papers and headings in the text cannot be the antecedents of pronouns.

NO ANTECEDENT

**Glaciers**

They are rivers of ice, with movement measured in inches per day instead of miles per hour. . . .

REVISED

**Glaciers**

Glaciers are rivers of ice, with movement measured in inches per day instead of miles per hour. . . .

## ❑ EXERCISE 3

ref 12g

Revise the following passage to ensure that all pronoun references are clear.

**The Typewriter Keyboard**

The most conventional one is called "Qwerty," after the first six keys of the third row from the bottom. It was designed in 1873 to slow typists down, because the keys stuck if they went too fast.

Sticking keys are no longer a problem, and a better system is needed. Patented in 1936, the Dvorak-Dealy keyboard reduces fatigue and increases speed, which makes it more efficient. The most commonly used keys are on the second row from the bottom—vowels and punctuation on the left, consonants on the right. This reduces the distance that the fingers must cover. In fact, with the Dvorak-Dealy system, typists' fingers travel about one mile a day; with the Qwerty system, they move their fingers about eighteen miles a day.

With the increase in computer use, more and more people are learning to type. Perhaps if manufacturers would offer the Dvorak-Dealy system as an alternative keyboard, it would be possible that someday all typists would change to it.

# 13

pn
agr
13a

# Pronoun-Antecedent Agreement

A pronoun must agree in number with its antecedent—that is, the noun or noun phrase that the pronoun refers to. A singular antecedent requires a singular pronoun; a plural antecedent, a plural pronoun.

SINGULAR ANTECENDENT/ SINGULAR PRONOUN: The amethyst is usually purple or bluish-violet; it is a semiprecious stone made from a variety of quartz.

PLURAL ANTECEDENT/ PLURAL PRONOUN: Amethysts are usually purple or bluish-violet; they are semiprecious stones made from a variety of quartz.

When revising, be sure that the pronouns agree with their antecedents. In most cases, you simply find the antecedent and check to see whether it matches the pronoun in number. If the number of an antecedent is not obvious, the following guidelines will help you choose the appropriate pronoun.

## 13a Antecedents Joined by *And*

Usually, antecedents joined by *and* require a plural pronoun.

PLURAL PRONOUN: The wombat and the bandicoot carry their young in pouches.

In two instances, however, antecedents joined by *and* require a singular pronoun.

- When the antecedents refer to a single person, place, thing, or idea

SINGULAR PRONOUN: The judge and executioner eyed his victim impassively.

SINGULAR PRONOUN: The candidate loudly supports law and order—as though it were debatable.

- When *each* or *every* precedes the compound

SINGULAR PRONOUN: Each hot spell and each rainstorm took its toll on my dwindling vegetable garden.

SINGULAR PRONOUN: Every retired bronc rider and calf roper in the Southwest had paid his entry fee.

## 13b Antecedents Joined by *Or/Nor*

When singular antecedents are joined by *or/nor,* use a singular pronoun. When plural antecedents are joined by *or/nor,* use a plural pronoun.

SINGULAR PRONOUN: The field judge or the back judge blew his whistle.

PLURAL PRONOUN: Neither the Russians nor the Chinese sent their delegations.

When one antecedent is singular and the other plural, the pronoun agrees with the nearer antecedent. To avoid an awkward sentence, place the plural antecedent nearer the pronoun.

AWKWARD: Neither my grandparents nor my mother would sign her name to the petition.

REVISED: Neither my mother nor my grandparents would sign their names to the petition.

## 13c Indefinite Pronouns and Sexist Language

A common problem in pronoun-antecedent agreement occurs with indefinite pronouns that can refer to people: *anybody, anyone, each, either, everybody, everyone, neither, nobody, no one,* and *none.* In casual conversation, speakers often use the plural pronoun *their* with these indefinities:

INFORMAL: Everyone in the auto-repair clinic provides their own tools.

This construction, however, is not acceptable in formal prose. *Everyone* is singular and requires not only a singular verb but also a singular pronoun. In the past, writers used *he, him,* or *his* to refer to both males and females.

OUTDATED: Everyone in the auto-repair clinic provides his own tools.

Today, the use of a masculine pronoun for both men and women is considered sexist language and should be avoided. (See 32e.) One alternative is to change the antecedent, the verb, and the pronoun to the plural.

PLURAL CONSTRUCTION: Participants in the auto-repair clinic provide their own tools.

Another alternative is to use both a masculine and a feminine pronoun.

SINGULAR CONSTRUCTION: Everyone in the auto-repair clinic provides his or her own tools.

Remember, however, that frequent use of both masculine and feminine pronouns is awkward and wearisome. If you do not want to switch to the plural, you should eliminate pronouns where possible.

AWKWARD: Everyone in the auto-repair clinic provides his or her tools so that he or she can work individually with instructors. The clinic, however, furnishes the vehicles needed by everyone for his or her hands-on training.

REVISED: Everyone in the auto-repair clinic provides the tools for working individually with instructors. The clinic, however, furnishes the vehicles needed for hands-on training.

## 13d Generic Nouns and Sexist Language

Sexist language can be a problem when nouns are used generically to refer to all members of a group—*the astronaut* can refer to all astronauts, *the writer* to all writers, *the swimmer* to all swimmers, *the police officer* to all police officers. Even though these generic

pn
agr
13e

nouns refer to more than one person, they require singular pronouns. Formerly, writers used *he, him, his,* which were supposed to refer to both sexes. Today, the use of masculine pronouns to refer to both males and females is unacceptable. (See 32e.)

OUTDATED: The astronaut must begin his training long before a flight.

You can make such a sentence acceptable by including both the feminine and the masculine pronoun or by rewriting the sentence with plural nouns and pronouns. Or you can eliminate the pronoun altogether.

SINGULAR PRONOUNS: The astronaut must begin his or her training long before a flight.

PLURAL PRONOUN: Astronauts must begin their training long before flights.

NO PRONOUN: The astronaut must begin training long before a flight.

## 13e Collective Nouns As Antecedents

Collective nouns—such as *audience, jury, orchestra, committee, family*—are singular when they refer to a group as a unit and plural when they refer to the individual members in the group. Therefore, depending on their meanings, collective nouns may require singular or plural pronouns.

GROUP AS A UNIT: The family incorporated itself for tax purposes.

INDIVIDUAL MEMBERS: The family are squabbling over their grandfather's estate.

If *the family are* sounds peculiar to you—as it does to many people—you can always supply a subject that is clearly plural.

PLURAL SUBJECT: The members of the family are squabbling over their grandfather's estate.

### ❑ EXERCISE 1

**Rewrite the following sentences to make pronouns and antecedents agree and to avoid sexist language.**

1. Each salesperson and each manager must submit their job description annually.

2. Neither the faculty members nor Dean Harper gave their approval to the new curriculum.
3. Everyone on board the ship had saved money for more than five years to pay for their passage.
4. A civil engineer should make sure that he has a thorough knowledge of architectural history.
5. When the jury delivered their verdict, reporters raced from the courtroom.
6. Did the popcorn or the pretzels have its ingredients listed on the package?
7. Both the angler fish and the stargazer have "lures" to attract its prey.
8. Every citizen should keep informed about how their tax money is spent.
9. A nurse under stress may do their job inefficiently and unsafely.
10. The Cadillac or the Buick is supposed to have their transmission fixed today.

## ❑ EXERCISE 2

Revise the following passage to ensure that pronouns and antecedents agree.

Because Shakespeare wrote for his audience, we can learn much about his plays by looking at the people who attended the Globe Theater. The average theatergoer did not question the social or political system, in which everyone knew their place. They had inherited a belief in an ordered universe. And yet that order was threatening to collapse. Both the aristocrat and the commoner in Shakespeare's day began to think that his ordered world might be shattered.

This conflict was partially responsible for the excellence of Shakespeare's work. Theodore Spencer suggests that great tragedy is written in periods when a person's patterns of behavior and their beliefs are threatened. Probably neither the theatergoers nor Shakespeare realized how soon their social order would collapse. But they were aware of the conflict. And in the conflict were some of the components of Shakespeare's remarkable plays.

## ❑ EXERCISE 3

Revise the following passage to eliminate sexist language. Make sure that in your revision each pronoun agrees with its antecedent.

The Cooperative Education Program allows the student to alternate his academic study with periods of work related to his major. Trained advisors assist the student in securing employment that will provide him with practical work experience as well as financial aid to support his education. Any student with an overall GPA of 2.50 is eligible to enter the program after he has completed forty-five hours. An applicant should submit the names of four character references, including at least one member of the business community, who must write his assessment of the student's employment potential.

# 14

# Case of Nouns and Pronouns

Nouns and pronouns have **case,** that is, different forms for different functions. Most pronouns and all nouns change form only in the possessive—the case that expresses such ideas as ownership *(your phone),* authorship *(Ann's poetry),* measurement *(week's pay),* and source *(president's power).* A few pronouns have three cases.

| *Subjective* | *Objective* | *Possessive* |
|---|---|---|
| I | me | my/mine |
| he | him | his |
| she | her | her/hers |
| we | us | our/ours |
| they | them | their/theirs |
| who | whom | whose |
| whoever | whomever | |

The subjective forms of these pronouns are used as subjects and subject complements, sometimes called predicate nominatives.

> We fed the animals a high-protein diet. [subject]
>
> The first guest to arrive was she. [subject complement]

The objective forms are used as objects and as subjects and objects of infinitives.

> The voters will never elect him. [direct object]
>
> The new hospital gave them hope. [indirect object]
>
> I felt the painting looking at me. [object of preposition]
>
> My manager wanted me to hire them. [subject and object of infinitive]

In addition to case, some pronouns have forms made with the suffixes *-self* and *-selves: myself, yourself, himself, herself, itself, ourselves, yourselves, themselves.* These forms are used in two ways.

- As reflexives: objects that rename subjects

  She corrected herself.

  The winners congratulated themselves.

  I was ashamed of myself.

- As emphatics: pronouns that repeat, for emphasis, the nouns or pronouns they refer to

  The owner himself waited on tables.

  You must write the letter yourself.

  They catered the party themselves.

Although use of incorrect pronoun case does not ordinarily mislead the reader, it is considered nonstandard. Therefore, when you revise your papers, check the case of pronouns carefully. The following guidelines should help you choose the appropriate forms.

## 14a Case in Compound Constructions

Compounding in no way affects the case of a pronoun. When in doubt about which case is appropriate, simply drop all other elements in the compound construction. Then you can readily determine the correct form.

> The Senator hired Mary and (I or me). [You would write *The Senator hired me,* not *The Senator hired I.* Thus, the correct sentence is *The Senator hired Mary and me.*]

> Both his brother and (he or him) attended Yale. [You would write *He attended Yale,* not *Him attended Yale.* Thus, the correct sentence is *Both his brother and he attended Yale.*]

In a compound appositive, pronoun case depends on the use of the word that the appositive renames. An appositive renaming a subject or subject complement is in the subjective case; an appositive renaming an object or object complement is in the objective case.

> The centers, Hackett and he, were benched for fighting. [*Hackett and he* renames the subject, *centers.* Thus, the pronoun is in the subjective case.]

The cabin was built by three people—Craig, Ray, and me. [*Craig, Ray, and me* renames *people,* the object of the preposition *by*. Thus, the pronoun is in the objective case.]

Compounds that often cause mistakes contain pronouns in the first person singular. Always use *me* as the object of any preposition, regardless of the context.

NONSTANDARD: Just between you and I, the credit union is in financial trouble.

CORRECT: Just between you and me, the credit union is in financial trouble.

Use the pronoun *myself* only as a reflexive or an emphatic. Never use *myself* when the subjective or objective case is called for.

NONSTANDARD: Brett and myself had dinner at Antoine's.

CORRECT: Brett and I had dinner at Antoine's.

NONSTANDARD: The coach saw Lee and myself at the party.

CORRECT: The coach saw Lee and me at the party.

### ❑ EXERCISE 1

**For each sentence, choose the pronoun in the appropriate form.**

1. According to the *Old Farmer's Almanac,* which my father and (I, me) have always relied on, March 5 will be flannel-pajama weather.
2. In the Chinese restaurant, Luke and (I, myself) got the same fortune cookie message: "Big Luck to Big Tippers."
3. My grandmother decided to divide her property between (he, him) and (I, me).
4. The credit for the team's performance must go to two people, the coach and (he, him).
5. The attendant told Mr. Ford and (she, her) that the flight had been delayed.

## 14b Pronoun Case after *Be*

In conversational English, most people use pronouns in the objective case as complements of *be*.

INFORMAL: It's me.

INFORMAL: That's him.

Although the objective case is appropriate in conversation, the subjective case is required in formal writing.

FORMAL: The first dignitary presented at state occasions was always he.

FORMAL: The only medical doctor in the county was she.

### EXERCISE 2

**In each sentence, choose the form of the pronoun appropriate in formal writing.**

1. It wasn't (I, me) who recommended the course.
2. The best violinist in the orchestra is (she, her).
3. The employee who most often used the microfiche machine was (he, him).
4. It was (they, them) who wrote the script.
5. They discovered that it was (I, me) who had called.

## 14c *Who/Whom* and *Whoever/Whomever*

Although the form *whom* is not common in conversation, you should observe the case distinctions between *who/whoever* (subjective case) and *whom/whomever* (objective case) when you write or speak in formal English.

To use the forms correctly, you must determine the pronoun's use in its own clause—whether independent or dependent. You can make this determination by the following method.

1. Isolate the pronoun's clause, and ignore the rest of the sentence.
2. Put the parts of the isolated clause in normal sentence order (subject + verb + other elements).
3. Substitute pronouns to see which fits. If you would normally use *he, she,* or *they,* choose *who* or *whoever.* If you would normally use *him, her,* or *them,* choose *whom* or *whomever.*

A few sample sentences will illustrate the method.

(Who/whom) did you contact?

You did contact who/whom?

You did contact him.

Whom did you contact?

These are the recruits (who/whom) we think will go to OCS.

Who/whom will go to OCS?

They will go to OCS.

These are the recruits who we think will go to OCS.

The newspaper always attacks (whoever/whomever) the governor appoints.

The governor appoints whoever/whomever.

The governor appoints her.

The newspaper always attacks whomever the governor appoints.

### ❑ EXERCISE 3

**Insert *who, whoever, whom,* or *whomever* in each of the following sentences. (Remember to base your decision on the use of the pronoun in its own clause.)**

1. The conference will be attended by those __________ teach psychology in senior colleges.
2. The position should be filled by someone __________ our clients will trust.
3. Show this pass to __________ is at the gate.
4. He is the actor __________ they say the director slapped.
5. The delegation met with the Prime Minister, __________ they assumed was in a position to make decisions.
6. Do you know someone __________ we can ask?
7. You can get through a class reunion by saying "You look fantastic!" to __________ you don't remember.
8. My grandmother knew a man __________ groomed Teddy Roosevelt's horse.
9. __________ stole my car now owns a gas guzzler that breaks down every fifteen miles.
10. __________ did he say wrote that novel?

## 14d Case in Elliptical Clauses

Dependent clauses introduced by *than* or *as* are often elliptical—that is, some parts are not stated but understood (7d). When an elliptical clause contains a pronoun, you might have to fill in the missing parts to determine the pronoun's case. For example, suppose you were trying to decide whether to use *she* or *her* in the following sentence: *Her parents seemed younger than. . . .* Completing the sentence will tell you which form is correct.

ELLIPTICAL: Her parents seemed younger than she.

COMPLETE: Her parents seemed younger than she seemed.

In some elliptical clauses, either subjective or objective case is possible. Be sure to choose the pronoun form that conveys the intended meaning.

ELLIPTICAL: The skiing lessons helped Joan more than I.

COMPLETE: The skiing lessons helped Joan more than I helped Joan.

ELLIPTICAL: The skiing lessons helped Joan more than me.

COMPLETE: The skiing lessons helped Joan more than they helped me.

ELLIPTICAL: Her friends annoy me as much as she.

COMPLETE: Her friends annoy me as much as she annoys me.

ELLIPTICAL: Her friends annoy me as much as her.

COMPLETE: Her friends annoy me as much as they annoy her.

### ❑ EXERCISE 4

**Supply the correct pronouns in the following sentences. If either the subjective or objective case is possible, explain why.**

1. Anyone in the department can edit the report as well as (I/me).
2. A monarchy is not an appropriate government for people such as (they/them).
3. She writes about Jefferson as well as (he/him).
4. Mr. Thames, rather than (she/her), should present the achievement award.
5. We understood their ideas better than (they/them).

## 14e Possessive Case with Gerunds

A gerund is the *-ing* form of a verb functioning as a noun (5c). In formal prose, nouns and pronouns acting as determiners for gerunds must be in the possessive case: *my singing, Frank's passing, their whispering*. In conversation, you might say, "I don't mind him spending the money." But you should write, "The public objected to his spending money on state dinners"—because it is the spending that the public objects to, not him. *His* identifies whose spending it was.

INFORMAL: The listeners quickly tired of the candidate evading the issue.

FORMAL: The listeners quickly tired of the candidate's evading the issue.

INFORMAL: The security office objected to them parking in the fire lanes.

FORMAL: The security office objected to their parking in the fire lanes.

## ❑ EXERCISE 5

Make the following sentences formal. Change nouns and pronouns to the possessive case where necessary.

1. The lecturer discussed Napoleon crowning himself emperor.
2. The reader tires of him constantly whining about life's injustices.
3. We are concerned over the project getting funded.
4. The State Department objected to them traveling to Libya.
5. Your host will appreciate you arriving on time.

## ❑ EXERCISE 6

Revise the following passages to correct any errors in noun or pronoun forms.

1. Whenever my neighbors get a new dog, they get a terrier who they always name Fido. This habit is almost as old-fashioned as my father naming his dog Rover. One man who I know called his dogs clever names like Go Away and Let Go. Between you and I, these silly names would embarrass any decent, self-respecting dog. Then, there are the American Kennel Club members, to who we are indebted for such names as Jo-Ni's Red Baron of Crofton, Sir Lancelot of Barvan, and St. Aubrey Dragonora of Elsdon.

My brother and me have a solution to all this nonsense. We favor names like Sam and Jake for our dogs. You can't find more sensible names than them, and sensible animals deserve sensible names.

2. We began the study in fall 1985 at the University Sleep Center. The subjects were divided into two groups—one monitored by Dr. Patricia Goldin and myself, the other by a team of Austrian researchers. The participants who Dr. Goldin and me worked with were all under thirty years of age. None of the subjects objected to us monitoring them breathing during deep and twilight sleep. The subjects who we monitored recorded their breathing habits during waking hours. Dr. Goldin divided the collected data between the Austrian team and I for analysis.

adj/adv
forms
15a

# 15

# Nonstandard Adjective and Adverb Forms

Adjectives and adverbs are modifiers—that is, they describe and qualify other elements of sentences. Adjectives modify nouns and pronouns. Adverbs modify verbs, adjectives, other adverbs, and whole clauses. (See Chapter 3.) Many adjectives and adverbs have characteristic forms. Confusion or misuse will produce **nonstandard adjective and adverb forms.**

## 15a Confusion of Adjectives and Adverbs

Be careful not to substitute adjectives for adverbs. A few adjectives and adverbs (such as *fast, early, late*) share identical forms. However, the adjective and adverb forms of most modifiers are different. In fact, many adverbs are formed by adding *-ly* to adjectives. For example, *serious* and *perfect* are adjectives; *seriously* and *perfectly* are adverbs.

| | |
|---|---|
| ADJECTIVE SUBSTITUTED FOR ADVERB: | We talked serious about our future. |
| REVISED: | We talked seriously about our future. [adverb modifying *talked*] |
| REVISED: | We had a serious conversation about our future. [adjective modifying *conversation*] |

ADJECTIVE SUBSTITUTED FOR ADVERB: He recited the speech perfect.

REVISED: He recited the speech perfectly. [adverb modifying *recited*]

REVISED: His speech was perfect. [adjective modifying *speech*]

You probably have little difficulty with modifiers such as *serious/seriously* and *perfect/perfectly*. However, because of a conflict between conversational and written English, a few pairs of modifiers are particularly troublesome.

awful/awfully | most/almost
bad/badly | real/really
good/well

The adjective forms of these modifiers should be used after linking verbs such as *feel, taste, sound,* and *smell.*

ADVERB SUBSTITUTED FOR ADJECTIVE: I feel badly.

REVISED: I feel bad.

If you have problems with any of these troublesome modifiers, look them up in "Glossary of Usage" at the end of this book. There they are defined, and their appropriate uses are discussed and illustrated.

## ❑ EXERCISE 1

**Choose the correct adjective or adverb for each sentence. When in doubt about the correct choice, look up the options in the Glossary.**

1. The linguini tastes (good, well).
2. I feel (bad, badly) about the mistake.
3. The health farm is a (real, really) expensive resort.
4. It (most, almost) always rains during the first two days of our annual rodeo.
5. The child reads exceptionally (good, well).
6. The steak was (bad/badly) burned.
7. If we are going to perform well, we must practice (regular, regularly).
8. She spoke so (quiet/quietly) that I could not hear her.
9. The employees felt (bitter/bitterly) about the layoff.
10. Our test was (awful/awfully) hard.

## 15b Inappropriate Comparative and Superlative Forms

Most adjectives and adverbs have three forms, or degrees. The positive form is the simple form of the modifier. The comparative form (expressed by *-er, more,* or *less*) is used to compare two items. The superlative form (expressed by *-est, most,* or *least*) is used to compare more than two items. (See 3c for discussion and examples.)

Do not use the comparative form to refer to more than two items or the superlative to refer to only two.

INAPPROPRIATE COMPARATIVE: Jones is the more interesting of all the lecturers.

REVISED: Jones is the most interesting of all the lecturers.

INAPPROPRIATE SUPERLATIVE: We should buy the fastest of the two printers.

REVISED: We should buy the faster of the two printers.

Avoid double comparisons—the use of *more* or *most* with another comparative or superlative modifer. Sentences containing double comparisons are nonstandard.

DOUBLE COMPARISON: This summer is more hotter than the last.

REVISED: This summer is hotter than the last.

DOUBLE COMPARISON: The most unusualest piece in the collection was an ebony necklace.

REVISED: The most unusual piece in the collection was an ebony necklace.

Some adjectives, called *absolutes,* cannot logically express degree. For example, one thing cannot be more first than another nor more infinite: something is either first or not, either finite or infinite. About other adjectives, however, there is disagreement. Some people claim that perfection, uniqueness, and correctness can be approximated. Thus, one thing can be more perfect, more unique, or more correct than another. Other people apply strict logic: something is either perfect or imperfect, unique or not unique, correct or incorrect.

Because many readers disapprove of the comparison of absolutes, you can always insert *more nearly* before the adjective.

QUESTIONABLE COMPARISON: The second portrait is a more perfect likeness than the first.

REVISED: The second portrait is a more nearly perfect likeness than the first.

### ❑ EXERCISE 2

**In the following sentences, correct any errors in the comparative and superlative forms of adjectives and adverbs.**

1. German shepherds are the more dependable of all the popular guide dogs for the blind.
2. The Smithsonian is the most complete of the two museums.
3. The grass on the front lawn is deader than that on the back.
4. The new missile is more faster than its predecessor.
5. The mainest thing to remember is that the clutch doesn't work.

## 15c Inappropriate Demonstratives

The demonstratives (*this, that, these,* and *those*) can function not only as pronouns but also as determiners—*this concept, that tablet, these entries, those mistakes*. Only two problems are usually associated with these modifiers.

- The use of *them* in place of *these* or *those*

NONSTANDARD: Them shoes were half price.

REVISED: Those shoes were half price.

- The use of *these* instead of *this* before a singular noun like *kind, sort, type*

NONSTANDARD: These kind of flowers bloom twice a year.

REVISED: This kind of flower blooms twice a year.

REVISED: These kinds of flowers bloom twice a year.

### ❑ EXERCISE 3

**Revise the following passage to correct any adjective or adverb errors.**

It used to be real awkward for me to leave a party. I would have the most hardest math test the next day and need to study, but I couldn't find a polite way to leave. Every time I was the first person to go, people would say they felt badly that I did not have a good time or that I should wait to hear their new guitar. These kind of remarks drove me crazy.

For a while, I tried two excuses. The best one was that I had to leave to let my dogs out of the house. The worst was that a spell of nausea had overtaken me very sudden. But no one took them excuses serious.

The silly thing is that most of the time, people don't actually care when I leave. They are merely being nice. So now I simply leave rapid before anyone notices that I am gone.

dm/mm
16

# 16

# Dangling and Misplaced Modifiers

The function of modifiers is to describe other words—to qualify, limit, intensify, or explain them. Thus, modifiers and the words they describe form a close relationship, which must be immediately clear to readers. When a modifier is not clearly related to any other word in its sentence, it is called **dangling.**

DANGLING PHRASE: To have a successful camping trip, the right equipment must be packed.

REVISED: To have a successful trip, campers must pack the right equipment.

DANGLING CLAUSE: When covered with a fine white ash, the chicken should be placed on the grill.

REVISED: When the coals are covered with a fine white ash, the chicken should be placed on the grill.

When a modifier seems to relate to the wrong element in a sentence, it is called **misplaced.**

MISPLACED PHRASE: He led me to a corner table with a sneer.

REVISED: With a sneer, he led me to a corner table.

MISPLACED CLAUSE: We cooked fresh vegetables on an old wood stove that we had picked that morning.

REVISED: On an old wood stove, we cooked fresh vegetables that we had picked that morning.

Both types of faulty modification can create awkward and confusing constructions. Therefore, when you revise your writing, be sure to eliminate dangling and misplaced modifiers.

## 16a Dangling Modifiers

Although any modifier can dangle, the problem occurs most commonly with verbal phrases and elliptical clauses. (See Chapter 5 and 7d.)

### (1) Dangling verbals: participles, infinitives, and gerunds

When a verbal phrase modifier begins a sentence, the verbal should refer to the subject of the following clause. Without this logical connection between the verbal and the subject, the modifier dangles. To revise an introductory dangling verbal, you can make the logical connection between verbal and subject, or you can eliminate the verbal.

DANGLING PARTICIPLE: Scoring a touchdown in the last seconds, the game was won 6–0.

REVISED: Scoring a touchdown in the last seconds, the team won the game 6–0.

REVISED: The team won the game 6–0 with a touchdown in the last four seconds.

DANGLING INFINITIVE: To restore the damaged wood, a special chemical was used.

REVISED: To restore the damaged wood, they used a special chemical.

REVISED: A special chemical restored the damaged wood.

DANGLING GERUND: In deciding the case, illegally obtained evidence was used.

REVISED: In deciding the case, the judge used illegally obtained evidence.

REVISED: The judge's decision was based partially on illegally obtained evidence.

Less common is a dangling modifier in the middle or at the end of a sentence. If the relationship between actor and action is not immediately clear, the sentence will be weak or confusing. To revise this kind of dangling structure, you can make a clear connection between the verbal and a preceding noun or pronoun, or you can eliminate the verbal.

DANGLING GERUND: My dexterity improved by practicing the piano.

REVISED: I improved my dexterity by practicing the piano.

REVISED: Piano practice improved my dexterity.

DANGLING PARTICIPLE: The evidence showed an increase in the water-pollution level, concluding that the habitat might endanger waterfowl.

REVISED: The evidence showed an increase in the water-pollution level, suggesting that the habitat might endanger waterfowl.

REVISED: Because the evidence showed an increase in the water pollution level, researchers concluded that the habitat might endanger waterfowl.

A few verbals do not dangle, even though they do not modify a specific noun. These include nominative absolutes (5d) as well as common expressions that modify whole sentences (*considering, assuming, to conclude, to tell the truth,* and so forth).

NOMINATIVE ABSOLUTE: The swing set finally assembled, Father lay down in complete exhaustion.

COMMON EXPRESSION: Considering the expense, the trip isn't worth it.

COMMON EXPRESSION: To tell the truth, an independent candidate would have a good chance.

## ❑ EXERCISE 1

**Rewrite the following to correct the dangling verbal phrases.**

1. **Caught in a rip current, it is important for a swimmer not to panic.**
2. **Enough French can be learned to ask common questions by using a conversation guide.**
3. **Beating Milwaukee, a well-deserved trophy was won by the Celtics.**
4. **By awarding scholarship money, potential nurses will be encouraged.**
5. **Adequate funds must be available in campaigning effectively for a candidate for governor.**

6. Blowing from the north, the bay was kicking up whitecaps from the wind.
7. To learn more about the Loch Ness monster research, annual reports of the Loch Ness Phenomena Investigation Bureau can be studied.
8. To be an effective chip, most experts say that it must operate in either parallel or serial mode.
9. By blending Hollywood glamour and soul music, the direction of American music has been changed by Motown.
10. Based on this growing interest, the department has become more specialized.
11. After ascending the English throne, French became the language of government.
12. To avoid confusion, it is necessary to organize the balance sheet properly.

## (2) Dangling elliptical clauses

In an elliptical clause (7d), the subject and a form of the verb *be* are sometimes omitted. If an elliptical dependent clause is correctly constructed, its omitted subject is the same as the subject of the main clause.

ELLIPTICAL: While attending Radcliffe, she began her autobiography. [*She was* is omitted after *while*.]

ELLIPTICAL: Although responsible for the crash, the air controller refuses to accept any blame. [*The air controller is* is omitted after *although*.]

An elliptical clause dangles when the omitted subject is not the same as the subject of the main clause. To correct a dangling clause, you can make the subject of the main clause the same as the omitted subject of the elliptical clause. Or you can rewrite the sentence to avoid the ellipsis.

DANGLING CLAUSE: While living in Tahiti, rich tropical settings were painted by Gauguin.

REVISED: While living in Tahiti, Gauguin painted rich, tropical settings.

REVISED: In Tahiti, Gauguin painted rich, tropical settings.

DANGLING CLAUSE: If dissatisfied with a product, a complaint should be made.

REVISED: If dissatisfied with a product, the consumer should complain.

REVISED: The consumer who is dissatisfied with a product should complain.



## ❑ EXERCISE 2

**Revise the following sentences to eliminate dangling elliptical clauses.**

1. **Once redecorated, there was a pleasant atmosphere in the office.**
2. **Although annoyed by his attitude, his argument was convincing.**
3. **When repeating the story, a few details were added to make it more gruesome.**
4. **While making the meringue, the pie should be set aside to cool.**
5. **If enrolling in the class, it is recommended that you know Fortran.**

# 16b Misplaced Modifiers

A modifier can be positioned so that it seems to modify the wrong word or phrase. It is possible to misplace any sort of modifier—a word, a phrase, or a clause.

## (1) Misplaced words

The most commonly misplaced words are "qualifiers," such as *only, nearly, simply, almost, even,* and *just.* In speech, these words usually occur before the verb, regardless of what they modify. In written English, however, you should place qualifiers immediately before (or as near as possible to) the words they modify.

MISPLACED: He only died yesterday.

REVISED: He died only yesterday.

MISPLACED: The students just pay one-third of the cost.

REVISED: The students pay just one-third of the cost.

Misplacement of words other than qualifiers often leads to ambiguity.

AMBIGUOUS: Follow the instructions for installing the antenna carefully. [*Carefully* can modify either *follow* or *installing*.]

REVISED: Follow carefully the instructions for installing the antenna. [*Carefully* modifies *follow*.]

REVISED: Follow the instructions for carefully installing the antenna. [*Carefully* modifies *installing*.]



## (2) Misplaced prepositional phrases

You should place prepositional phrases as near as possible to the words or elements they modify because placement affects the meaning of sentences.

The researchers studied aggressive behavior in Washington. [*In Washington* modifies *behavior*.]

The researchers in Washington studied aggressive behavior. [*In Washington* modifies *researchers*.]

Misplacing a prepositional phrase can produce a sentence that is unclear or even silly.

MISPLACED: The computer contained the voting statistics we had collected on the hard disk.

REVISED: On the hard disk, the computer contained the voting statistics we had collected.

MISPLACED: Heinrich planned to conquer France on his deathbed.

REVISED: On his deathbed, Heinrich planned to conquer France.

## (3) Misplaced clauses

Dependent clauses should refer clearly and logically to the words that they modify. In some sentences, you can move misplaced dependent clauses near the words they modify. In other sentences, you may have to rewrite to eliminate the misplaced clauses.

MISPLACED: The archeologists found at the site a ceramic pot they had been digging in for two years. [Clause modifies *pot*.]

CLAUSE MOVED: The archeologists found a ceramic pot at the site they had been digging in for two years. [Clause modifies *site*.]

MISPLACED: Because of his allergies, he could not drive a tractor in a hayfield that was not air-conditioned. [Clause modifies *hayfield*.]

CLAUSE ELIMINATED: Because of his allergies, he could not drive an un-air-conditioned tractor in a hayfield. [*Un-air-conditioned* modifies *tractor*.]

### (4) Squinting modifiers

"Squinting" modifiers are misplaced in such a way that they can modify either the preceding or the following elements.

SQUINTING: The courses he teaches frequently have been cancelled. [*Frequently* modifies either *teaches* or *have been cancelled*.]

REVISED: The courses he frequently teaches have been cancelled. [*Frequently* modifies *teaches*.]

REVISED: The courses he teaches have been cancelled frequently. [*Frequently* modifies *have been cancelled*.]

SQUINTING: They told him after the meeting to submit a proposal. [*After the meeting* can modify *told* or *to submit*.]

REVISED: After the meeting, they told him to submit a proposal. [*After the meeting* modifies *told*.]

REVISED: They told him to submit a proposal after the meeting. [*After the meeting* modifies *to submit*.]

## ❑ EXERCISE 3

**Rearrange or rewrite the following sentences to eliminate the misplaced and squinting modifiers.**

1. We went to a movie about a criminal that was considered controversial.
2. The Sahara Desert is the largest desert in the world, which stretches across North Africa from the Atlantic Ocean to the Dead Sea.
3. Mrs. Jones decided to hang two swords that had belonged to her father on the wall.
4. The soap opera that we watch often has characters suffering from amnesia.
5. McLemore wrote that the computer would probably arrive on Tuesday in a letter.
6. The fisherman decided on the dock to clean the fish.
7. A therapy session will be held for students who have crises from 5:00 to 7:30 p.m.
8. The Nobel Prize winner for chemistry almost received enough money to retire.
9. The sailboat moving through the water slowly came into view.
10. As an adult dog, I expect my golden retriever to be well mannered and obedient.
11. Johnson tried always to have a lot of money in his account.
12. The police officer who was summoned immediately arrested the suspect.

13. The author said that he opposed taxation on property in the first chapter.
14. The computer only has one disk drive.
15. My instructor gave the class notes on how to design a title page that I now had to consult.

## ❑ EXERCISE 4

**Revise the following passages to eliminate dangling and misplaced modifiers.**

1. For a ranch hand, a cowboy hat is practical. Using a cowboy hat for a variety of everyday needs, life can be simplified. When wearing the hat, the sun cannot burn the skin. Filled with water, a drinking cup is made. Also, when on horseback, a hat can be used as a whip.
2. Bad dreams about school are common. Entering the classroom to take a final, suddenly horror strikes. The dreamer is wearing no clothes. In another typical dream, the dreamer only gets to class to find the door locked. People have said often in their dreams that they oversleep and miss all their exams. Or while racing through the halls, there is the sudden realization that a forgotten research paper is due.

# 17

# Shifts



A **shift** is an unnecessary change from one kind of construction to another—for example, from present to past tense, from active to passive voice, from singular to plural. Any kind of shift hampers communication by focusing the reader's attention on the syntax rather than on the message. Thus, when revising, watch for shifts that you may have created in early drafts when you were concentrating on ideas rather than grammatical structure.

## 17a Shifts in Verb Tenses

Because of the variety of possible contexts, it is difficult to make rules about the sequence of verb tenses. Nevertheless, any tense shifts must be logical so that the reader can follow the movement of your prose. (See 4c.)

### (1) Present and past tenses

Sometimes, the first sentence in a passage establishes a time context—either present or past. Once established, the time should not shift illogically between the present and past tenses.

MIXED TIME: My brother collects [present] used furniture, not antiques. He thinks [present] that the prices of antiques are [present] so high that used furniture is [present] a good buy. Also,

shft 17a

he enjoyed [past] repairing and refinishing bargains that he picked up [past] in places like auctions and garage sales.

CONSISTENT PRESENT TIME: My brother collects used furniture, not antiques. He thinks that the prices of antiques are so high that used furniture is a good buy. Also, he enjoys repairing and refinishing bargains that he picks up in places like auctions and garage sales.

CONSISTENT PAST TIME: My brother collected used furniture, not antiques. He thought that the prices of antiques were so high that used furniture was a good buy. Also, he enjoyed repairing and refinishing bargains that he picked up in places like auctions and garage sales.

## (2) Perfect tenses

The perfect tenses allow a writer to record layers of time—to show the relationship between the time of one occurrence and the time of another. In general, use the present perfect and past perfect tenses as follows.

- Use the present perfect tense (*have/has* + past participle) along with present tense or time.
- Use the past perfect tense (*had* + past participle) along with past tense or time.

MIXED TIME: Obviously, the architect's travels have influenced [present perfect] his work. All his designs reflected [past] the houses he has visited [present perfect] in Tokyo.

CONSISTENT PRESENT TIME: Obviously, the architect's travels have influenced [present perfect] his work. All his designs reflect [present] the houses he has visited [present perfect] in Tokyo.

CONSISTENT PAST TIME: Obviously, the architect's travels had influenced [past perfect] his work. All his designs reflected [past] the houses he had visited [past perfect] in Tokyo.

The future perfect tense (*will* + *have* + past participle) is rarely used because the simple future (*will* + base form) is usually adequate. The future perfect is appropriate, however, when the context includes another future time expressed by a present tense verb or by an adverb of time.

MIXED TIME: The game will have begun [future perfect] by the time we will arrive [future].

REVISED: The game will have begun [future perfect] by the time we arrive [present].

REVISED: The game will have begun [future perfect] by dark [adverb].

## 17b Shifts with *Can/Could* or *Will/Would*

Conversational English allows a casual use of the auxiliaries *can, could, will,* and *would.* But in written English, the conventions for the use of these words are rather strict. In general, follow these guidelines.

- Use *can* with *will* and *could* with *would.*
- Use *can* and *will* with present tense and time.
- Use *could* and *would* with past tense and time.

SHIFTED: If I could borrow a car, I will go to the dance.

CONSISTENT: If I could borrow a car, I would go to the dance.

CONSISTENT: If I can borrow a car, I will go to the dance.

SHIFTED: Jaffe predicts [present] that current trends could double the shortage in ten years.

CONSISTENT: Jaffe predicts [present] that current trends can double the shortage in ten years.

CONSISTENT: Jaffe predicted [past] that current trends could double the shortage in ten years.

SHIFTED: If the trees are cut down [present], the house would lose its charm.

CONSISTENT: If the trees are cut down [present], the house will lose its charm.

CONSISTENT: If the trees were cut down [past], the house would lose its charm.

## 17c Shifts in Mood



The indicative is the verb mood most common in prose. But sometimes, for special meanings, you use the imperative or the subjunctive mood. (See 4f.) You can mix moods when the logic of a passage demands the shift, but an unnecessary or illogical shift results in awkward prose.

SHIFTED: If I were [subjunctive] an honor student and I was [indicative] ready to graduate, I would apply to a medical school.

CONSISTENT: If I were [subjunctive] an honor student and I were [subjunctive] ready to graduate, I would apply to a medical school.

SHIFTED: In one day, eat [imperative] no more than 30 milligrams of cholesterol, and you should drink [indicative] no more than 4 ounces of alcohol.

CONSISTENT: In one day, eat [imperative] no more than 30 milligrams of cholesterol, and drink [imperative] no more than 4 ounces of alcohol.

CONSISTENT: In one day, you should eat [indicative] no more than 30 milligrams of cholesterol, and you should drink [indicative] no more than 4 ounces of alcohol.

## 17d Shifts in Voice

The term *voice* refers to whether the subject of a sentence performs the action (active voice) or receives the action (passive voice). (See 4e.) You should not shift, without good reason, between active and passive voice— particularly within a sentence. A shift in voice usually results in an awkward and cumbersome sentence.

SHIFTED: In the eighteenth century, Noah Webster set out [active] to make American English independent from British English; and through his books, great influence was exerted [passive] on the language.

CONSISTENT: In the eighteenth century, Noah Webster set out to make American English independent from British English; and through his books, he exerted great influence on the language.

## ❑ EXERCISE 1

Revise the following sentences to correct shifts in verb tense, auxiliaries, mood, and voice.

1. The dictionary lists the most common part of speech first, and the most frequent meaning is given as the first definition.
2. In Spanish, *macho* is an adjective meaning "manly"; *machismo* was a noun that meant "masculinity."
3. If the diver were equipped with the new tank, he can stay underwater for eight hours.
4. The litigants will have spent thousands of dollars before an agreement will be reached.
5. In emergencies, pause, and then you should take a couple of deep breaths.
6. By providing a puppy with the proper atmosphere, you can promote good habits; and then trainability can be established.
7. If I can go to bed earlier, I would get more done during the day.
8. In reviews, critics usually point out when actors had overplayed scenes.
9. The doctor suggested that lowering my salt intake will reduce hypertension.
10. In Orwell's *1984*, the government plans an official Newspeak dictionary, which was supposed to free the world of words like *justice, morality,* and *science.*

# 17e Shifts in Number

The term *number* refers to singular (one) and plural (more than one). You should not shift carelessly between singular and plural nouns that should have the same number.

SHIFTED: Beekeepers wear protective veils over their face.

REVISED: Beekeepers wear protective veils over their faces.

SHIFTED: Frequently, a person exercises to relieve stress. As a result, people sometimes become psychologically dependent on excessive exercising.

REVISED: Frequently, people exercise to relieve stress and, as a result, sometimes become psychologically dependent on excessive exercising.

## 17f Shifts in Person

shft 17g

The term *person* refers to first person (*I, we*), second person (*you*), and third person (all other pronouns and all nouns). Shifts in person usually involve *you* and a noun. If you are directly addressing your reader, you can revise these shifts by using *you* consistently. However, if you are referring to a group of people in general, revising in the third person is the better solution.

SHIFTED: Off-campus students should use the bus system because you get frustrated trying to park every day.

REVISED IN SECOND PERSON: If you live off campus, you should use the bus system because you will get frustrated trying to park every day.

REVISED IN THIRD PERSON: Off-campus students should use the bus system because they get frustrated trying to park every day.

### EXERCISE 2

**Revise the following sentences to correct any shifts in person and number.**

1. Don't submit your manuscripts in ornamental binders; students should put their manuscripts in plain folders or boxes.
2. A traveler should consult several guides. Travelers who do no research are sure to miss many opportunities.
3. These four courses require a one-hour lab.
4. You will find the microcomputer especially valuable when you prepare proposals. The writer can easily pull together previously stored data.
5. At first, math teachers objected to the student use of pocket calculators. Now, however, a math teacher usually sees the value of one.

## 17g Shifts between Direct and Indirect Discourse

In direct discourse, the exact words of a speaker or writer appear in quotation marks: *Truman said, "If you can't convince them, confuse them."* In indirect discourse, the words of a speaker or writer are not reported exactly, and the quotation marks are omitted: *Tru-*

*man said that if you can't convince people, you should try to confuse them.* A shift from one type of discourse to the other can create an awkward, unbalanced sentence.



SHIFTED: The reporter said, "I would rather write about steeplechases than football games," but that his editor would not approve.

The reporter's words should be stated in either direct or indirect discourse.

DIRECT DISCOURSE: The reporter said, "I would rather write about steeplechases than football games, but my editor wouldn't approve."

INDIRECT DISCOURSE: The reporter said that he preferred to write about steeplechases rather than football games but that his editor would not approve.

## 17h Mixed Constructions and Faulty Predication

When the structure of a sentence shifts so that the subject and predicate do not fit together grammatically, the result is called a *mixed construction.* One kind of mixed construction occurs when the writer sets out to state a reason or a definition and begins with an expression such as the following.

The reason is because
Something is when
A place is where

In these cases, the words *because, when,* and *where* introduce adverb clauses. However, a sentence expressing a reason or definition should state that one thing is equivalent to another. Any structure following the verb *be* must therefore be either a noun, a noun phrase, or a noun clause beginning with *that.* One way to revise these mixed constructions is to place a noun or noun equivalent after the *be* verb. Another way is to rewrite the sentence with a verb other than *be.*

SHIFTED: The reason tuition increased was because enrollment dropped.

REVISED WITH NOUN CLAUSE: The reason tuition increased was that enrollment dropped.

shft
17h

REVISED WITH VERB CHANGE: Tuition increased because enrollment dropped.

SHIFTED: A malapropism is when a person misuses a word humorously.

REVISED WITH NOUN PHRASE: A malapropism is the humorous misuse of a word.

REVISED WITH VERB CHANGE: A malapropism results when a person misuses a word humorously.

SHIFTED: Farm clubs are where players train for the major leagues.

REVISED WITH NOUN PHRASE: Farm clubs are training grounds for the major leagues.

REVISED WITH VERB CHANGE: At farm clubs, players train for the major leagues.

Another kind of structural shift occurs when a writer loses control of the structure in midsentence and mixes incompatible parts. These shifts can result not only in awkward sentences but also in sentences that make no sense.

The various ways in which structures can be mismatched are not entirely predictable. Most mismatches occur in rough drafts written in haste. You should, therefore, read drafts carefully in order to revise any shifts in structure. Also, if you have trouble revising structural shifts, review Chapter 7.

MISMATCHED SUBJECT AND PREDICATE: Fraternities that were banned on campus were an issue loudly debated.

REVISED: The banning of fraternities on campus was an issue loudly debated.

SENTENCE WITH NO SUBJECT: Currently, with the lack of security, causes financial losses from computer crime.

REVISED: Currently, the lack of security causes financial losses from computer crime.

MISMATCHED MODIFIER: Maturity is the stage that a person accepts responsibility.

REVISED: Maturity is the stage at which a person accepts responsibility.

A third kind of sentence shift, faulty predication, results when the predicate does not logically fit the subject. For example, in the following sentence, the subject, *study,* cannot perform the action of the verb, *concluded.*

> The study concluded a need for the early identification of alcohol abuse.

When revising a faulty predication, change the sentence to make a logical connection between the parts.

| | |
|---|---|
| FAULTY PREDICATION: | The use of plastic wrap can melt in microwave ovens if the wrap contacts hot food. |
| LOGICAL CONNECTION: | Plastic wrap can melt in microwave ovens if the wrap contacts hot food. |
| FAULTY PREDICATION: | Tanning oils have shifted their sales efforts to appeal to the public's fear of skin cancer. |
| LOGICAL CONNECTION: | The manufacturers of tanning oils have shifted their sales efforts to appeal to the public's fear of skin cancer. |
| FAULTY PREDICATION: | His attitude was filled with arrogance and disrespect. |
| LOGICAL CONNECTION: | His attitude was arrogant and disrespectful. |

## ❑ EXERCISE 3

**Revise the following sentences to correct the shifts in direct/indirect discourse and in mixed constructions and faulty predications.**

1. The Renaissance was when people began to emphasize classical art and culture.
2. Garbage as an energy source is a capacity to save money.
3. The reason for the boycott was because the company charged too much rent.
4. The lady protested indignantly, "What do you mean, you won't take dogs" and that her Fifi would never stay in a kennel.
5. Poor attendance and bad reviews were the early cancellation of the play.
6. Women, growing in numbers in the police force, the improvement has produced results.
7. The reason he quit his job was because he wanted to move to Florida.
8. The reduction of the car's weight is an idea that will reduce gasoline use.

9. She feels that by working at two jobs would make enough money to buy a motorcycle.
10. Every year, gun control laws get more heated.

## ❑ EXERCISE 4

Revise the passage to eliminate shifts. The shifts may occur in tense; with *can/could, will/would;* in mood, voice, number, or person; between direct and indirect discourse; and in mixed constructions and faulty predication.

There is a movement today to make the curricula of schools more demanding. The reason is because American schools are now being compared to the rigorous Japanese schools and were found lacking. Therefore, students cannot find crib, or gut, courses as easily as you once could. Supposedly, credit once could be gotten by students for Basketweaving 101 or Relaxation I. Now, such courses are rare. With a careful strategy, however, you could still find a few courses that will not strain your brain or tax your time.

First, a student can find out which courses would be recommended for the athletes. For example, if you had heard a geology course referred to as "Rocks for Jocks," you know it has possibilities. Also, another possibility might be a course for elementary education majors. At registration, look for a course in poster painting or construction paper art.

Also, you can search for files and guides kept by organizations. One fraternity's file is named "Micks," short for Mickey Mouse. According to one member, "The Micks file is the one most often used" and that it is constantly kept up to date.

Another strategy is where you look for special kinds of titles in the school catalog. With something called "Highlights of . . . " is a good bet. The use of "Basics of . . . " and "Fundamentals of . . . " also explains that the courses probably required little effort.

Since the search for crib courses has gotten harder, use these suggestions to ensure a painless education. If a student cannot locate enough easy courses to fill out a schedule, you might have to break down and study.

# 18

# Split Constructions



A **construction** consists of two or more grammatical items related in some way—subject and predicate, auxiliary and main verb, verb and direct object, and so on. No rule forbids splitting a construction with a modifier or modifiers, but you should be cautious. Some splits result in blurred meaning and awkward constructions.

## 18a Split Subjects and Verbs

Subjects and verbs do not always appear next to each other; modifiers or other elements may interrupt the construction. Be sure, however, that the interruption is not so long that it distracts a reader or creates a cumbersome structure. You can often revise a sentence with a split subject and predicate by moving the intervening element.

SPLIT: The language, with a simple sound system of only five vowels and seven consonants, is easy to learn.

REVISED: With a simple sound system of only five vowels and seven consonants, the language is easy to learn.

In some cases, you can restructure the sentence to position the subject and verb closer together. In the following sentence, for example, the long interruptive element can be rewritten as the predicate.

SPLIT: Our campus newspaper, which caricatures such groups as graduate students, athletes, sorority and fraternity members, and independents, is edited by two promising comedy writers.

REVISED: Our campus newspaper, edited by two promising comedy writers, caricatures such groups as graduate students, athletes, sorority and fraternity members, and independents.

Another possible solution is to divide a cumbersome construction into two separate sentences.

SPLIT: Shopping malls, which have grown from clusters of shops to elaborate structures with fountains, exotic plants, restaurants, and theaters, have led the American consumer to associate buying with entertainment.

REVISED: Shopping malls have grown from clusters of shops to elaborate structures with fountains, exotic plants, theaters, and restaurants. These extravagant centers have led the American consumer to associate buying with entertainment.

## 18b Split Verbs and Complements

Sometimes a modifier separates a verb from its direct object or subject complement—elements that complete the verb's meaning. When a verb and its completer are separated unnecessarily, the interruptive element should be moved to another place in the sentence.

SPLIT: The marathoner injured, during the last race, his left foot.

REVISED: The marathoner injured his foot during the last race.

SPLIT: No one knows, although some historians estimate about 5,000, exactly how many soldiers the Germans lost on D-Day.

REVISED: Although some historians estimate about 5,000, no one knows exactly how many soldiers the Germans lost on D-Day.

## 18c Split Verbs

The verbs in many sentences are not single words but phrases: *would improve, will be moving, has been profiteering, could have been defined*. Frequently adverbs occur between the parts of a verb phrase. In fact, sometimes the natural place for an adverb seems to be within, rather than before or after, a verb phrase.

The issue was hotly debated.

Experts are now predicting a rise in prices.

The new drug will not produce any side effects.

Nevertheless, you should not split a verb phrase awkwardly with a long modifier, especially a prepositional phrase or a clause.

SPLIT: The insurance company is, regardless of the number of people involved in an accident, required to pay each one.

REVISED: Regardless of the number of people involved in an accident, the insurance company is required to pay each one.

SPLIT: A conversion will, when the plates are in metric measurement, give the needed dimensions.

REVISED: A conversion will give the needed dimensions when the plates are in metric measurement.

## 18d Split Infinitives

An infinitive is the *to* form of a verb: *to go, to understand, to be*. In a split infinitive, the *to* is separated from the verb itself: *to sometimes go, to not so clearly understand, to soon be*. In general, you should avoid splitting infinitives—particularly with long modifiers—since the split can create awkward constructions.

SPLIT INFINITIVE: The robot's three-pronged finger arrangement allows it to with a great deal of accuracy pick up objects.

REVISED: The robot's three-pronged finger arrangement allows it to pick up objects with a great deal of accuracy.

Even splitting an infinitive with a short modifier can sometimes create an awkward rhythm.

SPLIT INFINITIVE: Don Knotts' portrayal of Deputy Barney Fife seems to never lose popularity.

REVISED: Don Knotts' portrayal of Deputy Barney Fife seems never to lose popularity.

Of course, you cannot always avoid splitting an infinitive because of the normal patterns of the language. In the following sentence, for example, *more than* cannot be moved.

NORMAL SPLIT: We expect our profits to more than double next year.

Other times, you may want to split an infinitive to ensure your intended meaning or to avoid an awkward sentence rhythm. For instance, the following split infinitive is acceptable.

ACCEPTABLE SPLIT: The task force met to quickly assess the extent of the oil spill.

If you try to avoid the split by placing *quickly* in front of *to,* you change the meaning of the sentence.

CHANGED MEANING: The task force met quickly to assess the extent of the oil spill.

If you place *quickly* after *assess,* you create an awkward structure.

AWKWARD STRUCTURE: The task force met to assess quickly the extent of the oil spill.

## ❑ EXERCISE 1

**Revise the following sentences to eliminate awkward and unclear split constructions.**

1. If you default on mortgage payments, the lender can, according to the general rule of mortgage law, foreclose on your property.
2. Warm Springs, Georgia, where Franklin D. Roosevelt went to try to recover the use of his legs in the warm baths, is now a rehabilitation center.
3. Whatever the English architects imported, they changed it to, with great inventiveness, fit the British climate and temperament.
4. The first mechanical adding machine was, surprisingly in 1642, invented by Blaise Pascal when he was just a teenager.
5. The focus of genetic research in agriculture has been to safely increase yield and to effectively make plants resistant to disease and damage.
6. To make computer chips, engineers first draw, by hand or by a computer, maps of the electrical circuit.
7. Cats and villagers in the 1950s in Japan developed after eating fish contaminated by mercury from a chemical plant a nervous disorder dubbed the "dancing cat" disease.
8. Elvis Presley was, according to Tom Wolfe, a "Valentino for poor whites."

9. Rudolf Flesch, the author of numerous books on reading and what Flesch calls "readability," has devised a formula that measures the reading level of prose.
10. Portions of the Conewago River were unable to satisfactorily support the reproduction of trout.



## ❑ EXERCISE 2

Revise the passage to eliminate awkward or unclear split constructions. You may decide that some of the split constructions are acceptable.

In high school, I, with insistence from my parents, took French. I had no idea why they had at this time demanded that I learn a foreign language. No one around me spoke French. Anyway, I obediently enrolled, but there was no incentive to industriously and enthusiastically study. France was very far away, and I had in my wildest dreams no idea of ever meeting a native.

I, you might guess, did not apply myself to learning. I did, however, come to intensely love the sound of French; it can make the dullest statements sound romantic and interesting. But I after weeks and weeks of struggling could never master the *r* in the throat or the *n* or *m* in the nose. Another problem was in some spoken phrases that the French run words together. For example, *les hommes* (*the men*) when it is spoken sounds like *layszumm.*

I could manage to without difficulty learn vocabulary like *boeuf* for *beef, porc* for *pork,* and *juin* for *June.* But other words were with my limited effort much harder to learn.

The worst problem was that the nouns are masculine or feminine. *The book* (*le livre*) for some very strange reason is masculine; *the chair* (*la chaise*) for an equally strange reason is feminine.

This summer I have a chance to visit Paris, and I, with real regrets about not studying, will have to probably depend on sign language and pity from the French to survive.

inc
19

# 19

# Incomplete Constructions

In some sentences, a word or words needed for grammatical completeness may not appear. The omission does not always detract from the meaning. For example, the following sentences would be perfectly clear even if the words in brackets were omitted.

> Did you think [that] we weren't coming?
>
> The police made the arrest while [they were] on a routine inspection.
>
> Zombies have always frightened me more than werewolves [have frightened me].

Sometimes, however, an omission makes a sentence confusing.

CONFUSING: She writes more often to her representative than you.

POSSIBLE MEANING: She writes more often to her representative than you do.

POSSIBLE MEANING: She writes more often to her representative than she does to you.

When a reader doesn't know exactly what the writer has left out, the construction is not acceptable. You can easily correct **incomplete constructions** by adding the necessary words.

## 19a Omissions in Compound Constructions



Make sure that the omission of a necessary part of a compound expression does not obscure structure or meaning.

| | |
|---|---|
| OMISSION OF DETERMINER: | My teacher and counselor advised me to study physics. [*My teacher and counselor* could refer to one person or two.] |
| REVISED TO MEAN ONE PERSON: | My teacher counseled me to study physics. |
| REVISED TO MEAN TWO PEOPLE: | My teacher and my counselor advised me to study physics. |
| OMISSION OF PART OF VERB: | I have never and will never be interested in the stock market. [*Been* must follow *have*.] |
| REVISED: | I have never been and will never be interested in the stock market. |
| OMISSION OF PART OF IDIOM: | The bright lights detract and ruin the effect of the display. [*From* must follow *detract*.] |
| REVISED: | The bright lights detract from and ruin the effect of the display. |

## 19b Omitted *That*

Frequently, the word *that* can be omitted from the beginning of a noun clause without any loss of meaning.

The players believed [that] they would win.

In some sentences, however, the omission will cause the main clause and the noun clause to fuse. Readers cannot tell where one clause ends and the other begins. For instance, in the following sentence, the subject of the second clause looks like the object of the first clause.

| | |
|---|---|
| OMISSION OF THAT: | He noticed the mistake worried me. |
| REVISED: | He noticed that the mistake worried me. |

### ❑ EXERCISE 1

inc
19c

Revise the following sentences by completing the compound constructions or by inserting *that* wherever necessary.

1. John Brookings added the loans by the bank had been excessive.
2. Many consumers are insisting and purchasing foods low in sodium, sugar, and fat.
3. The recent graduates said when they tried to get jobs, they had no success.
4. The budget cuts have proved the answer can come from financial control.
5. The writer and director we heard speak last year in New York will both be on the panel.
6. The course included familiarization and qualification on the M-16.
7. I read the indictment was not made public for three weeks.
8. The hotel has not and does not plan to charge guests for telephone calls.

## 19c Incomplete Comparisons

Omissions frequently occur in comparisons, and usually a reader can fill in the missing word or words with no difficulty.

> This route is as long as that one [is long].
>
> The copies from this machine are darker than those [copies are dark].
>
> The weather is hotter this week than [it was] last [week].

In some comparative constructions, however, the omissions cause the comparison to be incomplete. For example, in clauses beginning with *than* or *as,* an omission can create ambiguity. A reader cannot with certainty fill in the missing word or words.

INCOMPLETE: Stray dogs are friendlier to me than my roommate.

POSSIBLE MEANING: Stray dogs are friendlier to me than my roommate is.

POSSIBLE MEANING: Stray dogs are friendlier to me than they are to my roommate.

Also, in *than* or *as* clauses, the omission of *other* may cause something to be illogically compared to itself. For example, in the following sentence, the omission suggests that Texas is not a state.

INCOMPLETE: Texas produces more oil than any state.

REVISED: Texas produces more oil than any other state.

A double comparison requires the three conjunctions *as . . . as . . . than*—for example, "The pig is *as* smart *as,* if not smarter *than,* the dog." The omission of the second *as* makes the first comparison incomplete.

INCOMPLETE: Aiken's autobiography is as successful, if not more successful than, Adam's.

REVISED: Aiken's autobiography is as successful as, if not more successful than, Adam's.

Incomplete comparisons may also result from unexplained modifiers. Modifiers like *best, worst, cutest,* or *sweetest* should be completed.

INCOMPLETE: *Gone with the Wind* is the best movie.

POSSIBLE MEANING: *Gone with the Wind* is the best movie ever made.

POSSIBLE MEANING: *Gone with the Wind* is the best movie I have ever seen.

In informal conversation, a speaker sometimes uses *so, such,* or *too* as an intensifier without explaining results—*so nice, too hard.* In formal English, however, these modifiers signal comparisons or measurements, and the omitted explanation leaves the idea incomplete. A writer, therefore, must either complete the comparison or use a true intensifier like *very* or *extremely.*

INCOMPLETE: The noise of the plane was so loud.

REVISED: The noise of the plane was so loud that we could not hear what was said.

REVISED: The noise of the plane was extremely loud.

In addition, an omission may cause the illogical comparison of two different classes of entities. For example, in the following sentence, the writer has compared a technique to a contender.

INCOMPLETE: His technique for throwing the discus is unlike any other contender.

REVISED: His technique for throwing the discus is unlike any other contender's.

REVISED: His technique for throwing the discus is unlike that of any other contender.

## ❑ EXERCISE 2



Make the changes necessary to eliminate any confusion that results from incomplete or illogical comparisons.

1. The computers at the library work so slowly.
2. They installed the most sophisticated stereo equipment.
3. The Washington Monument is nearer the Mall than the Lincoln Memorial.
4. Louisiana's shrimp season begins earlier than other Gulf states.
5. The Sears Tower in Chicago is taller than any building in America.
6. The jazz performance was such a brilliant one.
7. Cheese has far more fat.
8. The volcano is as dangerous, perhaps even more dangerous than, Mt. St. Helens.
9. The damage done by the water was more serious than the wind.
10. Few candidates have had their campaigns aided by as influential a politician as Mayor Nelson.

## ❑ EXERCISE 3

Revise the following passage to eliminate incomplete constructions.

Horse racing is more harmful to horses than any sport. I once considered it exciting, but now I have come to realize profits are more important to owners than the horses.

Races are scheduled so often. The owners do not take into consideration the general health of the horses may be endangered by fatigue. Even bad weather does not often cause cancellation of races.

Sometimes the racetrack surface is too hard. Horses' legs are more fragile than many other animals. Numerous injuries are caused and result from this physical abuse. Drugging horses is crueler. I have noticed drugs like narcotics are still used at many racetracks. The horses run unaffected and unaware of pain.

Probably some owners treat their horses humanely. But others have never and will never consider the welfare of their horses to be as important, or more important than, profits.

# 20 Parallelism



Sentences frequently contain lists of two or more items. Such items in a sequence must be parallel; that is, they must have the same grammatical structure. The following examples illustrate parallel sequence.

| | |
|---|---|
| 2 Noun Phrases: | The best beer has both natural ingredients and natural fermentation. |
| 3 Prepositional Phrases: | The Shakespeare company has traveled not only to city theaters and to college campuses but also to small communities. |
| 4 Verb Forms: | "Uncooperative" computers have been riddled with bullets, burned up with gasoline, stabbed with screwdrivers, and hammered with shoes. |
| 3 Noun Clauses: | We now know that sleep has at least four depths, that dreaming is most intense in the period of rapid eye movement, and that sleep deprivation is dangerous. |

Be sure to make items parallel in a compound structure, a series, a list, or an outline. A mixture of grammatical structures lacks logic and symmetry.

## 20a Parallelism in Compound Structures

// 20a

The two items in a compound structure must be grammatically the same: *pencil* and *paper, working* and *playing, to search* and *to find, when they read* and *when they listen*. Although the two items are most often linked by *and*, there are several other ways to connect them.

- Compounding with coordinating conjunctions (*and, but, or, nor, yet*)

The elements on either side of a coordinating conjunction must be the same grammatical construction.

NOT PARALLEL: The heat wave will increase the demand for electricity and causing power outages. [*And* joins a verb phrase to a participial phrase.]

REVISED WITH 2 VERB PHRASES: The heat wave will increase the demand for electricity and will cause power outages.

NOT PARALLEL: The bicycle path should be located along Route 234 or to follow the Pendleton River. [*Or* joins a prepositional phrase to an infinitive phrase.]

REVISED WITH 2 PREPOSITIONAL PHRASES: The bicycle path should be located along Route 234 or beside the Pendleton River.

- Compounding with correlative conjunctions (*not only . . . but also, not . . . but, either . . . or, neither . . . nor, both . . . and*)

Whatever grammatical element follows the first part of a correlative conjunction must also follow the second part.

NOT PARALLEL: I will either leave from National Airport or from Dulles. [*Either* is followed by a verb; *or* is followed by a prepositional phrase.]

REVISED WITH PARALLEL PREPOSITIONAL PHRASES: I will leave either from National Airport or from Dulles.

NOT PARALLEL: The reporter wondered both what the lawyer had meant and the need for reporting the remark. [*Both* is followed by a noun clause; *and* is followed by a noun phrase.]

REVISED WITH PARALLEL NOUN CLAUSES: The reporter wondered both what the lawyer had meant and whether the remark should be reported.

NOT PARALLEL: We not only want to visit the Corcoran Gallery but also the Hirshhorn Museum. [*Not only* is followed by a verb; *but also* is followed by a noun.]

REVISED WITH PARALLEL NOUN PHRASES: We want to visit not only the Corcoran Gallery but also the Hirshhorn Museum.

- Compounding with other connecting words (*not, as well as, rather than, less than, more than, from . . . to, instead of*)

Some words and phrases create compound structures in the same manner as the coordinating conjunctions: they must join elements with the same grammatical structure.

NOT PARALLEL: We should advertise the car wash rather than to be overlooked by potential customers. [*Rather than* joins a verb phrase to an infinitive phrase.]

REVISED WITH PARALLEL VERB PHRASES: We should advertise the car wash rather than be overlooked by potential customers.

NOT PARALLEL: The reporter has covered the trial from the swearing in of the jury to when the judge sentenced the murderer. [*From . . . to* joins a noun phrase to a subordinate clause.]

REVISED WITH PARALLEL NOUN PHRASES: The reporter has covered the trial from the swearing in of the jury to the sentencing by the judge.

NOT PARALLEL: My history teacher is guilty of telling about past events instead of an explanation of them. [*Instead of* joins a gerund phrase and a noun phrase.]

REVISED WITH PARALLEL GERUND PHRASES: My history teacher is guilty of telling about past events instead of explaining them.

// 20b

### ❑ EXERCISE 1

Find and correct any examples of faulty parallelism in compound structures.

1. The book is divided into two sections—the first focusing on individuals and the second examines generalizations.
2. We wrote a letter intended to eliminate the confusion and which was apparently not received.
3. In temperament, not how he appeared, he resembled his mother.
4. The story is not only puzzling but also disturbs the ordinary reader.
5. As a fly ball is hit, a fielder must judge where the ball will come down and how fast to run to get there.
6. Future space explorations will require flights not of days but years.
7. I would rather suffer through a boring lecture than to miss out on important information.
8. We neither have the time nor the means to learn German before our trip.
9. The book covers information from the discovery of the site to when the artifacts were displayed in the Egyptian museum.
10. The campers were either in their cabins or eating in the mess hall.

## 20b Parallelism in Series, Lists, and Outlines

A sequence of more than two items may appear within a sentence or in a list with one item under the other. All the items, no matter how many, must be the same grammatical structure.

NOT PARALLEL: The students go to the clinic to get vitamins for anemia, for aspirins for headaches, or just counseling. [The series contains an infinitive phrase, a prepositional phrase, and a noun phrase.]

REVISED WITH SERIES OF NOUN PHRASES: The students go to the clinic to get vitamins for anemia, aspirins for headaches, or counseling for their emotional problems.

NOT PARALLEL: I asked the curator whether the museum was well funded, about the style of paintings it featured, and to supply the names of its patrons. [The series contains a noun clause, a prepositional phrase, and an infinitive phrase.]

REVISED WITH SERIES OF CLAUSES: I asked the curator whether the museum was well funded, what style of paintings it featured, and if he would supply the names of its patrons.

NOT PARALLEL: The members decided to fulfill these responsibilities:

1. Meet with parents and guardians
2. Meet with interested citizens
3. Answers to questions from the news media
4. A record of responses to telephone calls

[The list contains two verb phrases and two noun phrases.]

REVISED WITH SERIES OF VERB PHRASES: The members decided to fulfill these responsibilities:

1. Meet with parents and guardians
2. Meet with interested citizens
3. Answer questions from the news media
4. Record responses to telephone calls

NOT PARALLEL: **Slang: Its Useful Purposes**

I. Slang used to identify social groups
II. To enliven language
III. Slang gives us new names
IV. Euphemisms for things that are unpleasant or offensive

[The outline contains a noun phrase, an infinitive phrase, an independent clause, and a noun phrase.]

REVISED WITH SERIES OF SENTENCES: **Slang Serves Useful Purposes.**

I. Social groups use slang as a sign of identification.
II. Slang develops to enliven language, to eliminate monotony.
III. Slang gives us names for new things, such as physical objects or social movements.
IV. Slang supplies euphemisms for unpleasant or offensive actions and places.

REVISED WITH SERIES OF NOUNS: **The Usefulness of Slang**

I. In-group identification
II. Variety
III. Names for new things
IV. Euphemisms

## EXERCISE 2

Correct the faulty parallelism in the following sentences.

1. I find your continuing chauvinistic attitude offensive, sophomoric, and simply displays the worst taste.
2. Computers are capable of programming, remembering, scanning, and they can sort information.
3. The author is a distinguished journalist, lecturer, and has written over fifteen books.
4. The most successful adults have learned to channel their energy, to empathize with others, and they fit into a suitable society.
5. A marketing research analyst has these duties:

   designing marketing research studies
   to interpret research results
   operating a research data retrieval system
   an analyst must monitor existing products

## EXERCISE 3

Fill in the blanks with words parallel to the other words in the sequences.

1. The songs have typical themes—broken hearts, lonely nights, and ________________.
2. The program traces not only how we got involved in Vietnam but also ________________.
3. A path winds through the woods, along a stream, and ________.
4. The store sells expensive but ________________ books.
5. At the school I will learn either to use the word processor or ______.
6. He has a reputation for working hard but ________________.
7. Many people do not know what a quark is or ________.
8. I will take a cut in pay rather than ________________.
9. _____ and when you use credit cards, you must take special care not to overextend yourself financially.
10. How you take a photograph, not ______, will determine the quality of the result.

## ❑ EXERCISE 4

Revise the following passage to remove any faulty parallelism.

In football games, the job of the officials is not easy. They must be ready to react to such confusing plays as blocked kicks, fumbled snaps and catches, goal line plays, end zone plays, and whether a player is eligible. They must be aware both of when a foul occurs and where the ball is at the time of the foul.

Officials not only must know all the rules but also be able to remember them instantly. They must cope with such complicated infractions as these:

an illegal block by the fair catch caller
when a player runs into or either roughs the kicker or holder
when a player bats the ball forward in the field of play or backward out of the end zone
a noncontact interference with the opportunity to catch a kick

No official can stop the game, get out the rule book, studying the details, and then calling the play.

The officials' job, though, is not just to call the plays on the field; officials must also deal with the players themselves. Players frequently play very aggressively, not in a cooperative mood. Officials must make sure that all players are under control and respecting the whistle which signals the end of a play. To ensure this control, officials must stay alert and being able to move quickly to the location of the infraction. Either the players must respond to this authority or be removed from the game.

The next time you disagree with an official or hear one booed by fans, take pity. It's hard work.

# Review Exercise

Revise the following compositions to remove all grammatical and structural errors. As you read, look specifically for

fragments (frag)
comma splices (cs)
fused sentences (fs)
subject-verb agreement errors (s-v agr)
nonstandard verb forms (vb)
pronoun reference errors (ref)
pronoun-antecedent agreement errors (pn agr)
pronoun case errors (case)
dangling or misplaced modifiers (dm/mm)
adjective-adverb confusion (ad)
split constructions (split)
shifts (shift)
faulty parallelism (/ /)
incomplete constructions (inc)

1. I began reading those "romance novels" last summer that are sold in drugstores and quick-stop groceries. Finally, after three months, I realized both that these books all tell the same story and have the same characters.

Readers are first introduced to the heroine, who they are supposed to identify with. On page one, you see her in shabby clothing however, we know she was born an aristocrat because of her "aristocratic brow and regal bearing." As our story opens, we discover our heroines family is down on their luck. Although the young lady has been forced to work as a governess or music teacher to support an invalid mother or father. The family have rich (but haughty) relatives.

Now the hero. He, of course, is one of the rich and haughty relatives who has shunned the heroines family. But the relationship is distant enough for him to marry the heroine eventually. The hero had black hair—and plenty of it. He also has black, "mocking" eyes and with muscles that show through his clothes.

When the hero and heroine meet, this happens. She is rude to him because he is real arrogant, he is charmed by her "spirit." The plot unfolds. The heroine both despises and yearns for the hero. He, after becoming fatally smitten with her charms, "determines to have her." The reason is because she is "in his blood." In some of these kind of novels, the characters engage in steamy love scenes. In others, the author demurely notes when the heroine is near the hero, her "pulse quickens alarmingly." In the end, it's all the same. Hero marries heroine. Hero becomes doting wimp, heroine becomes rich.

After reading these literary clones, a plot of my own begun to take shape. Author of books tell same story over and over to wimpy readers; author gets rich.

2. King Louis XIV of France commissioned La Salle to explore the Mississippi River and claim its great valley for France. La Salle organized an expedition in Canada and started down the Mississippi River in February 1682. La Salle's expedition, like many before and after it, made not only important discoveries but also encountered many misadventures and tragedies.

When La Salle reached the mouth of the river on April 9, 1682. He then planted the French flag and proclaimed that all lands of this great river valley belonged to Louis, King of France. In his honor, he named the new lands "Louisiana."

La Salle's next job was to fortify the mouth of the river to keep other nations out. After returning to France for supplies, soldiers, and men, the plan was to sail back to the mouth of the river by way of the Gulf of Mexico. Events begun to go awry immediately, on the trip the Spanish captured one of La Salle's four ships. Then, La Salle, suffering from a near fatal illness and misled by erroneous information about winds and currents in the Gulf, sailed too far west and misses the mouth of the river. Instead, they landed at Matagorda Bay on the Texas coast.

La Salle's troubles multiplied. Attempting to make camp ashore, he lost many of his provisions when his supply ship ran aground. Local Indians attacked his camp, and also his hunting parties were harassed. Sending one of his two remaining ships back to France, La Salle set out cross-country with a small party of twenty men, he hoped to locate the mouth of the river. Unable to find it, he returned to his camp to learn that his only remaining ship had been run aground and destroyed.

Now stranded, he set out to feel his way toward Canada. On the way, his crew was weary, and La Salle became more despondent almost to the review

point of madness. This caused the crew to mutiny. After an argument, they murdered La Salle's nephew and two aides. Then to conceal these murders, he was killed. They buried him in the wilderness and walked back to Canada. Only five of the men made it to Canada. On the Texas coast, the settlers, who La Salle had left behind, were wiped out by the Indians and because they got diseases. France's first attempt to settle the Gulf Coast ended in failure.

# PART III

# Punctuation and Mechanics

Punctuation and mechanics are signals that work together with words and structures to create meaning. With the aid of these signals, readers anticipate, link, separate, stress, de-emphasize, and characterize ideas according to a writer's wishes. In fact, readers rely so heavily on these marks that their misuse can distort or obscure intended meaning. Therefore, to communicate clearly, you must use punctuation marks and mechanics according to standard practice.

# 21

# Commas

, 21a

The most versatile of all punctuation marks, **commas** enclose, separate, and set off information. Because commas indicate sentence structure and meaning, their use is essential to clear writing.

## 21a Commas between Independent Clauses Joined by Coordinating Conjunctions

One way to join two independent clauses is with a comma and a coordinating conjunction (*and, but, or, nor, for, so,* and *yet*).

> The Vice President will arrive at 9:30, and the commissioning of the battleship will begin at 10:00.
>
> The regular edition of the dictionary is twelve volumes, but the compact edition is only two.
>
> I have to maintain a C average, or my parents will make me pay for my own courses.
>
> All the dormitories were full, so we were housed temporarily in local motels and hotels.

You may omit the comma when the independent clauses are very short and parallel in structure and when the conjunction is *and, but, or,* or *nor.*

> The lights are off and the door is locked.

You should, however, always include the comma when the conjunction is *for, so,* and *yet*. Because these conjunctions can function as other parts of speech, the comma prevents misreading. For example, in the first sentence of the following pair, *for* seems to be a preposition; in the second, the comma makes clear that *for* is a conjunction.



MISLEADING: They went back home for their roots were there.

CLEAR: They went back home**,** for their roots were there.

In the first sentence of the next pair, *yet* seems to be an adverb of time; in the second, *yet* is clearly a conjunction.

MISLEADING: We didn't want to go yet we thought it was our duty.

CLEAR: We didn't want to go**,** yet we thought it was our duty.

NOTE: When independent clauses are long or contain internal punctuation, you may prefer to join them with a semicolon and a coordinating conjunction to show the major break in the sentence. (See 22c.)

> If you approach the colt slowly, talking in a calm voice, you can gain his confidence**;** but if you move abruptly or speak sharply, he will bolt.

## ❑ EXERCISE 1

**In the following passage, insert commas where they are needed between independent clauses.**

**In the 1950s, there were a number of "quiz" shows on television. Contestants displayed a breadth of knowledge but most won very little money. Winning the game by displaying one's knowledge was the point. Now the quiz shows are gone and in their place have come "game" shows. Contestants don't need any knowledge to play yet they must have the ability to jump up and down and squeal. With this talent, they can win thousands of dollars or they can drive away in Cadillacs.**

## ❑ EXERCISE 2

**Join each of the pairs of sentences with a comma and an appropriate coordinating conjunction (*and, but, or, nor, for, so,* and *yet*).**

1. **Classes were dismissed at noon. By 1:00, the campus was deserted.**
2. **I dropped out of school temporarily to get some experience in the business world. To put it another way, I ran out of money and had to work for a while.**

3. We stayed in Florida for an entire week. The sun never came out once.
4. This course has no prerequisite. It can be taken anytime during the program.
5. In the past, children of divorced parents were said to come from "broken homes." Now these children are said to belong to "single parents."



## 21b Commas after Introductory Prepositional Phrases, Verbals, and Dependent Clauses

An introductory or dependent clause appears at the beginning of a sentence or another clause—either independent or dependent. For a discussion of verbals, dependent clauses, and independent clauses, see Chapter 5 and Chapter 7.

### (1) Introductory prepositional phrases

A comma usually follows a long introductory prepositional phrase (a preposition and its object) or a combination of phrases.

| | |
|---|---|
| INTRODUCING A SENTENCE: | At yesterday's press conference, the coach denied the NCAA charges of recruiting violations. |
| INTRODUCING A DEPENDENT CLAUSE: | The local television station announced that as a result of a recent campaign, the city government had agreed to improve the public bus service. |
| INTRODUCING A SENTENCE: | After a bizarre wedding ceremony in the health spa, the couple jogged off into the sunset. |
| INTRODUCING A SECOND INDEPENDENT CLAUSE: | The well-known *couturiers* once catered to the idle rich, but with so many women now in the business world, designers are taking a more practical approach to fashion. |

If a prepositional phrase is short and does not interfere with ease of reading, you can omit the comma.

By 1862 the pony express was no longer in existence.

At twilight we always heard the whippoorwill.

## ❑ EXERCISE 3

**In the following sentences, place commas where needed after introductory prepositional phrases.**

1. In my family public displays of affection were discouraged.
2. During droughts the plant's roots reach deeper into the ground.
3. As an entering freshman I was intimidated by my professors, but after one semester in school I realized that most of them are helpful and not fearsome.
4. A representative of the group stated that without a good bit of government aid many area farmers would lose their farms this year.
5. By noon electricity had been restored.

### (2) Introductory verbals and verbal phrases

You should place a comma after an introductory verbal (participle, infinitive, or gerund) or verbal phrase, regardless of its length.

| | |
|---|---|
| PARTICIPIAL PHRASE INTRODUCING A SENTENCE: | Built in 1752, Connecticut Hall is the oldest building on the Yale campus. |
| PARTICIPIAL PHRASE INTRODUCING A SECOND INDEPENDENT CLAUSE: | He swung the door open; then realizing his error, he stammered and backed from the room. |
| INFINITIVE PHRASE INTRODUCING A SENTENCE: | To avoid the crowds, I did my Christmas shopping in September. |
| GERUND PHRASE INTRODUCING A SENTENCE: | By encroaching on the dense woods, we have greatly reduced the wild-turkey population. |

Use a comma even after a single introductory participle or infinitive.

| | |
|---|---|
| PARTICIPLE INTRODUCING A SENTENCE: | Exhausted, she fell asleep on the chair. |
| INFINITIVES INTRODUCING A FIRST AND SECOND INDEPENDENT CLAUSE: | To jitterbug, you must tense your arm muscles, but to waltz, you must relax them. |

## ❑ EXERCISE 4

**In the following passage, insert commas where needed after introductory verbal phrases.**

To solve the pollution problem each of us must accept our individual responsibility, and we might as well start with the kitchen sink, the place where most people store their household cleaners. By throwing away bottles and cans of hazardous, toxic, and corrosive cleaners we pollute the garbage and then a landfill. Leaking from the landfill the waste comes back home in the drinking water.

Through advertising manufacturers lead us to believe that we need powerful chemical cleaners in our homes. However, these cleaners are not really necessary. To clean ovens all we need is a mixture of salt and baking soda, both natural abrasives. Vinegar can replace ammonia-based cleaners for floors. Sprinkled with dry cornstarch and then vacuumed carpets become as fresh as those cleaned with commercial carpet cleaner. We can all help decrease pollution; by using the products on our kitchen shelves instead of those under our kitchen sinks we can be more responsible citizens.

### (3) Introductory adverb clauses

Most introductory clauses are adverb clauses, introduced by subordinate conjunctions such as *after, although, as soon as, because, before, even though, if, once, since, unless, when, where, while*. (See 7c.1.) Usually, a comma should separate an introductory adverb clause from the rest of the sentence.

> Although hypnosis now has a recognized place in medicine, the technique has its opponents.
>
> Unless the student newspaper can generate more advertising, readers will have to pay fifty cents per issue.
>
> When a tuning fork is struck, the tone remains always the same.

A comma should also follow an adverb clause that introduces a subsequent clause in a sentence.

> A baby is born with the language center in the left side of the brain, but if he or she suffers brain injury very early in infancy, the language center can shift to the right side.
>
> The power went out because when I plugged in the coffeepot, I overloaded the circuit.

After a short introductory clause that does not interfere with ease of reading, you can omit the comma. Nevertheless, the comma is always appropriate.

CORRECT: When it snows I get depressed.

CORRECT: When it snows, I get depressed.

## ❑ EXERCISE 5

**In the following passage, insert commas where needed after introductory adverb clauses.**

**Even though the birthrate is increasing over half the population of the United States will soon be over fifty years of age. If we are to deal successfully with this new trend we must rethink our attitudes toward aging. In the past, most of us have believed that when we reach fifty we should also have reached all our goals. We cannot afford, however, to have 50 percent of our citizens without goals, without direction, without interest in the future. Life after fifty can be full of challenge and growth. But how?**

**Where there is learning there is growth. Once we stop trying to educate only our youth and start trying to educate the entire population we will make progress. Continued learning—at all ages—is the key to a full life and to a vital citizenry. As we have always heard youth can accomplish much with education. The same is true of those no longer young.**

### (4) Introductory noun clauses

Normally, a noun clause used as an object or complement follows the verb and should not be separated from the rest of the sentence with a comma. (See 7c.3.)

COMPLEMENT: People can be whatever they want to be.

DIRECT OBJECT: The group automatically opposes whomever labor supports.

When the normal order is reversed and the noun clause is introductory, it should be followed by a comma.

INTRODUCTORY COMPLEMENT: Whatever people want to be, they can be.

INTRODUCTORY OBJECT: Whomever labor supports, the group automatically opposes.

NOTE: A noun clause that functions as the subject of a sentence should not be followed by a comma.

Whatever you prefer is acceptable to me.

## ❑ EXERCISE 6

**Put commas after the introductory noun clauses serving as objects and complements but not as subjects.**

1. Whoever wishes to enjoy a cruise must also enjoy close quarters.
2. Whatever he said his assistant echoed.
3. Whomever the governor appoints the legislature must approve.
4. Whatever the animal is trained to be it will be.
5. Whatever the omens foretold was not questioned.



## 21c Commas to Set Off Nonrestrictive Elements

The terms *nonrestrictive* and *restrictive* usually refer to adjective clauses, verbals and verbal phrases, and appositives (words and phrases that rename or restate). A nonrestrictive element is not essential to the meaning of its sentence. In other words, readers do not need the element to identify the word or phrase it follows. By setting off a nonrestrictive element with commas, you point to its nonessential role in the construction.

NONRESTRICTIVE CLAUSE: A widely cultivated fruit is the strawberry, which belongs to the rose family.

NONRESTRICTIVE VERBAL PHRASE: Pompeii, covered by volcanic ash, was sealed for almost 1,700 years.

NONRESTRICTIVE APPOSITIVE: Lister, a physician at Glasgow University, founded antiseptic surgery.

In contrast, a restrictive element is essential to the meaning of its sentence. Readers use the element to identify the word or phrase it follows. The absence of commas around a restrictive element points to its essential role in the construction.

RESTRICTIVE CLAUSE: The rose that I prefer is the edible strawberry.

RESTRICTIVE VERBAL PHRASE: The volcanic ash covering Pompeii sealed the city for almost 1,700 years.

RESTRICTIVE APPOSITIVE: Antiseptic surgery was founded by the physician Lister.

Several techniques will help you determine whether an element is restrictive or nonrestrictive.

### (1) Look for the introductory words in clauses.

- A clause that begins with *that* is retrictive.

  The Warren Report summarizes the events that relate to John F. Kennedy's assassination.

Athletes should eat foods that are high in complex carbohydrates.

- A clause with no introductory word is restrictive.

  The lands Alexander conquered stretched from Greece to northwestern India. [*That* is understood before *Alexander*.]

  The artists we admire usually startle or amuse us. [*Whom* or *that* is understood before *we*.]

- A clause that begins with *which* is usually nonrestrictive.

  The area is famous for its pink grapefruit, which is unusually sweet.

  Her hobbies, which included rock climbing and camping, led to her career as a forest ranger.



### (2) Look for proper nouns.

An element following a proper noun is usually nonrestrictive.

One of Europe's most effective monarchs was Elizabeth I, who successfully overcame religious strife, a bankrupt treasury, war with France, and the Spanish Armada.

The Dalmatian, also called the coach dog, closely resembles a pointer.

The best known American clown was probably Emmett Kelly, the forlorn tramp.

### (3) Look for elements that can refer to only one possible person, place, or thing.

These elements are nonrestrictive.

My family hero is my mother's mother, who once rode a horse from Dallas to San Francisco.

His first, car, purchased from a neighbor for $300, was a 1958 Pontiac.

I was craving my favorite cold-weather food, vegetable soup.

### (4) Look for appositives introduced by *or.*

Use commas to show that these nonrestrictive elements explain or define the nouns they follow. Without commas, the appositives will seem to be alternatives in *either/or* compounds. In the following sentence, for instance, *body language* defines *kinesis*. If the comma were removed, the sentence would erroneously suggest alternatives, *either body language or kinesis.*

The company trains all its personnel in kinesis, or body language.



### (5) Check intended meaning.

Occasionally, an element can be either nonrestrictive or restrictive, depending on the writer's intent. In these cases, punctuation must indicate the meaning. For example, the first sentence below, with commas, means "All politicians sacrifice integrity for power, and all are dangerous." In contrast, the second sentence, without commas, means "Some politicians sacrifice integrity for power, and those particular politicians are dangerous."

NONRESTRICTIVE: Politicians**,** who sacrifice integrity for power**,** are dangerous.

RESTRICTIVE: Politicians who sacrifice integrity for power are dangerous.

Similarly, different punctuation in the next two sentences produces different meanings. The writer of the first sentence has only one daughter; the writer of the second, more than one daughter.

NONRESTRICTIVE: I spent Christmas with my daughter**,** who lives in Miami.

RESTRICTIVE: I spent Christmas with my daughter who lives in Miami.

## ❑ EXERCISE 7

**In the following sentences, enclose the nonrestrictive clauses and phrases with commas.**

1. James Savage who was my Shakespeare professor won the bass fishing rodeo for five straight years.
2. Students taking the word processing course must schedule laboratory time once a week.
3. Chicken soup sometimes called homemade penicillin actually has medicinal effects.
4. The musician Dylan seemed to be at odds with the poet Dylan.
5. The Civil War or the War of the Rebellion settled the question of whether a state could secede.
6. The first-string quarterback who sprained his knee in the first game was out for the season.
7. There is a proverb that states, "Never eat at a place called Mom's and never play cards with a man named Doc."

8. Registration reminded me of the U.S. Army whose motto is "Hurry up and wait."
9. The student a computer buff since high school was arrested for selling bootlegged software.
10. Everyone I knew on the entire campus had gone home for the holidays.



## ❑ EXERCISE 8

Combine each of the following pairs of sentences into one sentence containing a restrictive or nonrestrictive element. Indicate restrictive elements by the absence of commas and nonrestrictive elements by the presence of commas.

EXAMPLE: One of the jewels in the Triple Crown is the Kentucky Derby. The Derby is the best-known horse race in the country. → One of the jewels in the Triple Crown is the Kentucky Derby, the best-known horse race in the country.

1. Rhode Island is the smallest state in the Union. It is also an important industrial area.
2. The royal palm is a tropical tree. It resembles a pillar with a crown of leaves at its top.
3. The shallot is the best of the sauce onions. It is especially good in wine cookery.
4. I don't like digital watches. They look like machines instead of jewelry.
5. My father has an excellent sense of direction. He can find his way through any city with ease.
6. I try to take courses from certain professors. These professors don't assign research papers.
7. The game of hockey began in the 1800s. It became the national sport of Canada by the 1900s.

## ❑ EXERCISE 9

Insert commas to enclose the nonrestrictive elements in the following passage.

The authenticity of Robin Hood who was a legendary English hero has been much disputed. He was popularized as Locksley a character in Sir Walter Scott's fiction. But Robin appeared long before that. A few early historians have made claims that he lived in the 1100s. Also, he was mentioned in *Piers Plowman* a work written in the late 1300s. Furthermore, one of the earliest ballad collections that has been preserved is *Lytell Geste of Robyn Hoode* which was printed in 1495.

In most sources, Robin lives in Sherwood Forest which is located in Nottinghamshire. He leads a band of colorful outlaws who spend their time robbing the rich and giving to the poor.

**Probably not much of the myth is true. Yet Robin's "grave" is supposedly located in Yorkshire where his bow and arrow are exhibited.**

, 21d

## 21d Commas between Items in a Series and between Coordinate Adjectives

### (1) Items in a series

A series is a list of three or more parallel structures—three or more nouns, adjectives, verb phrases, prepositional phrases, dependent clauses, independent clauses, and so on. Ordinarily, you should use commas to separate items in a series. (If the series items themselves contain commas, use semicolons. See 22d.)

ADJECTIVES: We are looking for someone reliable, efficient, and versatile.

NOUN PHRASES: When in doubt about the procedure, consult the lab manual, the operational instructions, or the student assistant.

DEPENDENT CLAUSES: When I returned to my room, I found that my roommate had eaten lunch on my bed, that one of his friends had spilled coffee on my history notes, and that another friend had borrowed my sports jacket.

INDEPENDENT CLAUSES: The roots absorb the water from the soil, the sapwood carries the water to the leaves, and the leaves make food for the tree.

Some writers, particularly journalists, omit the comma before the conjunction and the last element in the series. However, omission of this comma can sometimes cause misreading.

UNCLEAR: The Grievance Committee met with three petitioners, two students and a faculty member.

The reader cannot know whether the committee met with six people or with three. But proper punctuation can make the meaning clear.

CLEAR: The Grievance Committee met with three petitioners, two students, and a faculty member. [six people, listed as items in a series]

CLEAR: The Grievance Committee met with three petitioners: two students and a faculty member. [three people, presented as an appositive following a colon]



## ❑ EXERCISE 10

**In the following sentences, insert commas between items in a series.**

1. As a child, he liked to read stories about the American wilderness the exploration of the frontier and the Indian wars.
2. The primary staples of their diet were cornbread chicken rice and gravy.
3. I buy clothes that are washable wrinkle-free and reduced.
4. Either the schedule was wrong the train was late or I was in the wrong terminal.
5. The elegant auction featured diamond jewelry ancient jade statues and furniture.

### (2) Coordinate adjectives

Coordinate adjectives can be rearranged and can be logically connected by *and*. In the absence of *and*, commas should separate coordinate adjectives.

COORDINATE: He liked to play tennis on a shady, secluded court.

REARRANGED: He liked to play tennis on a secluded, shady court.

CONNECTED WITH *AND*: He liked to play tennis on a shady and secluded court.

Noncoordinate adjectives, which can be neither rearranged nor connected with *and*, should not be separated by commas.

NONCOORDINATE: He liked to play tennis on an old clay court.

IMPOSSIBLE: He liked to play tennis on a clay old court.

IMPOSSIBLE: He liked to play tennis on an old and clay court.

When an adjective phrase contains both coordinate and noncoordinate adjectives, the same principle applies: commas should appear in positions where *and* could be inserted.

COORDINATE AND NONCOORDINATE: I was met at the door by two large, shaggy, playful Irish setters.

POSSIBLE: I was met at the door by two large and shaggy and playful Irish setters.

IMPOSSIBLE: I was met at the door by two and large and shaggy and playful and Irish setters.



### EXERCISE 11

In each series of modifiers, insert commas between coordinate adjectives but not between noncoordinate adjectives.

1. a spacious elegant Italian provincial house
2. the first four years of school
3. a smooth delicate cheese sauce
4. a cold gray rainy afternoon
5. many happy carefree lazy summer vacations

### EXERCISE 12

In the following passage, insert commas between items in a series and coordinate adjectives.

When taking photographs with people as subjects, most amateur photographers do not pay enough attention to the horizon the position of the subjects or the framing. You can easily solve these problems.

First, make sure that the horizon is not tilted that it does not dominate the picture and that it does not split the picture in half. Next, position your subjects so that the picture seems evenly lit. Place subjects where the sun hits them from the side put them in the shade against an uncluttered background or put them in filtered muted lighting.

Finally, check the edges of the photograph fill the whole area with what you are shooting and eliminate as much background as possible. To make your subject or subjects more interesting, include something interesting in the foreground: a tree branch to suggest depth a stream that leads from the foreground to the background or a fence that the eye can follow.

## 21e Commas in Place of Omitted Words

When consecutive clauses have parallel structure and common vocabulary, a comma can replace the verb or part of the predicate.

Rankin received 312 votes; Jenkins, 117. [The comma replaces *received*.]

The older sister wanted to be an actress, and the younger sister, a doctor. [The comma replaces *wanted to be*.]

The first question was on the prose of the eighteenth century; the second, on the poetry; and the third, on the drama. [The commas replace *was*.]



## ❑ EXERCISE 13

**In the following sentences, use commas to indicate where verbs or parts of predicates have been omitted.**

1. An African bull elephant weighs from 12,000 to 14,000 pounds; an Asian bull from 7,000 to 12,000.
2. The Brontë sisters shocked readers with their unusual stories: Emily with the eerie *Wuthering Heights;* Charlotte with the independent heroine of *Jane Eyre.*
3. The northern trade route ran from China across central Asia to Byzantium; the southern route from China to the Red Sea and overland to the Nile and northern Egypt.
4. During the day the temperature is over ninety; at night under sixty.
5. The ancestry of a purebred horse is traced through a single breed; the ancestry of a thoroughbred horse to three Arabian stallions—Darley Arabian, Godolphin Barb, and Byerly Turk.

# 21f Commas to Set Off Parenthetical, Transitional, and Contrastive Elements

## (1) Parenthetical elements

A parenthetical element is a structure that could be enclosed in parentheses without changing the meaning of the sentence. The element can occur within a sentence and interrupt the structure abruptly, or it can appear at the end of a sentence and serve as a concluding remark. In either case, use a comma or commas to set off the element from the rest of the sentence.

| | |
|---|---|
| INTERRUPTING THE SUBJECT AND VERB: | The coach, according to informed sources, intends to leave after this season. |
| INTERRUPTING THE VERB AND OBJECT: | The bank officers said, believe it or not, that they had accurately reported the assets. |
| INTERRUPTING THE VERB PHRASE: | She was not, strictly speaking, managing the estate. |

CONCLUDING REMARK: Salaries have not improved at all during the last three years, at least not as far as the clerical staff is concerned.



## ❑ EXERCISE 14

**In the following sentences, insert commas to set off parenthetical elements that function either as interrupters or as concluding remarks.**

1. **You should write a note after a job interview regardless of whether you want the job to thank the interviewer for his or her time.**
2. **Diary keeping at least for many people is a way of comparing dreams and realities.**
3. **The stereo speakers according to the instructions should be about 20 feet apart.**
4. **The reporter refused to reveal her sources because she wanted to protect their safety or so she said.**
5. **Wrinkles as a general rule are caused by the breakdown of collagen and elastin in the skin.**

### (2) Transitional expressions

Transitional expressions, or conjunctive adverbs, are words and phrases such as *however, therefore, for example, in conclusion, accordingly, nevertheless, in addition,* and so on. (See chart of transitional expressions on p. 412.) You should set off these expressions with commas.

Houseplants available at nurseries can be expensive and, in addition, difficult to grow. Therefore, people without green thumbs are often reluctant to spend money to watch their purchases wither and die. There is, however, a solution for people who want to grow plants with little expense or effort—the avocado.

The seed of a well-ripened avocado planted in porous soil will sprout and produce a good-sized plant in a few weeks. An avocado plant grown in the house will not, of course, flower or bear fruit. Nevertheless, it will provide inexpensive, luxurious, and trouble-free greenery.

## ❑ EXERCISE 15

**Use commas to set off the transitional expressions in the following passage.**

While looking at some old photograph albums that had belonged to my mother, I was struck by how carefully she had documented her life. First there was her young adulthood with friends; then there were the early years of her marriage; and finally there were the stages of her children's lives. For example I saw her at high school dances and college football games. I saw her on her honeymoon at Niagara Falls. I saw my brother and me as infants, toddlers, grammar school brats, and teenagers.



Most of the pictures of course were amateurish. In addition many were blurred with age. Nevertheless that photograph album brought whole lives into focus. And more particularly it brought only the good times back. Consequently looking at the snapshots made me feel that life had been good to my mother and to her children.

As a result I have determined to take more photographs. I will naturally embarrass my children by running around with a camera, leaping from behind potted palms to immortalize them with a click. They will however thank me when they grow up—just as I now thank my mother.

## (3) Contrastive elements

Elements that contrast with whatever has preceded usually begin with words like *not, never, but, unlike,* and *rather than.* Normally, you should set these elements off with commas.

> It was the beginning**,** not the end**,** of the social upheaval.
>
> Our codes of conduct in those days were dictated by our peers**,** never by our parents.

You may omit the commas when the contrastive elements are not abrupt. To emphasize the elements, however, always include the commas.

> NOT EMPHATIC: The speech was informative but tedious.
>
> EMPHATIC: The speech was informative**,** but tedious.

## ❑ EXERCISE 16

**In the following sentences, enclose the contrastive elements within commas whenever necessary.**

1. Lately, it seems that football not baseball is the national pastime.
2. Living in Los Angeles unlike living in New York requires a car.
3. They provide guides for tours but only for walking tours.
4. The reflexive of *they* is *themselves* never *theirselves.*
5. This manual is a complete but not very readable guide to organic gardening.

## 21g Commas to Set Off Interjections, Words in Direct Address, and Tag Questions



### (1) Interjections

An interjection is an exclamation with no grammatical connection to the rest of the sentence. You may punctuate an interjection as a separate sentence with a period or an exclamation point. Or you may punctuate it as part of another sentence by setting it off with a comma or commas.

> Well, the time has finally come to act.
>
> His costume was, no kidding, a shower curtain.

### (2) Words in direct address

You should always set off words in direct address, which name whomever or whatever is spoken to.

> Excuse me, sir, is this the plane to Denver?
>
> Sit and beg, Butch.

### (3) Tag questions

Tag questions appear at the end of statements and ask for verification. Always set these questions off with commas.

> The budget was balanced, wasn't it?
>
> She did not ask for a second opinion, did she?

### ❑ EXERCISE 17

**In the following speech, insert commas to set off interjections, words in direct address, and tag questions.**

Ladies and gentlemen may I have your attention please. Thank you for coming tonight to hear our candidate for governor. Usually, all politicians are alike. We know how they operate don't we? They make promises they don't keep in return for our contributions—which they do keep. Well this candidate is a bit different. He's going to tell us what he might be able to do as governor. He isn't going to tell us thank goodness what he promises to do. And wonder of wonders he isn't going to ask us for any money. So friends please help me welcome this unique candidate won't you?

# 21h Commas in Special Contexts: in Dates, Places, Addresses; in Numbers; with Titles of Individuals; with Quotation Marks



## (1) Dates, places, and addresses

The commas in dates, places, and addresses serve to isolate each item for the reader.

Month day, year,

> She graduated on May 22, 1986, from Loyola University. [commas before and after the year when the day is given]

Day month year

> She graduated 22 May 1986 from Loyola University. [no commas when the day precedes the month]

Month year

> She graduated in May 1986 from Loyola University. [no commas when the day is unspecified]

City, state,

> We surveyed the voters in St. Louis, Missouri, two weeks before the election. [commas before and after the names of states]

Street address, city, state zip code,

> Ship the package to 1110 East Marina Road, Dallas, TX 75201, within ten days. [comma between street address and city; comma between city and state; no comma between state and zip code; comma between zip code and material that follows]

## (2) Numbers expressing amounts

Commas indicate thousands and millions in numbers of five or more digits. Many people also prefer commas in four-digit numbers.

> Last year the company sold 2,165 records; this year they sold 1,926,021.

## (3) Titles of individuals

A title following a name should be set off with commas.

Applications for the summer co-op program should be sent to Kathryn McLeod, travel director, or to Carl Jenkins, personnel director.

, 21h

Usually, *Jr.* or *Sr.* following a name is set off with commas. Some people, however, prefer to omit the commas, and you should honor that preference.

Mr. and Mrs. James W. Marcott**,** Jr.**,** hosted the reception.

James Hillery Godbold Sr. donated the funds.

## ❑ EXERCISE 18

**In the following letter, use commas to punctuate dates, addresses, numbers, and titles.**

9781 Ironwood Drive
Birmingham Alabama 35201
June 11 1992

Mr. Arnold Bennett President
Bennett and Hughes
8581 Indian Wood Road
Nashville Tennessee 37219

Dear Mr. Bennett:

On June 10 1992 we surveyed the proposed site for the bridle paths. The 10112-acre site can accommodate 23 miles of paths. The terrain seems ideal, varied but not dangerous. The area is scenic, with diverse plant life, small streams, and outcrops of rock.

We suggest that you have a feasibility study done to determine whether tourist access to the area is sufficient. We can recommend a reputable firm in Nashville, with an excellent history in feasibility and marketing studies. For information, write to

Donald Shaw
Adams and Cromwell
1919 University Place
Nashville TN 37219

Sincerely yours,

L. Brett Carter

L. Brett Carter

### (4) Direct quotations

Commas should set off a grammatically independent quotation from the words that identify its source. When a comma and a closing quotation mark occur together, the comma comes first.

> "You can't expect to hit the jackpot**,**" said Flip Wilson, "if you don't put a few nickels in the machine."
>
> "The results of the tests are insignificant**,**" according to Dr. Landrum.
>
> "It was a perfect title**,**" Dixon thought, "in that it crystallized the article's niggling mindlessness, its funereal parade of yawn-enforcing facts, the pseudo-light it threw upon non-problems." (Kingsley Amis)

A comma is not appropriate when a quotation is an integral part of the sentence structure.

> Ayn Rand defined civilization as "the progress toward a society of privacy."
>
> Who said that for every credibility gap, there is a "gullibility fill"?

, 21i

## ☐ EXERCISE 19

**Insert commas where appropriate to set off quotations from the words that identify their source.**

1. "Remember that as a teenager" Fran Lebowitz said "you are in the last stage of your life when you will be happy to hear that the phone is for you."
2. According to H. L. Mencken "For every human problem, there is a neat, plain solution—and it is always wrong."
3. The report showed that employees were very dissatisfied with the classification system. Quite a few comments addressed that subject. For example, one employee said "The job levels are totally unfair, and moving from one level up to another is virtually impossible." Another complained "The salary increments for some levels do not allow for cost-of-living raises, much less for merit raises." Many employees felt that job levels did not reflect the responsibilities of the positions. "I am an assistant to two coordinators" said one person "and my responsibilities are administrative. Yet, the Office of Personnel classifies me as a clerk-typist, and I am paid accordingly."

## 21i Commas to Ensure Intended Reading

In some instances, commas are necessary simply to prevent misreading. For example, in the following sentence, the comma indicates that *can try* is not a unit.

CONFUSING: Employees who can try to carpool twice a week.

CLEAR: Employees who can, try to carpool twice a week.

In other instances, commas create stylistic effects. For example, the commas in the next two sentences are not grammatically necessary; instead, they indicate pauses and create a reading different from the usual.



"There is no safety in numbers, or in anything else." (James Thurber)

The child had never had a guardian, and never had a friend.

## ❑ EXERCISE 20

**In the following sentences, insert commas for clarity.**

1. No matter how late the message was welcome.
2. To the Burgundian beer drinkers are contemptible.
3. Any unlikely event that would destroy carefully laid plans if it did occur will occur.
4. With the extras added on the car can be purchased for about $23,000.
5. Those who can perform; those who cannot criticize.

# 21j Inappropriate Commas

Commas are inappropriate in the following situations, except when necessary to ensure proper reading.

- Between major sentence elements—such as subject and predicate, verb and object, items in a verb phrase

INAPPROPRIATE: Several people on horseback, suddenly appeared at the bridge. [separation of subject and predicate]

REVISED: Several people on horseback suddenly appeared at the bridge.

INAPPROPRIATE: Conner realized, that he wanted to go home. [separation of verb and object]

REVISED: Conner realized that he wanted to go home.

- Between two items joined by a coordinating conjunction or correlative conjunctions unless those items are independent clauses

INAPPROPRIATE: The road began at the edge of the field, and ended abruptly in the middle. [separation of two verbs]

REVISED: The road began at the edge of the field and ended abruptly in the middle.

INAPPROPRIATE: We hoped the commission would prohibit not only channelization, but also the planting of kudzu. [separation of two objects]

REVISED: We hoped the commission would prohibit not only channelization but also the planting of kudzu.



INAPPROPRIATE: Most critics agreed that the plot relied too heavily on coincidence, and the director relied too heavily on special effects. [separation of two dependent clauses, with *that* understood after *and*]

REVISED: Most critics agreed that the plot relied too heavily on coincidence and the director relied too heavily on special effects.

- After the final adjective in a series

INAPPROPRIATE: He wore a cheap, shabby, and ill-fitting, suit.

REVISED: He wore a cheap, shabby, and ill-fitting suit.

- After a coordinating or a subordinating conjunction

INAPPROPRIATE: We ate at a terrible restaurant that featured waffles and, fried seafood.

REVISED: We ate at a terrible restaurant that featured waffles and fried seafood.

INAPPROPRIATE: Nothing grows in that section of the yard because, there is too much lime in the soil.

REVISED: Nothing grows in that section of the yard because there is too much lime in the soil.

- Between an indirect quotation and the rest of the sentence

INAPPROPRIATE: The author said, that the historical data had been carefully researched.

REVISED: The author said that the historical data had been carefully researched.

## ❑ EXERCISE 21

**Remove any inappropriate commas from the following sentences.**

1. **The ball seemed to float toward the goalposts and, then remain stationary for several seconds.**

2. The book that he assigned us, was too technical for novices.
3. My feet were sore, my back was aching, and, my head was swimming.
4. The announcement said, that the winner had been disqualified, and that the race would be rerun.
5. The realtor felt, that the property was valuable.
6. I think baton twirling is silly, although, I realize it takes a good bit of skill.
7. It was a slow, lazy, meandering, stream.
8. The dancer was not only graceful, but also remarkably athletic.
9. I thought I heard someone scream, that the stadium was on fire.
10. The people who lived next door, had eight cats and six dogs.



## EXERCISE 22

In the following composition, insert commas where they are needed, and delete commas where they are inappropriate. Some of the commas are properly placed.

Getting a summer job takes a good bit of planning, that must not be overlooked. First you must consider what kinds of jobs you are qualified for. For example if you cannot type you can rule out not only a secretarial position, but also a receptionist position which almost always involves some typing. Or if you are under twenty-one you cannot expect to land a job, that requires you to handle alcoholic drinks. In other words you must realistically assess your possibilities.

After this assessment you should consider whether there are any jobs you are simply unwilling to undertake. For example if you are not willing to work late at night on weekends and on the Fourth of July you should not apply at fast-food restaurants. No, a better job for you would be, with a local government, which would ensure you regular hours, and vacations on holidays.

When you have your abilities and preferences in mind the next step is to get yourself ready to accept responsibility. Come to terms with the fact that you cannot miss work because of late-night partying and you cannot expect other employees to do the work, that you have been hired to do. You must act, in other words like a mature responsible adult.

Once you are ready, psychologically ready to work you can begin your search. First you should check all want ads bulletin boards and radio programs that list jobs. Also you should register with the local state-employment agency for this service will not charge a fee for a job search. In addition if you can afford the cost you should apply with private employment agencies which usually charge a percentage of the first, month's salary.

The next step is, to contact people in your community who might act as references and recommend you to prospective employers. Everyone has heard that old expression, "It isn't what you know that counts; it's whom you know." It does matter of course what you know but it also matters whom you know. A phone call, or letter from someone a prospective employer knows, can help you land the job you want.

With luck and effort you can obtain some job interviews. When you do be sure to take plenty of time to prepare for each interview: anticipate possible questions, practice answering them, learn all you can about the job and the company or agency and arrive neatly groomed in an attractive no-nonsense outfit.

Finally take Winston Churchill's advice and, "never, never, never, never give up." You may search for several weeks before getting a job or you may not find one at all. The experience you gain and the contacts you make however will teach you a great deal and you will probably have better luck the next summer.

# 22

# Semicolons

; 22a

**Semicolons** are marks of punctuation weaker than periods but stronger than commas. Basically, there are two positions for semicolons: between independent clauses and between items in a series that contain commas. In each position, the semicolon occurs between coordinate elements—that is, elements of the same grammatical construction.

## 22a Semicolons between Independent Clauses Not Joined by Coordinating Conjunctions

Independent clauses can be joined in a variety of ways, depending on the ideas expressed. (See 33a.1.) The semicolon is a logical choice when the ideas in each clause seem fairly equal and balanced. For example, in the three sentences that follow, the semicolon functions like the conjunction *and*.

> The left brain controls the right side of the body**;** the right brain controls the left side.
>
> Shakespeare's vocabulary included about 20,000 words**;** Milton's included about 11,000.
>
> Lights went out**;** elevators stopped**;** traffic stood still.

The semicolon is also an option when none of the coordinating conjunctions (*and, but, or, for, nor, so, yet*) seems to express the appropriate relationship.

> The bus was a bizarre sight**;** it lurched, swayed, and heaved itself forward like a drunk.
>
> Their motive was not money**;** it was something far more interesting than that.
>
> Benjamin Franklin carried out a number of experiments with lightning**;** in one of them, he passed an electric current through a chain of six men.



Semicolons should not be overused within a single passage. They are more noticeable than commas and thus should be used sparingly, lest they lose their effect.

OVERUSED: Bluegrass is an old-timey sound from Virginia, Tennessee, and Kentucky; it is the most traditional form of country music. Now the bluegrass festival has become a popular entertainment; families pack picnic lunches to spend the day listening to professionals and amateurs play. Some fans listen to the performances on the stage; others wander about enjoying the impromptu sessions on the grounds.

REVISED: An old-timey sound from Virginia, Tennessee, and Kentucky, bluegrass is the most traditional form of country music. Now the bluegrass festival has become a popular entertainment. Families pack picnic lunches to spend the day listening to professionals and amateurs play. Some fans listen to the performances on the stage**;** others wander about enjoying the impromptu sessions on the grounds.

## ❑ EXERCISE 1

**Complete each sentence by adding an independent clause after the semicolon.**

1. The weather is very strange; ______________________________ .
2. One of our coaches resigned; ______________________________ .
3. The birthday party was unusual; ______________________________ .
4. Eating at fast food places can lead to bad habits; ____________________ .
5. When we are children, Christmas is magic; ____________________ .

## 22b Semicolons between Independent Clauses Joined by Transitional Expressions

; 22b

When two independent clauses are joined, their relationship is often signalled by a transitional expression, such as *however, therefore, also, nevertheless, for example, consequently,* or *instead.* (See p. 412 for a more complete list.) These expressions are not grammatical conjunctions but adverbs modifying the entire clause. Thus, in the absence of a true conjunction, the semicolon joins the clauses.

> People under stress report long, complex dreams**;** however, people with placid lives report dreams that are uneventful and usually uninteresting.
>
> Each year the group publishes a list of words and phrases that should be banned from the language**;** for example, one year it listed "at this point in time" and "have a nice day."

The difference between a transitional expression and a conjunction can be illustrated very simply: a transitional expression can be moved about in a clause; a conjunction cannot.

POSSIBLE: We feared that computers would increase unemployment**;** instead, they have created more jobs.

POSSIBLE: We feared that computers would increase unemployment**;** they have, instead, created more jobs.

POSSIBLE: We feared that computers would increase unemployment**,** but they have created more jobs.

IMPOSSIBLE: We feared that computers would increase unemployment, they have, but, created more jobs.

### ❑ EXERCISE 2

**Combine each of the following pairs of independent clauses into a single sentence. Use a transitional expression with the second clause, and punctuate the sentence correctly.**

1. **The academic standards in the school are extremely high. Most of the graduates receive scholarships to good colleges.**
2. **A "cruise control" is useful for a steady highway speed. You should use it only on level roads.**

3. Cooking in front of television cameras can be embarrassing. I have seen cooks spill batter all over the stove, drop food on the floor, and cover up mistakes with bunches of parsley.
4. I want to get a roommate who makes up the bed. I filled out a questionnaire to help determine roommate compatibility.
5. The women's basketball team lost their first twelve games. They won the thirteenth game by one point.



## 22c Semicolons between Independent Clauses Joined by Coordinating Conjunctions

Ordinarily a comma appears between two independent clauses joined by a coordinating conjunction (*and, but, or, nor, for, so, yet*). However, when the first independent clause contains commas, a semicolon clarifies the structure.

UNCLEAR: Of the 11,000 men who encamped at Valley Forge, only 8,000 came with shoes, and only 8,000 survived.

REVISED: Of the 11,000 men who encamped at Valley Forge, only 8,000 came with shoes**;** and only 8,000 survived.

UNCLEAR: The books effectively deal with systems and languages such as UNIX, BASIC, PASCAL, C, COBOL, but these books cost approximately twenty dollars each.

REVISED: The books effectively deal with systems and languages such as UNIX, BASIC, PASCAL, C, COBOL**;** but these books cost approximately twenty dollars each.

When only one comma occurs in the first independent clause, you can use a comma or a semicolon with the conjunction. Either of the following versions is appropriate.

By purchasing a month-long pass for the train, travelers can save five dollars**;** but a year-long pass will save ninety dollars.

By purchasing a month-long pass for the train, travelers can save five dollars**,** but a year-long pass will save ninety dollars.

### ❑ EXERCISE 3

**Combine each of the following pairs of independent clauses into a single sentence. Join the clauses with a coordinating conjunction and the appropriate punctuation.**

1. In *I Had Trouble in Getting to Solla Sollew,* the hero, burdened by the troubles of life, goes in search of a city where people have no troubles. After many adventures, he realizes no place is trouble-free.
2. Blenders, food processors, and instant food have eliminated most slicing, dicing, and pureeing. The time required for putting together a meal seems the same.
3. Executives, managers, and employees were questioned about "flextime." All replied that the system works well.
4. In 1910 most American immigrants were Italians. In 1983 America had immigrants from 183 countries, the largest group from Mexico.
5. The story of the woman with multiple personalities shows the disease's brutal cause, bizarre symptoms, and strange development. The story is not ever sensationalized.



## 22d Semicolons between Items in a Series with Internal Punctuation

Ordinarily commas separate items in a series.

> We subscribe to *Time, Newsweek,* and *Harper's.*

If, however, the items themselves contain commas, semicolons are required to mark the separation.

UNCLEAR: The train stops in Birmingham, Alabama, Atlanta, Georgia, Charlotte, North Carolina, and Charlottesville, Virginia.

REVISED: The train stops in Birmingham, Alabama**;** Atlanta, Georgia**;** Charlotte, North Carolina**;** and Charlottesville, Virginia.

UNCLEAR: The most significant dates of the Civil War were April 12, 1861, July 3, 1863, April 9, 1865.

REVISED: The most significant dates of the Civil War were April 12, 1861**;** July 3, 1863**;** and April 9, 1865.

UNCLEAR: The participants in the exhibit are Judi Parker, who paints in watercolor, Simon Rogers, who is a potter, and Peter Mondavian, who sculpts in transparent plastic.

REVISED: The participants in the exhibit are Judi Parker, who paints in watercolor**;** Simon Rogers, who is a potter**;** and Peter Mondavian, who sculpts in transparent plastic.

## 22e Inappropriate Semicolons



Avoid semicolons in these positions:

- Between elements that are not coordinate

INAPPROPRIATE: Only 7 plays by Sophocles now exist; even though he supposedly wrote 124.

REVISED: Only 7 plays by Sophocles now exist**,** even though he supposedly wrote 124.

- Before a list

INAPPROPRIATE: I have checked the following sources; encyclopedias, almanacs, indexes, and abstracts.

REVISED: I have checked the following sources**:** encyclopedias, almanacs, indexes, and abstracts.

REVISED: I have checked the following sources—encyclopedias, almanacs, indexes, and abstracts.

### ❏ EXERCISE 4

**Complete each sentence by adding a grammatically coordinate element.**

1. Tennis was once a game played by the upper classes; ______________ .
2. You can attend jazz festivals at the college on Sunday, June 24; on Friday, June 29; or ______________ .
3. Some used cars are good buys; ______________ .
4. Dr. Bertram Strass, a lecturer in Romance languages and literature, will speak at the meeting this week; and ______________ .
5. Applicants must be able to type 80 words a minute; communicate effectively, both in speech and writing; and ______________ .

### ❏ EXERCISE 5

**Revise the following sentences by inserting semicolons where needed and deleting them where inappropriate.**

1. Western languages contain a prejudice against left-handedness, for example, *sinister* and *gauche* are words for "left."
2. Since 1960, the Cuban government has severely curtailed the rights of its citizens, and since 1962, the United States has imposed an economic embargo on the Castro regime.

3. We have tickets for *La Traviata* on Tuesday, July 31, *Rigoletto* on Wednesday, August 29, and *Carmen* on Saturday, September 1.
4. Flashing a wide grin; the applicant tried to hide his nervousness.
5. According to a study of more than 300 adults; men cry about once a month, but women cry five times more often.
6. The new animals in the zoo are an elephant, donated by Sri Lanka, a Bengal tiger, purchased with funds, and an aardwolf, loaned by the San Diego Zoo.
7. Sherwood Anderson named his book of stories *The Book of the Grotesques,* however; his publisher changed the title to *Winesburg, Ohio.*
8. Most people who use personal computers for jobs such as word processing, bookkeeping, or filing don't program their computers, instead, they buy prewritten software.
9. The guide lists the major excavation sites around the world; where ongoing digs are uncovering secrets of ancient civilizations.
10. "The Star-Spangled Banner" is hard to sing; but most people don't want it changed.

## ❑ EXERCISE 6

In the following passage, insert semicolons where necessary between items in a series and between independent clauses.

People who have trouble sleeping and people who keep odd hours have seen, I'm sure, a variety of Frankenstein films on television. The monster that started this trend took shape in Switzerland in 1816 at a gathering made up of Shelley, the poet, Mary, his future wife, and Lord Byron. To get through the wet, cold winter, the three wrote ghost stories, but the only memorable work produced was Mary's *Frankenstein.* The two famous poets wrote nothing significant, Mary, however, produced a masterpiece.

Most of the Frankenstein films that appear on television bear little resemblance to the original. The book dramatizes the horror that results when human beings assume God's creative power, but most Frankenstein films dramatize silliness. You can see such ridiculous versions as *Frankenstein and the Monster from Hell,* with the doctor running an insane asylum, *Frankenstein Conquers the World,* with an overgrown monster terrorizing Tokyo, *Frankenstein's Daughter,* with a ridiculous female robot, and *Frankenstein Meets the Space Monster,* with an interplanetary robot gone amuck.

# 23

# Colons



Although the **colon** is used in diverse constructions, it has only two basic purposes: to point ahead and to separate. No matter what its purpose, the colon has a formal and official tone.

## 23a Colons before Lists

A colon sometimes announces that a list will follow. Usually, the list is written not as a tabulation but as a continuation of the sentence. However, in scientific, technical, and business writing, the list is often separated from the sentence and itemized down the page.

NONTECHNICAL WRITING: Several American writers have died young without completing work they had started**:** F. Scott Fitzgerald, Nathanael West, and James Agee.

TECHNICAL WRITING: According to sports psychologists, athletes can improve their performances by several techniques**:**

1. goal setting
2. mental practice
3. relaxation

Most experts agree that a complete sentence should precede a colon. In fact, writers often precede a list with an expression like *the following* or *as follows* in order to avoid splitting elements, such as a verb or preposition from its object.

SPLIT: We visited: Athens, Kusadasi, Rhodes, and Heraklion.

REVISED: We visited the following places**:** Athens, Kusadasi, Rhodes, and Heraklion.



SPLIT: The root *carn* appears in: *incarnation, carnage,* and *carnival.*

REVISED: The root *carn* appears in the following words**:** *incarnation, carnage,* and *carnival.*

## 23Colons before Appositives That End Sentences

An appositive renames and identifies another sentence element, as *pitcher* renames *Satchel Paige* in the following example.

> Satchel Paige, a great pitcher, entered the major leagues at the age of 42.

An appositive at the end of a sentence introduced by a colon creates drama or emphasis.

> Seventy years after the hoax of the Piltdown Man, a surprising new suspect has been found**:** Sir Arthur Conan Doyle.
>
> All the evidence points to the same conclusion**:** that a vast source of oil exists in the area.

## 23c Colons between Independent Clauses

Usually, two independent clauses are joined with a comma and a coordinating conjunction or with a semicolon. On occasion, however, the second clause explains or illustrates the first clause or some part of it. A colon between the two clauses can indicate this special relationship. If the second clause is a formal statement or principle, you may capitalize the first word.

> Galileo discovered that Copernicus was correct**:** The earth was not the center of the universe.
>
> The most exciting shot in volleyball is the spike**:** one team tries to drive the ball across the net at up to 110 miles an hour.

## 23d Colons before Grammatically Independent Quotations

A grammatically independent quotation is a complete sentence or several complete sentences. Ordinarily a comma separates the quotation from the rest of the sentence, but when the quotation is especially long and when the tone is formal, a colon may separate the two.

> In a radio address on April 7, 1932, Roosevelt made a statement that still seems modern**:** "These unhappy times call for the building of plans . . . that build from the bottom up and not from the top down, that put their faith once more in the forgotten man at the bottom of the economic pyramid."

> In 1945 Einstein wrote optimistically**:** "I do not believe that civilization will be wiped out in a war fought with the atomic bomb. Perhaps two-thirds of the people of the earth might be killed, but enough men capable of thinking, and enough books, would be left to start again, and civilization could be restored."

## 23e Colons between Titles and Subtitles

A colon separates a title from a subtitle.

> *The Masks of God**:** Creative Mythology*
>
> *Famine on the Wind**:** Plant Diseases and Human History*
>
> "Boomerang**:** The Stick That Returns"
>
> "*Timon of Athens**:*** A Reconsideration"

## 23f Colons in Correspondence

Several elements in business correspondence contain colons.

> Salutation
>
> Dear Ms. Plavin**:**
>
> Attention or subject line
>
> Attention**:** Dr. Grace Fortune

Subject: Reassignment of Duties

Headings in memoranda

To: Part-Time Employees

From: Milton Greenberg, Personnel Director

Date: May 3, 1993



## 23g Colons with Numerical Elements

In several types of numerical sequences, colons separate the parts—hours from minutes, chapters from verses, and numbers in ratios.

| | |
|---|---|
| 5:30 P.M. | Psalms 29:2 |
| 10:00 A.M. | 4:3 |

## 23h Inappropriate Colons

Do not use a colon between the following elements.

- An independent and a dependent clause or phrase

INAPPROPRIATE: I have received only one response to my letters: although I wrote to twenty companies.

REVISED: I have received only one response to my letters, although I wrote to twenty companies.

- The parts of a phrase—for example, a verb and its complement, a preposition and its object, or *to* and the rest of the infinitive

INAPPROPRIATE: Is acid rain ruining: our gardens, our lakes, our farms?

REVISED: Is acid rain ruining our gardens, our lakes, our farms?

INAPPROPRIATE: Please send catalogues to: Carolyn Hacker and Stephen Hastings.

REVISED: Please send catalogues to Carolyn Hacker and Stephen Hastings.

INAPPROPRIATE: They are planning to: secure funds and send out a request for bids.

REVISED: They are planning to secure funds and send out a request for bids.

## ❑ EXERCISE

To improve clarity in the following sentences, add missing colons, remove incorrect colons, or change existing marks to colons.



1. The first electronic computer required: 17,000 vacuum tubes, 70,000 resistors, 10,000 capacitors, and 6,000 switches.
2. Our textbook for the course is *The Americans A Social History of the United States, 1587–1914.*
3. He was dressed in the standard school attire corduroy slacks, button-down Oxford shirt, and Shetland sweater.
4. During the nineteenth century, one man stands out for the influence he had on other writers Emerson.
5. Dorothy L. Sayers explained the appeal of mystery novels this way "Death seems to provide the minds of the Anglo-Saxon race with a greater fund of innocent amusement than any other single subject . . . the tale must be about dead bodies or very wicked people, preferably both, before the Tired Business Man can feel really happy."
6. Language can be ranked by its acceptability into these levels

   | | |
   |---|---|
   | 1. standard or formal | 4. jargon |
   | 2. informal | 5. nonstandard |
   | 3. slang | 6. taboo or vulgar |

7. I am qualified in: COBOL, FORTRAN, and UNIX.
8. The candidates grappled over issues that especially concern women, equal opportunity, equal pay, abortion, old-age security.
9. The research points to a great improvement, to an immunization against colds.
10. The best travel guides are: Michelin, the Blue Guide, and Fodor's.
11. A single basic fact governs encoding; a computer stores only numbers.
12. They are trying to grow the following vegetables, corn, tomatoes, radishes, and broccoli.
13. These extensions of the Blue Ridge Mountains are names enshrined in American folklore, the Great Smokies, the Balsams, the Nantahalas.
14. The envelope had this notation "Attention A Human Being."
15. Sometimes a copy of a book by a living author can be a collector's item *Poems* (1934), William Golding's first book, sold recently for $4,000.

# 24

# Dashes, Parentheses, and Brackets

24a

**Dashes, parentheses,** and **brackets** primarily enclose information, isolating it from the rest of a sentence. But the effect of these three marks of punctuation is somewhat different. Dashes emphasize the elements they enclose. Parentheses de-emphasize interrupters and nonessential elements. Brackets usually enclose clarifications, especially in direct quotations.

## Dashes

### 24a Dashes to Set Off Appositives Containing Commas

An appositive is a word or phrase that renames or restates. Dashes set off an appositive containing commas so that a reader can see where it begins and ends. As the examples show, an appositive may appear in the middle of a sentence, at the end, or at the beginning.

CONFUSING: A number of the Founding Fathers, Jefferson, Madison, Adams, Hamilton, were extremely intellectual.

REVISED: A number of the Founding Fathers—Jefferson, Madison, Adams, Hamilton—were extremely intellectual.

CONFUSING: The pitcher can throw a variety of breaking pitches, curves, screwballs, and knuckleballs.

REVISED: The pitcher can throw a variety of breaking pitches—curves, screwballs, and knuckleballs.

CONFUSING: A poet, dramatist, novelist, essayist, historian, Voltaire has been an influential figure in the history of thought.

REVISED: A poet, dramatist, novelist, essayist, historian—Voltaire has been an influential figure in the history of thought.

## 24b Dashes to Set Off Nonrestrictive Modifiers Containing Commas

Ordinarily commas set off a nonrestrictive modifier, whether a clause or a phrase. (See 21c.) When the modifier itself contains commas, however, dashes can make its boundaries clear.

> Jules Feiffer—who has produced cartoons, novels, plays, and screenplays—uses humor to reflect human folly.
>
> By the eighteenth century, riddles—written, at least—were becoming less suggestive and vulgar.

### ❑ EXERCISE 1

**In the following sentences, insert dashes to set off appositives and nonrestrictive modifiers that contain commas.**

1. **The tennis instructor, a short, skinny, agile fellow, was visibly agitated by my incompetence.**
2. **Karl, who had recently read *The Jewel in the Crown, Gandhi,* and *The Blood Seed,* claimed to be an expert on India.**
3. **Blacks, Jews, Catholics, southerners, women, people of minority groups are sought out for political endorsements.**
4. **The editorial, which attacked university policies on housing, meal tickets, and zoning regulations, was written by a freshman.**
5. **The book contains reminiscences by a wide range of people, journalists, musicians, artists, critics, and teachers.**

## 24c Dashes to Emphasize Sentence Elements

Dashes can emphasize any kind of construction (a word, a phrase, or a clause) that can be set off or separated from the rest of the sentence.

We have noticed a persistent quality in the lives of famous people—confidence.

They were stealing—via computer—hundreds of thousands of dollars in goods and services.

In *Walden,* Thoreau tells how he built his cabin—down to the cost of the nails.

Most people who read food magazines never cook anything by the recipes—they're too difficult.

## 24d Dashes with Interrupters

Dashes effectively set off an element that interrupts the continuity of prose, separates the essential parts of a sentence pattern, or breaks a piece of dialogue.

The author was sitting—slouching, really—on the sofa.

"I never knew—well, I don't suppose it matters now."

"But not—I really wouldn't call the move a mistake."

### ❑ EXERCISE 2

**To emphasize elements and to set off interrupters, insert dashes or change existing marks to dashes.**

1. Human beings, of whom there are today close to five billion, rely primarily on plants for food.
2. On the Fourth of July we had fireworks, not sparklers or Roman candles, but a large professional extravaganza.
3. Just below Lee Highway, parallel to it, in fact, is Arlington Boulevard.
4. He was, it was now unmistakably clear, a coward.
5. The subway travelers have a high tolerance level for trash, dirt, and graffiti (or they have no alternative transportation).
6. "He's, oh, my heavens, he's already here."
7. Finally (I think it was in October, or maybe November) he went to see a doctor.
8. Eakins' portraits are honest, honest in the external details and honest in the psychological characterization.
9. The riddle was a conundrum, that is, a riddle that depends on a pun.
10. The article was about America's biggest business, food.

## Parentheses

## 24e Parentheses to Enclose Interrupters

Parentheses isolate and de-emphasize elements that interrupt a sentence or passage. Interrupters may be explanations, illustrations, or clarifications. They may be single words, phrases, or even whole sentences.

> Since 1603, the royal arms of Britain have been supported by the English lion (dexter) and the Scottish unicorn (sinister).
>
> KYB CHG (Keyboard Change) allows an operator to change the keyboard arrangement.
>
> Monticello (pronounced *Montichel'lo* in the Italian way) was built on a Virginia hilltop Jefferson's father had left him.

When one whole sentence interrupts another, the interrupter neither begins with a capital letter nor ends with a period.

> After the Civil War, gangs of homeless burglars (they called themselves "yeggs") rode the freight trains, robbing and stealing along the way.

When a whole sentence is inserted between sentences, the interrupter begins with a capital letter and ends with a period. The final parenthesis follows the period.

> In his early youth Wordsworth was an enthusiast for the French Revolution. (He had been influenced by the ideas of Rousseau.) But as he grew older, he became increasingly conservative.

## 24f Parentheses for References to Pages, Figures, Tables, and Chapters

Parentheses can enclose references to specific pages, to relevant figures or tables, or to different chapters. The following examples illustrate the two ways to make these references: inside a sentence or as a separate sentence.

> A map of the river shows where each aquatic plant still grows (45).
>
> James McNeill Whistler is considered the forerunner of abstract art. (See pp. 52–76.)

The inertial reel makes seat belts lock up automatically (see the accompanying diagram).

Safes fall into two types: fire-resistant safes for records and burglar-resistant safes for money. (See figs., p. 167.)

[ ]
24g

## EXERCISE 3

**Use parentheses to add at an appropriate place the information specified for each sentence.**

**EXAMPLE: The new mapmaking technique for the oceans has uncovered previously unknown seamounts. [Explain that seamounts are underwater volcanoes.] → The new mapmaking technique for the oceans has uncovered previously unknown seamounts (underwater volcanoes).**

1. **Generally, two-way or three-way speakers will sound better than single-cone. [Explain that two-way is coaxial; three-way, triaxial.]**
2. **T. E. Lawrence published an account of his World War I adventures in *The Seven Pillars of Wisdom.* [Add that the account was published in 1926.]**
3. **VLSI research is helping speed up the evolution of microprocessors. [Explain that VLSI means "Very Large-Scale Integration."]**
4. **The few players who engage in serious tournament chess are mainly concerned with strategy. [Instruct readers to refer to Chapter 16.]**
5. **The exhibit at the Anacostia Neighborhood Museum is *Black Wings,* about black American aviators. [Add the dates July 2–August 5.]**
6. **New York City, which is surrounded by major tomato-growing regions, depends mainly on California and Mexico for its tomatoes. [Explain that the regions are New Jersey, Long Island, and upstate New York.]**
7. **The goldsmith said that for $4,200 he could design the trophy. [Add the comment "That's not a bad price."]**
8. **I am an admirer of the work of Leonard. [Add the comment "More accurately, I am a fan."]**

# Brackets

## 24g Brackets around Insertions in Direct Quotations

Exact quotations taken out of context often contain pronouns without clear references, terms needing explanation, or names without identification. In such situations, you can insert clarifications in brackets after the unclear word or phrase. Or you may replace the unclear word or phrase with the bracketed clarification.

> De Tocqueville wrote, "They [the Americans] have all a lively faith in the perfectibility of man."
>
> or
>
> De Tocqueville wrote, "[The Americans] have all a lively faith in the perfectibility of man."
>
> The author points out, "The Countess of Lovelace [Byron's daughter] met Babbage and soon became the first computer programmer."
>
> or
>
> The author points out, "[Byron's daughter] met Babbage and soon became the first computer programmer."



You may also use brackets to insert corrections in direct quotations.

> Harry Truman wrote a letter to his daughter on March 19, 1956, saying, "If you don't trust the people you love . . . you'll be the unhappiest and [most] frustrated person alive."

Instead of adding a correction, a writer can insert *sic* in brackets following the error to show that it appeared "thus" in the source.

> From Hyeres, Fitzgerald wrote Thomas Boyd: "Zelda and I are sitting in the Café l'Universe writing letters . . . and the moon is an absolutely *au fait* Mediteraenean [sic] moon with a blurred silver linnen [sic] cap . . . we're both a little tight and very happily drunk."

To emphasize an element in the source being quoted, you may italicize (or underline) the element and insert an explanation in brackets.

> According to the article, "As a society, we need to grapple with the *real* problem—which is the lack of consensus—not about public education, but over what public education should be about [italics mine]."

## 24h Brackets for Parentheses inside Parentheses

On the very rare occasions when parentheses are required inside parentheses, brackets replace the inner set.

Most psychologists believe that phobias are stress related. (But a recent study **[**1984**]** suggests that agoraphobia may have biological origins.)

[ ]
24h

## ❑ EXERCISE 4

Use brackets to add the explanations and insertions specified for each sentence.

1. According to the explanation, "Teletext magazines consist of 100 to 5,000 "frames' of graphics and information." [Explain in the previous quote that "frames" means the same thing as "video screens."]
2. Sir Herbert Read wrote of "the no-man's-years between the wars." [Indicate that these "years" are 1919–1939.]
3. According to the newspaper, "The police and 'volunter' auxiliaries surrounded the statehouse and checked identifications and otherwise harassed the protesters." [Show that it was the newspaper that misspelled *volunteer.*]
4. According to Bruce Catton, "This four-year tragedy . . . is the *Hamlet* and *King Lear* of the American past." [Indicate that by "tragedy" Catton means the Civil War.]
5. About a possible operation her father needed, Virginia Woolf wrote in a letter that "any operation however slight . . . must be bad when you'r old." [Show that it was Virginia Woolf who misspelled *you're.*]

# 25

# Periods, Question Marks, and Exclamation Points



**Periods, question marks,** and **exclamation points** are called end (or terminal) marks because they appear primarily at the ends of complete sentences. The period most commonly occurs after sentences and abbreviations. The question mark occurs mainly after a direct question. Exclamation points are common only in advertising copy, warnings in instructions, and dialogue.

## Periods

### 25a Periods as End Punctuation

Periods follow several types of complete sentences.

STATEMENTS: Mardi Gras is the last day before Lent.

COMMANDS: Use linseed oil on saddles and bridles.

INDIRECT QUESTIONS: He asked whether we had a reservation.

After polite requests, usually in correspondence, you may use either a period or a question mark.

Would you please send me your brochure on wildflowers.

Would you please send me your brochure on wildflowers?

To set off a mild interjection, you may use either a period or a comma (21g.1).

> Well. Hindsight is always 20–20.
>
> Well, hindsight is always 20–20.



## 25b Periods in Outlines and Displayed Lists

Periods follow numbers and letters in displayed lists, unless the numbers and letters are enclosed in parentheses.

Cathedrals
I. Types of Cathedrals
  A. Palace Churches
  B. Abbeys
II. Famous Cathedrals
  A. French Cathedrals
  B. English Cathedrals
  C. Italian Cathedrals

The report should include the following:

1. Abstract
2. Introduction
3. Procedure
4. Discussion
5. Conclusions and recommendations

## 25c Inappropriate Periods

Do not use periods in the following situations.

- After a period marking the end of an abbreviation

INAPPROPRIATE: The ceremony began at 3:00 P.M..

REVISED: The ceremony began at 3:00 P.M.

- After words and phrases in displayed lists

INAPPROPRIATE

Improperly canned foods can spoil for four reasons:

1. growth of yeasts and molds.
2. growth of bacteria.
3. presence of enzymes.
4. process of oxidation.

Revised

Improperly canned foods can spoil for four reasons:

1. growth of yeasts and molds
2. growth of bacteria
3. presence of enzymes
4. process of oxidation



## EXERCISE 1

**Revise the following sentences so that the periods are used correctly.**

1. **The tourists always ask when they can see the ghosts that haunt the castle?**
2. **She said calmly, "Sorry I didn't mean to upset you."**
3. **Garden flowers fall into three categories:**
    1. **annuals.**
    2. **biennials.**
    3. **perennials**
4. **Chinese art was flourishing by the time of the Shang dynasty, about 1500 B.C. to 1028 B.C..**
5. **Would you please send a transcript of my grades to the address listed below?**

# Question Marks

## 25d Question Marks As End Punctuation

The question mark is used as end punctuation in several different constructions.

- After direct questions

    When is the off-season in Florida**?**

- After sentences with tag questions

    September is unusually hot, isn't it**?**

- After elliptical questions in a series

    Should politicians be required to reveal all the details of their private lives**?** Why**?** And to whom**?**

## 25e Question Marks within Sentences



Direct questions usually appear alone.

What will be won**?**

On rare occasions a direct question appears, not alone, but as the subject of a sentence.

What will be won**?** was on their minds.

In this case, the question mark emphasizes the question. Be careful, however, to avoid using a question mark if the question is indirect and cannot appear separately.

INAPPROPRIATE: What we can gain by further negotiation? is the first question.

REVISED: What we can gain by further negotiation is the first question.

REVISED: What can we gain by further negotiation**?** is the first question.

A question mark can also express doubt about a fact such as a date, a place, a statistic, and the like.

The first edition of the novel (1918**?**) was banned in the United States.

The most famous of the Cleopatras (VII**?**) lived from 69 to 30 B.C.

### ❑ EXERCISE 2

**Revise the sentences so that question marks are used correctly both at the ends of sentences and within sentences to show emphasis or doubt.**

1. What does rattlesnake taste like.
2. Is the telephone company our servant, our partner, our master, or merely off the hook.
3. The founding fathers did believe in separation of church and state, didn't they.
4. The Trojan War (in the 1200s B.C.) was fought between Greece and the city of Troy. [Indicate that the date of the war is doubtful.]
5. How can we make retirees feel productive is not adequately discussed.

## Exclamation Points

### 25f Exclamation Points in Dialogue



An exclamation point is used in dialogue to indicate that the speaker is shouting or expressing intense feelings.

> "Stop**!**" the engineer shouted. "There is a unicorn on the tracks**!**"
>
> "Shut up**!**" she said between clenched teeth. "Just shut up**!**"

### 25g Exclamation Points with Interjections

Interjections are expressions of emotion, such as *well, goodness, oh,* and *whew*. You can punctuate a mild interjection with a period or a comma.

> Well**.** I suppose we could reconsider the matter.
>
> Oh**,** he does not understand.

When the interjection expresses strong emotion, however, you can use an exclamation point.

> Well**!** You've said quite enough.
>
> Whew**!** That car barely missed me!

### 25h Exclamation Points for Emphasis

Exclamation points are often used in warnings to catch the reader's attention and help prevent accidents.

> WARNING**!** DO NOT USE NEAR OPEN FLAME**!**

In prose, exclamation points can emphasize something astonishing or ironic.

> New pesticides arrive at the rate of five hundred a year**!**
>
> If we are lucky, we will have to battle only mosquitoes and ignorance**!**

You should, however, use exclamation points for emphasis very, very sparingly. When overused, they lose their dramatic effect.

Inexperienced writers sometimes try to convey enthusiasm by using exclamation points and vague words such as *great, wonderful, marvelous,* and *perfect.* Specific details, however, are more convincing than exclamation points, as the following two passages illustrate.



INEFFECTIVE: My favorite place to visit in winter is Rancho Mirage in the California desert. The scenery is marvelous! And the weather is great!

REVISED: My favorite place to visit in winter is Rancho Mirage in the California desert. The town is set in a lush oasis surrounded by a stark desert and rugged mountains. The temperature gets up to about 80 degrees during the day and down to about 60 degrees at night.

Another ineffective use of the exclamation point is to stress the importance of an idea. A better technique is to use words and phrases that express more specifically the degree of the idea's importance. Compare these sentences.

VAGUE: We must revise the nursing curriculum!

REVISED: One of our major goals should be to revise the nursing curriculum.

REVISED: Our primary concern should be the revision of the nursing curriculum.

REVISED: Until we revise the nursing curriculum, we can make no progress at all.

## ❑ EXERCISE 3

**Improve the following sentences by eliminating exclamation points. Replace vague words with specific details or add words and phrases that express the importance of the ideas.**

1. The party was fabulous!
2. The paper should be a five-page discussion of American transcendentalism. It must have a thesis supported by concrete details!
3. We must take steps to conserve energy!
4. Last Saturday's game was the greatest I have ever seen!
5. After spending hours at registration, I finally managed to get a perfect schedule!

# 26

# Apostrophes

’ 26a

**Apostrophes** have three functions—to form possessives, to allow contractions, and in a few contexts to precede *s* in plurals. By far the most common of the three, however, is to indicate possession.

## 26a Apostrophes to Indicate Possession

The grammatical term *possession* refers to such relationships as ownership, origin, and measurement—*Claudia's house, the professor's approval, a week's vacation*. Some pronouns have special possessive forms: *my/mine, our/ours, your/yours, his, her/hers, its, their/theirs, whose*. Nouns and all other pronouns are made possessive by the addition of an apostrophe plus *s* or simply an apostrophe.

The general rules for showing possession with apostrophes follow.

- Add *'s* to most singular nouns and to singular indefinite pronouns.

  doctor → doctor's diagnosis

  novel → novel's plot

  Don Quixote → Don Quixote's quest

  Ross → Ross's boat

  Ms. Jones → Ms. Jones's office

everybody → everybody's responsibility
someone → someone's parking space
neither → neither's fault



- Add ' to singular proper names when the addition of another *-s* would make pronunciation peculiar or difficult.

  Jesus → Jesus' teachings
  Moses → Moses' leadership
  Aristophanes → Aristophanes' plays
  Xerxes → Xerxes' conquests

- Add ' to plural nouns that end in *s.*

  teachers → teachers' pay
  drivers → drivers' training school
  six months → six months' pay
  trees → trees' roots

- Add *'s* to plural nouns that do not end in *s.*

  oxen → oxen's yokes
  children → children's art
  bacteria → bacteria's behavior
  alumni → alumni's involvement
  sheep → sheep's pasture

- Add *'s* or ' to the last word of a compound noun or pronoun.

  editor in chief → editor in chief's opinion
  attorney generals → attorney generals' decisions
  no one else → no one else's business

- Add *'s* or ' to the last name only to indicate joint possession.

  Lebanon and Syria → Lebanon and Syria's disagreement
  Crick and Watson → Crick and Watson's discovery
  juniors and misses → juniors and misses' department

- Add *'s* or ' to each name to indicate individual possession of more than one noun.

  the mayor and governor → the mayor's and governor's policies
  the Falcons and Saints → the Falcons' and Saints' schedules

## EXERCISE 1

In the following sentences, change each underlined phrase to a comparable possessive containing an apostrophe.

EXAMPLE: The border guard examined the visa of every tourist. → The border guard examined every tourist's visa.

1. The face of Medusa turned people to stone.
2. The waterfront of San Francisco attracts many visitors.
3. The weather can affect the emotions of anyone.
4. He lost his pay for a whole week.
5. The seismograph measured the intensity of the earthquakes.
6. People have always been fascinated by the love affair of Antony and Cleopatra.
7. The dressing rooms of the singers and the dancers were beneath the stage.
8. The press attacked the policy of the secretary of state.
9. One of the discoveries of Archimedes was the principle of buoyancy.
10. The new shop specializes in games for children.
11. The book by James Fallows is about Japan.
12. The schools in both cities lack adequate funds.
13. A hog belonging to our neighbors was killed in the tornado.
14. The meaning of the hieroglyphics was deciphered in 1822.
15. The landscape in Kansas is an expanse of tall grass.



## EXERCISE 2

Insert apostrophes where necessary to indicate possessive nouns.

*Hibernation* is a general term describing an animals sleeplike state during particular times of the day or year. "True" hibernation occurs only in warm-blooded animals that hibernate to avoid winters harsh temperatures and reduce the need for food. The ground squirrel, for example, is a true hibernator. In winter, the squirrels body temperature falls close to that of the surrounding air and its heartbeat is extremely slow. The true hibernators sleep, however, is not very deep; the animal is only napping and can rouse itself whenever it chooses. Other kinds of hibernation include the butterflys cocoon state, the bats daytime sleep, the hummingbirds night trance, and the desert snakes dormancy when water is scarce.

# 26b Apostrophes to Create Contractions

In contractions, the apostrophe takes the place of omitted letters, numbers, or words.

| | |
|---|---|
| it's = it is, it has | goin' (dialect) = going |
| who's = who is, who has | don't = do not |

| | |
|---|---|
| they're = they are | won't = will not |
| I'll = I will | would've = would have |
| '65 = 1965 | we'd = we would |
| rock 'n' roll = rock and roll | o'clock = of the clock |



Remember that *till, though,* and *round* are all words, not contractions. Do not write *'till, 'though,* and *'round.*

## 26c Apostrophes to Indicate Plurals of Letters and Words Used as Words

Whenever possible, form the plurals of letters or words used as such in the usual way—by adding an *s*. Sometimes, however, the *s* alone is not clear; then you should add an apostrophe plus the *s*. Lowercase letters, some capital letters, and abbreviations containing periods usually require an apostrophe before the *s*.

APOSTROPHE PLUS *S*: He has earned two M.A.'s.
NO APOSTROPHE: Only GIs are eligible.

APOSTROPHE PLUS *S*: She writes her *m*'s and *n*'s alike.
NO APOSTROPHE: He has mastered the three Rs.

APOSTROPHE PLUS *S*: Three COS's were stamped on the package.
NO APOSTROPHE: There are two YMCAs in the city.

APOSTROPHE PLUS *S*: You have used too many *and*'s.
NO APOSTROPHE: They are packaged in twos and threes.

## 26d Inappropriate Apostrophes

Do not use apostrophes in the following situations.

- Within a word, even though the word itself ends in *s*

| NONSTANDARD POSSESSIVE | REVISED |
|---|---|
| Charle's | Charles's |
| Jone's | Jones's |
| the Raider's | the Raiders' |

- In the plural of an ordinary word

| NONSTANDARD PLURAL | REVISED |
|---|---|
| tomato's | tomatoes |
| price's | prices |

- In the possessive forms of personal pronouns and in the possessive form of *who.* All personal pronouns and the pronoun *who* form possessives without the apostrophe.

| Nonstandard Possessives | Revised |
|---|---|
| it's or its' | its |
| her's or hers' | hers |
| your's or yours' | yours |
| our's or ours' | ours |
| their's or theirs' | theirs |
| who's | whose |

NOTE: Readers are especially confused by the incorrect use of *it's* and *who's* as possessives. Remember that *it's* and *who's* are contractions for *it is* or *it has* and *who is* or *who has*; they are never possessives.

Nonstandard: Do not buy the album; it's lyrics are not worth hearing more than once.

Revised: Do not buy the album; its lyrics are not worth hearing more than once.

Nonstandard: They discussed Planet 10, who's existence has been suggested by irregularities in the orbits of Uranus and Neptune.

Revised: They discussed Planet 10, whose existence has been suggested by irregularities in the orbits of Uranus and Neptune.

## ❑ EXERCISE 3

**Edit the following passage for incorrect or missing apostrophes.**

**I edited my manuscript about Democratic conventions during the 1960s with the help of a software program named Grammatik, who's purpose is to point out possible grammatical and punctuation errors. Grammatik even makes suggestion's for correcting these errors. Its a very effective program; it doesn't overlook much. It found two *ms* in *ommitted,* a missing apostrophe in *didnt,* an unnecessary apostrophe in *her's,* several unnecessary commas, and about seven examples of wordiness. It also pointed out that I had used in the text fifteen *very*s and ten *however*s. Grammatiks skills improved the accuracy of the paper. It's thorough checking surprised me. Now that Ive improved the manuscripts grammar, punctuation, and style, I need a software program to help with the content.**

“ ”
27a

# 27

# Quotation Marks and Ellipsis Marks

Although quotation marks and ellipsis marks have several uses, these marks appear most often in quotations, reproductions of someone's exact words. **Quotation marks** show the beginning and end of the citation. **Ellipsis marks** indicate where a part or parts of the original statement have been deleted.

## Quotation Marks

### 27a Quotation Marks to Enclose Direct Quotations

Direct quotations of a few sentences or lines should be enclosed in quotation marks. The identifying expressions, such as *the source said* or *according to the source,* appear at the beginning, middle, or end of the quotation and should not be enclosed inside the quotation marks.

> According to George Marshall, “The refusal of the British and Russian peoples to accept what appeared to be inevitable defeat was the great factor in the salvage of our civilization.”

> “The refusal of the British and Russian peoples to accept what appeared to be inevitable defeat was,” George Marshall maintained, “the great factor in the salvage of our civilization.”

"The refusal of the British and Russian peoples to accept what appeared to be inevitable defeat was the great factor in the salvage of our civilization," George Marshall reported in 1945.

Quotation marks also should enclose a part of a quoted statement.



George Marshall reported that Britain's and Russia's refusal to accept defeat in World War II was "the great factor in the salvage of our civilization."

George Marshall pointed out that Britain's and Russia's refusal to accept "inevitable defeat" in World War II saved civilization.

You should not use quotation marks when a quoted passage is long, that is, more than four typed lines or more than forty words. Instead, you should set up the passage as a "block," separate from the text, with each line indented. (See 41i.1.)

Also, do not use quotation marks with an indirect quotation, one in which the source is paraphrased.

George Marshall pointed out that in World War II Britain and Russia saved civilization by refusing to give up.

On some occasions, a quoted passage may itself contain a quotation. If a quoted passage already contains quotation marks, double marks (". . .") surround the whole passage, and single marks (' . . . ') surround the inside quotation. On a keyboard, make the single quotation marks with the apostrophe key.

ORIGINAL: His situation reminds one of a line, a plea really, from Maurice Sendak's harrowing slapstick fantasy *Higglety Pigglety Pop!*: "There must be more to life than having everything." (Leonard Marcus)

QUOTATION: Marcus points out that the child's situation reminds him of a "plea . . . from Maurice Sendak's harrowing slapstick fantasy *Higglety Pigglety Pop!*: 'There must be more to life than having everything!' "

## 27b Quotation Marks with Other Punctuation Marks

When closing quotation marks appear with other marks of punctuation, strict conventions govern the order.

### (1) Quotation marks with the period and the comma

A closing quotation mark should follow a period or comma. This rule applies even when closing quotation marks are both single and double.

> The judge who handled the case referred to the problem that "most defendants are indigents without easy access to assistance."
>
> "I've never seen a 3-D movie," she insisted.
>
> After finishing "The Headless Cupid," he read "The Famous Stanley Kidnapping Case."
>
> The book pointed out that "Japan is creating enormous research and industrial centers called 'technopolises.'"

EXCEPTION: When a parenthetical citation intervenes, the quotation mark should precede the citation, and the period should follow.

> Stendhal conducts "the rites of initiation into the nineteenth century" (Levin 149).

### (2) Quotation marks with the semicolon and the colon

A closing quotation mark should always precede a semicolon or colon.

> Many people in business and government use jargon and "acronymese"; in fact, they often leave ordinary people totally in the dark.
>
> He said, "The work must be finished on time"; and he meant it.
>
> The sign listed the scheduled performances of "Mostly Mozart": July 19, July 27, and August 2.
>
> According to the report, "Japan is shifting to a basic research phase": no longer will Japan be dependent on borrowed findings.

### (3) Quotation marks with the question mark, exclamation point, and dash

The quotation mark should follow a question mark, exclamation point, or dash that punctuates the quoted material.

> The advertisement asked, "Why give the common, when you can give the preferred?"

At the end of the game, the happy fan shouted, "Time to celebrate, man!"

He said, "No—" and was immediately interrupted.



A closing quotation mark should precede a question mark, exclamation point, or dash that punctuates the unquoted part of the sentence.

Which character says, "I am a feather for each wind that blows"?

Don't ever write an antiquated expression like "heretofore"!

"These"—he pointed to a tray of snails—"are delicious."

Sometimes both the quoted and unquoted material in a sentence are questions. In these cases, the closing quotation mark should follow the question mark.

What poem asks, "And by what way shall I go back?"

Did you ask, "Was H. L. Mencken from Baltimore?"

On rare occasions, a sequence may include a single quotation mark, a double quotation mark, and a question mark.

The professor asked the class, "Who wrote 'Ozymandias'?"

In this example, the single quotation mark should go first because the title it encloses is not a question; the question mark should go next because the quoted material, not the unquoted, is the question; and the double quotation mark should go last to conclude the quote.

## ❑ EXERCISE 1

**Correct any quotation marks that are positioned incorrectly in relation to other marks of punctuation.**

1. In none of the many novels and stories about Sherlock Holmes did he once say, "Elementary, my dear Watson".
2. Over 100 years ago, Chief Sealth of the Duwamish tribe said, "The White man must treat the beasts of this land as his brothers. What is man without the beasts?"
3. In Faulkner's story "The Bear", the hunted animal, when fatally wounded "fell all of a piece, as a tree falls."
4. How did the instruction manual say to answer the question "Is this to be installed on an MP/M system?"
5. The teacher shouted to the now intimidated student, "You cannot have forgotten the entire multiplication table!"

6. I lay awake all night wondering, "Before that enormous crowd, will I remember all the words of 'The Star-Spangled Banner'?"
7. It is redundant to write "from whence"; *whence* means "from where."
8. According to the author, Caesar was "a nobleman of surpassing prestige and authority (Kahn 56)."
9. Langston Hughes wrote about the nature of the blues: "The music is slow, often mournful, yet syncopated, with the kind of marching bass behind it that seems to say, 'In spite of fate, bad luck, these blues themselves, I'm going on!' "
10. According to the guide, "The preposition *in* means 'located or being with,' but it also quite correctly means 'moving or directed inside': for example, *going in the house* or *dived in the water.*"

## ❑ EXERCISE 2

Incorporate the quotation into sentences according to the instructions.

QUOTATION: In dealing with the future . . . it is more important to be imaginative and insightful than to be one hundred percent "right." (Alvin Toffler, *Future Shock*)

1. Quote the entire statement, placing "according to Alvin Toffler" at the beginning.
2. Quote the entire statement, placing "Alvin Toffler wrote in *Future Shock*" at the end.
3. Quote the entire statement, inserting "Alvin Toffler has written" after *future* and before *it.*
4. Quote the entire statement, placing "Was it Alvin Toffler who wrote" at the beginning.
5. Paraphrase all of the statement, making it into an indirect quote. Give credit to Toffler.

## 27c Quotation Marks in Dialogue

When a dialogue with two or more speakers is represented on paper, the exact words of the speakers are placed inside quotation marks. Ordinarily the spoken words are interrupted with comments that set the scenes, identify the speakers, and create the tone. You must separate these comments from the spoken dialogue, as in the following excerpt from Joseph Conrad's "An Outpost of Progress."

> "Is this your revolver?" asked Makola, getting up.
>
> "Yes," said Kayerts; then he added very quickly, "He ran after me to shoot me—you saw!"
>
> "Yes, I saw," said Makola. "There is only one revolver; where's his?"
>
> "Don't know," whispered Kayerts in a voice that had become suddenly very faint.



You indicate every change of speaker by a new paragraph with quotation marks before and after the speech. To show that one speaker continues for more than one paragraph, place a quotation mark before each paragraph, but place the closing quotation mark only after the last paragraph. The following example includes two paragraphs containing the words of one speaker. Notice the omission of the quotation mark at the end of the first paragraph.

> The professor gave us instructions before we began to dig for dinosaur remains: "In digging for bones, you will excavate in one small area, moving earth bit by bit with an ice pick. If you are not careful, you could accidentally sweep away bones.
>
> "Always remember that dinosaurs deserve this care. They roamed the earth for 140 million years. Humans have so far only survived 4 million."

## 27d Quotation Marks in Titles

Ordinarily, the way a title is marked tells a reader whether the title refers to a whole work or to only part of a larger work. Titles of collections and long works, such as anthologies and novels, appear in italics (or underlining). Titles of short works, such as short stories and poems, appear in quotation marks. In general, italicize titles found on the covers of published works, and enclose in quotation marks titles found within the covers. (For a complete discussion of italics, see 28a.)

| | |
|---|---|
| SHORT STORY: | "Her Sweet Jerome," from *In Love and Trouble* |
| SHORT POEM: | "Terrence, This Is Stupid Stuff," from *A Shropshire Lad* |
| ESSAY: | "Sootfall and Fallout," from *Essays of E. B. White* |
| ARTICLE: | "The Mystery of Tears," from *Smithsonian* |
| EDITORIAL: | "Facts and Figures for the President," from the *Fort Wayne News-Sentinel* |

CHAPTER: "Velikovsky in Collision," from *Ever Since Darwin*

TV EPISODE: "A Sound of Dolphins," from *The Undersea World of Jacques Cousteau*

SONG: "It Ain't Necessarily So," from *Porgy and Bess*



### ❑ EXERCISE 3

**Insert quotation marks wherever necessary in the following sentences.**

1. The Haunted and the Haunters is a spine-tingling ghost story.
2. One of Ogden Nash's poems is titled At Least I'm Not the Kind of Fool Who Sobs, What Kind of Fool Am I?
3. On Muzak, Johnny Mathis was singing Winter Wonderland.
4. The essay entitled The Blues: A Poetic Form analyzed the music of twelve blues singers.
5. In the *Washington Post* Friday, the editorial, Federal Officials Shirk Duty, was particularly critical of Congress.

## 27e Quotation Marks around Words Used in Special Ways

Quotation marks can show that words have been used in a special sense—for an ironic effect, with a twist of meaning, or as words. Make sure, however, that an enclosed word is indeed used in a special way. If it is not, the quotation marks will mislead readers.

> She insisted that the graduates from "her" school would never do such a thing.
>
> The report contained the "facts" of the case.
>
> When people talk about the movie, they use words like "strange," "haunting," and "weird."

### ❑ EXERCISE 4

**Explain the reasons for the quotation marks in the following sentences.**

1. On the Scrabble board, the tiles spelled out "SCOWLS," "SOBS," and "POOLS."
2. The dump calls itself a "restaurant" and the mush it serves "food."
3. The child cannot pronounce "aluminum."

4. The artist was "discovered" when he was fifty years old.
5. His only "exercise" is opening and closing the refrigerator door.
6. The advertisement maintains that the film is "art."

## 27f Inappropriate Quotation Marks



Avoid quotation marks in the following instances.

- Around the title of a composition when it appears on a title page or on the first page of a manuscript

INAPPROPRIATE: "A Hero for Today"

REVISED: A Hero for Today

- Around a nickname used in place of a name

INAPPROPRIATE: In the 1950s, "Fats" Domino was one of the big names in rock and roll.

REVISED: In the 1950s, Fats Domino was one of the big names in rock and roll.

- Around a slang or a trite expression used for lack of a more effective one

INAPPROPRIATE: "Last but not least," we must consider the endangered species.

REVISED: Finally, we must consider the endangered species.

- Around *yes* and *no* unless you are writing dialogue

INAPPROPRIATE: Answer "yes" or "no."

REVISED: Answer yes or no.

### ❑ EXERCISE 5

**Correct any errors made in the use of quotation marks.**

1. The first novel Mark Twain wrote was "The Adventures of Thomas Jefferson Snodgrass."
2. In Liverpool, a cat is a moggy.
3. The editorial, A Step Toward Success, says that the program is "an investment in future security;" however, I am not sure the program is that valuable.
4. The line "In my beginning is my end" appears in the poem *East Coker* from the book "Four Quartets".

5. Have you ever heard of a turtle called a "cooter?"
6. According to Edith Hamilton, Greek mythology developed when "little distinction had been made . . . between the real and unreal".
7. Was the actor in the right place on the stage when he said, "What's here? a cup, clos'd in my true love's hand?"
8. "Don't touch the"—it was too late.
9. "Duke" Wayne had his best role when he played "Rooster" Cogburn in "True Grit."
10. Victory is "just around the corner" and "almost in our grasp."

## Ellipsis Marks

## 27g Ellipsis Marks to Show Omissions

Ellipsis marks are a sequence of spaced periods that indicate an omission in a direct quotation. The number of periods you use depends on what has been omitted.

### (1) Omission within a single sentence

To show an omission within a single sentence, use three periods with a space before, between, and after each period.

ORIGINAL QUOTATION

"For the root of genius is in the unconscious, not the conscious, mind." (Dorothea Brande, *Becoming a Writer*)

QUOTATION WITH ELLIPSIS MARKS

Dorothea Brande wrote, "For the root of genius is in the unconscious . . . mind."

### (2) Omission at the end of a sentence

To show an omission at the end of a sentence, use a sentence period followed by three spaced periods.

ORIGINAL QUOTATION

"Most people who bother with the matter at all would admit that the English language is in a bad way, but it is generally assumed that we cannot by conscious action do anything about it." (George Orwell, "Politics and the English Language")

Quotation with Ellipsis Marks

According to Orwell, "Most people who bother with the matter at all would admit that the English language is in a bad way. . . ."

NOTE: When the quotation is obviously a fragment of the whole, you do not use ellipsis marks at the end.

Quotation without Ellipsis Marks

Orwell comments that most people concerned about English think it's "in a bad way."

## (3) Omission of a whole sentence or several sentences

If an omission involves a whole sentence or several sentences, use four periods—the period of the last sentence quoted plus the three spaced periods showing ellipsis.

Original Quotation

"Children are a relatively modern invention. Until a few hundred years ago they did not exist. In medieval and Renaissance painting you see pint-size men and women, wearing grown-up clothes and grown-up expressions, performing grown-up tasks." (Shana Alexander, "Kid's Country")

Quotation with Ellipsis Marks

As Shana Alexander points out, "Children are a relatively modern invention. . . . In medieval and Renaissance painting you see pint-size men and women, wearing grown-up clothes and grown-up expressions, performing grown-up tasks."

## (4) Omission at the beginning of a quotation

Do not use ellipsis marks to show an omission at the beginning of a quotation; instead, work the quoted words into your own syntax. The absence of an initial capital letter shows that the whole passage is not included. Also, when the quotation is obviously a fragment of the whole, you do not use ellipsis marks at the end.

Original Quotation

"America's group of republics is merged in one, in the eyes of the world; and, for some purposes, in reality: but this involves no obligation to make them all alike in their produce and occupations." (Harriet Martineau, *Society in America*)

QUOTATION WITHOUT ELLIPSIS MARKS

Martineau wrote in 1834 that the merging of America's republics "involves no obligation to make them all alike."



### (5) Omission of a line or lines of poetry

Use a line of spaced periods to show the omission of one or more lines of poetry. Remember that when you quote several lines of a poem, you should show them indented and formatted as in the original, without quotation marks.

ORIGINAL QUOTATION

> Power, like a desolating pestilence,
> Pollutes whate'er it touches; and obedience,
> Bane of all genius, virtue, freedome, truth,
> Makes slaves of men, and, of the human frame
> A mechanized automaton.

QUOTATION WITH ELLIPSIS MARKS

Shelley writes in "Queen Mab":

> Power, like a desolating pestilence,
> Pollutes whate'er it touches; and obedience,
> . . . . . . . . . . . . . . . . . . . . .
> Makes slaves of men, and, of the human frame
> A mechanized automaton.

## 27h Ellipsis Marks to Show Interruption in Dialogue

In dialogue, ellipsis marks can show interruption of a thought or statement.

"Well, Judge, I don't know **. . .** " and whatever he meant to say trailed off into silence.

"That car costs forty thousand **. . .** uh **. . .** forget it."

### ❑ EXERCISE 6

**Use ellipsis marks to show the omissions indicated.**

1. According to H. L. Mencken, "To be in love is merely to be in a state of perceptual anaesthesia—to mistake an ordinary young man for a Greek god or an ordinary young woman for a goddess." [Omit all of the sentence after "anaesthesia."]
2. Edith Hamilton has written: "Five hundred years before Christ in a little town on the far western border of the settled and civilized world, a strange new power was at work. Something had awakened in the minds and spirits of the men there which was so to influence the world that the slow passage of long time, of century upon century and the shattering changes they brought, would be powerless to wear away that deep impress. Athens had entered upon her brief and magnificent flowering of genius which so molded the world of mind and spirit that our mind and spirit today are different." [Omit the second sentence.]
3. Leslie Fiedler writes of Faulkner's writings: "The detective story is the inevitable crown of Faulkner's work; in it (the stories in *Knight's Gambit* and *Intruder in the Dust*) many strains of his writing find fulfillment, not least his commitment to the 'switcheroo' and the surprise ending." [Omit the part of the quotation in parentheses.]
4. In "The Second Coming" Yeats writes:

   Turning and turning in the widening gyre
   The falcon cannot hear the falconer;
   Things fall apart; the centre cannot hold;
   Mere anarchy is loosed upon the world,
   The blood-dimmed tide is loosed, and everywhere
   The ceremony of innocence is drowned;
   The best lack all conviction, while the worst
   Are full of passionate intensity. [Omit lines 4, 5, and 6.]

5. At 5:30 Mountain War Time, when the Atomic Age began, "At that great moment in history, ranking with the moment in the long ago when man first put fire to work for him and started on his march to civilization, the vast energy locked within the hearts of the atoms of matter was released for the first time in a burst of flame such as had never before been seen on this planet." [Omit the beginning of the quote through "civilization."]

ital
28a

# 28

# Italics/Underlining

Italic type slants to the right. Without this special typeface, writers preparing manuscripts by hand or with ordinary typewriters must substitute underlining for italics to distinguish such things as titles, foreign words, special names of vehicles, and words used as words. **Italics** or **underlining** can also show readers when to stress words that convey especially important ideas.

## 28a Italics/Underlining in Titles

Titles are marked either with quotation marks (27d) or with italics. As a general rule, italics are used for complete works; quotation marks, for parts of works. If you underline to represent italics, do not break the line. An unbroken line displays the title as a single unit and facilitates reading.

Although publishers do not always agree about when to use italics and when to use quotation marks, it is common practice to italicize the following kinds of titles.

Books and book-length poems

The Red Badge of Courage

The Short Stories of Saki

Four Screen Plays of Ingmar Bergman

Don Juan

Plays and movies

Othello

Crimes of the Heart

Dr. Strangelove

Reports and long pamphlets

*Handbook of Utilization of Aquatic Plants*

*A Nation at Risk: The Imperative for Educational Reform*

Newspapers, magazines, and journals
(Predominant practice is not to italicize the word *the* beginning a title.)

the *Washington Post*

the *New Republic*

*Art in America*

*Journal of Dental Research*

Operas, symphonies, ballets, albums

Verdi's *Rigoletto*

Bach's *Well-Tempered Clavier*

*Horowitz at the Met*

Paul Simon's *There Goes Rhymin' Simon*

Television and radio series

*The Shadow*

*The Jack Benny Show*

*Star Trek*

*Masterpiece Theatre*

Paintings and sculpture

*Absinthe Drinkers* by Degas

*Guernica* by Picasso

*Sky Cathedral* by Louise Nevelson

*Three Way Piece No. 2* by Henry Moore

NOTE: Remember to consider the punctuation following a title.

Italicize punctuation that is part of a title.

They are acting in *Who's Afraid of Virginia Woolf?*

Do not italicize sentence punctuation that follows a title.

Have you ever read *Babbitt*?

Do not italicize an apostrophe or an apostrophe plus an *s* that is added to a title.

*The Counterfeiters'* plot
*Time*'s editorial



EXCEPTIONS: Do not italicize the following titles.

Names of standard dictionaries and encyclopedias unless referred to by their formal names

Webster's Dictionary (*Webster's Third New International Dictionary*)

Random House Dictionary (*The Random House Dictionary of the English Language*)

Americana (*Encyclopedia Americana*)

Names of standard religious books

Bible

Koran

Talmud

Directories and catalogs

Atlanta Telephone Directory

JC Penney Catalog

The title of a composition when it appears on a title page or at the top of the first page of a manuscript

The Trouble with Television

The Unforgettable Miss Sternberger

## 28b Italics/Underlining for Words, Numbers, and Letters Used as Such

When a word, letter, or number refers to itself rather than to its usual meaning, italics alert readers to this special use. Compare, for example, the following two sentences. In the first, *dog* has its usual meaning of canine animal; in the second, it refers to the word *dog*.

> The dog barked.
>
> Dog comes from Anglo-Saxon.



Compare the use of *225* in the next two sentences. In the first, *225* refers to a quantity; in the second, it refers to the number itself.

> We planted 225 tulip bulbs in front of the courthouse.
>
> Someone had written 225 in the wet cement.

Often this special use is signalled by the insertion of "the word," "the letter," "the number," or some other appropriate description.

> In a legal document, the word said refers to something or someone previously mentioned.
>
> His shirts are monogrammed with the letters HCC.

Even when the signal is not present, it can be easily supplied.

> He says you know after every sentence.
>
> He says the words you know after every sentence.
>
> Southerners sometimes drop a final r.
>
> Southerners sometimes drop a final r sound.
>
> The British put two e's in judgment.
>
> The British put two letter e's in the word judgment.

NOTE: Words that refer to themselves can appear in quotation marks instead of italics. (See 27e.)

## 28c Italics/Underlining for Sounds

Italicize sounds that are represented by words or combinations of letters.

> The music had a recurrent ta ta ta tum refrain.
>
> With a woosh-thump, the golf club sent the white ball over the fairway.

## 28d Italics/Underlining for Foreign Words



Italicize foreign names of the scientific genus and species of animals and plants.

> The new threat to the marsh is *Hydrilla verticillata*, which can choke out all other life.

Italicize foreign words that are not considered part of the vocabulary of English.

> People assume that movies with gladiators, casts of thousands, and elaborate costumes must *ipso facto* be bad.
>
> On the ship we ate in the tourist-class *salle à manger*.

Some foreign words are in such common use that they are now considered English. For example, words such as *ex officio, ballet, connoisseur,* and *debut,* though originally Latin and French, no longer need italicizing. When you are sure a word of foreign origin is familiar to your audience, you need not italicize it.

## 28e Italics/Underlining for Vehicles Designated by Proper Names

Italicize the proper names of ships, aircraft, and spacecraft.

> U.S.S. *Iowa*
>
> *Challenger*

## 28f Italics/Underlining for Emphasis

You can italicize words for emphasis, but you should use this device in moderation. Overuse negates its impact.

> The department's expenditures are edging toward the 300-*billion*-dollar mark.
>
> She works all day as a secretary, and she still *likes* to type.

## ❑ EXERCISE

Underline any words that should be italicized.

1. The Statue of Liberty, a book by Marvin Trachtenberg, tells the fascinating story of Bartholdi's efforts to "glorify . . . Liberty."
2. Lewis and Clark brought back from their western expedition the Columbian lily (Fritillaria pudica).
3. The child kept throwing rocks into the lake—kerplunk, kerplunk, kerplunk.
4. Many people object to using the masculine pronoun he to refer to both sexes.
5. He was wearing a trenchcoat straight out of Casablanca.
6. Lequesne pronounced the finished statue his chef d'oeuvre.
7. Chess was his only love. [emphasis on *only*]
8. Stamma labeled the vertical rows of the chess board from a to h.
9. Some newspapers use pontiff as a synonym for pope.
10. Watteau's The Embarkation for Cythera is filled with angels and happy, elegant people.
11. She is supposed to be a femme fatale in The Young and the Restless.
12. Civilization has made some progress. [emphasis on *has*]
13. The word check is abbreviated + in algebraic notation.
14. Toe shoes were first used in the ballet La Sylphide.
15. On the program were Mozart's Jupiter Symphony and Rachmaninoff's Prelude in G Minor.

- 29a

# 29

# Hyphens and Slashes

Unlike other punctuation marks such as commas and semicolons, **hyphens** and **slashes** never signal sentence structure. Instead they function on the word level—hyphens to create compound words and slashes to show alternatives and make combinations.

## Hyphens

### 29a Hyphens in Compound Nouns and Verbs

Compound nouns and verbs are formed in various ways. Some are hyphenated *(safe-conduct);* others are written together *(safeguard);* still others are written separately *(safe hit).* Often the hyphens distinguish between a noun and verb form, but even so, you cannot be sure which form contains the hyphen.

| | |
|---|---|
| has-been (noun) | has been (verb) |
| send-off (noun) | send off (verb) |
| single-space (verb) | single space (noun) |
| black-market (verb) | black market (noun) |

There is one fairly consistent tradition: hyphenated nouns can show the dual nature of jobs and roles.

actor-director
player-coach
clerk-typist
secretary-treasurer
city-state
restaurant-lounge

Otherwise, your only guide for hyphenating nouns and verbs is an up-to-date dictionary. Although all dictionaries do not agree, they at least provide authority for whatever practice you follow.



### ❑ EXERCISE 1

**Should the following compounds be hyphenated, fused into one word, or left as two separate words?**

1. machine gun (verb)
2. machine gun (noun)
3. drop off (verb)
4. drop off (noun)
5. field test (verb)
6. field test (noun)
7. eye opener (noun)
8. eye lash (noun)
9. light year (noun)
10. light plane (noun)

## 29b Hyphens in Compound Modifiers

You should hyphenate a compound modifier preceding a noun so that readers will immediately understand that the modifier forms a single unit and a single concept. For example, *30-gallon cans* refers to cans that hold 30 gallons, whereas *30 gallon cans* refers to 30 cans that hold one gallon.

four-glass sets
man-eating clams
double-spaced lines
above-mentioned facts
long-remembered story

If a compound modifier does not appear before a noun, omit the hyphen or hyphens.

HYPHENATED: Fire destroyed the sixteenth-century building.
NOT HYPHENATED: The architecture was sixteenth century.
HYPHENATED: The machine registers only low-frequency sounds.
NOT HYPHENATED: The sounds should be low frequency.

HYPHENATED: I own a one-and-a-half-year-old beagle.

NOT HYPHENATED: The beagle is one and a half years old.

A few compound modifiers preceding nouns are exceptions to this practice. You should not hyphenate a modifier made of an *-ly* adverb plus another word.



carefully written paper

highly successful restaurant

badly designed building

Also, do not use hyphens when a compound modifier is obviously a unit, as in the case of a modifier made from a proper noun, a foreign expression, or a standard compound noun.

Red Cross office

*prima facie* evidence

child welfare payment

When two compound modifiers have a word in common *(three-column and five-column charts),* the common word need not appear but once *(three- and five-column charts).* Notice, however, that you should retain the hyphen in each piece of the compound.

whole- or half-year lease

forty- or fifty-thousand dollars

10-, 12-, and 15-pitch typefaces

American-bred, -owned, and -trained colt

## 29c Hyphens with Some Prefixes

Most prefixes are attached directly to the base word, but *self-* and *ex-* are attached with hyphens.

| | |
|---|---|
| self-defense | ex-champion |
| self-education | ex-clerk |
| self-conscious | ex-husband |

Use a hyphen when a prefix is attached to a proper noun (easily identified by its capital letter).

non-European pre-Columbian
mid-Atlantic anti-Communist
neo-Platonic un-American

Sometimes a hyphen is necessary to distinguish words that would be otherwise identical.

recover re-cover reform re-form
prejudicial pre-judicial extraordinary extra-ordinary

When reading is complicated by a repeated letter or by two vowels in a row, use a hyphen to separate the prefix from the base.

non-nuclear pro-union
anti-inflation semi-independent

Many words with repeated letters that were once hyphenated are now written solid—for example, *preempt* and *reentry*. A current dictionary will usually illustrate acceptable spelling.

## 29d Hyphens in Numbers

Use a hyphen with the following numbers.

- Spelled-out numbers from twenty-one to ninety-nine, whether they appear alone or as part of a larger number

  Alexander the Great died when he was only thirty-two.

  Thirty-two hundred of the automobiles were recalled.

- Spelled-out fractions, unless either the numerator or denominator already contains a hyphen

  One-fourth of those surveyed had voted.

  The arrow missed by two thirty-seconds of an inch.

- A range of numbers

  During the years 1975–1981, the building served as the library.

  See pages 25–96.

## 29e Hyphens for Word Divisions at the Ends of Lines

Writers sometimes hyphenate words at the ends of lines in order to align the right margin. Words split between two lines, however, usually distract readers and slow down their reading pace. In addition, frequent hyphenation makes a paper look messy. If you must hyphenate, follow these guidelines.

- Divide words only between syllables. If you are not sure of the divisions, either do not divide the word, or look for the correct syllabication in the main entry of a dictionary.
- Consider pronunciation. *Chemotherapy* makes more sense divided *chemo·therapy* than *chem·otherapy; fra·ternity* seems preferable to *frater·nity.*
- Do not leave one letter on a line by itself. For example, *a·like* and *tax·i* should not be divided.
- Do not divide the last word on a page. It is inconvenient to turn the page to find the rest of the word.

### ❑ EXERCISE 2

Supply any missing hyphens in the following passage.

Many people, enjoying the resurgence of a 4,500 year old game, are kicking around a golfball size object. Although kickball games have long been popular, a new version was invented by John Stalberger of Portland, Oregon. In order to rehabilitate a badly injured knee, he gave soccer style kicks to a mini size ball. After Stalberger introduced his "footbag" to people at a state fair, the game grew in popularity. Two companies, which started producing the footbag, got in a patent controversy but made an out of court settlement. The companies' products are somewhat different. One markets a four paneled footbag; the other, a two piece version. Other companies now have similar products—one an eight dollar fire engine red bag with a devil logo. Now there are even championships in which contestants play a sort of tennis and a sort of volleyball game over a 5 foot high net.

# ❑ Slashes

## 29f Slashes between Alternatives

A slash between words can show alternatives—*and/or, he/she, pass/fail.* The mark replaces the *or* that would otherwise be needed to separate the alternatives.

radio/television

A.M./P.M.

animal/vegetable

In informal or technical papers, the slash is acceptable; in formal or nontechnical papers, the *or* is preferred.

## 29g Slashes for Making Combinations

Combinations of words or numbers in compounds and sequences sometimes contain slashes.

Dallas/Fort Worth

*The MacNeil/Lehrer News Hour*

20/20 vision

4/21/81

1984/85

poet/critic/scholar

## 29h Slashes between Lines of Poetry

Two or three lines of poetry can be quoted in their original form or in prose form (incorporated into a sentence, from margin to margin). When the prose form is used, slashes show the poetic line divisions.

> Byron writes in *Don Juan,* "'Tis strange, but true; for truth is always strange;/ Stranger than fiction: if it could be told,/ How much would novels gain by the exchange!"

## 29i Slashes for Fractions

When a fraction is written in numerals, a slash separates the numerator from the denominator: *1/3, 3/5, 5/12.*

## ❑ EXERCISE 3

Wherever possible, substitute slashes in alternatives, combinations, or fractions. Assume that the context for these sentences is informal or technical.



1. The agency will provide car or bus transportation to the site of the ceremony.
2. WXTR AM or FM will have regular progress reports from the football coaches.
3. Interest rates have gone up three-tenths of a percent.
4. The Biloxi and Gulfport area is one of the fastest growing areas on the Gulf Coast.
5. If a person writes a company about a billing error, the company must acknowledge his or her letter within thirty days.

# 30

# Abbreviations and Numbers



The appropriate use of **abbreviations** and **numbers** depends in large part on their context. Abbreviations are appropriate in some circumstances; full words, in others. Sometimes, numbers should be expressed in words: other times, numerals are required. The following discussion outlines the conventions and describes the contexts that govern them.

## Abbreviations

## 30a Abbreviations vs. Full Words

Some abbreviations are so standard that the full form almost never appears. Others, however, may be used only in certain instances.

### Titles and ranks

Use the abbreviations *Mr.*, *Mrs.*, and *Ms.* when they appear before names. (*Miss* is not an abbreviation and is not followed by a period.)

Use the abbreviations *Jr.* and *Sr.* when they appear as part of a name: *Joseph W. Alsop, Jr.* The full words are appropriate only on formal invitations.

You may abbreviate *doctor* when the title appears before a name: *Dr. Williams.*



You may abbreviate civil and military titles when they appear before a full name but not when they appear before a last name alone.

ACCEPTABLE: Lt. Gov. John Bird, Col. Betty Morden

ACCEPTABLE: Lieutenant Governor Bird, Colonel Morden

UNACCEPTABLE: Lt. Gov. Bird, Col. Morden

You may abbreviate *Reverend* and *Honorable* when they precede a full name and do not follow *the*. Do not, however, abbreviate these titles when they precede a last name alone or when they follow *the*.

ACCEPTABLE: Rev. Donald Yanella, Hon. Ann Lott

ACCEPTABLE: Reverend Yanella, the Honorable Ann Lott

UNACCEPTABLE: Rev. Yanella, the Hon. Lott

### Degrees and certifications

You can abbreviate scholarly degrees *(B.A., M.S., Ph.D.)*. Remember that when a degree follows a name, no other title should precede the name.

ACCEPTABLE: Alice M. Cotton, Ph.D.

UNACCEPTABLE: Dr. Alice M. Cotton, Ph.D.

### Time, days, and months

Abbreviate time designations, such as *A.M., P.M., EST, CDT, A.D., B.C.* Remember that *A.D.* precedes a year and *B.C.* follows.

ACCEPTABLE: The Han dynasty lasted from 202 B.C. to A.D. 220.

UNACCEPTABLE: The Han dynasty lasted from 202 B.C. to 220 A.D.

In prose, always write out the names of days and months.

ACCEPTABLE: The ship sails on Friday, January 13.

UNACCEPTABLE: The ship sails on Fri., Jan. 13.

### Latin expressions

Except in extremely formal papers, use abbreviations for Latin expressions such as *i.e., e.g., vs.,* and so forth.

### Acronyms and familiar initials

The full forms of initials pronounced as words (acronyms) are almost never written out: *sonar, ZIP, COBOL, Alcoa, NASA, snafu.*

Neither are the full forms of many familiar initials. *UFO, ESP, IQ, ID, R.S.V.P., IBM, FBI, NBC.*



### Reference notations

Abbreviate words such as *page(s), figure, edition,* and *volume* when they appear in bibliographies and documentation: *pp. 13–26, fig. 4, 3rd ed., Vol. 1.*

### Geographical locations

In general, do not abbreviate geographical locations except in addresses. In any context, however, you may write *Washington, D.C.,* and *U.S.* when it is used as an adjective but not as a noun.

ACCEPTABLE: U.S. currency
ACCEPTABLE: currency in the United States
UNACCEPTABLE: currency in the U.S.

### Addresses

In formal letters, do not abbreviate words such as *street, avenue, road,* and *building.* Also, when a compass direction precedes a street name, it is part of the name and not abbreviated: *49 Northwest Farris Street.* When a compass direction follows a street name, it indicates a city's section and is abbreviated: *49 Farris Street, NW.*

In all but the most formal business letters, you have the option of abbreviating the names of states with the two-letter codes designated by the U.S. Postal Service.

| | | | |
|---|---|---|---|
| Alabama | AL | Illinois | IL |
| Alaska | AK | Indiana | IN |
| Arizona | AZ | Iowa | IA |
| Arkansas | AR | Kansas | KS |
| California | CA | Kentucky | KY |
| Canal Zone | CZ | Louisiana | LA |
| Colorado | CO | Maine | ME |
| Connecticut | CT | Maryland | MD |
| Delaware | DE | Massachusetts | MA |
| District of Columbia | DC | Michigan | MI |
| | | Minnesota | MN |
| Florida | FL | Mississippi | MS |
| Georgia | GA | Missouri | MO |
| Guam | GU | Montana | MT |
| Hawaii | HI | Nebraska | NE |
| Idaho | ID | Nevada | NV |
| New Hampshire | NH | South Carolina | SC |

| | | | |
|---|---|---|---|
| New Jersey | NJ | South Dakota | SD |
| New Mexico | NM | Tennessee | TN |
| New York | NY | Texas | TX |
| North Carolina | NC | Utah | UT |
| North Dakota | ND | Vermont | VT |
| Ohio | OH | Virgin Islands | VI |
| Oklahoma | OK | Virginia | VA |
| Oregon | OR | Washington | WA |
| Pennsylvania | PA | West Virginia | WV |
| Puerto Rico | PR | Wisconsin | WI |
| Rhode Island | RI | Wyoming | WY |



## 30b Punctuation and Capitalization in Abbreviations

Because the use of periods with abbreviations changes from time to time, you should check current practice in an up-to-date dictionary. There you will find that some abbreviations contain periods *(Dist. Atty., Sept., R.S.V.P.),* some have optional periods (*ft.* or *ft, lb.* or *lb, E.S.T.* or *EST*), and some have none.

Chemical symbols: Cu, N, Zn, Au

Acronyms: NATO, UNESCO, CORE

Military terms: POW, USA, GI

Points of the compass: NE, NW, SE

States in Postal Service abbreviations: HI, OH, AZ, OK

In general, the capitalization of an abbreviation reflects that of the full word: *GOP (Grand Old Party), Ph.D. (Doctor of Philosophy), hwy. (highway), Btu (British thermal unit).* But capitalization of a few abbreviations cannot be predicted by the capitalization in the full words: *eV (electron volt), a.m.* or *A.M. (ante meridiem), A.D. (anno Domini), n.d.* or *N.D. (no date).* When you are unsure of capitalization, check a recent dictionary.

### ❑ EXERCISE 1

**Make any necessary corrections in the use of abbreviations.**

1. The oldest house in town is at 120 W. Harbor Street.
2. My uncle used to tell stories about his war buddy, Sgt. Dumcke.
3. Miss. Ramsey was the most feared teacher in our grammar school.
4. The board elected James Ogden, Senior, as its president.
5. His case was heard by the Hon. Lucille Godbold.
6. The textile workers have launched an advertising campaign featuring products made in the U.S.
7. The Romans invaded Britain in B.C. 55 and again in 43 A.D.
8. The first lecturer will be Dr. Charles Shields, Ph.D.



### ❑ EXERCISE 2

Eliminate any inappropriate abbreviations in the following passage.

The Germans used submarines, called U-boats, to enforce a naval blockade of Eng. in the Atl. The U.S. had to keep the sea lanes open for supplies and for a possible invasion. The German submarines, traveling in "wolf packs," moved to the American East Coast. On Jan. 12, 1942, they opened an offensive off Cape Cod, MA, and soon after inflicted heavy destruction from Canada to Jacksonville, FL. From Jan.-Apr. 1942, almost 200 ships were sunk. Then Adm. Doenitz, the German commander, moved farther south and torpedoed 182 ships in May and June. Adm. King organized small escort vessels into an interlocking convoy system to combat the Germans. The convoy system, well-equipped destroyers, and radar-equipped planes eventually controlled the menace.

# ❑ Numbers

## 30c Numbers Expressed in Numerals

According to the Modern Language Association (MLA) and the American Psychological Association (APA), the following numbers are always expressed in numerals, never in words.

- All numbers 10 and above

  I ordered 15 cases of jelly beans but received only 12.

  The hurricane damaged over 500 homes.

- All numbers below 10 that are related to numbers above 10 and presented in the same paragraph

  Last year the class attracted 4 students; this year the number has grown to 27.

They were feeding 5 cats, 4 dogs, 6 horses, and 14 boarders.

- Numbers in dates and addresses

  On June 31, 1989, the couple moved to 520 State Street.

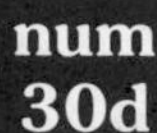

- Exact amounts of money

  Each participant is charged $7.50.

  The starting salary is $21,000.

- Sections of books and page numbers

  Chapter 2 ends on page 9.

- Numbers that accompany abbreviations and symbols

  The temperature was 8° F at 6:30 A.M.

  Take I-59 to New Orleans.

  Less than 8% of the group successfully quit smoking.

- Measurements and statistics

  Only 6 percent of the applicants qualified for aid.

  The final score was 6 to 3.

  The diameter of the table was 5 feet 4 inches.

  This soup contains 9 grams of fat per serving.

- Fractions, decimals, ratios, and mathematical functions

  They had restored about 4/5 of the Indian mound.

  Of the respondents, .08 percent were married.

  Add water to the mixture at a ratio of 3:2.

  Multiply the result by 5.

## 30d Numbers Expressed in Words

Use words to express numbers used in the following circumstances.

- Numbers from 1 to 9 (EXCEPTIONS: See 30c for numbers always expressed in numerals.)

  We spent eight weeks studying Chaucer.

  The wreck involved four cars and two trucks.

- Numbers that begin sentences

Six hundred and fifty people attended the meeting.

Forty-five copies of the questionnaire were distributed, and 32 were returned.

- Infrequent use of numbers



If only a few numbers occur in a document, you can write out those that require only one or two words and use numerals for those that require more than two words.

Park officials report that approximately 6,525 campers have used the area in the last twenty-two months. As a result, the water table has dropped below normal, and wildlife is threatened. The agency now proposes to phase out all camping over the next year and allow hiking only.

## 30e Mixed Numerals and Words

For clarity and ease of reading, use a combination of words and figures in two circumstances.

### Adjacent modifiers

When two separate numbers make up adjacent modifiers, you should express one number in numerals and one in words. Usually, the first number should be a word; but if this number is large, you can express it in numerals and use words for the second number.

We need ten 12-foot planks.

They bought 5,000 thirteen-cent stamps.

### Large rounded numbers

Because million and billion require so many zeros when expressed in numerals, readers find it easier to comprehend a combination of numerals and words.

We cannot expect a city government to accommodate 8 million people.

The debt was an awesome 5 billion dollars.

## ❑ EXERCISE 3

Revise the following passages so that numbers are expressed appropriately.

num 30e

1. Although the first guns with revolving cylinders had been made three hundred years earlier, Sam Colt got an American patent in eighteen thirty-five. Colt was a good businessman as well as an inventor. For example, in the Seminole Indian War, he sold officers all the five-shot Colt pistols that he had and fifty eight-shot rifles. Colt then developed the six-shot gun and established a factory with a production line. By eighteen fifty-seven, his factory was producing two hundred and fifty pistols a day.

2. Jane Hook is indeed a prolific mystery novelist. She has written 5 novels in the last 4 years. 3 of the mysteries are set in a hospital—a good background since Hook was for 15 years a hospital administrator. The other 2 novels also touch on real experiences; 1 is built around a psychiatric symposium, and the other has a 36-year-old nurse as the protagonist. The novels tend to be longer than the average mystery. The shortest of the 5 is 255 pages, and the longest is 420 pages.

# 31

# Capital Letters

cap
31a

Primarily, **capital letters** signal the beginnings of sentences and designate proper names and official titles. The practice of capitalizing the first word of a sentence is simple and stable. But the practice of capitalizing proper names and titles is more complex; authorities disagree, and conventions change. Furthermore, a word may be capitalized in one situation but not in another. The solution to most problems of capitalization, however, can be found in a standard up-to-date dictionary or a handbook like this one.

## 31a Capitalization of First Words

Capital letters signal the start of something new.

- In general, capitalize the first letter of the first word of the following.

### A complete sentence

Students broke the security of the computer system.

Does Assateague Island have nude beaches?

EXCEPTION: You should not capitalize a sentence's first letter when the sentence appears inside parentheses within another sentence.

The school's decision surprised everyone (he was, after all, a star player).

A quotation that begins a new sentence

Macbeth asks, "Will all great Neptune's ocean wash this blood clean from my hand?"

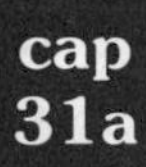

NOTE: When the quoted sentence is split, only the first word begins with a capital letter.

"In a real dark night of the soul," Fitzgerald writes, "it is always three o'clock in the morning."

If the quotation does not begin a new sentence, the first word is not capitalized.

Mussolini believed that only war put "the stamp of nobility upon the peoples who have the courage to face it."

Every line in a traditional poem even when the word does not begin a new sentence

But words are things and a small drop of ink,
Falling like dew upon a thought, produces
That which makes thousands, perhaps millions, think.

From Byron's *Don Juan*

The first word in every entry in an outline

**Japanese Military Operations in Indochina**

I. Military reasons for the operations
II. Entry of the Japanese
  A. Occupation of Laos
  B. Occupation of Vietnam
  C. Occupation of Cambodia
III. Japanese wartime bases
IV. Surrender to the Allied forces

The first word of a letter's salutation and complimentary close

| | |
|---|---|
| My dear Sir: | Yours truly, |
| To whom it may concern: | Sincerely yours, |

- You have the option of capitalizing or not capitalizing first words in these cases.

### A series of elliptical questions

Does an office this small really need a copier? Two word processors? A switchboard?

Is the book a novel? an autobiography? a travelogue?



### A formal statement after a colon

The lesson we learned was this: Work helps keep juveniles out of trouble.

Orson Welles' reputation is a mystery: he is considered a genius on the basis of one work—*Citizen Kane.*

### Each item in a list

The benefits include:

| | |
|---|---|
| Life and medical insurance | Investment programs |
| Accident insurance | Retirement program |

The test determined the car's

| | |
|---|---|
| (1) reliability | (3) performance |
| (2) comfort | (4) economy |

## 31b Capitalization of Proper Names and Proper Adjectives

Proper nouns are the names of specific persons, places, and things. In general, you should capitalize these nouns and the adjectives derived from them.

| | |
|---|---|
| France | French culture |
| Colombia | Colombian coffee |
| Jefferson | Jeffersonian ideals |
| Henry James | Jamesian story |

The following categories illustrate the kinds of words considered proper nouns and adjectives.

| | |
|---|---|
| NAMES OF PEOPLE AND ANIMALS—REAL AND FICTIONAL: | Gerry Wieland, Jean Kindelberger, Tom Sawyer, Trigger, Gargantua |
| PLACE NAMES—NATURAL AND ARTIFICIAL: | Venus, Africa, Potomac River, Montpelier, Union Station, Statue of Liberty |

cap 31b

| | |
|---|---|
| ORGANIZATIONS—GOVERNMENT, BUSINESS, SOCIAL: | Department of State, Committee for Economic Development, Milwaukee Chamber of Commerce, National Council of Churches |
| HISTORICAL NAMES: | Elizabethan Age, Tonkin Resolution, Truman Doctrine, Battle of Wounded Knee, Renaissance |
| RELIGIOUS TERMS: | God; He, His, Him [referring to God in a religious context]; Buddhism; Shinto; Palm Sunday, Ramadan |
| NAMES IN EDUCATION: | California Polytechnic State University, Basic Writing II, World History 101, Rhodes Scholarship, Scholastic Aptitude Test |
| AWARDS, MEDALS, PRIZES: | National Book Award, Pulitzer Prize, Good Conduct Medal, Medal of Honor |
| CALENDAR TERMS—DAYS, MONTHS, HOLIDAYS: | Monday, August, Veterans Day, Bastille Day |
| PRODUCT NAMES—TRADE NAMES AND SPECIFIC NAMES: | Renault Alliance, Ford Mustang, Soyuz T-5, Frigidaire, Ivory soap [The common term of a product's name is usually not capitalized.] |
| ETHNIC TERMS—NATIONALITIES, RACES, LANGUAGES: | English, Japanese, Serbian, Sioux, Indo-European |
| SCIENTIFIC TERMS—CLASSIFICATIONS (EXCEPT SPECIES) AND CHEMICAL ABBREVIATIONS: | *Equidae, Bovidae, Canis rufus, Alligator mississippiensis,* O [oxygen], Au [gold] |

Also, you capitalize nicknames or substitutes for proper names.

| OFFICIAL NAMES | SUBSTITUTES |
|---|---|
| New York City | Big Apple |
| Missouri | Show Me State |
| Earl Hines | Fatha Hines |
| William Warren | Grandfather (but *my grandfather*) |
| Mayor Stone | Mayor |

Some words derived from proper nouns, however, are no longer capitalized; others are capitalized at times. For example, the word *maverick* (derived from the name of Senator Samuel A. Maverick of Texas) is not capitalized; the word *draconian* (derived from the Athenean lawgiver Draco) is sometimes capitalized and sometimes not. Check current practice in an up-to-date dictionary.

No Longer Capitalized
boycott (after C. C. Boycott)
bourbon (after Bourbon County, Kentucky)
quixotic (after Don Quixote)

Sometimes Capitalized, Sometimes Lower Case
Platonic/platonic (after Plato)
Scotch/scotch (after Scotland)
Herculean/herculean (after Hercules)



## 31c Capitalization of Titles of Honor or Rank

Always capitalize titles of honor or rank—governmental, military, ecclesiastical, royal, or professional—when they precede names. When these titles do not precede names, you usually do not capitalize them.

Capital: In Texas, <u>Governor</u> Miriam A. "Ma" Ferguson served from 1925–27 and from 1933–35.

No Capital: Miriam A. "Ma" Ferguson of Texas served as <u>governor</u> of Texas after her husband was impeached.

Capital: In 1863, <u>General</u> William S. Rosecrans fought at Chickamauga.

No Capital: William S. Rosecrans, a <u>general</u> with the Union army, fought at Chickamauga.

Capital: After retiring, <u>Professor</u> Deutsch went into politics.

No Capital: After retiring, Dr. Deutsch, a <u>professor</u> of American history, went into politics.

You may, however, capitalize a few titles even when they do not precede names: President, Vice President, and the titles of other important members of the government. Either capital or lowercase letters are correct, but be consistent throughout a composition.

Taft, the largest man ever to serve as <u>President</u> (or <u>president</u>), weighed over 300 pounds.

Elihu Root, Secretary of State (or secretary of state) under Theodore Roosevelt, won the 1912 Nobel peace prize.

Margaret Chase Smith, the Senator (or senator) from Maine, campaigned for the Republican presidential nomination in 1964.



## 31d Capitalization of Academic and Professional Degrees

Capitalize academic and professional degrees only when they appear immediately after a name or when they are abbreviated.

Capitals: George Pratt, Doctor of Laws, died last year.

Capitals: George Pratt, LL.D., died last year.

No Capitals: George Pratt earned his doctor of laws degree in 1932.

Capitals: Doris Leigh completed her B.A. degree in 1912.

No Capitals: Doris Leigh completed her bachelor of arts degree in 1912.

Capitals: Lee Wallerstein, CPA, made the audit.

No Capitals: An independent certified public accountant made the audit.

## 31e Capitalization in Titles of Written Material and Artistic Works

Although there are various styles for capitalization within titles, the Modern Language Association (MLA) calls for capitalizing these words:

- The first word [When *the* is the first word of a periodical, it is dropped from the title, e.g., *Washington Post,* not *The Washington Post.*]
- The last word
- Every noun, pronoun, verb, adjective, adverb, and subordinating conjunction
- Any word that follows a colon, dash, or question mark

The following words are not capitalized unless they are the first or last words of a title.

- Articles [*a, an, the*]
- Coordinating conjunctions and prepositions
- The infinitive marker [*to*]



When you use the MLA system, you must determine the part of speech of each word in a title. In the following examples, notice especially that *or* is a coordinating conjunction, *if* is a subordinating conjunction, *to* is an infinitive marker, and *with* is a preposition.

> "Tall Talk: Half-Truth or Half-Lie"
>
> "Well, If I Called the Wrong Number, Why Did You Answer the Phone?"
>
> *A World to Win*
>
> *Still Life with Clay Pipe*

A frequent variation of the MLA system is to capitalize subordinating conjunctions and prepositions that have four or more letters. If you prefer this variation, you would capitalize, for example, the subordinating conjunctions *when, unless,* and *because,* but not *if.* You would capitalize the prepositions *with, between,* and *toward,* but not *in, out,* and *of.*

## 31f Capitalization in Some Abbreviations

Times of day are written A.M. and P.M. or a.m. and p.m. In print, these abbreviations are usually in small capitals. A few other abbreviations are capitalized even though the terms they replace are not, for example *T.V.* or *TV* (for *television*), *B.A.* (for *bachelor of arts*), *R.R.* or *RR* (for *railroad*), *POW* (for *prisoner of war*), *NE* (for *northeast*), *O* (for *oxygen*), A.D. (for *anno Domini*).

## 31g Capitalization of *I* and *O*

The pronoun *I* is always capitalized, even when it is a part of a contraction—*I'm* or *I've.* The expression *O* is capitalized, except when spelled *oh.*

## 31h Inappropriate Capitals

cap 31h

You should not capitalize the following words.

- Common nouns, even when they appear in phrases that contain capitals

  American history
  Epson computer
  Maxwell House coffee
  French poodle

- Words referring to areas of study, unless they are titles of specific courses

| Capitals | No Capitals |
|---|---|
| Economics 302 | economics |
| Algebra II | algebra |
| Studies in British Literature | literature |
| Introduction to Computing | computer science |

  NOTE: The names of languages are proper and are always capitalized: *French, English grammar, Chinese literature.*

- Words expressing family relationships, like *mother, father, aunt, uncle, grandmother,* and *grandfather,* unless they precede or substitute for names

  Capital: We learned to garden by helping Uncle Will.
  No Capital: We learned to garden by helping our uncle.

  Capital: When she was sixty-five, Grandmother bought a Porsche.
  No Capital: When she was sixty-five, my grandmother bought a Porsche.

- The words *north, south, southwest,* and so on when they refer to compass directions (These words are capitalized when they refer to regions.)

  Capital: The North won the Civil War.
  No Capital: Drive north.

  Capital: The first Europeans to explore the Southwest were the Spaniards.
  No Capital: The area lies southwest of here.

- Seasons, unless they are personified

  CAPITAL: "Come, gentle Spring! ethereal Mildness! come."
  NO CAPITAL: You plant the seeds in the spring.

- *Earth, moon,* and *sun* except when these words are used in connection with named planets (and without *the*)

  CAPITAL: Mercury and Venus are closer to the sun than Earth is.
  NO CAPITAL: The earth is the fifth largest planet.

  CAPITAL: The distance of Earth from Moon is 238,857 miles.
  NO CAPITAL: In an eclipse, the moon is too small to hide the sun.



## ❑ EXERCISE

**In the following sentences, correct any incorrect capitalization.**

1. As early as 1500, the English Bulldog was bred to bait bulls.
2. The president attacked the "demagoguery" of the speech made by the Communist speaker.
3. A Federal indictment was issued by U.S. attorney J. Frederick Motz.
4. The Bulgarian Government was accused of condoning drug trafficking.
5. A majority of republicans joined the democrats in support of a resolution sponsored by a senator from Maine.
6. The Commission recommended that High School students study English, Math, Science, Computer Science, and Foreign Languages.
7. The east-west conflict was aggravated by the unexpected announcement of increased Military spending.
8. Husbands and Wives may file a Tax Return jointly.
9. This Summer, the Chester public library announced that three Personal Computers could be checked out and taken home.
10. A pamphlet entitled "Life Insurance: Facts You Need to Know" explains the three basic types of Life Insurance policies.
11. The chief psychoactive ingredient in Marijuana *(Cannabis Sativa)* is delta-9-tetrahydrocannabinol, or thc.
12. Silver coins have gradually disappeared; during the Winter of 1970, the Government removed all silver from the Half Dollar.
13. The St. Lawrence seaway extends from the Atlantic ocean to the Western end of Lake Superior and allows ocean carriers to enter the midwest.
14. In the first Moon landing, Armstrong and Aldrin collected 48.5 Lbs. of rock and soil.
15. Have you seen *Go Tell It on the Mountain,* a tv adaptation of James Baldwin's Novel?

cap
31h

16. The Association has registered 661 varieties of trees; a holly is the smallest, and a sequoia is the largest.
17. "To make his magic, fiction, look real," Nabokov has said, "The artist sometimes places it . . . within a definite, specific historical frame."
18. For lunch we ate chicken cooked in a Dutch oven, French fries, and a salad with Russian dressing.
19. The constitution provided for a census every ten years to determine the number of Representatives who would go to congress from each state.
20. "Beauty: a Combination From Sappho" is a translation by Rossetti of a lyric composed in the sixth century b.c.

# Review Exercise



Correct the punctuation and mechanics in the following passages.

1. Horror films long a popular genre explore the supernatural the inexplicable and the evil all to terrify viewers relentlessly. The first attempts at provoking fear were not true horror films all the mystery was logically explained at the finish. In three classic films however no rational explanation is offered or even can be.

In 1930 Universal studios made a film about a blood drinking count, who could return from the dead Dracula. In this film directed by Tod Browning vampires travel the globe the dead live the innocent die and the irrational seems real. Audiences can find little comfort even a stake through Draculas heart cannot stop the malignant forces.

The next important horror film was directed by James Whale a british stage director. This film Frankenstein became a classic with it's brilliant performance by Boris Karloff as it's horrifying but tragic monster. The plot of the film 1931 is familiar. The brilliant Dr. Frankenstein succeeds in creating a living creature out of piece's of the dead. After killing the doctors assistant the monster escapes from the castle. Like Dracula this monster kills the innocent, and has been resurrected periodically in sequels.

The only other horror films that have ever rivaled Dracula and Frankenstein in importance are the films about Wolf Man. Introduced to the screen by Henry Hull the first werewolf film was The Werewolf of London 1934. The figure of a werewolf or lycantrope derived from the legends of central Europe where people had long heard tales of a man who changed to a wolf at every full moon, and stalked and killed victims through the night. In the future we will probably continue to see films containing these classic horror film monsters who's mysterious illogical existence continues to fascinate us.

review

2. When Columbus landed in Cuba the natives told him about "a sort of grain called maiz." In the New World corn, or maize, had long been a staple crop. And it still is. Today the U.S.s per capita consumption of corn or food derived from corn is more than 3 lbs a day and the U.S. grows so much corn it can export a 3rd of the crop. Corn has been an extremely reliable crop no famine has ever decimated the U.S. as wheat and potato famines have decimated other country's.

As a food corn lends itself to wide variety. When Cortes entered Mexico in 1519 tortillas formed the basis of the Mexican diet. South Americans also prepared tamales, the equivalent of the european meat pie and chinese spring roll. Early American settlers survived partly on hominy grits succotash and cornpone all derived from corn. It was even possible to make maize beer but this drink was never as popular in America as it was in Peru and Brazil. somewhat later the richer American People could afford wheat the poorer ones ate a lot of cornmeal mush and johnnycakes.

Today we still eat all these ancient dishes, however in addition we depend heavily on meat, that comes from animals nourished by corn. We drink whiskey, made from fermented corn. And we use corn oil cornstarch and corn sweetener in innumerable products.

# PART IV

# Style

A writing style results from a number of details: vocabulary, sentence length, sentence patterns, figures of speech, sound and rhythm. Often these details are spontaneous choices—a reflection of the writer's personality, education, and experience. But reliance on spontaneous decisions will not always produce effective writing. Developing a good prose style requires thoughtful choices of words and sentence structures.

# 32

# Word Choice

wd
style
32a

The English language has borrowed extensively from other languages. The result is an enormous vocabulary of some million words, many with similar meanings. *Roget's Thesaurus,* for example, lists almost 100 synonyms for *insane* and over 150 synonyms for *destroy.* From this abundance, writers choose the words that best fit intended meaning and individual styles.

## 32a Levels of Formality

Each time you write, you should decide whether to use a formal or an informal voice. The decision depends on your purpose and your audience. (See 35a, 35b, and 35c.) A formal voice is appropriate for business correspondence, reports, research papers, and articles in scholarly journals—documents in which writers distance themselves personally from readers. On the other hand, an informal voice is appropriate for purposes such as humorous writing, advertising, and articles in popular magazines—material in which writers try to establish a personal relationship with readers. Thus, you should use a formal style to establish a polite, professional relationship with a reader and an informal style to establish a friendly, conversational relationship.

The degree of formality or informality is established in large part by vocabulary. Words derived from Anglo-Saxon (Old English) seem more informal and conversational than words derived or borrowed from other languages. For example, the Anglo-Saxon derivatives *lucky, get, buy,* and *crazy* seem less formal than their synonyms derived from Greek and Latin: *fortunate, obtain, purchase,* and *demented.* Likewise, the English words *therefore* and *masterpiece* are less formal than their Latin counterparts *ergo* and *magnum opus.*



Clipped forms are more informal than full forms. For example, *pro, ad,* and *deli* are more informal than *professional, advertisement,* and *delicatessen.* Likewise, contractions *(can't, isn't, it's)* are more informal than uncontracted forms *(cannot, is not, it is).*

First person *(I, we)* and second person *(you)* are less formal than third *(one, the writer, the student).* If you are writing about yourself, *I* certainly seems more natural than *one* or *this writer.* If you are addressing the reader personally, *you* seems natural. Avoid, however, using *you* to mean people in general. (See 12c.)

Slang is informal—sometimes, very informal—and its appearance in formal documents can reduce them to the absurd. Imagine, for example, coming upon this sentence in a university bulletin: "Students with wheels should boogie on over to the security office and get a decal." On the other hand, a carefully chosen slang expression can make prose more interesting, vivid, or efficient. "Razzmatazz" is more interesting than "a flashy display." "Bug a telephone" is more vivid than "equip a telephone with a microphone." "Computer nerd" is certainly more efficient than "a person who forgets the social amenities in an obsession for computers." Remember, however, that an abundance of slang will make prose seem silly. Furthermore, the meanings of slang expressions are frequently unstable, changing unpredictably from time to time and audience to audience.

Choosing a formal or informal voice is often arbitrary; in many circumstances, readers will accept either. But whichever you choose, you should maintain it consistently throughout a composition. Notice how the voice in the following passage seems to shift from formal to informal and back to formal. As a result, the reader gets mixed signals about the writer's attitude.

SHIFTED

> If a person has no computer experience, shopping for a personal computer is very frustrating—primarily because the novice and the

sales personnel do not use the same vocabulary. A salesperson will toss off a lot of stuff about memory, hard disks, and menus. And the novice will stand by nodding wisely but without a clue. This problem could be overcome if sales personnel were taught to explain in nontechnical terms the capabilities of the equipment they sell.

A consistent voice—either informal or formal—makes clear the writer's attitude.



INFORMAL

If you have no computer experience, shopping for a personal computer is a nightmare—primarily because the computer-impaired and the salespeople don't speak the same language. A salesperson will toss off a lot of stuff about memory, hard disks, and menus. And you will stand there nodding like an idiot but without a clue. This problem could be overcome if salespeople were taught to talk in plain English.

FORMAL

If a person has no computer experience, shopping for a personal computer is very frustrating—primarily because the novice and the sales personnel do not use the same vocabulary. A salesperson will casually discuss memory, hard disks, and menus. And the novice will stand by nodding wisely but understanding nothing. This problem could be overcome if sales personnel were taught to explain in nontechnical terms the capabilities of the equipment they sell.

Remember that when you adopt a voice, you should maintain it consistently throughout a composition. Otherwise, your reader will not know how to react.

## ❑ EXERCISE 1

**Revise the following passages to make the formality of the vocabulary consistent.**

1. There are few aficionados of checkers. Most people think of checkers as a game for small fry. But this game can bring jollity and challenge even to the intelligentsia. Players can toil for years trying to divine the moves and can cram from hundreds of tomes that contain the lore of checkers masters. The competition at times gets fierce; it's no place for sissies with butterflies. One game played by virtuosos lasted seven hours and thirty minutes only to end in a draw.

2. You'll love the yummy cuisine you find all over New Orleans—especially the seafood. The oysters in an elegant café like Antoine's can be the

**pièce de résistance of a lavish supper—something that will really fill the bill. Whenever you're looking for a bellyful of sumptuous chow, you might consider the trout Véronique at the Hotel Pontchartrain or the shrimp rémoulade at Arnaud's.**

## 32b Precise Prose



In conversation, you can be somewhat relaxed about the words you choose because a listener can stop you and ask for clarification. Furthermore, you can watch the listener for signs of confusion, and you can restate or clarify as you go along. But in writing, you have no such opportunities. Your language should be as precise as possible to ensure that your reader understands exactly what you mean. This precision rests primarily on vocabulary. To control the meaning of your prose, you should carefully consider the meanings of words—both their denotation and connotation. And you should try to strike the right balance between the general and the specific, between the abstract and the concrete.

### (1) Denotation and connotation

The denotation of a word is the dictionary definition, the word's meaning devoid of any emotional association. The word *penguin* denotes a flightless marine bird; the word *piano* denotes a familiar keyboard instrument. If you want to use a word recently acquired or found in a thesaurus, make sure you know the word's denotation. Archie Bunker got laughs by saying, "You're invading the issue"; and Dizzy Dean was famous for remarks like "The players went back to their respectable bases." Except for an intentional comic effect, however, such mistakes (malapropisms) will ruin your credibility.

In addition to denotation, you should consider whether a word has connotation—that is, whether it evokes an emotional response. For example, to most readers, *home* seems more personal and secure than *house.* When we think of a house, we usually envision a building. But we think of home as more than a building: It is family, childhood memories, friends, and even an entire community. Consider the word *spy.* It evokes the image of an unsavory character, probably a traitor. But *secret agent* calls up James Bond, the dashing hero, using wit and muscle to overcome evil. The denotation of *suave* is "smoothly gracious or polite; polished." The connotation suggests a man—one who is perhaps continental. On the other hand, *sophisticated* suggests either a man or a woman—worldly wise and refined. *Peril* seems more serious and more imminent than *danger; zealot,* more fanatical than *enthusiast; naked,* more stark than *nude.*



Keep in mind that many words have emotional associations, and try to choose vocabulary that will convey exactly the meaning you intend.

## ❑ EXERCISE 2

Consider the following pairs of words. How do the connotations of each differ? In other words, what emotional responses do you associate with each?

1. curious/nosey
2. skinny/thin
3. melody/tune
4. chauffeur/driver
5. fiddle/violin
6. movie/film
7. orchestra/band
8. mob/crowd
9. dine/eat
10. lawn/yard
11. cuisine/food
12. attire/clothes

## ❑ EXERCISE 3

Discuss the effect that each word in the parentheses would have on the sentence as a whole.

1. As the kayak rushed uncontrollably through the white water, I felt as if I were being (thrown, rocketed, cast, hurled) into space.
2. The fans (swarmed, flocked, gathered, thronged) around the winning baseball players.
3. To escape to a more exciting world, Tom reads only spy (books, novels, thrillers, adventures).
4. The initial deposit can be as low as $250, and depositors earn market rates on all balances no matter how (tiny, little, small, puny).
5. Someone had hurriedly (written, printed, lettered, scrawled) "wash me" in the dust (enshrouding, covering, blanketing, coating) the truck.

## ❑ EXERCISE 4

Change any words that are inappropriate to the context because of their connotations.

**If you are toiling to become fit, you can try several schemes to lose poundage and to gain robustness. First, limit the time you spend ogling TV or availing yourself of video games. Whenever feasible, get out of the house and frolic, walk, or jog. Second, avoid sumptuous repasts. Eat plenty of legumes and fruit. Little food and lots of exercise will give birth to results.**

## (2) General and specific words



General words refer to classes or categories *(magazine)*; specific words refer to particular members of a class or category *(Newsweek)*. Whether a word is general or specific is sometimes relative. For example, *media* is more general than *magazine,* and *last week's Newsweek* is more specific than *Newsweek.* The following lists illustrate a gradual progression from general to specific.

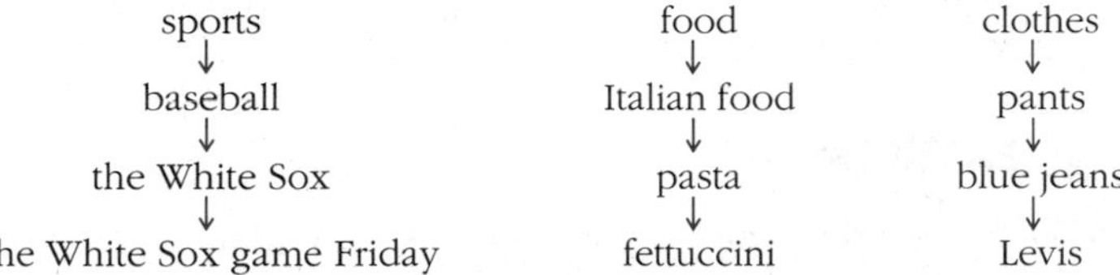


When you write, you should try to balance the general with the specific because both are inherent in the way we think. In other words, we sometimes reason by induction—moving from specific instances to find a generalization. For example, a person who sneezes every time a cat appears will conclude that he or she is allergic to cats. At other times, we reason by deduction—applying a general principle to a specific instance. A person who has an established allergy to cats and who suddenly begins sneezing will deduce that there is a cat in the area.

As we think and reason, we move back and forth from induction to deduction, from specifics to generalities. If you use both general and specific words when you write, readers are more likely to follow your reasoning process and thus more readily grasp your meaning. Suppose, for example, that you want to make the point that children learn valuable social skills in kindergarten. Relying exclusively on either general or specific words will obscure the point.

Too General: Kindergartens benefit children by allowing interaction in a social environment. In kindergarten, children lose some of their egocentric perspective and learn to tolerate the needs and feelings of others.

Too Specific: In kindergartens, children must share blocks, desks, and coloring books. Therefore, children learn not to snatch a toy that someone else is playing with. They also learn to say "please" and "thank you."

A mixture of general and specific words can convey the general idea and clarify it with details.



Mixed Use: Kindergartens benefit children by teaching them valuable social skills. For example, they learn to share desks, toys, and the teacher's attention. They learn that saying "please" and "thank you" is more pleasant and productive behavior than fighting and crying.

When you write, use general words for summing up and explaining; use specific words for supporting and detailing. This way, readers will understand not only what your conclusions are but also how you arrived at them.

## ❑ EXERCISE 5

**Rewrite the following passages to make the generalities more specific whenever appropriate. You may invent any specific details necessary to enliven the prose.**

1. One incident involved a student found carrying a deadly weapon on the school premises. The problem was handled by the proper authorities, who expelled the student and referred him to a court. The person in charge of the occurrence said that the learning environment could not tolerate such dangerous behavior and that the perpetrator should be rehabilitated, not just punished by removal from the scene.
2. The team was ranked high in the polls early in the year. As the season began, the team started off by losing several games. Evidently, those working with the players did not do a good job. The players had problems that were not solved by any of the measures taken. The team continued to lose, and at the end of the disastrous season, the staff made plans to improve the situation next year.

## (3) Abstract and concrete words

Abstract words denote ideas, qualities, feelings—anything that has no physical existence. Concrete words denote specific realities—anything that can be seen, touched, heard, smelled, or tasted. Although both kinds of words appear in most prose, an overreliance on abstract terms can mask meaning and bore readers. For example, suppose you were defining the abstract concept of frustration.

You could clarify the concept and enliven the discussion with a description of frustrating incidents—a traffic jam, a computer that refuses to compute, a test unrelated to lectures or reading assignments.

A good way to see the difference between abstract and concrete terms is to pair the two in sentences like the following.

> Happiness is a cancelled 8:00 class on a cold, rainy morning.
>
> Luxury is the smell of leather upholstery in a new Ferrari.
>
> Panic is realizing that next Wednesday's test is this Wednesday.



In each of these sentences, the quality of the abstract word is made real by the concrete and familiar example.

If your prose seems impersonal and vague, try adding concrete facts, instances, and examples that will enliven, enrich, and clarify your meaning.

### ❑ EXERCISE 6

**Pick five of the following abstractions and supply a concrete representation.**

EXAMPLES: **terrorism ⟶ the hijacking of the *Achille Lauro***
**restraint ⟶ refusing a chocolate eclair because of a diet**

1. **fright**
2. **pollution**
3. **ambition**
4. **poverty**
5. **optimism**
6. **relaxation**
7. **power**
8. **invigoration**
9. **speed**
10. **difficulty**

## 32c Vigorous Prose

To put some vigor and energy into your writing, you must think honestly about your subject. Otherwise, you may be tempted to rely on tired expressions repeated so often that they have become meaningless. You may also be tempted to avoid speaking directly about an unpleasant or controversial subject and thus create dull and lifeless prose. You do not have to be a professional writer to express yourself with energy and directness. But you do have to think honestly and speak honestly.

## (1) Clichés

Clichés are expressions, perhaps once vivid but now stale from overuse. A cliché conveys a superficial thought—if indeed it conveys any thought at all. In fact, it usually detracts from the point. To recognize clichés, question the effectiveness of overly familiar expressions, and look for certain clues. One clue is that clichés often contain repeated sounds.

| | |
|---|---|
| tried and true | takes the cake |
| black and blue | no great shakes |
| worse for wear | rhyme or reason |
| betwixt and between | rise and shine |
| super duper | wishy-washy |

Another clue is that clichés are frequently comparisons, such as metaphors and similes. (See 33d.) But instead of being fresh and interesting, these comparisons have become overly familiar and boring.

out in left field
chip on his shoulder
dropped like a hot potato
as cool as a cucumber
like a bolt from the blue
right in there pitching

Some clichés neither contain repeated sounds nor express comparisons. They are merely combinations that for some reason catch on and then are repeated again and again.

| | |
|---|---|
| agonizing defeat | cruel fate |
| crushing blow | a bang-up job |
| stifling heat | one in a million |
| hardened criminal | rude awakening |
| not half bad | agree wholeheartedly |

If you do not think honestly about a subject, you may find yourself relying on clichés. Consider, for example, this passage on holiday stress.

> To me, the Christmas holidays are stressful because I always wind up rushing around at the last minute trying to find the perfect gifts for

> friends and relatives. Between shopping, cooking, cleaning, and going to parties, I never find the time for rest and relaxation before I have to return to the hectic pace of school.

The writer has not really thought about the subject but has merely strung clichés together *(wind up, rushing around at the last minute, the perfect gifts, rest and relaxation, hectic pace)*. As a result, the passage is lifeless. Avoiding the clichés would encourage the writer to say something more interesting and vigorous.



> I would like to go home for Christmas to a quiet house where I could recover from the constant pressure of school deadlines. Instead, I go home to chaos. I plunge into department stores crowded with tired, irritable shoppers and search for gifts among the overpriced junk. I spend hours helping my parents to cook rich, fatty foods and to clean greasy, gunk-encrusted pans. I try to find rest in a house filled with breakable decorations and visiting children. No wonder the holidays cause stress.

You can, of course, use a cliché that has exactly the right meaning. But you would be wise to follow the lead of William L. Shirer and let the reader know you are not using the expression naively. In his autobiography, *Twentieth Century Journey,* Shirer remarks of his adventures as a foreign correspondent, "To say that 'there is no substitute for experience' may be indulging in a stale cliché, but it has much truth in it."

## ❑ EXERCISE 7

**In the following passages, strings of clichés create a dull and lifeless style. Rewrite the passages so that they have energy and meaning.**

1. A good friend is always tried and true, ready and willing to help in time of need. Whether you need a helping hand or just a pat on the back, a real friend will provide. If you get into serious trouble, false friends will drop you like a hot potato. But a real friend will stick by your side. A good friend is one in a million.
2. The ball was snapped into the hands of the eagerly awaiting quarterback, who then handed off quick as a wink to the halfback. Like greased lightning, the halfback sprang through a gaping hole in the line. Lo and behold, this brilliant performance was cut off in midstream by fate in the form of a tackler big as all outdoors. The ball popped loose into the waiting hands of an offensive lineman who lumbered 20 yards into the end zone, thus snatching victory from the jaws of defeat.

## (2) Euphemisms

The etymology of *euphemism* points to its meaning; in Greek *eu* means "good" and *pheme* means "speech." Thus, a euphemism is the substitution of a polite or inoffensive term for one that might be considered coarse or unpleasant. For example, you would probably be more comfortable writing *senior citizen* rather than *old person* or writing *disabled* rather than *crippled*. Many euphemisms like these result from a natural and well-intentioned motive—to make reality seem less harsh and cruel. But when euphemisms distort or glorify the ordinary, they can be dishonest and pretentious. A government that supports assassination might call it "neutralization"; a jeweler who sells rhinestones might advertise "faux diamonds"; a person who deals in pornography might describe the books and movies as "adult."



Dependence on euphemisms creates a weak style that evades the reality of its subject. For example, in the following passage, the subject is hidden behind indirect euphemisms *(peer pressure, experiment with artificial stimulants, social isolation, mental and physical disorders)*.

> Students are constantly under peer pressure to experiment with artificial stimulants. Those who resist the pressure will often suffer social isolation. Those who succumb to the pressure, however, can suffer serious physical and mental disorders.

The euphemisms in the passage weaken the urgency of the problem. Without the euphemisms, the dangers become real, and the real has impact and vigor.

> Students are constantly pressured by their classmates to drink and take drugs. Those who resist the pressure will often lose friends and invitations. Those who do not resist, however, can lose their minds or even their lives.

Whenever possible, avoid dishonest and evasive language. Use, instead, direct and vigorous expressions. The list that follows suggests possible substitutions for some common euphemisms.

| *Euphemisms* | *Direct Expressions* |
|---|---|
| correctional facility | prison |
| previously owned cars | used cars |
| depopulate | kill |
| revenue enhancements | taxes |
| mobile manor | trailer park |
| interred | buried |

| | |
|---|---|
| nonpassing grade | failing grade |
| preneed arrangements | funeral arrangements |
| sanitary engineer | garbage collector |
| horticultural surgeon | tree trimmer |

## ❑ EXERCISE 8

**Identify the euphemisms in the following passage. When you think they are deceptive or pretentious, make substitutions.**



When your beloved lifetime companion, having passed through the golden years, reaches the time to pass onward to the final resting place, consider the facilities of the Bow Wow Perpetual Interment Memorial Garden. We offer the full gamut of prearrangement option plans for such eventualities. A ceremoniously frocked mortician will deliver individualized obsequies for each doggie you lose. Come visit the resting places and slumber chambers for your dear beloved departed companions.

# 32d Cluttered Prose

If you have ever tried to make sense out of tax instructions or an insurance policy, you know how frustrating cluttered prose can be. Readers should not have to sort through unnecessary words and confusing phrases, searching for meaning. Good writing is clear; the meaning comes through readily. So when you revise, remember to clear out the clutter that results from gobbledygook, surplus words, and dense noun phrases.

## (1) Gobbledygook

There is a widespread movement in government and business to eliminate gobbledygook, also called jargon, bureaucratic language, double-talk, officialese, federalese, and doublespeak. This language is full of abstractions, indirect words, and convoluted constructions; it is devoid of humanity and sensitivity. You can recognize gobbledygook by its pomposity and wordiness.

GOBBLEDYGOOK: The committee must implement the operationalizing of those mechanisms and modes of activity and strategies necessary to maintain the viability of the institution's fiscal management operations.

REVISED: The committee must take measures to ensure the institution's financial security.

The success rate of the "plain English" movement is not impressive, probably because the causes of gobbledygook have not been eliminated (and possibly cannot be). Gobbledygook flourishes for a variety of reasons: its writers have nothing substantive to say; they do not fully understand their subjects; they try to protect themselves from criticism of their ideas; they do not really want anyone to understand what they say; they believe, rightly or wrongly, that the inflated prose impresses readers.



Some of the words and phrases popular in gobbledygook follow. You should avoid them and use instead their "plain" counterparts.

| *Gobbledygook* | *Plain English* |
|---|---|
| initiate | begin |
| terminate | end |
| utilize | use |
| transmit | send |
| administrate | administer |
| notate | note |
| orientate | orient |
| summarization | summary |
| origination | origin |
| routinization | routine |
| pursuant to | according to |
| cognizant of | aware of |
| conversant with | familiar with |
| inoperative | broken |
| at this point in time | now |
| prior to | before |
| subsequent to | after |
| a majority of | most |
| a number of | many, some |
| of considerable magnitude | large |
| as a means of | for |
| as a result | so |
| at the rate of | at |
| due to the fact that | because |
| for the purpose of | for |
| in connection with | about |
| in the interest of | for |
| in such a manner as to | to |
| in the neighborhood of | about |

When readers must struggle to glean sense from a passage, the consequences of gobbledygook are always annoyance and frustration. But when the struggle takes place in documents relating to business, medicine, insurance, and taxes, the consequences can endanger the economy and the public well-being. As William Zinsser comments in *On Writing Well,*

> What people want is plain talk. It's what the stockholder wants from his corporation, what the customer wants from his bank, what the widow wants from the Government office that is handling her Social Security. There is a yearning for human contact and a resentment of bombast. Any institution that won't take the trouble to be clear and personal will lose friends, customers and money.



## ❑ EXERCISE 9

**Identify the gobbledygook in the following passage and rewrite in plain English.**

**It has been shown at this point in time that contributions to the community improvement fund have fallen short of expectations. We had envisionized reaching our goal during the course of our fund-raising drive to accumulate the optimum number of contributions. Even though we utilized all feasible resources subsequent to the initiation of the drive, the requisite amount of money has not materialized, and we find ourselves with a deficit of considerable magnitude. It is clear that a plan of action must be activated that will minimize our problems. We must be cognizant of improved techniques that can expedite our endeavors in the future.**

### (2) Surplus words, or redundancies

Surplus words congest prose with redundancies and meaningless clutter. Without thinking, people often use phrases like these: *past history, blue in color, playground area.* Yet, some of the words in these phrases are unnecessary. History is always in the past; blue is a color; and a playground is an area. As the following passage demonstrates, surplus words add nothing to prose except flab.

SURPLUS WORDS: Our future plans are to add workshops in the areas of accounting, the method of maintaining automobiles, and the process of organic gardening. Instructors will begin with the basic fundamentals and then advance forward at a rate acceptable to individual persons enrolled. The end result will be a kind of class-directed learning technique.

Cutting the surplus away allows the ideas to emerge from the flab.

REVISED: We plan to add workshops in accounting, automobile maintenance, and organic gardening. Instructors will

> begin with the fundamentals and advance at a rate ac ceptable to the individuals enrolled. The result will be class-directed learning.

Listed are some familiar redundancies.



| | |
|---|---|
| any and all | 4:00 P.M. in the afternoon |
| basic fundamentals | free gift |
| completely finished | full and complete |
| consensus of opinion | future plans |
| crisis situation | important essentials |
| different individuals | in actual fact |
| each and every | modern world of today |
| educational process | personal friend |
| end result | reduce down |
| final outcome | true facts |

## ❑ EXERCISE 10

**Remove the surplus words from the following passage.**

**I read the other day that in actual fact 47 percent of American adults cannot swim. The final outcome of not being able to swim could be drowning. Each and every year thousands of people drown. In my personal opinion, teaching their children to swim should be a first priority of all parents. The effort would be small in size compared with the end result—protection from drowning. Also, by means of being able to swim, any and all people can enjoy different varieties of water sports like surfing and scuba diving. Since the benefits range all the way from safety to pleasure, the ability to swim is absolutely essential.**

### (3) Dense noun phrases

The compounding of nouns has long been a tendency in English. The language is full of such noun combinations as *tennis court, china cup, lawn mower,* and *garden party*. These compounds are more economic and sound more like English than *court for tennis, cup made of china, mower for lawns,* and *party in a garden*.

Three or more nouns, however, may produce a compound so "dense" that the reader has trouble deciding what modifies what. For example, consider the noun phrase *campus sorority standards board*. A reader must guess at the meaning: A standards board for campus sororities? A sorority standards board located on campus? A standards board made up of members of campus sororities? Adding an adjective even further confounds readers: *new campus sorority standards board.* What is new? The campus? The sorority? The standards? The board?

You can sometimes clarify a dense phrase by the use of hyphens. Also, you can always rewrite part of the structure as a modifying phrase. The following examples demonstrate the two techniques.



| | |
|---|---|
| DENSE PHRASE: | new employee investment policy |
| CLARIFIED WITH HYPHEN: | new employee-investment policy |
| CLARIFIED WITH HYPHEN: | new-employee investment policy |
| DENSE PHRASE: | government industry regulations |
| CLARIFIED BY REWRITING: | government regulations for industries |
| CLARIFIED BY REWRITING: | regulations for government industries |
| DENSE PHRASE: | Nevada historical artifacts conference |
| CLARIFIED BY REWRITING: | conference in Nevada on historical artifacts |
| CLARIFIED BY REWRITING: | conference on historical artifacts found in Nevada |

### ❑ EXERCISE 11

**Clarify the following dense noun phrases by using hyphens or by rewriting.**

1. **book sales conference**
2. **former patient payment plan**
3. **baboon heart transplant**
4. **last chapter conclusions**
5. **new high school student fitness program**

## 32e Discriminatory Language

Most readers resent discriminatory language, even when they are not members of the group referred to. As a writer, you should examine your language for bias. The appearance of sexual, ethnic, racial, or other biased terms not only will offend readers but also will undermine your credibility and authority.

Of course, most writers avoid language that is deliberately offensive and openly prejudiced. Sometimes, however, discriminatory language is subtle and easily overlooked. Therefore, you should check your writing to make sure you have not inadvertently included language that seems thoughtless or insensitive.

**wd style 32e**

1. Do not point out a person's race, age, gender, religion, ethnic background, or appearance unless it is pertinent to the subject being discussed.

For example, in a description of a skater's form and technique, the person's religion or race would probably not be pertinent. An analysis of prose style should not include the writer's age unless it is obviously significant. An argument about a mayor's policies should not automatically refer to the mayor's gender. A discussion of a person's work should not include irrelevant remarks about clothes, hairstyle, or physical characteristics.

2. Choose terms with care when you write about such emotionally charged subjects as gender, ethnicity, race, religion, physical or mental ability, or sexual orientation.

Try to use the terms currently preferred by the group you are discussing. Avoiding negative designations is usually easy; most people know which words demean or degrade deliberately. At times, however, the preferred terms are difficult to discover because preferences change. *Lunatic asylum,* for instance, gave way to *insane asylum,* in turn replaced by *mental hospital; slow students* became *students with a learning disability.* You may have to look to the news media, language authorities, or the groups themselves for current designations.

In addition, be careful about substituting hollow euphemisms for negative terms. Writers sometimes tend to avoid the offensive by using terms that are indirect at best and dishonest at worst. Drug addicts, for instance, are euphemistically called *individuals with chemical dependency;* handicapped people are called *differently abled.* Whenever possible, avoid extremes and seek out neutral terms that are accurate and honest, not timidly euphemistic, insensitive, or rude.

3. Avoid stereotypes.

Do not assume, for example, that certain groups of people all have inherent personalities or capacities—that some are arrogant, some deferential, some lazy, some industrious, some smart, some stupid. Generally, avoid any kind of typecasting—such as *the ab-*

*sent-minded professor, the dumb athlete, the forgetful senior citizen, the jolly, fat person.*

Also, do not assign stereotypical features to a region or to people of a region: *the backward South, the bland Midwest, prudish New Englanders, brusque Germans.*

4. Avoid language that generalizes about male and female roles or characteristics.



- Do not assume that doctors, bosses, pilots, and professors are men and that nurses, secretaries, flight attendants, and teachers are women. In general, you should not point out the gender of a professional person: for example, *a lady executive, a woman astronaut, a male nurse, a man hairstylist.*
- In the interest of fairness, use the same kind of language for the same characteristics in males and females. For example, do not call a male *angry* and a female *upset* or a male *commanding* and a female with the same personality *bossy.* On the other hand, do not belittle the *male ego* and praise a female with *self-esteem.*
- Use parallel terms to refer to males and females. *Man* is parallel to *woman, boy* to *girl,* and *gentleman* to *lady. A man and his wife* is not parallel; *a husband and wife* or *a couple* is preferable. A man's given name and a woman's married name are not parallel. Instead of writing *Dan Blake and Mrs. Richard Mullins,* write *Dan Blake and Amy Mullins.*

5. When reasonable substitute forms exist, do not use masculine nouns or pronouns to refer to groups that include women.

- Most masculine nouns have neutral substitutes. You need not go to the extreme of writing *huperson* for *human* or *freshperson* for *freshman.* When possible, though, use neutral terms.

| ***Example*** | ***Neutral*** |
|---|---|
| **manpower** | **personnel** |
| **foreman** | **supervisor** |
| **mailman** | **mail carrier *or* postal worker** |
| **fireman** | **fire fighter** |
| **early man** | **early humans** |
| **Congressmen** | **members of Congress** |

- Unless you are sure you are writing to a man, do not use *Dear Sir* as the salutation of a business letter. Instead, write *Dear Sir or Madam,* use a personalized greeting, or write a simplified letter with no salutation (see 45a). The *Dear Sir* salutation reflects a male-dominated business world and could easily offend the very person being asked for a favor.

- Referring to males and females with the pronouns *he, him,* and *his* is viewed today as outdated. Often, you can substitute compounds like *he or she* and *her or him,* but repeated use of these compounds in a passage sounds unnatural. The following techniques can help you avoid awkward repetition.

**wd style 32e**

Make the noun antecedent and the pronouns plural.

EXAMPLE: Each student must bring his own blue book.

NEUTRAL: All students must bring their own blue books.

Change the masculine pronoun to an article *(a, an, the).*

EXAMPLE: Everyone was struggling with his assignment.

NEUTRAL: Everyone was struggling with the assignment.

Change clauses to phrases.

EXAMPLE: When each contestant arrives, he will be given the rules.

NEUTRAL: After arriving, each contestant will be given the rules.

6. Remember that prejudice is unfair and offensive even when directed against those considered the majority or the privileged.

The audiences you address will frequently include white males; Anglo-Saxon Protestants; people with some degree of money, power, and social advantages. As a writer, you should not alienate any readers by making potentially inaccurate generalizations. Therefore, avoid blanket assumptions about such groups as sorority and fraternity members, people who attend private schools, or men in civic organizations.

## ❑ EXERCISE 12

**Find terms that might replace the following words and phrases.**

1. Latino
2. cripple
3. old man and old lady
4. the working man
5. policeman

## ❑ EXERCISE 13

Examine the following sets of terms and discuss how you think people might react to them. Would an audience find them acceptable, unacceptable, current, or unfashionable? Would different audiences react differently?

1. black, Afro-American, African-American, Negro
2. Native American, American Indian, Amerind, Abo-American (Aboriginal-American)
3. handicapped, physically impaired, physically challenged
4. WASP, Caucasian, white, Anglo
5. poor students, exceptional students
6. drunks, alcoholics, people with alcohol dependency



## ❑ EXERCISE 14

Without using compounds *(she or he, him or her)*, eliminate the discriminatory nouns and pronouns from the following passage.

Sales brochures can be of great value to a salesman. They are useful for distribution to potential customers who ask him about his company or its products. If the brochure looks professional and sophisticated, the salesman can give it to one of the girls at the front desk to ensure that he will get to see the right man in the company.

## ❑ EXERCISE 15

Would the blanks in the following sentences be more typically filled with *he* or with *she?*

1. ______ needs a raise to help support a family.
2. ______ does not need a raise because ______ is married and has additional income.
3. ______ is very attractive—competent, tough, decisive.
4. ______ is very attractive—diplomatic, polite, adaptable.
5. ______ is getting married; ______ will no longer be dependable.
6. ______ is getting married; ______ will now be more settled.
7. ______ is not in at the moment; ______ is probably at a meeting.
8. ______ is not in at the moment; ______ is probably taking a break.
9. If ______ is not at home on Saturday night, ______ is likely to be out drinking beer.
10. If ______ is not at home on Saturday night, ______ is likely to be at a concert.

# 33

# Sentence Style

sent
style
33a

A good prose style is smooth, clear, and interesting. These qualities rarely appear in a rough draft. Instead, they result from thoughtful revising—from deliberate polishing of sentence structure to achieve variety, emphasis, and clarity; from heightening the effect with sound, rhythm, and figures of speech. In other words, good style requires finding clear and interesting structures to replace those that may be confusing or monotonous. The sections that follow offer some suggestions to help you revise prose by choosing structures that effectively express your ideas. Because many of the techniques require you to be familiar with phrase and clause structure, you may wish to review Chapter 5 and Chapter 7.

## 33a Variety

Although the number of possible sentences in English is infinite, the number of possible clause patterns is limited. (See 7a.) In fact, most sentences have the underlying pattern *subject + verb + object* or *complement*. If nothing is added to these basic patterns, the result is monotonous, choppy prose—one short, simple sentence after the other. In the following passage, for example, all the sentences are short and simple. To make things worse, they all begin in the same way, with the subject followed immediately by a verb.

CHOPPY: Wilson was born an aristocrat. He was brought up in a conservative family. He was trained as a Hamiltonian. He became the greatest leader of the plain people since Lincoln.

The original version, in Morison and Commager's *The Growth of the American Republic,* is vastly superior.

ORIGINAL: Born an aristocrat, bred a conservative, trained a Hamiltonian, he became the greatest leader of the plain people since Lincoln.



The basic pattern of this sentence is very simple: *he became leader* (subject + verb + complement). But the three introductory modifiers give the sentence an interesting structure and sound not found in the choppy passage.

Even a series of fairly long sentences can be as monotonous as choppy prose if the structures never vary. The following passage, for example, consists only of independent clauses joined by *and* or *but.* In addition, each clause begins with the subject and verb.

MONOTONOUS: George Pratt compared the horses' footfalls, and he made an interesting discovery. The two horses seemed to run at the same speed, but Secretariat covered more distance per stride. Secretariat covered 23.8 feet per stride, and Riva Ridge covered 23.2 feet.

Variations can eliminate the monotony. Notice that in the revised version, not only the structures but also the beginnings of the sentences are varied.

REVISED: By comparing the horses' footfalls, George Pratt made an interesting discovery. Although the two horses seemed to run at the same speed, Secretariat covered more distance per stride than Riva Ridge—23.8 feet versus 23.2 feet.

Variety in sentence structure, however, does not guarantee good writing. Even when sentence structure is varied, prose can sound monotonous if each sentence begins with the subject and verb of the main clause.

MONOTONOUS: Science recognizes a number of differences between men and women. Men are physically stronger, for example, whereas women have more physical stamina. Men have more genetic defects and weaker immune systems although women are more prone to phobias and depression. Neither sex should feel superior or inferior. The differences fit together like the pieces of a jigsaw puzzle, and they create the whole picture of human beings.

The monotony can be eliminated by beginning some of the sentences with modifiers.



REVISED: Science recognizes a number of differences between men and women. For example, whereas men are physically stronger, women have more physical stamina. Although men have more genetic defects and weaker immune systems, women are more prone to phobias and depression. But neither sex should feel superior or inferior. Like the pieces of a jigsaw puzzle, the differences fit together to create the whole picture of human beings.

Following are some techniques for combining ideas and structures through coordination and subordination. Practicing these techniques will help you learn to manipulate—and thus to vary—sentence structure and sentence beginnings. With a knowledge of how to combine ideas in different ways, you can avoid simplistic and repetitious expression of thought.

## (1) Combine independent clauses through coordination.

The most effective way to join two independent clauses depends on the relationship between the ideas expressed in the clauses. If the ideas have a kind of equality, you can simply connect one clause to the other with a comma and the conjunction *and* or with a semicolon.

SEPARATED: In the early 1900s, cocaine was used in many patent medicines. It was even present in the original formula of Coca-Cola.

COMBINED: In the early 1900s, cocaine was used in many patent medicines, and it was even present in the original formula of Coca-Cola.

COMBINED: In the early 1900s, cocaine was used in many patent medicines; it was even present in the original formula of Coca-Cola.

Another way to show equality of ideas is to use the semicolon and a transitional expression such as *also, furthermore, in addition,* or *moreover.* The transitional expression can appear immediately after the semicolon or at some other appropriate place in the second clause.

SEPARATED: Pesticides have contaminated much of our groundwater. They have left residues on much of the food we eat.

COMBINED: Pesticides have contaminated much of our groundwater; in addition, they have left residues on much of the food we eat.

COMBINED: Pesticides have contaminated much of our groundwater; they have, in addition, left residues on much of the food we eat.



When clauses have a cause/effect relationship, they can be joined with a comma and the coordinating conjunction *so* or *for* or with a semicolon and a transitional expression such as *therefore, consequently, as a result,* or *thus.*

SEPARATED: His two interests were medicine and children. He became a pediatrician.

COMBINED: His two interests were medicine and children, so he became a pediatrician.

COMBINED: His two interests were medicine and children; consequently, he became a pediatrician.

Contrasting clauses can be joined with a comma and the coordinating conjunction *but, or, nor,* or *yet* or with a semicolon and a transitional expression such as *however, nevertheless,* or *on the other hand.*

SEPARATED: Augustus gave the Senate control of the peaceful provinces. He kept under his authority the unstable provinces of the frontier.

COMBINED: Augustus gave the Senate control of the peaceful provinces, but he kept under his authority the unstable provinces of the frontier.

COMBINED: Augustus gave the Senate control of the peaceful provinces; he kept under his authority, however, the unstable provinces of the frontier.

Other transitional expressions such as *for example, then,* and *in fact* link clauses. When clauses are joined with semicolons, these words can establish the relationship of the second clause to the first.

| | |
|---|---|
| SEPARATED: | An otherwise rational person often performs superstitious rituals. A baseball player may refuse to pitch without his favorite hat. |
| SECOND CLAUSE AS EXAMPLE: | An otherwise rational person often performs superstitious rituals; a baseball player, for example, may refuse to pitch without his favorite hat. |



| | |
|---|---|
| SEPARATED: | Her apartment was full of all sorts of animals. It seemed more like a pet store than a place to live. |
| SECOND CLAUSE AS REINFORCEMENT: | Her apartment was full of all sorts of animals; in fact, it seemed more like a pet store than a place to live. |

| | |
|---|---|
| SEPARATED: | To make the rock garden, cover the area with heavy plastic to keep out weeds. Add a layer of pea gravel for the base. |
| SECOND CLAUSE AS SECOND STEP: | To make the rock garden, cover the area with heavy plastic to keep out weeds; then, add a layer of pea gravel for the base. |

Alternatives can be emphasized by the correlative conjunctions *either . . . or* or *neither . . . nor.*

SEPARATED: The movies are getting sillier. Or I am getting more cynical.

COMBINED: Either the movies are getting sillier, or I am getting more cynical.

As the examples show, independent clauses are usually joined with conjunctions or with semicolons. Two less common devices are the colon and the dash. The colon indicates that the second clause explains or illustrates the first.

| | |
|---|---|
| SEPARATED: | The river was deceptively tranquil. Beneath the smooth, gently flowing surface were treacherous undertows. |
| SECOND CLAUSE AS EXPLANATION: | The river was deceptively tranquil: beneath the smooth, gently flowing surface were treacherous undertows. |

SEPARATED: The heat wave created a picnic atmosphere. Children played in the park fountains, while barefooted adults drank lemonade beneath shade trees.

SECOND CLAUSE AS ILLUSTRATION: The heat wave created a picnic atmosphere: children played in park fountains, while barefooted adults drank lemonade beneath shade trees.



Like the colon, the dash signals that the second clause explains the first or serves as an afterthought or addition to the first. Between independent clauses, the dash is a dramatic mark of punctuation, so you should use it sparingly. Overuse defeats the purpose.

SEPARATED: Cheerleaders are the most useless addition to football games. Their frantic efforts are almost totally ignored by the fans.

SECOND CLAUSE AS EXPLANATION: Cheerleaders are the most useless addition to football games—their frantic efforts are almost totally ignored by the fans.

SEPARATED: Ice cream doesn't taste as good as it did when I was a child. Spinach doesn't taste as bad either.

SECOND CLAUSE AS AFTERTHOUGHT: Ice cream doesn't taste as good as it did when I was a child—spinach doesn't taste as bad either.

The different techniques available for joining independent clauses allow you to clarify a relationship between ideas as well as to vary sentence structure. To make an effective choice, consider not only the need to avoid monotony but also the relationship you want to express.

### (2) Combine shared elements through coordination.

When two or more sentences share elements—such as subjects, predicates, or parts of predicates—you can avoid repetition and simplistic prose by compounding the common elements with simple coordinators like *and, but,* and *or;* with correlative coordinators like *not only . . . but also, either . . . or, both . . . and;* and with expressions like *in addition to, as well as, but not.*

SEPARATED: Garlic contains natural antibiotics. Onions also contain these substances.

COMBINED SUBJECTS: Garlic and onions contain natural antibiotics.

SEPARATED: The players didn't seem to understand what had happened. And the referees didn't either.

COMBINED SUBJECTS: Neither the players nor the referees seemed to understand what had happened.

SEPARATED: The Great Wall of China was built entirely by hand. It took hundreds of years to complete.

COMBINED PREDICATES: The Great Wall of China was built entirely by hand and took hundreds of years to complete.

SEPARATED: Leafy trees add beauty to your landscape. They also help lower your energy bill in the summertime.

COMBINED PREDICATES: Leafy trees not only add beauty to your landscape but also help lower your energy bill in the summertime.

SEPARATED: Your body requires the macronutrients (fats, carbohydrates, and proteins). It also requires the micronutrients (vitamins and minerals).

COMBINED DIRECT OBJECTS: Your body requires the macronutrients (fats, carbohydrates, and proteins) as well as the micronutrients (vitamins and minerals).

SEPARATED: He was willing to assume the privileges of the office. He was not, however, willing to assume the responsibilities.

COMBINED OBJECTS OF INFINITIVES: He was willing to assume the privileges of the office but not the responsibilities.

SEPARATED: She was a well-known jazz singer. She was also a well-respected portrait artist.

COMBINED COMPLEMENTS: She was both a well-known jazz singer and a well-respected portrait artist.



## ❑ EXERCISE 1

By applying the techniques just discussed, combine each of the following into a single sentence.

1. Some species of fish live many years in captivity. Others die in a year or so, either of old age or unknown causes.
2. A serious athlete must maintain a strict physical regimen. He or she must also maintain a strict mental discipline.
3. Apathy pervades this campus. Only a fraction of the student body votes in any election.
4. Reading a good daily newspaper will help you stay informed. Reading a good weekly news magazine will help you stay informed.
5. Honey Island Swamp once served as a hideout for pirates and bandits. The swamp was also a hideout for bootleggers and their whiskey stills.
6. The flowers have vanished. The tourists have vanished.
7. The boat circled back. It dropped anchor.
8. Technically, the term "shin splints" refers to pain along the lower, inner part of the leg. The term is often used to refer to any leg pain resulting from overuse.
9. Fireworks produce colorful displays of light and sound. Firecrackers produce monotonous noise.
10. The model ships were not just matchsticks glued together. They were tiny, ornate, meticulous creations.
11. The teacher calls on us to state the facts we have learned. We are also supposed to explain their significance.
12. His eyes began to adjust to the dark. He could see a shape emerging from the trees.
13. Shakespeare created heroes with flaws. He also created villains with consciences.
14. At some point, everyone yearns for a second chance. Few ever get one.
15. Nero could not have fiddled while Rome burned. Fiddles had not been invented.

### (3) Subordinate with adverb clauses.



One structure very useful for combining ideas is the adverb clause, which expresses time, place, cause, purpose, condition, manner, and contrast. The nature of the information in the adverb clause is clearly signaled through the use of an introductory subordinating conjunction such as *when, until, where, because, so that, if, as though, although,* and the like. (See 6b.3 and 7c.1.) Thus, adverb clauses can improve clarity in prose by flatly stating, through the subordinating conjunction, how one idea relates to another. In addition, since most adverb clauses can introduce sentences, they provide a way to vary sentence beginnings.

SEPARATED: Billie Jean King won nineteen tournaments in 1971. She became the first woman tennis player ever to earn $100,000 a year.

COMBINED: When Billie Jean King won nineteen tournaments in 1971, she became the first woman tennis player ever to earn $100,000 a year.

SEPARATED: Our school system offers almost no instruction in financial planning. Few of us learn to handle our finances in an intelligent manner.

COMBINED: Since our school system offers almost no instruction in financial planning, few of us learn to handle our finances in an intelligent manner.

SEPARATED: Mid-afternoon drowsiness is often called the "post-lunch dip." It occurs regardless of when, or if, we eat.

COMBINED: Although mid-afternoon drowsiness is often called the "post-lunch dip," it occurs regardless of when, or if, we eat.

### (4) Subordinate with adjective clauses.

The adjective clause can help eliminate the choppy prose that results from too much repetition of nouns and personal pronouns. In this structure, ideas are joined with relative words like *which, who/whom/whose, when,* and *where.* (See 2c and 7c.2.)

SEPARATED: The last stop on the tour was King's Tavern. This tavern was originally a hostel at the end of the Natchez Trace.

COMBINED: The last stop on the tour was King's Tavern, which was originally a hostel at the end of the Natchez Trace.

SEPARATED: Hamlin Garland spent his youth on farms in Wisconsin, Iowa, and South Dakota. He learned firsthand about grim pioneer life on these farms.

COMBINED: Hamlin Garland spent his youth on farms in Wisconsin, Iowa, and South Dakota, where he learned firsthand about grim pioneer life.

SEPARATED: I was forced to go to my first dance with Father's nephew, Talbot. His hair was longer than mine. And he danced like a trained bear.

COMBINED: I was forced to go to my first dance with Father's nephew, Talbot, whose hair was longer than mine and who danced like a trained bear.



## (5) Subordinate with verbal phrases.

The essential element in a verbal phrase is a verbal—a verb form *(to see, seeing, seen)* functioning as a noun, an adjective, or an adverb. In addition, a verbal phrase contains one or more of the following: a subject, object, complement, or modifiers. (See Chapter 5.) Subordinating with verbal phrases can eliminate repetition of nouns and personal pronouns and provide a source for varying sentence beginnings.

SEPARATED: The wedding date was already set. She felt compelled to go through with the marriage.

COMBINED: Having already set the wedding date, she felt compelled to go through with the marriage.

SEPARATED: You can dust the face lightly with a white, frosted powder. This procedure will produce a faint glow.

COMBINED: To produce a faint glow, you can dust the face lightly with a white, frosted powder.

SEPARATED: Vines covered the entire house. They almost concealed it from the casual observer.

COMBINED: Vines covered the entire house, almost concealing it from the casual observer.

## (6) Subordinate with appositives.

The appositive, one of the most versatile structures in prose, restates or renames a word or phrase. When immediately following the word or phrase it renames, the appositive adds information. When introducing a sentence, it serves as a descriptive lead-in to the subject and an unusual beginning for a sentence. And if postponed until the end of a sentence, it lends a bit of drama and suspense. The following examples demonstrate how the appositive works to make prose more efficient and structure more interesting.



SEPARATED: This automobile is an up-to-date mechanical achievement. It has a permanently engaged, all-wheel drive system.

APPOSITIVE INSIDE: This automobile, an up-to-date mechanical achievement, has a permanently engaged, all-wheel drive system.

SEPARATED: The Anchor Pub is the last survivor of the many Southwark taverns. It was built on the site of the Globe Theatre.

APPOSITIVE AT BEGINNING: The last survivor of the many Southwark taverns, the Anchor Pub was built on the site of the Globe Theatre.

SEPARATED: For the ten years of her imprisonment, Marie concentrated on revenge. It was the only thing that kept her alive.

APPOSITIVE AT END: Only one thing kept Marie alive for the ten years of her imprisonment: the thought of revenge.

Writers frequently use appositives to add ideas after an independent clause. Appositives like these can prevent short, repetitious sentences and vague pronoun references. One way to employ the technique is to repeat a word or words in the preceding structure.

SEPARATED: Chaucer tells us of a pilgrimage to the shrine of a saint. The pilgrimage is more social than religious.

COMBINED: Chaucer tells us of a pilgrimage to the shrine of a saint, a pilgrimage more social than religious.

SEPARATED: Our climate is precariously balanced. This means that a tiny variation in the earth's orbit could cause another ice age.

COMBINED: Our climate is precariously balanced—so precariously that a tiny variation in the earth's orbit could cause another ice age.

Another way to use the technique is to begin the appositive with a word or phrase that summarizes the preceding idea or ideas.

VAGUE PRONOUN: Health experts recommend that we decrease fat and increase fiber in our diets. This may lower our risk of cancer.

COMBINED: Health experts recommend that we decrease fat and increase fiber in our diets, two steps that may lower our risk of cancer.



VAGUE PRONOUN: Because so much of the business world now provides information rather than goods, many adults must return to school for retraining. This will change the recruiting tactics of universities.

COMBINED: Because so much of the business world now provides information rather than goods, many adults must return to school for retraining—a trend that will change the recruiting tactics of universities.

## EXERCISE 2

**Using some of the suggested subordinating techniques, combine each of the passages into a single sentence, eliminating choppy prose and vague pronoun reference.**

1. The bird-watchers all had binoculars hanging from their necks. The bird-watchers climbed hills and splashed through the swamps in search of the black-throated green warbler.
2. Lincoln rode into Springfield on April 15, 1837. He carried all he owned in his saddlebags.
3. Gardeners can buy software. This supplies such information as when, where, and what to plant in particular areas.
4. Nellie Bly once pretended to be insane. She had had herself committed to a mental hospital. Her purpose was to study conditions.
5. Advancement seemed to rest on flattering the executives. This was a policy designed to promote hypocrisy.
6. The woman died. She left her house and her money to her dog Teddy.
7. The five students were selling drugs. They were expelled from school.
8. A patient's mental attitude affects the chances for recovery. We cannot be sure that a good attitude will always effect a cure.
9. Da Vinci is recognized as one of the most versatile geniuses in history. He was a painter, a geologist, an astronomer, an inventor, a botanist, and a student of human anatomy.

10. The rock 'n' roll of the Tail Gators is often called "swampy." This refers to the warm and relaxed feeling of blues and folk music.
11. A red flag cannot anger a bull. Bulls are colorblind.
12. The man was brought to court. He claimed that someone had slipped a mysterious drug into his drink.
13. The stolen car was returned. Its owner found a note that said, "The brakes need attention."
14. Halloween used to be fun. It was ruined by the poisoned fudge and the needles in apples.
15. The Heimlich maneuver can be used on young people. Special care must be taken in using it on babies.



## ❑ EXERCISE 3

Improve the prose of the following passages by using the techniques for coordinating and subordinating previously discussed. With each passage, try several different ways of combining to achieve the most satisfactory results.

1. The dinosaurs may have died out because the earth was hit by a huge asteroid. The impact of the asteroid threw dust into the atmosphere. There was enough dust to block sunlight from the earth's surface. Then plant life was killed. Then the dinosaurs starved to death.

2. Many employers will not hire people without work experience. Perhaps employers should have apprentice programs. In apprentice programs, people could work part time. And they could work for lower pay than other workers. The apprentice program could count as job experience. The program could improve chances for employment.

3. George Bryan "Beau" Brummell inherited a moderate estate from his father. He set up lavish bachelor quarters in London. While he was in London, he influenced the style of men's clothing and manners for almost twenty years. Gambling and extravagant living bankrupted him. He fled to France to escape creditors in 1816. He was jailed for debt in France in 1835. He died in France in a mental institution.

4. During the seventeenth century many people were put to death. These people were accused of being witches. They were blamed for everything. They were blamed for bad weather, bad crops, diseases, and deaths. In England, Matthew Hopkins was a famous witch hunter. He called himself the "Witch Finder Generall." He claimed to have a list of witches. The list was given to him by the Devil. He and his aides went from town to town. They were searching for witches. They charged the townspeople money. Witch hunting was very profitable. Hopkins maintained that suspected witches

should take the "swimming test." In the "swimming test" the suspects were thrown into ponds or rivers. Floaters were judged to be witches. They were put to death. Sinkers were presumed innocent. By that time, though, they had probably already drowned.

### ❑ EXERCISE 4



**Improve the following passage by rearranging and rewriting to vary sentence beginnings.**

**I have gotten together with about a dozen friends every New Year's Day for the past few years. Our day begins with a lunch of ham and black-eyed peas, the traditional symbols of good luck for the coming year. We watch the college bowl games on television then from afternoon until night. We switch to pizza and old movies after the games are over. Our day finally ends with a familiar ritual. We write down our New Year's resolutions in a faded, old notebook; date them; and sign them. Someone in the group then turns to the beginning of the notebook and reads through all our past years' resolutions. We laugh and groan over our triumphs and failures. The new year seems to begin when I share with my friends this moment between the past and the future.**

## 33b Emphasis

Most of the sentences in a composition should be direct and unadorned with stylistic flourish. They should not have parts that are unusually long or artfully balanced. They should not call out to a reader for special notice. Sometimes, however, an idea warrants such notice. You can then create a dramatic structure by rearranging the parts of an ordinary sentence, by expanding a part beyond the reader's expectations, by building to a climactic conclusion, or by noticeably balancing the parts. These kinds of dramatic structures should appear sparingly because too many will make prose seem artificial and contrived. Used occasionally, however, and in the right situations, dramatic sentences will strengthen prose.

### (1) Periodic sentences

The most common kind of sentence is the "loose" construction, which begins with the main idea in an independent clause, followed by less-important details. This order is considered normal because English speakers seem naturally to progress from subject to verb to complement, with additions and modifiers tacked on. In the periodic sentence, the normal order is reversed, and the main idea is postponed until the end. A periodic order seems to hang the reader in suspension—anticipating the outcome.



LOOSE: This house was the last of the century-old buildings we had tried in vain to protect.

PERIODIC: Of the century-old buildings we had tried in vain to protect, this house was the last.

LOOSE: Don't order spaghetti when you go to an important business lunch, where you must present a neat, efficient, controlled image.

PERIODIC: When you go to an important business lunch, where you must present a neat, efficient, controlled image, don't order spaghetti.

When exaggerated, a periodic sentence calls attention not only to the idea at the end but also to the structure itself. In the following example, the writer begins with a long, detailed modifier, postponing the main idea until a final short clause, *the realities emerged.* The result is a fairly dramatic sentence that a reader will notice and enjoy.

> Through the motes of cracker dust, corn meal dust, the Gold Dust of the Gold Dust Twins that the floor had been swept out with, the realities emerged. (Eudora Welty)

In the next example, an introductory adverb clause and the parenthetical *you may ask* delay the point and thus add to the humor of the question—when it finally comes.

> If Man has benefited immeasurably by his association with the dog, what, you may ask, has the dog got out of it? (James Thurber)

In the following passage, two consecutive periodic sentences heighten the intensity of the writer's main idea: *the only difference between music and Musak is the spelling* and *it's all the same to me.*

> First off, I want to say that as far as I am concerned, in instances where I have not personally and deliberately sought it out, the only difference between music and Muzak is the spelling. Pablo Casals practicing across the hall with the door open—being trapped in an elevator, the ceiling of which is broadcasting "Parsley, Sage, Rosemary, and Thyme"—it's all the same to me. (Fran Lebowitz)

## ❑ EXERCISE 5

Rewrite these loose sentences as periodic.

1. She finally won a beauty contest after years of practice and coaching, after rigorous diets and plastic surgery, after countless attempts that ended in defeat.
2. The reality of our loss hit us when the dawn revealed the damage, when we found a burned shell instead of a house.
3. I entered a singing contest once in the sixth grade, although I cannot imagine why, since I could barely carry a tune.
4. Just give me an A rather than encouragement, advice, and study aids.
5. The star swept into the room wrapped in furs, signing autographs, posing for photographs, followed by a throng of admirers.



### (2) Cumulative sentences

The cumulative sentence is an exaggerated loose structure that piles up—or accumulates—structures at the end. One type of exaggeration is a long series of modifiers, like the *who* clauses in the following sentences.

> Grant was one of a body of men who owed reverence and obeisance to no one, who were self-reliant to a fault, who cared hardly anything for the past but who had a sharp eye for the future. (Bruce Catton)

A series of phrases at the end of a sentence can also produce a cumulative effect.

> This time the sorrel mare was in the lot before he heard it at all, the rider collarless and even bareheaded, trembling, speaking in a shaking voice as the woman in the house had done, his father merely looking up once before stooping again to the horse he was buckling, so that the man on the mare spoke to his stooping back. (William Faulkner)

In the next sentence, the writer begins with two main clauses and then tacks on a series of examples after the word *say*. The length of the structure and the number of details creates an attention-getting sentence.

> Summer will be admitted to our breakfast table as usual, and in the space of a half a cup of coffee I will be able to discover, say, that Ferguson Jenkins went eight innings in Montreal and won his fourth game of the season while giving up five hits, that Al Kaline was horse-collared by Fritz Peterson at the stadium, that Tony Oliva hit a single off Mickey Lolich in Detroit, that Juan Marichal was bombed

> by the Reds in the top of the sixth at Candlestick Park, and that similar disasters and triumphs befell a couple of dozen-odd of the other ballplayers—favorites and knaves—whose fortunes I follow from April to October. (Roger Angell)

### ❏ EXERCISE 6



**Make the loose sentences cumulative by adding structures onto each. If the beginnings do not stimulate ideas, substitute a few of your own.**

EXAMPLE: **The man was dressed like a gypsy. → The man was dressed like a gypsy, in a red silk shirt open to the waist, tight black pants, a bandanna on his head, gold loops in his ears, and a tight cummerbund circling his waist.**

1. **My favorite memories from childhood are summer afternoons.**
2. **The hamburger tasted like plastic.**
3. **My grammar school principal seemed frightening.**
4. **He wanted a wife who was like his mother.**
5. **I thought that college life would be fun.**

## (3) Climactic sentences

Another strategy for achieving emphasis is the climactic sentence, in which multiple ideas move up a scale—from less important to more important, from simple to complex, from the ordinary to the extraordinary. The climactic sentence can also build to a point, then shift suddenly from the literal to the ironic or from the normal to the unexpected. The effect is that the last idea expressed receives the most emphasis.

> The letter, written in pencil, expressed intense admiration, confessed regrets about the past, revealed deep sorrows—and was never mailed.
>
> Like us, stars have a cycle of life from birth, through youth and maturity, to decline and death.
>
> He fidgeted, took practice swings, spit, adjusted his clothes, kissed his bat, stepped into the batter's box, and struck out.

When the content lends itself to drama, the climactic sentence can be particularly effective, as the following sentence illustrates.

> Thus it is that the mouse seems always to dangle so languidly from the jaws, lies there so quietly when dropped, dies of his injuries without a struggle. (Lewis Thomas)

## ❑ EXERCISE 7

**Combine each of the following sets of sentences into one sentence with a climactic order.**

1. On the camping trip, our tent washed away in a flash flood. Also, the mosquitoes attacked us in swarms. The heat was unbearable. Our food spoiled.
2. The interviewer asked me what jobs I had held previously. She asked me if I were free for dinner. She asked me what salary I expected. She asked me what degree I held.
3. To prove he was as good a cook as my mother, my father prepared an elaborate dinner. He made Caesar salad. He concocted a flaming dessert which caught the tablecloth on fire. He fixed pork chops stuffed with raisin dressing.
4. Success is a matter of priorities. You must decide what you are willing to give up to attain your goals. You decide which goals are important to your success. You must decide what you consider success to be.
5. The child sat on Santa's lap. She pulled on his beard. She asked him for about a thousand dollars worth of toys. She said crossly, "You ain't my daddy." She stared at him hostilely.



### (4) Balanced sentences

A balanced sentence creates a symmetry—a noticeable and deliberate symmetry—achieved with parallel structure and often with repetition of key vocabulary. The "echo" of structure and words emphasizes the comparison or contrast of ideas.

> You cannot get a job without experience, and you cannot get experience without a job.
>
> From afar, the island looked like a tropical paradise of white sand and sparkling blue sea; up close, the island looked like a garbage dump of trash and polluted water.

When the structure and vocabulary of a sentence are perfectly balanced, the result can be quite dramatic. For example, the second sentence in the following passage has perfectly balanced independent clauses, with the subject and complement of the first clause *(seamen, gentlemen)* reversed in the second clause *(gentlemen, seamen.)*

> There were gentlemen and there were seamen in the Navy of Charles II. But the seamen were not gentlemen, and the gentlemen were not seamen. (Lord Macaulay)

Consecutive sentences can also be balanced; that is, a structure can be repeated and vocabulary carried over for two or more sentences in a row. In the next passage, the echo effect is created by the repetition of *when* clauses with *power* as the subject, followed by independent clauses with *poetry* as the subject.

> When power leads man toward arrogance, poetry reminds him of his limitations. When power narrows the areas of man's concern, poetry reminds him of the richness and diversity of his existence. When power corrupts, poetry cleanses, for art establishes the basic human truths which must serve as the touchstone of our judgment. (John Kennedy)



A balanced structure can highlight an idea or keep prose from sounding monotonous. Remember, however, that if overused, this kind of structure, especially when exaggerated, will seem pretentious and will rapidly wear on a reader's nerves.

## ❑ EXERCISE 8

**Revise the following sentences to create balanced structures by repeating structure and, where possible, key vocabulary.**

EXAMPLE: Although the plot of the mystery is ordinary, the book has unusual characters. → The plot of the mystery is ordinary, but the characters are extraordinary.

1. He knew when to give in. In addition, he also understood when he should give up.
2. Although he was friendly and outgoing in public, in private he was hostile as well as withdrawn.
3. The cost of one episode of *Miami Vice* was $1,500,000. The budget was $1,167,000 for running the entire Miami vice squad for a whole year.
4. To young people, the absence of pleasure is painful. The lack of pain, when people get older, is a pleasure.
5. Some people say that the clothes make the man. In my opinion, however, the man can have a beneficial effect on the clothes.

## ❑ EXERCISE 9

**Determine whether the following sentences are periodic, cumulative, climactic, or balanced.**

1. Integrity without knowledge is weak and useless, and knowledge without integrity is dangerous and dreadful. (Samuel Johnson)

2. There are, indeed, many other jobs that are unpleasant, and yet no one thinks of abolishing them—that of the plumber, that of the soldier, that of the garbage-man, that of the priest hearing confessions, that of the sand-hog, and so on. (H. L. Mencken)
3. Yet because the moth was so small, and so simple a form of the energy that was rolling in at the open window and driving its way through so many narrow and intriguing corridors in my own brain and in those of other human beings, there was something marvelous as well as pathetic about him. (Virginia Woolf)
4. The golf gallery is the Punchinello of the great sports mob, the clown crowd, an uncontrollable, galloping, galumphing horde, that wanders hysterically over manicured pasture acreage of an afternoon, clucking to itself, trying to keep quiet, making funny noises, sweating, thundering over hills ten thousand strong, and gathering, mousey-still, around a little hole in the ground to see a man push a little ball into the bottom of it with a crooked iron stick. (Paul Gallico)



## 33c Streamlining

Effective writing is easy to read. It allows a reader to move smoothly through sentences without laboring to discover structure and meaning. If your prose seems cumbersome and hard to read, you may be obscuring the meaning by packing too much into single sentences, by including too many empty or passive verbs, or by clouding the connection between subjects and verbs. Practicing the following techniques can help you streamline your writing and produce crisp, clear sentences that throw no obstacles in a reader's path.

### (1) Empty verbs and nominalizations

Empty verbs, such as *be, have,* and *make,* have little or no meaning themselves and must absorb meaning from their contexts. Since these verbs do not express action, they are frequently accompanied by a nominalization, that is, an expression of action in noun form. Using unnecessary nominalizations can result in cumbersome structures, as the following sentence illustrates.

> Rescue teams are making attempts to uncover the mine shaft, but authorities have no expectations of success.

Expressing the action in verbs rather than nouns tightens and streamlines the structure.

Rescue teams are attempting to uncover the mine shaft, but authorities do not expect success.

In revising, you should keep an eye out for nominalizations that weaken structure and pad your prose. The following pairs of sentences demonstrate how easily you can eliminate unnecessary nominalizations. Often the solution is simply to express the action in a strong verb or verbal. Notice that the revised versions are shorter and crisper.



ORIGINAL: We had hopes that the students would vote for the abolition of the curfews.

REVISED: We hoped that the students would vote to abolish the curfews.

ORIGINAL: The basis of the achievement of your goal is the development of a positive attitude.

REVISED: To achieve your goal, you must develop a positive attitude.

ORIGINAL: To make a discovery about how many people felt a necessity for longer lab hours, I made use of a simple questionnaire.

REVISED: To discover how many people needed longer lab hours, I used a simple questionnaire.

## ❑ EXERCISE 10

**Streamline the following passages by changing empty verbs and unnecessary nominalizations to strong verbs.**

1. In this morning's meeting, the club president made note of the number of people who were participants in the recreation program. She also made comments on the club's desire to offer support for the program next year. The treasurer then made the suggestion that we conduct a survey of members to find out how many have intentions of becoming participants next year.

2. Scientists hold the belief that the common cold is not a single disease. They have made the discovery that about 200 different viruses are the causes of infections. The experts, however, do not possess much knowledge about how colds are transmitted. Some have made the conclusion that the viruses can be transmitted through the air. Others believe that colds are the result of direct contact. In any case, since people cannot maintain isolation from others, they cannot find an escape from colds.

## (2) Weak passives

In an active sentence, the agent of the action appears in the subject position, and the receiver of the action appears as the direct object. In a passive sentence, this order is reversed. The receiver of the action appears in the subject position but still receives the action. The agent of the action can appear as an object of the preposition *by.*



ACTIVE: Locusts ruined their crops.

PASSIVE: Their crops were ruined by the locusts.

A passive sentence can be useful in certain situations. For example, sometimes a writer chooses the passive to emphasize the receiver of the action. The following pair of sentences illustrates the different emphasis found in active and passive constructions.

ACTIVE: The Etruscans and the Greeks influenced the earliest Roman sculpture.

PASSIVE: The earliest Roman sculpture was influenced by the Etruscans and the Greeks.

The active sentence focuses attention on the agents *(the Etruscans and the Greeks),* whereas the passive sentence focuses attention on the receiver of the action *(earliest Roman sculpture).*

Other times, a writer chooses the passive because the agent is unknown or unimportant in the context. In such cases, the phrase containing *by* or *with* and the agent is usually left out.

PASSIVE: The telephone lines were cut.

PASSIVE: Equity courts in the United States are called Courts of Chancery.

The passive may be preferable in some situations, but in others, it may be unnecessarily weak and wordy, especially when a *by* phrase supplies the agent. Active versions tend to be more concise, emphatic, and lively than their passive counterparts because the subject acts and the verb does not require the *be* auxiliary. Also, when the agent of the action figures significantly in the content, the active focuses a reader's attention on the right words.

WEAK PASSIVE: Booster cables should never be connected to a frozen battery by you.

ACTIVE: You should never connect booster cables to a frozen battery.

WEAK PASSIVE: The investors were swindled out of 10 million dollars by Arnold and Slack.

ACTIVE: Arnold and Slack swindled the investors out of 10 million dollars.

Compare the following two passages. The passive version obscures the important role of the host, calling attention instead to the result of his actions.



WEAK PASSIVE

Before a Japanese tea ceremony, the tea room and surrounding gardens are cleaned by the host. Then a fire is made in the hearth and the water is put on to boil. When the guests arrive, the tea bowl, tea caddy, utensils for tending the fire, incense burner, and other necessary tools are carried in by the host. After the tea is prepared in a historical ritual, each guest is served. Finally, all utensils having been removed, the guests are bowed to, the signal that the ceremony has been completed.

In contrast, the active version is livelier and emphasizes the importance of the agent (the host) in the action (the ceremony).

ACTIVE

Before a Japanese tea ceremony, the host cleans the tea room and surrounding gardens. Then he makes a fire in the hearth and puts the water on to boil. When the guests arrive, he carries in the tea bowl, tea caddy, utensils for tending the fire, incense burner, and other necessary tools. After preparing the tea in a historical ritual, the host serves each guest. Finally, he removes all utensils and bows to guests, the signal that the ceremony is over.

## ❑ EXERCISE 11

**Change the following passive-voice sentences to active. When no *by* or *with* phrase exists, you will have to supply an appropriate active-voice subject.**

EXAMPLE: **Piles of spicy crabs and boiled corn were eaten. → We ate piles of spicy crabs and boiled corn.**

1. **Hypnosis has been used by psychologists for more than a century.**
2. **The mountains were covered with snow.**
3. **Almost any plant can be composted for use in the garden.**
4. **Cheese was used as a food source more than 4,000 years ago.**
5. ***Mean Streets* was filmed by Martin Scorsese in New York City's Little Italy.**

6. The language in policies is being simplified by insurance companies.
7. Our lifestyles would be changed drastically by energy shortages.
8. The journal is published by a local press.
9. My bank was robbed this morning.
10. A touchdown was made in the last three seconds of the game.



## (3) Unnecessary *that, who,* and *which* clauses

When revising prose, look for adjective clauses that begin with *that, who,* or *which* followed by a form of the verb *be* (*that is, who are, which were,* etc.). Frequently, these are empty words that can be deleted. The deletion converts this kind of clause to a word or phrase—a more efficient structure.

UNNECESSARY CLAUSE: The teacher had a smile that was skeptical.

REVISED: The teacher had a skeptical smile.

UNNECESSARY CLAUSE: W. C. Fields often played swindlers who were dedicated to the rule "never give a sucker an even break."

REVISED: W. C. Fields often played swindlers dedicated to the rule "never give a sucker an even break."

UNNECESSARY CLAUSE: Radon, which is a radioactive gas that forms naturally underground, can seep into buildings.

REVISED: Radon, a radioactive gas that forms naturally underground, can seep into buildings.

## ❑ EXERCISE 12

**Streamline the following passage by eliminating any unnecessary *that, who,* and *which* clauses.**

**During the depression, a newspaper editor, who was from Oklahoma City, toured twenty states. In Washington, he reported his findings to a committee that was conducting hearings on unemployment. He told of conditions that were deplorable in the states that he had visited. He saw counties, which were once prosperous coal-mining regions, without a single bank. In Seattle, he saw women who were searching for scraps of food in refuse piles. He read of sheep raisers who were desperate and who were killing their sheep because they could get only a dollar a head. In the South, he saw**

**bales of cotton that were rotting in the fields. He sympathized with all these people who were victims of circumstances that were uncontrollable, and he warned the committee of conditions that were worsening.**

### (4) Excessive verb forms

sent style 33c

If a sentence seems congested and difficult to follow, check it to see whether it contains too many verb forms. Any verb form—main verb, infinitive, or participle—is the potential basis for a sentence. As a result, the addition of each verb form to a sentence complicates the structure. Consider, for instance, the following sentence with four verb forms.

> Residents who revel in the city's tradition of eccentricity expect 25,000 visitors to join in the dancing under the palm trees.

Embedded are four potential sentences.

> Residents revel in the city's tradition of eccentricity.
>
> Residents expect 25,000 visitors.
>
> The visitors will join in.
>
> The visitors will dance under the palm trees.

Because there are only four verbs, the sentence is not unduly complicated. But when too many verb forms are packed into a sentence, the structure will groan and collapse under its own weight. For instance, consider this sentence from a government document.

> Excessive Verb Forms
>
> After conducting surveys concerning public opinion toward automated highway systems, the department decided to abandon plans to allocate funds for studying such systems and is investigating mass transit systems that might help to alleviate congestion on highways leading into metropolitan areas.

Asking a reader to plow through eleven ideas in one sentence is simply asking too much. The solution is to split the sentence into smaller units and to eliminate some of the empty verbs that contribute nothing to the meaning. For example, *conducting surveys* can be expressed as *surveying; to allocate funds for studying* can be expressed as *to fund studies*. And because *decide to* and *help to* do not contribute information or clarity, they can be eliminated.

REVISED

After surveying public opinion toward automated highway systems, the department abandoned plans to fund studies of such systems. Instead, the department is investigating mass transit systems that might alleviate congestion on highways leading into metropolitan areas.

Now the first sentence has four verb forms, and the second has three. The result is a more streamlined passage that is easier to read.



## ❑ EXERCISE 13

**Streamline the following sentence by splitting it into more than one sentence and getting rid of any unnecessary words.**

**When Jones made the final shot that put the Knicks out in front just before the buzzer sounded to end the game, the excited fans were cheering and stomping so loudly that they did not realize that the official had blown the whistle to serve as a signal that someone had committed a foul and that the basket might possibly not count and the game could be lost.**

### (5) A clear connection between subject and verb

To understand a sentence readily, a reader must make a swift connection between the subject and its verb. If too many words intervene between the two, the vital connection is obscured, and the reader must grope for the sense. In the following example, 14 words intervene between the subject *(Second City)* and the verb *(has launched)*.

OBSCURE CONNECTION: Second City, originally a group of University of Chicago students who formed an improvisational repertory company, has launched an astonishing number of our best comic actors.

Since most sentences can be revised in several ways, the revision you choose depends on the meaning you want to convey. For instance, to emphasize *Second City,* the subject of the preceding example, you should probably leave it at the beginning—a place of emphasis. In this case, a possibility is to split the sentence. The original subject plus the intervening words could be made into a complete sentence. Adding a little transition between the two sentences would make their relationship clear.

CLEAR CONNECTION: Second City was originally a group of University of Chicago students who formed an improvisational repertory company. Since its origin, the group has launched an astonishing number of our best comic actors.

To emphasize *comic actors* instead of *Second City,* you could shift to a passive sentence. In this version, the original subject and intervening words move to the end, and the new subject *an astonishing number of our best comic actors* is now closer to its verb.



CLEAR CONNECTION: An astonishing number of our best comic actors have been launched by Second City, originally a group of University of Chicago students who formed an improvisational repertory company.

In the next example, 29 words separate the subject *(police officers)* from its verb *(are).*

OBSCURE CONNECTION: Police officers, who are apparently the only members of our society with legitimate excuses to use an assortment of deadly weapons and to drive fast with lights flashing and sirens blaring, are the favorite subjects of television writers.

Because the subject and the subject complement *(favorite subjects)* are interchangeable, switching the two elements can clarify the sentence.

CLEAR CONNECTION: The favorite subjects of television writers are police officers, who are apparently the only members of our society with legitimate excuses to use an assortment of deadly weapons and to drive fast with lights flashing and sirens blaring.

If this solution seems unappealing, an alternative is to rewrite the original intervening words as an adverb clause and move it to the beginning of the sentence. Thus, you bring together the subject and verb.

CLEAR CONNECTION: Because they are apparently the only members of society with legitimate excuses to drive fast, blare sirens, flash lights, and knock heads, police officers are the favorite subjects of television writers.

A compound subject, especially one containing modifiers, can be so cumbersome that the subject-verb connection is obscured.

OBSCURE CONNECTION: Osteoclasts, dismantling cells that destroy old bone, and osteoblasts, construction cells that help form new bone, combine to create a continuous remodeling process.



The complete subject contains the simple subjects *(osteoclasts, osteoblasts)* as well as the appositives *(dismantling cells, construction cells)* and adjective clauses *(that destroy . . . , that help . . .)*. This lengthy construction overwhelms the verb *(combine)*. One way to solve the problem is to move the shorter noun phrase from the end to the subject position.

CLEAR CONNECTION: A continuous remodeling process results from a combination of osteoclasts, dismantling cells that destroy old bone, and osteoblasts, construction cells that help form new bone.

Another way to clarify the connection between subject and verb is visual: parentheses can help the reader isolate the subjects and "read around" the appositives. Also, this solution eliminates four commas.

CLEAR CONNECTION: Osteoclasts (dismantling cells that destroy old bone) and osteoblasts (construction cells that help form new bone) combine to create a continuous remodeling process.

If the sentence still sounds cumbersome, it can be split, expanding the original subject to one sentence and the original predicate to another. Again, enclosing the appositives in parentheses reduces commas.

CLEAR CONNECTION: Dismantling cells (osteoclasts) destroy old bone, whereas construction cells (osteoblasts) help form new bone. This combination creates a continuous remodeling process.

As the examples demonstrate, the problem with long sentences is frequently not the length itself but rather the distance between the subject and the verb. Thus, when you revise your writing, pay attention to the subject-verb connection; make sure it is immediately clear. In the process, you will also streamline your prose, making it easier to read.

## ❑ EXERCISE 14



Streamline the following passage by making clear the connection between subjects and verbs.

The first American mule, bred two hundred years ago by George Washington from a Virginia mare and a Spanish jack named Royal Gift, a present from the King of Spain, began a revolution in draft animals. The mule, which is hardier than a horse, more resistant to disease, better able to tolerate intense heat, more sure-footed, and more intelligent, was invaluable before the Industrial Revolution. Mules cultivated cotton on southern plantations, toiled in coal mines, and transported goods across the desert. And of course, mules, which could carry weapons and supplies in terrain where trucks and jeeps were helpless to move, served in both world wars.

## ❑ EXERCISE 15

Using the techniques discussed in 33c, streamline the following passage.

The idea that Shakespeare's plays were written not by William Shakespeare himself but by some strange and shy genius hiding behind a pen name is one of the silliest literary theories ever to be proposed. "Real authors," from Ben Jonson and Christopher Marlowe to Queen Elizabeth and the Rosicrucians, are constantly being proposed by critics and amateur sleuths who believe that William Shakespeare was a simple-minded hick, who was possibly illiterate and did not have the background to make references to law, navigation, medicine, history, and court life, and that the records of Shakespeare's life are too scarce for someone who was so popular in his lifetime.

In fact, both of these ideas are invalid. First, Shakespeare's plays do not contain any information that would have been unavailable to any Elizabethan with a few books, and furthermore, the references made to geography and history are often mixed up and inaccurate; second, we know as much about Shakespeare's life as we know about the lives of many other famous Elizabethan authors whose work is not questioned.

The idea that some famous person would probably not have picked the name of an illiterate nobody to use as a pen name never seems to be considered by the "Shakespeare hunters."

## 33d Figures of Speech

Figures of speech communicate through comparison or association rather than through literal meaning. For example, the familiar expression *shed light on the matter* is not literal, but figurative. No reader would think of light in its actual sense of electromagnetic radiation. Instead readers make this association: *light* makes things clearer, more visible; therefore *shed light* means *make clear.* The concreteness and vividness of effective figures of speech can often communicate more directly and more intensely than abstractions and generalizations.



Probably the most common figures of speech are metaphor, simile, personification, and hyperbole. In a metaphor, two dissimilar things are said or implied to be the same. Thus, one thing (usually unfamiliar or abstract) becomes clearer because of its similarity with the other thing (usually familiar or concrete). For example, Churchill uses the concrete *tossing sea* and *firm ground* to contrast two abstract ideas.

> I pass with relief from the tossing sea of Cause and Theory to the firm ground of Result and Fact. (Winston Churchill, *The Malakand Field Force*)

In some metaphors the abstract ideas are not expressed but suggested. For example, Canby uses the concrete *fabric* to suggest the abstract idea of structure—something holding writing together. He uses *jelly* to suggest the idea of a formless mass—something without shape or structure.

> Without the support of reasoned thought the fabric of writing may collapse into a jelly of words. (Henry Seidel Canby, *Better Writing*)

Like the metaphor, the simile compares two dissimilar actions or things. Unlike the metaphor, the simile must include the comparative word *like* or *as*.

SIMILE WITH *LIKE:* Like a monster of the sea, the nuclear-powered research submarine NR-1 prowls the twilit depth of the Bahamas during a practice dive. (Emory Kristof, "NR-1, The Navy's Inner-Space Shuttle," *National Geographic*)

SIMILE WITH *AS:* Humor can be dissected, as a frog can, but the thing dies in the process and the innards are discouraging to any but the pure scientist. (E. B. White, "Some Remarks on Humor," *The Second Tree from the Corner*)

A personification is a special type of metaphor in which something not human (animal, object, place, idea) is given some human characteristic: *patient forest, marriage of flavors, eloquence of the museum, heart of the atom, sister continent.* In the following quotation, the writer personifies the winds:

> I'm alone here for much of the summer, these hot winds my only dancing partner. (Gretel Ehrlich, "A Season of Portraits")



A hyperbole is an exaggeration. For example, instead of being literal *(they spend too much money),* a writer can intensify the reader's awareness of size by writing a hyperbole *(the national defense budget couldn't pay their bills for one month).*

Although figures of speech are common in poetry and fiction, they should be used only sparingly in nonfiction. If you do use occasional figures of speech, try to avoid those that seem inappropriately exaggerated ("the fraternity system is a cancer, malignant and festering, which must be excised") or trite ("he is as stubborn as a mule"). Instead, try to choose those that help to clarify and enliven your writing.

## ❑ EXERCISE 16

**Identify the kinds of figurative language used in the following quotations.**

1. "The face of the sea is always changing. . . . Its aspects and moods vary hour by hour." (Rachel Carson, *The Sea Around Us*)
2. "Although one may fail to find happiness in theatrical life, one never wishes to give it up after having once tasted its fruits. To enter the School of the Imperial Ballet is to enter a convent whence frivolity is banned, and where merciless discipline reigns. (Anna Pavlova, "Pages of My Life," *Pavlova: A Biography*)
3. "The solar system as a whole, like a merry-go-round unhinged, spins, bobs, and blinks at the speed of 43,200 miles an hour along a course set east of Hercules." (Annie Dillard, *Pilgrim at Tinker Creek*)
4. "For a brief moment of time [clipper ships] flashed their splendor around the world, then disappeared with the sudden completeness of a wild pigeon." (Samuel Eliot Morison, *Maritime History of Massachusetts*)
5. "The fox was desperately close. Auntie Mame switched on the ignition and the car bounded forward just as a small cannon ball of black fur darted into the road. There was a terrible screech of brakes and I was thrown forward against the windshield. Then all hell broke loose.

Hounds, horses, and riders descended on us like an avalanche. Nearly three dozen riders were thrown, and two big bay mares rammed into the Dusenberg so hard the front fender and hood had to be replaced. A third mount was half in and half out of the back seat, whinnying horribly. All in all, there were more horses shot that day than at the Battle of Gettysburg." (Patrick Dennis, *Auntie Mame*)



## ❑ EXERCISE 17

Use your imagination to change the literal language of these statements to figurative language.

EXAMPLE: The sentence was long and confusing. → The sentence encircled and choked the meaning like a giant boa constrictor.

1. His opponent in the tennis match was fearsome.
2. The book was boring.
3. The plane ride was extremely rough.
4. Hate made him irrational.
5. The hurricane destroyed the town.

# 33e Sound and Rhythm

All human beings respond to the sounds of words and phrases. Children in the process of learning language constantly engage in sound play. They chant in games: *Red Rover, Red Rover, send Rachel right over; Cinderella, dressed in yellow, went upstairs to kiss her fellow.* They experiment with tongue twisters: *Peter Piper picked a peck of pickled peppers.* They show off with Pig Latin: *An-cay ou-yay eak-spay is-thay?* They delight in spoonerisms: *Mardon me padam; this pie is occupewed. Allow me to sew you to another sheet.*

Most adults rarely indulge in sound play just for fun, but they do respond to the music of the language. Television advertising, for instance, relies heavily on sound gimmicks to sell products and ensure that consumers remember brand names and slogans. Politicians use sounds and rhythmic patterns to capture the emotions of audiences. And of course, sound and rhythm help separate poetry from prose.

English speakers seem to respond to certain sounds in rather predictable ways. For example, /j/ and /ch/ often suggest noise *(jabber, jingle, chime, chirp)*. Short words that end in /p/, /t/, and /k/ have a crisp, staccato effect *(pop, tap, pat, whack)*. Repetition of /l/ can produce a liquid effect *(lily, lullaby, lyrical)*. The sequence of /uh/ or /ih/ plus an /f/ and a /y/ can make a word seem as light as air *(fluffy, puffy, whiffy)*.



In addition to individual sounds, the language also has phrasal rhythms that can wed sound to ideas. For example, phrases with lots of unstressed syllables seem to move fast: *It's funny how rapidly phrases go running along on the page.* Phrases made up mostly of stressed syllables seem to move much slower: *Like gunmen at high noon, some words walk slow.*

In the following excerpt from *An Essay on Criticism,* Alexander Pope admirably demonstrates how sound can reinforce sense. The first two lines state Pope's thesis—that a writer must deliberately make use of sound symbolism.

(1) 'Tis not enough no harshness gives offense,
(2) The sound must seem an echo to the sense:
(3) Soft is the strain when Zephyr gently blows,
(4) And the smooth stream in smoother numbers flows;
(5) But when loud surges lash the sounding shore,
(6) The hoarse, rough verse should like a torrent roar:
(7) When Ajax strives some rock's vast weight to throw,
(8) The line too labors, and the words move slow;
(9) Not so, when swift Camilla scours the plain,
(10) Flies o'er the unbending corn, and skims along the main.

In the third line of the excerpt, the repetition of /s/ suggests the sighing of the wind. In the fourth, the /sm/ and /st/ make silk-like sounds, and the long vowels in *smooth, stream, smoother,* and *flows* make the line flow slowly. The /g/, /sh/, and /r/ sounds in lines (5) and (6) echo the noise of the surf pounding the shore. Lines (7) and (8) have many more stressed than unstressed syllables and so seem to have *vast weight* and to *move slow*. In lines (9) and (10), the predominance of unstressed syllables makes words *skim along*. Thus Pope makes the sound *an echo to the sense.*

Another technique writers use for rhythmic effect is repetition of words and phrases. Consider Winston Churchill's famous "Dunkirk" speech before the House of Commons during World War II. The repetition of *we shall* and *we shall fight* sets up a cadence, culminating in the bold line *we shall never surrender.*

> We shall not flag or fail. We shall go on to the end. We shall fight in France, we shall fight on the seas and oceans, we shall fight with growing confidence and growing strength in the air, we shall defend our island, whatever the cost may be, we shall fight on the beaches, we shall fight on the landing grounds, we shall fight in the fields and in the streets, we shall fight in the hills; we shall never surrender.

In the next example, Adlai Stevenson not only repeats the words *rule* and *law* but also repeats a structure: compound nouns joined by *and*.



> As citizens of this democracy, you are the rulers and the ruled, the law givers and the law-abiding, the beginning and the end.

To achieve this moving passage about the carrying of the Olympic flame across the country in 1984, Lance Morrow uses sound to complement sense.

> The flame came fluttering out of the darkness into an early morning light. Americans in bathrobes would sometimes stand by the sides of two-lane roads, and as a runner carried the Olympic torch toward them, they would signal thumbs up and break the country silence with a soft, startling cheer. Their faces would glow with a complex light—a patriotism both palpable and chastened, a kind of reawakened warmth, something fetched from a long way back.

The passage begins with the repetition of /f/ sounds, suggesting softness, the way the flame must have looked in the *early morning light.* In the second sentence, Morrow uses a number of /s/ sounds, again suggesting softness. He ends the sentence with *a soft, startling cheer,* startling the reader with an unusual idea—that something soft can also be startling. The rhythm of the last sentence is made interesting by the three appositives after the dash, which have a chantlike quality. Also, the choice of the verb *fetched* is perfect. It is a crisp word, a no-nonsense word; and it is an old-fashioned word, appropriate for something from a long way back. The passage ends with three, single-syllable words to slow the movement, *long way back.* And the final word ends with the crack of a /k/.

As the examples indicate, effective writing is not merely clear and correct. It also sounds good. You may not be able to manipulate the sounds of the language with the expertise of the writers quoted here. You should, nevertheless, practice listening to what you write. Read it aloud. Try several versions. Pick the one that sounds the best, the one that is "an echo to the sense."

## ❏ EXERCISE 18

1. Rewrite these two sentences to make the sound echo the sense. Remember that unstressed syllables speed up the pace and stressed syllables slow it down.

   The small boy ran down the road so fast that the dust rose behind him like the wake created by a power boat.

   The moon came slowly up over the leafy trees, throwing a kind of eerie light over the garden where we sitting.



2. Try using sounds and rhythms in the following passage to suggest the light, airy quality of the comforter.

   The comforter that my grandmother gave me when I was fifteen was very large, but it weighed hardly anything. I would sleep under it and stay very warm, but I didn't feel like any weight was on my body.

3. Rewrite the following passage so that the rhythm suggests what the rider and horse are doing. The beginning of the passage should suggest a relaxed pace. Then the rhythm should get faster as the horse begins to run. Finally, the last sentence should reverse the pace and end with the word *Snip.*

   I spent my youth on a horse. His name was Snip. He was half quarter horse and half palomino. Whenever I was not in school, we would go off and spend the day in the hills and creeks. He would seem content enough while we were out, but at the end of the ride, when he could see the barn door, he would start to run. No pulling back on the reins could stop him. His shoulders would heave. His massive head would bob. He would breathe heavily. He would frantically try to lessen the distance between himself and the barn. He would go faster and faster headed home. I feel like Snip sometimes these days.

4. The rhythm of the following passage is choppy and abrupt. Try rewriting to suggest a floating cloud of pollen that spreads ominously like something in a horror movie.

   For many people, robins and jonquils are the first indications of spring. But for allergy sufferers, spring begins with an ominous cloud of yellow pollen. This pollen floats through the air. It is inside and outside. It covers cars. The pollen also gets on sidewalks and bushes. In the house it settles on bric-a-brac. As a matter of fact, it covers everything that doesn't move fast.

# Review Exercise

review

1. Improve the word choice in the following passages.

a. The physical requirements of a television news anchor are very rigid. First, he must be old enough to seem mature and young enough to seem with it. Second, he must have a face that will appeal to the man in the street, not too serious or grim but not too laid back. Third, he must be perfectly groomed, with every hair in place. Fourth, he can be neither skinny nor corpulent. In other words, his looks must appeal to every possible viewer—the corporate businessman, the housewife, the postman, the coed.

b. We have an uphill battle making asbestos contamination control efforts in virtually all sectors of the environment. Our tried and true methods of cleaning up have not always made the grade. Now we need to combine together to prioritize solutions. In the interest of the environment, we must eliminate the helter-skelter removal of asbestos materials. The public is aware of the problem and demands action but opposes any revenue enhancement at this point in time. Minimizing wastes and utilizing asbestos contamination abatement procedures are easier said than done. The safest techniques, needless to say, are also the most financially demanding, but it is better late than never.

c. In this day and age, the number of senior citizens has proliferated by leaps and bounds. The average life span was in the vicinity of fifty in 1910, but subsequent to improved quality of life, the old-timers can anticipate kicking up their heels till age seventy-five. Because of pensions and Social Security benefits, a number of these senior citizens will find rest and relaxation at a ripe old age in comfortable retirement villages. Lucky retirees, young in spirit, could spend their golden years in localities such as Saint Petersburg, Florida.

2. Improve the structures in the following passages by combining, separating, or rearranging structures; by streamlining to remove weak and wordy prose; and by changing the sound and rhythm.

a. In 1906, Upton Sinclair wrote *The Jungle.* He was only 28. The novel exposed the filthy conditions in Chicago's meat-packing industry. It was based on facts that were published in a 1904 study. The novel caused a furor. In the book, the main character is Jurgis Rudkus, a Slav immigrant. He goes to work in the Chicago stockyards. While he is there, he suffers the filth, disease, brutality, and helplessness of a typical packing worker. He and his wife, whose name is Ona, because of filthy working and living conditions, are attacked by disease; they are forced by their poverty to endure cold winters and flies in the summers. Eventually Ona dies in childbirth; previously, they had eaten bad food or, when Rudkus was laid off, no food. Because of the horrible working conditions that were exposed by the novel, reform was called for by many groups. The American Medical Association sought reform in the food industry. Theodore Roosevelt, as a result of the novel, began an investigation. As a result of the investigation, the Pure Food and Drugs Act was passed.

review

b. Two current issues that have led to an increased interest in mathematics are the feminist movement with its concern about women being excluded from many scientific or technical careers and educational reform with the general concern about students not getting the basic skills necessary to pursue advanced education. A person's attitude toward mathematics is what underlies both these issues. If a student has the expectation that mathematics challenges a person's highest creative abilities, helps a person to think clearly, provides good mental exercise, then this student's attitude will be an attitude that will probably lead to success. A student who has the belief that mathematics is busy work, that it is too hard, that it is too abstract will more than likely be a student who will not succeed in mathematics courses. Good mathematics students usually have the understanding that mathematics has been important to the advance of civilization; poor mathematics students do not have any realization of mathematics' value to society. The attitudes of these poor students are going to limit their opportunities for careers and make them anxious about mathematics for the rest of their lives. Not only should mathematical skills be taught by school teachers and other educators, but also attitudes toward mathematics should be emphasized.

c. In 1868, an act was passed by Congress that set forth the use of stamp taxes on liquor. The number of tax agents were increased, and the conflict between the moonshiners and the revenuers was started. Between 1880 and 1895, the number of seizures of moonshining stills was doubled. The confrontations, which sometimes reached the size of full-scale battles, caused carbines to be issued to the tax collectors and posses to be authorized. One of the severest battles that was ever fought between government agents and moonshiners occurred in 1878 in Overton County, Tennessee, where 10 government men were beseiged in a farmhouse by 25 moonshiners who were led by the notorious Campbell Morgan. Finally, a negotiated settlement that was reached made the specification that everyone would stop shooting and that Morgan would turn himself in—but not to the leader of the government men. A story that was developed about this time has a young revenuer who makes the discovery of a mountain shack ask a young boy about the whereabouts of his father. The boy replies that his father is away making moonshine. The agent, who offers to give the boy fifty cents to take him to the site, tells the boy, who holds out his hand, that the money will be given on their return. "I will take the money now," is what the boy says, "for you ain't coming back."

# PART V

# The Writing Process

No matter what the writing project, the process is essentially the same: thinking about a subject, finding an organization, producing a draft, revising until the final paper is satisfactory. This process, however, is not necessarily linear, with each stage completed before the next one begins. For instance, some writers think a subject through and then write an entire rough draft before revising. More commonly, writers think a while, write a while, think some more, revise parts of their work, think again, write again, and so on. Regardless of the sequence, it is important to work through the whole process.

# 34

# The Search for Ideas

search 34

Occasionally when you prepare to write, you have no subject at all in mind. Sometimes you have a subject, but you still do not know the best angle to take or the best focus to choose. At other times, you have an angle or focus, but you cannot envision the material that will best develop and support your ideas. In any case, when considering a potential subject, you need to discover what you already know about it and what material is available through research or personal experience to fill in the gaps. The most productive procedure is not to wait for inspiration but to stimulate thought by some technique that will activate and direct ideas.

One key to finding suitable subjects is to stay alert for something to write about. And let's face it—if you are in an English composition class, you will need something to write about. Try to develop the habit of looking at everything around you as a potential subject for writing. As your powers of observation and association improve, you should find that getting started becomes easier.

The following techniques can help you generate subjects and ideas about subjects. Some of these techniques use free association to generate ideas at random; others are more structured and channel ideas in controlled directions. Probably you will not use all the techniques suggested; different methods suit different personalities and different subjects. For example, freewriting seems aimless to some writers, whereas structured techniques seem too rigid to others. Just remember that if a technique is not productive in one instance, it might be in another—when you are in a different mood or when you have a different subject.

## 34a Journals

Keeping a journal does not mean keeping a record of your daily activities. Rather it means writing regularly about things that happen to you; things that puzzle, excite, anger, or depress you; things that make you laugh; things that interest you.

Whether for your eyes alone or for others', a journal can help your writing in several ways. First, you can structure your entries in any way you choose. You can try out techniques for getting ideas, write impressions, record anecdotes, or practice answering essay tests. Also, journal keeping helps you get used to putting words on paper and allows you to write without stress or fear of censure. Finally, a journal can function as a source of subjects for writing. You can record observations, immediate reactions, goals, frustrations, any of which might eventually be useful in a paper.



Although a journal may include any material you choose, journal keeping does require a certain discipline. For a journal to be useful, you must write in it regularly, preferably every day. So get a notebook that is portable and sturdy enough to hold up with lots of use. Many writers try to write at the same time each day, in the same place, for the same amount of time—say one hour. You may prefer, however, to write at different times of the day for different lengths of time.

Besides writing in your journal, you should read it regularly. You may find there some patterns that are revealing and productive. For example, if a certain person turns up again and again in your journal, perhaps you should consider that person's role in your life and write about it. If a certain problem keeps reappearing, perhaps you should write about its cause or its solution. In this way, your journal can be a source of specific subjects for writing assignments. Consider, for example, this journal entry, which led the student to write a paper on the most common types of phobias.

I was on an elevator today when a girl next to me had some kind of attack. She got faint and couldn't breathe — or felt like she couldn't. They said that she ~~happen~~ hyperventilated — couldn't get enough oxygen — or maybe she got too much, I forget which. She was OK. They said she had an anxiety attack caused by claustrophobia.

### EXERCISE 1

Keep a journal and write in it freely and frequently, even including material that at the time seems to lead nowhere. You never know what will be productive later on. The more you write, the more likely you are to find a good subject or to accumulate supporting details. Here are some suggestions about the sort of material you might include.



remembrances of early years
impressions of books or films
details about parties or vacations
descriptions of people at a concert, play, or athletic event
reactions to personal stories from a local newspaper
sketches of your family or friends
plans for the future
summaries of class discussions or conversations
opinions about current issues
ideas for improvements

## 34b Meditation

In writing, the term *meditation* usually refers to concentrated reflection. Some writers recommend sitting or lying down facing a blank wall so that nothing visual can interrupt the flow of thought. Such a drastic measure, however, may not be necessary for everyone. Some people can concentrate in busy environments, and many people do their best thinking while driving or jogging alone. So choose whatever place allows you to concentrate on your innermost thoughts.

If you have a subject, focus on that. If you do not have a subject, begin by picking a person, a place, an object, an incident, or an idea. Then let your mind move spontaneously from that initial point. Concentrate on what you are thinking, but do not try to direct your thoughts. If you come to some particularly interesting idea, focus on it and expand it.

Meditating has the advantage of being much faster than other techniques for getting ideas, simply because you do not have to write your thoughts down. But it has the disadvantage that you may forget some of your best material. A compromise is to talk into a tape recorder. This practice will slow you down only a bit and will preserve every strand of thought. Then you can listen to the meditation several times to find in it the most interesting or fruitful ideas, which you can record in your journal.

## ❑ EXERCISE 2

**Try meditation to find a subject for writing. If nothing comes immediately to mind, you might start by thinking about one of the subjects listed here. But do not try to stick to a topic. Just let your mind range wherever it will.**



**solutions to problems**
**moving to another place**
**past mistakes**
**the dangers of drugs**
**the worst jobs**
**the changing planet**
**future transportation**
**life without education**
**breaking up**
**breaking away**

## 34c Brainstorming

Brainstorming, a free-association technique, has proved successful in business, where members of a group get together to explore a topic or solve a problem—each person spontaneously contributing ideas that can stimulate other ideas.

Whether done in a group or alone, brainstorming should be completely unstructured. The theory is that structuring impedes the creative flow of ideas, whereas brainstorming allows the subconscious to release blocked ideas, no matter how irrelevant or silly they seem to be. If you try brainstorming, remember that you cannot predict which ideas will be useful. Consequently, you should jot down the ideas in words, phrases, sentences, doodles—anything that comes to you. After about ten minutes of brainstorming, go back through what you have written. Eliminate the extraneous, link related ideas, and think further about anything that strikes you as interesting.

Biology. Biology.
No time. 8:00 labs { Best part of lab— field trips
Hard work
Comp. tests { Worst-practicals

Weird [ Rewards? Satisfy curiosity
Social Life = ø
See nobody but other majors

search 34c

Looking over the brainstorming notes shown here, the writer noticed two related patterns: that the biology curriculum is difficult and that biology majors are a strange breed. From those two ideas, she wrote a character sketch of a typical biology major.

Sometimes brainstorming leads to a potential idea, but not to a fully realized one. In those cases, you can start over, using that idea to initiate another brainstorming exercise. You can repeat the process any number of times, each time exploring an idea in more depth or from a different perspective.

## ❑ EXERCISE 3

For ten minutes, brainstorm a topic by writing down anything that comes to mind. Begin with a topic such as one in the following list.

a favorite car
reasons that students drop out of college
problems in your community
the relationship between people and pets
a good job
the effect of abolishing grades
peer pressure on teenagers
gaining independence

After the ten minutes, read over your notes. Pick an idea or potential idea and repeat the process for another ten minutes to find at least one idea that might be developed into a complete paper. If you still have no idea for a paper, go through the process again or start over with another potential topic.

## 34d Clustering



In a variation of brainstorming, called clustering, ideas are linked through a graphic system of circles and arrows. To use this technique, start out by writing a topic, or "nucleus" word, in the middle of a blank page. Then, radiating out from the nucleus, write words that are suggested to you by the topic. Continue to write associations, circling each and linking it with an arrow to a related word, as shown here.

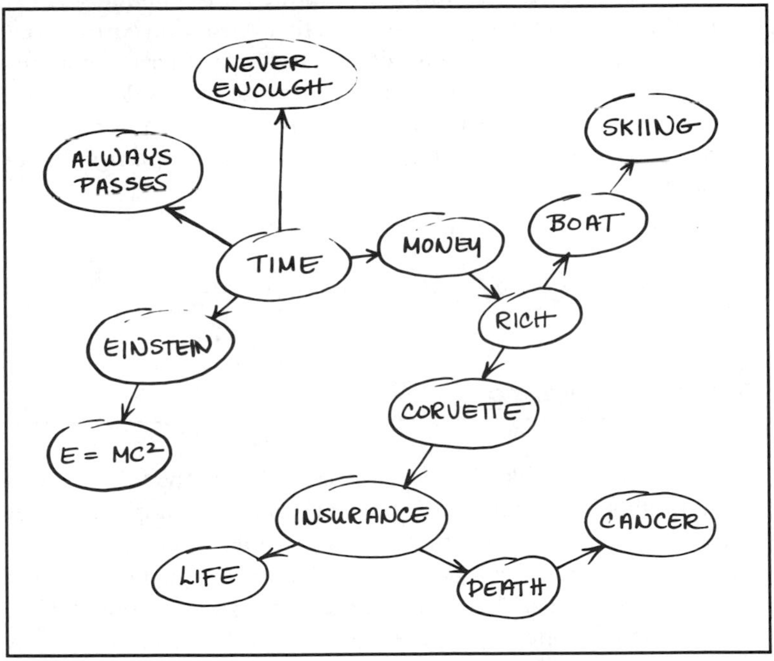

The point of clustering is to release the creative element of the mind. Usually, the system will, at some point, produce a subject for writing. For instance, in the preceding example, the writer saw in the clustering the possible subject of how the Corvette has changed over the years—suggested to him by the word *Corvette* and his nucleus word, *time*.

One advantage of clustering is that the jottings are not completely unstructured; the arrows show the directions of thought and ideas appear in related groups, any of which might be developed into a composition. Also, if a subject needs further development, it can become the nucleus of another clustering exercise.

### ❑ EXERCISE 4

search 34e

**Write the word *entertainment* in the center of a sheet of paper, circle it, and then use the clustering technique for ten minutes. Find a cluster that looks interesting, and write that cluster on a fresh sheet of paper. Repeat the clustering technique for another ten minutes. Then look over the pages for an idea that could be developed into a paper. If you find no idea, try the technique with other nucleus words such as *weather, noise, school, telephone, family, travel, cheating,* and *food.***

## 34e Freewriting

Freewriting is much like "talking on paper"—simply writing whatever thoughts occur, no matter how random or unimportant they may seem. Unlike brainstorming, which employs random jottings, freewriting is done in sentences or, at least, in constructions that express complete ideas. The technique serves several purposes. First, the very act of writing stimulates thinking. And many writers say that freewriting is like limbering up, like the finger exercises a pianist does before playing. Second, freewriting can turn vague ideas into visible words, thus indicating the potential of a subject.

While reading over some freewriting notes, a student writer found that she was interested in her second idea—that her computer science teachers discouraged working in groups, contrary to the actual practice of teamwork in the business world. She ultimately produced a paper arguing that the necessity for grades creates an artificial learning environment.

More and more projects are assigned for computer lab. a lot of people work on programs together – in groups. But most teachers would rather you didn't. I can't understand why because companies expect you to work in teams mostly. What I hate about lab is people laughing and acting stupid and silly at the next terminal to the one I'm using. Some people wear Walkman's to the lab to shut out the noise.



To use the technique, you should set some time or length limit on the process. When the limit is up, read what you have produced. If something interests you, you can use it as a starting point for another freewriting, or you can develop it with another method for getting ideas. Although freewriting may not produce polished prose, it can produce a number of ideas and occasionally a usable first draft.

## ❑ EXERCISE 5

For about fifteen minutes, write your thoughts as fast as you can, trying not to be critical or analytical. When you have lapses, scribble or write nonsense, but do not stop the momentum of putting something down on paper. To get started, you might pick an issue, such as one of the following.

smoking in public places
TV violence
crime prevention
consumer safety
prejudice
pollution
exercise and health
weaknesses in American schools
health services for students
traffic and parking problems
student employment

When time is up, read what you have written, and list any ideas that might serve as a subject or be useful in a paper.

## 34f Ladders

search 34f

Subjects like *cities, baseball,* or *movies* are too broad for a good paper, and ideas such as *friendship, warfare,* or *pollution* are too abstract. If you are struggling with unmanageable subjects such as these, you might want to construct ladders—graduated scales of words or ideas, beginning with the abstract or general and moving toward the concrete or specific.

By constructing ladders, you can discover concrete ways to talk about subjects. For example, the subject *cities* is entirely too general and unfocused. But if you think of *cities* as being on the top rung of a ladder, you can place a more specific subject on the next rung and continue down the ladder until a topic strikes you as a good one for a paper. Perhaps you move from *cities* to *New York* to *New York delis* and then end with the promising topic *New York-*

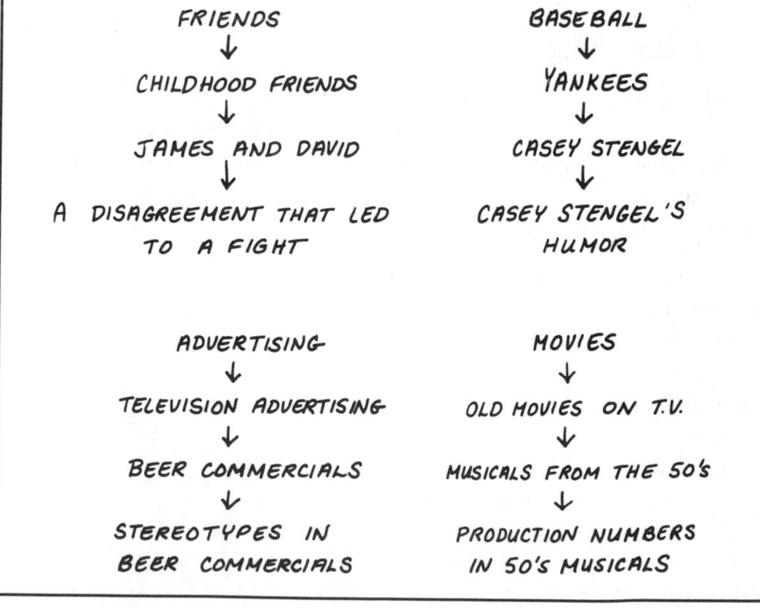

*style hero sandwiches.* With this topic you could, for example, classify the kinds of heroes, compare the New York hero with the New Orleans po'boy, or describe the process of assembling the ideal sandwich.

Notice how the ideas in the sample ladders progress toward manageable topics.



## ☐ EXERCISE 6

**For five of the following subjects, create ladders with four rungs, moving from the general or abstract to the specific or concrete.**

| | | | |
|---|---|---|---|
| humor | jealousy | games | conflict |
| contests | school | food | careers |
| television | celebrations | cars | hunting |

# 34g Questions

Because asking questions is one of the most natural mental processes, you may find it a comfortable and productive technique. Questions that naturally come to mind can get you started brainstorming, freewriting, or clustering. You can even keep a section in your journal for questions as they occur to you. At times questions may lead productively to a written composition.

Who is my most peculiar relative?
What kind of car would I like to own?
Where would I go on an ideal vacation?
When should a student decide on a major?
How does an automatic bank teller work?

If questions don't come immediately to mind, you can use the "journalistic questions." Reporters once claimed that the opening of a news story had to answer Who? What? When? Where? Why? How? These six questions, however, if answered superficially, may produce no more than a sentence.

> On November 8, 1989, the star basketball player at our school was indicted for betting on games in order to get money for drugs.

The sentence answers all six questions, but it does not establish a direction for a composition. A more productive use of the questions is to concentrate on one or two for a given subject. For example, the subject of corruption in college athletics might be explored with *why:* Why does a player risk a career by betting on a game? Or with *how:* How does a basketball player "throw" a game?

Questions can help you explore any type of subject—to find out how much you know about it or to narrow your focus sufficiently to deal with it in a concrete way. The following lists illustrate the kinds of questions that develop naturally from a general subject.



**An Object or Device** (for example, a Frisbee, a videotape machine)

What are its parts?
How is it used?
Are there categories of it?
What are people's opinions of it?
How did it originate?

**A Process** (for example, running a marathon, enlarging a photograph)

What are its steps or stages?
Is it difficult or easy?
Does it happen naturally?
What causes it?
What are its consequences?

**A Person** (for example, a relative, a typical school principal)

What does he/she do?
What does he/she look like?
What are his/her ambitions? Values?
How is he/she typical or unusual?
What do people think about him/her?

**A Place** (for example, the Vietnam War Memorial, a mountain lake)

What are its characteristics?
What places is it similar to or different from?
Why would someone want to go there or live there?
How is this place unusual? Special?

**An Event** (for example, the Chicago fire, a soccer match)

What caused it?
What did it cause?
How is it like other events?
Is it part of a trend or an isolated event?
What is its significance?

How could it have been avoided?
How did people respond to it?

**An Idea or Abstraction** (for example, homesickness, fascism)

What is its definition?
What is its significance?
What is it similar to or different from?
What is its history?
How has it affected society?

**A Problem** (for example, immigration, drugs)



What caused or causes it?
Who or what does it affect?
Where does it occur?
Is it social, political, financial, personal, or practical?
What is a possible solution?
What are the obstacles to a solution?
What would life be like without the problem?

**A Judgment or Opinion** (for example, "People who refuse to work should not be allowed to vote." "Public transportation should be free.")

How are the key words in it defined?
Is it logical?
Can it be proved?
What kind of evidence can prove or disprove it?
What are its consequences?
What are counterarguments?
What testimony can support it?

## ☐ EXERCISE 7

**Use questions to explore one topic in each category. Write four to six questions for each of the subjects you choose. From your questions, pick two that might be developed into a paper. (Remember that not all of the questions will be appropriate for every subject and that other questions can be added as they come to mind.)**

1. *object or device:* a painting, stereo, sculpture, motorcycle, lawn mower, typewriter, seashell, doll, toy, computer
2. *process:* painting a house, riding a skateboard, flying a kite, playing a particular card game, interviewing for a job, studying for a test, exercising
3. *person:* coach, preacher, teacher, relative, doctor, dentist, friend

4. *place:* your neighborhood, city, town, or state; a place of employment; your old grammar school; a video game arcade; a bowling alley; a golf course; a museum; a summer camp
5. *event:* rock concert, sporting event, trial, accident, college registration, initiation into a club, wedding, high school graduation, trip
6. *idea or abstraction:* pride, greed, ambition, confusion, misunderstanding, fear, frustration, peace of mind
7. *problem:* employment, housing, marriage, money, parents, transportation, crime, violence, overpopulation
8. *judgment or opinion:* The minimum wage law should/should not apply to those under twenty years of age. College athletes should/should not be required to take courses the semesters they compete. The quality of American cars is/is not equal to that of Japanese cars. Campus parking places should/should not be determined by lottery.



## 34h Classical Topics

In ancient Greece, rhetoricians and orators used the classical topics to help them develop lines of argument for persuasive speaking. In fact, the word *topic* comes from the Greek *topos,* which means "place"; thus, the classical topics were places to find arguments. Although used by the Greeks primarily for argument, the topics can effectively stimulate thought since they represent the way the mind works naturally to consider a subject.

| | |
|---|---|
| definition | saying what something is |
| comparison | saying what a subject is like or unlike |
| relationship | looking at causes and effects, antecedents and consequences |
| circumstance | exploring possibility or impossibility, past or future fact |
| testimony | discovering what is known, thought, and said about a subject |

Consider the subject "physical fitness." The topic *definition* suggests a look at its components (good muscle tone, low percentage of body fat, endurance, and so forth) or its types (fitness for the average person and fitness for an athlete in training). *Comparison* suggests an analogy to emotional and mental fitness or a contrast between a physically fit person and someone who is not. Comparison might also extend to comparing and contrasting degrees of physical fitness.

*Relationship* might lead to the causes of fitness or its effects. *Circumstance* can raise the question of the possible and impossible: what level of fitness is or is not possible for, say, a person who works every day in an office. It can also suggest a look at the past or the future, thus generating a question such as, "Were Americans more fit years ago?" or "Are we likely to be less fit in the future?"



The last classical topic, *testimony,* directs attention to research and data about the subject. It suggests finding out what authorities say about fitness, conducting an opinion poll on fitness, examining statistics to discover facts about the fitness of the general public or a certain group of people, or soliciting accounts of personal experiences with fitness. Finally, these data-gathering techniques might be combined for a fairly extensive investigation.

The classical topics probably will not help you find a subject, but once you have one, they will help you narrow the subject into something manageable and interesting.

## ❑ EXERCISE 8

**Use the classical topics to generate ideas about one of the following subjects. If none of the subjects appeals to you, use another. List at least one narrowed subject for each topic: definition, comparison, relationship, circumstance, and testimony.**

**the architecture in a particular region**
**space colonization**
**rock and roll**
**illiteracy**
**holiday depression**
**romance novels**
**fear of flying**
**racquetball**
**pornography**
**beauty pageants**

## 34i Reading and Listening

search 34i

When you are just getting started on a paper, your research is not structured library work but casual exploring—looking through newspapers and magazines, conducting informal interviews, listening to radio and television news and talk shows. A discussion with a student who is also a mother might lead to a paper comparing her problems with those of other students. A television discussion of prison conditions might lead to an argument for better vocational training for inmates. A look at classified advertisements could suggest a paper on selecting a good used car or managing a garage sale. A radio story on using dogs from an animal shelter for medical experimentation could lead to an argument against this practice or one vindicating the need for it.

The advantage of finding a subject through reading and listening is that in the process you also get a head start collecting usable details. Suppose, for example, you read in a magazine that only one-fourth of the electorate regularly vote. You might try to find out why this is so. You could begin by interviewing voters in your age group to discover what motivates them to vote or not to vote. You could look for a government document describing the voting trends for different age groups, economic groups, regional groups, or religious groups. If you decide to write on why students lack motivation to vote, you will have already collected some information from the interviews or from your reading.

### ❑ EXERCISE 9

**Find three potential subjects by reading, listening to radio, watching television, or talking to people. If a subject is too general or too abstract, you can use another technique such as brainstorming or asking logical questions to make the subject suitable.**

## The Computer Connection

Like pens, pencils, and typewriters, computers are tools to help writers turn thoughts into words. In fact, many writers believe that the computer may be the most flexible, adaptable writing tool ever invented. It is the easiest way we have for getting on paper the fragmented ideas and mental hopscotch that make up the writing process. With a computer, you can freely type your thoughts and ideas at random. You don't have to worry about their order or significance because with the touch of a few command keys, you can later add material, move sentences and paragraphs around, and type over errors. You can save anything useful and get rid of the rest. You can even throw material into a "wastebasket" file and retrieve it later if you change your mind.

### *Suggestions for Getting Ideas*

- Keep a journal in a separate file or on a separate disk, and add to it regularly. A computer journal has several advantages over a notebook. For instance, it saves time and storage space. In addition, a computer journal, because it is in a file, is more private than a notebook: nosy people cannot easily rummage through your personal thoughts without your consent.
- Try freewriting on the computer as a way to generate ideas for a paper. You can turn down the contrast on the screen so that you can't see what you're typing. This way, you won't be distracted from the flow of your ideas. After ten minutes, turn up the screen contrast and read through the results. If you find something that interests you, delete everything else, and freewrite again from that starting point.
- Anytime you get an idea for a paper, add it to an "idea" file. When it's time to begin a writing assignment, review your idea file for a suitable subject.
- Look for information to help you with a writing project through computer bulletin boards or electronic networks. Although a large number of people use computer networks for playing games and trading software, a growing number of writers are using networks to communicate about writing projects.
- You can use interactive software, if available, to stimulate your thinking about a subject. This software leads you through a dialogue. Questions appear on the computer screen, and you type in answers. One such program is Thoughtline.

*For reading:* Zinsser, William. *Writing with a Word Processor.* New York: Harper & Row, 1983.

# 35

# Decisions

decide
35a

After finding a subject and generating ideas about it, you are likely to have a jumble of facts and thoughts meaningful to you but to no one else. To make the jumble meaningful to a reader, you must go beyond the subject itself and consider your purpose, audience, and voice. Furthermore, you must narrow your subject to a thesis, or controlling idea, that can bring a composition into focus; and you must choose a pattern for structuring the composition. Of course, if the first thesis or pattern does not work, you can always change to another. But you should make tentative decisions. Planning helps you develop the composition and locate any gaps that must be filled by further thought or research.

## 35a Purpose

Purpose is an important consideration in writing, one that is closely tied to audience. Occasionally you might write for your own eyes alone. Normally, however, you write to an audience for a purpose. One simple but effective classification system divides purpose into four categories: *impression*, *information*, *argument*, and *entertainment.*

Of course, the purposes frequently are mixed; for example, an impression is often entertaining, and an argument must contain information. Nevertheless, most writing does have an overriding or dominant purpose, and that purpose helps to unify the writing. If your purpose is primarily to convey an impression, you reconstruct an emotional or physical experience from a subjective point of view. If you intend to inform, you communicate objective knowledge of such things as appearances, processes, or procedures. In argument, you use facts and reason to persuade your reader to agree with your opinion or to act as you have directed. To entertain your reader, you write to amuse, to excite, or to divert attention from weighty and serious matters.



Most often your purpose is predetermined. When your journal entries express your thoughts and feelings, then your purpose is impression. If you must write up a laboratory experiment or describe a field trip, your purpose is to convey information. The purpose of a proposal or a letter to a newspaper is usually to argue a point. Often in creative writing or in a journalistic feature story, you seek to entertain.

But sometimes your assignment is open-ended, and you can choose a purpose. Your choice controls, at least to some extent, the handling of the subject. Suppose, for instance, that you have decided to write about the parking problem on your campus. You could create an impression by describing the morning traffic snarl and the feelings of frustration and anger it produces in you. You could inform readers about the causes of the problem or argue that parking should be confined to off-campus lots, with shuttle buses provided for drivers. You could entertain your readers by describing the various strategies that drivers use to grab parking places.

Through your purpose, you transmit a message. If you have no clear purpose in mind, readers may not know whether you want them to laugh, to sympathize, to learn something, to be convinced, or to share an experience with you. If, however, your purpose is clear to you and you keep it in mind while you write, readers stand a good chance of getting the message.

## ❑ EXERCISE 1

**Usually, you can adapt a topic to any purpose. For example, you could write on the topic *SAT tests* with all four purposes.**

| | |
|---|---|
| **Impression** | **My fear when I took the SAT test** |
| **Information** | **Effective ways to study for the SAT test** |

| | |
|---|---|
| Argument | The SAT test is unfair to disadvantaged students. |
| Entertainment | Amusing strategies students use to prepare for the SAT test |

Try to adapt the following topics to two or more of the four purposes.

1. gang activities
2. computers
3. childhood games
4. classroom discipline
5. overpopulation
6. boxing
7. maps
8. horror movies
9. fast food
10. cowboy boots



## 35b Audience

Except in rare circumstances, such as keeping a diary or journal, a person writes for a reader or for readers, commonly called the audience. Too often, students write directly to their instructors, expecting them to fill any gaps in the information. Unless assigned to do so, however, you should not write to an instructor. Writing in a composition course serves as practice for the writing you will do beyond the classroom, and thus you should learn to address varied and realistic audiences.

An audience can be one person, several people, or a large number of people. The members of an audience may be well known to you or completely unknown. Further, an audience might be specific, such as members of an organization, or general, such as the readers of a newspaper.

No matter who your readers are, you have certain responsibilities toward them. You must, for example, abide by the conventions that readers expect. You cannot spell, punctuate, or construct sentences according to some unusual system of your own. Also, you must consider the distance between you and your readers. Unlike listeners, readers cannot observe your facial expressions, your gestures, and your tone of voice; therefore, you must make a special effort to be clear.

This distance also makes it necessary for you to consider the identity of your readers, a process usually called *audience analysis*. When you speak, your listeners are clearly defined: you can see them. But when you write, the audience is in your head, and you must concentrate on keeping a consistent image of who those readers are.

Audience analysis is particularly important in argument—for example, when you want a reader to believe you, to hire you, to support a cause or a candidate, or to buy a product. The more you know about your audience, the more likely you are to achieve the desired response. Thus, effective argument requires that you have a profile of your readers—their values, knowledge, and emotional involvement with the subject.



Of course, argument is not the purpose of all writing. Sometimes you write to say what you think or to get at the truth. In these cases, audience approval is a bonus but not the purpose of the writing. Still, it helps to know something about your audience. If you can assess how much your readers already know about the subject, you can avoid boring them with elementary information or confusing them with overly sophisticated material. In addition, knowing the educational or technical background of your audience helps guide your choice of vocabulary so that readers can understand what you say. After all, writing that communicates takes at least two: someone to send a message and someone to receive it. If you want to get your message across, you should pay attention to the audience receiving it.

## ❑ EXERCISE 2

**The following statements are all on the same subject—steroids. Their intended audiences, however, are different. What differences can you detect?**

1. "Throughout history athletes have looked for that extra edge that would assure them a superior performance in competition. For over three decades some have claimed to have found that edge through hormonal manipulation with chemical substances known as steroids."

2. "Experimental studies in both animals and humans have showed that steroids possess both anabolic and androgenic actions. The androgenic actions of steroids are those actions involving the development and maintenance of primary and secondary sexual characteristics, while the anabolic

actions consist of the positive effects of promoting protein synthesis and muscle growth."

3. "I was in bad shape, very bad shape. From the steroids. It had all come down from the steroids, the crap I'd taken to get big and strong and aggressive so I could play the game I love."

### ❑ EXERCISE 3



The following three passages are by the same author, John C. Lilly, and on the same subject, dolphins. What audience do you think Lilly was addressing in each?

1. "Eventually it may be possible for humans to speak with another species. I have come to this conclusion after careful consideration of evidence gained through my research experiments with dolphins."

2. "For picking up and transmitting the airborne voice output of the dolphin and the speech output of the human, either two Shure model 545 Unidyne II microphones were used or a model 545 plus a Lavalier model 560."

3. "Some of the sonic (audible to human beings) emissions of the bottlenose dolphin of the east coast of the United States (*Tursiops truncatus* Montagu) have been described."

## 35c Voice

As a writer, you must adopt an effective and appropriate voice through which you speak to the audience. If you are writing fiction, you can invent a voice—for example, that of an all-knowing creator or of a specific character in the fiction itself. But if you are writing nonfiction, the voices available to you are projections of your own different roles or personality traits. Depending on the occasion, you might speak as a friend, an impersonal observer, a concerned citizen, an antagonist, or an enthusiastic fan. Also, your voice may reflect traits or moods—serious, light-hearted, neutral, detached, energetic, or emotional.

For a formal paper, such as a research paper, you should write in the third person—that is, without using the first person *(I, we)* or second person *(you)*. A third-person voice helps establish a serious tone and a polite distance between writer and reader. For an informal paper, you can write in the first person, referring to yourself as

*I.* A first-person voice helps you establish a personal relationship with readers and seems more natural than calling yourself *one* or *this writer.*

SERIOUS, FORMAL VOICE IN THIRD PERSON

> One problem that plagues many students is burnout. This emotional state is usually associated with stress on the job, but it can also occur in school. Its most common symptoms are emotional exhaustion and negative attitudes. In addition, burnout can lead to depression, weight loss or gain, and physical illness.

LIGHT-HEARTED, INFORMAL VOICE IN FIRST PERSON



> I've read a good bit lately about burnout, an emotional state usually associated with stress on the job. But it seems that this problem can also occur in school, because I am certainly burned out. Have you ever considered how stressful it can be trying to dress appropriately for class, football games, volleyball games, pizza parties, cookouts, and formal dances? Just the sheer pressure of trying to find people to borrow clothes from has left me depressed. Also, the food I have eaten at all these outings has made me overweight. Both symptoms are sure signs of burnout.

The use of second person *you* is acceptable in informal papers if you are speaking directly to your reader, giving advice or instructions or sharing experiences. You must, however, be consistent. Notice how the voice changes from third to second person in the following passage.

MIXED THIRD AND SECOND PERSON

> Moving out of an apartment is always more trouble than the mover expects. He or she begins in a methodical manner, packing items neatly in sturdy boxes and labeling the boxes. After a day or so, you realize that you seem to have just as many unpacked items as you had to begin with. At this point, the mover panics and begins throwing items at random into garbage bags and pillow cases.

To use the second person in this case, you would need to establish the reader as someone who has moved or might likely move in the future. Then, you could speak directly to him or her.

CONSISTENT SECOND PERSON

> If you have ever moved out of an apartment, you know that the process is always more trouble than you expect. You begin in a methodical manner, packing items neatly in sturdy boxes and labeling the boxes. After a day or so, you realize that you seem to have just

> as many unpacked items as you had to begin with. At this point, you panic and begin throwing items at random into garbage bags and pillow cases.

Second person is tricky, and you should use it with caution. Be sure not to use it to place readers in a group to which they cannot belong. Consider this sentence, for instance.

> As a baseball pitcher, you must prepare yourself for a game not only physically but also mentally.



If the reader is not a baseball pitcher, the sentence is not logical.

A writer's voice (sometimes called a role, mask, stance, or persona) must sound sincere. For example, if you fake the voice of a person more sophisticated than you really are, you risk sounding phony or even silly. And by all means, avoid grafting onto your prose unfamiliar synonyms found in a dictionary or thesaurus. Although some synonyms can be used interchangeably, many cannot. You can substitute *parcel* for *package* without any change of meaning. You cannot, however, substitute *incapable* for *incompetent* even though the two words appear as synonyms in many dictionaries. *Incapable* means lacking ability or power; *incompetent* means unfit or unqualified for a job. Thus, while *He was incompetent on the job* makes sense, *He was incapable on the job* does not. Therefore, do not be satisfied merely to find synonyms. Look also for a word's full meaning and proper context. Certainly, you should add new words to your vocabulary, but you should not use them inappropriately to "elevate" your voice.

Whatever voice you choose must be consistent throughout an entire paper; one voice should not intrude on another. If you assume a distant and dignified voice in the beginning, do not insert a casual or personal remark. A technical paper, for example, is no place for a joke. Slang is inappropriate in a letter of application. Likewise, if you start out in a conversational voice, you should not suddenly become formal. For example, if you begin by calling yourself *I,* do not switch to *this writer.* Or if you have been using a humorous tone, do not suddenly become solemn.

Although various voices are possible, the choice you make is rarely arbitrary. A composition about possible nuclear war will not be written with the same voice as a composition about computer nerds. A letter to a newspaper requires a voice different from that of a letter to a friend. A reminiscence will not have the same voice as a theoretical argument. Your voice must fit its context—that is, the subject, the purpose, and the audience.

## ❑ EXERCISE 4

**For each passage, try to identify the writer's purpose (impression, information, argument, or entertainment). Then determine whether the passage is written for a general or a specific audience. Finally, describe the voice of each passage. Is it detached or involved? Solemn or humorous? Liberal or conservative? Formal or informal?**



1. The Pleistocene American mastodon, *Mammut americanum* . . . was quite large, reaching the size of our present day Indian elephant, perhaps even larger. The word *Mammut* means "earth burrower," and it can be traced back to the Middle Ages, when eastern European farmers found gigantic bones in their fields and believed that they belonged to some monstrous burrowing beast. (S. C. Knox and Sue Pitts)

2. Birth rates indicate that the number of high school graduates is decreasing and will not increase until 1998. Sociological studies show approximately 40 million adults in transition; these transitions include career change, unemployment, divorce, and widowhood. Furthermore, the median age in the U.S. is now 31. These demographic facts demonstrate clearly that the adult-student market in higher education is increasing. Thus, while you must continue to recruit students from the traditional-aged market, it is a serious mistake for you to concentrate all your efforts on that market. (B. Carter and C. Tullos)

3. Should your political opinions be at extreme variance with those of your parents, keep in mind that while it is indeed your constitutional right to express these sentiments verbally, it is unseemly to do so with your mouth full—particularly when it is full of the oppressor's standing rib roast. (Fran Lebowitz)

4. We found the cave up a side canyon, the entrance blocked with fallen boulders. Even to my youthful eyes it looked old, incredibly old. The waters and the frosts for centuries had eaten at the boulders and gnawed the cave. Down by the vanished stream bed a little gleam of worked flints caught our eye. (Loren Eiseley)

5. We are satisfied with justice, if the court knows what justice is, or if any human being can tell what justice is. If anybody can look into the minds and hearts and the lives and the origin of these two youths and tell what justice is, we would be content. But nobody can do it without imagination, without sympathy, without kindliness, without understanding, and I have faith that this Court will take this case, with his conscience, and his judgment and his courage and save these boys' lives. (Clarence Darrow)

### ❑ EXERCISE 5

Imagine a logical purpose, audience, and voice for the following subjects.

1. how to study for a history test
2. an improvement needed in your community
3. a holiday that should be added to your school's calendar
4. the safety of generic drugs
5. steps for avoiding a mugging
6. an evaluation of a textbook
7. an overrated entertainer
8. the car you would drive if money were no object
9. the season of the year you enjoy most
10. a subject that you find through such techniques as keeping a journal, brainstorming, or research



## 35d Thesis

By this time in the writing process, you have probably found a subject, perhaps through freewriting, brainstorming, asking questions, or one of the other techniques for getting ideas. Your subject may be very general (*fast food*) or somewhat specific (*a dieter's guide to fast food*). It may be a feeling (*frustration*, *grief*, or *satisfaction*). Or it may be an opinion (*The quarter system is better than the semester system*). Whatever your subject, you should refine it into a workable thesis—a specific statement that can control and direct a paper.

A thesis clarifies your subject and helps you make some initial decisions about the material you will include or exclude. Even though you are quite likely to revise your thesis or change it altogether as the paper progresses, you should not neglect this important step. The five questions that follow will help you test a thesis to make sure it is promising.

### (1) Is the thesis a complete idea?

Because the thesis states the point of your paper, it should be a complete idea. Otherwise, you will not know what direction you wish to take. Thus, a good first step for finding a thesis is to write a complete sentence about your subject. For example, *a degree in business* could become *A business degree is effective preparation for law school.*

### (2) Is your thesis compatible with your purpose?

If you want to convey an impression, your thesis should allow vivid description—for example, *The first time I saw a John Wayne movie, I found my childhood hero.* If you want to entertain with a humorous paper, your thesis should be one that promises a light- hearted approach, such as *One of the funniest old movies on television is "The Conqueror," starring John Wayne as Genghis Khan.* If you intend to inform, you should summarize the information that you mean to explain—*Although people associate John Wayne with heroes, he played a few memorable villains.*



If your purpose is to argue, your thesis must state a debatable opinion or a judgment. For example, you cannot argue a fact, such as *John Wayne was a popular movie star.* Wayne was indeed a popular star, and a counterview is impossible. Also, there is little point in arguing a generally accepted idea, such as *John Wayne was a popular actor because the role of the two-fisted hero appealed to the American public.* On the other hand, an unexpected viewpoint can produce an interesting argument: *Much of John Wayne's popularity as an actor resulted from his outspoken patriotism in real life.*

### (3) Is the thesis clear and specific?

A vague thesis cannot control material much more effectively than a simple topic. For example, consider this thesis: *Studying a foreign language is a good idea.* It does not indicate who is studying what language. Furthermore, since the word *good* can have any number of meanings, the sentence is not much more specific than *studying a foreign language.* A better thesis is a specific statement such as *Taking French helped me understand the grammar of English.* This thesis can control the subject and thus the choice of materials. When you formulate a thesis, make a specific statement and avoid vague words such as *good, bad, excellent, terrible,* and *nice.* Unless a thesis can exert control, it is of very little use.

### (4) Will the thesis lead to a paper of an appropriate length?

Suppose that you are assigned a paper of approximately 500 words and that you choose the thesis *In recent years, advertising has be-*

*come more and more suggestive.* This statement is much too broad. It indicates that you will look at all forms of advertising over a period of time. A more specific statement could narrow the subject to one particular type of current advertising: *Magazine advertisements for men's cologne rely on suggestive images to sell the product.* This thesis could be adequately supported in 500 words.

It is also possible to narrow a subject too much. For example, you would not get very far with the thesis *The parking problem on campus is caused by a shortage of spaces.* Once you establish that the number of available parking spaces exceeds the number of cars, you have proved your point. But with an expanded thesis, like *The parking problem could be alleviated by a more efficient use of space,* you could use the figures on available spaces and cars to help support your recommendations.



### (5) Is your thesis supportable?

Sometimes a thesis that sounds reasonable initially will turn out to be insupportable for one reason or another. Perhaps the thesis is not logical—for instance, *Good eating habits will prolong life.* A person can eat properly and still die very young from a disease or an accident. A more supportable thesis is *Good eating habits will increase mental and physical stamina.* Or perhaps the thesis is simply too dogmatic—for instance, *There are three causes of depression.* Scientists who have researched depression for years are uncertain about all of its causes; therefore, this idea cannot be supported. A more reasonable thesis is *Depression can be caused by stress, loneliness, or poor health.* This thesis does not rule out other causes; it simply addresses three.

After you have settled on a possible thesis, you can start assembling material to support it. If you have used some of the techniques for finding something to write about (Chapter 34), you can sort through your collection of notes and select those that are pertinent. Or if you have already written a first rough draft, you can rewrite it with your thesis in mind. Further, if you plan to write an argument, you can list evidence for and against your thesis. The result will be a kernel that you can develop into a complete paper.

Of course, as you develop a draft, you may find that your thesis does not work very well. Perhaps you do not have enough material to support the idea. Perhaps the thesis is too broad to control material or too narrow to produce more than a paragraph or two. Or perhaps you change your opinion while writing the paper. Instead of struggling with an unsatisfactory thesis, revise it to suit the material you want to include. Or abandon the thesis altogether and find another. In fact, you may have to try several times to find something that works, but the search will be worthwhile in the long run. With a good thesis, one you can effectively support, you are much more likely to write a good paper. Notice that in the composition-in-progress (Chapter 38), the student writer changed and refined the thesis several times throughout the drafts of the paper. The thesis does not appear in its final form until the fourth and last draft.



The examples that follow show how several student writers moved from a topic to a thesis specific enough to control the content of a paper.

1. The student first narrowed the general topic *detective novels* to *the settings of detective novels.* In her first attempt at a thesis, she wrote *In detective novels, the setting is usually important.* This thesis, however, was too broad for the length of the paper assigned. She narrowed the thesis to *In Elmore Leonard's "La Brava," the setting is very interesting.* Since the word *interesting* did not offer much direction, she tried again and produced the workable thesis *In Elmore Leonard's "La Brava," readers learn about the Miami that tourists never see.*

2. The student wanted to discuss *the advantages of word processing over typing* and began with the sentence *Word processing is better than typing.* He then rejected this vague thesis and wrote *Because a word processor encourages revision, its use can improve composition grades dramatically.* When he tried to write a rough draft, however, he found that he had little to say, since revision naturally improves papers and thus grades. The thesis was too narrow. He then wrote *Using a word processor can improve grades.* In his paper, he was able to discuss the advantages of revising compositions, typing lecture notes, and producing attractive out-of-class assignments.

3. The student wanted to write on *fly fishing* and first formulated the vague thesis *Fly fishing is a good sport,* which offered no direction for the paper. She then tried *Fly fishing requires more skill than any other type of fishing.* This idea proved unsatisfactory not only because it was too broad but also because it would be very hard to support. Next, she formulated the supportable thesis *Fly fishing is a difficult sport.* And finally, she revised the sentence to give direction to the paper: *Fly fishing is a difficult sport because it requires physical skill, concentration, and practice.*



4. Disgusted with his roommate for watching television constantly, the student writer chose the subject *couch potatoes.* In his irritation, he tried the thesis *Couch potatoes are lazy* and then *Couch potatoes are stupid.* Since neither statement was supportable, he tried *Most television programming is so boring that a couch potato must have a problem very much like a drug addiction.* He realized, however, that he did not know enough about drug addiction to support the position. At this point, he reconsidered his subject. Primarily, the irritating roommate watched situation comedies. The writer then abandoned his original idea and found a productive thesis: *The plots of current family-comedy shows are essentially "Leave it to Beaver Revisited."*

5. The writer began with the subject *the importance of studying computer science* and then changed it to *the advantages of studying computer science.* She first tried the thesis *Students who understand computers have more career options than those who do not.* In writing a first draft, however, she found that she had not fully considered what she meant by "understand computers." The draft moved from students with expertise in theory and design, to students with programming skills, to students with computer literacy. She revised her thesis to state *Computer literacy is an advantage in almost any profession.* She was then able to define "computer literacy" and discuss its advantages to people in fields such as accounting, law, marketing, food services, and office management.

These experiences show the importance of finding a suitable thesis. If the student writers had spent less time looking for a productive thesis statement, they would have had much more trouble producing a satisfactory paper.

### The Computer Connection

A computer helps you not only to get thoughts down on paper but also to make decisions. How should you handle your raw material? What should you keep or cut? How should you organize? What should you emphasize? Because adding, deleting, and rearranging is easy, you can experiment with different purposes, voices, and thesis statements to see which best suit your material. You can then print a hard copy of the different versions and compare them.

***Suggestions for Making Decisions***

- Type an idea for a subject and then brainstorm to find a thesis statement that might lead to a rough draft.
- Write a rough draft with a definite purpose in mind—impression, information, argument, or entertainment. If your purpose doesn't seem to fit the subject, switch to another purpose and redraft.
- After you complete a rough draft, try different versions with different voices. Print the versions to see which you prefer.
- If you use a computer program with multiple windows, you can keep notes or old versions in one window while at the same time composing in another.

*For reading:* Banks, Michael and Dibell, Ansen. *Word Processing Secrets for Writers.* Cincinnati: Writer's Digest Books, 1989.

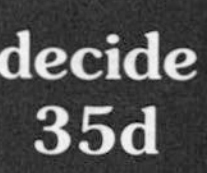


## ❑ EXERCISE 6

Which of the following do not meet the requirements for a suitable thesis? For each unacceptable thesis, state which requirements are lacking.

1. Telecommunications is an interesting field of study.
2. Although Frank Lloyd Wright made his reputation as an innovator, he was actually an imitator.
3. The four types of stress are mental, physical, chemical, and thermal.
4. A rumor circulated in 1978 that a fast-food chain put earthworms in hamburger meat to increase the protein content.
5. All nature is not beautiful.
6. Astrological profiles are silly.
7. Advice from a freshman in college to a high school student.
8. More marriages would survive if people signed premarital contracts.
9. Although many viewers love Mayberry in the *Andy Griffith Show,* few of them would like to live there.
10. Rock stars go to extremes to be different.

## ❑ EXERCISE 7

Write a thesis for five of the following subjects. Instead of simply turning each phrase into a sentence, narrow the subject by making a specific statement.

EXAMPLE: Cooking as a hobby → Learning to cook is an effective way to improve your social life.

in search of a decent hamburger
Tarzan as a romantic hero
how computers are changing society
status symbols in the middle class
the ultimate stereo equipment
the hardships of a tourist
part-time jobs for the untrained
magazines and their intended audiences
advice about studying
economizing in college
unsympathetic teachers
living alone
romance through personal advertisements
self-defense for women
telephone options



# 35e Patterns

Sometimes the best pattern for a paper is implicit in the thesis. *There are only three types of bartenders* leads naturally into classification. *I survived rush week* suggests a narrative that outlines events. *The campus parking problem could be solved by increased rates for permits* could take the form of problem/solution. A comparison/contrast pattern is an obvious plan for *Solar energy is more practical in the southern United States than in New England*. Enumeration of evidence is the likely development for *Air travel has its inconveniences*.

When a method of development is not implicit in the thesis, you must consider among possible patterns. For example, suppose your thesis were *Ulysses S. Grant was a weak president*. You could contrast Grant to strong presidents. You could treat his policies in a cause/effect pattern or illustrate his character with one detailed narrative. Or you might classify Grant's failings into two categories: his failure to stand up to radicals in Congress and his failure to police corruption among his associates. You could then enumerate examples under each category.

Each of the patterns can serve to shape an entire paper or one section of a paper. At times, the patterns seem to overlap rather obviously. However, they are presented not as pure forms but only as methods to help you frame and direct ideas.



### (1) Description

Description is the presentation of details that create a verbal picture of what something is or appears to be. Many of the papers you write in a composition class are likely to require some description. Obviously, you should not include all the details possible. Instead, you should select those details that best characterize what you are describing. Also try to strike a good balance; too few details will communicate little to the reader, and too many will obscure the picture.

Once you have decided which details to include, you must find some way to arrange them. One possibility is to organize spatially, from top to bottom, left to right, far away to close up—so that the reader sees the picture as though a video camera were ranging over the scene. Spatial arrangement works well for descriptions of buildings, bridges, parks, works of art, and scenes in nature. You can also move from positive to negative features or negative to positive. For example, you might present a favorite old car by first describing its good points and then its bad or vice versa. Or you can arrange details from the more obvious to the less obvious, describing your grandfather, let us say, first with those details obvious to anyone and then with subtle traits known only to people close to him.

Often your subject and the point you want to make about it will guide your choice. Often more than one option will seem logical. Whatever the arrangement, the details should be organized, not presented merely at random.

### (2) Narration

Narration tells a story, recounts events, or outlines the stages of a process. The arrangement of the actions can be strictly chronological, without interruptions, in the order in which they occurred or do occur. The arrangement can also be predominantly chronological, interrupted with flashbacks to previous actions. Or it can be episodic, with actions grouped into incidents not necessarily sequential.

Narration is a good scheme for recounting an experience or relating an anecdote, such as an uncomfortable job interview or a trip that turned into a comedy of errors. Narration is also a logical pattern for explaining a process, such as how a chemistry experiment works or how to rappel down a mountainside. When you choose narration to structure a paper, take special care to include only the details that advance the story or the account of the procedure. Extra information causes the reader to ask the deadly question, "So what?"



### (3) Enumeration

In enumeration, details are listed to support the thesis of a whole paper or the topic sentence of a paragraph. The details may be anything appropriate to the subject—facts, statistics, examples, precedents, or testimony. Suppose, for example, you have this thesis: *Vigorous exercise can help reduce stress.* You could enumerate statistics from studies that support your position and testimony from people who have overcome stress by exercise. Or consider this idea: *Art and theater majors dress differently from other students on campus.* You could enumerate the types of clothes that will prove your point.

Writers disagree about the best order for enumeration. Some prefer the order of increasing importance, in which the most important items come last. Others, arguing that readers remember best what they read first, position items in order of diminishing importance. In any case, all agree that the most important items should not be put in the middle.

### (4) Comparison/contrast

Comparison/contrast shows how things are similar or different. This technique is appropriate for a thesis such as *"Gone With the Wind" and "So Red the Rose" deal similarly with the destruction of the planter class after the Civil War.* With this thesis, the paper would probably minimize differences and highlight similarities. On the other hand, a paper with the thesis *The parent-child relationship in single-parent families differs radically from that in two-parent families* would emphasize differences.

Comparison/contrast is an obvious pattern for presenting a conflict—for example, the feud between farmers and cattlemen in the American West, conflicting arguments about the theme of *Macbeth,* or the ideology of the Republican Party as opposed to that of the Democratic Party. When the purpose is to argue, the paper supports one side of the conflict. When the purpose is to inform, the paper describes the conflict without taking sides.



The two most common arrangements for a comparison/contrast pattern are *block* and *alternating.* Suppose, for example, you were comparing an article in *Reader's Digest* with the original to determine how an article can be simplified and shortened in a digested version. In the block arrangement, you would first discuss one version of the article, including each point of comparison and contrast, and then move to the other version, discussing the same points. In the alternating arrangement, you would organize the paper according to the points of comparison, with the two versions under each point. The following outlines help clarify the difference between the methods.

BLOCK ARRANGEMENT

1. Original version of magazine article
   1.1. Length
      a. The whole article
      b. Paragraphs and sentences
   1.2. Vocabulary
   1.3. Effect
2. *Reader's Digest* version of magazine article
   2.1. Length
      a. The whole article
      b. Paragraphs and sentences
   2.2. Vocabulary
   2.3. Effect

ALTERNATING ARRANGEMENT

1. Length
   1.1. The whole article

- a. Original version
- b. *Reader's Digest* version
- 1.2. Paragraphs and sentences
  - a. Original version
  - b. *Reader's Digest* version
2. Vocabulary
   - 2.1. Original version
   - 2.2. *Reader's Digest* version
3. Effect
   - 3.1. Original version
   - 3.2. *Reader's Digest* version

**decide 35e**

For most subjects, the alternating arrangement works best. It allows you to bring close together the similarities and differences so that a reader need not think back to another part of the paper to make mental connections. The block arrangement, on the other hand, works well when the comparison is very simple and does not depend on details.

## (5) Classification

In classification, items from a general category are grouped into smaller categories on the basis of selected principles. As the following list suggests, any number of subjects can be classified.

Melville's novels might be classified by their subject matter—those primarily autobiographical and those allegorical.

Comic strips might be classified by type of satire—social or political or both.

Sports commentators might be classified according to attitude—the ex-jock, the statistician, and the fan.

Sleeping bags might be classified by their fill—those containing down, Dacron, or polyurethane foam.

Watches might be classified by the image they produce—professional, trendy, ostentatious, macho.

The structure of a classification paper grows naturally out of the subject matter. Each class constitutes a section (a paragraph or more) of the final composition.

## (6) Illustration

An illustration is an example that makes a generality specific or an abstraction concrete. The illustration may be a narrative, a description, a fact, or anything that makes an idea graphic or real.

An entire paper built on one extended illustration usually takes a narrative form. For example, an argument that criminals should work to compensate their victims might narrate one incident, from the commission of a crime through a successful program of compensating the victim to the criminal's rehabilitation.

On the other hand, a paper built on a series of illustrations usually has an enumeration pattern. A writer could enumerate the examples of Muhammad Ali, Joe Louis, and Sonny Liston to support this thesis: *Boxing should be outlawed because of the brain damage suffered by participants.*



### (7) Definition

A word can be defined with a synonym (*probity* means "honesty") or with a formal explanation that puts the item defined into a general class, or genus, and then differentiates it from other members of that class: "A *misanthrope* is a person [general class] who hates humanity [differentiation]." Obviously, when an entire paper is devoted to definition, the subject must be expanded with other structures. For example, "What is a soap opera?" might be answered by a variety of methods.

| | |
|---|---|
| CLASSIFICATION: | the types of soap operas |
| COMPARISON/CONTRAST: | the ways in which soaps differ from other television forms |
| ILLUSTRATION: | the use of one popular soap opera or several to exemplify the form |

### (8) Analysis

Since the term *analysis* means breaking a whole into component parts, a number of rhetorical patterns could be considered analytical. In narration, events are broken into time segments; in classification, subjects are partitioned into categories; in comparison/contrast, subjects are divided into similarities and differences.

As a separate pattern of development, however, analysis refers to an orderly examination of constituents. Writers frequently have the task of analyzing a poem, a play, a mechanism, a system, a process, or collected data. The purpose of such an analysis is to bring a systematic understanding to a subject. For example, an analysis of a poem could examine the theme, the voice, the figurative language, and the sound pattern. An analysis of an insect might include these components: physical description, life history, habitat, enemies. An analysis of the process for tracing an ancestor might include interviewing relatives, checking local records, and reading genealogical collections.

### (9) Problem/solution



The logic and simplicity of the problem/solution pattern make it easy to design: identification of a problem and presentation of a solution. A paper with this pattern can either emphasize the problem or the solution or give equal time to both.

A problem/solution pattern is common in arguments, where the thesis often includes both problem and solution. *The overpopulation of cats and dogs should be controlled by law,* for instance, contains the problem (overpopulation of cats and dogs) as well as the solution (control by law). Both the problem (traffic flow and automobile accidents) and a solution (a bridge over an intersection) are stated in this thesis: *A footbridge should be built over the Moncrief Avenue–Carpenter Street intersection to facilitate traffic flow and reduce accident risk for pedestrians.*

### (10) Cause/effect

The cause/effect pattern is a versatile structure. A paper can begin with a cause and lead up to the effect, begin with effect and then explain cause, or shift back and forth between the two. This pattern is an obvious structure for papers on historical events but is by no means limited to discussions of the past. The structure is effective for discussions of conditions and results (if certain conditions are present, certain results can be expected) and speculations about the future (if certain trends continue, certain events are likely to occur).

The following titles suggest the range of subjects that can be organized in a cause/effect pattern as well as the emphasis a writer can impose on a subject.

The Common Causes of High Blood Pressure

The Effects of Custer's Recklessness on the Disaster at Little Big Horn

Tactics for Getting a Raise

The Future of Mount St. Helens

Telling the Truth Got Me into Trouble

You, Too, Can Have a Well-Behaved Dog

Too Many Hours in Front of a TV

If you decide to use the cause/effect pattern, be sure that your logic is sound. In other words, a preceding event does not necessarily cause the one that follows. Furthermore, many events and trends have multiple and complex causes. For advice on examining causes, see "Post Hoc Reasoning" and "Oversimplification of Cause" in the chapter on "Argument and Critical Thinking."



## ❑ EXERCISE 8

**What pattern or patterns are suggested by each of the following controlling ideas?**

1. Four strategies will help you remember names and faces.
2. Michael Cimino's eccentric personality made *Heaven's Gate* a synonym for disaster in the film industry.
3. Some theorists believe that most human behavior is learned, whereas others believe that humans are biologically programmed for particular behavioral patterns.
4. During his boxing career, Muhammad Ali's charisma was as remarkable as his physical prowess.
5. Over one hundred years of struggle preceded the opening of the Panama Canal in 1920.
6. The establishment of a food plaza would help attract shoppers to the depressed downtown area.
7. The compulsive consumer is a recognizable species.
8. This year's coverage of the Super Bowl typified excessive network hype.
9. Hollywood's biblical epics are more fantastic than religious.
10. Painting with watercolors is a better hobby than painting with oils.
11. Gardening programs in housing projects discourage vandalism.
12. Blue jeans can be classified by their purpose: to be practical or to be fashionable.
13. In exercise classes, differences between personality types are exaggerated.
14. There are three components of an effective letter of application.
15. Everyone needs to take a few business courses.

# 35f Outlines

Once you have settled on a subject and have a tentative pattern in mind, it is wise to work from some sort of plan, whether sketchy or carefully detailed. Before writing a plan, or outline, you should review any notes or material you have on hand so that you do not overlook information worthy of inclusion. Also, if at this point you need more material, you can return to techniques such as brainstorming or freewriting to refresh your memory or stimulate new thinking.



Whether you write a rough outline or a structured one depends on your personal work habits or on your assignment. Even if a structured outline is called for, most people begin with a rough outline and then refine it—usually after the paper has been completed so that changes made during the writing stage appear in the finished outline.

## (1) A rough outline

A working outline need not be formal, with a system of Roman and Arabic numerals, upper- and lowercase letters, and parallel grammatical structures. Instead, it can be "rough," with the emphasis on order and content rather than form and parallelism. A rough working outline should be finished enough to reveal the omission of necessary information, the presence of superfluous material, the compatibility of the parts of the composition, and the logic of sequences. Such an outline can also help a writer to evaluate a plan.

- Is the plan one the audience can follow?
- Does the thesis require further narrowing or expanding?
- How much more material must be collected?
- Is there time to collect the material?
- Are the resources available?

For example, suppose you were structuring a paper around the thesis *The problem with dogs is mainly a problem with their owners.* You might first jot down possible segments, such as these.

| | |
|---|---|
| barking all night | leash laws |
| roaming loose | strays |

overpopulation    vicious
good companionship

At this point, you should check the list for segments that should be omitted, combined, or added. The preceding list contains segments that overlap: *roaming loose* overlaps *leash laws; strays* overlaps *overpopulation. Good companionship* does not fit and should be omitted. And *disease* is a promising subject to add. Thus a working outline might look like this.

1. barking all night
2. roaming loose
3. overpopulation
4. vicious animals
5. disease



If the rough outline has too many divisions, you may need to narrow your focus. If the outline has divisions that do not seem to go together, your thesis is probably weak, and you should change it before moving ahead. If nothing seems to work, you can go back to the techniques for getting ideas and look for new material, a new thesis, or a new subject.

### (2) A structured outline

If you prefer to go beyond a rough outline to make a more structured plan before beginning a draft, you can make a topic, a sentence, or a paragraph outline. The topic outline helps ensure a logical sequence, predict paragraphing, and speed up production of a first draft. In addition, a topic outline can serve as a table of contents if the assignment requires one. A sentence outline can suggest topic sentences for paragraphs and blocks in the paper. A paragraph outline, almost a rough draft of the paper itself, is rare because few writers are prepared to develop ideas at the same time they are organizing the topic with an outline. Instead, most outlines develop gradually, progressing in detail and size as the subject is developed and the necessary information is accumulated.

Although a numbering system is not necessary for working outlines, some writers prefer to use one. A numbering system reveals the relationships between parts and the volume of material necessary to develop the subject. Two systems work well: the traditional system (Roman numerals and Arabic numerals and letters) and the decimal system.

**Traditional System**

Thesis: College professors fall into four basic categories: the Students' Pal, the Scholar, the Entertainer, and the Eager Beaver.

I. The Students' Pal
  A. Youthful clothes
  B. Casual classroom presentation
    1. Informal manner
    2. Use of students' first names
    3. Tendency to give high grades
  C. Social life with students
    1. Inclusion of students in faculty activities
    2. Invitation to his/her home
    3. Teacher/student leisure activities

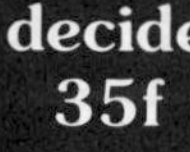


II. The Scholar
  A. Lack of attention to clothes
  B. Serious classroom attitude
    1. Emphasis on lecturing
    2. Lengthy discussion tests
    3. Preoccupation with specialized material
  C. Lack of interest in student activities
III. The Entertainer
  A. Eccentric clothes
  B. Entertaining classroom performance
    1. Lectures that resemble comedy monologues
    2. Emphasis on anecdotes and jokes
    3. Unpredictable, clever tests
  C. View of students as audience
IV. The Eager Beaver
  A. Conventional clothes
  B. Exuberant (but misguided) classroom presentation
    1. Cheerleader attitude
    2. Emphasis on class discussion and group projects
  C. Tendency to pout if students do not respond

**Decimal System**

Thesis: Social problems can hurt a student's schoolwork.

1. Poverty
  1.1. Inadequate resources
    1.1.1. Lack of supplies
    1.1.2. Lack of equipment
    1.1.3. Incomplete library

- 1.2. Poor diet
  - 1.2.1. Inability to concentrate
  - 1.2.2. Lack of stamina
  - 1.2.3. Frequent illness
- 1.3. Necessity for part-time jobs
  - 1.3.1. Long hours
  - 1.3.2. Inadequate sleep

2. Drugs and alcohol
   - 2.1. Lack of motivation
   - 2.2. Detriment to health
   - 2.3. Influence on truancy
3. Family Problems
   - 3.1. Parental divorce
     - 3.1.1. Anxiety
     - 3.1.2. Distraction from schoolwork
   - 3.2. Parental disinterest
     - 3.2.1. Lack of supervision
     - 3.2.2. Lack of regular hours



## ❑ EXERCISE 9

**Outlines can reveal problems with the subject of a proposed paper, the content, and the organization. What problems do the following outlines reveal?**

There are obstacles to the widespread use of the bicycle as transportation in the U.S.

Distances
Automobile and truck traffic
Bicycle use in Europe
Thievery

Since their introduction, Christmas cards have changed.

1. Now cards are often humorous.
2. Cards reflect sophisticated production techniques.

Unlike previous painters, impressionistic painters painted everyday pastimes.

1. Edouard Manet's *Boating*
2. August Renoir's *Rower's Lunch*
3. Claude Monet's interest in light and color
4. Edgar Degas' *Carriage at the Races*
5. Earlier artists' emphasis on noble and classical subjects

Advertising about weight reduction is often deceptive.

—Promise of immediate results
—Promise of sexual attractiveness
—Implication of effortlessness
—Misleading testimonials
—Medical jargon
—Exercising unnecessary
—Magical foods or pills

Some inventions have changed civilization.

I. Early Inventions
 A. Bow and Arrow
 B. Drill
 C. Wheel
 D. Plow
II. The Printing Press
III. The Industrial Revolution
 A. Steam Engine
 B. Power Loom
IV. Leonardo da Vinci's Inventions
V. Gunpowder
VI. Recent Inventions

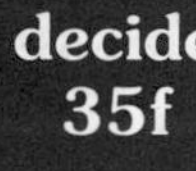


## ❑ EXERCISE 10

Write working outlines to develop three of the following ideas.

1. The Japanese education system is more rigorous than the American system.
2. People can be classified by the kinds of vacations they take.
3. Seeing a movie in a theater is a different experience from seeing one on television.
4. Christmas is typically a time of stress.
5. Some college classes make me wonder what I'm paying for.
6. The problem with television is that it makes us too passive.
7. Magazine racks in stores tell us something about interests of Americans.
8. Women's clothes are designed for ultrathin models, not for normal figures.
9. Consequences for misbehavior change as one grows older.
10. Elaborate weddings are a waste of money.

## The Computer Connection

Computers cannot write for you, but they can help you plan writing strategies and organize material. The structure of your paper will probably go through many stages, evolving as your ideas take shape. The computer makes it easy to experiment with alternatives as you look for a suitable structure.

### *Suggestions for Working with Structures*

- Start by making a list of major topics, arguments, or incidents you want to cover. Add subtopics as they occur to you, delete items, or shift the order.
- Experiment with more than one pattern or structure for the composition. For example, you might create two outlines—one in a cause/effect pattern, another in an illustration pattern—and then see how your material adapts to each structure. Which structure seems to strengthen or enhance the material? Do you need to find better supporting material or examples? Flag sections that need work.
- Some of your best ideas for examples, titles, transition lines, or opening anecdotes may come at inconvenient moments. Don't try to work them into the material right away; instead, create a "junk" file of random material and call it up as needed.
- Don't delete early versions of outlines or other material. If you keep a record of different attempts, you can return to them to retrieve information that looks better in retrospect.

*For reading:* Moberg, Goran G. *Writing on Computers in English Composition.* New York: The Writing Consultant, 1986.

# 36

# Paragraphs



At some point in the composition process, you must move from the planning stage to the writing stage. You must get your ideas down on paper. It is at this stage that some people develop "writer's block": they stare helplessly at empty white paper—and it stares back. The mind goes completely blank or rejects every idea that surfaces.

If you should experience this inertia, two tactics may help overcome it. First, get away from the blank paper for a while and do something else. Sharpen pencils, buy new paper, clean your room, jog, or read. Second, remember that you are not trying to produce a finished product in one sitting. Instead, you are simply trying to produce a rough draft, something to work from. Try writing rapidly to keep the momentum going. Once in rough form, the first draft can be changed, supplemented, and polished.

Some writers spend most of their time on preliminaries; they think through a subject, make plans, and take notes. Then they write the entire composition and revise it. Other writers think, write, and revise intermittently—working back and forth, weaving a composition piece by piece. No single system works for every person. If you have no established pattern for the drafting process, you might want to experiment to see what works best for you. When you find something that feels comfortable and that works well, you can stick with it.

Regardless of the drafting technique you prefer, your goal is to produce a series of segments that fit together within the overall structure of the whole paper. These segments are the paragraphs, the units of information that together develop the paper's thesis.

Drafting your paper paragraph by paragraph allows you to focus all your attention on developing each segment of information.

## 36a Body Paragraphs



The body of a composition, between the introduction and conclusion, contains the material that supports the thesis. This material must be presented in logical segments, or paragraphs. When you draft the body, think of the paragraphs as "mini-compositions" with internal structures similar to the structures of full papers. In other words, the details in a paragraph support a central idea just as the evidence of a whole paper supports its thesis.

In the drafting stage, you should not expect to produce a series of classic paragraphs, each with exemplary unity, coherence, and development. If you do, you can get bogged down, lose spontaneity, and forget where you are headed. The timc to cnsure each paragraph's unity, development, and coherence is during revision. You can then make sure that each paragraph is unified, that all its details relate to a single idea. You can check each paragraph's development to be sure that sufficient details cover the topic. And you can add any necessary transition to achieve coherence. (See Chapter 37, "Revision.")

### (1) Paragraphs with topic sentences

A useful way to construct a paragraph is to think in terms of a topic sentence, one that states the point of the whole paragraph. The traditional paragraph begins with a general statement, or topic sentence, which is subsequently supported or developed by discussion, illustration, or examples. This organization works especially well for inexperienced writers; it improves coherence and unity because the details are all related to the stated idea. Furthermore, as the following paragraph illustrates, placing the thesis at the beginning ensures its emphasis.

Topic Sentence at the Beginning

> Hypnosis can control people's vision. For example, if you were hypnotized and I told you a snake was slithering across the floor, you would not only believe me, you would actually perceive the snake as real. If I told you that there was no desk in the room, you could look right at it and not see it.

The topic sentence can occur not only at the beginning of the paragraph but also within the paragraph or at the end. These variations can relieve the monotony of a series of paragraphs, each beginning with a topic sentence.

Topic Sentence at the End

According to a survey, 50 percent of the prisoners convicted of murders, rapes, robberies, and assaults had been drinking before committing their crimes. Sixty percent of these prisoners had been drinking very heavily. Obviously, drinking is closely related to violence.



Topic Sentence in the Middle

For years, whenever I tried jogging, it turned out to be a painful struggle. So I quit, tried again, quit, and on and on. But now, I have discovered the answer. I never jog alone. Jogging with others somehow makes the torture bearable. Talking gets my mind off what I'm doing, and suffering with others is better than suffering alone.

In another variation of paragraph development, writers do not state the topic sentence but rely altogether on the content to indicate the central idea. For example, the idea of the following paragraph, though not stated, is obviously that baseball fans are fickle.

Topic Sentence Unstated

When a baseball team is winning, fans swarm into the stadium, enthusiastic cheers fill the air, good seats go only to those who buy tickets far in advance. When a team begins to lose, the stands are half empty, the silence broken only by catcalls, boos, and moans. With homers, high batting averages, and sparkling defensive plays, the players are magnificent heroes. In a slump, they turn suddenly into hopeless bums.

When the supporting material is lengthy, a block of several paragraphs may develop a single topic sentence. For example, in a rather long article on golfer Jack Nicklaus, this three-paragraph block develops the single topic sentence stated at the beginning of the first paragraph.

Topic Sentence for a Block of Paragraphs

*topic sentence*

In a word, Nicklaus has the ideal temperament for a golfer, and, combined with his physical stamina and phenomenal will to win, it helps to explain the miracles he has performed at many critical moments. Let me briefly describe three that come to mind.

*preview of organization*

In the playoff for the 1970 British Open at St. Andrews, he held

*first example*

a one-shot lead over Doug Sanders as they came to the eighteenth, a straightaway par 4 only 354 yards long. When there is a good following wind, as there was that afternoon, a big hitter like Nicklaus can drive the green. Sanders, with the honor, played a fine tee shot that ended up a few yards short of the green. Nicklaus then removed the sweater he was wearing—he did not mean this action to be as dramatic as it was—and swatted a huge drive dead on line for the pin. He had, in fact, hit the ball too well. It bounced onto the green and rolled over the back edge into some fairly high rough. Sanders had his birdie all the way, so it was up to Nicklaus to get down in two to win. From a difficult downhill lie in the rough, he played a delicate wedge chip that stopped eight feet from the hole. His putt looked as if it might be slipping a shade too much to the right, but it caught a corner of the cup and fell in. By and large, Nicklaus has been a very solid putter throughout his career—an invaluable asset.



*second example*

In the 1972 U.S. Open, at Pebble Beach, Nicklaus, with two holes to go, apparently had the championship won, for he led the nearest man by three strokes. Still, anything can happen on the last two holes at Pebble Beach. The seventeenth, a par 3, 218 yards long, is tightly bordered on the left by Carmel Bay, and the green is severely bunkered. With the wind in his face, Nicklaus chose to play a 1-iron. He ripped a beautiful shot through the wind which almost went into the hole on the fly. The ball landed inches short of the cup, bounced up and struck the flagstick, and came to rest inches away. He tapped it in for his birdie, and that was that.

*third example*

Three years later, in the Masters, Nicklaus was involved in a tremendous battle in the fourth, and last, round with Johnny Miller and Tom Weiskopf. Throughout the long afternoon, all three played some of the most spectacular golf shots imaginable, and the outcome was not decided until the final green, where both Miller and Weiskopf, who were the last twosome, missed makable birdie putts that would have tied them with Nicklaus. In retrospect, Nicklaus had played the winning shot on the sixteenth. When he came to that hole, a 190-yard par 3 over one of the largest and loveliest water hazards in golf, he trailed Weiskopf by a stroke. The pin was set that day, as it usually is on the fourth round of the Masters, in the hardest position—near the front of the narrow terrace at the back right-hand corner of the green. It takes a superlative shot, with true backspin on it, to hit and hold that terrace, because there is little margin for error: a large bunker sits in wait just beyond the green. Nicklaus, going with a 5-iron, played a so-so shot that ended up on the left side of the green well below the slope of the terrace and some forty feet from the pin. He took a long time studying his putt, to make certain he had read the line correctly. He then rapped the ball firmly up the slope and watched it break some eighteen inches to the left in a gradual curve and dive into the cup. That birdie put him in a tie for the lead with Weiskopf, and when Weiskopf three-putted the sixteenth for a bogey 4, Nicklaus was out in front to stay. (Herbert Warren Wind, "Mostly About Nicklaus," *The New Yorker*)

## EXERCISE 1



**Identify the topic sentences of the following passages. If no topic sentence is present, state it in your own words.**

1. In high school classes, students are expected to follow instructions unquestioningly. The main emphasis is on behavior and order. On tests students are required to repeat information or to check true-false answers. Curiosity and originality are discouraged. In fact, America's schools are breeding conformity.

2. When I visit a museum containing antique clothing, I am amazed at the difficulties people in the past must have had dressing. Everything was fastened by ties or buttons, no snaps and no zippers. All the clothes look very uncomfortable—constrictive, stiff, and layered. The shoes for the right and left feet were identical. I'm told that it wasn't until the mid-nineteenth century that shoes were designed to fit the different shapes of both feet.

3. Adults returning to school must sacrifice time with their families and sometimes sacrifice their accustomed standards of living. They often suffer doubts about their skills because of long periods of scholastic inactivity. Also, they may feel out of place surrounded by the younger students.

4. My childhood friends were called Boopie, Boo, Puddin, Cooter, and Bobo. At age twenty, these people are still known as Boopie, Boo, Puddin, Cooter, and Bobo. If anyone called them Susan, Marshall, Helen, Edward, or Chester, they probably wouldn't know immediately who was being addressed. Nicknames are hard to get rid of, especially in a small town. You might be able to move away and use the name on your birth certificate, but at home you will always have to answer to a nickname.

5. Customers who order pizza to be delivered to their homes or dormitory rooms have peculiar senses of humor. Some call in orders for places and rooms that don't exist. Others give addresses of people who have not ordered pizzas. Once, three drivers from three pizza restaurants showed up at the same time at the same house, and no one who lived there had placed the order.

Some customers also find it hilarious to order strange combinations like triple anchovy, triple shrimp, and triple jalapeño peppers. Others order weird proportions like one-third ham and sausage, one-third ham and hamburger, and one-third hamburger and sausage, mushrooms on the third with ham and sausage, peppers on the third with ham and hamburger, olives and onions on the third with hamburger and sausage, and hold the cheese.



## (2) Paragraph patterns

Like an entire composition, an effective paragraph or block of paragraphs has its own logical purpose and pattern. In fact, you can structure a paragraph or block of paragraphs with the same techniques available for whole papers—description, narration, comparison/contrast, classification, and so forth. (See 35e.)

The point of the paragraph determines the pattern or patterns you can choose. For example, if the paragraph exists to relate an incident, the pattern will more than likely include narration, leading from one occurrence to another. If the point of the paragraph is to show similarities and differences, a comparative pattern is a logical choice. Whatever the dominant point may be, some pattern or combination of patterns can accommodate its development.

### Description

You use description when you want to create an image that the reader can envision. The following paragraph, for example, paints a picture of a movie mummy that for years haunted the writer.

> It was the mid-1940s. I had just seen a movie about a mummy. I don't remember the name of it. Just the image, so powerful even still, of a man wrapped in grayish cloth around his ankles, legs, body up to the top of his head. Eyes and mouth exposed, one arm drawn up against his chest, elbow close to his side, hand clawed. The other arm dangling alongside the leg that dragged. Several strips of cloth hung loosely from that arm, swaying with each step-drag, step-drag. I don't remember where he was coming from or going to in the movie. It doesn't really matter. I knew that he was coming for me. (Frank Langella, "The Monsters in My Head," *New York Times Magazine*)

### Narration

For an event, anecdote, or story, you write a narrative. A paragraph with a narrative arrangement moves from one occurrence to another, usually in chronological order. The following paragraph narrates two early electrical experiments.

> The Abbé Noilet assumed the post of "official" electrician to Louis XV and arranged the spectacle of an electric discharge passed through 180 soldiers of the guard, all of whom leapt as one man into the air. An even more spectacular performance was arranged by him at the Couvent de Paris. Here, he assembled 700 monks in line, each joined "electrically" to his neighbour by means of a bit of iron wire clasped in either hand. The circuit was completed by having the monks at the end joined to the prime conductor and the condenser by a similar means. At the moment of discharge, to the great joy and amusement of the king and retinue, although to the discomfort of the monks, the 700 monks, like the 180 soldiers, leapt into the air with a simultaneity of precision outrivalling the timing of the most perfect corps de ballet. (I. B. Cohen, *Benjamin Franklin's Experiments*)



### Enumeration

Many paragraphs have an enumerative pattern. Anytime you need to present several facts or details to back up a general statement or to make a point, you use enumeration. This pattern is similar to a list, with examples itemized throughout the passage. In the following paragraph from a paper on the foolish ways people treat pets, the student writer enumerates details found in advertisements for boarding kennels.

> With family vacation plans that did not include pets, I began to search for a painless way to part company with two dogs and a cat. The Yellow Pages revealed surprising choices: a ranch, a motel, an inn, an academy, a country club, and even an animal kingdom. Our pets could luxuriate at the Pet-otel, at Paradise for Pets, at Pleasant Valley, or better yet, at Rhapsody Acres. The only ominous sounding place was the Dog House. At one of these places with "best friends" enjoying "tender loving care," the "furry four-footed companions" are provided with heated and air-conditioned accommodations, grooming, styling, and trimming. In another, they are entertained by music in "new, modern facilities with a skylighted atrium." One place transports its guests in a "pet taxi" and provides "dating." While dogs enjoy a "country atmosphere," cats step into a "jungle motif." It all sounds so appealing that my family's vacation

plans paled in comparison. If it weren't for the plucking and ear tattooing, I might have considered joining the animals.

### Comparison/Contrast

A paragraph can be structured around comparison (similarities) or contrast (differences) or both—whatever is appropriate or instructive. You could, for example, write about a local basketball player's skills by comparing them with the skills of a well-known player. Or you could write about a new breed of cat by contrasting the characteristics to existing breeds. In the following paragraph, the writer uses contrast to emphasize the qualities of the village of Greenwich.



> Greenwich was a Williamsburg with a difference: it wasn't dug out of the ground and rebuilt. There was another difference too: it didn't have that unnaturally genteel, sanitized look of the Virginia village that turns it into a museum. Surely, the first Williamsburg must have been a knockabout frontier town, a place of skullduggery and war, where the laundry got hung out and dogs pissed in the muddy lanes, where the scent of dung and wet horses was strong. To resurrect that town and playact the past is a good thing for Williamsburg. But it wasn't the way of Greenwich. Hidden in the tall marsh grass of the coastal lowland, the whilom seaport that once rivaled Philadelphia was remarkable. (William Least Heat Moon, *Blue Highways: A Journey Into America*)

### Classification

Classification is a scheme that organizes a subject—such as people, events, or ideas—into characteristic groups on the basis of some similarity the members share. You use classification whenever you need some sort of scheme for discussing a subject composed of many items. Obviously, you cannot discuss all boats, all computers, or all Italian food. Therefore, you group the items in categories to give your subject some order. In this paragraph, the writer classifies the residents of Venice, California, into workers and nonworkers.

> The residents of Venice fall into two groups: those who work and those who don't. The latter includes senior citizens, drifters, drug addicts, would-be moviemakers, and aging hippies and surfers who have made a cult of idleness and pleasure. The other group includes lawyers, dentists, real estate brokers, accountants. Many are workaholics, attached to their jobs as they are to nothing else. They

> work nights and weekends, eat fast food while driving to and from their work, and live alone, longing, in the silence before falling asleep, for connection. (Sarah Davidson, "Rolling Into the Eighties," *Esquire*)

### Illustration

A paragraph developed by illustration supplies evidence to back up a general statement or an abstraction. The evidence may be a narrative, a description, or enumerated examples—any information that helps to prove the truth of the paragraph's central idea. In the following passage, the student writer uses a narrative about a friend to illustrate his point.



> Even if a player makes it to the pros, he cannot be certain of a long career. Injuries frequently ruin dreams. A talented player from my hometown was drafted by the New England Patriots. After one season, he became a key part of the Patriots' defense. Then in one game, he injured his knee, was never able to rehabilitate it, and was out of a job.

### Definition

A paragraph can define a key term so that readers can better understand the entire composition. You will find definition especially useful when a term is confusing or has no universally accepted meaning. Here a student writer tackles the difficult term *humanities.*

> Any course that focuses on the meaning, purpose, and values of human life is a humanities course. The humanities include primarily history, literature, philosophy, language, and anthropology. Unlike the sciences that search for facts about the concrete world, the humanities interpret life. The humanities ponder the mystery of human existence; the sciences try to remove it.

### Analysis

A paragraph developed by analysis explores a subject by probing beneath its surface. The paragraph examines the units (parts, ingredients, characteristics, causes) that make up the larger whole. A machine, a person's behavior, an event, a book, a war, an idea—anything that can be divided into components can be analyzed. The student writer of the following paragraph analyzes the formula of the classic western by discussing its three components.

A classic western of the *High Noon* school has three interlocking components. First, it has a hero of amazing purity and innocence. A thought inappropriate for Sunday school class has never flitted across his brain. The second necessary ingredient is an evil for the hero to battle and overcome. The evil can be represented by one person, several people, or a whole town. The third piece of the puzzle is a woman, who may or may not be a victim of the evil. Her primary purpose in the story is to beg the hero not to battle the evil and thus allow him to say, "A man's got to do what he's got to do."

### Problem/Solution



Paragraphs developed with a problem/solution pattern usually begin with a statement of a problem and then move to a solution. With this structure, you can propose a solution or discuss one that already exists. Here a student writer starts with the conflict between academics and athletics and ends with a proposal for eliminating the conflict.

In many American colleges football players fail academically. These campus heroes may perform poorly in the classroom, but no matter, just as long as they perform brilliantly on the playing field. Many people lament the unfairness, the immorality, the waste of such a system. But at most schools academic reforms have been unsuccessful and are probably impossible. The solution is to stop deceiving ourselves. These players don't always go to school to learn. Instead, they are gambling on becoming professionals. Therefore, schools should give them up as students and hire them as athletes. In that way, they could enroll in classes if they wanted to, but they would not have to. In a sense, the team would be owned as a financial and promotional investment. If we can divorce academics and athletics, we can eliminate the hypocrisy and probably improve both.

### Question/Answer

A question/answer pattern generally begins with a question and moves to an answer. Clearly, this strategy for paragraphs cannot be used throughout a paper; it would become monotonous. On occasion, however, when you are supplying information, the pattern can be effective, as this paragraph illustrates.

Why do we stand aside and let someone older or more important go through the door first? Because in early history it was sensible for the strongest man to leave the castle first, since there was always a possibility he would be met with arrows, armed opponents, or the rebellious peasantry waving pitchforks and scythes. Gradually, a certain honor descended upon this position. It was assumed that the most important person was also the strongest, and even if he wasn't, he could hardly deny it. Many a lord must have wished somebody else would take his place as the first man to ride out through the gates, but since honor was involved, his rank demanded that he accept it. Eventually it became, of course, purely honorific, as is the custom of offering the honor to somebody else, in the knowledge that he will refuse it. Even today men can still waste several minutes offering each other the honor of being the first to leave a meeting through a revolving door ("after you"; "no, no, after *you*"), and no doubt the same tedious politeness took place in the castle keep, with the difference that the first one out might have to fight for his life. (Michael Korda, "The Hidden Message of Manners," *Success!*)



### Cause/Effect

Whenever your subject matter contains information that relates to a cause and an effect, you can begin with the cause and move to the effect or reverse that order. When the subject matter contains a sequence of causes and their effects, you trace the relationships, as the following paragraph does.

Professional athletes are sometimes severely disadvantaged by trainers whose job it is to keep them in action. The more famous the athlete, the greater the risk that he or she may be subjected to extreme medical measures when injury strikes. The star baseball pitcher whose arm is sore because of a torn muscle or tissue damage may need sustained rest more than anything else. But his team is battling for a place in the World Series; so the trainer or team doctor, called upon to work his magic, reaches for a strong dose of butazolidine or other powerful pain suppressants. Presto, the pain disappears! The pitcher takes his place on the mound and does superbly. That could be the last game, however, in which he is able to throw a ball with full strength. The drugs didn't repair the torn muscle or cause the damaged tissue to heal. What they did was to mask the pain, enabling the pitcher to throw hard, further damaging the torn muscle. Little wonder that so many star athletes are cut down in their prime, more the victims of overzealous treatment of their injuries than of the injuries themselves. (Norman Cousins, "Pain Is Not the Ultimate Enemy," *Anatomy of an Illness*)

### Combined Patterns

Many paragraphs involve more than one pattern. The next paragraph primarily describes the "insularity," or isolation, of the people in California's Central Valley. The writer structures the information around a topic sentence and illustrates her point with a short narrative. At the end she includes an ironic contrast of Modesto and Merced.

> U.S. 99 in fact passes through the richest and most intensely cultivated agricultural region in the world, a giant outdoor hothouse with a billion-dollar crop. It is when you remember the Valley's wealth that the monochromatic flatness of its towns takes on a curious meaning, suggests a habit of mind some would consider perverse. There is something in the Valley mind that reflects a real indifference to the stranger in his air-conditioned car, a failure to perceive even his presence, let alone his thoughts or wants. *topic sentence* An implacable insularity is the seal of these towns. *narrative* I once met a woman in Dallas, a most charming and attractive woman accustomed to the hospitality and social hypersensitivity of Texas, who told me that during the four war years her husband had been stationed in Modesto, she had never once been invited inside anyone's house. No one in Sacramento would find this story remarkable ("She probably had no relatives there," said someone to whom I told it), for the Valley towns understand one another, share a peculiar spirit. They think alike and they look alike. I can *contrast* tell Modesto from Merced, but I have visited there, gone to dances there; besides, there is over the main street of Modesto an arched sign which reads:
>
> WATER—WEALTH
> CONTENTMENT—HEALTH
>
> There is no such sign in Merced. (Joan Didion, "Notes from a Native Daughter," *Slouching Towards Bethlehem*)

draft 36a

## ❑ EXERCISE 2

Identify the organizational patterns used in each of the following paragraphs.

1. I keep emphasizing how dramatically things have changed; this is necessary because the scale of change is so enormous that it is far too easy to under estimate it. A useful analogy can be made with motor cars to put things in perspective. Today's car differs from those of the immediate postwar years on a number of counts. It is cheaper, allowing for the ravages of inflation, and it is more economical and efficient. All this can be put down to advances in automobile engineering, more efficient methods of production, and a wider market. But suppose for a moment that the automobile in-

dustry had developed at the same rate as computers and over the same period: how much cheaper and more efficient would the current models be? If you have not already heard the analogy the answer is shattering. Today you would be able to buy a Rolls-Royce for $2.75, it would do three million miles to the gallon, and it would deliver enough power to drive the *Queen Elizabeth II.* And if you were interested in miniaturization, you could place half a dozen of them on a pinhead. (Christopher Evans, *The Micro Millennium*)



2. The expansion of English around the world has been matched by the infiltration of English words into the vocabularies of dozens of other countries. Japanese sports fans talk knowledgeably of *beisuboru* and *garafu* (golf) over glasses of *koka-kora;* Spanish speakers, sometimes stimulated by too many *cocteles*, wax frenetic over *futbol,* while their newspaper *columnistas* deplore the spread of *gangsterismo.* West German newspapers run *Reporten* of legislative *Hearings* on *das Fallout* and *die Recession,* and cover *Press Konferenzen* complete with *no Komment* and *off die Rekord;* in France, *teenagers* (pronounced "teenahz*hair*") wearing blue *djins* buy *hot dogues* from street vendors. (Robert Claiborne, *Our Marvelous Native Tongue*)

3. Did you ever wonder why Mr. Rogers can do a children's television show day after day after day with the same kind, loving, gentle, understanding, and perfectly rational demeanor? Has it ever struck you as slightly odd that he can relate warmly and patiently to children with nary a whine or a whimper to say nothing of a scream? One day recently I finally discovered it's because he rarely has a child on his show. All his children are located conveniently thousands of miles away from him on the other side of the television screen. (Will Manley, "Facing the Public," *Wilson Library Bulletin*)

4. In academe, the number of courses on medieval subjects has been on the rise for several years, as has the number of students taking them. According to a survey by the medievalists Christopher Kleinhenz and Frank Gentry, during the decade ending in 1980 thirty-seven new scholarly journals specializing in the Middle Ages commenced publication. Since 1970, attendance at the annual conference of the Medieval Institute, at Western Michigan University, in Kalamazoo, has swelled from 800 to almost 2,000, making it the largest medieval *congressus* in the world. (Cullen Murphy, "Nostalgia for the Dark Ages," *Atlantic*)

5. The printed page was itself a highly specialized (and spatialized) term of communication. In 1500 A.D. it was revolutionary. And Erasmus was perhaps the first to grasp the fact that the revolution was going to occur above all in the classroom. He devoted himself to the production of textbooks and to the setting up of grammar schools. The printed book soon liquidated two thousand years of manuscript culture. It created the solitary student. It set up the rule of private interpretation against public disputation. It established

the divorce between "literature and life." It created a new and highly abstract culture because it was itself a mechanized form of culture. Today, when the textbook has yielded to the classroom project and the classroom as social workshop and discussion group, it is easier for us to notice what was going on in 1500. Today we know that the turn to the visual on one hand, that is, to photography, and to the auditory media of radio and public address systems on the other hand, has created a totally new environment for the educational process. (Marshall McLuhan, "Sight, Sound, and the Fury," *Commonweal*)

6. Although I didn't realize it at the time, scientists generally divide into two camps, abstractionists and experimentalists. The theorists and the tinkerers. Especially in the physical sciences, the distinction can be spotted straight off. It has since been my observation that, in addition to their skills in the lab, the latter group (particularly the males) can fix things around the house, know what's happening under the hood of a car, and have a special appeal to the opposite sex. Theorists stick to their own gifts, like engaging themselves for hours with a mostly blank sheet of paper and discussing chess problems at lunch. Sometime in college, either by genes or accident, a budding scientist starts drifting one way or the other. From then on, things are pretty much settled. (Alan Lightman, "A Flash of Light," *Science 84*)



## (3) Order of details

A well-structured paragraph or block of paragraphs, no matter what its purpose, contains details that require a systematic arrangement. Usually, the best strategy is a progressive order—spatial, chronological, climactic, general to particular, or particular to general. An order, however, should not be so constrictive that it forces information into an artificial mold. Instead, the order should direct the flow of ideas, provide control over details, and help the reader understand how one point leads to the next.

### Spatial Order

In paragraphs with a spatial order, the details of a specific space are arranged so that readers get a visual impression of it. The arrangement can follow the movement of the eye up, down, across, or around. In the following example, the writer uses spatial order to describe the photographic blowups behind the bar at Gipper's Lounge near Notre Dame University.

> This was in the Holiday Inn about three furlongs from the campus on the road to Niles, Michigan. Six days a week the Fight-

ing Irish and other refreshments are available here in Gipper's Lounge, a shrine dedicated to the memory of George Gipp, the patron saint of football and eight-ball pool at Notre Dame. Walls of the lounge are covered with photographic blowups of football plays and players. Three dominate the decor: behind the bar stands the Gipper himself, half again larger than life, wearing the soft leather headgear and canvas pants favored by all-America halfbacks around 1920; at his right is a huge head shot of Frank Leahy, the late, great coach; at Gipp's left, Harry Stuhldreher, Jim Crowley, Elmer Layden and Don Miller sit astride four plow horses. The riders wear football regalia with cowled woolen windbreakers, and each has a football tucked under an arm. (Red Smith, "Rum + Vodka + Irish = Fight," *The Red Smith Reader*)



### Chronological Order

Chronological order presents a sequence in time, arranging events in the order in which they took place. In the following paragraph, for example, the student writer recounts the stages in a trend.

I am one of those "reentry" students who figure prominently in education statistics these days. Many of us are women in their late thirties and early forties, divorced, with children ages six to fifteen. Most of us experienced the "women's movement" and had our "consciousness raised." We gained self-esteem, thought independent thoughts, and encouraged our children to overcome the male/female stereotyped roles. Then our husbands became successful and left us for younger women without raised consciousnesses. They also left us with children without raised consciousnesses. Worst of all, they left us with employers without raised consciousnesses, who expect women to work for less pay than men. And so, we went back to school.

### Climactic Order

One kind of climactic order moves from material of lesser importance to that of greater importance. Another kind describes small components and then moves to the whole, as does this paragraph on an ant colony.

Still, there it is. A solitary ant, afield, cannot be considered to have much of anything on his mind; indeed, with only a few neurons strung together by fibers, he can't be imagined to have a mind at all, much less a thought. He is more like a ganglion on legs. Four ants together, or ten, encircling a dead moth on a path, begin to look more like an idea. They fumble and shove, gradually moving the food toward the Hill, but as though by blind chance. It is only when you watch the dense mass of thousands of ants, crowded together around the Hill, blackening the ground, that you begin to see the whole beast, and now you observe it thinking, planning, calculating. It is an intelligence, a kind of live computer, with crawling bits for its wits. (Lewis Thomas, "On Societies as Organisms," *Lives of a Cell*)

### General-to-Particular Order

General-to-particular order begins with a general statement and moves to specific details. This order conforms to the traditional paragraph, in which the topic sentence, or general statement, appears first and is followed by support, or particular details. For example, the first sentence of the following paragraph is a very general statement. The next two sentences restrict the topic a bit, and the last sentence gives particular examples.



> Hollywood appears to be running out of new ideas. In the last few years, the number of remakes, sequels and readily-recognizable spinoffs of established winners has easily exceeded the tally of truly original concepts. Every blockbuster success inevitably spawns a host of shabby imitations. *The Exorcist* begat *Abby, The House of Exorcism, Beyond the Door* and *The Manitou; Jaws* begat *Tentacles, Tintorera the Tiger Shark, Marko-Jaws of Death, Barracuda* and *Orca; Star Wars* begat *Star Crash, Laserblast* and *Battlestar Galactica.* (Harry and Michael Medved, "The Biggest Ripoff in Hollywood History," *The Golden Turkey Awards*)

### Particular-to-General Order

Particular-to-general order begins with specifics and moves to a general statement, like this passage from an essay on the evolution of behavior. This order is natural when the writer wishes to postpone the topic sentence until the end of the paragraph.

> A whale's flipper, a bat's wing and a man's arm are as different from one another in outward appearance as they are in the functions they serve. But the bones of these structures reveal an essential similarity of design. The zoologist concludes that whale, bat and man evolved from a common ancestor. Even if there were no other evidence, the comparison of the skeletons of these creatures would suffice to establish that conclusion. The similarity of skeletons shows that a basic structure may persist over geologic periods in spite of a wide divergence of function. (Konrad Z. Lorenz, "The Evolution of Behavior," *Scientific American*)

## ❑ EXERCISE 3

Suggest strategies that you could use to develop the following subjects into paragraphs or blocks.

1. the expense of owning a dog
2. the monotony of American motels
3. American beer versus imported beer
4. types of parents
5. the consequences of sleeping late
6. T-shirt messages
7. the problems of working students
8. a tour of your hometown
9. effective excuses
10. the appeal of professional wrestling



## ❑ EXERCISE 4

Choose three topics (topics of your own or from Exercise 3), and develop each in a paragraph or block of paragraphs using one of the suggested strategies or a combination of strategies.

# 36b Introductory Paragraphs

The introduction to a paper makes a commitment to the audience by establishing the subject as well as the purpose and voice. In other words, the introduction tells the audience what to expect throughout the rest of the paper.

You can draft the introduction to a paper at any point during the writing process, depending on your preference. You may want to write it first, using it as a way to generate momentum. Or you may want to write it last, tailoring it to fit the body of the composition. Actually, you can compose the introduction any time an idea strikes. Regardless of when you write the introduction, however, remember that it is the first thing the audience reads, and it should make a favorable impression.

Often a technique for an introduction develops naturally out of the subject matter. If not, you can consult the techniques and examples that follow for ideas. Notice that some of the sample introductions are very brief and simple, whereas others are a bit more complex.

### (1) Stating the thesis, or controlling idea

An introduction can state or imply the thesis that the paper will support. This technique makes the point of the paper clear to the audience from the start. In the introductory paragraph that follows, the final sentence is the thesis of the entire article.

> Some call it the Dawn of a New Computer Age. Others call it the Post-Industrial Revolution. Still others call it the Age of Knowledge. Whatever the name, computers have entered another period of change in which they will be transformed, not simply improved. During the next decade or so, computers will be constructed differently and will operate differently. Most importantly, they will begin to reason and apply logic. These developments will not merely produce a dramatic change in the role of computers worldwide; they will cause a dramatic effect on society as well. (Deb Highberger and Dan Edson, "Intelligent Computing Era Takes Off," *Computer Design*)



### (2) Describing the problem

A logical introduction for a problem/solution paper is a description of the problem. The following introduction, for instance, describes the loss of the wilderness, the environmental problem that the paper addresses.

> They are best seen not on foot or from outer space but through the window of an airplane: the newly cleared lands, the expanding web of roads and settlements, the inexplicable plumes of smoke, and the shrinking enclaves of natural habitat. In a glance we are reminded that the once mighty wilderness has shriveled into timber leases and threatened nature reserves. We measure it in hectares and count the species it contains, knowing that each day something vital is slipping another notch down the ratchet, a million-year history is fading from sight. (Edward O. Wilson, "Million-Year Histories," *Wilderness*)

A statement of the problem often serves as the introduction to a literary paper. Here Bruce Morton begins with the problem: scholars agree that Fitzgerald was the model for a Hemingway character, but they do not explain why. The rest of the paper is Morton's solution—a theory that explains Hemingway's motive.

> Bruccoli, Lefcourt, and Lewis have all made credible cases for F. Scott Fitzgerald being the prototype for Francis Macomber in Hemingway's short story, "The Short Happy Life of Francis Macomber."

> Cumulatively, their cases based on similarities in name, character, and biography seem irrefutable. What, however, has not been heretofore established is why Hemingway chose to "go after" Fitzgerald in such a manner at that particular time. (Bruce Morton, "Hemingway's 'The Short Happy Life of Francis Macomber,'" *The Explicator*)

### (3) Stating the conflict

A paper addressing a conflict often begins with a summary of both sides of the issue. In the following introduction, a student writer describes the conflicting attitudes of the farmer and the conservationist toward the coyote.



> The coyote, always a symbol of freedom and wildness on the prairie, has lately become the focus of a controversy. Ranchers are blaming the coyote for killing baby farm animals, especially lambs. These ranchers claim that the coyote is contributing greatly to their financial ruin. In the coyote's defense, members of wildlife conservation groups claim that ranchers' losses are not serious and that the ecological balance is in danger because of the poisons and traps ranchers are using to kill coyotes.

### (4) Establishing a larger context

An introduction can put a subject into perspective by placing it within a larger context. In this introduction to a piece on aerial acrobatics, the student writer begins with the origins of flight and then narrows the subject to aerial acrobatics.

> When Orville Wright first flew in 1903, the problem was staying in the air; the first successful flight lasted only twelve minutes. To direct the plane right or left, he had to move his hips from side to side. Obviously, Wright's plane had little maneuverability. Early flights mainly moved straight ahead or wherever the winds blew the planes. Gradually, improved technology contributed speed, distance, and control. Finally, daredevils were inspired to try stunts. In 1913, a plane flew upside down. In 1914, a plane "looped the loop" one thousand times, did a tail spin, and flew inside a building. That was the beginning of aerial acrobatics.

### (5) Sketching the background

A sketch of the subject's background can supply interesting information while focusing the audience's attention. Here the writer introduces a report on the safety of aspartame by briefly sketching the development of the sweetener.

It's one of the food industry's great success stories. A chemist working on an ulcer medicine during the 1960s casually licks the powder on his finger and finds it sweet. Nearly 20 years later the substance, aspartame, sweetens foods such as breakfast cereal, chewing gum, cocoa, instant iced tea, and whiskey sour mix. As Equal, it's a granulated sugar substitute; as NutraSweet, it sweetens Diet Coke, Diet Pepsi, and Diet Seven-Up. (William F. Allman, "Aspartame: Some Bitter with the Sweet," *Science 84*)

## (6) Giving an overview

An overview tells the reader what the writer will cover and usually in what order. For example, this author leads readers to expect a paper with four major sections, outlined in the last sentence.



Freeze-dried, spray-dried, or vacuum-dried? Aluminum, plastic, or polypropylene? Wee-Pak, small pack, or six-pack? Every hiker has experienced the utter bewilderment of standing before an array of backpacking foods and trying to choose among them. The products all blend together, a jumble of colors, shapes, and sizes.

Not all commercially prepared lightweight foods are the same, however. There's a world of difference in price and content, for example, between "beef Stroganoff with noodles" and "Stroganoff sauce with beef and noodles," or between "chicken/vegetable stew" and "vegetable stew with chicken." One package will instruct you to add boiling water, while the contents of another will require some cooking. To select the items best suited to your palate, your nutritional needs, and your pocketbook, four things need to be considered: dehydrating methods, ingredient combinations, label information, and meal preparation. (Lois Snedden, "Dried and True: The Lowdown on Lightweight Foods," *Sierra*)

## (7) Catching the audience by surprise

Writing meant to entertain or persuade often begins with an introduction that surprises or shocks the reader. Here Michael Arlen catches the reader's attention with his unconventional attitude in "Ode to Thanksgiving."

It is time, at last, to speak the truth about Thanksgiving, and the truth is this. Thanksgiving is really not such a terrific holiday. Consider the traditional symbols of the event: Dried cornhusks hanging on the door! Terrible wine! Cranberry jelly in little bowls of extremely doubtful provenance which everyone is required to handle with the greatest of care! Consider the participants, the merrymakers: men and women (also children) who have survived passably well throughout the years, mainly as a result of living at considerable distances from their dear parents and beloved siblings, who on this feast of feasts must apparently forgather (as if beckoned by an aberrant Fairy Godmother), usually by circuitous routes, through heavy traffic, at a common meeting place, where the very moods, distempers, and obtrusive personal habits that have kept them all happily apart since adulthood are then and there encouraged to slowly ferment beneath the cornhusks, and gradually rise with the aid of the terrible wine, and finally burst forth out of control under the stimulus of the cranberry jelly! (Michael Arlen, "Ode to Thanksgiving," *The Camera Age*)



## (8) Identifying the source of interest

A writer's interest in a subject may spring from anywhere—from a book, an incident, a news report, a personal involvement, a casual conversation. Here, a student writer introduces a paper on "The Home Kitchen and a Happy Childhood" by summarizing a survey on carryout food.

It looks as if people are giving up cooking, even when they eat at home. In a recent magazine survey of 5,000 people, 43 percent got carryout food primarily from fast-food restaurants, 28 percent from restaurants, and 21 percent from supermarkets. Only 8 percent of those surveyed did not purchase carryout food at all. These statistics suggest that the availability of pre-prepared food could make home kitchens obsolete. If so, childhood would be drastically altered, and for the worse.

## (9) Presenting an antithesis

An argument often begins with the antithesis—the idea contrary to the thesis. This technique allows a writer to set up the opposition and then attack it. The following introduction, for example, presents a misconception about the microelectronics industry. The rest of the paper argues that the industry's traditionally clean reputation is deceiving.

When the microelectronics industry was launched about 20 years ago, it was hailed as a clean industry that would pose few health and safety problems to its workers, and even fewer to the surrounding environment. Most people assumed microelectronics would entail processes similar to those of conventional electronics. They envisioned large numbers of workers quietly soldering conductive wires onto printed circuit boards. And because the slightest bit of dust could not be permitted to contaminate the semiconductor chip, the major product of this industry, the companies' operations appeared even cleaner than anticipated. Workrooms were thoroughly ventilated with filtered air and workers wore white gowns, head coverings, and gloves. (Joseph LaDou, "The Not-So-Clean Business of Making Chips," *Technology Review*)



### (10) Defining a term

You should avoid the time-worn beginning, "Webster's dictionary defines such and such as. . . . " However, you can begin by defining a key term, particularly one not fully defined in a dictionary. Here a student writer begins a composition with an original definition of *redneck.*

> The name "redneck" was derived from the burned necks of farm workers. It later came to refer to poor whites in the South. Today, however, the redneck is not confined to any area of the United States or to any economic group. No, the redneck is a universal character—an insensitive and ignorant boob who is proud of the insensitivity and the ignorance.

### (11) Relating an anecdote

An anecdote can lead an audience into a subject. For example, this writer uses an amusing story to introduce a discussion of the relationships between humans and animals.

> A sidewalk interviewer asking people their beliefs about when human life begins, so the story goes, accosted a prosperous-looking man on his way out of a bank. "I'll tell you when life begins," the man answered. "It begins when the last kid is out of college and the dog has died."
>
> A lot of people would argue with his second condition for life's onset, and some of them are scientists opening up a brand-new field: human-animal relationships, specifically regarding pets, or companion animals as they came to be known in the immediately spawned jargon. This new field is of interest to me because by various avenues of accretion—most of them having to do with a collapse of willpower on my part—my house contains, at last count, 42 companion animals. This may seem excessive, but the findings of

> students of human-animal relationships have persuaded me that this immoderation will in fact redound to my continuing health, both physical and mental. (Jake Page, "Companion Animal Therapy," *Science 84*)

### (12) Asking a question

Asking a question or two that the rest of the paper will either answer or address can stimulate the reader's curiosity. Here, a student introduces a research paper with a question that most people would like answered.



> At 10:15 P.M. on April 14, 1865, while watching a play at Ford's Theatre in Washington, D.C., Abraham Lincoln was hit by an assassin's bullet. The next morning, without regaining consciousness, Lincoln died. Almost two weeks later, his assassin, John Wilkes Booth, surrounded in a tobacco shed, was shot to death. Eight other people were implicated in the assassination, tried before a military commission, and found guilty. One of these was a woman named Mary Surratt. Ever since, a question has nagged at America's conscience. Was Mary Surratt guilty?

### (13) Using a quotation

Sometimes a quotation is a natural way to introduce a paper. In fact, a statement by someone else may be the stimulant that first suggests a topic. A quotation by Samuel Johnson, for instance, led a student writer to a paper about overrated foods.

> According to Samuel Johnson, "A cucumber should be well sliced, and dressed with pepper and vinegar, and then thrown out, as good for nothing." I don't know why Johnson had such a dislike for the cucumber. Cucumber slices are delicious in salads and on sandwiches. However, there are other foods that do deserve scorn and yet for some reason are held in high esteem. Instead of cucumbers, I would like to see these foods "thrown out, as good for nothing."

### (14) Using a combination of strategies

It is not uncommon for writers to combine introductory techniques. In the following example, notice how the writer begins with a conflict of opinion about *The Duchess of Malfi,* then asks a question, and answers it with her thesis.

Despite William Archer's famous diatribe against the unrealistic aspects of *The Duchess of Malfi,* the play continues to fascinate readers and playgoers alike—and to make them angry. Critical opinion on it has developed into an almost furious quarrel over the motivation of its characters, the validity of its action, the meaning of its key phrases, and the overall philosophy behind it. The Duchess herself has been described as everything from a medieval saint to a modern bitch, while the question of Ferdinand's incestuous longing has generated as much serious discussion as is usually reserved for the personality of an historical figure. Why all this controversy over what might seem like a typical Jacobean horror play? There appears to be something in Webster's dark world that lies too close to the bone for critical comfort, something as uncertain in our own minds as in the play itself. (Phoebe S. Spinrad, "Coping with Uncertainty in the *Duchess of Malfi,*" *Explorations in Renaissance Culture*)



## ❑ EXERCISE 5

In each of these introductions, identify the technique or techniques used.

1. Introduction to an essay on the frequency of new discoveries in anthropology

My first teacher of paleontology was almost as old as some of the animals he discussed. He lectured from notes on yellow foolscap that he must have assembled during his own days in graduate school. The words changed not at all from year to year, but the paper got older and older. I sat in the first row, bathed in yellow dust, as the paper cracked and crumbled every time he turned the page.

It is a blessing that he never had to lecture on human evolution. New and significant prehuman fossils have been unearthed with such unrelenting frequency in recent years that the fate of any lecture notes can only be described with the watchword of a fundamentally irrational economy—planned obsolescence. Each year, when the topic comes up in my courses, I simply open my old folder and dump the contents into the nearest circular file. And here we go again. (Stephen Jay Gould, "Bushes and Ladders in Human Evolution," *Ever Since Darwin*)

2. Introduction to a report on theories about bird migration

The melancholy appearance of geese passing south under low autumn skies is as much a mark of the turning seasons as the first robin of spring. Some of us pay more attention to these things than others, but few are more drawn to the seasonal movement of birds than ornithologists who have for years been attempting to understand one of migration's most vexing riddles: How do birds know which way to go? (Patrick Cook, "How Do Birds Find Where They're Going?" *Science 84*)

3. Introduction to an essay on American wastefulness

Cans. Beer cans. Glinting on the verges of a million miles of roadways, lying in scrub, grass, dirt, leaves, sand, mud, but never hidden. Piels, Rheingold, Ballantine, Schaefer, Schlitz, shining in the sun or picked by moon or the beams of headlights at night; washed by rain or flattened by wheels, but never dulled, never buried, never destroyed. Here is the mark of savages, the testament of wasters, the stain of prosperity. (Marya Mannes, "Wasteland," *More in Anger*)



4. Introduction to an article on a new fishing boat

It never fails. As soon as times get better, everyone starts introducing newer, bigger boats. In one sense that's good for you, the boatman, for it allows you a more diverse arena in which to make your selection.

But unfortunately, another side darkens this new prosperity. Occasionally, such new boats are born of a haste to fill a perceived void in the manufacturer's line, and the final product shows it. Even worse, we see special-purpose boats—sportfishermen, for example—being introduced by companies lacking the experience or expertise to build them. (Richard Thiel, "Tiara 3600 Pursuit," *Boating*)

5. Introduction to a humorous essay on the struggle between people and things

Inanimate objects are classified into three major categories—those that don't work, those that break down and those that get lost. (Russell Baker, "The Plot Against People," *New York Times*)

6. Introduction to a report on the dialects of bees

For almost two decades my colleagues and I have been studying one of the most remarkable systems of communication that nature has evolved. This is the "language" of the bees: the dancing movements by which forager bees direct their hivemates, with great precision, to a source of food. In our earliest work we had to look for the means by which the insects communicate and, once we found it, to learn to read the language.

Then we discovered that different varieties of the honeybee use the same basic patterns in slightly different ways; that they speak different dialects, as it were. This led us to examine the dances of other species in the hope of discovering the evolution of this marvelously complex behavior. Our investigation has thus taken us into the field of comparative linguistics. (Karl von Frisch, "Dialects in the Language of Bees," *Scientific American*)

## ❑ EXERCISE 6

Write introductions suitable for papers on two of the following subjects. If none of the subjects seems appealing, supply two of your own.

a proposal for changes in NFL rules
a formula for writing horoscopes and never being wrong
folk remedies that work
the etiquette of coed dormitories
a classification of recreational vehicles by types of owners
effective ways to fight depression
types of television game shows
body building: for men only?
ridiculous Christmas presents
the expense of entertainment
strange pets
shopping by mail-order catalog



## 36c Concluding Paragraphs

A paper should never end suddenly, as if the writer were interrupted and never returned to finish. Instead, the paper should come to some recognizable end, some logical stopping place. Papers sometimes end with the last frame in a time sequence, such as the last stage in a process or the final event in a narration. Other papers end with a concluding sentence or two. Still others end with fully developed paragraphs that contain summaries, recommendations, forecasts, or warnings. The length and formality of a conclusion depend on the length and formality of the whole composition as well as on the subject matter.

A conclusion is your last opportunity to influence the reader. Thus, you should make this segment as effective as possible. If you have trouble concluding a paper, look at the following strategies. One of them might be an appropriate choice.

### (1) Returning to the thesis

Writers frequently begin with the thesis, or controlling idea, explore it in the body, and conclude by restating it. The major advantage of this structure is its clarity—a reader learns right away exactly what the point is, sees its development, and is reminded of it again in the conclusion. The following introduction and conclusion demonstrate this "envelope" pattern. Notice how the writer restates while avoiding boring repetition.



**From time to time, forgeries make the news: Hitler's diaries, George Washington's signature, a note by Shakespeare, an autobiography by Howard Hughes. Today, technology has made handwritten forgeries much easier to detect. But at the same time it has improved the techniques used by the forgers themselves.**

* * *

Detecting forgeries has moved from fingerprint powder and magnifying glasses to sophisticated analyses by such devices as ultraviolet light, infrared spectroscopy, and electrostatic detection apparatus. However, in a continuing contest with criminologists, criminals also are applying the technology, especially with copying machines and computer-generated documents. The important question is whether or not the technology of detection can keep pace with the technology of making forgeries.

## (2) Making a recommendation

A recommendation often serves as the conclusion for a paper comparing products, processes, or courses of action. The recommendation may be very specific or rather general. This conclusion, for example, ends a paper that compares brands and types of sleeping bags. The recommendation here is general, suggesting a plan, rather than specific, recommending a particular kind of bag.

When looking at sleeping bags, draw on your personal knowledge of what has worked for you in the past. If you are inexperienced, you will need to talk with salespeople and get their recommendations. You may want to ask them what kind of sleeper they are and what kind of bag they use. Get a number of opinions before you make up your mind, and remember that every recommendation is a *guess*.

The way you sleep at home can be important. If you like to sleep in an all-pervading warmth, then you are a cold sleeper and should try to err on the warm side. If you like your skin slightly cool while you sleep, then you are a warm sleeper who can get away with a cooler and lighter bag. Sufficient warmth during sleep is a valuable commodity. So plan for the bad, and your experiences will always be good. (Mike Scherer, "Choosing Your Dream Sleeping Bag," *Sierra*)

## (3) Summarizing major points

Many conclusions summarize the major points previously presented, thereby reminding readers of what they have read and reinforcing the significant ideas. This kind of conclusion works well for long, complex papers. Summaries are rarely called for in short papers, however, where readers have no trouble remembering what has been said. In the following conclusion, the writer condenses the content of her lengthy paper into three paragraphs. The phrase *in short* cues readers that a summary is about to begin.



*summary of section on creation of wastes*

In short, inventing and manufacturing new products has far outpaced our knowledge and ability to handle the detrimental wastes. Our scientists created new ideas that manufacturers forged into bright new products—and few had the foresight to wonder what would happen to all those ugly and poisonous wastes.

*summary of section on water pollution*

The brilliant technology that has produced astounding new products is now facing the problems of where to put the harmful wastes. And now all of civilization is paying the price—a growing crisis in the quality of our water.

*summary of section on need for a solution*

Indeed, all Americans are paying the price of living in an affluent and polluted society: a growing crisis in the quality of our water. We are finally beginning to realize that much more work, planning, and money are needed to help ensure the health of human beings, the beauty and purity of our waters, and the sanity of our nation. (Barbara Tufty, "Uses, Abuses, and Attitudes," *American Forests*)

## (4) Ending with a quotation

A paper can end with a quotation—sometimes made by a famous person, sometimes by a person who has figured in the discussion. You can use this technique if the quotation is effective and appropriate, but you should not search through a book of quotations and use something only vaguely related to your point. In the following conclusion, the writer quotes a woman who is trying to save an old frontier town from destruction. In this quotation, Janaloo Hill explains what motivates her great effort to preserve a very small and remote place.

Each year the greasewood takes root in the dry red earth and covers up just a little bit more of the rock foundations that were once Shakespeare, New Mexico. The graves of the old pioneers are threatened with obliteration now by new ditches, dug for the newly dead. Some folks in Lordsburg want the old ones moved out. "They don't know who they are, anyhow," the Hills say.

But in this place 90 miles north of the Mexican border in a corner of New Mexico so remote that the only people likely to come through here are travelers en route to somewhere else, two women will continue to work toward the preservation of this lonely, historic domain.



"All we're doin' here is getting out and doin' what needs to be done. A lot of people wouldn't use their own money on something like this," Janaloo admitted in a moment's acknowledgement of her rather novel existence before returning to her chores. "But you can only eat so much and drink so much . . . so why not do something that might last after you?" (Patricia Leigh Brown, "Shakespeare," *American Preservation*)

## (5) Giving warning

A conclusion can serve as a vehicle to warn readers against some action or the lack of it. Here the writer warns readers against the dangers of categorizing people.

Indeed, it is my experience that both men and women are fundamentally human, and that there is very little mystery about either sex, except the exasperating mysteriousness of human beings in general. And though for certain purposes it may still be necessary, as it undoubtedly was in the immediate past, for women to band themselves together, as women, to secure recognition of their requirements as a sex, I am sure that the time has now come to insist more strongly on each woman's—and indeed each man's—requirements as an individual person. It used to be said that women had no *esprit de corps;* we have proved that we have—do not let us run into the opposite error of insisting that there is an aggressively feminist "point of view" about everything. To oppose one class perpetually to another—young against old, manual labour against brain-worker, rich against poor, woman against man—is to split the foundations of the State, and if the cleavage runs too deep, there remains no remedy but force and dictatorship. If you wish to preserve a free democracy, you must base it—not on classes and categories, for this will land you in the totalitarian State, where no one may act or think except as the member of a category. You must base it upon the individual Tom, Dick and Harry, on the individual Jack and Jill—in fact, upon you and me. (Dorothy Sayers, "Are Women Human?" *Unpopular Opinions*)

### (6) Making a forecast

Often writers use the concluding paragraph or paragraphs to make a forecast. In this conclusion of a discussion of wine making, the writer predicts future improvements in the quality of wine.

> Improvement in the quality of wine has been accelerating since the end of World War II, dramatically so within the past ten years. Today we truly live in a golden age of wine. One is tempted to wonder how wines can be improved. To answer with certainty is, of course, impossible, but it seems reasonable that new types of wines will be developed, that the quality of everyday wines will continue to improve, and that these everyday wines will become even better bargains than they are at present. Vintage wines will become even finer as the many dedicated enologists who make them find the best varieties of grapes for each microclimate and apply the appropriate sciences in their vineyards and wineries. (A. Dinsmoor Webb, "The Science of Making Wine," *American Scientist*)



### (7) Calling for further study

Writers often use the conclusion to call for additional work or investigation. In this essay on the neglect of education, the student concludes by proposing a study to eliminate the problem.

> The cries of alarm throughout the state about the weaknesses in the educational system should be heeded. Although the problems have resulted from many years of neglect and disinterest, we must very quickly figure out specific ways to raise educational standards. An intensive study to find remedies is essential before any improvement can occur.

### (8) Showing applications

A paper that details an investigation often concludes with suggestions for possible applications of the study's findings. This report on student alcohol abuse, for instance, concludes with some practical ideas for student programs.

> What seems to be needed is an early identification process that will focus on the behavioral consequences of drinking. For example, in this sample the negative consequences were in direct proportion to the severity of the drinking. By identifying problem drinkers early, based on their behavior, student personnel staff may be able to provide resources and programs for these students.
>
> The identification process should focus on the behavioral manifestations of drinking rather than on drinking itself, because most students deny that they have a drinking problem. Programs designed for alcohol abuse should focus on students who: (a) are caught abusing alcohol; (b) while under the influence of alcohol, cause physical damage in the community or on the campus; (c) are identified as problem drinkers (e.g. through peer evaluation and referral); and (d) volunteer to participate. These programs should include a carefully designed network of components such as testing and evaluation, alcohol awareness groups, Alcoholics Anonymous meetings, and personal counseling. (T. A. Seay and Terrence D. Beck, "Alcoholism Among College Students," *Journal of College Student Personnel*)



## (9) Using a hook

A hook is a specific detail, example, or anecdote on which a writer "hangs" a larger subject. The writer begins with the hook and returns to it at the end of the paper. William F. Buckley, Jr., for example, uses an incident on a train to introduce an essay on the American tendency to tolerate inconvenience without complaining.

> It was the very last coach and the only empty seat on the entire train, so there was no turning back. The problem was to breathe. Outside, the temperature was below freezing. Inside the railroad car the temperature must have been about 85 degrees. I took off my overcoat, and a few minutes later my jacket, and noticed that the car was flecked with the white shirts of the passengers. I soon found my hand moving to loosen my tie. From one end of the car to the other, as we rattled through Westchester County, we sweated; but we did not moan.

At the conclusion, Buckley returns to the incident of the train to "frame" the essay.

When our voices are finally mute, when we have finally suppressed the natural instinct to complain, whether the vexation is trivial or grave, we shall have become automatons, incapable of feeling. When Premier Khrushchev first came to this country late in 1959, he was primed, we are informed, to experience the bitter resentment of the American people against his tyranny, against his persecutions, against the movement which is responsible for the great number of American deaths in Korea, for billions in taxes every year, and for life everlasting on the brink of disaster; but Khrushchev was pleasantly surprised, and reported back to the Russian people that he had been met with overwhelming cordiality (read: apathy), except, to be sure, for "a few fascists who followed me around with their wretched posters, and should be horse-whipped."

I may be crazy, but I say there would have been lots more posters in a society where train temperatures in the dead of winter are not allowed to climb to 85 degrees without complaint. (William F. Buckley, Jr., "Why Don't We Complain?" *Esquire*)



## ❑ EXERCISE 7

What typical concluding strategies or combination of strategies do you find in the following passages?

1. Technology and discoveries have radically changed dentistry. Children no longer have cavities as they once did, and adults no longer lose their teeth. Also, the equipment dentists use is costing more and more. Thus, students looking for a profitable profession should look toward other fields, not toward dentistry.

2. Over the years, a London art dealer collected the 425 photographs contained in this interesting but expensive album. Pictured are not only famous artists such as Whistler, Sargent, and Degas but also their friends and followers. The vivid likenesses bring the Victorian era to life; *The Victorian Art World* is well worth its price.

3. But before tanning salons can be considered safe, studies must be done on the long-range effects of ultraviolet A-rays on the human body.

4. In summary, many experts recognize six types of intelligence: linguistic, musical, spatial, logical/mathematical, kinesthetic, and personal. And as the case studies above demonstrate, parents should encourage their children's strengths and not worry unduly about weaknesses. As Dr. Wilkerson puts it, "People aren't happy doing things they don't do well."

5. So if your medical problem is not an emergency, compare several doctors. Ask where they went to medical school. Find out if they have up-to-date equipment. Check to see if their office personnel are pleasant and efficient. Investigate their fees. Surely you should spend as much time shopping for health care as you do for a car.

## ❏ EXERCISE 8

Write a suitable conclusion for two of the following papers.



1. A paper that evaluates a current movie
2. A paper that develops the following controlling idea: Attitude affects one's success in school.
3. A paper that attempts to solve the problem of massive unemployment among young people
4. A paper on dictionaries and books of synonyms; the paper begins with Mark Twain's statement, "The difference between the almost right word and the right word is the difference between the lightning bug and the lightning."
5. A paper that contains evidence that acid rain is damaging our land and water life, eroding our structures, and even threatening our health

## The Computer Connection

Many people feel they must draft compositions in some special way; they can write only on a yellow legal pad, in a Big Chief tablet, with a newly sharpened Faber pencil, at a desk, on a couch. Most habits, however, are simply the result of familiarity. If you have never tried drafting on a computer, experiment with the technique. A little practice may convince you that the computer is a very comfortable way to write. Knowing that you can easily make changes lessens tension and helps keep you in an experimental frame of mind.

### *Suggestions for Drafting Paragraphs*

- If you lack typing skills, use computer software designed to teach the keyboard or improve typing speed. The better you type, the more easily you can use the computer for drafting compositions. Available for this purpose are numerous software programs such as *Type Right, Typing Made Easy,* and *Typing Instructor.*
- Type a topic sentence and see whether the details and explanations follow naturally. Later, if necessary, you can delete, move, or change the topic sentence; but by writing it first, you may gain momentum.
- Type each paragraph straight through so that you do not lose your train of thought. If you feel compelled to stop often to correct typographical or grammatical errors, darken your screen or avoid looking at the monitor. You can correct errors during revision.
- Print out your paragraphs frequently. If you lose momentum, you can sometimes regain it by reading a printed version of your work.
- Try printing each paragraph on a separate page. Then when you revise the composition, you can read several different arrangements to determine which sounds best.

*For reading:* Schwartz, Helen J. *Interactive Writing: Composing with a Word Processor.* New York: Holt, Rinehart and Winston, 1985.

# 37

# Revision

revise 37

Revision is an integral part of the writing process. Too often inexperienced writers neglect this task altogether or confuse it with proofreading for spelling and typographical errors. It is only through revising, however, that ragged drafts are transformed into a finished product.

Just for the moment, think of writing as analogous to building a house. The structure takes shape piece by piece. It begins with a plan; moves through a number of messy stages while the foundation, walls, and roof go up; and finally emerges with plaster, paint, plumbing, and doors that do not squeak. Once the process is complete, no one sees the concrete that was repoured, the windows that were rehung, or the tile that went back to the factory. A writer is at once an architect, contractor, plumber, electrician, brick mason, paperhanger, and all the other laborers. The reader is the buyer; all he or she has to do is admire the finished construction. You do not want the buyer to say, "What a lot of trouble this was," but rather, "What a good job this is."

Some writers correct and revise their prose as they write. Others write very fast and revise the whole work afterward. Still others revise and correct obvious problems while drafting a paper and postpone careful examination until a draft is complete. Use whatever method suits you. But if possible, take a break before attempting to revise a draft you have just completed. You should find some mental or physical activity to divert your attention from the paper. Or if time allows, put the work aside for a day or several days. These tactics help you develop objectivity so that you can return to the manuscript as a reader rather than as the writer. Only then can you see weaknesses that you did not suspect in the composition stage. Other good editing schemes are reading your draft aloud and letting others read and critique your work. Also if possible, you should type your drafts. No matter how poor the typing, you will be able to edit a typed draft much more carefully than a handwritten draft.

Because of their speed and efficiency, computers and word processors greatly facilitate revision. Editing with a word processing program has obvious advantages over manual editing. Letters, words, lines, and paragraphs can be deleted at the punch of a button. Material can be inserted anywhere and moved effortlessly from place to place. A writer with a word processor can tinker with the text and compose in stages, letting the computer do the cutting and pasting typical in manual editing.



Another advantage of word processing is that every change can be made without retyping the entire paper. The writer thereby avoids typographical errors that can appear with each subsequent retyping. Thus, final drafts are less likely to be marred by last-minute corrections made in pen.

In addition to the purely mechanical advantage of word processing, software programs can help locate misspellings, incorrect punctuation, and inappropriate usage. Some programs even provide statistical information about repetition of words and phrases, sentence length, passives, nominalizations, and the like. The danger, of course, is that writers may want to rely entirely on the machine to improve their weaknesses. But the machine can only offer suggestions. It is the writer who must make the decisions.

Whether your draft is handwritten, typed on a conventional typewriter, or produced on a word processor, the time necessary for revising a draft depends on the individual. Nevertheless, you should devote as much effort to the revision process as time will allow. Effective revision involves several readings; few writers can concentrate on all types of problems at the same time. A methodical procedure is first to revise content, then to evaluate coherence, next to improve style, and then to check for grammatical and mechanical errors. Finally, if your paper is typed, you must proofread for typographical errors. In general, the following sections follow this procedure, guiding you through revision from larger to smaller units.

## 37a Unity

In a unified paper, both the whole and each part work together to develop a single idea. The following outline and paragraph illustrate how the details of a whole composition and one of its paragraphs are related—the outline covering a number of choices faced by a novice cyclist, the paragraph covering one of the choices. No details on either level stray from the point.



THESIS: People just getting into cycling face a bewildering array of choices.

I. Type of bike
   A. Touring bikes
   B. Racing bikes
II. Number of gears
III. Tires
   A. Tubulars
   B. Clinchers
IV. Optional equipment
   A. Helmet
   B. Gloves
   C. Shorts ←
   D. Shoes

Should you buy cycling shorts? Salespeople will tell you that you certainly cannot do without the skin-tight, knee-length, Italian-style shorts. They will also point out that ordinary shorts are totally unsuitable—irritating seams, the wrong cut and fabric. Cycling shorts have no center seam to chafe the legs, and some even come lined with chamois to eliminate friction. But is all this necessary for anyone but a professional? For the ordinary rider these shorts would be like a Mets uniform for playing sandlot baseball, full pads for touch football, and spiked track shoes for a 20-minute jog. If you are not planning to enter the World Cycling Championships, you can easily forego the shorts, that is, unless your main goal is to look as though you are in training for the Championships.

When checking for unity, begin with the overall structure and then look at each separate paragraph. Unless your paper is unified around a clear thesis, there is little point in concentrating on the details that make up the paragraphs.

### (1) Is the thesis clear?

Your paper should have a thesis either clearly stated or clearly implied. You should be able to find the stated thesis or formulate one from your material. In the event you cannot discover a thesis, you may have chosen a subject that doesn't interest you or that you don't know enough about. If so, return to Chapter 34, "The Search for Ideas," and begin again. This process is not as bad as it sounds. It is sometimes easier to change your subject completely than to struggle with one that is not productive.



### (2) Does everything in the paper relate directly to the thesis?

One of the best ways to check the overall structure is to construct an outline from your draft or to reexamine an already existing outline. This technique can reveal places where a paper has diverged from its thesis. If you find material that is off the subject, you should remove it. You may be reluctant to delete material that you have labored to collect and struggled to write. Nevertheless, if any part of the draft might distract the reader from the thesis or is obviously irrelevant to your subject, get rid of it. Notice how the student writer of the composition-in-progress (Chapter 38) abandoned material as the paper progressed from draft to draft.

### (3) Does each paragraph have unity?

The parts of a unified paragraph should develop a single idea. A paragraph with a topic sentence that expresses the central idea is less likely to contain extraneous details than a paragraph without a stated topic sentence.

When you revise your paper on the paragraph level, you should first locate each paragraph's topic sentence or determine the central idea or purpose. Then you should delete any material that is unimportant or irrelevant.

The following paragraph begins with a clear topic sentence but shifts to another subject in the underlined sentences.

> Rain forests, such as those in South America and Africa, contain more plant and animal species than does any other area in the world. For example, more bird species have been identified in a wildlife preserve in Peru than in the entire United States. <u>If the habitat is not protected, the bird species will eventually vanish.</u> At least 700 different tree species have been found in one forest in Borneo. That same number exists in the whole of North America. One river in Brazil contains more species of fish than all the rivers of the United States together. <u>If nothing is done to prevent these rain forests from being cleared, untold numbers of plants and animal species will certainly become extinct.</u>



The subject is clearly the abundance of species in rain forests; but in the third and last sentences, the writer strays to the subject of extinction. Fortunately, deletion of the two sentences on extinction can solve the problem without destroying the paragraph. Sometimes, however, revision requires a restructuring of the topic sentence, further research, or deletion of the entire paragraph.

## 37b Development

Development refers to the way a whole composition or a single paragraph elaborates or builds on a thesis or topic. If an idea is developed, it is supported by a sufficient number of details, examples, illustrations, or reasons. When you revise a paper, you should check for the presence of these specifics. The length of a composition or paragraph is not always a good indication. A fairly long unit that contains nothing but general statements may still be lacking. Satisfactory development demands specifics—but only logical inclusions. Do not throw in irrelevant details that distort your logic.

### (1) Does the paper contain enough information to develop the thesis?

Check your introduction. Does it claim that you will discuss more than your paper delivers? If you find the information in the body insufficiently developed, you can produce more ideas with tactics such as brainstorming, clustering, and asking questions. Or you can gather additional material through research—reading, interviewing, or observing.

### (2) Is each paragraph fully developed?

When you check each body paragraph, look for the topic sentence, or, if the topic sentence is not stated, think of what it would be. Then ask yourself if your reader would accept or understand the statement. If there is the least chance the reader would not, you probably should add supporting or explanatory information. A paragraph like the following lacks full development.



> "The Star-Spangled Banner," though very hard to sing, should not be replaced. Its complexity somehow makes it challenging; singers must take it seriously. Surely, every patriotic American would sorely miss the roll of the drum and the words "O'er the land of the FREE and the HOME of the BRAVE."

The cure for an underdeveloped paragraph is usually to add more details. The student who wrote the preceding paragraph improved it by explaining why the music is hard to sing and why it should not be replaced by another song.

> "The Star-Spangled Banner," though very hard to sing, should not be replaced. Who cares if singers strain their vocal chords over high notes, low notes, and extreme tonal combinations? Its complexity somehow makes it challenging; singers must take it seriously. To do away with this tradition would be like moving Washington, D.C., to Nebraska, eating spaghetti on Thanksgiving, or changing the N.Y. Mets to a soccer team. The song is history. We can share with Francis Scott Key the dramatic moment when, after the bombardment of Fort McHenry, the flag still flew. Surely every patriotic American would sorely miss the roll of the drum and the words "O'er the land of the FREE and the HOME of the BRAVE."

Brevity is not necessarily a sign that a paragraph is underdeveloped; writers sometimes include a short paragraph to add variety to prose or to emphasize material. Usually, however, material that develops one idea should be combined in one paragraph. For example, the following paragraphs are unjustifiably short. They all develop the same idea—that Nancy Drew has changed since the writer's childhood reading. Combining the material will create one well-developed paragraph.

> Nancy Drew has changed a great deal since the early books. No longer is she poking around in attics hunting for clues. In current books, she taps into electronic systems, reads videotaped ransom notes, and uses cellular phones and computers.
>
> Old radio shows are now rock bands; jewel thieves are now traitors selling secrets to foreign countries. Nancy now drives a blue Mustang, wears designer jeans, and uses credit cards. She even gets involved in romances.
>
> One thing, however, has remained the same: she always solves the mystery.



## 37c Coherence

Coherence in prose refers to a smooth and logical arrangement of the parts. Sometimes coherence is spontaneous, with the flow of ideas creating a natural sequence. More often, however, this spontaneity does not occur, and you must work to interlock the pieces smoothly and logically. The task requires the effective arrangement of the paragraphs as well as adequate connection between sentences and paragraphs. Checking your draft against the following questions will help you find weaknesses and achieve coherence.

### (1) Is the overall organization effective?

Even though an initial plan for organization seems sound, it may not produce a well-arranged composition, and you may have to reorganize the paragraphs. You should probably begin by taking a critical look at the overall composition. Does the body of the paper fulfill the promise of the introduction? For example, if the introduction suggests that the paper will illustrate the genre of the paperback romance with a single novel, the body should not instead classify the characters. Or if the introduction promises to analyze the novel's components, the body should not concentrate primarily on plot to the exclusion of characters, setting, and so forth.

After you look at your overall scheme, you may want to rearrange paragraphs to achieve the most logical or effective order of information. This procedure is sometimes called "cutting and pasting" and, in fact, is frequently accomplished in just this way. You can cut your paper into paragraphs and glue or tape them on paper in the desired order. Or you can write each paragraph on a separate page and then work out the best arrangement. And of course, if you use a word processor, you can move whole blocks of the draft around with ease. If you have trouble deciding on the best order, you might try writing alternative outlines to see which seems most effective.



In the sample first draft that follows, a student summarizes information about human memory. Put together from notes taken in psychology classes and material in a psychology textbook, the draft is a hodgepodge of facts not yet arranged coherently.

## Draft 1: No Coherence

One of the most amazing abilities of the human mind is memory. In about three pounds of brain, we store all kinds of information, such as multiplication tables, the sound of a car engine, the smell of a steak cooking, and the knowledge of how to ride a bicycle.

In spite of recent discoveries and theories, no one really knows how memory works. Many researchers believe that memory is the new frontier in science. Some researchers believe that to understand memory is to understand human beings.

Short-term memory usually lasts 15 to 20 seconds and allows us to look up a telephone number and remember it long enough to dial it. *information sep-arated from re-lated informatic*

Many scientists are now working on the physical nature of memory, the biochemical processes that occur in the brain when information is stored. *material to be developed or deleted*

One theory about long-term memory is that our memories change as we add information. Once we make some change in a memory, the original is lost. This process is probably what happens when we revise a childhood memory with what adults tell us about the experience. We create a memory of a memory.

Two kinds of long-term memory are "declarative" and "procedural." Declarative memory involves facts, such as names, dates, places, and statistics. Procedural memory involves activities, such as doing a dance step, shooting a basketball, and tying shoes.

Our moods seem to influence what we remember. If we learn something while in a sad mood, we will remember more of the information when we are sad. *material to be developed or deleted*

Some experts believe that memory is closely tied to language. We cannot remember what we cannot talk about. We cannot remember a coat we had before we knew the word <u>coat</u>. Other experts say "nonsense." Very small babies can remember faces, voices, movements, colors, and sounds. One explanation is that babies have procedural memory but not declarative memory. Some researchers think that declarative memory does not develop until about the age of two.

Our ability for long-term memory seems unlimited. The memories stored in long-term memory seem permanent. *misplaced material*

Short-term memory cannot hold a great deal of information. If we hear someone list numbers or words, we very quickly lose track and can remember only a few in the right order. *misplaced material*

The student writer produced a second draft of the paper by cutting and pasting the first draft, deleting some material, and rearranging the rest. The result suggests an organization: comparison and contrast of short-term and long-term memory.

## Draft 2: Overall Coherence Improved by Deleting and Rearranging Paragraphs

One of the most amazing abilities of the human mind is memory. In about three pounds of brain, we store all kinds of information, such as multiplication tables, the sound of a car engine, the smell of a steak cooking, and the knowledge of how to ride a bicycle.

Short-term memory usually lasts 15 to 20 seconds and allows us to look up a telephone number and remember it long enough to dial it.

*material on short-term memory brought together*

Short-term memory cannot hold a great deal of information. If we hear someone list numbers or words, we very quickly lose track and can remember only a few in the right order.

Our ability for long-term memory seems unlimited. The memories stored in long-term memory seem permanent.

One theory about long-term memory is that our memories change as we add information. Once we make some change in a memory, the original is lost. The process is probably what happens when we revise a childhood memory with what adults tell us about the experience. We create a memory of a memory.

Two kinds of long-term memory are "declarative" and "procedural." Declarative memory involves facts, such as names, dates, places, and statistics. Procedural memory involves activities, such as doing a dance step, shooting a basketball, and tying shoes.

*material on long-term memory brought together in logical arrangement*

Some experts believe that memory is closely tied to language. We cannot remember what we cannot talk about. You cannot remember a coat you had before you had the word coat. Other experts say "nonsense." Very small babies remember faces, voices, movements, colors, and sounds. One explanation is that babies have procedural memory but not declarative memory. Some researchers think that declarative memory does not develop until about the age of two.

In spite of recent discoveries and theories, no one really knows how memory works. Many researchers believe that memory is the new frontier in science. Some researchers believe that to understand memory is to understand human beings.

*second paragraph of first draft moved to end*

### (2) Is the organization within paragraphs effective?

Once you are satisfied with the overall scheme and the ordering of the major pieces of a paper, you can turn your attention to the individual paragraphs. You can treat each piece as a mini-composition and determine whether its pattern is an effective vehicle for the information and purpose. If you are not satisfied with the patterns, you might look over the methods suggested for organizing paragraphs in Chapter 36, "Paragraphs."



### (3) Is there adequate connection between sentences and paragraphs?

After you have revised the arrangement of the sections, you can provide connectors, or "links," to establish internal coherence. For example, you can link ideas and prevent unnecessary repetition by using pronouns such as *this, these, some, most, others, each, both, either, who,* and *which*. You can show the relationship between ideas with coordinating conjunctions: *and, but, or, for, nor, so,* and *yet*. You can use subordinating conjunctions, such as *although, because, if, when,* and *where*. (Section 7c.1 lists the subordinate conjunctions and their appropriate uses.) Another effective way to clarify the connections between ideas is to use transitional expressions such as *therefore, for example, in fact,* and *finally*. The following chart lists the common transitional expressions and their uses.

**Transitional Expressions**

| *To Express* | *You Can Use* |
|---|---|
| Contrast | however, on the other hand, on the contrary, in contrast, still, nevertheless, regardless, instead |
| Cause/effect | therefore, thus, consequently, for this reason, as a result, otherwise, thus, then, accordingly |
| Time sequence | first, second, third, next, last, finally, afterward, now, then, again, soon, formerly, eventually, subsequently |
| Restatement | in other words, in short, in summary, that is, again |
| Emphasis | in fact, indeed, of course, certainly, after all, surely, actually |
| Addition | furthermore, moreover, likewise, also, in addition, besides |
| Summary | in conclusion, on the whole, all in all, in summary |
| Example | for example, for instance, specifically |

By comparing the two paragraphs that follow, you can see how the addition of links improves coherence.

WITHOUT LINKS

My father likes to point out that he got his first car at age twenty. I got a car at age fifteen. I like to point out that his needs were very different from mine. Towns used to be organized around neighborhoods. My teen-aged father was within walking distance of almost every place he wanted to go. His high school was only four blocks from his house. After school, he could walk ten minutes to the local hamburger joint. He could find most of his friends there. To see a movie, he could walk a few blocks to pick up his best friend. They could be at the movie within a half-hour.

I need a car to get almost anywhere I want to go. My high school is seven miles from my house. Local hamburger joints in my hometown have been replaced by fast-food establishments. Fast-food establishments are usually located on frontage roads alongside superhighways. Movies are now in suburban malls. My friends and I must arrange a meeting place. We usually must drive at least a half-hour to get there.

The next time my father brings up the subject of cars, I am going to offer him a deal. I will give up my car. He will transport me. I will even pay for the gas. I suspect he and I will be very grateful for my car.



WITH LINKS

My father likes to point out that he got his first car at age twenty, yet I got a car at age fifteen. I like to point out his needs were very different from mine. Because towns used to be organized around neighborhoods, my teen-aged father was within walking distance of almost every place he wanted to go. For example, his high school was only four blocks from his house. After school, he could walk ten minutes to the local hamburger joint, where he could find most of his friends. If he wanted to see a movie, he could walk a few blocks, pick up his best friend, and be at the movie within a half-hour.

On the other hand, I need a car to get almost anywhere I want to go. My high school is seven miles from my house. Local hamburger joints in my hometown have been replaced by fast-food establishments, which are usually located on frontage roads alongside superhighways. Furthermore, movies are now in suburban malls. Consequently, my friends and I must arrange a meeting place and usually drive at least a half-hour to get there.

The next time my father brings up this subject, I am going to offer him a deal. I will give up my car if he will transport me. In fact, I will even pay for the gas. I suspect we both will be very grateful for my car.

In addition to eliminating repetition, the demonstrative pronouns *this, these, that,* and *those* are useful in phrases that summarize.

> Each year the federal government gives away millions of dollars in grants that allow researchers to investigate such issues as whether a lower ratio of students to teachers increases learning, whether the weather affects mood, and whether "the girls really do get prettier at closing time." Almost everyone already knows that the answer to these questions is "yes." Yet the taxpayer must foot the bill for this nonsense.

revise 37c

If you need more information on linking words and phrases, refer to the following chart.

**Linking Words and Phrases**

| *For Information On* | *Consult* |
|---|---|
| Demonstrative Pronouns | 2b |
| Relative Pronouns | 2c |
| Indefinite Pronouns | 2e |
| Conjunctions | 6b, 7c(1) |

In addition to words and phrases, a whole sentence can link what has gone before to what follows.

> Surimi, an imitation crab product, was first developed by the Japanese. Made of fish, it is extruded into a tube shape and topped with red food coloring. The Japanese are now exporting vast quantities of surimi to the West. Americans in the fishing industry, however, are countering this market with their own tactics. They are now exporting real crabmeat to Japan. In fact, about 50 percent of U.S. crabmeat is purchased by the Japanese.

To see how internal coherence works, consider the third draft of the student paper on memory. Although the parts of the second draft were logically arranged, they did not seem to cohere. In the following version, notice how the addition of the underlined "links" improves coherence, tightens structure, and allows some of the paragraphs to be combined.

## Draft 3: Internal Coherence Improved by "Links"

One of the most amazing abilities of the human mind is memory. In about three pounds of brain, we store all kinds of information, such as multiplication tables, the sound of a car engine, the smell of a steak cooking, and the knowledge of how to ride a bicycle.

But memory involves more than just this long-term storage. Short-term memory usually lasts 15 to 20 seconds and allows us to look up a telephone number and remember it long enough to dial it. This type of memory cannot hold a great deal of information. For example, if we hear someone list numbers or words, we very quickly lose track and can remember only a few in the right order.

On the other hand, our ability for long-term memory seems unlimited, and the information stored there permanent. The permanence, however, may not be real. According to one theory, our memories change as we add information; and once we make some change in a memory, the original is lost. This process is probably what happens when we revise a childhood memory with what adults tell us about the experience. Thus, we create a memory of a memory.

Two kinds of long-term memory are "declarative" and "procedural." The first involves facts, such as names, dates, statistics. The second involves skills, such as doing a dance step, shooting a basketball, tying shoes.

This fact/skill division is at the center of a disagreement about language and memory. Some experts believe that we cannot remember what we cannot talk about. We cannot, for instance, remember a coat we had before we had the word coat. Other experts say this idea is nonsense because very small babies remember faces, voices, movements, colors, and sounds. A possible explanation for this puzzle is that babies have procedural memory but not declarative memory, which some researchers think does not develop until about the age of two.

In spite of recent discoveries and theories, no one really knows how memory works. Nevertheless, many researchers believe that memory is the new frontier in science. In fact, some believe that to understand memory is to understand human beings.

# 37d Style

To improve the style of a composition, you should look carefully at your word choice. Not only should the words you choose convey your meaning precisely, but also they should be appropriate to your purpose and audience. The trouble-shooting chart below will help you locate and revise problems with vocabulary.



**Trouble-Shooting Chart for Word Choice**

| *If You Have a Problem With* | *Consult Material On* | *Section(s)* |
|---|---|---|
| identifying audience | audience analysis | 35b |
| level of formality | formal and informal words | 32a |
| | voice | 35c |
| precise meaning | denotation and connotation | 32b(1) |
| | general and specific words | 32b(2) |
| | abstract and concrete words | 32b(3) |
| dull, trite vocabulary | clichés and euphemisms | 32c |
| bureaucratic language | gobbledygook | 32d(1) |
| | surplus words | 32d(2) |
| | dense noun phrases | 32d(3) |
| discriminatory language | sexist pronoun use | 13c, 13d, 32e |
| | stereotyping | 32e |

**The Computer Connection**

For finding synonyms, many people depend on a computer thesaurus. In fact, most word-processing programs now contain a thesaurus as a standard component. This added feature allows you to change a word that doesn't have quite the right meaning or the right sound.

**Suggestions for Using a Computer Thesaurus**

- If a thesaurus is not included in your word-processing program, you can add one with little cost or trouble.
- Typically, you place the cursor on the word you want to replace, and possible alternatives will appear on the screen.

- If a synonym is unfamiliar, you can call up its definition, provided that a thesaurus dictionary has been loaded. Not having a dictionary limits the value of a thesaurus; if a word is new to you, you cannot be sure it is the right one to use.
- The choice of vocabulary in a composition is yours, and the computer thesaurus will not always contain enough information to help you. Computer thesauruses are less extensive than regular dictionaries and do not always provide an acceptable substitution. For example, one computer thesaurus suggests as a synonym for the verbal *delegating,* the noun *diplomat.* To find a synonym with the right meaning, you often must use a regular thesaurus or dictionary.



In addition to word choice, good style depends on smooth, easy-flowing sentences. If parts of your composition seem choppy, labored, or awkward, the sentence structure may need revision. The following trouble-shooting chart will help you identify problem structures and improve them.

**Trouble-Shooting Chart for Sentence Structure**

| *If You Have a Problem With* | *Consult Material On* | *Section(s)* |
|---|---|---|
| monotonous or choppy prose | varying sentence lengths, structures, or beginnings | 33a |
| flat or unemphatic prose | dramatic structures | 33b |
| | figures of speech | 33d |
| cluttered or weak sentences | empty verbs and nominalizations | 33c(1) |
| | weak passives | 33c(2) |
| | unnecessary clauses | 33c(3) |
| | excessive verb forms | 33c(4) |
| | split subjects and verbs | 33c(5) |
| awkward prose | sound and rhythm | 33e |

**The Computer Connection**

As William Zinsser states, the word processor is "science's gift to the tinkerers and the refiners and the neatness freaks." And indeed, revision with a word processing program has obvious advantages over the manual process. You can delete letters, words, lines, and paragraphs at the touch of a key. You can insert material and move it effortlessly from place to place without making a mess of the manuscript. You can make and unmake changes without retyping the entire page or composition.

***Suggestions for Revising (continued)***

- Take advantage of the ease with which you can tighten prose by pruning unnecessary words and phrases. As author Garrison Keillor notes: "Word processors can be responsible for producing a great deal of flabby writing. The words come out . . . like toothpaste sometimes. There's no shortage of sheer wordage in America; more sentences are not what this country needs." The computer that helps produce flabby prose, however, can also help eliminate it.
- Create a "wastebasket" file to save material deleted from the text during revision. You'll feel more comfortable about making radical cuts if you know you can easily retrieve the material.
- Use a split-screen feature for calling up another file. You might, for example, display your outline on the top half of a horizontal split screen while revising a draft displayed on the bottom half. Or you might bring up an early draft of the paper on the same screen as the current version in order to compare the two.
- Print a hard copy of the text. Then revise it to correct any weaknesses in coherence, logic, or sentence structure. You can spot some weaknesses more easily on paper than you can on a screen.

*For reading:* Venolia, Jan. "Computer-Age Writing." *Rewrite Right!* Berkeley, California: Ten Speed Press, 1987.



## 37e Grammar, Punctuation, and Mechanics

Even when readers can figure out your meaning, errors in grammar, punctuation, and mechanics are distracting and undercut the merit of your composition. You will probably not locate these errors with a superficial reading. In fact, editing is very different from reading. When you read, your eyes jump from phrase to phrase; but when you edit, you must use some sort of scheme to make yourself focus on every word and structure. It is possible to slow down and control your eyes if you read the manuscript aloud or read it out of sequence, by page or by paragraph. A good plan for correcting errors in a composition is to check first for structural errors, then move to individual words, and finally look at punctuation and mechanics.

### (1) Structural errors

Prose is made up of structures—phrases and clauses that are combined to express ideas. Structural errors result if the phrases and clauses are not put together correctly. To help identify and correct possible structural errors in your prose, refer to the following chart.

| **Trouble-Shooting Chart for Structural Errors** | |
|---|---|
| ***If You Have Difficulty Answering the Question*** | ***Consult the Material In*** |
| Does every sentence have at least one independent clause? | Chapter 7, Clauses and Sentences<br>Chapter 8, Sentence Fragments |
| In compound sentences, are independent clauses correctly connected? | Chapter 9, Comma Splices and Fused Sentences<br>Chapter 21, Commas, 21a<br>Chapter 22, Semicolons<br>Chapter 23, Colons, 23c |
| Do the pronouns have clear antecedents? | Chapter 12, Pronoun Reference |
| Do any adjective or adverb modifiers have nothing to modify or seem to modify the wrong element? | Chapter 16, Dangling and Misplaced Modifiers |
| Are any constructions split apart by an interrupter that causes awkwardness or a lack of clarity? | Chapter 18, Split Constructions |
| Are any constructions incomplete because of an omission? | Chapter 19, Incomplete Constructions |
| Are the items in sequences parallel? | Chapter 20, Parallelism |



## (2) Errors in the forms of words

Nouns, pronouns, adjectives, adverbs, and verbs have a variety of forms that change or add meaning. After you have read a manuscript to check the sentence construction, you should read it again to inspect the forms of the individual words. This stage of the revising process requires you to shift your attention back and forth from individual words to the larger structures in which they fit. For example, to decide on the form of a pronoun, you must determine the meaning you need and the correct case form required by the structure. Try not to hurry this stage of revising. If you go methodically through the following chart, you will be less likely to overlook errors.

revise 37e

**Trouble-Shooting Chart for Errors in the Forms of Words**

| *If You Have Difficulty Answering the Question* | *Consult the Material In* |
|---|---|
| Are all plural noun forms correct? | Chapter 1, Nouns |
| Are there any nouns or pronouns (the personal pronouns or *who/whom*) with the wrong case? | Chapter 1, Nouns<br>Chapter 2, Pronouns<br>Chapter 14, Case of Nouns and Pronouns<br>Chapter 26, Apostrophes, 26a |
| Are the comparative and superlative forms of adjectives and adverbs standard? | Chapter 3, Adjectives and Adverbs<br>Chapter 15, Nonstandard Adjective and Adverb Forms |
| Is each verb in the correct form? | Chapter 11, Nonstandard Verb Forms |
| Is each verb in the appropriate tense? | Chapter 4, Verbs and Verb Phrases |
| Do the verbs agree with their subjects in number? | Chapter 10, Subject-Verb Agreement |
| Do the pronouns agree with their antecedents in number? | Chapter 13, Pronoun-Antecedent Agreement |
| Are there unnecessary shifts from one form to another? | Chapter 17, Shifts |

### (3) Errors in punctuation marks and mechanics

It is not usually productive to edit for punctuation and mechanical errors until fairly late in the writing process. Structures most likely will change from draft to draft, and sentences will be deleted during revision. There is no point in correcting punctuation and mechanics until you have decided definitely on content and structure. When you reach this stage, you can survey the conventions in Chapters 21 through 31 or refer to the following chart.

| **Trouble-Shooting Chart for Errors in Punctuation and Mechanics** | |
|---|---|
| *If You Have Difficulty Answering the Question* | *Consult the Material In* |
| Are commas omitted anywhere? before a coordinate conjunction between independent clauses? after introductory elements? around nonrestrictive elements? in dates or addresses? | Chapter 21, Commas, 21a–21j |
| Are commas placed where they should not be? | Chapter 21, Commas, 21j |
| Should any commas be changed to semicolons? | Chapter 22, Semicolons, 22a–22e |
| Are the colons, dashes, and parentheses used correctly? | Chapter 23, Colons<br>Chapter 24, Dashes, Parentheses, and Brackets |
| Are any apostrophes omitted or positioned incorrectly? | Chapter 26, Apostrophes |
| Are quotation marks placed correctly in relation to the other marks? | Chapter 27, Quotation Marks and Ellipsis Marks, 27b |
| Are hyphens used correctly in compounds? | Chapter 29, Hyphens and Slashes, 29a–29b |
| Are the right words capitalized? | Chapter 31, Capital Letters |



### (4) Spelling errors

Checking for spelling errors requires reading so slowly that your eyes fall on each individual word. A trick long used by typists is to read backward word by word, thus reading isolated words, not ideas. Another aid in detecting misspelled words is to be alert for those words that frequently cause problems—words such as *receive, occurred,* and *truly.* If you become sensitive to problem words, you can take special care to spell them correctly. Appendix

A, "Spelling," includes lists of problem words as well as patterns of the English spelling system.

Some writers are fortunate enough to work on a word processor and to have a software program that will check documents for spelling errors. Even so, programs that check spelling will not correct such problems as confusing *affect* for *effect* or *their* for *there*, since all these spellings are correct. For help with such word confusion you can use the "Glossary of Usage and Commonly Confused Words."



**The Computer Connection**

When you type your composition with a word processor, you usually have an efficient way to eliminate spelling and typing errors. Most word-processing programs have built-in spell checkers, which will check the spelling throughout an entire document or of just a single word. The computer can check hundreds of words so quickly that you won't have time to get up for a short break before it provides results.

***Suggestions for Using a Computer Spell Checker***

- Keep a dictionary handy; at times spell checkers suggest alternative spellings that are not useful. For example, one program was not sure that *ruff* was correct in *the queen wore a ruff around her neck.* The suggested replacement words were *buff, cuff, duff,* and *gruff*—all useless. A quick look in a conventional dictionary shows that *ruff* is the correct spelling.
- If your program allows, create a personal dictionary. Proper names, technical terms, and other words that are not in the computer dictionary can be placed in a customized list that will be checked by the program.
- Most spell checkers also check double words like *the the.* Sometimes you must command the checker to ignore double words in contexts where they are appropriate—for example, *they had had an accident in 1989* or *he favored the draft, draft exemptions, and an agricultural tax.*
- Computer dictionaries are much less extensive than regular dictionaries and are especially weak on word variations. For example, a list might contain *privateer,* but not *privateering.*
- Most spell checkers will not find words used in the wrong context. One checker noticed nothing wrong in *I appreciate your patients* and *Claude dies his hair.*
- WARNING: Do not depend totally on spell checkers for proofreading your papers. Although valuable, especially for finding typographical errors, they cannot find some kinds of mistakes and should be used as a backup only.

## EXERCISE 1

Two rough drafts of student papers follow. Revise each, using these questions as guides.

(1) Is the thesis clear?
(2) Does everything in the paper relate to the thesis?
(3) Is the organization clear?
(4) Is there adequate connection between sentences and paragraphs?
(5) Are there stylistic weaknesses?
(6) Are there errors in grammar, punctuation, and mechanics?
(7) Are there any spelling errors?



A.

Many people view retarded children as freaks. Some ignore these children. Some are even afraid of them. I must admit to having these feelings about retarded children when I first worked with them.

When I first worked with retarded children, I was nervous to say the least. I do not know what I expected the children to be like. I was not prepared for my first meeting with them. The children seemed shockingly pitiful. Some looked as if they were not even aware of their own existance. One child aimlessly walked in circles, another stood swaying from side to side. Children wildly ran around in another room and shouted at each other.

As an assignment for a child psychology class I had to spend twenty hours observing children. I decided to spend my time observing retarded children. I wanted to find out what they were really like. I wanted to know why I was afraid of retarded children.

The school for retarded children is well staffed. The teachers read to the children. They taught practical things like the meaning of traffic lights, the names of coins and bills in our currency system, and table manners.

As the days went by, I got aquainted with the children. They were not always easy to manage, but "normal" children are not easy to manage either. On one occasion I accompanied the class on a field trip to a fire station and to McDonald's. I was very apprehencive about going to eat at McDonald's. I kept wondering how the children were going to act in public. I was sure I would be embarrassed in one way or another but I was wrong. The children ate hamburgers and played on the playground as any other children would have done. They did not go wild as I had expected, they just had a good time. This surprised me.

I realized that those children, although handicapped, are not very different from other children. Sometimes a retarded child is good. Other times they are bad. They were no longer the wild demons of my first impression, they were just children.



B.

You might want to get rid of a roomate for a variety of reasons. You realy hate the person or you have a friend who needs a place to live and wants to move into your apartment with you or your roomate is a very nice person but never has any money and so cannot pay his share of the expenses. A good roomate is compatible with you, is always considerate, and is willing to compromise.

Their are a number of tactics you can use to get rid of an unwanted roomate. You need a carefully planned scheme that begins with little things and work up to more drastic measures. This keeps you from being any nastier than necessary. If the little measures work your roomate might leave while you can still be friends. If you are friends. Also the real nasty measures could lead to retaliation by physical violance or legal action. In stage one you can do little things such as leaving dirty dishes in the sink, filling up the refrigerator with specimens from your biology lab, taking long showers that use up all the hot water. You can also wet his toothbrush so that he will suspect you have been using it. And you can borrow his clothes and return them dirty.

If the tactics in stage one do not work you need to intensify your efforts. You must move from being annoying to being offensive. Such as getting a big, shaggy dog and letting it sleep on your roomates bed while he is gone. Or you can forget to give him phone messages from his girl friend, you can even ask her for a date. You can also borrow his car and use all the gas without filling it up.

If stage two does not get rid of him, you must now resort to drastic measures. Two sure fire strategies will finish him off. One is to leave a fake message to yourself on the answering machine. The message should be from a doctor and should go something like this: "Mr. Jones, I hate to inform you that the tests were positive. This disease is often fatal and highly contagious. You must see a specialist at once." If this does not work he is too insensitive to move on his own and you must move to the second strategie. Wait until he leaves for the weekend, put his belongings in the hall, and change the locks on your doors. Its hard to get a good roomate. You need to find someone you can get along with.



# 37f Titles

Almost every writing project requires a title. Depending on the kind of paper, the title might be simple, catchy, businesslike, or technical. In any case, the title should accurately reflect the purpose of the paper and the nature of the content.

## (1) Fit the title to the purpose of the paper

A title should not mislead the reader about the purpose of a paper. For example, a title such as "The Principles and Health Effects of Vegetarianism in the United States" suggests a serious study and is inappropriate for an informal, entertaining paper on vegetarians. On the other hand, "Confessions of a Sometime Vegetarian" leads the reader to expect an informal, entertaining paper. If you are unsure whether a title gives a false impression, whether its meaning is clear, or whether readers will be amused, use a simple, straightforward title, such as "Three Advantages of Vegetarianism."

For formal papers written to inform or persuade, you might want to use a title containing a colon. If so, give the general topic first, followed by the colon, and then restrict the topic in some way—with a statement of focus, with information about the type of paper, or with an explanation: "Right-Handedness: A Peculiarly Human Preference," "The Importance of Grades: A Survey of Student Opinion," "The Innovators: The Pioneers of Rock 'n' Roll." The colon seems to create a sense of authority and tightens the title's information.

### (2) Choose a title specific enough to be informative



A title should not be so general that it gives readers no idea about the content of a paper. For example, "Train Travel" is not very descriptive. More informative are titles like "Train Travel: A Superior Mode of Transportation," "Trains: Our Neglected Resource," or "Vacationing by Train in the West."

### (3) Avoid "cute" titles

As a general rule, you should avoid "cute" titles such as "A Hare-Raising Tale" for a paper about raising rabbits or "Everybody Out of the Pool!" for a paper about futile attempts at carpooling. For one thing, these titles promise clever papers, which you must then deliver. For another, readers are more likely to be annoyed than amused by strained attempts at cleverness.

## ❑ EXERCISE 2

**Point out which of the following titles would be effective for the papers described.**

1. "Running: A Form of Anorexia"
   a formal paper that examines obsessive running as an emotional problem
2. "The Inquisitive Eye"
   an informative paper about new equipment for amateur photographers
3. "Health Foods"
   an argument that a diet of "health foods" is no more nutritious than any sensible eating program
4. "How to Choose a Long-Distance Company"
   an informative guide comparing rates and services of long-distance telephone companies
5. "Confessions of a Fraidy Cat"
   an impression of the writer's first day in the first grade—the fears and trials

## ❑ EXERCISE 3

**Choose effective titles for the ineffective ones in Exercise 2.**

## 37g The Finished Paper

A few guidelines can help you prepare manuscripts, both typewritten and handwritten. The guidelines are by no means rules; other conventions and formats are also acceptable. For an assigned paper, the best approach, of course, is to ask what the instructor prefers.

### (1) Paper



#### Typewritten Papers

Use 8 1/2-×-11-inch, good grade, bond paper. If you use erasable bond, choose it carefully. Some erasable paper is very thin, and much of it smears easily. An alternative is to use nonerasable paper and correction liquid. Then you can photocopy your manuscript on good paper. The liquid will not show up on the copy, and the paper will look neat and clean.

#### Handwritten Papers

Use lined white paper, and write on only one side of each sheet. Avoid colored paper, paper with narrowly spaced lines, and paper larger or smaller than 8 1/2 × 11 inches. Also, do not turn in paper torn from a spiral notebook; the ragged edges not only look messy but also stick together.

### (2) Script

#### Typewritten Papers

Some typewriters and line printers produce unusual script, such as italic or something simulating handwritten script. But usually these fancy scripts are difficult to read. If you have a choice, choose a conventional script. Also, use a black ribbon new enough to leave a clear impression. And if you are typing on a typewriter, make sure the keys are clean so that they will not produce smudges and black dots for *o*'s.

#### Handwritten Papers

Use either dark blue or black ink, and make a conscious effort to write legibly. Avoid any personal handwriting quirks or frills, such as *i*'s dotted with circles, unusual capital letters, or anything that might interfere with clarity.

### (3) Margins

The usual rule of thumb is as follows.

*First page* Leave 2 to 3 inches at the top of the page, 1 inch at the bottom, 1 1/2 inches at the left side, and approximately 1 inch at the right.

*All other pages* Leave 1 1/2 inches at the top and left sides, 1 inch at the bottom, and approximately 1 inch at the right.



If you plan to put a cover on your paper, leave 2 inches on the left side of each page. The extra space will be taken up by the binding, and the margin will be left intact.

Indent paragraphs five spaces in a typewritten manuscript and about 1 inch in a handwritten manuscript.

### (4) Hyphenation

Readers do not expect the right margin of either a typed or handwritten manuscript to be perfectly straight. Therefore, you should hyphenate (divide) a word at the end of a line only when writing it out would make the margin extremely uneven. A somewhat uneven margin is not nearly so distracting as a series of hyphenated words down the right margin. When you must hyphenate, be sure to do so according to the guidelines in 29e.

### (5) Spacing

#### Typewritten Papers

Most instructors prefer that you double-space a typed paper so that they have room to write comments and make corrections. Single spacing is conventional for correspondence, some technical papers, items in an outline, and steps in instructions. If you do single-space the entire paper, remember to double-space between paragraphs.

#### Handwritten Papers

If you choose paper with lines at least 1/2 inch apart, writing on each line should leave ample space. Do not skip lines unless your instructor tells you to do so.

### (6) Pagination

Ordinarily, the first page of a paper is not numbered, but it is counted; so the second page is numbered 2. If instructed to number the first page, place the number at the bottom center of the sheet. Number the rest of the pages in the upper right corner, on the right margin and several spaces from the top of the page. Do not use hyphens, parentheses, or periods with page numbers unless instructed to do so.



### (7) Title page

If you include a title page, keep it simple: name, title of paper, date, and possibly the instructor's name and a course number or title. Place this information neatly on the page and resist any urge to "decorate." The example on page 431 is typical.

### (8) Proofreading and making corrections

Proofread your final copy to check for any remaining errors. The task is more difficult than it might seem because the content distracts the eye from superficial errors. To make errors more obvious, you can read the paper aloud, concentrating on each word; or you can read it backward line by line or word by word. You can also use a ruler or straight edge of some sort to isolate each single line of type.

Once you have found the errors, how do you correct them? Of course, if you write with a word processor, you can simply correct your errors on the disk and print a clean copy. If you use a conventional typewriter, you will have to use correction tape or fluid and perhaps photocopy your paper to get a clean copy. And if you hand-write your paper, you can make corrections neatly by using correction fluid to blot out errors and then rewriting. Ideally, you want to make your paper free of visible corrections.

But, of course, there is always that error you spot just before you turn your paper in. Make the correction neatly with ink as near the color of the original as possible. Remember, a reader will be prejudiced in favor of a neat paper and against a messy one.

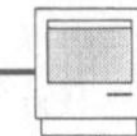

## The Computer Connection

The last step in the writing process is editing. In this step, you put the paper in its final form—the form your reader will see. If you want to make a good impression, you must produce an attractive document with a well-designed format. Also, you must remove any mechanical or typographical errors; they will distract your reader from the content, no matter how logical the organization or how smooth the prose. You've worked too hard so far to overlook this important step. And fortunately, the computer can do much of the work for you.

### *Suggestions for Editing*

**revise 37g**

- Use a display feature to format the text, and proofread it as it will appear on the printed page. This process allows you to avoid bad page breaks, to see where headings and titles might be separated from the text that follows, and to make sure that you have indented in all the right places.
- Using the cursor or the scroll function, scroll the text up from the end of your paper to the beginning. It's sometimes easier to catch errors when proofreading text backwards—word by word or line by line.
- Take advantage of the editing software currently available:

  a thesaurus that lists synonyms
  a spell checker that locates and corrects misspelled words
  a grammar checker that analyzes the reading levels of prose and looks for problems such as clichés
  a search-and-replace feature that enables you to correct repeated errors, update statistics, or replace a vocabulary item with a more suitable one. (If, for example, you decided to change the word *fireman* to *firefighter,* you would type the replacement word only once—and the computer would make the change throughout.)

- Don't rely entirely on the machine to correct errors and improve your prose. Computer editing functions are limited. Spell checkers, for example, flag any word that isn't in their memory. Furthermore, most of them don't catch errors such as *too* for *to* or *except* for *accept,* since these are not spelling errors. Grammar checkers don't know where you want to put commas. Nor can they choose words with the right connotations or sentence structures with the best effect. In the end, you are still the editor-in-charge.

*For reading:* Hult, Christine and Harris, Jeanette. *A Writer's Introduction to Word Processing.* Belmont, California: Wadsworth Publishing Co., 1987.

Shopping by Mail:

Convenience or Nuisance?

Alexandra Brooks

Professor Sheffield
English 101
September 15, 1988

Sample Title Page

## ❑ EXERCISE 4

Proofread the following paragraph. Look especially for

transposed letters
omitted letters
repeated letters
omitted words
repeated words
incorrect capital letters
incorrect punctuation or mechanics



In 1834, when Richard Henry Dana, Jr., was a a sophmore at Harvard, he cauught measles and consequently suffered serious eye trouble. Temporarilly unabel to use his eyes, he became an ordinary seaman, aboard the *Pilgrim* on its cruise from Boston around Cape Horn to California. In californa, Dana spent a year gathering animal hides. Then, he returned to Boston on the the ship *Alert,* attended The Harvard law School, and began work on a book basd on the journal he had kept during thhe voyage. In 1840, he graduated from law schoool and that same yaer published *Two Years Before the mast,* a realistic account of the suffering and grievances of ordinary seamen. Acccording Dana, the books purpose was to present "the life of a common sailor at sea as it really is—the light and the dark together.

# 38

# Composition-in-Progress

comp 38

In this chapter, a composition is shown in all its stages of development. It represents one student's efforts from an initial freewriting through the generation of ideas, a rough outline, and several drafts. The assignment was to write in one week a 300- to 500-word composition on any subject, addressed to a general reader. Thus, the writer was relieved of making decisions about audience but was faced with finding a subject, a purpose, a voice, and a structure.

Notice that once the writer found a subject, it did not change. Its development from draft to draft, however, changed radically. Also, notice that not until the third draft did a definite purpose, voice, and structure emerge.

The student began this assignment by freewriting these notes in ten minutes.

> I don't know what to write about. This better work. I have a Math test to study for. What can I eat tonight that would taste different? I've had it with greasy hamburgers, pizza, and fried chicken from take-out places. I need vegetables. Not those institutional vegetables. Like those green peas that look like shriveled marbles. Maybe if I cleaned this place up, it would help me think. The thing that would really help me think is if

that radio down the hall wasn't blasting my ear drums. Why is it that people with loud radios never consider whether everyone in ten blocks wants to hear the same music?

It's going to snow. Snow is nice when it first falls. But when it turns brown and slushy it isn't nice. It isn't romantic. It isn't a Hollywood set. It's just wet and cold.

I think I have "Math anxiety" I keep having that dream about Math class. People say it's common, that dream where you have a Math Test and you haven't been to class in weeks. Or maybe never. And you wander around a strange building looking for your classroom.



Looking back over the freewriting exercise, the writer saw a possible subject in the question *Why is it that people with loud radios never consider whether everyone in ten blocks wants to hear the same music?* This question prompted the writer to think about the subject "background noise." Viewing background noise as a problem, the writer then asked questions associated with problems (see 34g) and roughed out some answers.

What causes it?

Maybe fear of silence? Radios. Television. Stereos. Canned music.

Whom does it affect?

Me. Almost everyone in America. Families. Shoppers.

What does it affect?

Relaxation. Nerves. Stress.

Where does it occur?

Homes. Grocery stores. Department stores. Telephones. Restaurants. Elevators. Public recreation areas. Dormitories.

What is a possible solution?

Maybe education about the dangers of too much noise. Maybe health education classes. An individual can get away to the country sometime to escape the noise.

What would life be like without the problem?

We could hear the sounds of nature. The normal sounds of the city. We could relax.

The material generated by the questions and answers led to this working outline.

1. Background noise in the home
   television
   stereos
2. Background noise outside the home
   Muzak (canned music) in stores and businesses
   radios in public areas
3. Life without background noise

Writing rapidly, without concern for grammar, spelling, or mechanics, the writer then produced the following rough draft from the working outline.

### First Draft

> American society seems to be obcessed with background noise. Most households have at least one television set that plays whether anyone is watching. And many households have several television sets that run constantly. In addition, families with teenagers usually have the burden of loud stereos that compete with the television for your attention.
>
> But background noise is not confined to homes. Businesses like grocery stores, department stores, and resterants have piped in Muzak that plays constantly in the background. Also, individuals bring their radio to public recreation areas and play pop music that everyone else must listen to, whether they want to or not. It seems that if a sound system is not provided, people bring their own.
>
> It seems that Americans fear silence. But would life without background music be so bad? Without the constant blaring of local radio stations, we might be able to tune in the sounds of nature and everyday life. We could hear the quiet sounds of the woods, the sounds of the country side, the bustle of the city, the sounds of children at play. We could tune into life instead of radio and television.

*potential thesis*

*details supporting obsession with noise*

*potential thesis*

*potential thesis*

This first draft is rather unimpressive. There are three potential theses, and the composition lacks enough concrete details to catch a reader's attention. Nevertheless, the draft was certainly productive. It started the writer thinking about the subject and generating a few controlling ideas.

You will notice that the first draft has errors and misspelled words. At this stage, however, editing for grammar and mechanics would be a waste of time. Instead, the writer set the draft aside, reread it the next day, and made several decisions: (1) to deal only with music, not all background noise; (2) to expand the middle section with concrete details; (3) to expand the first idea in the third paragraph (fear of silence) into an introduction; and (4) to expand the description of the sounds of nature and everyday life. The second draft incorporated these changes.

## Second Draft

Our world is filled with uncertainties and dangers, so many that most people suffer from all kinds of fears. Some people fear cancer; some, nuclear war; some lonliness; some, not succeding in life. What it comes to is that people fear what may lay ahead as an obstacle to a long and happy life. All these fears are legitimate, I think. But there is one fear that has swept over our country that is not only ridiculous but is driving me crazy. The fear of one waking moment without background music.

*potential thesis*

Call a business and let the receptionist put you on hold; you will be treated to a tune that sounds like a combination of "My Beautiful Balloon" and Lawrence Welk playing a fox trot. Go the the track to jog and someone will have brought their radio blaring pop music for your listening pleasure. Stop at a traffic light in the summertime. Some person in the lane next to you will have his car radio on so high that you could not hear an eighteen wheeler bearing down on you from 30 feet away. Go to a swimming pool to relax in the sun. Stereo speakers will blast your brain with music to go crazy by. Babies for a 10-mile radius will wake screaming from their afternoon naps, while mothers of babies will tear their hair. Go out for a solitery lunch during exam week and try to cram in a few last minutes of study over your hamburger. Someone will put dozen coins in the juke box and start a series of country and western tunes that will wail the material you've learned right out of your head. Or a grocery store; the Muzak makes you feel as if you should be skating rather than walking through the aisles.

*details—types of background noise*

Where did this fear of silence come from? There was a time when people could tell where they were just from the sounds around them. In the woods, birds chirped, crickets

*details—description of life in the past.*

sang, frogs croaked, creeks babbled. In the fields, cattle bellowed or tractors chugged. In the suburbs, weed eaters whirred and backyard cooks called to each other from patio to patio. In the city horns honked, taxi drivers swore, subways roared.

But no more. I know the Constitution garantees us freedom of speech. But I don't believe it garantees freedom of noise.



Although the second draft is much better than the first, it has a number of problems. The introductory material on fear (which contains a potential thesis) is never developed, only mentioned briefly again at the beginning of the fourth paragraph. Furthermore, the voice in the introduction seems to change from serious to light.

In addition, the concrete details in the second paragraph have no logical organization, and they are made somewhat vague by the use of the indefinite *you*. The conclusion has no tight connection with the rest of the composition. And generally, the purpose and the structure are not clear.

The writer decided not to edit for grammar and mechanics at this point but to set the composition aside once again. Coming back later to the second draft, the writer made an important decision: to abandon the idea of fear and begin with the idea that in the past, people could hear the sounds of nature and life around them. This decision had several positive effects. It got rid of the weak introduction and the overly serious tone at the beginning. And it provided a "hook" for the conclusion: the last sentence of the next draft hooks back to the first sentence. Most significantly, the decision led the writer to a thesis: *Today, people cannot hear the sounds of life and nature because of constant background music.* The thesis suggested an overall chronological structure for the paper—what was in the past; what is in the present.

Another change vastly improved the composition. The writer condensed all the examples in the body of the paper into an "average day" and used a narrative in the first person (*I*). This change got rid of the vague *you* and gave chronological structure to the disjointed details. It also allowed an extension of the details to include a thwarted hiking trip—something personal and not generalized.

The use of the first person allowed the writer to develop the subject in a consistent voice: the narrator is frustrated, but not irate. The purpose and structure are also clear: to inform the reader of the problem, using the "average day" as illustration.

## Third Draft

*introductory paragraph on sounds of the past*

There was a time when people could tell where they were just from the variety of sounds around them. In the woods, birds chirped, crickets sang, frogs croaked, creeks babbled. In the countryside, cattle bellowed, tractors chugged, roosters crowed. In the suburbs, dogs barked, weed eaters whirred, and backyard cooks called to each other from patio to patio. In the city, horns honked, drivers swore, subways roared. Public parks rang with splashes of kids belly flopping in the pool, the twang of tennis rackets, the creaking of swings and see-saws.

*statement of thesis*

But no longer are our days filled with these sounds. That rich variety of sounds is now masked and our lives are filled with three audio backdrops: Muzak, country and western, and pop music. This came to me during an average day last summer.

*thesis supported with an illustration*

Early in the morning, I went to the track to jog and think peaceful thoughts. Someone had brought a radio blaring pop music for my listening pleasure. I went to the grocery store: the Muzak made me feel as if I should have been skating rather than walking down the aisles. On the way from the grocery store, I stopped at a traffic light. In the lane next to me, a high school boy had his car radio turned up so high that I would have been unable to hear an eighteen wheeler bearing down on me from 30 feet away. I went to a swimming pool to relax in the sun, stereo speakers blasted my brain with music to go crazy by. Babies for a 10-mile radius surely must have waked crying from their afternoon naps, while their mothers groan in frustration. I left the pool and went home to my little brother and his friends glued to a television rock video pulssating noise for several blocks around. I fled to my room and called a local employment office to check on my job applications. The receptionist put me on hold; I was treated to a tune that sounded like Lawrence Welk playing "My Beautiful Balloon." I went out for a hamburger, and the juke box was playing pop music so loud that the waitress had to read lips to take orders.

That night I determined to find some peace and quiet for at least a few hours. So the next day, I got my hiking gear and took off to the woods to rest my ears. After a few miles, I approached the spot where I used to sit and read to the quiet sounds of nature. But the woods were cleared, and construction workers were building a house, hammering and sawing to the rythms of a country and western station. Just over the hill, a family in a camper had brought along a radio that could pick up rock stations from Radio Free Europe. Sadly, I walked back to my car. Wondering whether there was any escape for me in a society full of music addicts.

The mystery I am unable to solve is this: Do the people who insist on providing me with this constant background music think they are doing me a favor? Or do they feel that their own desires take precedence over the desires of others? Or is it simply that they don't want to know where they are?

*conclusion "hooking" back to first sentence*

Looking over the third draft, the writer found problems with the thesis: "That rich variety of sounds is now masked and our lives are filled with three audio backdrops: Muzak, country and western, and pop music." First, the metaphor is illogical; lives are not filled with backdrops. Second, the thesis suggests a three-pronged organization that is not forthcoming. The writer simplified the thesis to read *That rich variety of sounds is now masked by constant background music.*

Now satisfied that the composition had a clear thesis, an appropriate voice, and a logical structure, the writer revised the paper sentence by sentence—correcting errors and improving style. The following is a final draft, complete with a title.

A Search for Silence

There was a time when people could tell where they were just from the variety of sounds around them. In the woods, birds chirped, crickets sang, frogs croaked, creeks babbled. In the countryside, cattle bellowed, tractors chugged, roosters crowed. In the suburbs, dogs barked, weed eaters whirred, and backyard cooks called to each other from patio to patio. In the city, horns honked, drivers swore, subways roared. Public parks rang with splashes of kids belly-flopping in the pool, the twang of tennis rackets, the creaking of swings and seesaws.

But no more. That rich variety of sounds is now masked by constant background music. This revelation came to me during an average day last summer.

*insertion of* revelation *clarifies a vague* this

*new thesis that more accurately predicts subject matter*

Early in the morning, I went to the track to jog and think peaceful thoughts. Someone had brought a radio blaring pop music for my listening pleasure. I went to the grocery store: the Muzak made me feel as if I should have been skating rather than walking down the aisles. On the way from the grocery store, I stopped at a traffic light. In the lane next to me, a high school boy had his car radio turned up so high that I would have been unable to hear an eighteen-wheeler bearing down on me from 30 feet away. I went to a swimming pool to relax in the sun. Stereo speakers blasted my brain with music to go crazy by. Babies for a 10-mile radius surely must have waked crying from their afternoon naps, while their mothers groaned in frustration. I left the pool and went home to my little brother and his friends glued to a television rock video

*comma splice corrected*

*tense shift corrected*

pulsating noise for several blocks around. I fled to my room and called a local employment office to check on my job applications. The receptionist put me on hold; I was treated to a tune that sounded like Lawrence Welk playing "My Beautiful Balloon." I went out for a hamburger, and the jukebox was playing pop music so loud that the waitress had to read lips to take orders.

*spelling error* (pulssating) *corrected*

That night I determined to find some peace and quiet for at least a few hours. So the next day, I got my hiking gear and took off to the woods to rest my ears. After a few miles, I approached the spot where I used to sit and read to the quiet sounds of nature. But the woods were cleared, and construction workers were building a house, hammering and sawing to the rhythms of a country and western station. Just over the hill, a family in a camper had brought along a machine that could pick up rock stations from Radio Free Europe. Sadly, I walked back to my car, wondering whether there was any escape for me in a society of music addicts.

*spelling error* (rythms) *corrected*

*repetition of* radio *eliminated*

*sentence fragment attached to preceding sentence*

The mystery I am unable to solve is this: Do people who insist on providing me with this constant background music think they are doing me a favor? Or do they feel that their own desires take precedence over the desires of others? Or is it simply that they don't want to know where they are?

# PART VI

# Special Writing Projects

Some papers have special purposes and special audiences. To carry out the purpose of a paper and to satisfy its audience, you must become familiar with the characteristics that make the paper unique. For example, an argument requires a conflict, and a research paper requires documentation according to rigid guidelines. A business letter follows a standard arrangement. A progress report requires specific content. Thus, when undertaking a special writing project, make sure you adhere to the expected conventions for the components and format.

# 39

# Argument and Critical Thinking

arg/
crit
39

Of all the writing projects you encounter in your academic and professional life, the most common is probably argument. If you propose that the data from a laboratory experiment or the symbols in a poem be interpreted in a certain way, you are arguing. If you recommend that your office purchase one computer rather than another, you are arguing. If you try to motivate people to stop littering, you are arguing. An argument can advance a theory, suggest a solution to a problem, or urge a course of action. Developing an argument can be a very gratifying process, for here you have the opportunity to express your own opinions rather than merely to report the ideas and opinions of other people. For the argument to be effective, however, you must proceed logically and objectively—from investigating the subject and gathering evidence to organizing materials and writing the paper. In other words, you must engage in critical thinking throughout the entire process.

The phrase *critical thinking* does not refer to criticizing in the negative sense. Rather, it refers to a systematic mental scrutiny of ideas and material. When most experienced readers and researchers read or listen to oral presentations, this scrutiny is automatic. First, they keep an open mind—prepared to accept new information and opinions. At the same time, they are cautious—alert to fallacious reasoning and to inaccurate, insufficient, and irrelevant evidence. They analyze the material, dividing it into component parts and separating opinions from facts. Furthermore, they question how the material relates to what they already know and what it means in a larger context. They separate the main ideas from the details and the useful ideas from the trivia. In other words, their thinking is disciplined. By manipulating the material, they control it intellectually.

Inexperienced readers and researchers, on the other hand, tend to take information at face value in its entirety. Often, they either accept the whole or reject it. These readers are not in control, and, consequently, the material is not very useful to them.

A simple analogy is that of horse and rider. The critical thinker is like the experienced rider, who uses reins and body movements to control the horse and put it through its paces—seemingly without effort. The inexperienced reader is like the city slicker at a dude ranch. As the old story goes, he gets on the horse, takes one rein in either hand, and waits. When nothing happens, he says to the horse, "Well. Commence."



If you are inexperienced in critical thinking, you do not have to sit there like the man on the horse. Fortunately, there is a procedure to guide you. With practice, you will develop the mental discipline necessary to use information to your advantage. As you work on an argument, follow the steps that guide experienced writers through the process: find a subject, sort out the conflict, frame a thesis, gather evidence, evaluate the evidence, and choose a structure for the material. In addition, make sure you have identified as clearly as possible the audience that will read your paper.

## 39a Subject

You can write an argument on virtually any subject as long as you know what you are talking about. Nothing fizzles so quickly as an argument put forth by a writer ignorant of the subject. You must choose a subject about which you are informed or can become informed. (See Chapter 34.) Also, your knowledge of the subject must extend beyond your own views to encompass all sides of the issue. You cannot write a successful argument unless you can understand the views of the opposition.

For this reason, it probably is not wise to write on a subject about which you are irrevocably prejudiced and therefore unable to think critically. Developing an effective argument requires that you examine an issue carefully, keep an open mind, and be prepared to change your own stand if the evidence points you in a new direction.

Your first step, then, is to consider subjects that you already know about or that you want to learn about. For example, if you are an experienced hunter, you might want to defend hunting against the critics who denounce it as cruel. On the other hand, if you morally oppose hunting but know little about it, you must be willing to do some preliminary research before you write—read articles that support and oppose the practice, talk to hunters, perhaps even interview a psychologist to find out what motivates hunters.

### ❑ EXERCISE 1



**List 10 subjects that you might want to develop for an argument. First, think about each subject in the list and discard any that you cannot consider objectively and critically, without prejudice. Second, consider the remaining subjects and discard any that do not interest you sufficiently to warrant the necessary research. Here are a few subjects just to get you started thinking: drunk-driving laws, "politically correct" speech, computer literacy, foreign-language requirements, salaries of professional athletes, early marriage, women in combat, drug testing.**

## 39b Conflict

After you have chosen several possible subjects, explore them as areas of conflict. You want a subject about which you can express an opinion, a judgment. Inherent in the subject must be the possibility of conflicting ideas, interpretations, or behavior.

If you can prove your position beyond any doubt, you do not have an opinion; you have a fact. For example, you cannot argue that teenage pregnancy is on the rise; this fact can be statistically proved or disproved. You could, however, argue about the primary reason for teenage pregnancy: lack of sex education, parental negligence, influence of television and movies on teenage mores, and so on. People will certainly disagree about the causes of the problem.

Likewise, you cannot argue something generally accepted, such as the idea that parental love is important to human beings.

Although the idea cannot be statistically established, few people would oppose it. On the other hand, you could argue an unorthodox view—for example, that absence of parental love often results in artistic, creative children. You would have to base your argument on psychological theories and on real-life experiences of artists and other creative people.

One good way to examine a subject for conflict is to ask questions. Consider for a moment the subject of requiring high school students to wear uniforms. Try throwing out random questions: What exactly is a uniform? What would be the effects of wearing uniforms? Who would benefit? How would students react at first? How would they react after a time? Why would someone advocate uniforms? What are the social implications? The political implications? How practical or impractical are uniforms?



You can use questions to explore any conflict. (See 34g.) The subject of athletic programs in college, for example, suggests a number of interesting questions. What is a student athlete? How many athletes are really students? How much time do they spend on academic courses? How many classes do athletes attend on the average? How many graduate from college? Which courses are most popular with athletes? Who benefits most from student athletics? Who suffers the most? The players? The coaches? The pro clubs? The college or university? Is the idea of student athletes a myth? Should we abandon the myth and pay the players? Should athletes be held to the same standards and rules as other students? Does an athletic program actually pay for itself?

You can also identify conflicts by looking for relationships. In the case of high school uniforms, you could explore, for example, the relationships between student dress and student behavior; between clothes and self-esteem; between provocative clothes and promiscuous behavior; between *macho* clothes and aggressive behavior; between clothes and social standing; between clothes and individualism.

In the case of student athletics, you could consider relationships such as those between academic involvement and athletic participation; between the student athlete and other students; between college athletics and professional sports; between coaches and their players; between college coaching and professional coaching; and between the lives of college superstars and average players.

Once you have generated some ideas about your subject, you can see conflicts more clearly. Begin by looking at all sides of the issue. What are the logical positions of each side—the pros and cons? For example, consider the pros and cons of the two subjects we have already explored.



**Pro: The case for uniforms**

Uniforms would eliminate some of the social disadvantages suffered by students who cannot afford expensive clothes.

Uniforms might discourage aggressive behavior. (People in dress shirts and ties might be less likely to wield knives than those in tee shirts and leather vests.)

Uniform dress might encourage students to concentrate on studies rather than on fashion statements.

Uniforms would save parents money, which they could contribute to such school improvements as laboratory equipment or air conditioning.

**Con: The case against uniforms**

Uniforms would not flatter some students' appearance and would thus cause loss of self-esteem and self-confidence.

Choosing clothes allows a young person to express individuality.

Uniforms would not eliminate status symbols. Wealthier students would still sport symbols such as cars, expensive haircuts, and designer shoes and sunglasses.

Parents would not likely contribute the saved money to the general needs of the educational system. The money would probably be spent on dress clothes, stereos, cars, and so forth for their children.

Members of ethnic groups could not express their cultural heritage through their style of dress.

**Pro: The case for college athletic programs**

Athletic programs provide scholarships and thus education for many students otherwise unable to attend college.

Student athletes can polish skills in an amateur arena and become professionals when they mature.

Athletic programs provide a bond between the school and the community.

Athletic departments do not ignore education; instead, they provide tutors for students with academic problems.

Student athletes are required to stay in shape; therefore, they are less likely than most students to indulge in drugs and alcohol.

**Con: The case against college athletic programs**

Student athletes do not actually receive an education because they are given special academic privileges, are steered into easy courses, and are not encouraged to graduate.

Athletic departments seduce athletes with false expectations. For example, student athletes rarely know that many "scholarships" are one-year grants renewable according to athletic performance or that only 1 to 2 percent of student football players go on to the pros.

Many college coaches, ambitious to be hired in a professional league, abuse student athletes with pain killers and unrealistic demands. Therefore, many athletes suffer physical damage.

Athletic departments have no interest in education; at one school, for example, the baseball team played over 60 games (most on the road) in four months—that is, in 80 classroom days.

Giving student athletes special privileges damages their ability to function in the real world.

By exploring conflicts, you learn whether you wish to pursue a subject and whether you need to fill in any gaps with some research. For the subjects of school uniforms and athletic programs, for example, you might want to find some case histories of people with experience. Also, you could look for magazine articles on the subject in the *Readers' Guide to Periodical Literature* or in other indexes. (See 40c.) In addition, you might take an informal survey of students to get their ideas.



### ❑ EXERCISE 2

**Consider once again your final list of subjects from Exercise 1. For each subject, ask questions and look for conflicting relationships. Pick two or more of the subjects that seem most promising and try to generate some statements on two sides of the issue.**

## 39c Thesis

Once you have considered the conflicts inherent in a subject and generated some statements on both sides of the issue, you should be able to formulate a thesis, the opinion you wish to argue. (Read about thesis statements in 35d.)

When formulating your thesis, consider whether a reasonable argument can be made against it and whether you could defend against that argument. Be sure to keep an open mind. You may want to change or modify your original position in order to develop a workable thesis—one that is clear and specific enough to allow intelligent debate. Let's suppose you want to formulate a thesis on the school uniform issue. Your argument will falter with a thesis such as *Requiring uniforms for high school students is a good (or bad) idea.* The words *good* and *bad* are too vague. They give no concrete base for support or defense, and thus the thesis lends no direction to the argument. Besides, examination of the conflict showed that uniforms are neither all bad nor all good.

Look back at the pros and cons on the subject. The pros suggest a tentative thesis such as this one: *Requiring uniforms in high school would eliminate the social discord among students and the financial burdens of parents.* The cons suggest something like this: *Requiring uniforms in high school would prevent students from expressing individuality and ethnic identification.* These statements are more specific but too sweeping. Obviously, uniforms would not eliminate all discord and financial burdens, nor prevent all individuality and identification. Each thesis would benefit from qualification: *Requiring uniforms for high school students would help to ease the social discord among students and the financial burdens of parents* and *Requiring uniforms for high school students would lower student morale by destroying a major avenue for individual and ethnic expression.*



Both theses now state a position and a line of defense. You may, of course, restate a thesis while you are drafting the paper. But you should at least begin drafting with a thesis that gives you a direction.

### ❑ EXERCISE 3

**In Exercise 2, you were asked to choose several subjects and generate statements on two sides of an issue. Look back over the pros and cons you generated for each subject. Then write two theses for each subject, one thesis based on the pros and one based on the cons.**

## 39d Kinds of Evidence

In settling on a thesis, you have already explored your subject and possibly even researched it. Now you must select the evidence to support your thesis. There are several different kinds of evidence—ranging from facts to informed opinions to logical reasons. No matter which kinds of evidence you have available, be sure to use a critical approach. Select only the evidence that is reliable and directly related to your thesis.

### (1) Facts and observations

Some facts are indisputable or easily verifiable. By consulting a dictionary or encyclopedia, for example, you can quickly identify the seventh vice-president of the United States or the date of the Wright Brothers' first successful flight at Kitty Hawk. Factual information commonly used as evidence, however, is usually a bit more complex. For example, you might want to use data that you or another researcher has obtained from laboratory experiments or mathematical calculations.

Some factual information is derived from observations—such as your own examination of a polluted beach, an archaeologist's description of an excavation site, a biologist's observations on insect damage to a forest, an eyewitness account of a riot, or a sociologist's case studies of child abusers.



A popular kind of factual evidence is information gathered in a survey. In fact, professional pollsters and researchers have so perfected their techniques that their statistics can be cited with confidence. If you do a survey yourself, explain your particular methodology so that readers can assess the reliability of your findings. Also, whether you survey by written questionnaire, telephone, or interviews, use the same questions for each respondent and phrase each question carefully. For advice for how to phrase survey questions, see 45c(2).

### (2) Informed opinions

The opinions of other people can serve as evidence for an argument. But those opinions should come from informed scholars or experts in the field you are discussing. For example, if you were supporting a claim that Shakespeare created roles especially for the actors in his company, you should cite a respected Shakespearean scholar or an expert in theater history. To locate reliable opinions, you will more than likely use the library. For a discussion of library resources and search techniques, see 40c–e.

When you use the exact words of an informed source, honesty requires that you quote faithfully. If you leave out parts of the quotation to save space or to eliminate the irrelevant, be especially careful not to distort the meaning. Notice the way the following quotations alter the meaning of the original statements.

DISTORTED: "Dwight Eisenhower was one of the outstanding leaders in . . . this century."

ORIGINAL: Dwight Eisenhower was one of the outstanding leaders of the Western world in this century.

DISTORTED: "Scientific news is . . . a random collection of amazing facts."

ORIGINAL: Scientific news is too often presented as a random collection of amazing facts that at best have little, if anything, to do with the real world.



Before you quote sources in your paper, read 27a, 27b, and 27g on quotation marks and ellipses and 40h on avoiding plagiarism.

## (3) Logical Reasoning

Basically, there are two kinds of logical reasoning: induction and deduction. Inductive reasoning involves using specific instances to arrive at a general principle. If you get sick every time you eat cheese, yogurt, ice cream, or butter, you will eventually induce that you are allergic to dairy products. Conversely, deductive reasoning involves using a general principle to predict a specific instance. If you know that you are allergic to dairy products, you will deduce that Aunt Martha's peach ice cream will make you sick.

We move back and forth between the induction and deduction easily and constantly. Take, for example, the idea that a high-fat diet and lack of exercise contribute to heart disease. Medical researchers studied thousands of individual heart patients (the specifics) to reach this conclusion (the general principle). You might use the general principle as evidence that physical education and nutrition classes are essential to the public schools. And you might deduce that students who attend these classes will live longer and healthier lives.

Although both kinds of logic are quite natural and ordinary, they can mislead you to false conclusions, and you should be cautious when using them to support an argument. To guard against the common pitfalls in induction and deduction, see the discussions of hasty generalization and of non sequitur in the next section, "Evaluation of Evidence."

A special kind of logic is the analogy, a comparison between two different things and the suggestion that what is true of one is true of the other—for example, what is true of the computer is also true of the brain; what was true of the Roman Empire is also true today. Obviously, since the two things being compared are not alike, the conclusion is at best a probability. Therefore, you should qualify a conclusion drawn from analogy with a word such as *probably, usually,* or *in some instances.* Notice how the word *usually* in the following statement improves the acceptability of the analogy: The economy is like a complex piece of machinery; therefore, when something goes wrong, we usually have a difficult time finding the cause.



### ❑ EXERCISE 4

**Explain what kind of evidence you would look for to support the following claims.**

1. Children watch too much television.
2. Television preachers depend more on showmanship than on theology.
3. Both Aldous Huxley in *Brave New World* and George Orwell in *1984* warn of the loss of individual freedom.
4. In political campaigns, advertising should be controlled to make campaigning equable for all candidates.
5. The school year should be lengthened.
6. If soil erosion is not controlled, successful agriculture is doomed.
7. Patients should assume some responsibility for their own treatments and not rely solely on doctors.
8. Some people treat their animals like children.
9. Many popular video games have violent or destructive themes.
10. The violent and destructive themes of many video games lead to antisocial behavior.

## 39e Evaluation of Evidence

As you gather evidence, you must think critically about its quality and question whether to include it in your argument. Through constant skepticism and criticism, you can weed out material that is inaccurate, irrelevant, unclear, or illogical. You can also determine whether the material is sufficient to convince readers to agree with you or to act as you wish.

Thinking critically about your evidence requires thoughtful reading and scrutiny. It requires systematic judgment. Most experienced readers and writers have developed a system that they use naturally and instinctively. Inexperienced readers and writers must consciously and deliberately analyze their evidence. If you are inexperienced or need to ensure the quality of the material you use, learn to question. Questioning truth, accuracy, or value is the essence of intellectual discipline. Five questions typify the habit of thinking critically about what you read and hear. By asking these questions, you can better evaluate your evidence.



### (1) Is the evidence accurate?

Inaccurate evidence will quickly undermine an argument. Whether the evidence is primary (direct observation) or secondary (someone else's account), it must be accurate. You know the accuracy of your own observations, but you must assess the accuracy of statements made by others. When you read or listen to others, look for several telling characteristics.

Is the source full of facts or full of opinions? A fact is something that has actually happened or that is really true (verifiable); an opinion is a belief that is potentially right or wrong. For example, that the climate is warming in certain parts of the globe is a fact verifiable by recorded data. Currently, however, scientists differ in their opinions about the reasons for the warming trends. A source long on opinions and short on facts is suspicious. There is little value in opinions unsupported by either facts or a sufficient number of examples or illustrations. Of course, if the source is a proved expert, the opinion is backed up by reputation—a career involved in gathering information. Nevertheless, most real experts are careful to support their opinions with sufficient factual data.

What does the tone of the work tell you? If the tone is more emotional than rational, you should beware of using the source as evidence. Material that seems too angry, too sentimental, or too dogmatic reveals a questionable source. Some display of emotion may be appropriate, yet when it is excessive or not balanced with reason and moderation, it should be viewed with suspicion. Likewise, the tone of your own argument should be rational. For such subjects as abortion, capital punishment, gun control, and religion, emotions must be held in check. When writers feel very strongly about a subject, they naturally tend to dramatize. If you cannot present a rational argument on a strongly held conviction, you probably should avoid writing about it.

A source that includes discriminatory language is usually a poor source of evidence. Slurs against women, particular races, places, and groups indicate a source that lacks objectivity. Often this kind of language takes the form of loaded, abusive language such as *religious fanatic, bleeding-heart liberal, knee-jerk conservative, egghead, male chauvinist pig*. (See 32e.) Prejudice in a source or in your own prose can alienate readers at the very time that the purpose should be to win their confidence.



In determining whether a source is accurate, you should also consider the quality of the research. Is the source well documented? Accurate material is not necessarily documented; however, documentation indicates the origin of the information and may give clues to its accuracy. Sometimes the reputation of the publisher can indicate reliability. What is the date of the publication? Some information—particularly on scientific and technical subjects—ages poorly. New research often makes earlier data obsolete. Questioning the research will not ensure the accuracy of a source but will help you avoid weak evidence.

## ❑ EXERCISE 5

**Which of the following statements are facts? Which are opinions? Which are opinions backed up by facts?**

1. Some people have rejected supermarket fruits and vegetables and instead buy from organic farmers, health-food stores, and food co-ops.
2. Edgar Allan Poe's dark view of the world can be traced to his mother's early death.
3. Food commercials are a dieter's enemy. They try to make food look delicious, fun to eat, and healthful.
4. *The Great Escape* contains unrealistic touches. In it, Steve McQueen, accompanied by the dramatic strains of the music score, vaults barbed-wire fences on his motorcycle.
5. Al Capp not only created the funny comic strip *Li'l Abner* but also wrote very humorous prose.
6. For the study of birds, the contributions of amateurs can be important.

Amateurs can contribute to science by keeping detailed field notes about their observations of such information as bird behavior, numbers seen, weather, and terrain.

7. After their 1944 assassination attempt failed to kill Hitler, Ervin von Witzleben and General Karl-Heinrich von Stulpnagel were executed.
8. In America, drinking water is not harmful; wells and reservoirs are either naturally clean or are clarified. Filters in homes are therefore unnecessary.
9. By one estimate, less than 10 percent of America's 85 million bicycle riders wear helmets.
10. Used cars can be risky buys. A fair price is uncertain; odometers can be doctored to hide the mileage; damage can be camouflaged with fresh paint and polish; and little can be done in case you buy a lemon.

arg/ crit 39e

## ❑ EXERCISE 6

Assess the accuracy of the following passages. Is the tone rational? Is bias present? Is there evidence of research?

1. Before the South seceded from the Union, William S. Barry became absorbed in the contemplation of the great question of disunion, whose rapid approach his sagacity foresaw; and as it rolled its huge proportions to the brow of the political horizon, he became more and more convinced that, though beast it might be, it was far preferable to that *monstrum horrendum, informe, ingens,* of Northern fanaticism, whose ravages threatened the destruction of every Southern interest and Southern right. Mr. Barry was not a disunionist *per se,* and had used his best endeavors to stay the storm, so long as he considered an effort to do so consistent with manhood and honor.

2. Sport fishing may be changing. People once felt compelled to return to dock with as many fish as the boat could hold. They never thought about the waters getting overharvested. Nowadays, a new phase may be developing. More and more people believe that a fish is too valuable to catch just once, that catch-and-release is essential if the resources of our waters are to be protected. Recently on a chartered trip, after a long struggle, a young boy pulled on board a large king mackerel. After the congratulations, he said, "Hurry, we've got to throw it back before it suffers." No one suggested keeping the fish. No one suggested a victory photo. The thrill was in the catch and in seeing the fish swim vigorously away. Perhaps we are learning to conserve our marine resources.

3. The feminist movement has completely ruined American society. Feminists constantly spout accusations that everything demeans women. They have encouraged women to dress like men and to go to work and aban-

don their family responsibilities. Feminists complain that they have no equality, but in truth they have instead too much equality. They are now suffering stress, alcoholism, and even heart attacks. They have alienated men to the point that marriage and children will never be possible. They should look around and see the damage that the movement has caused before it's too late.

4. The available information reveals considerable variety in the way steroids are taken. Both the amount and kinds of drugs taken differ. In a study of the drugs taken by competitive bodybuilders from Kansas and Missouri, Tricker, O'Neill, and Cook (1989) discovered that individual use ranged from one to fifteen different types of steroids. Pope and Katz (1988) reported that doses vary; some athletes take as much as 100 times the amount called for when the drug is taken as a legitimate medicine. Many athletes also "stack" drugs, taking several at once—from two to as many as six—and they administer the drugs both orally and by injection (Gaines, 1991).



### (2) Is the evidence relevant?

Successful arguments stick to the issue at hand; they do not shift from the real issue to focus on irrelevant material. Sometimes writers include irrelevant material in order to pad an argument—either to disguise a lack of hard evidence or to avoid the trouble of searching for the right kind of evidence. Other times, writers shift focus in order to involve the reader emotionally in the issue or to create a diversion. Padding is easy to recognize in your own work or in that of others: the writing veers off in an unexpected direction. Emotional appeals and diversions are less obvious, and you must be alert to recognize them in your sources as well as to avoid them in your own writing. Some of the most common are appeals to tradition, irrelevant testimonials, appeals to popularity, ad hominem attacks, straw man positions, and red herrings.

#### Appeal to Tradition

Possibly the most common way to shift an issue is to appeal to the cultural conditioning of a group—the traditions, the customs, the common heritage. Suppose, for example, a paper considers whether women in the armed services should be sent into combat. To sway an American audience *against* the idea, a writer might invoke the "wisdom of the Founding Fathers, who did not call to war our mothers, our sisters, and our daughters." This kind of rhetoric paints a picture of wise, white-wigged statesmen guarding the future flowers of the nation's motherhood. To sway an audience *toward* the idea, a writer might discuss the "pioneer woman, fighting side by side with her husband to protect the home and family." This scenario paints a picture of a strong, handsome woman, bonnet askew, aiming a rifle through a cabin window at marauders. Both of these pictures contain honored traditions in our culture and thus evoke powerful emotions. But in reality, neither of these pictures is directly relevant to the issue of whether contemporary women should be sent into combat.



### Irrelevant Testimonial

Advertisers frequently cite the testimony of a celebrity to support a claim: a football star touts a deodorant soap, an actress starts every day with Brand A coffee, a tennis pro gets her stamina from Brand X cereal, a talk-show host drives only a certain kind of car. The audience is expected to transfer approval of the celebrity to approval of the product. In the manner of advertisers, writers sometimes try to support an argument with quotations from inappropriate people—citing a popular novelist on a point of law, for example. You should reject this evidence and avoid this practice. Use only relevant testimonials: the knowledge and opinions of experts in the field in question.

### Appeal to Popularity

In advertising, the appeal to popularity is rampant: X is popular; therefore, X is good. Television viewers see cheering crowds rushing deliriously toward a plastic building where beautiful girls in cute hats smile, sing, and dispense processed chicken nuggets. Viewers, of course, are supposed to feel that they are missing out unless they join the fun and hurry on down to Chickie Doodle. In politics, the tactic is usually called "the bandwagon." Voters are encouraged to "get on the bandwagon and vote for the people's choice." The implication is that the candidate's popularity indicates his or her merit.

In arguments, the tactic usually results in asserting that many wrongs make a right. For example, one might attempt to justify cheating on income taxes or insurance claims by stating that "everyone does it." History clearly demonstrates that popular ideas are not necessarily good ideas. Alert readers will reject evidence that shifts support from legitimate proof to the numbers of proponents.

### Ad Hominem Attack

Avoid evidence containing ad hominem attacks, a personal attack on an individual's character rather than on his or her position. A common form of ad hominem attack is guilt by association. In this ploy, a speaker or writer tries to associate someone with an idea or with another person that the audience finds distasteful. Politicians favor this tactic, identifying their opponents with characters that voters reject. For instance, a gubernatorial candidate might attempt to associate his or her opponent with a member of organized crime. Likewise, a writer might attempt to discredit an argument merely by associating its proponents with an "ultraconservative" political group. Of course, people can be judged to some extent by the company they keep. Nevertheless, you should judge an opponent's position on its own strength and not resort to such smear tactics.



### Straw Man Position

Altering the opposing view to make it easier to attack is creating a straw man. Suppose, for instance, a writer is arguing for a flat-rate tax system in which each individual pays 10 percent of total income with no deductions. The writer could set up a straw man position like this one: "A graduated tax system benefits only the rich, since they are the only taxpayers who can take advantage of large deductions." It is easy, of course, to attack a system that benefits only the rich. But the evidence oversimplifies the graduated tax structure. For example, a deduction system can encourage individuals and businesses to make contributions to charities, universities, hospitals, medical research laboratories, and other institutions that benefit the whole society at all economic levels. The straw man (graduated tax = pro-rich) is easy to attack, but it is also irrelevant.

### Red Herring

*Red herring* is an old hunting term that refers to dragging a herring across a trail to divert the hounds from their prey. The term refers to a diversionary tactic, a dodge that switches the issue. For example, suppose a writer argues that Medicare has increased the cost of medical examinations and uses as support the claim that medical doctors are wealthy because they overcharge their patients. Even if the writer could prove that claim, it would not prove that Medicare escalates health-care costs. It would merely divert the argument into a vaguely related area.

## ❑ EXERCISE 7

Identify the types of emotional appeals and diversions that appear in the following statements.

1. Do-gooders who oppose capital punishment should have to pay for the expense of keeping a prisoner on death row.
2. The government of South Africa has been accused of despotism, but the country has been more economically successful than other African nations.
3. There is nothing wrong with buying research papers. If it were wrong, there would be no established businesses providing this service.
4. William Faulkner was an alcoholic; therefore he cannot be included in a discussion of serious writers.
5. It is not fair to make food manufacturers list all the ingredients included in a product. Consumers do not understand all the items being listed anyway.
6. All books containing any references to illegal drug use must be removed from public school libraries because we must teach wholesome American values to our children.
7. Soap operas must have some redeeming qualities because their ratings are extremely high.
8. Lie-detector tests are reliable. That fact was published by a nationally known newspaper.
9. It is un-American to favor gun control.
10. You cannot totally trust the lawyer's motives in the antiobscenity case; his wife once posed for *Playboy.*



### (3) Is the evidence sufficient?

To support a claim or a belief, a writer must include sufficient evidence. But how much is enough? Unfortunately, there are no clear-cut guidelines for deciding. The subject usually determines the amount of evidence you need. For example, in an argument about the harm that results from wearing walkabout radios and stereos, only two reasons might support the claim—that they damage hearing and make the wearers insensitive to dangers such as cars and trains. These two reasons may be sufficiently convincing if they, in turn, are backed up by expert testimony, illustrations, and examples. On the other hand, if an argument asserts that inbreeding is ruining the health of pedigreed dogs, a discussion of the deafness and skin ailments of the Dalmatian is not enough. Many more examples and expert testimony would have to be added.

### Hasty Generalization

When a writer bases a claim on too little evidence, the problem is called a hasty generalization—a result of not thinking critically. Hasty generalizations are easy to recognize in everyday conversation. After the purchase of one lemon, the buyer concludes that all similar cars are bad. On the basis of one victory, fans predict a winning season for the local football team. In written arguments, the hasty generalization is usually a bit less obvious. For example, a writer might conclude that the entire South is rapidly entering the economic mainstream by examining only the economy of Atlanta. A typical kind of hasty generalization occurs when a writer bases a broad conclusion on a nonrepresentative survey. For instance, after interviewing 25 acquaintances in a women's dormitory, a writer might claim that American college students favor nongraded courses. But 25 students are not likely to represent the attitudes of all American students—and certainly not 25 of the same sex who all attend the same university and live in the same dormitory. Broad conclusions can be drawn only from surveys that elicit information from a representative sample, one that is a microcosm of the group in question.



If the evidence is limited, but it is all that can be collected, a writer must be honest. For example, from a survey of only 50 people, you may not claim that Americans are dissatisfied with their medical system. A careful writer would simply state that in a limited survey of 50 people, the respondents expressed dissatisfaction with their medical system. Though not as sweeping or forceful as the general claim, the limited claim has credibility.

## ❑ EXERCISE 8

**Which of the following statements are generalizations based on inadequate evidence?**

1. Diets do not work because a survey showed that 200 people who lost weight on diets eventually gained the weight back.
2. Vitamin C does not help colds; I took 250 milligrams for a month and still got a cold.
3. I thought I was drinking Coca-Cola, but I was told the drink was Pepsi; the two drinks taste exactly alike.
4. To determine the speed of the computer printers, we measured the time necessary to print a 170-word letter. We performed the test on 12 print-

ers—4 laser printers, 4 ink-jet printers, and 4 dot-matrix printers. The laser printer proved to be the fastest, even faster than the dot-matrix models in their draft mode.

5. Barley can lower your cholesterol levels. Scientists at the University of Wisconsin found that chickens fed a barley-based diet had cholesterol levels in their flesh that were 30 percent lower than chickens fed the usual corn-based diet.
6. According to a study which traced the smoking habits of 25,000 people over a period of 10 years, 75 percent of those who quit smoking relapsed within a year.
7. Shakespeare could not have been the author of the works attributed to him. The real author was well traveled and showed detailed knowledge of Venice in *The Merchant of Venice.* During his life, Shakespeare never left England.
8. Many people still believe that President Roosevelt knew beforehand about Japanese plans to attack Pearl Harbor. Yet no credible evidence has ever been discovered to support that claim.



### (4) Is the language clear?

Effective evidence must be written clearly. If the meaning of your sources is not clear to you, do not use them as evidence. Material in such sources as scholarly journals and technical publications is frequently incomprehensible to the average person. If you find your sources difficult, use a dictionary to look up the meanings of words and break down long, complex sentences into short segments. If you still cannot understand the information, you must locate material that has been restated for lay people, or you must change the subject of your argument.

In evaluating the quality of evidence, be alert to the problem of imprecise language. The meanings of terms should be clear and consistent. Abstract words pose a particular problem; words like *freedom, justice, success,* and *happiness* mean different thing to different people and thus must be defined or avoided.

Also, words should not refer to more than one thing at a time. This problem, called ambiguity or equivocation, is sometimes used deliberately to confuse unwary readers. For example, advertisers often use the expression *natural* to mean both "something in nature" and "something desirable." They make much of natural ingredients, which the audience is supposed to interpret as preferable to unnatural ingredients, whatever that means. In an argument, the "nature = good" theme could be used to argue that human beings have always engaged in warfare; therefore, war is part of human nature; therefore, war is natural; therefore, we should not bother to strive for peace. But not everything in nature is necessarily good—for example, tornadoes, earthquakes, and viruses. And furthermore, everything that happens in society is not necessarily part of the natural course of events. To eliminate such confusion in your arguments, always read carefully and always question the meanings of words.

## ❑ EXERCISE 9

The following statements make poor evidence because of the language. In each, determine whether the language is obscure, abstract, or ambiguous.



1. His intelligence scores are low; therefore, he cannot be expected to make an intelligent career decision.
2. If the Vietnam war had been fought fairly, America would have never lost.
3. Americans have the right to free speech. Therefore, I can say whatever I think.
4. Section 62e provides that a custodial account will be treated as a qualified trust if such custodial account would, except for the fact that it is not a trust, constitute a qualified trust and the custodian is a bank or other person who demonstrates that the manner in which the assets will be held will be consistent with the requirements.
5. College is a meaningful experience. Students learn a lot in college that they wouldn't otherwise learn. Students who want meaning in their lives should attend college.
6. Because of the economy, the company has been forced to make organizational changes. The chief executive has decided that an involuntary termination program will be needed to facilitate the corporate upturn. Some of the restructuring will involve involuntary separation, but the company plans to implement an enhanced separation policy whenever possible. The chief executive insists that the primary concern will be for the human resources of the company.
7. Run-to-run controls assure the accuracy or completeness of information received by a program. For example, following validation, control totals of valid transactions by transaction type are developed by the program which validated the transactions. Control records are written at the end of the transaction file containing the control totals by transaction type.
8. Today, technology has made our lives easier and healthier. People have the power and freedom to develop a better world. Without technological improvements, our world would be much slower.

### (5) Is the reasoning logical?

Think critically when you read and when you write. Carefully examine not only your sources but also your writing for any material that contains a logical fallacy—a flaw or slip in the reasoning process. In particular, watch for these common types of logical fallacies.



#### Post Hoc Reasoning

*Post hoc, ergo propter hoc* means "after this, therefore because of this." In the post hoc fallacy, a person reasons that simply because A preceded B, A caused B. For example, after the Civil War, small-scale subsistence farming was doomed. But it would be fallacious to blame the war. Although the war preceded the failure, it was not actually the cause; instead, economic and technological forces doomed subsistence farming. Sometimes post hoc reasoning neglects a common cause and assumes a cause and effect relationship between two events that actually have another cause. In the decade before the stock market crash of 1929, for instance, unemployment ranged from 1 1/2 to 4 million. But unemployment did not cause the crash. Both phenomena were part of a complex economic situation that existed in this country and abroad. The way to avoid this kind of logical fallacy is to learn as much as possible, given the time allowed, about the subject under discussion.

#### Oversimplification of Cause

People frequently oversimplify cause when they do not fully understand an issue. For instance, inflation is blamed on interest rates, declining literacy on television, a rising divorce rate on the women's movement. In fact, inflation, the quality of public education, and the status of marriage are complex issues. Many factors bear on each, and none can be explained as the result of one simple cause. Discerning readers recognize when a writer does not have a grip on the complexities of a subject.

#### Either/Or Reasoning

The either/or fallacy presents an argument as though there were only two alternatives. This kind of thinking results in bumper stickers like "America—Love It or Leave It," implying that to live in this country requires unqualified approval of everything that takes place here. Writers can also fall into this trap, oversimplifying an issue to include only two possible choices. For example, universities must either have open-admissions policies or enroll only the children of the rich. A high school can have either a good athletic program or a good academic program. Society must sanction either capital punishment or violent crime. In such cases, the either/or fallacy shifts an issue into too narrow a framework. In reality, few issues are so simple.

### False Analogy

A false analogy involves an assumption that because two things are alike in one way or in several ways, they are alike in some other regard. For example, just because both government and business have income and expenditures, there is no basis for concluding that government can be run in exactly the same way as a business. For one thing, a government is responsible for its unproductive members; business is not. Also, unlike business, government's purpose is not to make a profit. A notable false analogy was made by the Ayatollah Khomeini when explaining the Iranian government's execution of prostitutes, homosexuals, and adulterers:



> If your finger suffers from gangrene, what do you do? Let the whole hand and then the body become filled with gangrene, or cut the finger off?

Khomeini wanted the audience to reason thus: "disease in the body equals moral corruption in society. Thus, a moral society is achieved in the same way as a healthy body." The analogy, however, will not work. For one thing, doctors can identify gangrene with some certainty and agree on the necessity to remove a finger. But people rarely agree on what is immoral. For another thing, a person is not part of society in the same way that a finger is part of a body. A person (unlike a finger) has a mind, a personality, and rights.

### Begging the Question

Begging the question is a kind of circular reasoning: a writer or speaker "begs" the audience to grant at the outset that which is actually at stake. This kind of reasoning usually takes the form of a semantic trick. For example, readers might be asked to grant that "the unfair tuition increase should be repealed." Of course, readers will oppose anything unfair. The real issue is whether or not the increase is, in fact, unfair. This kind of circular reasoning often comes from people who are emotionally involved with their subjects and seek to involve their audience in the same way. Rhetoric typical of circular reasoning occurs in statements and questions such as these: "Immoral programs should not be shown on prime-time television." "How can we allow the murder of these innocent animals at slaughterhouses?" "We should not encourage violence in our youth by encouraging violent sports like football." People who use this rhetoric ask their audiences to grant that certain programs are immoral, that the slaughter of domestic food animals is murder, and that football encourages social violence—the very issues at stake. A writer may be able to beg the question with an uninformed, emotional audience, particularly an audience that already agrees on the issue. Informed readers, however, will not allow such tricks but instead will demand proof of claims.



Non Sequitur

The term *non sequitur* (Latin for "it does not follow") means that the conclusion does not follow from the argument. Thus, in a sense, any fallacy could be called a *non sequitur*. Usually, however, the term refers to a fallacy in an argument based on deduction—an argument in which a person deduces a conclusion from accepted premises.

**Logical Deduction**

| | |
|---|---|
| ACCEPTED PREMISE: | Students who miss more than ten class meetings without written permission from the dean will fail the course. |
| ACCEPTED PREMISE: | Maureen missed more than ten class meetings without written permission from the dean. |
| VALID CONCLUSION: | Therefore, Maureen will fail the course. |

**Non Sequitur**

| | |
|---|---|
| ACCEPTED PREMISE: | Students who miss more than ten class meetings without written permission from the dean will fail the course. |
| ACCEPTED PREMISE: | Maureen failed the course. |
| INVALID CONCLUSION: | Therefore, Maureen missed more than ten class meetings without written permission from the dean. |

Obviously, Maureen could have failed the course for poor grades, not for missing classes; therefore, the conclusion that she necessarily failed for missing classes does not follow.

Ordinarily in an argument, the premises and the conclusions are not set out formally as just shown. Instead, the non sequitur usually occurs in statements where some of the pieces of the argument are implied, as in the following examples:

NON SEQUITUR: Harry should be in politics because he has a good speaking voice. [A good speaking voice is an advantage to a politician. However, it does not follow that anyone with this characteristic should be in politics.]

NON SEQUITUR: My sister is good in math, so she must be smarter than I am. [The writer falsely assumes that mathematic ability is the only measure of intelligence.]

## ❑ EXERCISE 10



Point out the fallacy or fallacies in each of the following statements.

1. Since the security of our country is at stake, the CIA must have the freedom to collect information in any way necessary.
2. The rhino population has been affected either by poaching or by human encroachment.
3. The unreasonable medical fees of today's doctors should be subject to consumer protection laws.
4. The dodo was a species of bird that lived on the island of Mauritius in the Indian Ocean. The dodo could not fly and therefore became extinct.
5. We can improve our school system by giving up compulsory education. Then those who do not want an education can stay away, and the money can be better spent on the diligent students who remain.
6. The poor are deprived of necessities because of the money we have spent on space exploration.
7. Professor Brown gave no A's in Economics 101 last semester, so that course must be too hard.
8. The railroad system should be abolished because it is inefficient.
9. When a car has mechanical problems, we get a new one. In the same way, we should replace an employee with physical problems.
10. NASA should stop sending vehicles into space because every time one goes up, we have bad weather.

# 39f Structure

When you have tentatively settled on a thesis and chosen some supporting evidence, you can begin to assemble the components of the argument. Begin by writing down the thesis at the top of your paper. You can change the thesis, of course, as you draft your argument; but temporarily, you should use it as a guide to choose materials.

Under the thesis, list the pros (the evidence supporting your position) and cons (the evidence against your position). If the subject allows, you can pair points and counterpoints—pro/con, pro/con, pro/con. You should also list any concessions to the opposition or state any points of agreement. Use whatever system allows you to discover the strength of your argument. Then consider whether you still stand by your thesis. If not, rewrite it to reflect your defense.

With the components assembled, you can consider how best to organize the argument. The most common organizations are the classical structure, the discovery structure, and the Rogerian structure. You can follow one of the structures strictly; or you can use one simply as a guide to help you organize your material.



## (1) The classical structure

The most traditional structure for argument is the format used for oratorical debates by classical rhetoricians like Aristotle. Originally, the structure had six parts. The first (*exordium*) served to get the audience's attention and introduce the subject. The second (*narratio*) supplied any necessary facts or background. The third (*partitio*) stated the thesis and prepared the audience for the "partitioning," or organization, of the augment to come. The fourth (*confirmatio*) presented evidence in support of the thesis. The fifth (*refutatio*) attempted to disprove the views of the opposition. And the sixth (*peroratio*) summarized the argument and appealed to the audience for agreement.

Contemporary writers still use this logical and forceful structure with few modifications. The Latin headings, of course, are rarely used now; and the format is usually condensed to five parts. But the basic format remains popular.

*Introduction* describes the subject and states the thesis, usually at the end of the section.
*Statement of Fact* presents facts or background the reader needs to know to follow the argument.
*Proof* presents reasoning and evidence supporting the thesis.
*Refutation* explains why the opposing view is invalid.
*Conclusion* summarizes the major points of the argument.

In short papers, you need not include headings separating the sections. You can, nevertheless, use the structure the headings indicate.

If the classical structure does not exactly suit the materials in your argument, you can always modify it. Suppose, for example, you want to argue that the United States should increasingly develop community-supported agriculture. The most logical strategy would be to begin with the background since the idea is fairly new to this country.

> The idea for Community Supported Agriculture (CSA) has been implemented in Japan and Western Europe for about thirty years. Because farm land is scarce and food is expensive in these countries, people have long needed to work cooperatively. In a CSA arrangement, consumers from a community buy shares in a farm so that a farmer is guaranteed a market and shareholders are guaranteed fresh food they know is safe. Everyone works together to be self-sufficient.



Then you could present the proof that supports joint agriculture. You might, for example, write a paragraph discussing the benefits to farmers.

> Farmers get start-up cash from shareholders and thereby avoid the frustrating step of getting a bank loan that they must repay with interest. Also, the risk that farmers normally bear alone is now shared. In times of emergencies like floods and droughts, farmers can call on shareholders to pitch in and work to avert crops rotting in the field, weeds choking plants, or soil requiring mulch. Through participation, shareholders get a thorough education about farms and farmers. Consequently, farmers are no longer invisible members of the community; they gain standing and a well-deserved reputation for hard and essential work.

Additional sections of the argument could describe the benefits to consumers and the advantages of eliminating shipping and middlemen. A few illustrations of successful CSA projects would also help support the feasibility of this kind of farming.

If you have already listed the cons of the argument, you could check your list for any that seem persuasive. Then you could position the refutation at the end of the paper.

> The primary fear of farmers is probably that people will not participate. However, participation should not be a problem if farmers can adequately explain the system. In fact, many people who do not own land feel detached and dependent. They would probably welcome the change to become a part of the process, to see things grow, to taste fresh food free from unnecessary chemical additives. Thus, the key is explanation. Organizers must present a clear statement that includes details about cost per share and shareholder responsibilities. Also, they must be specific about what will be planted, which chemicals will be used, and how produce will be divided. The agricultural system is not easy to set up, but its rewards are worth the effort.



The classical structure can be fairly easily adapted to any subject. Here, for example, is another version of the format.

*Introduction* to subject and statement of thesis
*Concession* of any indisputable points
*Evidence* supporting the thesis
*Counterarguments* attacking the opposition's points
*Summary* of major points

Of course, when your subject warrants it, you can present just the essentials: an *introduction* to your subject and *statement of the thesis,* followed by the *supporting evidence.* Be sure, however, that you do not neglect other classical components if they would strengthen your argument.

### (2) The discovery structure

In the discovery structure, you invite the reader to explore a subject with you and finally to "discover" with you the natural, logical conclusions of your argument. Thus, your thesis appears in the middle or near the end of the paper. Although any argument can take this form, the discovery structure is a good choice when your subject is little understood. For example, to address a complicated problem such as disposal of nuclear waste, you could discuss alternatives and lead the reader to discover the most feasible.

Discovery is also a good choice when your position is likely to be unpopular. Suppose, for example, you want to argue this thesis: *Everyone between the ages of 18 and 21, except people in the military, should be required to work one year in community service.* Most people would react adversely to the idea because it suggests government infringement on individual freedom. By delaying the thesis, however, you could persuade an audience to consider, if not accept, the idea.

You could begin by discussing the problems that your proposal would help to solve. Your discussion could include some of the following ideas:

> Because of the military, the country seems fairly secure from outside threats; but our society is disrupted with a number of social problems. Too many of our young people have no family structure or supervision. Consequently, they drop out of school, thus losing any hope of meaningful jobs. Some escape into a world of drugs and crime. For some, gangs provide a substitute for family and the security of a group. Others live on welfare or on the street.
>
> As the population grows, the wear and tear on our physical and social environment increases. Litter proliferates; streets and highways are in disrepair; parks and other green spaces decay; schools and hospitals lack adequate staff and the money to provide it.
>
> Federal, state and local governments rely for funds on the already overtaxed white- and blue-collar workers, who now support the jobless, the homeless, and the elderly. Furthermore, as the economy slows and workers are laid off, the number of people with taxable income decreases.



You could support the discussion of problems with statistical details as well as demographic trends and predictions. You could also perhaps give case histories or hypothetical scenarios involving people affected by the problems.

Then you could introduce the importance of work to individual self-worth, supporting the claim with testimony from social workers or psychologists. Next, you could introduce the idea of a job corps and its many advantages to the participants.

> Working in meaningful jobs would give young people the supervision, the camaraderie, the self-discipline, and the social structure that many need so desperately. They would experience a sense of community and the pride that comes from accomplishment. Furthermore, participants would acquire skills in fields such as clerical work, carpentry, construction engineering, health care, recreation, forestry, and crime prevention.

You might also show how communities benefit.

> Schools, hospitals, parks, street and highway departments—all sorts of services would benefit from extra hands. Moreover, when people work toward improving the community, they better understand its problems and are less likely to demand instant solutions. Also, they develop community pride, which tends to discourage vandalism and crime.



You could use as supporting evidence the successes of communities and neighborhoods that have banded together to improve their collective lifestyle.

You could then move to your thesis, which the audience might now be prepared to accept or at least to consider. You could conclude by asserting that your proposal would be cost efficient: it would provide job training, reduce crime, and increase the number of productive citizens.

The strength of the discovery technique is that you delay the thesis until you can establish a background for its acceptance.

### (3) The Rogerian structure

The Rogerian argument was named for the psychologist Carl Rogers, who developed the strategy as a means of compromise between warring factions. According to Rogers, the purpose of many arguments should be not to win but rather to find the truth or to solve a problem. To use the Rogerian format, you structure your argument in five parts.

*Statement of the problem* explains the problem that led to the conflict.

*Opponent's position* gives an objective statement of the opposing view, without attacking it.

*Your position* gives an objective statement of your view.
*Areas of agreement* points out where the two sides agree.
*Resolution* suggests a compromise that solves the problem to the satisfaction of both sides.

Obviously, the strategy in the Rogerian structure is to concentrate on a solution rather than on victory. Thus, the format works well with emotionally charged subjects on which opposing sides can never agree completely—subjects such as abortion, pornography, and environmental issues. You would use a Rogerian argument to move the debate off the battleground of personal opinion and place it in an area of mutual benefit through cooperation.

You can also use the Rogerian structure for less controversial subjects. For example, suppose you wanted to argue that a business major is the best undergraduate degree for lawyers. You could begin by stating the problem: the quality of lawyers today is deteriorating. You could support this assertion with some sort of evidence—perhaps statements by judges or articles in periodicals, material that would be fairly easy to find in a library. Then, you could state the position of the side you oppose and move on to your thesis.



> Traditionally, law-school students have majored in liberal arts—usually political science, English, or history. However, that prelaw major is no longer relevant. Today, the primary legal problems are taxes, leases, mortgages, bankruptcies, and contracts—all involving knowledge of business. Therefore, the most valuable pre-law education would be in the business school of a university or college.

In the Rogerian structure, the next step is to point out areas of agreement. In this case, you could agree that liberal arts courses are important. Then you could move to the resolution—a compromise between the two pre-law curricula.

> Of course, lawyers deal primarily in words. Therefore, they must be able to write and speak well, and they must be able to comprehend what they read. Also, lawyers must understand politics and political theory. And they must have an overview of historical institutions and movements. Thus, the best pre-law curriculum is a business major with electives carefully chosen

from the school of liberal arts, electives that teach the specific skills and knowledge that lawyers need. The reverse would be impractical because a major in liberal arts would leave little time for important business electives.

Whichever structure you choose, you are not bound to it irrevocably. As you work through successive drafts of your paper, you may want to adapt the chosen structure to your particular subject. Or you may want to change to another structure altogether. Your goal is to write an effective argument, not to force your material into a specific format. Remember that the process of writing an argument is like the process of writing anything: one draft will not likely produce a good paper. You should expect to make changes as you develop and refine the argument.



### EXERCISE 11

**Propose two subjects that would lend themselves to the classical structure; two, to the discovery structure; and two, to the Rogerian structure. Formulate theses for any three of the subjects and work up rough outlines.**

## 39g Sample Argument

The student who wrote the argument that follows was appalled by the amount of garbage that accumulated around the dumpster and in the parking lot at his apartment complex. He began asking questions about the subject "garbage" and found the two most important to be "What produces the garbage?" and "What can reduce it?" He then looked for relationships and found several potential conflicts—between lifestyle and garbage reduction, between packaging and garbage reduction, between food preparation and garbage reduction. In the library, the student consulted a few periodicals, including *Environmental Action, EPA Journal, Consumer Reports,* and *Garbage.* His reading not only turned up ideas and facts for use as evidence but also suggested another conflict that eventually framed his argument: recycling and composting versus reuse.

Reuse: The Garbage Solution

Too much of the United States is covered with trash, and the problem is getting worse. Trash litters the scene from city streets to country roads, from beaches to mountains, from deserts to forests. Recently, volunteers picked up 250,000 pounds of trash from just 76 miles along the Louisiana coast (*Garbage,* September/October 1991). That amounts to 3,289 pounds of trash per mile. Neighborhood residents pile up trash in front of houses, assuming that when it is out of sight, it has in fact vanished. Communities face increasing mounds of trash and spend ever larger sums to build landfills and incinerators to dispose of waste—not always safely. Trains and barges loaded with municipal trash and waste roam the country searching for places to dump their loads. People must change their attitudes. They must become more conscious of the volume of trash and waste and work to reduce it.

Recently, recycling has become popular as the answer to the problem. Certainly, recycling helps reduce the volume of trash, but it is not a complete solution. For one thing, recycling can be bothersome, and everyone will not put forth the effort required. Materials must be separated into several containers—one for aluminum, one for paper, one for glass, one for cans, and one for plastic. Bottles and cans must be rinsed out. Often glass must be separated by color, and paper must be sorted by type.

In addition, the recycling process that works well for glass and aluminum does not work as well for paper, tin cans, and plastic. With each recycling, the quality of paper gets worse, and the process releases pollutants because of the presence of chlorine and toxic ink. The tin must be separated from the steel in tin cans, requiring extra cost. And according to *Consumer Reports* (October 1991), municipal programs only rarely recycle polypropylene, a thermoplastic resin used in packaging and coatings. The most serious drawback to recycling, however, is that alone it cannot sufficiently reduce the glut of trash that constantly accumulates.

Likewise, composting is not a solution. It can help remove

some kinds of garbage. For example, food scraps and yard clippings can be converted into valuable humus for soil replacement or enrichment. But on a large scale, there are serious problems with composting. Materials that are not completely degradable, such as the plastic in many disposable diapers, are not compostable. Also, there is the difficulty of separating organic from inorganic material and uncontaminated from contaminated wastes. In addition, composting can produce bad odors that nearby residents will probably not tolerate.

The only effective solution is to reduce the amount of trash that we generate at ever-accelerating rates. Changing habits and merchandising practices will not be easy, but change is essential.

First, we must reduce packaging. Too many products come in multiple layers of wrapping. A typical microwavable meal comes on a plastic tray, covered with a plastic wrap, all placed inside a paperboard box. One particular frozen dinner comes wrapped inside five different layers of plastic. Fresh fruits and meats are displayed on unnecessary plastic trays and wrapped with unnecessary plastic wrap. Small objects like cassette tapes generally come in elaborate packaging four times the product's original size. Matchbox cars, which originally came in matchboxes, are now sold in foot-long plastic boxes. Understandably, this kind of packaging helps prevent pilfering; but it also increases cost and waste. In a recent television advertisement, a deodorant company boasts about its environmental attitude by pointing out that its product does not come in a box. Perhaps this attitude will spread. Consumers obviously do not control packaging, but by complaining and boycotting, they can certainly influence manufacturers.

Second, consumers can stop buying products that can be used only once. Reusable cloth towels or sponges can replace paper towels, and cloth diapers can replace disposable diapers. Reusable glasses, cups, dishes, and cookware can replace throw-away plastic and styrofoam. People faced with the inconvenience of washing and cleaning will not welcome these changes; but if they can be impressed with the seriousness of the trash explosion, they can be persuaded to work a little harder to save the environment.

Third, there must be widespread use of returnable or refillable bottles. Of course, glass can be successfully recycled, but it must be ground up and reprocessed. Reuse would be much cheaper and more energy efficient. For the consumer, the most obvious advantage to reusable bottles is the refund upon return. But another advantage is that the liquid inside these thick bottles stays fresher, gets colder, and tastes better because it undergoes fewer chemical changes than liquid in flimsy disposables. And with a little imagination, we could eliminate the annoying accumulation of bottles: in Germany, for example, shoppers bring refillable milk bottles to the market and fill them with milk from a machine. Manufacturers can be persuaded to make the necessary changes if throwaways were taxed. Some states have already successfully levied taxes on wasteful containers. More states and the federal government should follow suit.

Through a concerted effort, we can and must reduce the amount of trash that is overwhelming our environment. Consumers must change their purchasing habits and throwaway behavior to reduce the amount of trash they produce. They must view reduction as more important than either recycling or composting. Business and industry must recognize the wastefulness of excessive packaging and throwaway products. Finally, community, state, and federal governments must promote awareness and effectively enforce a clean environment.

## ❑ EXERCISE 12

1. Find the thesis in the student argument. Does the writer state the thesis more than once? If so, where?
2. What is the purpose and effect of the first paragraph?
3. Point out the evidence that supports the thesis.
4. Are there any concessions to the opposition?
5. Does the writer include refutation?
6. Does the writer use the classical, the discovery, or the Rogerian structure? Or does he use a combination?

# 40

# Research Papers in Progress

res
40a

The process of writing a research paper is not very different from the process of writing any paper: choosing a suitable subject and a clear purpose, gathering information, organizing, writing, and revising. And like other kinds of papers, research papers do not always develop in a sequence; writers must often retrace steps or sometimes even start over. In other ways, though, writing research papers is different. Instructors who assign these papers expect effective use of the library; successful paraphrasing, summarizing, and quoting of sources; and the accurate use of some system for citations and references.

## 40a Subject

When undertaking a research paper, choose your subject very carefully. No amount of work can salvage a poor choice. Good subjects come from many kinds of stimuli: an instructor, a textbook, a television program, your own curiosity. If you keep a journal, you might find a suitable subject there. Otherwise, you might try freewriting, brainstorming, or asking questions. (See Chapter 34, "The Search for Ideas.")

Another approach is to go to the library and browse through the material. The news stories, articles, editorials, and letters in newspapers and periodicals are often good sources. Encyclopedias, almanacs, and other reference books contain vast amounts of information. Indexes list topics and titles. In fact, you never know where you might find a subject that will fire your enthusiasm.

When you are deciding on a subject, you should make sure that it fits several criteria.

- The subject must suit the audience.

Although you must satisfy your instructor's expectations, you do not write to the instructor personally. Instead, you usually address a general audience made up of such readers as college students or graduates. Therefore, the subject should be one that would interest intelligent readers.

- The subject must suit the assignment.



Consider the type of paper assigned, its expected length, and the kind of material available or required. You may be expected to argue a thesis or to accumulate information. You may be expected to write a short paper of about five pages or a longer one of about twenty pages. You may be expected to use a few sources or a comprehensive body of available material. All these considerations can affect the subject you choose.

- The subject must not be too difficult.

Many writers get in trouble because they tackle topics that interest them, only to discover that reading the available information is too difficult. For example, suppose a nonexpert wants to write a paper on cancer research but finds that most of the sources are technical and sound like this: "Mutation affecting the 12th amino acid of the c-H-ras oncogene product occurs infrequently in human cancer." If you lack the background to understand the material that covers your subject, you will have to find a less technical subject.

- The subject must not require that an excessive number of sources be checked.

For some subjects like *Buddhism* or *Shakespeare,* you could easily find more than one hundred books listed in a typical library catalog. You know you cannot possibly search the material adequately within a reasonable time. Whenever you find too much material in the library, you know you must limit or change your subject. Instead of beginning with a subject like *crime,* begin with *detectives in literature;* instead of *earthquakes,* begin with *earthquakes and building.*

- A sufficient amount of material on the subject must be available.

The number of sources you will need depends on your assignment, the amount of usable information in each source, and the expected length of the paper. You should abandon a subject if you fear that insufficient material is available to develop it thoroughly. If you look up a subject like *hijacking yachts* and you find only one source, you could shift to *hijacking airlines,* which is more extensively covered, or change directions completely.

- The subject should have key words associated with it.



Key words are specific terms associated with a subject. They are the words that researchers look up in catalogs and indexes in order to find material. Subjects without key words are very difficult to research. What words could you look up for the subject *the problem of inefficiency in business?* An excessively general word like *business* leads to sources on a multitude of unrelated subjects, and abstract words like *inefficiency* or *problem* will not even be listed in catalogs and indexes. You get better results with a subject like *the effect of television advertising on the food choices of children.* It suggests key words (*television, advertising,* and possibly *consumers*) that can lead to useful sources of information. You might look in reference books and indexes before you definitely settle on a subject; you will then be sure that the subject has indexed key words that can lead to material.

- The subject must not be excessively broad.

Sometimes, you do not know at the beginning of a writing project whether a subject is the right choice. Writers frequently envision one paper but later, particularly after outlining, realize the scope is entirely too broad. The writer of the paper on discrimination in Japanese business (pp. 543–550) intended at first to write about all the problems within the Japanese system—inhumane factories, inflexibility, stress, slow promotion, lack of creativity, and discrimination. Then the writer discovered that he had attempted too much. The paper would be longer than the requirement or time would allow. Therefore, he restricted the topic to only two points—the discrimination against men without the right connections and the general discrimination against women.

### ❑ EXERCISE 1

The following scenarios describe some of the circumstances that affect decisions about subjects for research papers. Judge the appropriateness of each subject in light of the criteria discussed in 40a.

1. The writer plans a 10- to 20-page paper on the errors made by Hitler in World War II but finds a 288-page book entitled *Hitler's Mistakes.*
2. The writer is taking an introductory course in biology and plans to write a five- to ten-page paper on the recent findings about genetic diseases. The sources contain terms such as *phenylketonuria, factor VIII replacement,* and *adenosine deaminase deficiency.*
3. The writer has a rather good understanding of computers and wants to write a 20-page paper about the advantages of computer use.
4. Because the writer once played Juliet in Shakespeare's *Romeo and Juliet,* she wants to know more about other female roles. She plans to write a 20-page paper on women in Shakespeare's plays.
5. The writer has heard of water pollution in other states and wants to find out the extent of this problem in his. A search of the library turns up only three articles, and one of them is eleven years old.



## 40b Purpose

A subject suitable for research has a clear purpose that will direct and limit the amount of material to be gathered. Without a clear purpose, a paper will likely contain bits and pieces of information that are only loosely tied together. For example, the subject *Meriwether Lewis* lacks purpose. What will be the point of the paper? What material will be included? On the other hand, the question *Was Meriwether Lewis murdered?* gives direction to the paper. The writer can concentrate on answering the question.

A good subject is inextricably linked to the purpose of the research. To stimulate and focus your research, you can look for a question that has not been definitively answered, an issue you feel strongly about, or scattered information that needs synthesizing.

### (1) Answering a question

One common stimulus for research is an intriguing question or mystery.

Was the Hindenburg sabotaged by enemy agents?

Why did the dinosaurs die out?

Can gorillas learn to talk?

Why did the poet Ezra Pound collaborate with the Fascists?

What produces the special sound of Stradivari violins?

The sample paper on Mark Twain (pp. 526–535) began with this sort of motivation. After reading in the *Oxford Companion to American Literature* that Mark Twain had left the Confederate army during the Civil War, the writer decided to find out why. If the purpose of your paper is to answer a question, you can support one answer or explore several possible answers.



### (2) Presenting an argument

Another logical purpose for a research paper is to present an argument. The sample paper on pages 543–550 argues that in the Japanese business world, discrimination exists against some men and most women. Throughout the discussion, the writer tries to convince readers that this opinion is sound.

If you decide to write an argument, first be sure that the subject is debatable. You should not try to argue an established fact or take a position that everyone would agree on. For example, you are not likely to generate much debate if you argue that Byron wrote poetry, that computer literacy is an asset, or that drunken drivers are dangerous. You could argue, however, that despite Byron's denial, the poem *Childe Harold's Pilgrimage* is autobiographical; that computer literacy should be required of all college graduates; that drunken drivers should be sentenced to perform public service rather than to serve time in jail.

Some subjects, even though arguable, have been overdone to the point that very little interesting or new can be written about them. You are wise to avoid topics like abortion, marijuana, and the death penalty unless you can contribute fresh ideas to these subjects.

### (3) Surveying the literature

Another common motivation for a research paper is to collect material and present a survey of the information available on a subject.

This type of paper (sometimes called a literature review, a narrative bibliography, or a bibliographic essay) can provide a great service to readers. Suppose a reader wants to know what has been written about the current condition of the prisons in Michigan. Ordinarily, getting that information would require hours of searching and reading. But a compilation of this information, succinctly and clearly presented, gives the reader a convenient shortcut. A survey paper might reveal the latest information on subjects such as nausea in space travel, the weaknesses of standardized tests, the use of animals in transplant research, or the critical reception of a novel. The sample paper on pages 558–564 surveys information available on taste research.



## ❑ EXERCISE 2

Answer the following questions to get an idea of how the purpose of a paper is linked to its subject.

1. What question or mystery is associated with three of the following? If you do not know, check in an encyclopedia or some other library source.

   the death of John F. Kennedy
   the events at the Alamo
   the building of the pyramids
   the identity of the dark lady of Shakespeare's sonnets
   water on Mars
   the meaning of dreams
   the Bermuda Triangle

2. What position could you argue in a research paper on three of the following issues? If necessary, use an encyclopedia or some other library source for background.

   the best Union Civil War general
   the turning point of the Kennedy-Nixon presidential campaign of 1960
   the causes of criminal behavior
   astrology's reliability
   immigration to America
   the guilt of Alger Hiss
   the Nagasaki bomb

3. Assume you must write a 10- to 20-page paper surveying the literature written on a particular subject. Which of the following subjects seem appropriate for such a paper?

**the ill effects of working long hours with a video display terminal (VDT)**
**interpretations of T. S. Eliot's "The Love Song of J. Alfred Prufrock"**
**developments in computer technology**
**conditions in the national parks**
**opinions about the acting ability of Clint Eastwood**

## 40c Preliminary Library Research



Whether you have a clear purpose or merely a tentative one, you must do preliminary library work to check its suitability, to put it in focus, and to make sure you can unify the diverse bits of information you will collect and assemble. Thus, at this point, you must go to a library and spend time searching, reading, and thinking.

In the library, you need to accumulate a bibliography (a record of the material you find) because later you will want to return to any relevant information. Also at this stage, you may take some preliminary notes on information that you are fairly sure you can use. Never trust your memory; as you move from source to source, you will forget many ideas and where you found them. Nevertheless, you should not mistake the preliminary stages of research with the actual note-taking stage. If you do, two problems may occur. First, you very possibly will end up throwing away notes you have laboriously written. Second, more likely, you may try to use your notes whether they fit or not, and the resulting paper will be a disconnected hodgepodge. To avoid these problems, you should read widely to focus the subject and weed out inappropriate material.

To begin your search of the library, you must understand what is housed there and how to retrieve whatever you need. In other words, you must know what kinds of sources exist and how they are organized.

### (1) Primary and secondary sources

Libraries have two types of material—primary and secondary sources. Primary sources are firsthand, original material such as eyewitness accounts, letters, diaries, original investigations, speeches, literary works, and autobiographies. Secondary sources are those that analyze, combine, or comment on other sources.

| *Primary Source* | *Secondary Source* |
|---|---|
| transcript of a trial | reporter's interpretation of a trial |
| Constitution | historian's analysis of the Constitution |
| poem | literary critic's explanation of a poem's meaning |
| data of a scientific study | textbook's discussion of the significance of a study |

Each type of material has its advantages. Secondary sources, which interpret and pull together other materials, can simplify your research and expand its breadth. Primary sources, on the other hand, can have greater immediacy and impact. Some subjects are best developed through primary sources; others through secondary; some require both types. Use whatever sources are appropriate and available.



## (2) Library organization

Although all libraries do not use the same system, they do share characteristics. All libraries have a central desk where you can get information and check out books; all libraries have some sort of reference area, which contains such works as encyclopedias, dictionaries, indexes, almanacs, and other research aids. All libraries have a catalog of holdings and specific areas for books and for periodicals. In addition, all libraries arrange books according to some numbering system, most often the Library of Congress system or Dewey Decimal System. The call number assigned to each book identifies its location and appears in the catalog and on the book. If you are unfamiliar with the library you plan to use, check signs, brochures, and handouts for information about locations. And when necessary, do not hesitate to ask questions of the librarians.

## (3) The reference area

Once you know general locations in the library, you then need to find specific resources. The reference area contains material that is absolutely essential in research. This area usually houses two kinds of material. The first includes encyclopedias, dictionaries, almanacs, and other general works that can provide you with an overview of a subject and help you find a supportable thesis. The second kind includes catalogs, indexes, and abstracts. These direct you to other books, articles, and reports that contain the information you will search for useful material.

### (4) General works

To find general information about your subject, you search the reference works that contain broad, comprehensive surveys. But first, you must determine which reference works will help you research your particular subject.



If you are new to library research, particularly in an academic or research library, you might find the following scenario helpful. Assume you enter the library and locate the reference area. You see hundreds of books. Which ones should you check? Although reference works are indexed by subject in the catalog, you might thumb through many cards or hunt through many lists unproductively. A better way is to figure out how your library's collection is organized. A library usually posts its numbering system, but if not, ask a librarian for help. The general works, like encyclopedias, are the easiest to find. They are marked with an A in a library using the Library of Congress system and with the numbers 000–099 in a library using the Dewey Decimal System. The other reference works also are arranged systematically by call number. For example, American history appears in the 970s in the Dewey system and under E or F in the Library of Congress system. Knowing the system, you can browse along the rows of books, looking for useful sources.

Another suggestion is to look at some of the following works. These reference works mainly provide an overview of a subject and suggest how to limit it. Sometimes they contain bibliographies that supply the names of pertinent books and articles. Although not exhaustive, the list indicates the kinds of material available in reference collections.

**Encyclopedias**
***General***

*Encyclopedia Americana*
*Encyclopaedia Britannica*
*Collier's Encyclopedia*
*New Columbia Encyclopedia*

***Humanities***

*Encyclopedia of American History*

*Encyclopedia of World History*
*American Political Dictionary*
*Encyclopedia of Philosophy*
*Encyclopedia of World Literature in the 20th Century*
*Worldmark Encyclopedia of the Nations*
*Readers' Encyclopedia*
*Encyclopedia of Science Fiction and Fantasy*
*Encyclopedia of Mystery and Detection*

**Social Sciences**

*International Encyclopedia of the Social Sciences*
*Encyclopedia of Sociology*
*Encyclopedia of Psychology*
*Encyclopedia of Social Work*
*Encyclopedia of Education*
*Encyclopedia of Advertising*

**Science and Technology**

*McGraw-Hill Encyclopedia of Science and Technology*
*Van Nostrand's Scientific Encyclopedia*
*Encyclopedia of the Biological Sciences*
*Encyclopedia of Chemistry*
*Encyclopedia of Computer Science*
*Grzimek's Encyclopedia of Ecology*

**Film and Television**

*Magill's Survey of Cinema*
*New York Times Encyclopedia of Film*
*Complete Encyclopedia of Television Programs, 1947–1979*
*New York Times Encyclopedia of Television*
*Focal Encyclopedia of Film and Television Techniques*

**Sports**

*Sportsman's Encyclopedia*
*Encyclopedia of the Olympic Games*
*Encyclopedia of Football*
*Official World Encyclopedia of Sports and Games*

**Art and Music**

*Encyclopedia of World Art*
*Britannica Encyclopedia of American Art*
*Encyclopedia of Painting*
*International Cyclopedia of Music and Musicians*
*World's Encyclopedia of Recorded Music*
*Encyclopedia of Pop, Rock, and Soul*

### Biographies

#### *General*

*Who's Who in America*
*International Who's Who*
*Who's Who (British)*
*Dictionary of American Biography*
*Dictionary of National Biography (British)*
*Webster's Biographical Dictionary*
*Current Biography*
*New York Times Biographical Service*
*Biography and Genealogy Master Index*

#### *Specialized*

*Contemporary Authors*
*Twentieth Century Authors*
*American Men and Women of Science*
*Biographical Dictionary of Scientists*
*Dictionary of Scientific Biography*
*Who's Who in Rock*
*Who's Who in Horror and Fantasy Fiction*

### Handbooks and Manuals

*Oxford Companion to English Literature*
*Oxford Companion to American Literature*
*Historian's Handbook*
*Handbook of Chemistry and Physics*
*Engineering Manual*
*Occupational Outlook Handbook*
*United States Government Manual*
*TV Facts*
*Filmgoer's Companion*
*Oxford Companion to Sports and Games*

### Atlases and Gazeteers

*Atlas of the Universe*
*National Geographic Atlas of the World*
*Oxford Economic Atlas of the World*
*Times Atlas of the World*
*Webster's New Geographical Dictionary*

### Almanacs and Yearbooks

*Facts on File*
*Statesman's Year-Book*
*Statistical Abstract of the United States*
*World Almanac and Book of Facts*

*Yearbook of the United Nations*
*Americana Annual*
*Britannica Book of the Year*
*Broadcasting Yearbook*

## (5) Keywords



To find material on a subject, you must check lists of sources—catalogs, indexes, and abstracts. There, you find subjects listed in alphabetical order under headings, called *keywords,* or *descriptors.* Sometimes you must look under not just one keyword but several.

You can find the keywords that may lead you to sources by checking in the volumes entitled *Library of Congress: Subject Headings.* For example, to find out what is known about how people taste food (the topic of the sample research paper on pp. 558–564), the researcher looked up *taste* and found the entry shown in Figure 1. It lists keywords that can be searched manually in the catalogs, indexes, and abstracts. You can also find keywords for computer searches in thesauruses such as the *Thesaurus of ERIC Descriptors.*

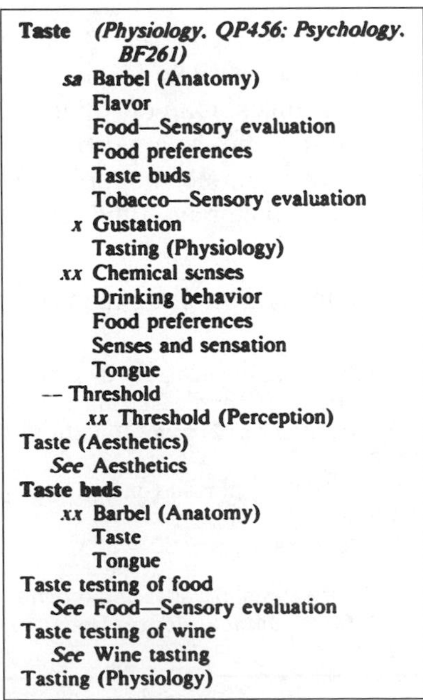

**Taste** *(Physiology. QP456: Psychology. BF261)*
*sa* **Barbel (Anatomy)**
**Flavor**
**Food—Sensory evaluation**
**Food preferences**
**Taste buds**
**Tobacco—Sensory evaluation**
*x* **Gustation**
**Tasting (Physiology)**
*xx* **Chemical senses**
**Drinking behavior**
**Food preferences**
**Senses and sensation**
**Tongue**
**— Threshold**
*xx* **Threshold (Perception)**
**Taste (Aesthetics)**
*See* **Aesthetics**
**Taste buds**
*xx* **Barbel (Anatomy)**
**Taste**
**Tongue**
**Taste testing of food**
*See* **Food—Sensory evaluation**
**Taste testing of wine**
*See* **Wine tasting**
**Tasting (Physiology)**

**Figure 1** Keywords relating to *taste*

## (6) Catalogs

Once you know keywords, or subject headings, that could lead to useful sources, you should look in your library's main catalog, a primary aid for locating material. Catalogs vary from library to library. Some are the traditional files, alphabetically arranged drawers with each item listed on an index card. Increasingly files are computerized or copied on microfilm. Some catalogs contain all the library's holdings; others contain only lists of books, not periodicals.

res 40c

Whatever its format, a catalog will contain three entries for every work—title, author, and subject. Sometimes the entries are separated into different files, with titles in one, authors in another, and subjects in yet another. Other times all entries (title, author, and subject) are arranged alphabetically in one file. At this point, since you are looking for information on a subject, you will look primarily at the subject file for sources. In a traditional card catalog the subject cards contain the information shown in Figure 2. A computerized catalog using the Library of Congress system lists the works available (Figure 3) and then gives more detailed information about selected items (Figure 4).

A "bibliography" notation means that the work contains a list of additional sources on the same subject. A bibliography can save you time since someone else has already gone through the catalogs and indexes compiling sources. One drawback is that you do not always know how thorough the list is. Also, these lists are not always up to date. However, they can supply very useful supplements to your own list of materials. Bibliographies also may be

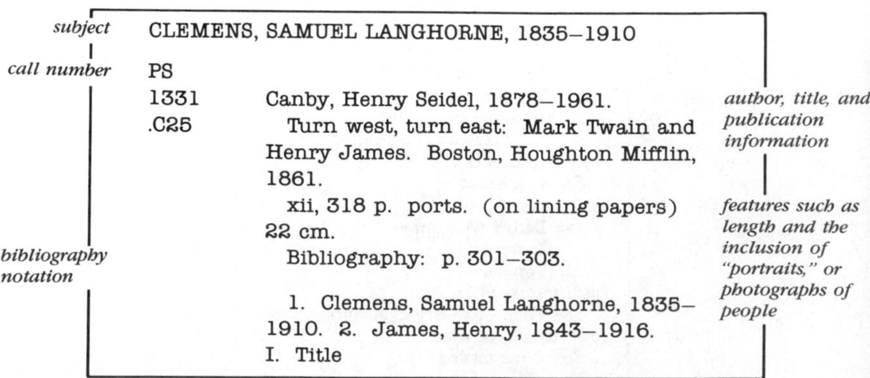

subject
CLEMENS, SAMUEL LANGHORNE, 1835–1910
call number
PS
1331
.C25
Canby, Henry Seidel, 1878–1961.
Turn west, turn east: Mark Twain and Henry James. Boston, Houghton Mifflin, 1861.
xii, 318 p. ports. (on lining papers) 22 cm.
Bibliography: p. 301–303.
1. Clemens, Samuel Langhorne, 1835–1910. 2. James, Henry, 1843–1916. I. Title
author, title, and publication information
features such as length and the inclusion of "portraits," or photographs of people
bibliography notation


**Figure 2** Subject card

```
FILE:LCCC; TITLE/LINE-SET 3
                              ITEMS 10-15 OF 277
10.  62-19224: Smith, Henry Nash. Mark
       Twain. Cambridge, Belknap Press
       of Harvard University Press,
       1962. ix, 212 p, 25 cm. LC CALL
       NUMBER: PS1331 .S55 1962
11.  63-11599: Smith, Henry Nash. Mark
       Twain. Englewood Cliffs, N.J.,
       Prentice-Hall, 1963. 179 p, 22 cm.
       LC CALL NUMBER: PS1331 .S548 1963
12.  64-21709: Duckett, Margaret. Mark
       Twain and Bret Harte. Norman,
       University of Oklahoma Press,
       1964. xiii, 365 p, illus., ports,
       23 cm. LC CALL NUMBER: PS1333 .D8
13.  65-20437: Salsbury, Edith Colgate.
       Susy and Mark Twain. New York,
       Harper & Row, 1965. xvii, 444 p,
       illus., ports, 25 cm. LC CALL
       NUMBER: PS1332 .S3
14.  66-11966: Cox, James Melville. Mark
       Twain. Princeton, N.J., Princeton
       University Press, 1966. viii, 321
       p, 23 cm. LC CALL NUMBER: PS1331
       .C6
15.  66-17603: Kaplan, Justin. Mr.
       Clemens and Mark Twain. New York,
       Simon and Schuster, 1966. 424 p,
       illus., ports, 24 cm. LC CALL
       NUMBER: PS1331 .K33
READY FOR NEW COMMAND OR NEW ITEM NBR (FOR
NEXT PAGE, XMIT ONLY)
```

**Figure 3** Partial printout of works available

```
     66-17603    ITEM 15 OF 277 IN SET 3  (LCCC)

Kaplan, Justin,
  Mr. Clemens and Mark Twain, a
    biography. New York, Simon and
    Schuster, 1966. 424 p. illus., ports,
    24 cm.
LC CALL NUMBER: PS1331 .K33
DEWEY DEC: 817.4 B
SUBJECTS (INDX): Twain, Mark-1835-1910
NOTES:
  Bibliographical references included
    in "Notes" (p. 389-410)
READY FOR NEW COMMAND
```

*author, title, and publication information*

*call numbers*

*bibliography notation*

**Figure 4** Detailed information about #15 (Figure 3)

listed in encyclopedias, other reference books, and specialized volumes such as the *Bibliographic Index* (1937–) and the *World Bibliography of Bibliographies* (1939–). *The Subject Guide to Books in Print* (*BIP*) and the *Cumulative Book Index* (*CBI*)—both comprehensive bibliographies of books—may be worth checking for sources on your subject.

If you use other researchers' bibliographies or comprehensive bibliographies of published books, you may find that your library does not own the books you want. In this case, you might consider getting the books on loan from another library, if the service is available. However, before you order a book on interlibrary loan, you might check the *Book Review Digest,* where you can find book reviews describing many publications. The information there will give you a good idea whether a wait for the material is worth the time, especially since the wait may be lengthy.



### The Computer Connection

Although the electronic, paperless library envisioned by many futurists is not here, you can expect to find more and more libraries with computer systems. Because of the cost, all libraries will not have the newest technology, but several large research libraries have provided online computer searches for about 10 years. The most common online system available today is the catalog of a library's holdings, called an OPAC (online public-access catalog). Searching the catalog with a computer eliminates the tedious job of thumbing through cards stuffed in cramped drawers. In addition to OPAC, you may also find other computerized resources, such as encyclopedias, dictionaries, thesauruses, and lists of quotations.

#### *Suggestions for Using Online and Ondisc Reference Material*

- Use the computer catalog, when available, to save time. The computer will usually print out a list and eliminate the need to copy entries. A big advantage of an online catalog is that with a modem, you can conduct your search on a home computer.
- You can make a computer search even if you have little experience. Computers are getting more user-friendly, and directions for using them are fairly short and simple.
- Be sure to learn the dates covered in any database you use. Frequently, online material will be the most recent. If you are searching for old sources, you may have to use printed material.
- Learn to use Boolean searches to speed up your work. To link ideas, you type AND between two terms—*suicide* AND *students* or *steroids* AND *athletes.* To search alternative terms, you type OR between them—*high schools* OR *secondary education* or *health* OR *wellness.* To exclude unwanted sources, you type NOT—*pollution* NOT *noise* or *drugs* NOT *medical.*

- Don't hesitate to ask librarians for assistance; large research libraries employ people trained in online searches.
- Learn about hypertext; an opportunity to use it would be interesting and profitable. In hypertext, several sources are linked. When the technology becomes generally available, you can move at will back and forth among many sources—for example, from a book to an encyclopedia to a dictionary, and on some systems even to a recording or film.

*For reading:* Auster, Ethel, ed. *The Online Searcher.* New York: Neal-Schuman Publishers, 1990.

## (7) Indexes and abstracts

The library's catalog helps you locate books rather quickly, but the material on many subjects will come mainly from periodicals—journals, magazines, and newspapers. A search of periodicals is essential to ensure that you have not overlooked valuable information.



No matter what subject you are researching, you will probably find it covered in some index. Many indexes provide general coverage; many others are very specialized, covering publications in only one area, such as in ecology, biography, or physics. Some indexes give only publication information; others also provide summaries, or abstracts.

But be forewarned; you cannot rush to the library and complete your work in an hour. Many searches require a time-consuming examination of the printed indexes. Usually you must check several different periodical indexes and many volumes of each index. If you are trying to locate very current information, the issues may not be bound or cumulatively indexed. Consequently, you may have to search a number of unbound monthly issues. Although a search of the periodical indexes takes time, much valuable information could never be located without their help. Even if your library provides a computer search of the indexes, you must allow enough time to complete it. You may need an appointment with a librarian to do a thorough search of the right data bases.

### Searches of printed indexes and abstracts

Most students search the indexes shelved in the library. The advantage of such a search is that students have a degree of control. They can pick the indexes that cover material within their level of expertise, and they are free to shift and change the focus of their research as it progresses.

If you are not familiar with the indexes in the library, there are several things you can do. One is to consult *Guide to Reference*

*Works,* edited by Eugene Sheehy. This guide lists general and specialized indexes that contain information for the social sciences, the humanities, history, or the pure and applied sciences. You can also ask reference librarians for advice and browse the shelves in appropriate sections.

*General Indexes and Abstracts* For material on most topics, people usually start with a search of *Readers' Guide to Periodical Literature.* It indexes articles in popular periodicals such as *Time, Esquire,* and *Psychology Today.* For newspaper articles, most people use the *New York Times Index,* and for government documents, the *Monthly Catalog of United States Government Publications.* If your paper involves a person, you will want to search the *Biography Index.* An excellent starting place for topics related to science and technology is the *General Science Index;* most of the sources indexed there are clear to people without a technical background.

*Specialized Indexes and Abstracts* After checking in the general works, you should then turn to more specialized indexes. The following list contains indexes you will find valuable for the humanities, social sciences, and science and technology.

### Humanities

*International Index* (1907–1965)
*Social Sciences and Humanities Index* (1965–1974)
*Humanities Index* (1974–)
*MLA International Bibliography* (1921–)
*Essay and General Literature Index* (1900–)
*Historical Abstracts* (1955–)
*America: History and Life* (1964–)
*Music Index* (1949–)
*Art Index* (1929–)
*Book Review Index* (1905–)

### Social Sciences

*Social Sciences and Humanities Index* (1965–1974)
*Social Sciences Index* (1974–)
*Sociological Abstracts* (1975–)
*Psychological Abstracts* (1975–)
*Business Periodicals Index* (1958–)
*P.A.I.S.* (*Public Affairs Information Service*) (1915–)
*Index to Legal Periodicals* (1886–)
*Criminology and Penology Abstracts* (1961–)
*Education Index* (1929–)
*Current Index to Journals in Education* (*CIJE*) (1969–)
*American Statistics Index* (*ASI*) (1973–)

## Science and Technology

*Applied Science and Technology Index* (1958–)
*Biological Abstracts* (1926–)
*Biological and Agricultural Index* (1947–)
*Chemical Abstracts* (1907–)
*Engineering Index* (1906–)
*Computer and Control Abstracts* (1966–)
*Computer Literature Index* (1980–)
*Cumulated Index Medicus* (1960–)
*Hospital Literature Index* (1955–)
*Technical Book Review Index* (1935–)

If you are using an index for the first time, you may need an explanation of its format and any unfamiliar abbreviations. You can find instructions and explanations by consulting the information that usually appears at the front of each issue. Most indexes are not difficult to use; they generally follow a format similar to the one illustrated in Figure 5 from the *Readers' Guide*.

res 40c

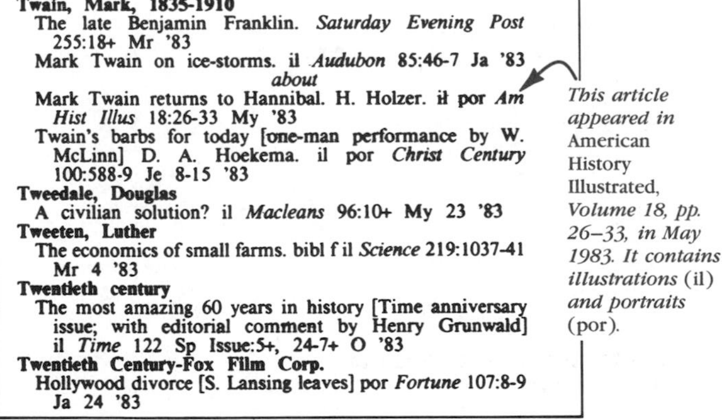
**Twain, Mark, 1835-1910**
The late Benjamin Franklin. *Saturday Evening Post* 255:18+ Mr '83
Mark Twain on ice-storms. il *Audubon* 85:46-7 Ja '83
*about*
Mark Twain returns to Hannibal. H. Holzer. il por *Am Hist Illus* 18:26-33 My '83
Twain's barbs for today [one-man performance by W. McLinn] D. A. Hoekema. il por *Christ Century* 100:588-9 Je 8-15 '83
**Tweedale, Douglas**
A civilian solution? il *Macleans* 96:10+ My 23 '83
**Tweeten, Luther**
The economics of small farms. bibl f il *Science* 219:1037-41 Mr 4 '83
**Twentieth century**
The most amazing 60 years in history [Time anniversary issue; with editorial comment by Henry Grunwald] il *Time* 122 Sp Issue:5+, 24-7+ O '83
**Twentieth Century-Fox Film Corp.**
Hollywood divorce [S. Lansing leaves] por *Fortune* 107:8-9 Ja 24 '83

*This article appeared in* American History Illustrated, *Volume 18, pp. 26–33, in May 1983. It contains illustrations* (il) *and portraits* (por).

**Figure 5** Excerpt from *Readers' Guide*

### Computer searches of indexes and abstracts

Many indexes are now listed in databases, which can be searched by computer in a fraction of the time it would take a person to use the paper versions. Some computer searches of indexes are free or inexpensive; researchers with an appropriate computer terminal can conduct a search themselves by following simple instructions. However, many databases are limited in scope—for example, they may include only popular periodicals, and they may cover only a limited number of years. If you conduct an online search, be sure to check the scope of the database.

Some libraries provide searches of commercial databases, but a search may cost about ten dollars or more, depending on the amount of information printed out. In many cases, the printouts are so thorough that the sources listed are unavailable in the average library. For specialists, who must thoroughly search the literature, the procedure can be invaluable; for undergraduates, however, a search of commercial files is not always advisable.

A computer search of the Magazine Index (MI), using the keyword "taste research," turned up ten sources. Figure 6 shows three of these sources. Of the ten, only one contained the kind of information that the student writer could use in her paper (pp. 558–564). Notice that the entry from the printout gives the name of the periodical and all the information needed to locate the article precisely. In addition, the entry shows that the full text of the article is in the computer's database. If the library did not have the periodical, the student could have gotten the article on a computer printout, but usually at a cost.



```
5/3/1
2005589  DATABASE: MI File 47
  New tastes for seniors. (loss of sense
    of taste)
  Berton, Paul
  Maclean's 98 P60(1) Dec 16 1985
  CODEN: MCNMB

5/3/2
1919336  DATABASE: MI File 47 *Use Format
  9 for FULL TEXT*
  A question of taste in space.
  Savold, David
  Science '85 v6 p86(2) March 1985
  illustration; photograph
  AVAILABILITY: FULL TEXT Online
  LINE COUNT: 00054

5/3/3
1905946  DATABASE: MI File 47
  Space taste. (loss of sense of taste
    during space flight)
  Engler, Nick
  Omni v7 p31(1) May 1985
  CODEN: OMNIDQ
  COLLECTION 28E4318
  illustration; photograph
  AVAILABILITY: COLLECTION 28E4318
```

*source used in paper (pp. 558–564)*

**Figure 6** Printout from computer search

## ❑ EXERCISE 3

Answer these questions about your library.

1. Where is the reference area?
2. Which numbering system does your library use?
3. Where are the encyclopedias?
4. Where are the general biographies?
5. Where are the atlases?
6. Where are the almanacs?
7. Is your library's catalog a single alphabetical file or are the subject, title, and author files separated?
8. Is the catalog computerized?
9. Where is the *Library of Congress: Subject Headings?*
10. Where are the microfilms?
11. Where is the *Readers' Guide to Periodical Literature?*
12. Where is the *New York Times Index?*
13. Where is the *Monthly Catalog of United States Government Publications?*
14. Where are the specialized indexes and abstracts?
15. Does your library provide a computer search of the indexes?



## ❑ EXERCISE 4

By using the resources of your library, find answers to the following questions. List the sources you used to find the answers.

1. What is the largest state east of the Mississippi?
2. Who wrote *Old Possum's Book of Practical Cats?*
3. Whose pseudonym was Diedrick Knickerbocker?
4. Who is the only President buried in Washington, D.C.?
5. What are quarks and squarks?
6. What is an example of a Spoonerism?
7. Who was Laodamia?
8. Who won the men's and women's singles competition at Wimbledon in 1965?
9. What is the origin of the word *infantry?*
10. Who played the dwarf in the 1931 version of *Frankenstein?*

**The Computer Connection**

Consider the time it takes to search through yearly lists of periodical articles published in various indexes. Simply looking through the *Readers' Guide* alone is time consuming, and probably you must look through several additional indexes in compiling a bibliography for a single research project.

Computer searches can save you an enormous amount of time. Most libraries are constantly enlarging their capacity for online searches, so whenever possible, take advantage of computers for doing research. Not only is the computer search faster, but the computer will usually print out a list and save you copying time.

***Suggestions for Using Online or Ondisc Indexes***

- For your search, carefully select keywords, often called *descriptors.* It's better to check in a thesaurus, such as *Thesaurus of ERIC Descriptors* and *Thesaurus of Psychological Index Terms* to make sure a word is listed in the database. Without the best keyword, a researcher risks overlooking valuable sources or paying for useless lists.
- Locate newspaper articles by using such databases as the Information Bank (index to the *New York Times,* and many other important papers, including the *Washington Post* and *Los Angeles Times*), the Dow Jones News/Retrieval Service (index to the *Wall Street Journal* and *United Press International*), and NEWSEARCH (daily index of more than 2000 news stories, information articles, and book reviews).
- Search for popular magazine articles in the *Magazine Index* (MI) or the *Readers' Guide* (RG), if these are available on computer.
- Search for information in specialized fields by using such databases as ERIC (education), MLA Bibliography (language and literature), PsycINFO (psychology), PAIS (public affairs), Chemical Abstracts (chemistry), and BIOSIS (biology).
- Of special value are the databases that contain, in addition to the bibliographic entry, the full text, which you can get printed out. ERIC can print complete articles, and the Information Bank contains the complete articles from the *New York Times.*

*For reading:* Batt, Fred. *Online searching for end users: An Information Sourcebook.* Phoenix, Arizona: Oryx Press, 1988.



# 40d Working Bibliography

As you locate promising sources in the catalogs, indexes, and printouts, you should write down information such as author, title, publication, call number, volume, date, page number, the place where you found the citation—anything that will help you find the sources in the library. This information should be checked for accuracy when you use the work itself. You can also add any other information you need for documenting sources according to the style assigned by your instructor. In this way you can prevent having to go back to look up such details later on.

The traditional method for preparing a working bibliography is to put the information about each source on a separate index card like the one in Figure 7.

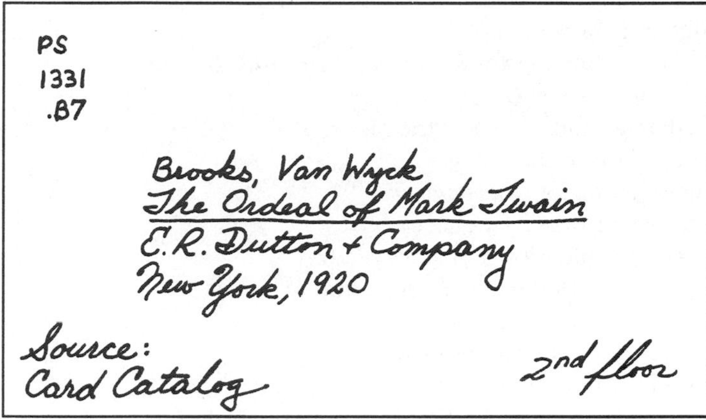

PS
1331
.B7
Brooks, Van Wyck
The Ordeal of Mark Twain
E.R. Dutton + Company
New York, 1920
Source:
Card Catalog
2nd floor


**Figure 7** Bibliography card



The advantage of using cards is that when you find a source unavailable or irrelevant, you can throw the card away; the stack that is left becomes your "working" bibliography—the sources you will examine closely for possible inclusion in your research paper. Also, you can shuffle the cards into either alphabetical order or the order of use so that you can easily type the reference page in your final paper.

## ❑ EXERCISE 5

**Pick one of the following subjects or choose a subject of your own. Do enough preliminary research to decide on a specific purpose: to answer a question, to argue a position, to review the literature. Then gather a working bibliography.**

**Union spies during the Civil War**
**Edgar Allan Poe's detective stories**
**The nutritional value of the hot dog**
**Pershing's pursuit of Pancho Villa**
**Zombies: fact or fiction**
**The perfume industry**

The death of Mountbatten
Nineteenth-century attitudes toward venereal disease
Voyager 2's pictures of Uranus
The authenticity of *Clan of the Cave Bear*
The death and resurrection of Sherlock Holmes
Computer chess champions
Symbolism in Hemingway's *The Old Man and the Sea*
The food of Classical Greece
Elizabethan attitudes toward the Moors
Bohemian Paris in the 1880s
The pirate utopia of Libertatia
Esperanto: a universal language
The flying machines of Paul MacCready
The meaning of Oedipus's self-blinding
The discoverers of penicillin
Computers in the movie industry
El Niño's effect on the weather
The condition of the bullet that killed President Kennedy



## 40e Locating Material

You do not have to accumulate a complete bibliography before you begin to locate the books, articles, and reports you have listed. In other words, if you notice a title that sounds interesting, find the source and read it. By reading widely as your paper takes shape, you will have options. The more you know about your subject, the better you will be able to control it: to narrow it, broaden it, shift the focus, or even abandon it altogether. And the sooner, the better.

To locate the sources you have listed, you must be familiar with the layout of your library and the system it uses. In some libraries, the shelves of books are open to users. In that case, you locate books by call numbers. If your library's books are in an area closed to general use, you write out call numbers, authors, and titles on slips of paper. Then a library employee gets the books for you. Special locations—such as specialized reading rooms and departmental libraries—will be noted in the catalogs, usually under call numbers. Be sure to write down these locations, and if necessary, use the library map to find the material.

Your library probably has a separate catalog—called a periodical file—that lists the available periodicals and their locations. The periodicals may be in a closed area, but often they are in bound volumes on shelves you can search. Unbound periodicals (current issues) are usually available in a reading area. Increasingly, periodicals are on microfilm or microfiche and must be read on special machines in a special room.

## 40f Working Outline



Once you have a working bibliography, you need to become increasingly selective about the materials you collect. At this point, you need to plan your paper, tentatively at least, with a working outline. (See 35f.) Then you can assess your subject and focus it more precisely. If you discover an overabundance of material, you will have to limit your subject further. If your sources cover entirely different points, unconnected to any central purpose, you must shift to the most interesting of the points or the point that holds the greatest promise of leading to a unified paper. And of course, if your outline looks short and incomplete, you will have to expand your subject or change it.

Even for a short paper, the working outline permits you to juggle several pieces of information, fitting them together in various combinations to achieve the best arrangement. New information that you gather can be added wherever it fits best. For information on traditional organizations, consult Chapter 35.

For some papers a working outline might be just a list of major points with the sources lined up underneath. As other sources are accumulated, they can easily be added at the appropriate points. The student writer of the sample paper on pages 526–535 began with this working outline.

```
Mark Twain: Civil War Deserter?
    1. coward
    2. humor
            Twain
    3. childishness
            Van Wyck Brooks
```

4. guilt
    Kaplan
    Mattson
5. family
    Webster

For other papers, the working outline might be a fairly elaborate list, including precise divisions and subdivisions along with the sources for developing several different ideas. An early outline of the student research paper that appears on pages 543–550 started out with these divisions.

Discrimination in Japanese Business

1. Japanese success
    A. In Japan
        Ouchi
        Lohr
    B. In America
        Wheelwright
2. Discrimination against men
    A. Education determines job
        Lohr, Ouchi
    B. Cliques
        Osako
3. Discrimination against women
    A. Education
        Forbis, Ouchi
    B. Traditional role
        Dillon, Osako
    C. Inferior work conditions
        Rehder, Ouchi
    D. Inferior jobs
        Dillon, Rehder, Osako



An outline can even guide a literature review in which the sources are presented in sequential order—one, two, three. The outline can show the division of material into segments and ensure a logical arrangement. The student writer of the paper on pages 558–564 began with a short list of the sources and their focus.

```
Taste Research: Advances and Problems
   1. food for the hungry—Mattell
   2. cause of obesity—Roper
   3. mechanism—Bartoshuk
   4. taste malfunction—Savold
```

When you write a working outline, let it remain flexible. Papers frequently take shape gradually, and new reading or thinking may make changes necessary. You may need to explore new directions even though your original outline does not provide for them. A new direction may turn out to be the key that will unify and improve your paper. Also, if one section of an outline grows disproportionate to the others, you might consider a paper devoted just to that point. For example, the sample paper on Japanese business discrimination (pp. 543–550) originally covered the broader subject of Japanese business problems, but the material on discrimination grew so large that it became the primary subject.



### ❑ EXERCISE 6

**Using the material from the bibliography you gathered for Exercise 5, write a working outline. Note any sections that seem to lack coverage in your sources, that seem to be getting out of control, or that need to be added or deleted.**

## 40g Note-taking

Once your paper's direction is established, you are ready to take notes and to decide how best to incorporate your sources into your paper. Note-taking is not an isolated stage in the process of writing a research paper. You can take notes at any point that you find information you want to remember. You will not necessarily use all your notes; but if you do not write down ideas, figures, and statements, you are likely to forget them or to forget where you read them. As you move from one source to another, your interest shifts, and you probably will not remember details about a source several readings back or several days before.

Since good notes can reduce masses of information to a manageable size, you should summarize source material whenever possible. If you are not sure how you will use a source in your paper, though, you can quote it fully or make a notation so that you can easily return to specific pages. One efficient method is to photocopy material and cut and paste it on cards for organizing. Cards are more easily grouped and shifted around than full-length sheets of paper. Whatever technique you prefer, always identify each note. A full reference is not necessary if it is on a card in your working bibliography. The author's name and the page number may be all that are needed for identification. Also, when possible, label the topic the information covers (Figure 8).

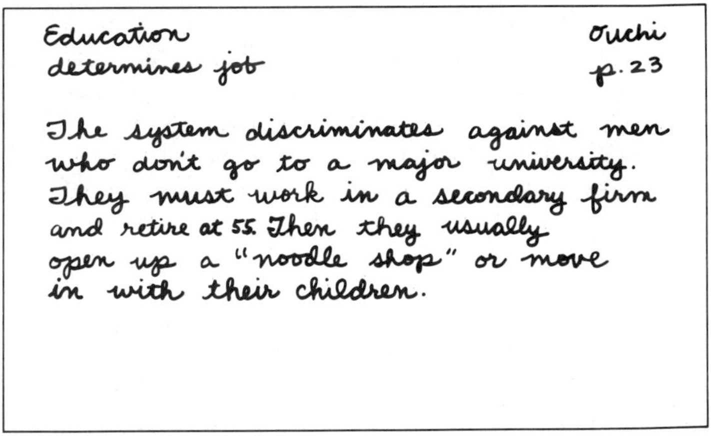

Education determines job — Ouchi p. 23

The system discriminates against men who don't go to a major university. They must work in a secondary firm and retire at 55. Then they usually open up a "noodle shop" or move in with their children.

**Figure 8** Note card

If your note does not fit your working outline, make adjustments. Either file the note separately as superfluous or change the outline to include the information on the note. But do not use a note just because you have gone to the trouble to take it. It could destroy the coherence of your paper.

# 40h Plagiarism

Plagiarism is deceiving the reader into thinking that the ideas or words taken from a source are your own. The word *plagiarism* comes from a Latin word that means "kidnapping," and in a sense plagiarism is a kind of kidnapping of material belonging to another.

Since plagiarism undermines learning and may even cause failure, why do people plagiarize? The answer varies. Some writers do not understand what plagiarism is; they simply do not know how to present material taken from another source. Other writers cannot effectively rewrite an original sentence or passage because they have not actually mastered the material. On the other hand, there are writers who deliberately plagiarize because they fear that they cannot produce a satisfactory paper and mistakenly believe that they can camouflage their weaknesses. In addition, poor time management can lead writers to plagiarize. Transforming a source into different words and a different style takes more time than copying. Consequently, writers who rush to produce a last-minute paper may plagiarize sources out of a sense of desperation. The solution is to realize that rewording sources is a time-consuming process and to allow ample time for careful paraphrasing.



### (1) Giving credit

Plagiarism can result from not giving credit to the person who thought of an idea, calculated statistics, made a discovery. You cannot pass off as your own another person's work. As these examples taken from the sample research papers indicate, you can easily give credit for ideas by including the name of the person who wrote the original or by referring the reader to a name or source in a list of references.

> Van Wyck Brooks in *The Ordeal of Mark Twain* blames Twain's desertion on an "infantile frame of mind."

> According to Ouchi (1981), women are considered temporary employees even though they may work for as long as twenty years at a job.

> But the problem remains, and all the astronauts can do at present is spice up with seasonings, like taco sauce (7).

In addition, you must show when you have used someone else's words. Quotation marks around the material let the reader know that a word, phrase, sentence, or short passage appeared in the original source. Long quoted passages are set off from the rest of the paper.

The only parts of a research paper that do not show credit to someone else are those parts written independently of any sources and those parts containing common knowledge (factual information known widely by educated people). For instance, you would not have to show the source of such information as the fact that Lincoln was president during the Civil War or that Shakespeare wrote *Hamlet.*

## (2) Paraphrasing carefully



Make sure that plagiarism does not result from the failure to paraphrase sufficiently, that is, to rewrite a passage in your own words and your own style. To paraphrase well, you must first understand the information in the source. If you do not understand what you are reading, you may need to abandon the subject and find one more general and less technical. Sometimes, though, you cannot abandon the subject. It may be assigned, or you may not have time to start over. If so, you should get help in understanding the material. You cannot accurately paraphrase prose you do not understand.

When you paraphrase, you must be sure that you have changed the prose from the original without any distortion of meaning. Compare the original paragraph that follows with the two unsuccessful attempts at paraphrasing. The plagiarized examples illustrate two extremes—first, a blatant copying of whole sections, and second, the retention of a few significant words and phrases.

Original Passage

The "injuries and insolencies" that caused conflict on the frontier were usually rooted in simple trespass either by English cattle or hogs onto the unfenced cornfields of the Indians or by the Indian habit of moving freely over open fields that the English regarded as sacred private property. (Robert M. Utley and Wilcomb E. Washburn, *Indian Wars*)

Plagiarized Version 1

Conflict on the frontier between the English and Indians was usually rooted in simple trespass either by English animals onto the unfenced cornfields of the Indians or by the Indian habit of moving freely over open fields that the English considered to be their own private property.

In the plagiarized version, the writer changed the opening words of the original but then with the exception of substituting "animals" for "cattle or hogs" and "considered" for "regarded" copied the rest of the passage almost word for word.

Plagiarized Version 2

Conflict on the frontier between the English and the Indians was usually rooted in a lack of respect for property. The English cattle and hogs were permitted to trespass on the unfenced cornfields of the Indians. The Indians trespassed freely on private property that the English regarded as sacred.



The second version is a better attempt, but its writer could still face accusations of plagiarism. The expressions "rooted in," "unfenced cornfields of the Indians," and "regarded as sacred" should have been changed. Neither example gives credit for the information. The next example is a more successful paraphrase that acknowledges the source in the rewording.

Successfully Paraphrased Version

Utley and Washburn maintain that the frontier conflict between the English and the Indians often had a simple cause—trespassing on the other's property. The English permitted their animals to wander on cornfields that the Indians refused to fence. The Indians, with little notion of private property, wandered freely over English fields.

Successful paraphrasing preserves the meaning of the original but changes its expression. If you find it difficult to change someone else's language, try this technique: read the source; then write down its meaning in your own words as if you are explaining to someone what you just read. Avoid looking back at the source. If you get confused, reread the material but write the paraphrase from memory. After the material has been paraphrased, check to see that it has these characteristics.

- The paraphrase accurately restates the meaning of the original.
- The sentence structure differs from that of the original.

- The paraphrase contains only the ordinary words or phrases appearing in the original.
- Any unique or distinctive expressions are changed or placed in quotation marks.

To paraphrase well, then, you must be able to understand the content, manipulate sentence structure, and distinguish between the words and phrases you can use and those you cannot. Words like articles, prepositions, conjunctions, and pronouns are obviously necessary, and you can use them without fear of plagiarism. You can use the source's nouns, verbs, and adjectives when they have simple denotations and no equivalent synonyms. Words such as *computer, tree, read, see,* and *green* have no ordinary substitutions. But words like *scintillating, bolster,* and *magnum opus* do.



Phrases that appear in an original source are usually distinctive and must be either rewritten or placed inside quotation marks. To protect yourself, always avoid duplicating phrases, except for common ones like *in school, blue sky, nuclear test site.* You certainly could not use phrases like the following without quotation marks.

a particularly sobering illustration
a transfer of coping skills
overly ambitious curriculum
the most pernicious of illusions
to cast in sharp relief

Remember that each person's writing style is distinctive, and a reader can detect a shift. A paper that begins simply and suddenly shifts into sophisticated prose is immediately suspicious. In the following passage, the style of the first paragraph is that of the average writer. The second paragraph shifts to a professional style.

> Political campaigns have become more and more like entertainment. To get elected, politicians advertise themselves like commercial products. The commercials do not say much. Instead, they have pictures, music, and slogans.
>
> What is happening is that the use of extended and complex language is being rapidly replaced by the gestures, images, and formats of the arts of show business, toward which most of the new media, especially television, are powerfully disposed. The

result is that in the political domain, as well as in other arenas of public discourse—religion and commerce, for example—Americans no longer talk to each other; they entertain each other.

## ❑ EXERCISE 7

Paraphrase each of the following passages and give credit to the source within the paraphrase.

1. Throughout the Middle Ages, and even later, it was widely believed that London had once been inhabited by giants, a legend which derived from the massive bones which were occasionally unearthed in and around the City. Sometimes these finds were put on display in City churches: during the sixteenth century, for instance, St. Mary Aldermary exhibited a huge thigh-bone, "more than after the proportion of five shank bones of any man now living," together with a twelve-foot drawing of a Goliath-like figure to assist the ignorant public in the work of reconstruction. (Robert Gray, *A History of London*)

2. A marathon is any kind of endurance contest—running, dancing, bicycling, flagpole-sitting. It is named for the narrow valley in Greece where in 490 B.C. the Athenians, under Miltiades, pinned down superior Persian forces so that they could not use their cavalry, and proceeded to slaughter them. The Persians lost 6,400 men in the battle; the Greeks, 192. Miltiades, fearing that Athens might surrender to Persian attack by sea in ignorance of the victory at Marathon, dispatched Pheidippides, his fastest runner, to take home the good news. Though nearly exhausted, having already run to Sparta and back, Pheidippides raced twenty-some miles to Athens, gasped out "Rejoice—we conquer!" and fell dead. (Willard R. Espy, *Thou Improper, Thou Uncommon Noun*)

res 40i

# 40i Using Sources

To use an idea in a paper, you have several options. The one you choose is sometimes arbitrary and sometimes dependent on matters such as the style, content, and importance of the source.

### (1) Quoting a passage

Be cautious about using too many direct quotations. You do not want your paper to be a series of quotations interspersed with short passages of your own prose. Instead, quote material when you want to emphasize it or when it is so well stated that a restatement would diminish its effect. There is no point in quoting material with ordinary content and style. Also, never quote directly simply to avoid the trouble of paraphrasing.

Short quoted passages are enclosed in quotation marks. (You can find guidelines in Chapter 27.)

> As David Osborne observes, "We have developed one new technology after another—from videocassette recorders to machine tools to semiconductors—only to watch the Japanese take the market from us."

res 40i

Long quotations, more than 4 typed lines, are usually blocked, that is, indented on the left side and set off from the rest of the paper. Quotation marks are omitted unless they appear in the original.

> David Osborne explains:
>
>> At the moment, we have a clear lead in the race to commercialize space. We have the space shuttle, and we will probably have a space station by 1995. But the experience of the past fifteen years is cause for concern. We have developed one new technology after another—from videocassette recorders to machine tools to semiconductors—only to watch the Japanese take the market from us. (57)

(See also the blocked quotations in the sample research papers, pp. 528 and 546.)

## (2) Mixing a quotation and a paraphrase

This technique is useful for passages that cannot be completely restated and for retaining any effective style in the original. Notice the way the following example quotes two phrases and paraphrases the rest.

> America leads "the race to commercialize space." The space shuttle and the strong possibility of a space station are evidence of our successful technology. However, developing technology is

not enough. In the past we have been successful "only to watch the Japanese take the market from us" (Osborne, 1985).

## (3) Paraphrasing a passage

Technically a paraphrase is about the same length as the original and is most useful for a passage full of relevant information. The following retains most of the original's details.

> According to Osborne (1985), in the attempt to make space commercially profitable, America is presently in the lead. The space shuttle and the strong possibility of a space station are evidence of our successful technology. However, developing technology is not enough. In the past, we have developed the technology but have lost the market to Japan.



## (4) Summarizing the passage

Summaries permit a writer to emphasize important ideas and to delete details. Furthermore, condensed material is less likely to be plagiarized. In the process of reducing the number of words, a writer is more likely to revise the sentence structure and vocabulary of the original. For example, the following version reduces the 67-word passage to 25 words.

> Although America has developed superior technology in the commercialization of space, we may, as we have in the past, lose the market to the Japanese (Osborne, 1985).

## ☐ EXERCISE 8

Take notes on the following passage as directed below.

There are, in fact, many puzzling features concerning sunspots, which may be answered once the causes of magnetic fields on an astronomic scale are worked out. For instance, the number of sunspots on the solar surface wax and wane in an eleven and one half year cycle. This was first established in 1843 by the German astronomer Heinrich Samuel Schwabe, who studied the face of the sun almost daily for seventeen years. Furthermore, the spots appear only at certain latitudes, and these latitudes shift as the cycle progresses. The spots show a certain magnetic orientation that reverses itself in each new cycle. Why all this should be so is still unknown. (Isaac Asimov, *Guide to Science*)

1. Quote the first two sentences.
2. Quote the second sentence and the last three sentences. Paraphrase enough remaining information for the note to make sense.
3. Paraphrase the entire passage.
4. Paraphrase the first sentence but quote the expression "puzzling features."
5. Summarize the entire passage.

## 40j Drafting the Paper

res 40j

The way you write the first draft depends on the time you have spent organizing and taking notes. If your notes are carefully composed and systematically arranged, much of the writing has already been done. If you have merely decided on the overall pattern and gathered together some of the material you will use in each section, you must move back and forth from your sources to your own composition. Most writers fall between the two extremes. The note-taking for some sections will be complete; for other sections, it will be unfinished, particularly if the writer is unable to visualize how the source might eventually be used.

Regardless of the stage at which you start to draft your paper, you must at this point focus your attention on the overall scheme—the organization of the whole, the introduction, the synthesis of the parts, the paragraph structures, and the conclusion.

### (1) Make sure your overall organization works effectively.

It is not too late to delete, add, or switch sections around. If you have not found the sources needed to back up a section of your plan, you should delete it. Of course, if the section is crucial, you can leave a gap to be filled after further investigation. Interesting material that you have located can be added to the working outline, but only if it really fits. Do not insert a source, no matter how interesting, if it does not support your overall purpose. As you begin to write, you sometimes discover that sections are not in the right order and must be moved to another place. In general, the drafting stage is not too late for changes in the organization.

### (2) Write an introduction that makes your purpose clear.

If, at this point, you have lost sight of a clear purpose, you should rethink the whole paper. Are you answering a question? Arguing a thesis? Reviewing the literature? Once the purpose is clear to you, you must make it clear to your readers. Some strategies for introductions are discussed in 36b, Introductory Paragraphs. You will also find in the discussion examples illustrating each strategy. Remember that the introduction establishes your reader's first impression of your skills and your subject. A poor first impression is unfortunately hard to change. Therefore, treat the introduction seriously. It does not matter when you write the introduction, but when you do, put into it your best effort.



### (3) Make sure your paper has coherence.

Make sure that you lead your reader smoothly not only from paragraph to paragraph but through each paragraph as well. In a typical paragraph you will have a topic sentence stating the point, and then you will use your sources to develop or substantiate that sentence. (For discussion and examples of paragraph organization, see 36a, Body Paragraphs.) Figure 9 shows how the writer combined three notes to create a single paragraph that explains the "traditional role that women play in Japanese society."

goal: marrige and motherhood Dillon p.22

Role influenced by society's belief that "marriage and motherhood" are the ultimate goal of women. Because of arranged marriages, anyone can get married. Extremely high marriage rate.

| Care of children | Dillon p. 23 |
|---|---|

Mothers are given the responsibility of child care. Most women stay home and don't seek jobs. New role: "education mothers"– help educate sons. Ed. very important to male's future. "Mothers play an important role (and live vicariously) through the career development of their sons."

| Care of sons and husband | Osako pp 17-18 |
|---|---|

Collective achievement more important than individual. "Therefore, a woman is considered more virtuous if she devotes herself to the advancement of other family members (notably sons and husbands) rather than pursuing her own career." [p. 18]

res 40j

Another reason for employment discrimination is the traditional role that women play in Japanese society. Their goals are "marriage and motherhood" (Dillon, 1983). The marriage rate is extremely high, and the care of children is the exclusive job of women. Consequently, women rarely seek employment. Instead, they remain at home and promote the education of their sons, since male children, if successful in school, may some day be successful in business. According to Dillon, "Mothers play an important role (and live vicariously) through the career development of their sons" (p. 23). Osako (1978) writes, "A woman is considered more virtuous if she devotes herself to the advancement of other family members (notably sons and husbands) rather than pursuing her own career" (p. 18).

**Figure 9** Three notes combined into paragraph

### (4) Use lead-ins to introduce sources.

When you incorporate quotations or paraphrased material into your paper, you usually introduce them so the reader knows where the borrowing begins. Some of the established lead-ins that signal the beginning of a source are these.

Vogel points out that . . .

According to Brooks . . .

Stuart Berg Flexner agrees that . . .

John Wain wrote that . . .

The verb tense of a lead-in depends on whether the statement or work is associated with the past or with the present. Work in science, technology, and the social sciences is frequently related to the time in which it occurred. Therefore, lead-ins are usually in the past tense or present perfect tense.



Darwin discovered . . .

The researchers have studied . . .

But some past events are considered a constant reality and are written about in the present tense. This "historical present" signifies that literary works or other documents are preserved and remain presently available or that a truth is unaffected by time.

Chaucer writes . . .

The Constitution guarantees . . .

Sometimes present and past tenses are mixed, as for example, in a passage about both Shakespeare the man and Shakespeare's drama.

Shakespeare left [past tense] his wife only his "second-best bed"; nevertheless, in his dramas, he shows [present tense] a great deal of respect for women.

Similarly, in a report of a scientific or technical investigation, the data might be presented in the past tense and the conclusion in the present.

> In the study the salinity measured [past tense] 3.5 percent. The results show [present tense] that the salinity of the bay increased [past tense] during the two years studied.

### (5) Write a suitable conclusion.

Several different strategies for conclusions can effectively end a research paper: a return to the thesis, a summary of the major points, a recommendation, or a call for further study. For a more complete list of strategies and for descriptions and examples, see 36c.

# 41

# Research Papers and Documentation

doc 41

At one time, writers regularly documented papers by placing a superscript (raised) number after each paraphrase, summary, and quotation taken from a source. Then they identified the source in a note at the bottom of the page or the end of the paper. Also they added a bibliography, a list of all the sources used throughout. Thus, the paper was heavily documented. In fact, each source was really listed twice—once in a note and once in the bibliography. Even though this style is still used in some disciplines, the duplication and the problems with typing and printing costs have brought about some changes. Most publications now use a simplified style in which the sources are listed only once, at the end. Either the content of the paper or a notation in parentheses indicates which source from the list has been cited.

You can find an appropriate documentation style in several ways. First, there are style guides published for a number of disciplines. Among the most popular are these.

*MLA Handbook for Writers of Research Papers*. 3d ed. New York: Modern Language Assn. of America, 1988.

*Publication Manual of the American Psychological Association*. 3d ed. Washington: American Psychological Assn., 1984.

*CBE Style Manual: A Guide for Authors, Editors, and Publishers in the Biological Sciences*. 5th ed. Bethesda: Council of Biology Editors, 1983.

*Handbook for Authors of Papers in American Chemical Society Publications*. Washington: American Chemical Soc., 1978.

*Chicago Manual of Style*. 13th ed. Chicago: U of Chicago P, 1982.

Second, you can follow the style of documentation used by a scholarly journal. Third, you are sometimes required to use guides supplied by instructors, businesses, or agencies. Unless you have special instructions or unusual problems, however, you can find the information needed for documentation in the following explanation of the three most common styles: the MLA style, the APA style, and the number system. Use whichever style you are assigned or prefer.

# 41a MLA Documentation

doc 41a

The popular MLA style of documentation is detailed in the *MLA Handbook for Writers of Research Papers.* The following description presents the most common uses of sources and the most commonly used forms. Whenever you need special information not covered here, consult the *MLA Handbook.* For the style in a complete paper, see "Mark Twain: Civil War Deserter?" (section 41b).

## (1) MLA documentation inside the paper

In the text of a paper, you must show exactly where borrowed material came from—no matter whether it is a paraphrase, summary, or quotation. In the MLA style, the name of the author of the source and usually the page number indicate where the material came from. The *MLA Handbook* specifies the placement and conventions of the documentation.

1. The author's last name and page or pages can appear in parentheses. Note that no comma separates the two and that the parentheses are inside the sentence.

   When Orion left for Nevada, Twain went with him (Mack 47–49).

   For two or three authors, give the last name of all authors—(Murray and Boston 124) or (Dunn, Frye, and Franklin 74). For more than three authors, give only the first author's last name and the abbreviation for "and others," *et al.*—(Sargent et al. 39).
2. When the author's name appears in the sentence, the page numbers go in parentheses.

   Thus, to Kaplan the story is intended to help remove the burden of guilt (322–25).

3. When a source ends with a quotation, the parentheses go after the quotation mark but before the period.

   He also writes that the war had not yet turned the "green recruits" from "rabbits into soldiers" (265).

4. A secondhand quote, one taken from a secondary not a primary source, is indicated this way.

   Mark Twain called John Wanamaker "that unco-pious butter-mouthed Sunday school-slobbering sneak-thief" (qtd. in Kaplan 319).

## (2) MLA documentation at the end of the paper



At the end of a paper, in "Works Cited," you list in alphabetical order all the sources you have cited. (See the example at the end of section 41b.) The components of your citations—their arrangement, capitalization, punctuation, mechanics, and spacing—must follow the specifications of the MLA style guide. The following chart explains the MLA specifications for the major components of the most commonly used sources—books as well as periodicals (journals, magazines, and newspapers).

**The Major Components of MLA Citations**

**Author**

One author

- Reverse names (last name first).
- Place a period at the end.

Example: Boswell, James.

Two or three authors

- Reverse name of only first author.
- Separate names with comma or commas.
- Place an *and* before last name.
- Place a period at the end.

Example: Hunt, Ray C., and Bernard Norling.
Example: Watts, Frank, Edward Norton, and Charles Lexington.

More than three authors

- Name first author only.
- Follow with a comma and *et al.* ("and others").

Example: Bates, Richard M., et al.

<table>
<tr><td>Title</td><td>Book<br>• Underline with a solid line.<br>• Place a period at the end.<br><br>Example: <u>A Combat Artist in World War II</u>.<br><br>Periodical Article<br>• Place in quotation marks.<br>• Place a period at the end (before the quotation mark).<br><br>Example: "Reactionary Rhetoric."<br><br>Periodical<br>• Underline with a solid line.<br>• Place no period at the end.<br><br>Example: <u>American Journal of Science</u></td></tr>
<tr><td>Publication Information</td><td>Book<br>• Give the city, a brief form of the publisher's name, and year of publication.<br>• Place a colon after the city, a comma after the publisher, and a period at the end.<br><br>Example: New York: Knopf, 1976.<br><br>Journal<br>• Give the volume number (arabic numeral), year of publication, and inclusive page numbers.<br>• Place the year in parentheses.<br>• Place a colon after the last parenthesis.<br>• Place a period at the end.<br><br>Example: 52 (1981): 75-79.<br><br>Magazine and newspaper<br>• Omit the volume number.<br>• Give date (day/abbreviated month/year) and inclusive page numbers.<br>• For pages that are not consecutive, give first page number and a plus sign (21+).<br>• Place a colon after the year.<br>• Place a period at the end.<br><br>Example: 20 Mar. 1988: 4-9.<br>Example: 9 June 1982: 12+.</td></tr>
</table>

doc 41a

In formatting the major components, you also must pay attention to the spacing. When typing "Works Cited," double-space every line. Indent the second and subsequent lines of a reference five spaces. In general, MLA calls for you to space twice after periods and once after other marks of punctuation. The following chart of basic forms illustrates complete entries and their proper spacing.

| Basic Forms in MLA Style | |
|---|---|
| **Book** | Ryan, Cornelius. A Bridge Too Far. New York: Simon, 1974.<br>Nie, Norman, et al. Statistical Package for the Social Sciences. New York: McGraw, 1975. |
| **Journal** | Sewall, Richard B. "The Tragic Form." Essays in Criticism 4 (1954): 345-58.<br>Higgs, E. S., and J. P. White. "Autumn Killing." Antiquity 37 (1963):282-89. |
| **Magazine** | Edwards, Mike. "Kabul." National Geographic Apr. 1985: 494-505.<br>Landau, Jon. "In Praise of Elvis Presley." Rolling Stone 23 Dec. 1971: 72. |
| **Newspaper** | Cooke, Robert. "A Circus in Old Carthage: Curses and Chariots." Atlanta Constitution 4 June 1985: A4. |

doc 41a

In addition to the basic forms used most of the time, there are some variations used occasionally. The following list includes variations of the basic forms and also special forms such as encyclopedia articles, government documents, radio and television programs, films and videotapes, interviews and lectures.

## Additional MLA Citation Forms

EDITED BOOK

Hofstadter, Richard, ed. Great Issues in American History. New York: Vintage, 1958.

Michaels, Leonard, and Christopher Ricks, eds. The State of Language. Berkeley: U of California P, 1980.

Prinz, Martin, et al., eds. Guide to Rocks and Minerals. New York: Simon, 1978.

CHAPTER, STORY, OR OTHER PART OF A BOOK

Stafford, Jean. "The Echo and the Nemesis." The Collected Stories. New York: Farrar, 1970. 35–53.

Malory, Sir Thomas. "Isolde the Fair." *The Works of Sir Thomas Malory.* Ed. Eugene Vinaver. London: Oxford UP, 1954. 276–331.

FOREWORD AND PREFACE

Gardner, John. Foreword. *Becoming a Writer.* By Dorothea Brande. 1934. Los Angleles: Tarcher, 1981.

Tannahill, Reay. Preface. *Food in History.* By Tannahill. New York: Stein, 1973.

MULTIVOLUME WORK

Brown, T. Allston. *A History of the New York Stage.* 3 vols. New York: Blom, 1903.

In the citation in the text, the volume is followed by a colon, then the page number, as in (3:136).



MULTIVOLUME WORK WITH A SEPARATE TITLE FOR EACH VOLUME

Malone, Dumas. *The Sage of Monticello.* Vol. 6 of *Jefferson and His Time.* 6 vols. Boston: Little, 1981.

REPUBLISHED WORK SUCH AS A PAPERBACK EDITION

Faulkner, William. *Absalom, Absalom.* 1936. New York: Vintage, 1972.

TRANSLATION

Euripides. *Alcestis.* Trans. William Arrowsmith. New York: Oxford UP, 1974.

LATER EDITION

Gould, James A., ed. *Classic Philosophical Questions.* 2nd ed. Columbus: Bobbs, 1975.

BOOK WITH A TITLE WITHIN THE TITLE

Martin, Jay, ed. *A Collection of Critical Essays on "The Waste Land."* Englewood Cliffs: Prentice, 1968.

Paul, Henry N. *The Royal Play of* Macbeth. New York: Macmillan, 1950.

WORK WITH CORPORATE AUTHOR

Lunar & Planetary Institute, Houston. *Basaltic Volcanism on Terrestrial Plants.* Elmsford: Pergamon, 1982.

ENCYCLOPEDIA ARTICLE

Bay, Christian. "Civil Disobedience." International Encyclopedia of the Social Sciences. 1968 ed.

"Perkins, Maxwell Evarts." Encyclopedia Americana. 1985 ed.

GOVERNMENT DOCUMENT

Cong. Rec. 25 Jan. 1940: 698–99.

United States. Historical Section, Army War College. Order of Battle of the United States Land Forces in the World War (1917–19). Washington: GPO, 1931.

United States. Cong. Staff Investigative Group to the Committee on Foreign Affairs. The Assassination of Representative Leo J. Ryan and the Jonestown, Guyana Tragedy. 96th Cong., 1st sess. H. Doc. 223. Washington: GPO, 1979.



ARTICLE IN A SCHOLARLY JOURNAL

Frye, Northrop. "Varieties of Literary Utopia." Daedalus 94 (1965): 323–47.

When the journal's page numbers run consecutively throughout the year, only the volume number, the year, and the page numbers are listed.

Hytier, Adrienne. "The Battle in Eighteenth-Century French Fiction." Eighteenth Century Life 8.3 (1983): 1–13.

When each issue of the journal begins with page 1, the volume and also the issue must be listed. A period separates the volume number from the issue number.

ARTICLE IN A MAGAZINE OR NEWSPAPER, NO AUTHOR

"Ponzi Is Gone but His Game Goes On." U.S. News & World Report 10 Jan. 1985: 14.

"Pan Am Charts a Course for Europe, 1939." Wall Street Journal 26 May 1989: B1.

EDITORIAL AND LETTER

Fowler, Elaine W. Letter. Washington Post 1 Mar. 1975: A19.

"Manuage." Editorial. New York Times 2 June 1985: E22.

BOOK REVIEW

Costello, Bonnie. "The Fine Art of Remembrance." Rev. of The

Collected Prose, by Elizabeth Bishop. Partisan Review 52.2 (1985): 153–57.

Radio and Television Program

Ciardi, John. Morning Edition. Natl. Public Radio. WNYC, New York. 20 May 1985.

"The Sleeping Sharks of Yucatan." The Undersea World of Jacques Cousteau. Dir. Philippe Cousteau. Prod. Andy White. A Marshall Flaum Production in Association with the Cousteau Society and MPC-Metromedia Producers Corporation and ABC News. WFAA, Dallas. 4 June 1975.

Computer Software



Tobias, Andrew. Managing Your Money. Computer software. MECA, 1986.

MathCAD. Vers. 2.0. Computer software. Mathsoft, Inc., 1987. IBM PC, 512KB, graphics card, disk.

Material from a Computer Information Service

Webre, Elizabeth C. An Annotated Bibliography of Children's Books with Cajun Themes. ERIC, 1988. ED 299 569.

Film and Videotape

2001: A Space Odyssey. Dir. Stanley Kubrick. MGM, 1968.

Introduction to Chimpanzee Behavior. Videocassette. National Geographic Society, 1977. 23 min.

Interview or Lecture

Edwards, Sylvia. Personal interview. 8 Dec. 1986.

Moorman, Charles. Lecture. London. 21 July 1985.

Schoenecke, Michael. "Political and Social Ideology in Jack London's Science Fiction." The 23rd Annual Northern Great Plains History Conference. Eveleth, MN, 23 Sep. 1988.

### Typing with MLA style

- Use good quality paper, $8\frac{1}{2} \times 11$ inches, and standard type.
- If your instructor requests a final outline, it should precede the paper. The outline page should not be numbered.

- Use no title page. Instead type identification information at the top left corner of the first page. Center the title. Follow the example, page 526.
- Use 1-inch margins on all sides.
- Double-space the entire paper including the list of references at the end.
- Number the first page with the numeral 1 in the top right-hand corner, ½-inch from the top of the page. Starting with page 2, type in this same position your last name and the page number.
- Do not hyphenate words at the ends of lines.
- Block long quotes of more than four typed lines. They should be double-spaced and indented ten spaces from the left margin and none from the right. See the quotation on page 529.
- Type the references in alphabetical order on a separate page. Title the page "Works Cited." Type the first line of each reference against the left margin. Indent other lines five spaces. If you have more than one entry by the same author, do not repeat the author's name. Use instead three hyphens. For example:

Mangelsdorf, P. C. "The Domestication of Corn." Science 143 (1969), 538–45.

---. Plants and Human Affairs. Bloomington: Indiana UP, 1952.

# 41b Sample Research Paper Using MLA Style

1" from top of p

Olivia Guest

Professor Dugan

ENG 102

April 30, 1992

Mark Twain: Civil War Deserter?

I. Introduction--Shannon's accusations about Twain's cowardice during the Civil War

II. Explanation in the autobiography

III. Descriptions in "History"

  A. Humorous description

  B. Indictment of war

IV. Accusations of childishness

  A. Van Wyck Brooks

  B. <u>New York Times</u>

  C. Support from "History"

V. Antiwar explanation

  A. Support of explanation

    1. Justin Kaplan

    2. J. Stanley Mattson

  B. Refutation of explanation--Maxwell Geismar

VI. Divided sympathies

  A. Twain's divided sympathy

    1. Connection to the South

    2. Connection to the North

  B. Missouri's divided sympathy

    1. Minimal interest in the war

2. Opposition to secession

3. Confusion illustrated in "History"

VII. Other influences

A. Interest in the continent

B. Orion's influence

VIII. Desertion as a common occurrence

A. Bell Wiley's statistics

B. Twain's description of camp life

Guest 1

*½" from top of page*

Mark Twain: Civil War Deserter?

*centered title*

On January 25, 1940, Representative Shannon of Missouri insisted that his state did not want any of the recently issued stamps commemorating Mark Twain. According to Shannon, Twain had disgraced Missouri during the Civil War. Soon after Twain had joined the Confederate forces under a Colonel Jack Burbridge and had been made a lieutenant, Twain deserted. In Shannon's version of what had happened, "A Minie ball came whizzing past his ears, and [Twain] started running. He ran; and, oh, how fast he did run. He never stopped until he got to Keokuk, Iowa. Colonel Burbridge fought 4 years in the Southern Army; Mark Twain about 4 minutes." Shannon concluded his criticism by quoting Captain Billy Ely, who had been company commander of the Burbridge Brigade, "I can say to my fellow Missourians that we had but one coward in our whole group, and his name was Samuel L. Clemens" (Cong. Rec. 698-99).

*background established*

*brackets to indicate insertion*

Shannon's version of Mark Twain's military career is not completely accurate, but it does bring up some interesting questions. What was Twain's position during the Civil War? Why did he desert? When we look to Twain himself, we get very little reliable information. In his autobiography we learn that the war interrupted his career as a river pilot. Then he devotes only two sentences to the whole war episode:

*purpose: to find out wh[y] Twain dese[rted]*

> In June I joined the Confederates in Ralls County, Missouri, as a second Lieutenant under General Tom Harris and came near having the distinction of being captured by Colonel Ulysses S. Grant. I resigned

*quotation o[f] more than 4 lines indent[ed] 10 spaces from left margin*

Guest 2

*name and page number on every page*

> after two weeks' service in the field, explaining that I was "incapacitated by fatigue" through persistent retreating. (102)

*page number after period and 2 spaces*

Another version of his career as a soldier appeared first in 1884 in Century Magazine as "The Private History of a Campaign That Failed." However colorful and interesting this account, it is probably more fictional than factual. According to William J. Kimball, "Exactly what happened in the summer of 1861 is probably beyond recovery, but the 'History' is obviously not an accurate account" (382). In the tale Twain tells of kids who join together to play soldier in a real war. They spend their time for the most part avoiding the Union forces they are supposed to be locating. The story contains several very humorous descriptions: the pretentious Dunlap, who changed his name to d'Un Lap; the uncooperative mules and horses, which constantly threw and bit their riders; the men, who rolled down hills in mud, slept in a corn crib, and were captured by dogs ("the most mortifying spectacle of the Civil War"). No one would cook, and no one would take orders.

*quotation marks around a short quotation*

In addition to the humor, the story also contains a very moving and dark episode in which Sam Clemens thinks that he has shot an innocent stranger. He writes:

> And it seemed an epitome of war; that all war must be just that--the killing of strangers against whom you feel no personal animosity; strangers whom, in other circumstances, you would help if you found them in trouble, and who would help you if you needed it. (263)

Guest 3

Several people have tried to explain Mark Twain's war experiences with less prejudice than Representative Shannon. In fact, together they help to sort out the confusion we feel about Twain's actions.

*transitional paragraph*

Van Wyck Brooks in The Ordeal of Mark Twain blames Twain's desertion on an "infantile frame of mind." Brooks maintains that Twain's independence from his mother's "leading strings" was so ill developed that he "slipped back into the boy he had been before." Brooks writes that we can see in the "History"

*combination of three sources by paraphrasing and quoting*

> a singular childishness, a sort of infantility, in fact that is very hard to reconcile with the character of any man of twenty-six and especially one who, a few weeks before, had been a river "sovereign," the master of a great steamboat, a worshipper of energy and purpose. (74-75)

In the New York Times a response to Representative Shannon's attack also points out that although at the time of his desertion Twain was 26, "mentally he was not yet 21" ("Ranger of Hannibal"). In "History," one of Twain's remarks supports this view. After he has become disillusioned with war, Twain comments, "It seemed to me that I was not rightly equipped for this awful business; that war was intended for men, and I for a child's nurse" (263). He also writes that the war had not yet turned the "green recruits" from "rabbits into soldiers" (265).

*title used when author unknown*

Justin Kaplan in his biography Mr. Clemens and Mark Twain writes that the episode of the killing of the stranger in "History" gave Twain a justification to desert. Now because of

*two conflicting sources*

Guest 4

the nightmarish killing, even though fictional, Twain was able to condemn war as dreadful. Thus, to Kaplan the story is intended to help remove the burden of guilt (322-25). J. Stanley Mattson also supports the view that the story is antiwar and that Twain is a pacifist. He writes, "It directs an arsenal of grape-shot at the entire concept of the glory of war" (794). Maxwell Geismar in Mark Twain: An American Prophet argues that although the story brings out the horror of war, its overall intention is to be humorous--"humor, yes. Guilt, no!" And Mark Twain left service with about half of the company simply because the "war was a disappointment" (129-30).

*parentheses inside the periods*

Perhaps more plausible than desertion because of exhaustion, childishness, or the inhumanity of war are explanations based on considerations of family, friends, and locality. Twain's sympathies leaned toward the South; he had recently spent time in Louisiana. When he returned to Missouri, he hid out for a while fearing he would be forced to pilot a Union gunboat. Twain's aunt wrote that when a friend suggested a Confederate company, Twain "accepted at once" (Webster 60). However, his brother Orion, to whom Twain was very close, favored the Union side. Showing how divided Mark Twain was, his aunt wrote:

*transitional sentence*

*author's name in parentheses when not in text*

> He loved his country's flag and all that it symbolized. . . . I know he would gladly have given his life for his country, but he was a Southerner, his friends were all Southern, his sympathies were with the South. It was the same problem that Robert E. Lee and thousands faced. (Webster 62)

The divided sympathies and possible indifference of Twain were typical of the feeling in Missouri as a whole. The interest in the war was minimal; "most Missourians probably would gladly have watched the war from the sidelines, waiting to study the meaning of its outcome" (Nagel 128). Voters (70 percent) favored compromise. Lincoln received only 10 percent of the votes. In a special 1861 convention, only 30,000 votes out of 140,000 cast favored secession. Despite the opposition, Missouri entered the war favoring the Union; three-fourths of the soldiers fought for the Union (Nagel 128-29). At the beginning of the "History" Twain writes of "a good deal of confusion in men's minds" and "a good deal of unsettledness, of leading first this way, then that, then the other way" (243). He tells that his pilot-mate and he were "strong for the Union." Then they both became rebels. Later the friend switched again and was piloting a federal gunboat (244).

Henry Seidel Canby expresses Twain's dilemma this way: Twain was "Southern in manners and Northern in mind." But Canby offers another dimension to the problem. Twain was really not interested in North or South, but it was "the continent that excited and persuaded him" (26). About this same time, Twain's brother Orion, a lawyer who had campaigned to get Lincoln elected President, got appointed Secretary of the Nevada Territory. When Orion left for Nevada, Twain went with him (Mack 47-49). Delancey Ferguson reports that "Orion wanted to stop his brother's dallying with the Southern cause" (65).

Guest 6

To people today, desertion seems a terrible crime and cowardly act. But during the Civil War, it was very common. Bell Wiley in The Common Soldier of the Civil War points out that many soldiers unlawfully left camp. He estimates deserters at 100,000 for the Confederate forces and 200,000 for the Federals. Wiley attributes the large numbers of desertions to the monotony of camp life (63). Twain writes in "History":

> We stayed several days at Mason's; and after all these years the memory of the dulness [sic], the stillness, and lifelessness of that slumberous farm-house still oppresses my spirit as with a sense of the presence of death and mourning. There was nothing to do, nothing to think about; there was no interest in life (257).

sic *in brackets to indicate spelling error in the original*

From a historical perspective, Twain's desertion was not unusual. Because of Twain's closeness to Orion, the decision to leave for Nevada was not surprising. No one should hastily condemn Twain without considering the complexity of the desertion.

*conclusion—reasons for Twain's desertion were complex*

Guest 7

Works Cited

Brooks, Van Wyck. The Ordeal of Mark Twain. New York: Dutton, 1933.

Canby, Henry Seidel. Turn West, Turn East: Mark Twain and Henry James. Boston: Houghton, 1951.

Clemens, Samuel L. The Autobiography of Mark Twain. Ed. Charles Neider. New York: Harper, 1959.

---. "The Private History of a Campaign That Failed." The American Claimant and Other Stories and Sketches. New York: Harper, 1897.

Cong. Rec. 25 Jan. 1940: 698-99.

Ferguson, Delancey. Mark Twain: Man and Legend. Indianapolis: Bobbs, 1943.

Geismar, Maxwell. Mark Twain: An American Prophet. Boston: Houghton, 1970.

Kaplan, Justin. Mr. Clemens and Mark Twain. 1966. New York: Pocket, 1968.

Kimball, William J. "Samuel Clemens as a Confederate Soldier: Some Observations about 'The Private History of a Campaign That Failed.'" Studies in Short Fiction 5 (1968): 382-84.

Mack, Effie Mona. Mark Twain in Nevada. New York: Scribner's, 1947.

Mattson, J. Stanley. "Mark Twain on War and Peace: The Missouri Rebel and 'The Campaign That Failed.'" American Quarterly 20 (1968): 785-94.

Nagel, Paul C. Missouri: A Bicentennial History. New York: Norton, 1977.

*all materia[l] double-spa[ced]*

*hyphens to indicate sa[me] author as above*

*volume, ye[ar,] pages*

Guest 8

*author unknown; work alphabetized by title*

"Ranger of Hannibal." New York Times 7 Feb. 1940: 20.

Webster, Samuel Charles, ed. Mark Twain, Business Man. Boston: Little, 1946.

Wiley, Bell. The Common Soldier of the Civil War. New York: Scribner's, 1975.

# 41c APA Documentation

Many disciplines follow the APA style of documentation developed by the American Psychological Association. This style appears in publications in such fields as psychology, education, sociology, political science, and geography. Also, many other disciplines in science, technology, and business use the same system with minor variations. The style is commonly known as the name-year system because each citation includes the author's name and the year of publication, a most important bit of information to researchers in these fields.



## (1) APA documentation inside the paper

In this system there are several ways to acknowledge sources within the paper's text.

1. The author's last name and the year of publication appear in parentheses. The parentheses are placed inside the sentence; a comma follows the author's name.

   America has lost superiority to Japan in the production of cars and consumer electronics and may soon lose its advantage in such industries as computers (Lohr, 1984).

   Sometimes you must place in the parentheses more than one author's name. For two authors, insert both last names, separated by an ampersand (&)—(Baron & Hall, 1980). For three to five authors, give all authors in the first reference (Wilson, Allen, Lakoff, & James, 1979); and in subsequent references, give the first author followed by *et al.*—(Wilson et al., 1979). For six or more authors, always give only the first author and *et al.*—(Linn et al., 1989).

2. The author's name is in the sentence, and the year goes in parentheses.

   Dillon (1983) describes the jobs available to women as low-paying, boring, repetitive, and unskilled.

3. Both author's name and the year appear in the sentence.

   In 1975, Forbis gave these statistics.

4. For a quotation, a page number appears in addition to name and year. The parentheses containing the identifying information should be

placed immediately after the quotation marks. Any punctuation that the sentence requires (period, comma, and so on) follows the parenthesis.

> Because of information about Japanese success, the United States has come to realize that "Japanese productivity has successfully challenged, even humiliated, America in world competition" (Bowman, 1984, p. 197).

> As Rehder (1983) points out, "Here women receive low wages, little job security, and less opportunity for training or educational development" (p. 43).

The page number for a blocked quotation also appears in parentheses but follows the period that ends the last sentence. See the example (p. 546) that ends

> . . . cram courses represent a multibillion-dollar industry. (p. 23)

doc
41c

## (2) APA documentation at the end of the paper

In the APA style, you list the cited sources at the end of the paper in a section entitled "References." As the list on page 550 illustrates, the sources are alphabetized. When you use the APA style, you must arrange the major components of each entry according to specifications. The following chart illustrates the formats of the most commonly used sources—books and periodicals (journals, magazines, newspapers).

| The Major Components of APA Citations | |
|---|---|
| **Author** | One author<br>• Give last name first.<br>• Use initials instead of full first and middle names.<br>Example: Clark, M. V.<br>Two or more authors<br>• Give last name and initials of all authors, no matter how many.<br>• Separate names with commas.<br>• Place an ampersand (&) before the last author. |

Example: Romer, M. A., & Shapiro, C. B.
Example: Bond, G. T., Gardner, H. L., Hart, F. C., & Magee, T.

**Date**

Book and journal

- Place the year of publication (in parentheses) after the author's name.
- Place a period at the end.

Example: (1954).

Magazine and newspaper

- For monthly publications, give the year and month (in parentheses) after the author's name.
- For weekly publications, give the year, month, and day (in parentheses) after the author's name.
- Place a comma after the year.
- Place a period at the end.

Example: (1978, January).
Example: (1986, August 15).



**Title**

Book

- Underline with a solid line.
- Capitalize only first word (title and subtitle) and proper nouns.
- Place a period at the end.

Example: Centuries of childhood: A social history of family life.

Periodical article

- Use no quotation marks or underlining.
- Capitalize only first word (title and subtitle) and proper nouns.
- Place a period at the end.

Example: The problem of perfection.

Periodical

- Underline with a solid line.
- Capitalize conventionally (see 31d).
- Place a comma after the title.

Example: Natural History Magazine,

**Publication Information**

Book

- After the title, give the city and a brief form of the publisher's name.
- Place a colon after the city and a period at the end.

Example: New York: Macmillan.

Journal

- Place the underlined volume number (arabic numeral) after the title; follow with a comma.
- Give inclusive page numbers.
- Place a period at the end.

Example: 3, 197-209.

Magazine and newspaper

- Omit the volume number.
- Give inclusive page numbers
- Place p. before one page number and pp. before more than one.
- Place a period at the end.

Example: p. B1.
Example: pp. 12-24.



In documenting references, you need to remember a few specifications about spacing. For student papers, APA allows single spacing in an entry but requires double spacing between entries. You should space twice after a period and once after other marks of punctuation. The first line is against the margin; any subsequent line is indented 3 spaces. The full forms of the most commonly used kinds of sources appear below.

**Basic Forms in APA Style**

| | |
|---|---|
| **Book** | Grotjohn, M. (1957). Beyond laughter. New York: McGraw-Hill.<br>Tiger, L., & Fox, R. (1971). The Imperial Animal. New York: Holt. |
| **Journal** | Bond, D. (1985). Ocean incineration of hazardous wastes: An update. Environmental Science and Technology, 19, 487-497.<br>Lockard, J. S., McDonald, L. L., Clifford, D., & Martinez, R. (1976). Panhandling: Sharing of resources. Science, 191, 406-408. |
| **Magazine** | Paul, C. K. (1979, October). Satellites and world food resources. Technology Review, pp. 18-29. |
| **Newspaper** | Witcher, G. (1989, May 22). Smart cars, smart highways. The Wall Street Journal, p. B1. |

In the *Publication Manual of the American Psychological Association*, there are numerous variations of these basic forms, most of which are reproduced below. If your source does not fit any of these categories, consult the manual.

### Additional APA Citation Forms



EDITED BOOK

Kleinmuntz, B. (Ed.). (1970). Concepts and the structure of memory. New York: Wiley.

Maccoby, E. E., Newcomb, T. M., & Hartley, E. L. (Eds.). (1985). Readings in social psychology. New York: Holt, Rinehart and Winston.

PART OF A BOOK

Lewin, K., Dembo, T., Festinger, L., & Sears, P. S. (1944). Level of aspiration. In J. McV. Hunt (Ed.), Personality and the behavior disorders. (pp. 333–378). New York: Ronald.

VOLUME OF A MULTIVOLUME WORK

Gibb, C. A. (1969). Leadership. In G. Linzey and E. Aronson (Eds.), Handbook of social psychology (Vol. 4, pp. 205–282). Reading, MA: Addison-Wesley.

LATER EDITION

Boshes, L. D., & Gibbs, F. A. (1972). Epilepsy handbook (2nd ed.). Springfield, IL: Thomas.

WORK WITH CORPORATE AUTHOR

League of Women Voters of the United States. (1969). Local league handbook. Washington, DC: Author.

ENCYCLOPEDIA ARTICLE

Hodge, R. W., & Siegel, P. M. (1968). The measurement of social class. In D. L. Sills (Ed.), International encyclopedia of the social sciences (Vol. 15, pp. 316–324). New York: Macmillan.

GOVERNMENT DOCUMENT

President's Committee on Mental Retardation. (1976). Mental retardation: The known and the unknown. Washington, DC: U. S. Government Printing Office.

Bormuth, J. R. (1969). Development of readability analyses (Univ. of Chicago Final Report No. 7–0052). Washington, DC: U. S. Office of Education.

ARTICLE IN A SCHOLARLY JOURNAL

Wright, P. (1960). Two studies of the depth hypothesis. British Journal of Psychology, 60, 63–69.

The volume number, not the issue number, is used when the journal is numbered continuously through the year.

Kaplan, B. M. (1985). Zapping—the real issue is communication. Journal of Advertising Research, 25(2), 9–12.

The volume number and the issue number are given when each issue begins with page 1.



ARTICLE IN A MAGAZINE OR NEWSPAPER, NO AUTHOR

Tale of the tape. (1989, May 29). Sports Illustrated, p. 14.

Pan Am charts a course for Europe, 1939. (1989, May 26). The Wall Street Journal, p. B1.

EDITORIAL AND LETTER

South Africa: Whites vs. apartheid. (1979, January 5). The Christian Science Monitor, p. 15.

Weinberg, G. L. (1985, June 18). Hitler remark on Armenians reported in '39 [Letter to the editor]. New York Times, p. A26.

BOOK REVIEW

Robinson, P. (1985, April). Freud's willful secretary [Review of Acts of will: The life and work of Otto Rank]. Psychology Today, pp. 69–71.

ABSTRACT

Pippard, J., & Ellam, L. (1981). Electroconvulsive treatment in Great Britain. British Journal of Psychiatry, 139, 563–568. (From Psychological Abstracts, 1982, 68, Abstract No. 1567)

MATERIAL FROM A COMPUTER INFORMATION SERVICE

Mazor, A. Y., & Mazor, S. R. (1983). Children's Ability to Draw Inferences from Text. Wisconsin Center for Education

Research, Madison. (ERIC Document Reproduction Service No. ED 239 239).

FILM

Kramer, S. (Producer), & Benedek, L. (Director). (1951). Death of a salesman [Film]. Columbia.

INTERVIEW

Anderson, A., & Southern, T. (1958). [Interview with Nelson Algren]. In M. Cowley (Ed.), Writers at work (pp. 231–249). New York: Viking.

If the interview is not published, it does not appear in "References." Instead, the text of the paper should clarify the interview's nature and date.

doc 41c

## Typing with APA style

- Use standard-sized (8½-×-11-inch) bond paper and standard type.
- Use a title page.
- Use 1½-inch margins on every page. The top margin of the first page of text may be wider.
- Double-space the paper. Student papers may have single-spaced references but with double spaces between them.
- Do not hyphenate words at the end of lines.
- Start numbering with the title page (page 1) and number the remaining pages consecutively.
- Block long quotations of more than forty words. Indent the left margin five spaces. In student papers, the entire block may be single-spaced. See the example, page 548.
- Type references on a separate page in alphabetical order. Title the reference page "References." Type the first line of each source against the left margin; indent other lines three spaces. For more than one entry by the same author, repeat the author's name.

# 41d Sample Research Paper Using APA Style

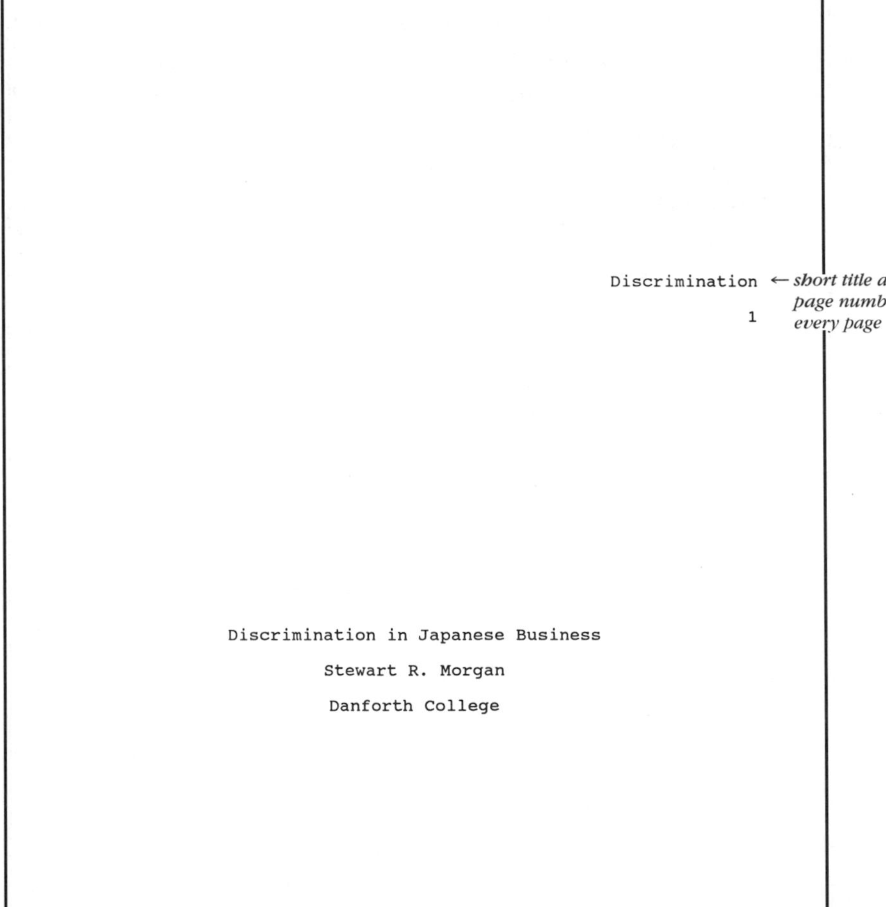

Discrimination ← *short title and page number on every page*
1

Discrimination in Japanese Business

Stewart R. Morgan

Danforth College

Discrimination

2

Outline

I. Japanese success

 A. Progress in Japan

 B. Progress in America

II. Problems despite the success

III. Discrimination against men

 A. Educational requirements

 B. University cliques

IV. Discrimination against women

 A. Educational limitations

 B. Traditional male business environment

  1. Importance of "group"

  2. Importance of a homogeneous system

  3. Importance of fraternizing

 C. Women's traditional role

  1. Marriage and motherhood

  2. Importance of sons and husbands

 D. Inferior work conditions

  1. Temporary work

  2. Lack of job security

 E. Inferior jobs

  1. Forbis' statistics

  2. Typical jobs

Discrimination in Japanese Business

*title repeated*

Japan has progressed from 260 years of feudalism to become a leading industrial nation (Rehder, 1983). Since World War II, Japanese productivity has increased four times as much as that of the United States (Ouchi, 1981). Although Japan is no larger than California, it now produces about 10% of the goods and services in the world. America has lost superiority to Japan in the production of cars and consumer electronics and may soon lose its advantage in such industries as computers (Lohr, 1984).

*author's name in parentheses when omitted from text*

Japanese businessmen have even made an impact on American companies. Steven Wheelwright (1981) tells the story of Matsushita's purchase of a Motorola TV assembly plant, which was troubled with problems such as 150 defects for every 100 sets it assembled. Under the guidance of Matsushita, the plant "increased its productivity by 30% and reduced its defects to fewer than 4 per 100 sets" (p. 67). Even with this improvement, according to Wheelwright, the Motorola plant still cannot equal similar Japanese plants, which have defect rates averaging only 0.5% or less.

*year in parentheses when author's name is in text*

*page number for a direct quotation*

Because of information about Japanese success, the United States has come to realize that "Japanese productivity has successfully challenged, even humiliated, America in world competition" (Bowman, 1984, p. 197). Also because of the growing reputation for Japanese business achievement, many American companies are trying to adopt Japanese methods into their management policies. However, American managers should be aware of several problems. In Japan, men in business are discriminated against occasionally, but women are discriminated against most of the time. And this discrimination is not at all compatible with American values.

In the Japanese system, children, both male and female, are rigorously educated from nursery school through the university. Lohr (1984) describes the system as extremely competitive and stressful:

*educational system desc[r] with three sources—o[n] quoted and summarize[d]*

> It is a system that emphasizes learning by rote, brute memorization, as the means to achieving high scores on standardized tests. Students, some of them as young as 3 years old, are sent to special schools to master test-taking tactics. These cram courses represent a multibillion-dollar industry. (p. 23)

After graduation the top male graduates of the best schools get the best jobs and form an "elite corps" (Bowman, 1984, p. 201). According to Ouchi (1981), the system discriminates against males who don't go to a major university. They usually find work in a secondary firm and at age 55 (the Japanese retirement age), open a "noodle shop" or move in with their children (p. 23).

A male who does graduate from the "right" university can get ahead through "informal clique networks" that are common in businesses. An older employee who graduated from the same university becomes a sponsor. According to Osako (1978), men without sponsors have little chance for respectable promotion.

The system also widely discriminates against women. Forbis (1975) points out that although both men and women go to college, women usually go to two-year colleges while men go to four-year universities. According to Rehder (1983), "Women graduates, regardless of their talent or level of academic achievement, remain outside the mainstream of corporate or government career opportunities (p. 43). Ouchi (1981) says bluntly, "Probably no form of organization is more sexist or racist than the Japanese corporation" (p. 92).

Bowman (1984) points out that in Japan "the basic social unit . . . is the group rather than the individual" and that in industry a major objective is to develop an "organizational cohesiveness" (p. 199). Ouchi (1981) believes that it is this attitude, rather than a belief in male superiority, that excludes women from employment. He maintains that Japanese organizations are "homogeneous social systems" and reject women because they are "different" (p. 92). He gives as an example a case in which an employer must choose between two equally qualified people--one male, one female. The employer, because of inexperience in evaluating females, would naturally choose the male; "no one in his right mind will choose an uncertainty over a certainty" (pp. 91-92). Osako (1978) observes that a woman is rarely part of a group unless she goes to bars with her male colleagues. Few women in Japan fit into this kind of setting.

Another reason for employment discrimination is the traditional role that women play in Japanese society.

Their goals are "marriage and motherhood" (Dillon, 1983). The marriage rate is extremely high, and the care of children is the exclusive job of women. Consequently, women rarely seek employment. Instead they remain at home and promote the education of their sons, since male children, if successful in school, may someday be successful in business. According to Dillon, "Mothers play an important role (and live vicariously) through the career development of their sons" (p. 23). Osako (1978) writes, "A woman is considered more virtuous if she devotes herself to the advancement of other family members (notably sons and husbands) rather than pursuing her own career" (p. 18).

Because of the possibility of marriage and family, working women are considered temporary employees (Rehder, 1983). According to Ouchi (1981), female employees are considered temporary even though they may work as long as 20 years at a job. Consequently, they have very little job security and are the first to be laid off in slack periods.

Dillon (1983) describes the jobs available to women as low-paying, boring, repetitive, and unskilled. In 1975, Forbis gave these statistics:

> Women dominate such jobs as nursing, stenography, textile spinning and weaving, and telephone operation, but they constitute only 8 percent of doctors, one-half of 1 percent of lawyers, and 1 percent of civil servants in managerial jobs. Women comprise half of elementary school teachers, but only 1 percent of all elementary school principals. (p. 35)

*quotations o[f] more than 2[...] words single-space[d] indented 5 s[...]*

According to Dillon, women from poor families end up in jobs with low prestige, like nightclub hostesses. A job like a department store sales clerk is not secure; clerks must retire at age 30 "when their physical attractiveness begins to wane" (p. 23). If women do get jobs, the work will likely be in Japan's "second economy" in small companies or cottage industries. As Rehder (1983) points out, "Here women receive low wages, little job security, and less opportunity for training or educational development" (p. 43). In fact, as Margaret Shapiro (1988) observes, although 40% of the work force is female, women have the lowest salaries and the worst jobs--"often wearing office uniforms with aprons to run errands and pour tea."

*four sources blended with quotations and summaries*

Therefore, while the Japanese system works with some success in Japan, Americans would find many of the practices unacceptable. Most Americans would object to the rigor of an educational system that depends heavily on entrance examinations, a hiring and promotional system based on favoritism, and an employment system that discriminates against women in all of its phases.

*a summary of points made in the main body*

Discrimination

8

*references single-spaced within items, double-spaced between*

References

Bowman, J. S. (1984). Japanese management: Personnel policies in the public sector. Public Personnel Management, 13, 197-247.

Dillon, L. (1983). Career development in Japan: Its relation to Japanese productivity. Journal of Career Education, 10, 22-26.

Forbis, W. H. (1975). Japan today: People, places, power. New York: Harper.

Lohr, S. (1984, July 8). The Japanese challenge: Can they achieve technological supremacy? New York Times Magazine, pp. 18-23, 37-41.

Osako, M. M. (1978). Dilemmas of Japanese professional women. Social Problems, 26, 15-25.

Ouchi, W. G. (1981). Theory Z: How Americans can meet the Japanese challenge. Reading, MA: Addison-Wesley.

Rehder, R. R. (1983). Education and training: Have the Japanese beaten us again? Personnel Journal, 62, 42-47.

Shapiro, M. (1988, February 9). In Japan, the sun still rises: Woman's main role remains housewife. The Washington Post, pp. A1, A16.

Wheelwright, S. (1981). Japan--where operations really are strategic. Harvard Business Review, 59, 67-74.

*volume numb[...] underlined, p[...] numbers*

# 41e Documentation with the Number System

Many papers and books are documented with the number system, popular primarily in science and technology. In this system, a number (placed in parentheses, in brackets, or above the line) marks each place where an outside source is used. A list of all sources appears at the end of the paper, either in alphabetical order or in the order of appearance in the work. The numbers in the text correspond with the numbers in the list of sources.

Although there are several versions of the number system, they are all similar. With a few modifications for student papers, the following version is the one used by *Science*, the publication of the American Association for the Advancement of Science.



## (1) Number-system documentation inside the paper

To follow the number system used in *Science*, you insert inside parentheses the numbers that indicate sources. You number your references in the order of their first mention: the first source you use is numbered (1), the second, (2), and so on. If you repeat a source in your paper, however, do not give it a new number. Instead, repeat the number used previously for that source. The numbers in the text can appear in two positions.

1. The number appears at the end of the borrowed material. Note that the number is placed within a sentence.

   With research, however, scientists may be able to make these foods "taste right" and thus significantly increase the food supply in countries with shortages (2).

2. When the author's name or the name of a source appears in a sentence, the number directly follows the name.

   According to Linda Bartoshuk (4), one of these controversies goes back to the last century.

## (2) Number-system documentation at the end of the paper

The numbers in the paper refer to references listed at the end of the paper in a section named "References" or "References and Notes."

The sources in the reference list should be in the order of their appearance in the text. Do not, however, list references more than once, even though they were used more than once in the text. While the numbers in the text appear in parentheses, the numbers in the reference list do not. Instead, they are followed by a period.

In addition to the sources, the list can also include comments not wanted in the text of the paper. For an example, see note 5, in the reference list on page 564. When a note or notes appear, the list is titled "References and Notes."

The following chart illustrates the way *Science* formats the components of the most commonly cited sources—books, journals, magazines, and newspapers.

doc 41e

**The Major Components of Citations in *Science***

**Author**

One author

- Use initials for given names.
- Use full last names.
- Place a comma at the end.

Example: R. Shiller,

Two authors

- Use initials and last names.
- Separate two names with *and*.
- Place a comma at the end.

Example: S. LeRoy and R. T. Porter,

Three to five authors

- Use initials and last names.
- Separate names with commas.
- Place a comma at the end.

Example: T. Marsh, S. D. Voss, M. B. Gorin, G. Andrews,

More than five authors

- Use initials and last name of first author.
- Follow name with *et al.*
- Place a comma at the end.

Example: P. Shapiro et al.,

**Title**

Book

- Capitalize traditionally (see 31d).

| | |
|---|---|
| | • Underline with a solid line.<br>Example: Principles of Rice Production<br>Periodical<br>• Capitalize traditionally.<br>• Underline with a solid line.<br>• Abbreviate titles of more than one word if you know the abbreviation or have looked it up in an index such as *Applied Science and Technology Index.*<br>Example: Sci. Am.<br>Example: Science |
| **Publication Information** | Book<br>• Give the publisher, place of publication, and date in parentheses.<br>• Separate the three items with commas.<br>• Place a comma after the last parenthesis.<br>• Give the page numbers preceded by the abbreviation p. or pp.<br>• Place a period at the end.<br>Example: (Wiley, New York, 1981), pp. 247-251.<br>Journal or magazine<br>• Give the volume number in bold type. If you have no bold type, underline the volume number with a wavy line.<br>• Place a comma after the volume.<br>• Give the first page number.<br>• Give the year; month and year; or day, month, and year in parentheses.<br>• Place a period at the end.<br>Example: **259,** 72 (1988).<br>Example: **25,** 15 (May 1980).<br>Newspaper<br>• Give the date (day/month/year) followed by a comma.<br>• Give the page number or numbers preceded by the abbreviation p. or pp.<br>Example: 5 June 1984, p. 1. |

doc 41e

These components fit together to form complete entries, illustrated in the following chart.

**Basic Forms in *Science* Style**

| | |
|---|---|
| **Book** | 1. B. Vladeck, *Unloving Care* (Basic Books, New York, 1980), p. 123.<br>7. A. Atkinson and J. Stiglitz, *Lectures on Public Economics* (McGraw-Hill, New York, 1980). |
| **Journal or Magazine** | 3. D. T. Krieger et al., *Nature* **298,** 468 (1982).<br>9. R. Davis, K. Kahn, D. A. Barber, M. Ebert, N. T. S. Evans, *Tech. Rev.* **58,** 39 (August 1960). |
| **Newspaper** | 2. E. Hersher, San Francisco *Chronicle*, 18 March 1989, p. A16. |



If you look at a reference list in *Science*, you will see the occasional use of *ibid* (the abbreviation of the Latin *ibidem*, meaning "in the same place"). *Ibid.* is used like a ditto mark to replace repeated information. For example, if two entries in a row cite the same journal, *ibid.* replaces the journal's name or the name, volume, and year.

6. A. E. Gill, *J. Phys. Oceangr.* **13,** 586 (1983).
7. D. E. Harrison and P. S. Schopf, ibid. **14,** 923 (1984).
8. M. C. Cane, *Science* **222,** 1189 (1983).
9. E. M. Rasmusson and J. M. Wallace, ibid., p. 1195.

Obviously, the use of *ibid.* saves space and thus cost. However, since space is not a problem in student papers, it is not essential to use *ibid.* The information can instead be repeated.

In addition to the basic forms used in the reference list, *Science* also contains special forms to cover a variety of sources, for example, parts of books, edited works, multivolume works, translations, and government documents.

### Additional Citation Forms from *Science*

#### Edited Book

9. B. Gray, Ed., *For-Profit Enterprise in Health Care* (National Academy Press, Washington, DC, 1986), p. 187.

7. O. A. Jones and R. Endean, Eds., Biology and Geology of Coral Reefs (Academic Press, New York, 1974), pp. 205–245.

CHAPTER

3. P. Gilman, in The Physics of the Sun, P. Sturock, Ed. (Reidel, Hingram, Mass., 1985).

LATER EDITION

6. J. D. Jackson, Classical Electrodynamics (Wiley, New York, ed. 2, 1975), pp. 672–679.

CORPORATE AUTHOR

4. U. S. Senate Committee on Aging, Aging America: Trends and Projections (Dept. of Health and Human Services, Washington, DC, 1988).
5. National Research Council, Oil in the Sea (National Academy Press, Washington, DC, 1985).



ONE VOLUME OF A MULTIVOLUME WORK

2. R. A. Norberg, Swimming and Flying in Nature (Plenum, New York, 1975), vol. 2, pp. 763–781.

REPRINTED WORK

9. D. R. Griffin, Listening in the Dark (Yale Univ. Press, New Haven, 1958; reprinted by Dover, New York, 1974).

TRANSLATION

7. E. S. Carlos, translator, The Sidereal Messenger of Galileo Galilei (Dawsons, London, 1880), pp. 70–71.

GOVERNMENT DOCUMENT

11. Statistical Abstract of the United States, 1983–84 (Department of Commerce, Washington, DC, 1983).
12. House Committee on Appropriations, Department of Labor, Health and Human Services, and Education, and Related Agencies Appropriations Bill, 1983, 97th Cong., 2nd sess., 29 September 1982, H. Rep. 894, p. 26.
13. Annual Report: Commissioner of Internal Revenue (US Internal Revenue Service, Washington, DC, 1985), p. 70.

REPORT

5. R. V. O'Neill and D. E. Reichle, Dimensions of Ecosystem Theory (Oak Ridge National Laboratory Publication No. 1355, Oak Ridge, TN, 1980).

ARTICLE IN JOURNAL OR MAGAZINE

9. L. Lewin, T. Eckels, L. Miller, New Engl. J. Med. **318,** 1212 (1988).

When the periodical's page numbers run consecutively throughout the year, only the volume number, beginning page number, and year are listed.

10. E. N. Parker, Sci. Am. **249,** 44 (August 1983).

11. S. L. Montgomery, Petroleum Bull. **3** (no. 4), 2 (1986).

doc 41e

When each issue of a periodical begins with page 1, you can add the month or day and month to the parentheses, or you can add the issue number in parentheses following the volume number.

ARTICLE IN A NEWSPAPER, NO AUTHOR

14. Anchorage Daily News, 19 April 1984, p. A-1.

ABSTRACT

10. J. B. C. Jackson, Bull. Mar. Sci. **23** (1973). [Abstract 10211, from Biol. Abstr. **59,** 1023 (1975)].

UNPUBLISHED MATERIAL

15. C. Sullivan and M. Perkins, unpublished observations.

16. B. K. Siesjo, personal communication.

### Typing with the number system

- Use standard paper (8½-×-11-inch bond) and type.
- Use a title page.
- Leave margins of 2.5 centimeters.
- Double-space the entire paper.
- Number the title page page 1. Type the title in the middle of the page. See the example, page 558.
- If you include an abstract, place it on page 2, and begin the text on page 3. Without an abstract, begin the text on page 2. Starting with the title page, place your name and the page number on each page.

- Do not hyphenate words at the ends of lines.
- Type references on a separate page entitled "References and Notes" or simply "References," if you have no notes. The items in the list are not in alphabetical order; instead, the items are listed in the order in which the citations appear in the text. All entries are numbered. For correct format, see the examples, page 564. When you have more than one reference by the same author in sequence, list the author once. In the subsequent entry, type a five-space line instead of the name. For example:

9. M. N. Cornforth and J. S. Bedford, Science **222,** 1141 (1983).

10. ———, Chromosoma **88,** 315 (1983).

# 41f Sample Research Paper Using the Number System

Pat Hogue
1

*author's n[ame] and page n[umber] on every p[age]*

Taste Research: Advances and Problems

Professor Wilford

English 102

## Outline

I. Introduction--A survey of the literature on the subject of taste research reveals not only a lack of knowledge but also considerable disagreement.

II. Research could increase the food supply by making potential food tasty.

III. Research could help explain the causes of obesity.

   A. "Learned satiety" helps normal people associate taste with calories and nutrition.

   B. Obese people may lack "learned satiety."

   C. Obese people may disregard "learned satiety."

IV. The mechanism of taste is disputed.

   A. The nature of the four tastes is disputed.

      1. Some believe in four distinct tastes.

      2. Some believe that tastes are a "continuum."

   B. Researchers disagree about the reaction of nerve fibers.

      1. The "pattern theory" was accepted until the 1970s.

      2. The "labeled-line coding" theory is disputed.

      3. The code has not been discovered.

V. The cause of taste malfunctions is disputed.

   A. As the cause, Henkin supports zinc deficiency.

   B. <u>Nutrition Reviews</u> disputes zinc therapy.

   C. The cause of taste malfunctions in space is unknown.

*introductory paragraph o[n] importance [of] subject*

On the surface, the taste of food may seem a trivial issue, but it could have widespread importance. Because taste determines which foods are eaten and which avoided, it may affect both personal health in developed countries as well as the food shortage in many underdeveloped countries. A survey of the research on taste reveals not only a significant lack of knowledge on the subject but also considerable disagreement on how taste functions. According to Phyllis E. Lehmann (1), taste research has been "long relegated to the back burner of scientific and medical research," but now taste is being investigated. Despite research, however, crucial questions are still unanswered.

*citations numbered i[n] sequence; parentheses [precede] the punctua[tion]*

The need for research into the connection between taste and the chemical structure of compounds has been attested to by Dr. Morley R. Kane, recipient of the Underwood-Prescott Memorial Award for contributions to the advancement of food science. According to Kane, at present there exist many potential foods that could feed the undernourished, but these foods are judged unpalatable. With research, however, scientists may be able to make these foods "taste right" and thus significantly increase the food supply in countries with shortages (2).

Taste research is also important in areas without food shortages. In Western society, too many people suffer from obesity. T. J. Roper (3) in <u>New Scientist</u>, cites studies indicating that normal people seem to associate the taste of food with its caloric and nutritional value. Called "learned satiety," this ability enables them to predict

*reference to content not[e]*

the amount of a particular food they want in a particular circumstance. Given a cafeteria setting, for example, most people can "decide whether to opt for salad or for sausage, egg, chips, and beans." Yet this kind of judgment fails obese people. One theory discussed by Roper is that they cannot make the association between amount of food and calories. Another theory is that obese people can make the right association, but for some reason, like a love of sweets, ignore it. Both theories have supporting evidence, but neither has been proved.

Other disputed theories involve the mechanism of taste itself. According to Linda Bartoshuk (4), one of these controversies goes back to the last century. Some current researchers agree with nineteenth-century physiologist Hjalmar Oehrwall, who maintained that the four tastes--sweet, salty, sour, and bitter--were completely distinct. Others agree with Friedrick Kiesow, a nineteenth-century German psychologist, that tastes are not separate but a continuum like a color spectrum. The argument has not been settled.

Taste researchers also disagree about the way nerve fibers react to the four tastes. Does a single nerve fiber react to only one of the four tastes or to more than one? If a fiber reacts to more than one taste, how does the brain know which taste to register? As Bartoshuk (4) explains, the "pattern theory," accepted until the 1970s, maintained that fibers respond to more than one taste and that a complex pattern of reactions permits the brain to get a specific message. A later refinement of the pattern theory is called "labeled-line coding." In this hypothesis, some fibers respond to more than one of the tastes, but each fiber is sensitive primarily to one of the tastes. Bartoshuk (4) writes about labeled-line coding, "There is no definitive proof that this view of taste is correct." Lehmann (1) supports the idea that some kind of "special code, which scientists are not yet able to 'crack,' tells the brain whether the taste is salty or sweet or whether the smell is roses or sulfur from a nearby coal-burning plant."

*two sources summarized quoted*

Another area of ongoing research is the problem of taste malfunctions. Scientists do not know what causes in some an absence of taste and in others a serious distortion (5). Robert Henkin, of the Georgetown University Medical Center, heads the only taste and smell treatment center in the world. Although Henkin cannot determine the cause for disorders in 19 percent of his patients, he believes most disorders were caused by flu, head injuries, or allergies. He further believes that about a third of his patients suffer from a zinc deficiency and respond when administered a supplement (1), but an article in Nutrition Reviews (6) concluded that "no scientific basis exists for administering zinc sulfate therapeutically for treating ordinary taste and smell dysfunctions."

*reference to content note*

*two conflicting sources cited one sentence*

In addition to questions about taste on earth, scientists find that taste presents problems in space. To the astronauts, food tastes different than it would on earth. No one knows why, although studies were done on Skylab in 1973 and 1974

Pat Hogue 6

and on Challenger in 1984. Russian studies of the unpleasant tastes of food in spacc have also been inconclusive. Theories blame nasal congestion in zero gravity, air currents in space, and changes in saliva. But the problem remains, and all the astronauts can do at present is spice up with seasonings, like taco sauce (7).

*conclusion on the importance of continued research*

To date, scientists face a multitude of unanswered questions about taste. However, continued research should result in worthwhile knowledge that could help us solve problems of world hunger, personal health, and even space travel.

Pat Hogue 7

References and Notes

1. P. E. Lehmann, Sciquest **54**, 7 (March 1981).

2. J. I. Mattill, Tech. Rev. **81**, 82 (February 1974).

3. T. J. Roper, New Scientist **101**, 30 (29 March 1984).

4. L. Bartoshuk, Psychol. Today **14**, 48 (September 1980).

5. Taste and smell disorders, called "anoemia," are considered serious handicaps to daily life. In fact, victims of these disorders can now claim disability under the Worker's Compensation Law and through the Veteran's Administration (1).

6. Nutr. Rev. **37**, 283 (1979).

7. D. Savold, Sci. 85 **6**, 86 (March 1985).

*double-spac… throughout*

*volume num… boldfaced*

*note 5 adds information writer does … include in th… body*

*information content note taken from … 1, P. E. Lehm…*

## ❑ REVIEW EXERCISE

"Kubla Khan" by Samuel Taylor Coleridge has received a great deal of attention because of the many mysteries associated with the poem: Is the poem really a dream? When was it written? What does it mean? Material written in an attempt to answer these questions is extensive. Therefore, for a short paper, a writer would have to treat a limited part of the poem. The following excerpts from books and articles on the poem cover only one of the poem's images—"Alph, the sacred river." To practice paraphrasing, documenting, and integrating sources, write a paper on the various interpretations of the meaning of the river. Follow this procedure.

Read the poem and the excerpts. (Any information explaining the contexts for the excerpts will appear in brackets.)
Take notes by any method you think appropriate—by paraphrasing, summarizing, quoting, or by a combination of methods.
Write a short paper, blending the material into a coherent whole.
Document all sources by some acceptable system.



Kubla Khan

In Xanadu did Kubla Khan
A stately pleasure-dome decree:
Where Alph, the sacred river, ran
Through caverns measureless to man
    Down to a sunless sea.
So twice five miles of fertile ground
With walls and towers were girdled round:
And here were gardens bright with sinuous rills,
Where blossomed many an incense-bearing tree;
And here were forests ancient as the hills,
Enfolding sunny spots of greenery.

But oh! that deep romantic chasm which slanted
Down the green hill athwart a cedarn cover!
A savage place! as holy and enchanted
As e'er beneath a waning moon was haunted
By woman wailing for her demon-lover!
And from this chasm, with ceaseless turmoil seething,
As if this earth in fast thick pants were breathing,
A mighty fountain momently was forced:
Amid whose swift half-intermitted burst

Huge fragments vaulted like rebounding hail,
Or chaffy grain beneath the thresher's flail:
And 'mid these dancing rocks at once and ever
It flung up momently the sacred river.
Five miles meandering with a mazy motion
Through wood and dale the sacred river ran,
Then reached the caverns measureless to man,
And sank in tumult to a lifeless ocean:
And 'mid this tumult Kubla heard from far
Ancestral voices prophesying war!
    The shadow of the dome of pleasure
    Floated midway on the waves;
    Where was heard the mingled measure
    From the fountain and the caves.
It was a miracle of rare device,
A sunny pleasure-dome with caves of ice!



    A damsel with a dulcimer
    In a vision once I saw:
    It was an Abyssinian maid,
    And on her dulcimer she played,
    Singing of Mount Abora.
Could I revive within me,
Her symphony and song,
To such a deep delight 'twould win me,
That with music loud and long,
I would build that dome in air,
That sunny dome! those caves of ice!
And all who heard should see them there,
And all should cry, Beware! Beware!
His flashing eyes, his floating hair!
Weave a circle round him thrice,
And close your eyes with holy dread,
For he on honey-dew hath fed,
And drunk the milk of Paradise.

**Sources**

Excerpts from John Livingston Lowes, *The Road to Xanadu,* published by Houghton Mifflin, Boston, 1927.

[Lowes maintains that the poem actually came to Coleridge in a dream in which images from books he had read blended. Two of these books were travel books—William Bartram's, which describes an isle of palms in Florida, and James Bruce's, which describes the Nile River. From numerous other sources such as Pausanias and Virgil, Coleridge would have learned the myths of the sacred Nile and Alpheus, both which supposedly ran underground from Asia.]

*Excerpt 1:* Of one thing, then, we may be certain: impressions of Bartram's "inchanting little Isle of Palms" were among the sleeping images in Coleridge's unconscious memory at the time when "Kubla Khan" emerged from it. (p. 365)

*Excerpt 2:* One of the books most widely read at the close of the century was James Bruce's *Travels to Discover the Source of the Nile,* and Coleridge knew it well. (p. 370)

*Excerpt 3:* The vivid images of fountains in Florida and Abyssinia, with their powerfully ejected streams, have coalesced in the deep Well and risen up together, at once both and neither, in the dream. And by virtue of that incomprehensible juggling with identities which is the most familiar trick of dreams, "the sacred river" is the Nile—while at the same time it is *not.* Only in a dream, I once more venture to believe, could the phantasmagoria . . . have risen up. (p. 372)



*Excerpt 4:* Above all, what lost suggestion underlies that most mysterious of appellations, "Alph"? (p. 387)

*Excerpt 5:* And that myth of the subterranean-submarine passage of the Nile from Asia through to Africa Coleridge certainly knew. It is needless to conjecture how often, in "the wide, wild wilderness" of his early reading, he had met it. (p. 388)

*Excerpt 6:* Bartram's subterranean caverns and the mythical abysses of the Nile are two of a kind. It would be next to impossible for Coleridge to read of either without some reminiscence of the other. And the two were probably associated in his memory long before the moment of the dream. (p. 391)

*Excerpt 7:* There was another storied river which sank beneath the earth, and flowed under the sea, and rose again in a famous fountain. As was inevitable, it was constantly associated with the legendary Nile. And Coleridge, like every schoolboy, knew it [the Alpheus]. (p. 393)

*Excerpt 8:* [A chapter of a work by Seneca] contains a vivid picture of the "lifeless ocean" and the "sunless sea" out of which such rivers as the Nile and the Alpheus rise, and to which they return. (p. 395)

*Excerpt 9:* Passages [that Coleridge had read] had telescoped in the dream, so there seem to have merged linked reminiscences of the Alpheus and the Nile. And by one of those puckish freaks of the dream intelligence which are often so preternaturally apt, "Alpheus" has been docked of its syllabic excess, and dream-fashioned, as "Alph," into a quasi-equivalence with "Nile." (p. 396)

Excerpts from Wylie Sypher's article "Coleridge's Somerset: A Byway to Xanadu," which appeared in the *Philological Quarterly,* volume 18, October 1939, pp. 353–356.

[Coleridge was influenced by the terrain of the land around Somerset in England, particularly by caverns at Cheddar Gorge and by a dramatic cavern named Wookey Hole.]

*Excerpt 1:* Coleridge had visited Cheddar long before "Kubla Khan" was written, and the supposition that its "deep romantic chasm" influenced the imagery of the poem seems allowable. (p. 358)

**doc 41f**

*Excerpt 2:* Then too, hidden streams, like those in "Kubla Khan," did and do well up in Cheddar gorge; in fact, the river at the mouth of the chasm debouches from an underground rivulet through sundry fissures. . . . Nevertheless, the "pleasure domes," the "caves of ice," the river sinking in tumult, and the "caverns measureless to man" more probably originate, in part, in that fantastic grotto of Wookey (or Ochey) Hole, five miles from Cheddar and a mile from Wells. To presume that Coleridge did not know of Wookey or that he had not read of it or visited it is far more unwarranted than to suppose the opposite. (p. 359)

*Excerpt 3:* Coleridge may also have read Samuel Bowden's description of the subterranean river at Wookey in his *Poems* (1754). Bowden links this river with the Nile and the Alpheus, which admittedly suggested to Coleridge the name of his sacred river Alph. (p. 361)

Excerpt from G. Wilson Knight, *The Starlit Dome,* published by Oxford University Press, London, 1941.

*Excerpt:* There is a "sacred" river that runs into "caverns measureless to man" and a "sunless sea." That is, the river runs into an infinity of death. The marked-out area through which it flows is, however, one of teeming nature: gardens, rills, "incense-bearing" trees, ancient forests. This is not unlike Dante's earthly paradise. The river is "sacred." Clearly a sacred river which runs through nature towards death will in some sense correspond to life. I take the river to be, as so often in Wordsworth (whose *Immortality Ode* is also throughout suggested), a symbol of life. (p. 91)

Excerpts from Humphry House, *Coleridge,* published by Rupert Hart-Davis, London, 1953.

*Excerpt 1:* "Kubla Khan" is a poem about the act of poetic creation. (p. 115)

*Excerpt 2:* The precision and clarity of the opening part are the first things to mark—even in the order of the landscape. In the center is the pleasure-dome with its gardens on the river bank: to one side is the river's source in the chasm, to the other are the "caverns measureless to man" and the "sunless sea" into which the river falls: Kubla in the center can hear the "mingled measure" of the fountain of the source from one side, and of the dark caves from the other. The river winds across the whole landscape. (p. 116)

*Excerpt 3:* Its [the river's] function in the poem is clear. The bounding energy of its source makes the fertility of the plain possible: it is the sacred given condition of human life. By using it rightly, by building on its bank, by diverting its water into his sinuous rills, Kubla achieves his perfect state of balanced living. It is an image of these non-human, holy, given conditions. It is not an allegorical river which would still flow across the plain if Kubla was not there. It is an imaginative statement of the abundant life in the universe, which begins and ends in a mystery touched with dread, but it is a statement of this life as the ground of ideal human activity. (p. 121)



*Excerpt 4:* For this is a vision of the ideal human life *as the poetic imagination can create it.* (p. 122)

Excerpt from Douglas Angus's article "The Theme of Love and Guilt in Coleridge's Three Major Poems," *Journal of English and Germanic Philology,* volume 59, 1960, pp. 655–668.

*Excerpt:* One of the most mysterious images in "Kubla Khan" is the strange river that dominates the landscape of the first half of the poem. It is too strange a river and takes on too great a role in the poem to be simply a river. Its mysterious name, Alph, its equally strange origin, the fact that it is sacred, its odd course, first meandering lazily, then sinking into caverns measureless to man, all suggest hidden meanings. But the river is a very familiar symbol of life, as the common phrase "the stream of life" implies. William Steckel in his extensive study of dreams discusses the river as a symbol of the dreamer's life at great length, and Freud mentions particularly the frequency with which concealed and underground waterways seem to symbolize in dreams the womb and sexual apparatus of the body. In the poem it is tied in with the familiar symbols of birth (the laboring fountain) and of death (the sunless sea where all rivers end); moreover, its early mazy, meandering, open course is suggestive of childhood before the complications of repressions turn life inward. This course lasts for five miles (such measurements are nearly always a symbol of time according to Freud) before it sinks into the caverns measureless to man, a wonderful way of saying symbolically that the center of life has shifted below the consciousness. (p. 664)

Excerpts from George Watson's article "The Meaning of 'Kubla Khan,'" *Review of English Literature,* volume 2, January 1961, pp. 21–29.

*Excerpt 1:* What is "Kubla Khan" about? This is, or ought to be, an established fact of criticism: "Kubla Khan" is a poem about poetry. (p. 23)

*Excerpt 2:* Though the whole design is of course artificial—an enclosed park centering upon a palace or "stately pleasure-dome"—it contains within itself, as its unique possession, something utterly natural and utterly uncontrollable: the sacred river itself, for the rest of its course subterranean, bursts into the light at this point and flows violently above ground before sinking back. It is for this reason, evidently, that the tyrant chose the site for his palace, which stands so close to the water that it casts its shadow upon it and is within earshot of the sound of the river, both above and below ground. And these two noises, we are told, harmonise. (pp. 24–25)

*Excerpt 3:* The vast power of the river is allowed to rise, but only "momently," and then sinks back into silence, "a lifeless ocean." This is not the River of Life. It is the river of poetry—the poetry of imagination which, under the old order, had been debased into a plaything and allowed its liberty only when properly "girdled round." The passage that describes the river as it rushes above ground is dense with the imagery of the violent reshaping of dull matter, like the "essentially vital" power of the imagination working. . . . So many rivers and springs of classical mythology are associated with poetry that there is nothing remote or improbable about Coleridge's imagery here. (p. 29)

doc 41f

**Excerpts from Marshall Suther, *Visions of Xanadu,* published by Columbia University Press, New York, 1965.**

*Excerpt 1:* For once, virtually everything is in agreement. . . . The sacred river is the river of Life. (pp. 211–212)

*Excerpt 2:* The sacred river Alpheus seems the most likely origin of the name, and the poem is relevantly enriched if the associations clinging about the fabulous river in the many works where Coleridge was likely to have encountered it at least hover in the background of the reader's mind. (p. 212)

# 42

# Essay Examinations

exam 42a

Essay examinations require students to write answers in composition form. These examinations usually do not allow enough time for the normal writing process of getting ideas, organizing, writing several drafts, and revising. Therefore, instructors do not expect essay examinations to be as well written as papers that have been drafted and redrafted. They do, however, expect informed and logical answers with reasonably correct grammar, mechanics, and punctuation.

## 42a Effective Studying

When you study for essay examinations, you should anticipate possible questions, a much easier job than you might expect. The typical essay question calls for specific material treated in a particular way. For example, if you are studying short stories, your instructor might choose two and ask you to compare and contrast the main character in each. Or if you are studying different types of human cultures, your instructor might want you to classify them. Or if you are studying the American Revolution, your instructor might ask you to discuss the effects of Thomas Paine's pamphlets on public sentiment. In other words, an instructor will not want you to write random notes on everything you have studied. Instead, he or she will phrase questions to direct the content and organization of the answers. Usually, a question will specify a certain organizational technique: analysis, cause/effect, classification, comparison/contrast, defense, definition, explanation, evaluation, illustration, interpretation, or summary.

Following is a list of these organizational techniques along with a description of what they ask you to do and sample test questions. If you become familiar with the typical phrasing of essay questions, you will be able not only to anticipate the questions but also to organize material in preparation for tests.



ANALYSIS: Divide into components a theory, philosophy, process, device, literary work, or event.

SAMPLE QUESTIONS: "Analyze the process of mitosis." "What are the four major components of a computer system?"

CAUSE/EFFECT: Point out the reasons that something happened or will happen, or show what resulted from an event or what might result from a set of conditions.

SAMPLE QUESTIONS: "What were the major causes of World War I?" "Discuss the social effects of the Industrial Revolution."

CLASSIFICATION: Divide into types or categories whatever you are studying—people, events, theories, trends, practices, processes, literary works, or works of art.

SAMPLE QUESTIONS: "Classify the forms of city government." "Discuss the major subtypes of schizophrenia."

COMPARISON/CONTRAST: Show significant similarities and differences between theories, literary works, eras, cultures, processes, productions, or people.

SAMPLE QUESTIONS: "Compare and contrast the two young heroes of *The Catcher in the Rye* and *Huckleberry Finn*." "How does state government differ from federal government?"

DEFENSE: Support or justify an idea, movement, procedure or decision.

SAMPLE QUESTIONS: "Defend the following statement: To some extent, our language determines the way we think." "Support the notion of group personality."

| | |
|---|---|
| DEFINITION: | Define or explain a theory, process, term, or philosophy. |
| SAMPLE QUESTIONS: | "Define 'transcendentalism.'" "What is an 'excited' atom?" |
| EXPLANATION: | Use generalizations and supporting details to make clear an idea, theory, process, or interpretation. |
| SAMPLE QUESTIONS: | "Discuss the impact of the Civil War on women in the North and South." "Explain Newton's First Law of Motion." |
| EVALUATION: | Make a judgment on the worth of an idea, trend, theory, procedure, literary work, or production. |
| SAMPLE QUESTIONS: | "Evaluate the validity of Margaret Mead's findings in *Coming of Age in Samoa*." "Is the movie *High Noon* an artistic triumph or a stock, sentimental western?" |
| ILLUSTRATION: | Give examples to clarify an idea, theory, practice, or type of literature. |
| SAMPLE QUESTIONS: | "Use three of the short stories you have studied this semester to illustrate the omniscient point of view." "Use Yorktown as a case study to discuss the movement toward British surrender." |
| INTERPRETATION: | Provide insight into the meaning of a literary work, work of art, theory, or law. |
| SAMPLE QUESTIONS: | "Interpret the symbolism in one of Salvador Dali's paintings." "Discuss Faulkner's short story 'The Bear' as a nature myth." |
| SUMMARY: | Condense the main ideas in the material. |
| SAMPLE QUESTIONS: | "Summarize the functions of money in society." "Briefly discuss how an anthropologist conducts a field study." |

exam 42a

## ❑ EXERCISE 1

**Which of the preceding techniques could be used to organize an answer to each of these essay questions? Sometimes, more than one pattern is appropriate.**

1. Discuss Gray's "Elegy Written in a Country Churchyard" as an example of "graveyard poetry."
2. What is the "greenhouse effect"?
3. Discuss the validity of the theory of Social Darwinism.
4. Briefly discuss the nature of urban crime and attempts to fight it.
5. What were the principal reasons for peasant uprisings in the fourteenth century?
6. Describe the main parts of a turbojet engine.
7. How did the lives of cattle ranchers on the Western frontier differ from the lives of farmers?
8. Support the "big bang" theory.
9. Interpret the light and dark imagery in Conrad's *Heart of Darkness.*
10. Why must cells have the processes of endocytosis and exocytosis?



## 42b Practice Examinations

While studying for essay examinations, you should apply the organizational techniques discussed in 42a to increase your comprehension of the material. Try to imagine possible essay questions and then write some practice examinations—probably the most important steps for success. Writing several essays such as your instructor might assign gives you practice in handling the material and in expressing your ideas about it. Just as important, the practice writing will help you remember the material.

Before you write, consider that your purpose is to inform and that your audience is a general reader. (For a discussion of purpose and audience in writing, see 35a and 35b.) Do not write to your instructor; you might be tempted to omit key information because the instructor already knows it. If you leave out essentials, your answer will be inadequately developed.

Next, find a thesis, or controlling idea, to direct your writing. Simply writing down random notes will not accomplish much. Instead, you need an idea to control your thoughts, your lecture notes, and the information in your textbook. (See 35d.) If the material you are studying does not suggest a direction, go back to the techniques and look for an idea something like the following.

> Basically there are four types of consciousness. (classification)
>
> *The Great Gatsby* illustrates life among the idle rich in the Jazz Age. (illustration)

Henry Clay wanted to be president of the United States but did not succeed. His combativeness caused his failure. (cause/effect)

Skinner's theories of behaviorism are outdated. (defense)

Once you have framed your thesis, make an informal outline or list of supporting evidence; then write the essay. You may have to write several drafts before you get a satisfactory product. But the rewriting helps you not only to remember the material but also to iron the wrinkles out of your logic, learn to spell unfamiliar words, and practice your prose.

If you do not have time to write essays, at least outline answers to several possible questions. Outlines will help you think about the material, find support for controlling ideas, and organize information.

Obviously, you cannot predict with certainty the questions on your test, but practice essays are never a waste of time—active studying is much more effective than passive studying. And after you have written the practice essays, you might want to read them into a tape recorder and play them back while tending to everyday affairs, such as exercising, cleaning up, or driving to class.



## 42c Taking the Examination

One of the greatest psychological blocks to writing good essay examinations is fear of running out of time. But here a cliché is worth remembering: "Haste makes waste." The following guidelines will help you use your time productively.

- Take the time to read the directions carefully.

Make sure you know whether you have to answer all the questions or whether you have choices. In addition, see if point values are given and plan to spend the most time on the questions with the most value.

- Carefully examine the wording of each question.

What does the question ask you to do? Compare? Contrast? Analyze? Classify? Evaluate? Illustrate? Define?

Outside of poor preparation, the most common cause of a weak examination essay is the failure to address the question as it is asked. Too often students want to write the information just as they studied it. But on an essay examination, an instructor usually wants to see whether students can think about the material and manipulate it in some special fashion.

If your instructor asks you to discuss the theme of a story, you will not get many points for a plot outline. If the question says "evaluate," a simple summary of the ideas will not be satisfactory. You should not expect to answer the questions just as you practiced. But you will frequently be surprised how much previous thinking and organizing can be incorporated into the examination.

- Find a thesis, a controlling idea.

A thesis will unify your essay by guiding the details you choose to incorporate.



- Spend a few minutes roughly outlining each major point and its support.

This tactic will help you find a logical organization before you write and prevent your leaving out anything important as you write.

- Address a general audience.

As you did with your practice essays, write to a general audience, not to your teacher. You must demonstrate the extent of your knowledge.

- Establish your point immediately.

Do not waste time preparing an elaborate introduction. A good way to begin is to state your thesis, or controlling idea, so that you and your instructor can see the point you intend to support.

- Include only those details that support your thesis.

Do not include something irrelevant just to show that you studied it. Extra material, no matter how interesting, will not help your grade. It will only skew your logic and confuse your organization.

- Make your support as specific as possible.

You should support the major points in your rough outline with concrete details. You cannot successfully support a generalization with nothing but other generalizations.

- Do not equate length and quality.

One of the major myths about essay tests is that instructors do not read the papers but merely look to see how long each answer is. Content is more important than length.

- Remember that you cannot separate a thought from its expression.

Grammar does count. So do punctuation and correct spelling. Poor prose gets in the way of your reader's understanding. Furthermore, bad writing makes a bad impression by directing the reader's attention to the writing faults rather than to the strength of the preparation and understanding.

- If possible, save a little time to proofread.

You do not always have the time, but you should try to go back over the essay once you have finished it. You might catch an error or an omission that really makes a difference.



## 42d Sample Essay Examinations

The two questions that follow are typical of essay examinations, the first from an English class, the second from a history class. For each question, you will find two answers—one unsatisfactory, the other satisfactory. Compare the answers and the analyses to see what distinguishes a good answer from a poor one.

ENGLISH QUESTION: Discuss the conflict in Thurber's story "The Catbird Seat."

ANSWER 1 TO ENGLISH QUESTION

The conflict in the story is between Mr. Martin and Mrs. Barrows. The president of the firm hires Mrs. Barrows to make changes in the business. She runs around the firm saying things about getting an ox out of a ditch and sitting in the catbird seat. She heard these things from the announcer of Dodger baseball games.

Mr. Martin becomes afraid that Mrs. Barrows will ruin his department, so he decides to kill her. Everyone knows that Mr.

Martin does not drink or smoke, so he buys a package of Camels and goes to Mrs. Barrows' apartment. He tries to find a murder weapon there, but he can't. So he drinks a drink and smokes a cigarette and tells Mrs. Barrows that he takes heroin. He even tells her that he is going to kill the president of the firm. Mrs. Barrows tells him to leave and goes into the office the next day and tells the president what Mr. Martin did at her apartment.

The president calls Mr. Martin in and asks him about what Mrs. Barrows has said. Mr. Martin says that he didn't do it. So, the president fires Mrs. Barrows.

The story teaches us that sometimes quiet people can be quite dangerous.



ANALYSIS OF ANSWER 1 TO ENGLISH QUESTION

The question asks the student to explain one element in the short story, the conflict. Thus, the answer should consist of a generalization (a thesis, or controlling idea), supported by details. But the writer ignores the question and gives instead a plot summary, probably the worst mistake that can be made in an essay about literature. Aside from the first sentence, the answer does not contain any discussion at all of the conflict. Thus, the essay does not tell the instructor whether or not the student understands either the idea of conflict in literature or Thurber's use of conflict in this particular story.

Next, the writer insists on finding a moral: "This story teaches us. . . ." The primary purpose of the story is to entertain. In the process, Thurber may show the reader something about human behavior, but he does not "teach."

Finally, the writer cannot remember the name of a significant character, referring to him as "the president of the firm." Although a good essay answer might contain a memory slip, in this case the omission simply confirms the low quality of the writer's presentation.

ANSWER 2 TO ENGLISH QUESTION

The conflict in the story occurs at two levels. First, it arises out of the war between Mr. Martin, a timid clerk at F. and S., and

Mrs. Barrows, a loud, crude woman employed as a special advisor to reorganize the business. Martin is happy with his files and the security he has gained from twenty years in the firm. Barrows rampages through the company, attacking departments and offending Martin with down-home remarks like "tearing up the pea patch" and "sitting in the catbird seat."

When Martin realizes that Barrows is about to attack his department, he devises a vague plan to kill her. But after he arrives at her apartment and can't find a suitable murder weapon, a better plan occurs to him. He drinks, smokes, claims to take heroin, and announces his plan to blow up his boss, Fitweiler, with a bomb.

The second level of the story's conflict occurs within Martin himself. He struggles to control his panic when he thinks Barrows will attack his department. He struggles to carry out the charade in her apartment without giving himself away. He struggles to maintain his composure when confronted with Barrows' accusations.



Both conflicts are resolved when Fitweiler believes Martin's quiet denial of the accusations. Barrows is carted off to a psychiatrist, and Martin is left "sitting in the catbird seat."

**Analysis of Answer 2 to English Question**

The second answer to the question is much better because the writer directly addresses the question and explains the conflict in the short story. The essay begins with the thesis, the idea that the story's conflict occurs at two levels. Then the writer takes up each level of conflict, one at a time, giving only those plot details that support and clarify the claim. Thus, the essay has a clear point and a logical organization. Furthermore, all the information directly supports the thesis. The essay ends with a short paragraph that points out the conflict's resolution and explains the story's title. An instructor can tell from this essay that the writer has read the story carefully, understands the concepts of conflict and resolution, and can apply the concepts to a particular piece of literature.

**History Question:** How did the roles of men and women in the city-state of Sparta differ from those in Athens?

ANSWER 1 TO HISTORY QUESTION

Sparta was a military state. Boys were taken from their families at age seven and put in companies of fifteen boys. They all ate their meals together. At age fifteen, the boys gave up all their clothes except one outer garment. They lived a very harsh and simple existence. They served on the police force from age twenty to thirty. At thirty, a male was considered a full citizen with all the rights of citizenship. At sixty, men retired from the military and either went into public service or trained boys for the military. Women, however, did not participate in the military and were well treated.



The men of Athens went through four stages of government. They were first ruled by a king, then by landowning aristocrats, then by a tyrant, then by the people. Athens was a democracy. However, Athenian women did not have any voice in the government. They were treated like slaves and foreigners.

ANALYSIS OF ANSWER 1 TO HISTORY QUESTION

Clearly the question calls for a comparison/contrast technique, and the writer at least makes some attempt to contrast the two societies. The answer includes the notion of the Spartan military state versus the Athenian democracy. However, the treatment of Sparta is twice as long as that of Athens. In fact, the writer devotes more time to the role of Spartan men than to the roles of Spartan women, Athenian men, and Athenian women combined. Furthermore, some of the details included in the discussion seem beside the point. For instance, the fact that Spartan boys had only one outer garment is interesting but does not shed much light on the differing roles of men and women. In short, this answer has no thesis, or controlling idea, to direct the choice of details and no balance among the parts of the essay.

ANSWER 2 TO HISTORY QUESTION

The social roles of Spartan men and women were very different from those of Athenian men and women. Sparta was a militaristic state in which men served the defense system for most of their lives. At age seven, boys were taken from home and placed in military companies, where they had only the bare necessities of life. Their education stressed discipline and physical skills. From twenty to thirty, Spartan men served as military police to keep the slaves in line. At thirty, they became full citizens; they could attend public meetings, hold public office, and marry. Because of their harsh military training, Spartan men were generally very conservative politically and had no interest in art and culture.

Athenian men set great store by political freedom and the enrichment of the human spirit. This attitude encouraged intellectual and artistic development. In fact, Athenian men were the cultural leaders of the Greek world. All classes of free men, not just aristocrats, participated in government and were interested in drama, art, and philosophy.



In view of these differences, one would expect the society of Athens to be more liberal toward women than that of Sparta. However, Athenian women had no legal or political rights. A woman could not hold public office or appear in court without a male representative. Also, a woman had to have a legal guardian, usually her husband or father; this guardian controlled her property and her behavior. Athenian women were forbidden not only to participate in the Olympics but even to attend the games. The Athenian philosopher Aristotle wrote that women were by nature inferior to men.

On the other hand, Spartan females had more freedom than any women in Greece. The girls participated in athletics. The women ran households and businesses. Some even became wealthy and powerful. In fact, it has been reported that two-fifths of all the land in Sparta was owned by women.

### Analysis of Answer 2 to History Question

This answer begins with a thesis that limits discussion to the "social roles" of men and women in Sparta and Athens. The essay has two main parts—first a contrast of men's roles and then a contrast of women's roles. The details included in each section support the controlling idea.

In addition, approximately the same number of details define the roles of Spartan men, Spartan women, Athenian men, and Athenian women. Thus the essay has a proper balance, with equal time devoted to each element of the question.

## ❑ EXERCISE 2

**Following are two answers to the essay question "Contrast the characters of Ralph and Jack and their roles in *The Lord of the Flies.*" Choose the better answer and defend your choice.**



ANSWER 1

Both Ralph and Jack try to be the leader of the island. First Ralph finds a conch shell and calls all the boys together, so they elect him their leader. Jack leads the choirboys and gets mad when he isn't elected. Ralph tells the boys that no one can speak at meetings unless he is holding the conch shell. He tries to establish order.

The boys use a pair of glasses to start a signal fire so they can be rescued, but they don't keep it going all the time. Ralph gets mad because the boys don't tend the fire and build shelters. Ralph wants the boys to behave in a civilized manner and use common sense. Also, Simon seems to like Ralph better than he likes Jack. Like Simon, Ralph tries to think of the welfare of the others. But he gradually loses control of the boys. Finally, they don't follow him any more.

Jack likes to hunt and kill pigs like a savage. Gradually, Jack gains control over the boys. By the end of the story, they see Jack as their leader and they try to hunt Ralph down and kill him.

Before the boys are able to kill Ralph, a naval officer appears. Ralph breaks down and cries.

ANSWER 2

Although Ralph and Jack have some qualities in common, they represent two different sides of human nature. Throughout the novel, Ralph seems to stand for order and reason. His right-hand man is

Piggy, the intellectual of the group. Ralph and Piggy take a practical approach to the predicament, trying to keep a signal fire going and to build shelters. They start the signal fire by using a lens of Piggy's glasses. The suggestion is that the glasses bring fire, or light, symbolic of knowledge.

Jack is also practical to a point. He organizes the hunters and kills wild pigs for food. But the killing of the pigs soon becomes a ritual. The hunters paint their faces with colored clay, and they dance and chant after the killings. Jack's right-hand man is Roger, a sadist and a murderer.

While Ralph tries to remain civilized, Jack reverts to savagery. Nevertheless, the two characters are not pure symbols of good and evil. Ralph joins in the attack on one of the boys during a ritual after a hunt, and there is a hint that he participates in the murder of Simon. On the other hand, Jack occasionally has a few misgivings about his violent acts.



On the whole, however, Ralph represents reason, order, and common sense. Jack represents irrational evil and savagery. The author seems to suggest that these two major characters represent the potential for good and evil that exists in all human beings.

# 43

# Critical Reviews

crit 43

Critical reviews explain and evaluate some form of scholarship, art, or entertainment, such as a novel, an art exhibit, a play, a movie, a concert, or a restaurant. Reviews published in newspapers, magazines, and journals help readers to decide whether to read a book; see an exhibit, play, or movie; or eat in a restaurant. While in school, you are not likely to write published reviews. You are likely, however, to write reviews as class assignments—reviews of novels, short stories, poems, plays, or nonliterary works.

Writing a critical review is similar to writing other kinds of papers. You must find a topic, generate ideas for its development, focus and structure your ideas, and write and revise until you produce a paper that satisfies the audience's expectations and needs. (See Chapters 34–38 for a discussion of the entire writing process.) In producing a critical review, however, you emphasize some parts of the process more than others. Usually, you will not have to search for a topic from a broad range of possibilities. Frequently, the topic is assigned. If you do have a choice of written works to review, your sources are still limited. Thus, you will probably spend less time looking for a topic but more time reading the work and researching the genre, the author, or the historical background.

## 43a Careful Reading

Never attempt to review material that you have not read carefully, preferably more than once. In the first reading, you should familiarize yourself with the work as a whole and determine the author's purpose. Every work has an underlying purpose that guides the author's choice of materials and method of presentation. For example, the writer of a science fiction novel may set out to comment on the problems of contemporary society by creating a bizarre world in the future. The writer of a book on criminal justice may intend to sketch a history of the penal system for students new to the field. The writer of a play might be trying a form of experimental theater.

After you have an overview, you should read the work again to look closely at the details. It is the details that will support your opinion of the work. Without reference to details, your review will be so general and superficial that it will lack credibility.



To be able to retrieve the details when you write the review, you must mark significant and supporting passages as you read. How you mark a work depends on whether you own it or not. If a work belongs to you, you can highlight the passages and annotate them in the margins. If a work belongs to another, you can take notes on cards or paper, making sure to include page numbers of specific passages that you may wish to mention or quote when you write the review. One effective technique is to use self-stick removable notes as tabs to mark your place. If you use medium- and large-size removable notes, you will have space for your annotations.

What should you mark? Mark passages that seem especially well written or badly written; you can use these passages in a discussion of style. Mark any puzzling passages so that you can later decide whether the problem lies in the way they are written or in the way they were read. Mark any repetitions; these may be a clue to meaning or purpose, or they may be tedious or unnecessary. Mark especially any statements that help to answer the questions in this section. These questions must be answered if your assessment of a work is to be competent and complete.

### (1) Fiction (novels and short stories)

Novels and short stories will require some interpretation of meaning on your part. For example, you must go beyond their plots to find the central idea or ideas. Usually, your assignment will specify how you are to approach a critical review of fiction. If not, the following questions and comments can guide your reading and note-taking.

When reviewing fiction, you must, of course, consider the plot—that is, what happens, how the events relate to each other, and how they relate to the work as a whole. But remember that you do not want to "retell" the plot of the work. Make notes summarizing only those events that will support the points you make about the work, and concentrate on other questions, such as these.

- What is the purpose of the work?



The purposes of literature range from a momentary escape from reality to a serious interpretation of human existence. If escape is the purpose, the reader gains an entertaining diversion that erases, at least partly, the pressures of life or the monotony of the usual. A common kind of escape literature is the paperback romance novel sold in supermarkets. In its extreme form, escape literature loses its appeal once the plot has been discovered. On the other hand, interpretive literature comments on life in a meaningful way and is worth reading many times to probe the meaning beneath the surface. Most good literature has elements of both escape and interpretation; it is both entertaining and illuminating at the same time. Nevertheless, one purpose is usually dominant. Knowing a work's dominant purpose helps you to gain an overall perspective of the work and to judge it effectively.

- What is the theme of the work?

The theme is the central idea of the work—a generalization about life. Do not confuse theme with moral; only in very simplistic writing can theme be expressed in a proverb such as "Virtue is rewarded" or "Absence makes the heart grow fonder." Instead, a theme is usually an insight into the nature of human beings and their relationships to themselves, one another, and the universe. Serious writers rarely try to "teach a lesson." Rather, they try to provide an experience—one with the complexities, quandaries, and emotions of real life. For example, a story about a disastrous Christmas dinner could examine the agonizing conflicts that can arise between parents and adult children. Or a story about a young, inexperienced soldier might make the reader feel the human fear of new responsibilities. When considering theme, you should also consider how it is supported by plot, character, setting, point of view, and other details of the work.

- What are the conflicts in the work?

The plot usually arises from conflict between the protagonist (the main character) and the antagonist (an opposing force). The antagonist can be another character or characters, society, nature, or even some trait within the protagonist. Thus the conflict may be a clash of actions, ideas, or emotions.

- What is the point of view?

The term *point of view* refers to the perspective of the narrator. In general, there are four points of view: omniscient, limited omniscient, first person, and objective. With an omniscient point of view, the narrator is not a character in the story but rather an all-knowing presence who can see into the minds of characters, tell us what they think, and interpret their actions.



In a limited-omniscient point of view, the narrator has access to the thoughts of only one character. Thus, the narrator observes the actions of the remaining characters from this single perspective.

In first-person point of view, one of the characters tells the story (using *I*). The narrator may be a major or minor character, an active participant, or an observer. In any case, the narrator cannot enter the minds of other characters but can only speculate about their thoughts and motives.

Finally, with the objective, or dramatic, point of view, the plot unfolds as in a play—seemingly without a narrator. The reader is an observer of the action and has no access to the minds of any of the characters. Instead, the reader draws conclusions from what the characters do and say, not from what they think.

- How are the characters presented?

Characters are said to be flat or round, depending on their complexity. Flat characters are very simply drawn and can be very simply described—"a greedy, ambitious scoundrel"; "a country bumpkin"; "a scheming woman." Round characters are more lifelike, with the complexities of real people.

Another way to classify characters is to determine whether they are static or developing. A static character does not change from the beginning to the end of the story. The developing (or dynamic) character undergoes some change—large or small, good or bad—as a result of experiences.

- What motivates the characters?

The plot, of course, is what the characters do. Just as important is what motivates them. An omniscient narrator can explain the motives of all the characters but will not necessarily do so. When the point of view is limited omniscient, you may know the motives of one character but will have to infer the motives of the rest. When the point of view is first person, you must decide how much to trust the narrator: the character who tells the story may not understand himself or herself, much less the other characters. Finally, when the point of view is objective, you must infer all motivation from the characters' words and interaction. Thus, determining motivation may involve a good bit of interpretation on your part.



- What is the significance of the setting, that is, the time and place in which the story occurs?

Writers do not choose a setting at random, and you should consider the choice carefully. Try to evaluate what bearing the setting has on the conflict. If a primary conflict lies between the protagonist and society, the setting may be the antagonist, providing both the catalyst for action and the key to motivation. In any case, the setting will likely support the theme of the work, providing an appropriate backdrop for the struggles of the characters.

### (2) Drama

Drama is much like fiction; it has plot, characters, conflict, setting, and theme. Unlike fiction, however, drama is meant to be performed before an audience. And unlike fiction, drama allows only the objective point of view. Nevertheless, the playwright, like the fiction writer, strives to comment on human beings and their relationships to themselves, to each other, and to the universe. In broadest terms, the dramatist has two possible vehicles to convey this commentary: comedy and tragedy.

Basically, comedy may be romantic or satiric. Romantic comedy is usually lighthearted, involving one or more romantic entanglements, with the couple or couples united at the end. Satiric comedy holds characters up to ridicule and exposes their human weaknesses and vices. And of course, many comedies combine both the romantic and the satiric. Regardless of type, comedies usually end happily or at least with justice done. Moreover, comedies tend to emphasize the common foibles of humanity.

Tragedy, on the other hand, does not end happily. In a classic tragedy, the plot involves the "fall" of the main character (protagonist), who dies or loses something dear. The fall results from the combination of circumstances and human weakness (the "tragic flaw"). The audience tends to sympathize with the protagonist for two reasons. First, the fall is due to a weakness, not to a crime or vice. Second, the protagonist finally understands—but too late—the folly of his or her actions.

Because drama has many of the same characteristics as fiction, you must consider for a review some of the questions and comments from the preceding fiction checklist.



What is the purpose of the work?
What is the theme?
What are the conflicts?
How are the characters presented?
What motivates the characters?
What is the significance of the setting?

In addition, if you see the play performed, you can also consider these questions.

- Was the presentation realistic or nonrealistic?

Drama may be presented realistically—with sets, props, and costumes that attempt to re-create reality. Or it may be presented nonrealistically—on a bare stage, for example, or with sets, lighting, and costumes that suggest not reality but mood.

- How effective were the production techniques, such as stage sets, costuming, and lighting?

Often the production of a play can be as entertaining as the content itself. And unfortunately, poor production can ruin even the finest drama.

- How skillful were the actors?

Almost nothing can save a play performed by bad actors. On the other hand, skillful acting can sometimes save an otherwise mediocre work.

### (3) Poetry

To analyze a poem, you must read it a number of times, slowly and thoroughly, making sure that you completely understand all the vocabulary. Also, read the poem aloud several times and listen to it; poetry conveys meaning through sound as well as sight. It is impossible to describe in a few paragraphs the devices that help to create the sound and fabric of poetry—repetition, variation, rhythm, rhyme schemes, figurative language, images, symbols, allusions, and so forth. These devices can best be learned from a knowledgeable instructor or from a helpful guide such as Laurence Perrine, *Sound and Sense: An Introduction to Poetry.* In addition, the following questions and discussion suggest inclusions for a critical review of a poem.



- Who is the speaker?

The speaker of a poem is not necessarily the poet. Frequently, the speaker represents a type of person—rejected lover, dying man, soldier, mother, deposed ruler, traveler, patriot, prisoner. Unless you know who is speaking, you will not likely understand the poem or its purpose.

- What is the tone?

Through the speaker's vocabulary and sentence structure, the poet establishes a particular tone. The established tone may be, for example, scholarly or familiar, arrogant or folksy, playful or serious, bitter or thankful.

- What is the poem's purpose?

The purpose may be to express an emotion, a mood, or an idea. It may be to reveal human nature, describe a place, tell a story, or achieve some combination of purposes.

- What is the poem's form?

A poem may be a narrative—a story in verse. Or it may be a lyric—a verse that expresses emotions like grief or joy, creates a mood like foreboding or celebration, or develops an idea like fate's unfairness or the power of friendship. The form may be traditional—a sonnet, blank verse, couplets, quatrains (see the Glossary of Terms for explanations). Or the form may be free, following no set pattern of rhythm and rhyme.

- Do the sound and rhythm contribute to the purpose?

The sound and rhythm should be compatible with the emotion, mood, or idea of the poem. (See 33e.)

- What are the central images?

Images appeal to the senses, calling forth the sights, sounds, smells, tastes, and tactile impressions of the physical world: sun-baked, red clay hills; the blare of a dozen trumpets; heavy, cheap perfume; clammy, wet clay.

Poets use images not only to create physical experiences but also to establish moods. The image of spring flowers blowing in the breeze obviously creates a mood very different from that of rotting trees and stagnant water. When you are analyzing a poem, pay close attention to the images; they play an important role in the poet's message.



- Are there any symbols in the poem?

A symbol is an image that stands for an idea or a complex of ideas. Symbols are common in everyday life—for example, a flag often represents patriotism; a skull and crossbones, death; a lightbulb, the flash of inspiration.

Sometimes symbols are central to the meaning of a poem, as in Robert Frost's famous poem "The Road Not Taken." Walking through the woods, the speaker comes upon two diverging roads and chooses the "one less traveled by." The two roads are symbolic of the choices one must make in life. In this case, the symbol is the key to the poem's meaning.

Take care, however, not to read each image as a symbol. A symbol points to the meaning beneath the surface. Images are details that create realism or a mood but suggest nothing more. To distinguish between the two is not always easy. Some people exaggerate imagery, calling everything a symbol: a closed door symbolizes alienation; a fish, freedom; a star, the mystery that cannot be solved. Unless the image relates to the theme of a work, it is probably not a symbol. Instead, the image may be a literal detail meant only to add to the background.

- Is the language literal or figurative?

The language of poetry is often figurative rather than literal—that is, suggestive rather than straightforward. For example, T. S.

Eliot, instead of using a literal, factual description of fog, pictures a cat's languid and pervasive movements through the evening. When the meaning of a figure of speech is not obvious, the reader must interpret the meaning. (See 33d.) If a poem uses figurative language, you might want to comment in your review on whether a figure is fresh or stale, forceful or weak, effective or silly.

- What does the poem mean?

A poem's meaning derives from its many elements. A paraphrase (a literal rewording of what a poem says) may be an insufficient expression of the meaning. All the other elements—for example, the symbolism, the suggestions, the tone, and the figures of speech—contribute to meaning. Therefore, when you try to discover meaning, look at the poem as a whole, not at just an isolated element. And remember that some poems are very puzzling. Do not get discouraged. Even professional critics have difficulty with interpretation, and frequently they strongly disagree about the meaning of a poem. Some may interpret Herrick's "Corinna's Going a-Maying" as Christian; others, as pagan. Some interpret nature in Wordsworth's "Ode" as benevolent; others, as sinister. If after multiple readings you cannot figure out the meaning, just say so and explain why.



### (4) Nonliterary works

A nonliterary work will probably not require you to interpret meaning. In most cases, the author will strive to state the main ideas directly and support them with concrete details. As you read, you should keep the following key questions in mind. Responding to these questions will help bring logic and order to your notes and ultimately to your final draft.

- What is the purpose of the work?

The table of contents, if there is one, can help you determine purpose by revealing the work's overall organization and content. Also, the author or editor may state the purpose in preliminary pages (such as the preface or foreword) or in an introduction. If not, a first reading should tell you whether the author intended to inform, shock, expose, teach, entertain, or achieve some combination of purposes.

- Does the work have a thesis—that is, a controlling idea or a point of argument?

In much nonliterary writing, particularly in a short work such as an article or essay, the author argues a point of view or takes a position on an issue. You should be able to state this thesis, or position, so that you can judge whether or not the author has adequately proved or supported it. (See 35d.)

- Who is the intended audience?

Sometimes the introduction or the preliminary pages identify the intended audience. If not, you can usually determine the audience by evaluating the nature of the content, the technical or educational level of the vocabulary, and the sophistication of the writing style. You need to know whom the author is addressing if you are to judge the work's success.



- Is the presentation logical and each conclusion valid?

Works that set out to argue or explain must present information in a logical and orderly fashion; otherwise, readers will be confused. Evaluating the logic of the presentation can help you evaluate a work's clarity. An author's conclusions should be based on sound logic and concrete support. If you need help assessing these components, see Chapter 39.

- Is the style clear?

A poor writing style can mar a work no matter how logical its presentation or how valid the author's conclusions. As you read a work, notice the prose style. Is it smooth and easy to follow or is it awkward and confusing? If the prose style is distinctive in any way, you should note particularly characteristic passages for quoting. (See Part IV.)

## 43b Research

Before you write a review, you may want a better understanding of the literary terms used in criticism, or you may want more understanding of a genre—the type of work you are reviewing. If so, you can consult sources such as these.

### Dictionaries of Literary Terms

Deutsch, Babette. *Poetry Handbook: Dictionary of Terms*. 4th ed. 1982.
Fowler, Roger, ed. *A Dictionary of Modern Critical Terms*. 1973.
Frye, Northrop, Sheridan Baker, and George Perkins. *The Harper Handbook to Literature*. 1985.
Holman, C. Hugh. *A Handbook to Literature*. 4th ed. 1980.
Pech, John, and Martin Coyle. *Literary Terms and Criticism: A Student's Guide*. 1984.

### Fiction

Allen, Walter. *The Short Story in English*. 1981.
Booth, Wayne C. *The Rhetoric of Fiction*. 1983.
Brooks, Cleanth, and Robert Penn Warren, eds. *Understanding Fiction*. 3d ed. 1979.
Friedman, Norman. *Form and Meaning in Fiction*. 1975.
Perrine, Laurence. *Story and Structure*. 1959.
Shorer, Mark, ed. *Story: A Critical Anthology*. 2d ed. 1967.
Thurston, Jarvis A. *Reading Modern Short Stories*. 1955.



### Poetry

Brooks, Cleanth, and Robert Penn Warren. *Understanding Poetry*. 1960.
Kenner, Hugh. *The Art of Poetry*. 1959.
Perrine, Laurence. *Sound and Sense: An Introduction to Poetry*. 2nd ed. 1963.
Preminger, Alex, ed. *The Princeton Encyclopedia of Poetry and Poetics*. rev. ed. 1974.
Ribner, Irving, and Henry Morris. *Poetry: A Critical and Historical Introduction*. 1962.
Schneider, Elisabeth. *Poems and Poetry*. 1964.
Turco, Lewis. *The Book of Forms: A Handbook of Poetics*. 1968.

### Drama

Altenbernd, Lynn, and Leslie Lewis. *Introduction to Literature: Plays*. 1963.
Anderson, Michael. *Crowell's Handbook of Contemporary Drama*. 1971.
Arnott, Peter. *The Theater in Its Time: An Introduction*. 1981.
Barranger, Milly S. *Theatre Past and Present: An Introduction*. 1984.
Bierman, Judith, James Hart, and Stanley Johnson. *The Dramatic Experience*. 1958.
Kernan, Alvin. *Character and Conflict: An Introduction to Drama*. 1963.

### Nonliterary Works

Barzun, Jacques. *Simple and Direct*. 1975.
Booth, Vernon. *Communicating in Science: Writing and Speaking*. 1985.
Kostelanetz, Richard. *Essaying Essays: Alternative Forms of Exposition*. 1976.
Zinsser, William. *On Writing Well: An Informal Guide to Writing Nonfiction*. 1980.

You may want to research an author for pertinent biographical details that can contribute to an understanding of a work, details such as the social and political climate in which the author lived. In the reference section of libraries, you can find biographical works such as *Dictionary of American Biography, Current Biography, Contemporary Authors, Who's Who in America,* and *Biography Index*.



## 43c Writing the Review

Once you have carefully read the work you are reviewing, considered the questions that should be answered, made some notes, and done any pertinent research, you are ready to write the review. If your assignment tells you what to include, you should, of course, follow directions and design the review accordingly. If you have no specific guidelines, you can think in terms of what a reader might want to know. Imagine a reader who will use your review either to decide whether to read the work or to evaluate and understand it.

First, your reader will want to know what the work is about. One way to orient your reader is to include a short synopsis, or summary, of the work. Another way is to summarize and explain as your discussion progresses. Take care not to overdo the summary. Particularly avoid giving the entire plot of a work of fiction, paraphrasing a poem, or summarizing chapter by chapter a work that informs or instructs.

Include also the purpose of the work. Then you can move to the question central to critical reviews: How successfully does the work achieve its purpose? Suppose, for example, you are reviewing an article that classifies rock stars. If the author's purpose is to inform the reader in a serious manner, you must judge how valid the conclusions are, how accurately the types are depicted. On the other hand, if the purpose is merely to entertain, you need not dwell on the accuracy of the author's classification. Instead, you should decide whether the article is worth reading purely for entertainment.

Whatever your judgment about the success of the work, you must support it with concrete evidence. Here you can use your notes to cite certain characteristics of the work or particular passages that support your answer.

Many reviewers include a judgment of the value of the work. Should you choose to do so, avoid broad statements such as "This is the best book I have ever read" or "I did not enjoy this book." Instead make a specific statement that relates the work to the appropriate audience or occasion: "This novel is good escape fiction for a rainy afternoon but is not serious literature"; "Anyone wanting to learn to surf should buy this book"; "The work is valuable for upper-level chemistry majors but is too advanced for beginning students"; "The anthology of short stories includes something for everyone, from serious literature to light romance and humor." Where possible, support your judgment with evidence from the notes you took while reading. When your notes do not produce evidence, return to the work for supporting details or quotations.



Also, if you are familiar with other works by the same author or on the same subject, a comparison can be useful to the reader. For instance, you might note that although previous plays by an author were light-hearted humor, the one under review is cynical, almost bitter. Or in reviewing a "how-to" book on scuba diving, you might advise the reader that this work is superior or inferior to several others you have read.

## 43d Comparing Reviews

As the following examples of student reviews illustrate, there is no set format. However, a comparison of the examples will show that in spite of different styles, reviewers do try to tell readers what the work is about and give some general reaction to it, supported by concrete details.

To write the following review of Sinclair Lewis's novel *Main Street,* the student did some research into critical opinions of the work and took rather detailed notes while reading the novel. As a result, she was able to support her opinions with quotations both from critics and from the novel itself.

Sinclair Lewis's Main Street is a satirical portrait of a typical midwestern small town in the first half of the twentieth century. Lewis sees small-town American life as unrelieved boredom:

*statement of novel's purpose*

*general comment supported with direct quotation*

> It is an unimaginatively standardized background, a sluggishness of speech and manners, a rigid ruling of the spirit by the desire to appear respectable. It is contentment . . . the contentment of the quiet dead. . . . It is the prohibition of happiness. It is slavery self-sought and self-defended. It is dullness made God.

The novel revolves around Carol Milford, a young woman from Minneapolis. When the book opens, Carol is a college student with a vague dream of doing something important. She imagines, "I'll get my hands on one of those prairie towns and make it beautiful. . . . I'll make 'em put in a village green, and darling cottages, and a quaint Main Street!" Several years later, she marries Dr. Will Kennicott, a physician from Gopher Prairie, and sets off to fulfill her vague dream. Kennicott is a practical, hard-working man who wants to accumulate wealth, hunt and fish, and have an adoring wife to make his home his castle. He is a "booster," constantly describing Gopher Prairie as "up-and-coming," populated with "the best people on earth."

*details of plot to summarize novel's beginning*

The conflict is primarily between Carol and the town. The citizens of Gopher Prairie are motivated by "the desire to appear respectable" and controlled by fear of gossip. Above all, they are self-satisfied. Carol is dissatisfied, bored, and bewildered by the town's complacency. She wants to change things, to reform the town. She wants to make it prettier, more democratic, more sophisticated, more cultured. But

*statement of conflict*

*discussion of motivation*

Carol is not an effective reformer. She backs away from the slightest criticism and retreats into self-pity.

Carol finally leaves Gopher Prairie to work two years in Washington, D.C. But even there she is unhappy and unable to fulfill her romantic dreams of doing something important. Finally, she returns to Gopher Prairie, where nothing has changed, not even she.

*generalization supported with outside sources*

In spite of the dreariness of the plot and the setting, Main Street is an interesting novel because of Lewis's detailed description of the community. In fact, since the novel's publication (1920), critics have noted that Lewis's main strength is his attention to detail. In 1921, H. L. Mencken wrote, "The virtue of the book lies in its packed and brilliant detail. It is an attempt, not to solve the American cultural problem, but simply to depict with great care, a group of typical Americans." In 1935, Granville Hicks wrote, "If what one wants is a detailed, accurate record of the way people live, Lewis is the most satisfying of our authors." In 1961, Mark Shorer wrote, "The image of the American village that Lewis created through . . . details remains pretty much the image of the village that most of us still hold today." And in 1981, David Anderson wrote that Lewis's work has "the reality of the monograph, the field study, or the case history."

Regardless of the vivid details of the novel, the characters sometimes seem flat, more like caricatures than actual people. Lewis has populated Gopher Prairie with types:

*criticism of character presentation supported by sketches of the main characters*

Vida Sherwin—the local schoolteacher, a civic-minded do-gooder. Vida is one of the leaders of the women's study club, "such a cozy group, and yet it puts you in touch with all the intellectual thoughts that are going on everywhere."

Miles Bjornstram—the town atheist who enjoys shocking the solid citizens. "He was the one democrat in town."

Mrs. Bogart—a nosy, vicious gossip. "She was a widow . . . and a Good Influence."

Cy Bogart—the widow's son and the town bully. Because of Cy, a young schoolteacher, although innocent, is run out of town in disgrace.

Guy Pollock—a bachelor lawyer, a bookish, poetic man, who escapes Gopher Prairie by reading books.

Mrs. Luke Dawson—"wife of the richest man in town" and patron of the arts. "We're learning all of European Literature this year. The club gets such a nice magazine, Culture Hints, and we follow its program."

In conclusion, Main Street is a successful satire of small-town America. But in his attempt to satirize, Lewis has created types, not characters that hold the reader's attention as real people. Finally, the reader is as bored with Carol as Carol is with Gopher Prairie.

*conclusion—novel's purpose and reviewer's major criticism*

The following is a review of Eileen Power's *Medieval People.* Since the purpose of the book as well as the intended audience is stated in the Author's Preface, the student writer was able to evaluate the work on the basis of those statements. He also found in the Preface a list of Power's sources, which led to his only negative comment on the work.

In the Author's Preface to Medieval People, Eileen Power states that she intends to make the past "live again for the general reader more effectively by personifying it than by presenting it in the form of learned treatises." In Power's view,

*book's purpose from Preface*

> It is the idea that history is about dead people, or, worse still, about movements and conditions which seem but vaguely related to the labours and passions of flesh and blood, which has driven history from the bookshelves where the historical novel still finds a welcome place.

*In Medieval People*, she hopes to "interest for an hour or two the general reader, or the teacher, who wishes to make more concrete by personification some of the general facts of medieval social and economic history."

*brief summary c work*

To achieve her purpose, Power sketches the day-to-day life of various individuals in the Middle Ages. She treats Bodo, a peasant on a typical medieval estate; Marco Polo, the Venetian adventurer and trader; Madame Eglentyne, the prioress of a nunnery; a wife in a middle-class home; Thomas Betson, a wool merchant; and Thomas Paycocke, a clothier. In order to reconstruct the lives of these people, Power used actual historical records, such as the estate book of a medieval manor, chronicles of Polo's travels, a husband's instructions to his young wife on the subject of household management, family letters, records, and wills.

*claim that auth achieves her pur pose; details to support that claim*

Power has achieved her purpose. The sketches almost seem like short stories with interesting characters in believable settings. In the section on Bodo, the peasant, Power describes the different kinds of buildings and workers that existed on the manors as well as the kinds of work done and rents required. Also, she presents in detail a typical day in the life of Bodo and his wife and children. The section on Marco Polo describes not only Polo's travels but also his life as a young boy in the splendor of Venice. Through the prioress, the reader is told about the life of medieval nuns, including their rituals, eating and drinking habits, gossip, and even the sign language they used when observing hours of silence. The sketch entitled "The Menagier's Wife" describes the marriage of a middle-class man of about sixty to a young woman of fifteen. Much of the material was taken from a book the husband wrote as advice to his wife on everything from the proper behavior at church to ways for removing grease spots from clothing. From the sketches of the wool merchant and the clothier, the reader learns about business dealings, courtship, family life, and family quarrels.

The economic, political, and social events that often seem dull in textbooks become important as they touch the lives of individuals.

Because of her approach, Power does succeed in interesting a "general reader" not familiar with the field of medieval history. Her use of historical records, however, does present the general reader with one problem. She often quotes her sources in the original Latin or French without offering a translation either in the text or in the notes at the end of the book. To a reader like me, with no knowledge of foreign languages, this habit is a little annoying. I would like to know what those sentences mean. Nevertheless, in presenting six very real medieval people, Power gave me a great deal of information about life in the Middle Ages and a pleasant reading experience.

*negative comment on book's documentation*

*conclusion that work is successful*

In the review that follows, a student evaluates a scientific article from *Scientific American* entitled "The Fighting Behavior of Animals." To show an understanding of the article, the reviewer emphasizes its content, simplifying and summarizing the material.

"The Fighting Behavior of Animals" by Irenaus Eibl-Eibesfeldt is a very clear description of the ritualized fights between members of a single species. The author begins by explaining the purposes of aggression within a species. Fights spread animals out over a larger territory as the defeated moves away from the victor; also, fights permit the stronger animals to mate and thus improve the quality of the species in general. But the most interesting observation in this report is that these fights rarely result in deaths. In fact, to inflict death is not the purpose of the fighting at all. The author maintains that fighting is instead an inborn behavioral trait that has developed into a ceremony meant to improve the species, not to reduce its numbers.

*short summary of the article*

*statement of the author's thesis*

The author carefully supports this thesis with evidence from a number of different studies of aggressive behavior in many different animals: wolves, birds, marine iguanas, lava lizards, lizards of central Europe, fish, rattlesnakes, fallow deer, mountain sheep, wild goats, antelopes, and Norway rats. One of the most interesting of the studies is that of the rattlesnake because its bite could easily kill. Two snakes in combat perform a ritual similar to "Indian wrestling," in which the winner pins the loser and then permits an escape.

*details that support thesis*

In addition to the descriptions of animal behavior, this report links the meaning of animal behaviors to aggression in the human species. Many scientists have maintained that aggression is learned behavior and consequently can be eliminated by improvements in environment. Basing their findings on laboratory experiments with rats, these scientists concluded that a rat that experiences no aggression early in life will grow to be unaggressive. The implication is that human aggression could also be controlled environmentally. But Eibl-Eibesfeldt tested this theory by isolating rats for five to six months. When released, these rats performed the same aggressive rituals as nonisolated rats. Thus, the study supports the belief that aggression is "innate and fixed behavior." The author also backs up this conclusion by referring to another study supporting biological aggression. By stimulating specific areas of an animal's brain, the scientists were able to make the animal fight.

*interesting implications of the research*

The author concludes by stating that at one time humans very likely had these same aggressive and less lethal patterns. And although changed in form by man's complex society, "aggressiveness is deeply rooted in the history of the species and in the physiology and behavioral organization of each individual."

*brief conclusion: summarizes author's principal conclusion*

## ❑ EXERCISE 1

Following are three examples from *Choice,* a publication that reviews books for librarians. List the questions that each review answers, for example:

What is the purpose of the work?
How successfully does the work achieve that purpose?
What is the value of the work?
Is the organization logical?
How does the work compare with other works on the same subject or with other works by the same author?
Who is the intended audience?
How effective is the writing style?
What are the main strengths of the work?
What are the weaknesses of the work?
What are the author's qualifications?



JAMES, Harry C. Pages from Hopi history. Arizona, 1974.

The first full-length history of the Hopi, pueblo dwellers in Arizona. It should be of interest to the general reader as well as the specialist. James has been a friend and observer of the Hopi for over half a century and was a participant in some of the controversies he describes. After three chapters on their pre-history and clan organization, James presents a conventional survey of Hopi history. His sources were the annual reports of agents, prior studies of the Indians, and his own experiences among them. A serious omission from James' sources was the manuscript material in the National Archives. The result is a book valuable for the insights that only a scholar like James could bring to it, but lacking the depth and balance that a use of more archival material could have provided for the American period. The style is good except where marred by excessively long quotations.

BOGEN, Nancy. Klytaimnestra who stayed at home. Twickenham Press, 1980.

The first novel of a literary scholar and teacher, *Klytaimnestra who stayed at home* retells the story of the day of Agamemnon's return to his kingdom. Bogen's prose, straightforward and contemporary, successfully avoids any suggestion of the quaintly archaic. Reflecting the author's careful research, the numerous details of life among the ancient Greeks are vividly drawn and seem entirely authentic. Through shifting narrative viewpoint and interior monologue, Bogen fills out complexities of the story not found in Aeschylus's play. The result is highly imaginative. The novel, however, domesticates and "humanizes" the characters and story to the point of trivializing a great dramatic tragedy (the murder of Agamemnon, for example, is about as compelling as a man cutting himself shaving). All sense of grandeur and the tragic is missing. The work therefore reads like contemporary Gothic in the manner of John Gardner or Percy Walker. It can be recommended only for collections of popular fiction.

LAYZER, David. Constructing the universe. Scientific American Books, 1985.



The origin, dynamics, and structure of the universe are covered in this book by the well-known Harvard astronomer David Layzer, who has published extensively in this area and is well qualified to write such a book. Both Newton's theory of gravity and Einstein's theory of general relativity are covered in detail, and there is an interesting final chapter on modern cosmology. The writing, for the most part, is clear, and the book is illustrated with hundreds of diagrams and color photos. All in all it is a beautiful book. The major difficulty associated with it is the intended audience. It is not a textbook, yet algebra is used extensively; furthermore calculus is also used. There are detailed mathematical arguments that would bore the general reader. Although many with the appropriate background would no doubt enjoy Layzer's work, it is not a book for the general public but for the upper-division undergraduate student.

## ❑ EXERCISE 2

Write a review of one of the following.

a novel
a short story
a play
a poem
a textbook
a cookbook
any book or article on a subject of particular interest to you

# 44

# Business Letters



Telephones provide a quick and easy way to conduct business, but they are not always appropriate. Formal and official situations call for business letters, which provide written records of transactions. Through letters, people apply for jobs, request information, order goods, make complaints, and, in general, take care of financial and consumer affairs.

Unlike a school paper, which usually addresses a general audience, a business letter is normally written to a specific reader—the president of a company, a personnel director, a university registrar, a department manager, a bank officer, or the like. Thus, a business letter must observe the conventions of letter writing so that readers will not be offended or think the writer uninformed. These conventions may seem a bit demanding and strict. But a messy, poorly written letter creates a bad impression on the reader. On the other hand, a well-written, attractively presented letter often produces the desired results.

## 44a Conventions for Business Letters

Certain general requirements govern letters.

- Letters should follow an acceptable format; innovation and superfluous ornamentation are distracting.

- Writers should get directly to the point; readers usually get impatient with letters that are not concise and pertinent.
- The information in letters should be carefully organized. Readers should be able to distinguish between main and subordinate points without any difficulty.
- Letters should be typed or printed on a high-quality paper, preferably with a good machine. Pica type, or 10-pitch (10 characters per inch), is easier to read than elite, or 12-pitch.
- Letters should be impeccably neat and clean, unmarred by obvious erasures or corrections.

## (1) Styles of letters



The two basic styles of letters are the traditional and the simplified, illustrated on pages 612 and 615.

### The Traditional Letter

The traditional letter is the one used most often. It contains these mandatory parts.

a return address
a dateline
an inside address
a salutation
the message
complimentary close
the signature and the typed name

### The Simplified Letter

The simplified letter is similar to the traditional but omits the salutation, omits the complimentary close, and adds a subject line typed in all capitals. Consequently, it contains these parts.

a return address
a dateline
an inside address
a subject line
the message
the signature and the typed name

Although most readers still prefer the traditional letter, the simplified letter avoids a very common problem: the salutation to use when you do not know the name or sex of the reader. *Dear Sir* seems inappropriate if the reader is female. *Dear Sir or Madam* is awkward regardless of the sex of the reader. And *To Whom It May Concern* is stilted and annoying. The solution to the problem is to omit the salutation altogether. Thus, when you write to someone whose name or sex you do not know, the simplified letter is an effective option.

## (2) Components of letters

The components you choose for a letter depend largely on whether you write a traditional or a simplified letter. However, a few components such as an attention line, a subject line, and notations, are optional.



### Letterhead or return address

Business stationery often has a printed letterhead with the company's name, logo, address, and telephone number. If you do not use letterhead stationery, you should type a return address at which you can be reached. The return address does not include your name.

### Dateline

The date is typed under the letterhead or the return address. Either the month/day/year form (July 27, 1992) or the day/month/year form (27 July 1992) is appropriate. In formal letters, do not use abbreviations.

### Inside address

The inside address contains the name and full address of the person or organization receiving the letter.

### Attention line

An attention line, such as *Attention: Personnel Department,* directs a letter to a specific person or department. You use an attention line only when the letter is addressed to an organization. The line is typed in one of two places: under the organization's name in the inside address or between the inside address and the salutation.

### Salutation

If you know the name of the person you are writing, the salutation should include it, as in *Dear Ms. Lewis* or *Dear Dr. Craft.* If you do not know the name of the addressee, you can use a title if there is one, such as *Dear Personnel Manager* or *Dear Registrar.* If you know the sex of your reader, you can write *Dear Sir* or *Dear Madam.* If you know nothing about your reader, you can use the simplified style and omit the salutation.

### Subject line

In a traditional-style letter, a subject line is not always used. In a simplified-style letter, it is essential. It is usually capitalized and appears where the salutation would otherwise appear.

### Message



Since the message will be single-spaced with double spacing between paragraphs, you have the option of indenting paragraphs or not. No paragraph should be particularly long; in a letter, even a one-sentence paragraph is acceptable.

### Complimentary close

Use a closing traditional for business letters. The most common are *Yours truly, Respectfully yours, Sincerely, Sincerely yours, Yours sincerely,* and *Cordially.* Remember that the complimentary close is omitted in the simplified style.

### Signature

Do not forget to sign your letter. And if you send a photocopy, do not sign the original before you copy the letter; a copied signature does not look authentic. Sign the copy you send.

### Sender's typed name

Signatures are often illegible, so a typed name appears under the signature. You can also include a title if you have one. (See the student letter, p. 622.)

### Notations

Notations, typed several lines beneath the sender's typed name, display information such as the initials of the writer, the initials of the typist, an indication of enclosures, and a notice that copies have been sent to someone other than the addressee. This information can be presented in several different ways.

| | |
|---|---|
| INITIALS OF TYPIST: | btl, j |
| INITIALS OF WRITER AND TYPIST: | B:J, JSC/mj, EIH: JRS, HW: pm |
| ENCLOSURE: | Enclosure, Enc., 2 Enclosures, Check enclosed |
| COPY NOTICE: | cc Herbert Matthews, CC Personnel Office, cc: M. J. Dinther, CC: Mr. Austin |

## (3) Conventions for typing business letters

Readers will not take seriously letters that look careless and confusing. To ensure serious consideration of your message, you should follow a traditional typing style, punctuate conventionally, and position the letter attractively on the page.



### Typing Style

The full-blocked style, with all lines beginning at the left margin, is required in simplified letters. Many writers also prefer it for traditional letters since it is neat and easy to type. (See p. 615.)

Another possible typing style is the semiblocked style. In this style, the dateline, the complimentary close, and the writer's name begin at the center of the page. Paragraphs may be unindented, or they may be indented five spaces. The balanced appearance of the semiblocked letter makes this style very popular among typists. (See pp. 612 and 617.)

### Punctuation

You can punctuate your letter in two ways. You can omit punctuation at the end of the salutation and the complimentary close. Or you can place a colon after the salutation and a comma after the complimentary close.

### Spacing

If you have little experience typing letters, you may have difficulty positioning your letter on the page. For a balanced appearance, you should calculate the margins and the spacing between the components before you begin to type. Using the following chart can eliminate time wasted through trial and error. However, remember that you may need to make adjustments when you use the simplified style or stationery with a letterhead.

| Spacing For Letters | | | | |
|---|---|---|---|---|
| *Length* | *Margins* | *First Line of Return Address* | *First Line of Inside Address* | *Space for Signature* |
| Short (fewer than 100 words) | 2 inches | line 16–20 from top of page | 5–6 lines from date | 4–6 lines |
| Medium (100–200 words) | 1½ inches | line 11–15 from top of page | 4–5 lines from date | 4 lines |
| Long (more than 200 words) | 1 inch | line 8–10 from top of page | 2–3 lines from date | 3–4 lines |

let 44a

Many word processors can justify the right margin; that is, they space so that all the lines are the same length. Some readers think this uniformity makes a letter look as impersonal as a form letter, and some find unjustified text easier to read. Therefore, in most cases, you should not justify the right margin.

### (4) Conventions for typing envelopes

On a business envelope (9 1/2 × 4 1/8 inches), single-space your name and address in the upper left corner. Begin at about the third line down from the top, and indent five spaces from the left edge. Type the name and address of the person who will receive the letter about 14 lines from the top edge and about 4 inches from the left edge. If your envelope is smaller, adjust the spacing.

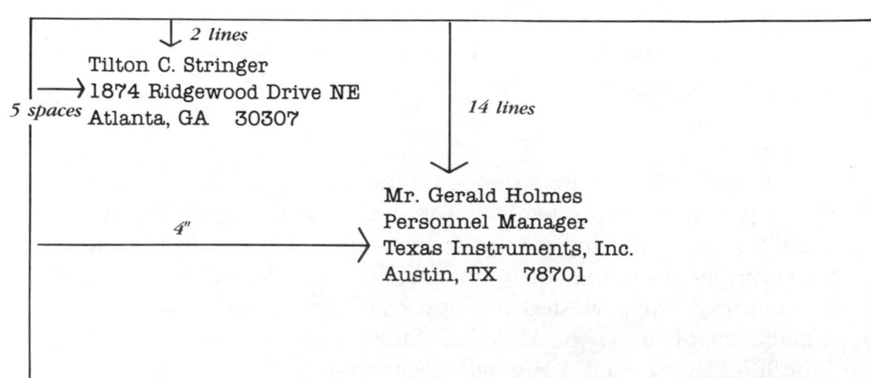

## 44b Types of Letters

Some of the most common types of letters are order letters, letters of complaint, letters of inquiry, and letters of application with résumés. Following are guidelines for composing each type of letter as well as examples that illustrate different letter types, lengths, and typing styles.

### Order Letter

Ordering by letter is a good way to purchase merchandise. Ordering by telephone is faster and simpler, of course, but a letter provides a written record that protects you against any mistakes the seller might make. The letter should clearly describe what you want to purchase, how you will pay for it, and if necessary, how you wish it to be delivered. The merchandise you order will determine exactly how you word the letter, but in most cases, you include the following information.



- A description of the item. Include whatever information is available and appropriate—name, price, model number, number of the catalog page showing the item, quantity, size, color, and so on.
- The method of payment (C.O.D., check, money order, or credit card). If you are paying by credit card, be sure to include the exact name that appears on the card, the card number, and the expiration date.
- The shipping instructions, if you have a choice in the manner of delivery. State whether you want the merchandise sent through the U.S. mail, air express, truck freight, a company such as UPS, or whatever.

The following order letter contains all the necessary information to produce satisfactory results.

### Sample Order Letter

Letter Style: traditional

Typing Style: semiblock with paragraphs indented

Length: short

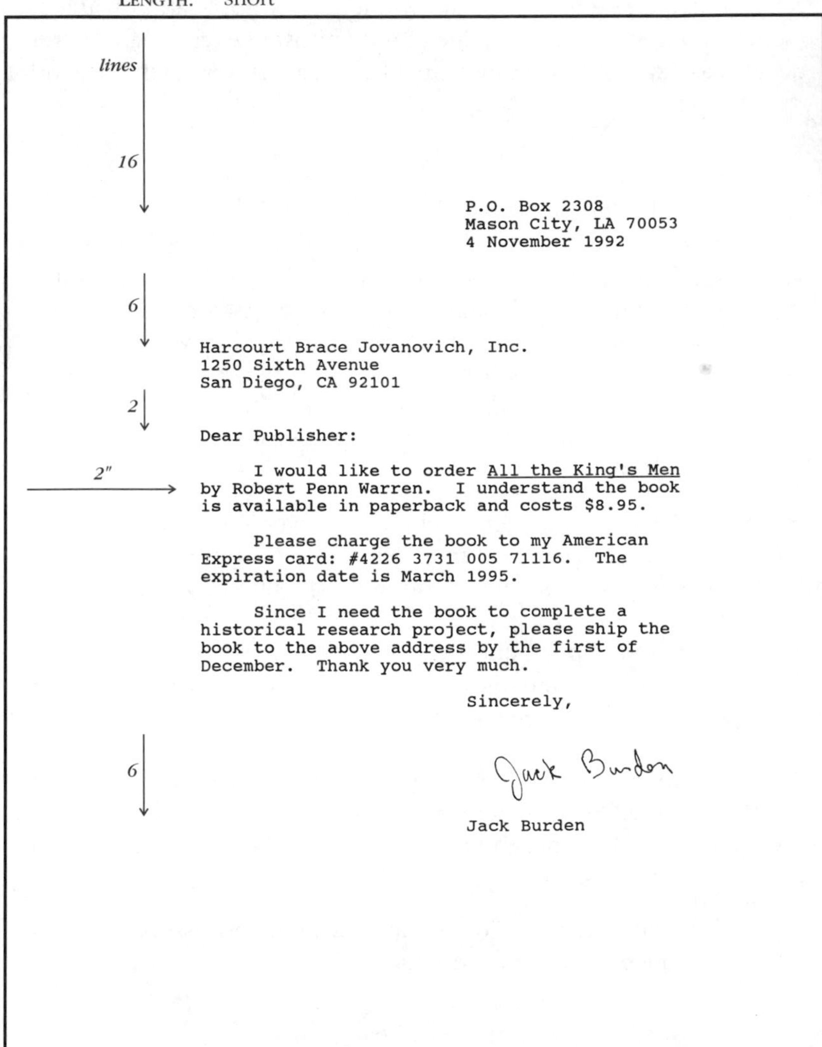



P.O. Box 2308
Mason City, LA 70053
4 November 1992

Harcourt Brace Jovanovich, Inc.
1250 Sixth Avenue
San Diego, CA 92101

Dear Publisher:

I would like to order All the King's Men by Robert Penn Warren. I understand the book is available in paperback and costs $8.95.

Please charge the book to my American Express card: #4226 3731 005 71116. The expiration date is March 1995.

Since I need the book to complete a historical research project, please ship the book to the above address by the first of December. Thank you very much.

Sincerely,

Jack Burden

Jack Burden

## ❑ EXERCISE 1

Write an order letter for a product or service such as one in the following list. Supply the necessary names, addresses, descriptive details, manner of payment, and shipping instructions.

| | |
|---|---|
| school catalog | camera |
| record album | pest-exterminating service |
| stereo speakers | housekeeping service |
| library card | government pamphlet on herb gardens |
| telephone answering machine | back issue of a magazine |
| vacuum cleaner | list of local computer dealers |
| VCR | replacement part for a bicycle |



### Letter of Complaint

A letter of complaint requests compensation of some kind: a refund, an adjustment, a replacement, better or faster service, or even an apology. Because anger or frustration usually prompts a complaint, this kind of letter can be difficult to write. First, to get results, the letter must be written in a calm, businesslike tone. Rudeness, offensive language, and sarcasm will only antagonize the reader and lessen the chances of success. Second, the letter must state the facts of the case clearly and objectively, without exaggeration. And finally, the letter must explain exactly how the writer expects to be compensated. If you need to write a letter of complaint, you might consider the following strategies before beginning a draft.

#### Identification of the Problem

Here you should include enough information for the reader to know exactly what you are finding fault with: an action or a behavior, a product, a service, a staff member, a store clerk, a company policy, or whatever. Include enough identifying details to rule out any confusion on the reader's part. For example, if you are complaining about behavior, you should be specific about what happened, when, and where. If you are complaining about a product, you should include identifying details, such as its model number, size, color, and date of order. If you are complaining about a service, you might explain what the service is supposed to do, where it is located, and who performs it. If you are complaining about a person, you should include his or her name and position.

#### Explanation of the Problem

Avoid vague complaints. Instead of saying that a product, service, policy, or person is unsatisfactory, you should describe the problem in enough detail that the reader understands what prompted your complaint. In other words, exactly what is wrong? You can also include here how you or others have been inconvenienced. Has the problem cost you money, time, or irritation? Be careful, however, not to include unnecessary details that make the letter overly long. Readers are much more likely to respond to efficient letters than to long-winded rhetoric.

#### Statement of Request



Ultimately, the purpose of a letter of complaint is to request compensation. A reader who does not know what your request is can hardly be expected to fulfill it. Therefore, state exactly what you want: a complete refund, a replacement for the product you received, an adjustment in your bill, an apology for rudeness, speedier service, or whatever remedial action seems appropriate and reasonable.

#### Conclusion

One good way to conclude a letter of complaint is to express confidence in the reader's integrity. In other words, you can conclude with a statement such as "I have always been satisfied with your company's service and feel certain that you will correct this error" or "We know that your agency will be concerned about this matter." Finally, you should thank the reader for attending to the problem as soon as possible.

## ❑ EXERCISE 2

**Write a letter of complaint about an action, behavior, product, service, policy, or person. The following list suggests some possible subjects for your letter. Supply any necessary details such as names, addresses, product or service description, the problem you have had, and the action you would like taken.**

**computer software that malfunctioned**
**article of clothing damaged by a laundry**
**unsatisfactory exercise machine**
**university policy that requires freshmen to live in dormitories**
**club policy that only children of members are hired for summer jobs,**

### Sample Letter of Complaint

Letter Style: simplified
Typing Style: block
Length: medium

*lines*

*13*

203 Fulbright Road
Little Rock, AR 72201
April 20, 1993

*5*

Environmental Protection Agency
401 M Street, S.W.
Washington, D.C. 20460

*3*

PROTECTION OF RAGLAND HILLS, ARKANSAS

*3*

Ragland Hills is a geologically unique area of approximately four hectares located about seven miles southeast of Woodson, Arkansas, on federal property. This area, with high hills and low ravines, is known for its diversity of wildlife.

*1½"*

For several years, motorcyclists have used Ragland Hills for motorcross dirt-bike riding. The motorcycles tear up the terrain, and many of the hills are now eroding rapidly. Also, the noise level disturbs the animals and could cause them to move into less suitable habitats.

I am confident that your agency will investigate this matter to determine the extent of the damage. If the severity of the damage is confirmed, you should take measures to ban motorcycles from the area. If action is not taken soon, the erosion and harm to the wildlife may well be irreversible.

*5*

Ruth Leland

RUTH S. LELAND

such as lifeguarding, waiting on tables, maintaining the golf course and tennis courts
car repair service that overcharged you
member of a library staff who was discourteous when you asked for help
salesperson who refused to exchange merchandise
city government's negligence in repairing streets
speed trap set by a state highway patrol

let
44b

## Letter of Inquiry

A letter of inquiry asks the reader to provide some particular information for a specific reason. For example, a letter might request details about a school, a product, or a subject being researched. Whatever the inquiry, the writer asks the reader to take the time and trouble to respond. Therefore, the letter must clearly state the purpose and express appreciation for any inconvenience to the reader. The guidelines that follow are applicable to any letter of inquiry you might have to write, regardless of the information you request.

### Introduction

In the introduction, you should introduce both yourself and your purpose. The reader will expect to know who you are and why you are requesting the information.

### Body

The body should state very clearly what information you need. Do not approach the reader with a vague request such as "Please send me all available information on. . . . " Instead, be reasonable and specific about what you want.

If you have several questions to be answered, number them and list them down the page. In this way, the reader can easily identify what information must be gathered for a reply.

### Conclusion

In the conclusion, you should offer to pay for the information, send a copy of the report you are writing, return the favor, or whatever is appropriate compensation for the reader's time. Also, you should thank the reader with some statement such as "Thank you for your time and consideration" or "I very much appreciate your time and effort."

A typical letter of inquiry is shown opposite.

## Sample Letter of Inquiry

**Letter Style:** traditional

**Typing Style:** semiblock with paragraphs not indented

**Length:** long

*lines*

*8* ↓

Box 7822
Peabody, Kansas 66866
21 September 1990

*2* ↓

Dr. Jayne McRaney
Bauer School of Nursing
Peabody, Kansas 66866

*2* ↓

Dear Dr. McRaney:

*2* ↓

The Student Nurses Association is planning to submit a proposal about the need for computer literacy among all undergraduate nursing students. Before we work any further on our proposal we want to investigate faculty reaction to our preliminary plan and to some possible alternatives.

Presently, nursing students at Bauer are not required to have computer literacy when they graduate. Further, because of curriculum requirements, students cannot find time to take a computer course as an elective. Consequently, most graduates suffer an educational deficiency that could affect their attractiveness in the job market. (See attached employment statistics.) Now, graduates of Bauer must get on-the-job training when they are already burdened with the uncertainties of a new job.

In view of this problem, I would very much appreciate your answering the following questions:

1. Would you support an undergraduate course in computer training?
2. If the course were instituted, should it be taught by an outside consultant or by a faculty member in the School of Nursing?
3. If the course were instituted, should it be a regular three-hour course or a workshop of some kind?

Thank you very much for your time and consideration. Your answers will help us determine the details for the final proposal concerning this problem. As soon as the proposal is complete, we will send you a copy.

*2* ↓

Sincerely,

*3* ↓

Harriet Manly

Harriet Manly
President

*2* ↓

Enclosure

## ☐ EXERCISE 3

Choose one of the following situations, and write a letter of inquiry. Provide any necessary information such as the name, address, and position of the person addressed in the letter.

1. Write a letter of inquiry asking about the work-study programs at your university. Request information about eligibility, available positions, and pay scale.
2. Write a letter of inquiry to a university or an agency asking for information about a workshop or continuing education course in a subject such as word processing, car repair, dance, carpentry, creative writing, ceramics, or any subject that particularly interests you. You might ask for details concerning subject matter, student participation, method of teaching, price, meeting times, and duration of the course.
3. Write a letter of inquiry to a faculty member requesting information about a project you are working on. For example, you might ask a history professor to supply reliable sources that you can use to research a historical figure or event. You might ask a science professor to suggest a method for conducting an experiment. You might ask a law professor to comment on the best prelaw undergraduate degree.
4. Write a letter of inquiry to an employment service at your university or in your community asking for information about employment opportunities in a particular field, such as marketing, banking, landscaping, or any field that interests you.
5. Write a letter of inquiry to a state or federal agency, a chamber of commerce, or a travel bureau asking for information on a subject you are researching. You might ask about camping facilities, art exhibits, festivals, or concerts in the area. Or you might request information on water pollution, nutrition, gardening, conserving energy, or any other subject that might be written up in brochures and pamphlets.



### Letter of Application and Résumé

Although you can pay a firm to design a letter of application and résumé for you, preparing them yourself says something very positive about your independence, resourcefulness, and capability. In fact, if your letter and résumé demonstrate that you are not only qualified but also capable of effective writing, you will have a real advantage in the job market. On the other hand, if you submit poorly written documents, you will seem inattentive to details and lacking in communication skills—undesirable qualities for an employee. Thus, writing letters of application and résumés is a task you should take seriously. Do not let the brevity of the documents lead you to think they can be dashed off effortlessly. You should compose them carefully—selecting the right message and experimenting with different formats.

### Letter of Application

Like all business correspondence, a letter of application must follow the conventions for formal letter writing. (See 44a.) The finished document must be visually attractive—good-quality paper, readable type, no distracting errors or messy corrections. In addition, the document requires some special details and may even involve some background research. A sample letter of application is shown on page 622.

#### Researching the Employer



Before you write a letter of application, you would be wise to research the prospective employer. You want to sound as familiar as possible with such details as the names of departments, the specific kinds of work the employer does, and most important, the names of people who work there. If at all possible, you should address your letter to a specific person—the personnel director, the head of a department, or an officer. A letter addressed to an individual receives a much better reception than one impersonally addressed to *Dear Sir.* You can call a business and ask the operator or secretary to supply or confirm the name and the spelling. You can also find names and addresses through chambers of commerce and in professional directories in the library. Some of the library works you might consult are these.

*F & S Index of Corporations and Industries*
*Encyclopedia of Associations*
*Standard & Poor's Register of Corporations, Directors and Executives*
*Moody's Industrial Manual*
*Who's Who in Finance and Industry*
*Business Periodicals Index*

#### Composing the Letter

Once you complete the research, you are ready to write the letter itself. In clear prose, explain the kind of job you want, highlight your qualifications, and make yourself available for an interview. Application letters often contain only this information, separated into three paragraphs. However, if appropriate, you can also add the following.

the name of a person who recommended that you write
the way you found out about the job opening or the company
the reason you are interested in the work or the company
a statement expressing admiration for a company characteristic or policy
the relation of your education or experience to the job you seek
a reference to your résumé for details
a potential time for an interview

Whatever information you include, try not to exceed the length of one page. Although the letter should be short, write and organize it carefully. The letter gives you an opportunity to show that you can write skillfully—an asset that employers hold in high regard.

let 44b

### Résumé

Your résumé, or data sheet, should list your accomplishments at school and work. It must be persuasive so that the reader will want to hire you rather than someone else. Therefore, try to emphasize your strengths and minimize your weaknesses. One simple way to stress information is to position it first in the document and also first in each section. A sample résumé is shown on page 623.

Some résumé writers have difficulty squeezing their accomplishments into the recommended page or two. Others, less active, have difficulty stretching the résumé to one full page of qualifications. Thus, a single plan or design may not be appropriate for all. Choose whichever components and arrangements show your strengths.

#### Identification

Begin the résumé with your name, address, and telephone number. Some people also include their Social Security numbers.

#### Education

List any part of your formal education that would interest or impress an employer. Begin by listing your most recent education, and work backward. You can include these items in this section.

your school(s) (High school can be omitted unless you have notable achievements.)
your degree(s)
the date(s) you graduated or will graduate
scholarships and honors

the courses that are particularly related to the job you seek (possibly in a separate subsection called something like "Relevant Courses" or "Significant Courses")
your grades if they are above average
special training and conferences
any extracurricular activities that pertain to the job

EXPERIENCE

Organize your work history to emphasize your qualifications for the job you seek. Stress an important job by placing it first, and list the rest in descending order of importance. If no jobs warrant emphasis, list your experience in reverse chronological order, beginning with the most recent. For each job, you can describe the following, choosing an order that emphasizes the most impressive facts.



position held
employer
specific duties
accomplishments
dates of employment

PERSONAL DATA

In a separate section entitled *Personal* or *Personal Data,* you can include information such as height, weight, health, marital status, language proficiency, special skills, or travel experience—but include only information related to the job you seek. Except for special kinds of jobs, such information as height and weight is rarely relevant. Avoid any unnecessary references to race, religion, sex, and age. Ordinarily, photographs are not appropriate.

REFERENCES

You can handle references in several ways. If you are applying to only a few places, you can list several people who have agreed to write recommendations on your behalf. Always include their addresses and telephone numbers. If you are mailing out a large number of résumés, you should not list names. Instead you can write, "References available upon request," or you can file your recommendations with a placement bureau and write, "References on file at [the name and address of the bureau]." The advantage of a placement bureau is that it will send duplicates of your recommendations, and no one will have to write more than one letter.

## Sample Letter of Application

Route 3, Box 300 E
Florence, Texas 76527
March 10, 1990

Mr. A. H. Young
Director of Materials Research
Standard Chemical Company
1032 Columbus Drive
Minden, Louisiana 71209

Dear Mr. Young:

Dr. Thomas Shipley, chair of the Department of Chemistry at Packard Polytechnic College, recommended that I write to you. Dr. Shipley indicated that your firm was seeking a chemist experienced in the testing and formulating of adhesives, coatings, and polymer systems. I would like to apply for this job in the Research and Development Department.

In May 1990, I will receive from Packard Polytechnic College a B.S. degree in chemistry with an emphasis in polymers. I am active in the Polymer Science Club, attend all guest lectures and symposiums, and keep up with the latest techniques and developments in the field. My classes have given me practical laboratory experience, including the use of the latest laboratory equipment. Further information about my education and work experience is detailed in the enclosed resume.

I would appreciate the opportunity for a personal interview at your convenience. You can reach me at the above address or at (512)346-8673 between 3 and 5 p.m.

Sincerely yours,

Carol S. Culpepper

Ayn Rand

Atlas Shrugged

The Fountainhead

822-3074

## Sample Résumé

CAROL S. CULPEPPER
Route 3, Box 300E
Florence, Texas 76527
(512) 346-8673

EDUCATION

Packard Polytechnic College, Crockett, Texas
Bachelor of Science Degree in Chemistry, May 1990
Emphasis: polymer chemistry, polymer coatings, polymer processing
Senior research project: synthesis of polymeric composites

HONORS

Dean's List 1988-1990
Phi Theta Kappa (National Honor Society)
Polymer Science Merit Scholarship

ORGANIZATIONS

American Chemical Society (student affiliate)
Society of Plastics Engineers
Polymer Science Club

WORK EXPERIENCE

Chemistry lab assistant, Packard Polytechnic, 1988-1990
Duties included characterizing composites with viscosity studies, F. T. Infrared, and F. T. Nuclear Magnetic Resonance.

Pharmacy technician, Methodist Hospital, Florence, Texas, summers 1986-1988
Duties included filling orders, restocking, conducting inventory, and delivering IV solutions.

PERSONAL INFORMATION

Date of Birth: January 17, 1967
Language Proficiency: 3-year study of Spanish
1-year study of Latin
BASIC
Travels: United States, Mexico, Spain

REFERENCES will be furnished upon request.

## ❑ EXERCISE 4

1. Design a résumé that you could use in a general search for a summer job.
2. Write a letter of application in response to a newspaper advertisement for a specific job. Supply the necessary details such as the prospective employer's name and address, the job description, the name of the newspaper, and the date of the advertisement.
3. Prepare a résumé to accompany the letter in item 2.
4. Write a letter of application to a company that has not advertised an opening. Supply details such as the prospective employer's name and address, the kind of job you seek, the date you can be available for work, and whatever else is necessary for an effective letter.
5. Prepare a résumé to accompany the letter in item 4.

# 45

# Reports

Papers such as progress reports, proposals, investigation reports, and instructions are often referred to as business writing or technical writing, depending on the content. This kind of writing serves some specific and practical purpose. For example, the purpose of a progress report is to record the status of a project—to give information about work accomplished, problems encountered, and adherence to schedule. The purpose of most proposals is to solicit permission, business, or funds. An investigation report outlines the process of an investigation and presents the conclusions. Instructions detail the steps in a procedure for a reader who wants to perform them.



To achieve these purposes, most business and technical reports address not general but specific audiences: instructors, supervisors, customers, colleagues, employees, employers, stockholders, or funding agencies. Although you write some compositions for a general audience, you write a report with some particular reader or readers in mind. Also, reports look different from general-audience writing; they normally have formats with headings, numbering systems, and specified components—all designed so that a reader can retrieve information quickly and easily.

The following discussion treats some of the most common reports: their purposes, components, formats, and typical audiences.

## 45a Progress Reports

Progress reports are often essential to people involved in research or business projects. Whether submitted occasionally or at regular intervals, progress reports provide written records of the status of a project. These reports also allow directors or funders to supervise ongoing projects. Some businesses and funding agencies provide forms or standardized guidelines for progress reports. Others allow the writer to design the format. Either way, most progress reports include the following information.

- What has been accomplished
- What remains to be done
- What, if any, problems have been encountered
- Whether or not the project is on schedule
- Whether the budget, if any, needs adjusting



The differences among progress reports depend primarily on the type of project they describe. For example, suppose you were reporting to an instructor your progress on a chemistry research project. You might structure your report in the following manner.

1. Assignment
2. Experiments Performed
3. Equipment
    Equipment Used
    Additional Equipment Needed
4. Adherence to Schedule
5. Tentative Hypothesis

But in a report on an oral history project, you might employ very different headings, such as these.

1. Assignment
2. Library sources
    2.1 Work to Date
    2.2 Problems Encountered
    2.3 Future Work
3. Interviews
    3.1 Work to Date
    3.2 Problems Encountered
    3.3 Future Work

As these outlines indicate, a progress report allows you and your supervisor to evaluate your project and modify the procedure when necessary.

### ❑ EXERCISE 1

Write a progress report on one of the following subjects or on a subject of your own choice. The preceding outlines can suggest report components and headings, but you can use any format that serves your purpose effectively. Be sure to choose a specific reader, appropriate to the subject.

1. progress on a research paper
2. progress of a group to elect a candidate to a campus office
3. progress toward career goals
4. progress in writing a computer program
5. progress in a laboratory experiment



## 45b Proposals

People write proposals for a variety of reasons, such as obtaining permission, winning contracts, or securing funds. Whether simple or complex, all proposals submit a plan to be approved. A long, complex proposal usually appears as a formal report with a cover, a table of contents, lists of illustrations, a summary, and appendixes. These proposals are often written by a team of individuals with different kinds of expertise. A short or simple proposal usually appears in the form of a letter addressed to the person or group giving permission for a project. Regardless of length or complexity, however, most proposals contain these basic components.

- The problem that prompted the proposal
- The solution to the problem
- The procedure to be followed
- Any equipment, personnel, or facilities needed
- The budget

Suppose, for example, you were assigned to submit a proposal for a paper based on surveys and library research. A format like the following would allow your instructor to judge whether or not you should proceed as planned.

Proposal

To determine whether changes should be made in the premedical curriculum

Methodology

Research in written documents to collect information about premedical curricula at comparable universities

Survey of premedical faculty

Survey of premedical students

report 45b

Or suppose you rent an apartment in need of repair: inside walls need repainting; doors and windows need weather-stripping; back steps need replacing. You offer to make these repairs if the owner will waive three months' rent. The most efficient way to approach the matter is to submit a proposal describing your plan to the owner. You could follow a format something like this one.

Problem

Under this heading, you could describe the problems with the apartment and the repairs needed.

Solution

Here you could compare the cost of hiring you versus the cost of hiring someone else. You could also describe the materials needed and compare the cost of your providing them versus the owner's providing them.

Capabilities and experience

Here you could try to sell the owner on your ability to handle the job by describing your skills and past experience.

Time schedule

Because the owner would probably want some limit set on the time the job would take, you should establish a time schedule either for the entire job or for each specific task.

Budget

Your budget figures should be as precise as possible. The owner would more likely be cooperative if he or she knew exactly how much money would be spent and what it would be spent on.

## ❑ EXERCISE 2

Following are some suggestions for proposals. Choose one, or think of a subject of your own. Then write a proposal offering a solution to the problem.

1. Write a proposal to your campus housing department solving a problem at your dormitory (such as poor outside lighting, high noise level, or drafty windows).
2. Write to a prospective employer proposing to complete specific tasks—such as carpentry, gardening, housekeeping, or car repairs. Include both a time schedule and a budget.
3. Propose a change in the curriculum of your academic major. Address the proposal to the appropriate chair or dean.
4. You may have observed on your campus or near your residence a traffic problem, such as the need for a stoplight, for a footbridge over a busy intersection, or for increased parking facilities. Write a proposal to an appropriate department on campus or in your community and propose a solution.
5. Write a proposal for a project to raise funds for an organization such as a social club, a professional club, or a charity.



# 45c Investigation Reports

People conduct investigations to find answers to questions. Thus the purpose of an investigation may be to search for causes, effects, solutions, origins, characteristics, identities, trends—anything unknown that the investigator wants to know.

## (1) Framing questions for an investigation

Generally, the purpose of an investigation can be stated as a question. For example, you might conduct an investigation to answer such questions as these:

How can the congestion in the computer laboratory be eliminated?
What are the personality traits of a habitual cheater?
Who was responsible for the recent NCAA violation that resulted in the probation of a particular football team?
What are the latest trends in science fiction films?
Are self-service gasoline pumps accurate?

Whatever question you choose, make sure that you have the ability, the equipment, and the time to find the answer. Suppose, for instance, you ask the question "How pure is the water in the community water system?" If no test results are available to the public, you would have to conduct tests yourself or have them conducted—a task requiring time, equipment, and expertise. On the other hand, if data about the purity of the water are available, you could compare that data with government standards and draw some valid conclusions. Or suppose you want to know "How much student support exists for a new student union?" Unless you have the time and expertise to survey a representative sample of students on campus, the results of your poll will not reflect a cross-section of the student body. A better question might be "Do the students in Reed Hall support a new student union?" You might have the time to survey almost every student in one dormitory and draw some valid conclusions.



### (2) Collecting data

After your question is framed, you must collect pertinent data, that is, information to help answer the question. You can collect data in various ways. For example, you can generate information in a laboratory through experiment and observation. Or you can gather information from books, journals, newspapers, historical records, legal documents, diaries—any written material, whether published or unpublished. Also you can collect data in the "field." For example, to gauge the traffic passing through a certain intersection at noon, you could go there and count the vehicles. Or to collect data about the facilities in area water parks, you could visit the sites.

A particularly popular method of data collection is the survey—soliciting information from appropriate respondents by written questionnaires, by telephone polls, or by personal interviews. Investigators frequently survey experts. Swimming coaches, for example, would know how weight training affects a swimmer's performance. Florists or employees in plant nurseries could tell you what kinds of plants survive in a dimly lit dormitory or apartment. In other investigations, the respondents are not experts but rather the "subjects" of investigation. For a paper on the kinds of recreation currently in vogue on your campus, you would survey students. To find out whether residents in your apartment complex would pay for on-site day care, you would survey those with small children.

The validity of the survey results depends on a variety of factors. For instance, questionnaires or interviews must be designed to prevent ambiguous or slanted results, and the respondents must be willing to answer questions honestly. In addition, finding a "representative sample" is a complicated process involving mathematical formulas, demographic data, and statistical analysis—a process requiring special training and expertise. Nevertheless, you can gather data with a simple survey of a small number of respondents if you do not generalize too broadly from the results. Let us say that for an investigation of the exercise trends on campus, you survey 100 students at random. You find that 20 percent prefer jogging; 15 percent, racquetball; 5 percent, tennis; and so on. You could not claim that your percentages apply to the entire student body. To survey a representative sample, you would have to interview a microcosm of the student body, selected by sex, age groups, majors, regional backgrounds, and so forth. When you conduct a limited survey, make it clear to readers how you selected your sample, and do not suggest that the responses represent a larger group than they actually do.



Also, take care to phrase your questions carefully so that respondents will not be confused. Otherwise, you may collect misleading or useless data. The following guidelines will help you get good results.

- Define all necessary terms.
  If you are seeking opinions about the value of studying the humanities, you should define *humanities* to ensure valid responses.
- Ask only one thing at a time.
  Avoid phrasing items so that they ask two questions at once, such as "Did your high school prepare you for college English and college science?" The school could have prepared the respondent for one and not the other. Thus, you should ask two separate questions: "Did your high school prepare you for college English?" "Did your high school prepare you for college science?"
- Avoid leading questions.
  You should not lead your reader to a certain answer by asking a question like "Do you oppose the university's preferential treatment of athletes?" Because "preferential treatment" is gen-

erally undesirable, the phrase would lead most respondents to answer yes. A fairer question would be "Do you think the university gives preferential treatment to athletes?"

- Phrase questions in positive terms.
  Negative words unnecessarily complicate a question. Readers would be confused by the negatives *dis-* and *not* in this question: "Do you disapprove of not allowing parking on campus?" The question would be much clearer in positive terms: "Do you approve of the parking ban on campus?"
- Avoid ambiguous questions.
  In the question "Would a larger football stadium be beneficial?" a respondent might well wonder whether *beneficial* means beneficial to the school, to the athletes, to the fans, or to the respondent. More exact phrasing would eliminate the ambiguity: "Do you approve of enlarging the football stadium?"



### (3) Organizing investigation reports

Regardless of the data-collection method, an investigation report takes the form of a narrative that details the research. The following components are typical.

#### Introduction

The introduction states the purpose, defines the question or problem that prompted the research, and indicates the scope (or limits) of the investigation. In addition, the introduction can include the significance of the research.

#### Literature review

A literature review is a survey—usually very brief—of other reports, articles, or books pertinent to the subject. The literature review may be included in the introduction or treated under a separate heading. Either way, the review establishes the importance of the subject and provides a background for the question that will be answered. Further, the review demonstrates that the writer is familiar with other investigations on the subject and has not, out of ignorance, duplicated the work of others.

#### Methodology

The methodology section explains to readers how the research was conducted. This section should include enough detail so that a reader could duplicate the research; few people will have faith in the results of a study unless they know how it was conducted.

Possible headings for this component are *Materials and Methods, Sample Collection, Design of Study, Methodology, Procedure, Data Collection,* and *Analytical Technique.*

Results

The results are the pertinent data collected in the investigation. These may be presented in prose; in figures, graphs, charts, and drawings; or through a combination of techniques—whatever is clearest and most efficient.

Conclusions

The conclusions are the interpretation of the data, the generalizations about the findings. This section can include the significance of the work, its applications, and its limitations.



Recommendations

Some investigation reports contain recommendations. Depending on the kind of investigation conducted, the report might recommend that further research be done, that a procedure or policy be changed, that a plan be implemented, or that a product be selected.

In some cases, recommendation is the central purpose of investigation reports: researchers compare various alternatives according to a set of criteria. These papers resemble the articles in *Consumer Reports,* where researchers test several alternative brands of products against a set of criteria, such as cost, weight, maneuverability, maintenance, and durability. Then they recommend a best buy to consumers.

In reports with recommendations, readers must understand the criteria used to judge the alternatives. Otherwise, the recommendation will carry little weight.

### (4) Sample outlines for investigation reports

Although you can adapt headings to accommodate your own particular data collection and results, the basic components still appear. For example, if you were to investigate weight-loss groups and clinics through fieldwork and other research methods, your paper might have this format.

I. Introduction

Here you might state the question that prompted the investigation. Also, you could describe the scope of your report (i.e., set limits on the kinds of programs investigated). For example, you might have set out to find the best clinic in the area for a student or for people of a certain age.

II. Method

You would describe the way you conducted the research: whether you visited each group or clinic, talked to the directors, collected pamphlets and other literature, or participated in sessions.



III. Results

In this section, you might divide your data according to types of programs, such as commercial systems, private groups, and community services. These types could serve as convenient headings or subheadings in the report. You might even include a chart comparing the programs: requirements to enroll, types of diets, exercise regimens, success rates, prices, and so on.

IV. Recommendations

Here you might want to evaluate the programs and make recommendations to your readers. If you included a chart in "Results," you could base your recommendations on those facts and figures.

Another investigation report might use slightly different headings. For example, if you were to investigate a problem such as the cause of congestion in a computer laboratory, your format might look like this one.

I. Introduction

You could introduce the report with a description of the problem: extent of congestion, peak hours, ratio of equipment available to students needing equipment, and so on.

II. Data collection

In this section, you would include a description of the survey, both respondents polled and questions asked. For respondents, you could give the number surveyed, majors, classifications, or whatever is appropriate. Also you could include here either the questionnaire itself or a description of the questions.

III. Results

In this section, you would present your findings, that is, the survey results. A conventional technique is to list the questions and, under each, the responses either by percentage or head count—for example,

Approximately how many hours per week do you use the lab?

over 10 hours ........................................ 17%

6-9 hours ............................................... 27%

3-5 hours ............................................... 50%

less than 3 hours .................................... 6%

Or you could use a prose version.

When asked how many hours per week they used the laboratory, respondents answered as follows: 17% said over 10 hours; 27% said 6-9 hours; 50% said 3-5 hours; and 6% said less than 3 hours.

You may also show results in a table if you wish, using whatever format is clear and efficient.

IV. Conclusions

In the final section, you could interpret your findings. You might note anything your survey revealed about the lab congestion that was not obvious from simple observation. Also, you might suggest a possible solution to the problem.



## ❑ EXERCISE 3

Conduct an investigation to answer one of the following questions or a question of your own choice. Then write an investigation report detailing your findings.

1. What is the best buy in a personal computer for a student?
2. What kind of local facilities are available for boarding animals?
3. How does a particular program at your school (nursing or engineering, for example) compare with the same program at a comparable school?
4. Why do people join sororities and fraternities?
5. What are the best campsites within a 20-mile radius?
6. What work-study opportunities are available to students on your campus?
7. Which grocery store in your area has the best produce for the price?

8. What types of students on your campus take an interest in state elections?
9. What places in your community or on your campus ban cigarette smoking?
10. What are student attitudes toward standardized entrance examinations, such as ACT and SAT?

## 45d Instructions



The purpose of a set of instructions is to detail a procedure for readers who want to perform it. So before you write instructions, you must have a very clear picture of your readers. How familiar are they with the procedure already? What, if any, technical vocabulary and expertise must they have in order to carry out the instructions? As you draft the instructions, never lose sight of your readers. Remember, they are depending on you to guide them. Your mistakes will be their mistakes. The following tactics should help you write instructions that produce satisfactory results.

- Include all steps in the procedure.
- Indicate clearly all necessary tools and materials.
- Be sure to include any appropriate warnings, cautions, or notices.
- Write directly to your reader with imperative (command) verbs, and avoid the third person or passive voice when readers must perform the step. In other words, if you expect the reader to tilt a victim's head backward, do not write, "The victim's head should be tilted backward." Instead, write, "Tilt the victim's head backward."
- Design the layout to help rather than hinder readers. Leave enough space between each step and substep to separate them clearly. When steps must be completed in order, use a numbering system. Make warnings, cautions, and notices stand out. Enclose them in boxes or set them off with capital letters, stars, exclamation points, or some other visual device.
- Search your instructions for words and sentences that could possibly be ambiguous or misunderstood.
- Make sure you are not blinded by your own knowledge. Before doing a final draft, let someone unfamiliar with the procedure read your work or actually follow the directions. He or she might be able to discover weaknesses you have overlooked.

Basically there are two types of instructions, illustrated by the following examples. One type lists separate items of advice, to be carried out in no fixed order. For example, these instructions give general information on interviewing for a job but dictate no particular sequence.

How to Interview for a Job

A job interview can be the decisive difference between getting and not getting a job. To avoid a lost opportunity, you should take the following advice seriously.

Prepare for the interview by boning up on the company or the employer. Read the company's annual report or go to the library and consult the F & S Index of Corporations or the Business Periodicals Index.



Anticipate questions that could be asked. Practice answering difficult questions such as these: What are your long-term and short-term goals? Why did you choose this career? What is more important, the money or the work? Why should you be hired?

Ask the interviewer a few intelligent questions about the company. What are the company's plans? How does it test new products? How important is research and development?

Try to postpone talking about money and benefits until the end of the interview. Asking about these too early can make a bad impression.

Dress appropriately. Even companies with a casual dress code expect a male candidate in a conservative coat and tie and a female candidate in a tailored dress or suit.

Sit with correct posture. You don't want to look too casual or too insecure. Your body language should suggest that you are relaxed but interested and alert.

The other type of instructions, like the following, lists steps that must be followed in sequence—each step completed before the next one is begun.

The Rabbit-from-the-Hat Trick

In the most classic magic trick of all, the magician pulls a live rabbit out of a hat. The trick developed at a time when gentlemen in the audience wore tall silk opera hats. The magician could borrow a hat and thus dispel the suspicion of a secret compartment. Now, opera hats are obsolete, but any hat will work, even the magician's own hat, which the audience should be able to see is empty. The following set of instructions, based on suggestions by Harry Blackstone, Jr., will help aspiring magicians sneak a rabbit into an empty hat.



1. Hide the rabbit.
   1.1 Place onstage a chair with a solid back.
   1.2 Hammer a headless nail into the chair's back.
   1.3 Put a rabbit into a black cloth bag.
   1.4 Hang the bag on the headless nail so that it can be quickly scooped into the hat.
2. Create a diversion.
   2.1 Sneak a tightly rolled string of silk handkerchiefs tied together into the hat. The string should be at least 7 feet long.

   > Note: Blackstone suggests cutting the handkerchiefs in half diagonally to make the string long but not thick.

   2.2 "Palm" the tight roll of handkerchiefs in your hand and conceal it under the hat's brim as you show the inside of the hat to the audience.
   2.3 Reach into the hat with the hand containing the roll of handkerchiefs.

2.4 Begin to unroll the handkerchiefs and to pull them out.

2.5 Move to the chair. Let the handkerchiefs pile up on the seat.

2.6 Hold the last length of handkerchiefs high in the air; smile at the audience as if having successfully completed a trick.

3. Place the rabbit in the hat.

3.1 While the audience applauds and you drop the handkerchiefs onto the chair, move slightly back.

3.2 Putting the hat under the bag, quickly scoop the bag into the hat.

| Option: | Loose silk handkerchiefs can be concealed in the bag along with the rabbit and brought out at this point. These handkerchiefs can give you time to move away from the chair. |
|---|---|



4. Presto! Pull out the rabbit.

## ❑ EXERCISE 4

Write a set of instructions explaining some process you know well. The following list might suggest an idea.

How to develop film
How to shoe a horse
How to repot a plant
How to make a perfect omelet
How to assemble a stereo
How to choose skiing equipment
How to dissect a frog
How to execute a half gainer
How to eat steamed lobster
How to write a computer program
How to wax a surfboard
How to choose luggage
How to frame a drawing
How to conduct a garage sale

APPENDIX A

# Spelling

sp

The English spelling system is often criticized for its "inconsistencies," that is, for its failure to reflect pronunciation accurately. For example, the pronunciation of the word *answer* does not include a /w/ sound, and the pronunciation of the word *night* does not include either a /g/ or an /h/ sound. The sound "ah" can be spelled with an *a* (as in *father*) or an *o* (as in *not*). A *d* sometimes represents the sound /d/ (as in *bagged*) and sometimes the sound /t/ (as in *jumped*). In other words, many English words are not pronounced as their spellings might indicate.

One reason for the inconsistencies is the tendency of English to borrow words from other languages. These words, such as the French *naive* or the Dutch *yacht,* reflect the spelling systems of those languages rather than of our own. But receptiveness to foreign words is one of the strengths of English, making it flexible, adaptable, able to survive. Spelling peculiarities seem a small price to pay for that strength.

Another reason for inconsistencies in the English spelling system is the large number of regional dialects, which frequently have differing pronunciations of the same words. Thus, English spelling often seems to contradict phonetics. But it must. If our spelling were phonetic, English speakers from different regions would have to spell words differently. Consequently, a New Yorker would have to struggle to read an Atlanta newspaper, and written communication between an American and an Australian would require translation.

In addition, the pronunciation of English has changed throughout history. To reflect pronunciation accurately, spelling would have to change over the years, and these changes would create a very inefficient writing system. The written records of the past would too quickly become obscure: knowledge of law, history, and literature, for instance, would be available only to those who knew the old tongues.

Obviously, the primary requirement of a spelling system is not that it be logical but that it be as stable as possible from dialect to dialect and from era to era. Furthermore, it is imperative that you observe the system, no matter how illogical it seems. To most readers in the worlds of business, commerce, and scholarship, spelling is a mark of a person's education, sense of responsibility, and even intelligence. Therefore, you cannot afford to take a casual attitude toward spelling; it is to your professional advantage to take spelling seriously.

## Tips for Improving Spelling

Some people seem to have a natural talent for spelling, an ability that allows them to visualize words correctly. These people can simply look at commonly used words and know immediately if the spelling is correct. Thus, natural spellers rely on dictionaries to spell only unusual or technical words. But many people do not have this talent and instead must be always alert to the possibility of misspelled words in everything they write. If you fall into this second category of spellers, you may want to adopt some or all of the following five techniques for improving spelling.

**sp**

### 1. Use the Dictionary

The best way to solve spelling problems is to use a dictionary. Poor spellers often counter this suggestion with "If I don't know how to spell a word, I can't find it in the dictionary." This assumption usually is not true. With a few exceptions (such as *kn, ph, sc*), an initial consonant is almost always predictable. And initial vowels are almost as easy to predict as consonants—a word like *envision* may begin with either an *i* or an *e,* but it certainly is not likely to begin with an *a,* an *o,* or a *u.* Thus, finding the right section of the dictionary requires little effort. At that point, the word can be located rather quickly.

Suppose, for example, you want to look up the correct spelling of a common word like *concept.* From its sound, you can guess that the first letter is going to be *c* or *k.* The first vowel, if not *a,* is likely to be *o.* It is certain that an *n* will follow that vowel. Next comes an /s/ sound, rarely spelled any way except *s* or *c.* After that comes a sound usually represented by an *e.* Finally, the *p* and *t* are almost completely predictable. In summary, if *concept* is not in the *k*'s, it will certainly be in the *c*'s. And from that point, it should take only a few minutes to track the word down.

### 2. Practice Pronunciation

Once you have found a word in the dictionary, be sure you know exactly how to pronounce it. To fix the pronunciation in your mind, say the word aloud several times, pausing between syllables. Then say the word aloud a number of times without pausing. If you have difficulty understanding the pronunciation symbols of dictionaries, you might try the *Oxford American,* which uses an Americanized pronunciation key much simpler than those of most other dictionaries.

### 3. Practice Writing the Word

After you are sure of the pronunciation, write the word a dozen times or so. This practice not only will help fix the word in your motor memory but also will let you see how it looks in your own handwriting. If possible, also type the word a number of times to help you recognize it in print. When you know a word in sound, script, and type, you are not likely to forget how to spell it.

### 4. Keep a Word List

You might find it helpful to keep a list of words that you tend to misspell. You can include those words that instructors have marked on your papers as well as words you must frequently look up in the dictionary. Studying your list and using it when you edit papers will help you master the words you find particularly troublesome.



You can also consult lists of commonly misspelled words, such as those at the end of this chapter. You can single out the words you do not spell with confidence and add them to your individual list.

### 5. Study Spelling Patterns

Get familiar with spelling patterns, also called "spelling rules." Remember, however, that a rule in spelling is an observation—a description of a pattern that recurs in the language, not an iron-clad law never violated.

## Spelling Patterns

Inconsistencies do exist between the spelling system and the sound system. And bizarre spellings do occur, although usually with scientific terms, esoteric words, and proper names. But on the whole, patterns predominate.

### Silent *e* with Long Vowels

Many words end with an unpronounced letter *e*—commonly called "silent *e.*" Actually, the silent *e* is a key to pronunciation, as the following pairs of words illustrate.

| | |
|---|---|
| van/vane | lop/elope |
| gap/gape | dot/dote |
| spit/spite | occur/cure |
| forbid/abide | sum/consume |

The word pairs show that silent *e* follows a stressed (accented) syllable with a long vowel, a vowel that requires the muscles in the mouth to tense during pronunciation.

| | |
|---|---|
| *ee* in *theme* | *ay* in *mate* |
| *oo* in *rude* | *iy* in *bite* |
| *oh* in *hope* | |

The *e* may attach to a single-syllable word or to a word stressed on the last syllable.

The absence of the *e* on a stressed (accented) syllable indicates a short vowel. Short vowels like the following allow the muscles in the mouth to remain lax during pronunciation.

| | |
|---|---|
| *ih* in *fit* | *aw* in *bought* |
| *eh* in *bet* | *ah* in *spa* |
| *uh* in *cup* | *aeh* in *mat* |

The pattern is as follows.

- Stressed syllable with long vowel: silent *e* (*tape, ride*)
- Stressed syllable with short vowel: no *e* (*tap, rid*)

The rule does not apply when the stressed final syllable has

- More than one vowel in a row (*boom, appear*)
- More than one consonant in a row (*comb, dodge*)

sp

## ❑ EXERCISE 1

In each word, identify the final or only vowel sound as long or short. If the vowel is long, think of a companion word with a short vowel; if the vowel is short, think of a companion word with a long vowel.

EXAMPLE: *rob,* short; *robe,* long

1. din
2. note
3. cur
4. envelop
5. shine
6. cute
7. tot
8. hate
9. wine
10. fat

### Silent *e* with Suffixes

When a suffix is added to a word that ends in silent *e*, the *e* drops if the suffix begins with a vowel and remains if the suffix begins with a consonant

| Base | Suffix with Vowel Drop the *E* | Suffix with Consonant Retain the *E* |
|---|---|---|
| arrange | arranging | arrangement |
| like | likable | likely |
| sincere | sincerity | sincerely |
| name | naming | nameless |
| intense | intensify | intensely |
| tone | tonal | toneless |
| waste | wasting | wasteful |
| excite | exciting | excitement |
| love | lovable | lovely |

EXCEPTION: Three common exceptions to this pattern are *truly, argument,* and *judgment.*

sp

EXCEPTION: The letter *c* may represent the hard sound /kuh/ as in *cup* or the soft sound /s/ as in *supper.* The letter *g* may represent the hard sound /guh/ as in *gum* or the soft sound /juh/ as in *gentle.* With the suffixes *-able* and *-ous,* silent *e* is retained in two situations.

- After soft *c*: service/serviceable
  notice/noticeable
- After soft *g*: outrage/outrageous
  advantage/advantageous

## ❑ EXERCISE 2

For each base word, an appropriate suffix is listed. Indicate whether to drop or retain the *e* on the base word when adding the suffix.

1. argue + ment
2. encourage + ing
3. survive + al
4. immense + ly
5. use + ful
6. remove + able
7. face + less
8. whine + ing
9. trace + able
10. courage + ous

### Doubled Consonants with Verbs

With regular verbs, the past tense and past participle are made by adding *-d* or *-ed* to the base form. (See 4a.) The spelling pattern is as follows.

- When the verb ends in a stressed syllable and a single consonant, the consonant is doubled and *-ed* is added (*pin/pinned, uncap/uncapped*).

- When the verb ends in a stressed syllable and a silent *e*, a *-d* is added to the base (*dine/dined, escape/escaped*).

| BASE FORM | PAST FORM AND PAST PARTICIPLE |
|---|---|
| bar | barred |
| bare | bared |
| refer | referred |
| interfere | interfered |
| grip | gripped |
| gripe | griped |
| occur | occurred |
| cure | cured |
| mat | matted |
| mate | mated |

sp

The present participle is made by adding *-ing* to the base form of the verb. The spelling pattern is as follows.

- When the verb ends in a stressed syllable and a single consonant, the consonant is doubled and *-ing* is added (*pin/pinning, uncap/uncapping*).
- When the verb ends in a stressed syllable and a silent *e*, the *e* is dropped and *-ing* is added (*dine/dining, escape/escaping*).

| BASE FORM | PRESENT PARTICIPLE |
|---|---|
| bar | barring |
| bare | baring |
| refer | referring |
| interfere | interfering |
| grip | gripping |
| gripe | griping |
| occur | occurring |
| cure | curing |
| mat | matting |
| mate | mating |

## EXERCISE 3

Decide whether to double the last consonant when making the past tense and past participle (adding *-d* or *-ed*) and the present participle (adding *-ing*) of each verb.

1. dare
2. engage
3. gag
4. omit
5. smoke
6. embed
7. assume
8. hope
9. sum
10. bud

### Doubled Consonants with Prefixes, Suffixes, and Compounds

When a prefix ends with the same consonant that the base begins with, both consonants are retained.

| | |
|---|---|
| dis + satisfied | dissatisfied |
| over + rate | overrate |
| un + necessary | unnecessary |



When a suffix begins with the same consonant that the base ends with, both consonants are retained.

| | |
|---|---|
| mental + ly | mentally |
| stubborn + ness | stubbornness |
| heel + less | heelless |

When the first part of a compound word ends with the same consonant that the second part begins with, both consonants are retained.

| | |
|---|---|
| book + keeper | bookkeeper |
| beach + head | beachhead |
| room + mate | roommate |

## EXERCISE 4

Combine the following words, prefixes, and suffixes.

1. ir + responsible
2. awful + ly
3. under + rate
4. mis + spell
5. jack + knife
6. non + negotiable
7. dis + satisfy
8. fatal + ly
9. lamp + post
10. en + noble

### *I* before *e*

Almost everyone knows the "i before e" school rhyme:

"*I* before *e* except after *c*
or when the vowel sounds like *a* as in *neighbor* and *weigh.*"

The rule in this rhyme works with many *ie* words.

| | |
|---|---|
| achieve | relief |
| believe | thief |
| friend | view |

It also works with many *c* plus *ei* words.

| | |
|---|---|
| ceiling | deceive |
| conceit | perceive |
| conceive | receive |

And *ei* does appear in words that sound like *weigh*.

| | |
|---|---|
| eight | neighbor |
| feign | sleigh |
| freight | veil |

sp

But many words without the *c* or the *weigh* sound are spelled with *ei.*

| | |
|---|---|
| either | neither |
| foreign | seize |
| height | weird |

The rhyme does cover words like *believe* and *receive,* but it is not completely reliable. The best solution to the *ie/ei* problem is the dictionary.

## ❑ EXERCISE 5

Which of the following correctly spelled words follow the rules in the "*i* before *e*" school rhyme and which do not?

1. piece
2. receipt
3. leisure
4. friend
5. financier
6. yield
7. rein
8. protein
9. vein
10. foreign

### *-Cede, -ceed,* and *-sede*

Since *-sede, -ceed,* and *-cede* are pronounced identically, writers sometimes confuse them, spelling *proceed,* for example, as *procede.* Mastering the "cede" words, however, is a simple matter of memorizing the spelling of four words: *supersede, exceed, proceed,* and *succeed.*

> *Supersede* ends in *-sede.*
> *Exceed, proceed,* and *succeed* end in *-ceed.*
> All the rest end in *-cede: recede, secede, concede,* and so on.

### ❑ EXERCISE 6

Correct the incorrectly spelled "cede" words in the following sentences.

1. I was asked to intersede with the parents on behalf of the child.
2. Weight on the pulley should not exseed 50 pounds.
3. His bouts of depression were usually preceeded by visits from his creditors.
4. If the caution light comes, do not procede any farther.
5. In 1832, South Carolina threatened to sesede from the Union because of the national tariff.

sp

## Lists of Frequently Misspelled Words

Several lists of frequently misspelled words are grouped according to the characteristics that cause problems.

### Easily Confused Words

accept/except
advice/advise
affect/effect
all ready/already
all together/altogether
allusion/illusion
ally/alley
aloud/allowed
altar/alter
analysis/analyze
ascent/assent
assistance/assistants
board/bored
breath/breathe
bridal/bridle
capital/capitol
censor/censure
hear/here
heard/herd

choose/chose
cite/site/sight
cloths/clothes
coarse/course
complement/compliment
conscience/conscious
council/counsel
currant/current
dairy/diary
descent/dissent
device/devise
die/dye
ensure/insure
envelop/envelope
formally/formerly
forth/fourth
foul/fowl
prophecy/prophesy
quiet/quit/quite

idol/idle
incidence/incidents
its/it's
know/no
later/latter
lead/led
lessen/lesson
lightning/lightening
loan/lone
loose/lose
maybe/may be
moral/morale
muscle/mussel
naval/navel
paid/payed
passed/past
peace/piece
personal/personnel
presence/presents
principal/principle
right/write
road/rode
sail/sale
shone/shown
stationary/stationery
statue/stature
straight/strait
than/then
their/there/they're
through/threw
to/too/two
vain/vein
waist/waste
wait/weight
weather/whether
were/we're/where
which/witch
who's/whose
your/you're



### Frequently Mispronounced Words

| *Correct Spelling* | *Mispronunciation* |
|---|---|
| accidentally | "accidently" |
| athlete | "athelete" |
| barbarous | "barbarious" |
| disastrous | "disasterous" |
| February | "Febuary" |
| mathematics | "mathmatics" |
| miniature | "minature" |
| mischievous | "mischievious" |
| monstrous | "monsterous" |
| parliamentary | "parlimentry" |
| probably | "probly" |
| sophomore | "sophmore" |
| temperature | "temperture" |

### Words with *s, ss, c,* and *sc*

absence
accessible
adolescent
associate
conscience
conscious
ascend
assassinate
assistance
occasion
permissible
persistence

decision
descend
discussion
ecstasy
embarrass
expense
fascinate
insistent
license
mischievous
muscle
necessary
nuisance
physical
possession
reminisce
resistance
scarcity
sincerely
source
succeed
succession
suspicious
unconscious
unnecessary
vicious

### Words with *-able* or *-ible*

acceptable
admissible
advisable
believable
changeable
collapsible
comfortable
compatible
credible
dependable
edible
eligible
flammable
flexible
gullible
impossible
incredible
irresistible
irritable
likeable
movable
noticeable
peaceable
permissible
possible
probable
profitable
resistible
responsible
separable
visible

### Words with *-ence* or *-ance*

abhorrence
abundance
acquaintance
appearance
appliance
assistance
attendance
conference
deference
defiance
magnificence
dependence
difference
endurance
existence
guidance
independence
inference
insistence
intelligence
interference
prominence

maintenance
nuisance
occurrence
patience
permanence
persistence
preference
prevalence
providence
reference
resemblance
significance
surveillance
temperance
tolerance
vengeance

## ❑ EXERCISE 7

Correct any misspelled words in the following passages. When the spelling patterns will not solve the problem, consult a dictionary or the lists of frequently misspelled words.

1. Last month I applied for a credit card at a major department store. The application ask for information that was completly unecessary: my hieght, my wieght, my religous preferance, and outragous details of my personel life. I dutifuly filed out all the information. When I recieved the card, imagine my surprize to find that my name was mispelled and my address was incorect.

2. Whenever I vow to begin a regular exercise program, something happens to interfer with my plans. For example, last Sunday, the sun was shinning, the temperture was 75 degrees, and my midterm test were behind me. So I determined to improve my physicle condition. I dug out my sweat suit and joging shoes and set out for the track. But providance was all ready preparing to intervene. Half way to the track, I had a flat tire. By the time I had gotton the tire fixed, the sun was gone and my intrest in musel tone had vanished.

sp

APPENDIX B

# Dictionary Use and Vocabulary Development

Good dictionaries are among the writer's best resources. Dictionaries explain the meanings and trace the histories of words. They answer questions about spellings, pronunciations, and forms. They provide synonyms and sometimes indicate appropriate word use. Some dictionaries even contain guides to people and places, grammar and punctuation, colleges and universities, and signs and symbols. Using this valuable resource frequently and knowledgeably can improve both your understanding of language and your ability to use language effectively.



## The Development of the Dictionary

The dictionary developed into its present form fairly recently. Before the eighteenth century, no dictionary of the English language had been published. The only available publications similar to dictionaries were lists of unfamiliar words and English equivalents of foreign words. People had no convenient way to look up meanings, spellings, and pronunciations or to determine acceptable usage. Those who were not well educated had little chance to improve their literacy.

Finally, to meet the needs of an increasingly ambitious public, a dictionary resembling the ones we take for granted was published. In 1721, Nathaniel Bailey published the *Universal Etymological Dictionary of the English Language,* a revolutionary guide to pronunciation, usage, and etymology (word history), containing even quotations and illustrations. In 1755, Samuel Johnson's two-volume *Dictionary* appeared. Very much like Bailey's but much more influential, this dictionary improved definitions and etymologies by systematically illustrating meaning through quotations and by arbitrating disputed spellings and pronunciations.

From this time, dictionaries continued to evolve, improving techniques and scope. The culmination of dictionary making was the twelve-volume *Oxford English Dictionary*—so thorough that 70 years went by from its beginning in 1857 to its completion in 1928. In 15,487 pages this dictionary defined 414,824 words, illustrating their meanings with 1,827,306 quotations.

After America's independence from England, it was inevitable that an American dictionary would appear. In 1828, Noah Webster published *An American Dictionary of the English Language* with American spellings and pronunciations, references to America, and quotations from the Founding Fathers. Because of this dictionary, Webster's name now appears as part of the title of many dictionaries. This use, however, does not signify any direct connection with the early lexicographer. Because the name is now in the public domain, it can appear in any title.

Today, dictionaries fulfill two important purposes—to provide a guide to such practical matters as spelling, meaning, pronunciation, and usage and to represent the entire vocabulary of the English language. The latter purpose is fulfilled by the large unabridged dictionaries like *Webster's Third New International Dictionary* (about 450,000 entries), *The Random House Dictionary of the English Language* (about 260,000 entries), and *Funk and Wagnall's New Standard Dictionary of the English Language* (about 450,000 entries). The most comprehensive dictionary available is the second edition of the *Oxford English Dictionary* with its 22 volumes and half a million definitions. This dictionary is also available on a compact disk for use with a computer. For practical purposes, however, a desk, or college, dictionary (averaging about 160,000 entries) will answer typical questions.



## A Survey of Your Dictionary

To get the maximum benefit from a dictionary, you should read the introductory material. Although dictionaries are strikingly similar, there are differences. Whenever dictionary makers "abridge," or reduce, a dictionary from its potentially mammoth size, they obviously must leave something out. When you use a particular dictionary, you should know what has been included and what omitted. Some dictionaries cut down on the number of words or the number of definitions. Some dictionaries shorten or eliminate etymologies, coverage of synonyms, and appendixes. If a dictionary's introduction does not indicate omissions, you should check a few entries to see what they include. In addition, you can compare entries to those in other dictionaries.

You also should determine whether a dictionary is a single alphabetical list or whether some words, such as the names of people and places, have been taken out of the main section and listed in appendixes. For example, all entries in the *Oxford American Dictionary, Webster's New World Dictionary,* and the *Random House College Dictionary* are in one alphabetical list. *The American Heritage Dictionary* and *Webster's Ninth New Collegiate Dictionary* have divided lists with separate sections for biographical entries, place names, abbreviations, four-year colleges, and two-year colleges. In addition, some dictionaries provide a style manual, linguistic essays, and a guide to signs and symbols. Although most dictionaries of the same size and scope contain similar information, variations do exist.

## ❑ EXERCISE 1

Read the introductory material in your dictionary and answer the following questions.

1. When was your dictionary published?
2. Does your dictionary put names of places in the main list of words or in a special list?
3. If several definitions are given for a word, in what order are they listed?
4. What usage labels appear in your dictionary?
5. Does your dictionary contain usage paragraphs?
6. Does your dictionary contain lists of synonyms or paragraphs describing synonyms?
7. Does your dictionary give the etymology of words?



## Components of the Entries

Regardless of the variations among dictionaries, the components they include to explain a word are generally similar. All have the main entry, divided into syllables. All give pronunciations, identify the parts of speech, and list the inflected forms. And obviously, all define the entries. In addition, most dictionaries include etymologies, synonyms, illustrations of words in context, and usage notes. The example from *Webster's Collegiate* illustrates the typical components, which will be fully discussed one by one.

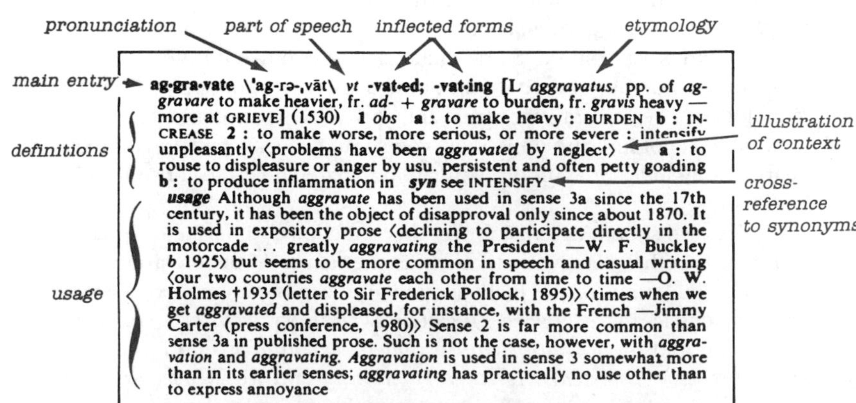


**ag·gra·vate** \'ag-rə-,vāt\ *vt* **-vat·ed; -vat·ing** [L *aggravatus,* pp. of *aggravare* to make heavier, fr. *ad-* + *gravare* to burden, fr. *gravis* heavy — more at GRIEVE] (1530) **1** *obs* **a** : to make heavy : BURDEN **b** : INCREASE **2** : to make worse, more serious, or more severe : intensify unpleasantly ⟨problems have been *aggravated* by neglect⟩ **a** : to rouse to displeasure or anger by usu. persistent and often petty goading **b** : to produce inflammation in ***syn*** see INTENSIFY

***usage*** Although *aggravate* has been used in sense 3a since the 17th century, it has been the object of disapproval only since about 1870. It is used in expository prose ⟨declining to participate directly in the motorcade . . . greatly *aggravating* the President —W. F. Buckley *b* 1925⟩ but seems to be more common in speech and casual writing ⟨our two countries *aggravate* each other from time to time —O. W. Holmes †1935 (letter to Sir Frederick Pollock, 1895)⟩ ⟨times when we get *aggravated* and displeased, for instance, with the French —Jimmy Carter (press conference, 1980)⟩ Sense 2 is far more common than sense 3a in published prose. Such is not the case, however, with *aggravation* and *aggravating*. *Aggravation* is used in sense 3 somewhat more than in its earlier senses; *aggravating* has practically no use other than to express annoyance

### The Main Entry

The main entry for a word, printed in boldface type, indicates spelling and syllabic division. Obviously, a primary use of the dictionary is to find out how to spell words. Usually, there is only one spelling, but occasionally more. When several spellings appear, the first listing is generally more common than the others. The syllabication shows where to divide the word when it must be hyphenated to fit the right margin of a manuscript. In most main entries, centered dots appear between all syllables except those with hyphens or those made up of more than one word.

Not every word is listed as a main entry. For example, the words *inaugurator, opportunely,* or *chauvinistic* are not separately listed. Instead they appear without definitions at the ends of these entries: *inaugurate, opportune, chauvinism.* These undefined words, or "run-on entries," are derived forms, such as adjectives made from nouns, adverbs made from adjectives, and nouns made from verbs. The meaning of a run-on entry is easily figured out from the definition of the main entry.

## ☐ EXERCISE 2

Which of the following are main entries in the dictionary? Which are run-on entries?

1. hindrance
2. instrumental
3. pinheadedness
4. radiantly
5. velvety
6. sectarianism
7. would-be
8. millennial
9. reptilian
10. scentless

### Pronunciation

Not all dictionaries use the same method to show the stresses and sounds of pronunciation. To understand the method in your dictionary, you should read the explanation in the introduction and follow the pronunciation key. In particular, dictionaries mark stress (or accents) differently. Some dictionaries show two levels of stress (strong and medium) with bold marks (**′**) and light marks (′); others use high-set marks \ˈ\ and low-set marks \ˌ\. Instead of stress marks, the *Oxford American Dictionary* uses boldface type for stressed syllables. Likewise, not all dictionaries symbolize sounds in the same way. Notice how differently these dictionaries represent the stresses and sounds of the verb *harass.*

| From *Webster's New World* | From *Webster's Collegiate* |
|---|---|
| **har·ass** (hə ras**′**, har′əs) | **ha·rass** \hə-ˈras, ˈhar-əs\ |
| From *Oxford American* | From *Random House* |
| **har·ass** (hă-**ras**, **har**-ăs) | **har·ass** (har′əs, hə ras**′**) |

People frequently assume that when a dictionary gives more than one pronunciation, the first is preferred. But most dictionaries are very cautious about prescribing preference. Instead, they try to present an objective description of language. Some dictionaries do, however, indicate when a word's pronunciation is not common; for example, *Random House* marks an infrequent pronunciation with the word *sometimes,* as in this guide to the pronunciation of *often.*

FROM *RANDOM HOUSE*

**of·ten** (ô′fən, of′ən *or*, *sometimes*, ôf′tən, of′-).

## ❑ EXERCISE 3

In a dictionary, look up the pronunciation of each of these words.

1. victuals
2. forehead
3. psalm
4. mischievous
5. salmon
6. vase
7. wash
8. corps
9. Cairo (Illinois)
10. Cairo (Egypt)
11. ignominy
12. subtle

dict

### Parts of Speech

Most parts of speech are labeled with traditional abbreviations: *adj., adv., conj., n., prep., pron.,* and *v.* or *vb.* Verbs may be further identified by type: *tr.* or *vt.* (transitive) and *intr.* or *vi.* (intransitive). Other labels that may appear are *interj.* (interjection), *aux.* (auxiliary verb), *def. art.* (definite article), *indef. art.* (indefinite article), *pref.* (prefix), and *suff.* (suffix).

The part-of-speech label can be very important because it tells which definition applies whenever a word can function as more than one part of speech. For example, *effect* can be a noun or a verb, and the definitions are not at all the same.

## ❑ EXERCISE 4

Name the different parts of speech listed in the dictionary for these words.

1. double
2. intellectual
3. round
4. well
5. up
6. over
7. once
8. besides

### Inflected Forms

The inflected forms of words are the different forms appropriate for different functions—such as the changes in verbs (*ride, rode, ridden*), the different degrees of adjectives and adverbs (*scary, scarier, scariest*), and the plurals of nouns (*heroes*). Many dictionaries omit these inflected forms when they are regular because users are not likely to look up this information. Other dictionaries, such as the *American Heritage,* give forms even when regular.

FROM *AMERICAN HERITAGE*

**a·brade** (ə-brād') *tr.v.* **a·brad·ed, a·brad·ing, a·brades.** To rub off or wear away by friction; erode. [Lat. *abradere,* to scrape off : *ab-,* off + *radere,* to scrape.]

## EXERCISE 5

By looking in a dictionary, answer the following questions about inflected forms.

1. What is the plural form of each of these words?

| | |
|---|---|
| datum | rabbi |
| formula | tornado |
| scarf | syllabus |
| navy | index |

2. What is the past form of each of these words?

| | |
|---|---|
| shrink | dive |
| cleave | cling |
| drag | drug |
| shine | work |

3. What are the forms for each of these adjectives and adverbs?

| | |
|---|---|
| long | well |
| noble | jolly |
| tacky | slow |
| sad | murky |



### Definitions

As a language evolves, so do the meanings of its words. Thus, words frequently have multiple meanings or shades of meaning. Lexicographers must decide which definitions to list, given the projected size of a dictionary. If a dictionary is a small paperback version, it obviously cannot include as many meanings as a large work. Logically, the rare and obsolete meanings will be sacrificed. Compare the entries from the paperback edition and the college edition of the *American Heritage Dictionary.*

FROM *AMERICAN HERITAGE,*
PAPERBACK EDITION

**dull** (dŭl) *adj.* **1.** Lacking mental agility; slow to learn. **2.** Not brisk; sluggish. **3.** Not sharp; blunt. **4.** Not intensely or keenly felt. **5.** Unexciting; boring. **6.** Not bright or vivid. **7.** Cloudy; gloomy. **8.** Muffled; indistinct. —*v.* To make or become dull. [< MLG *dul.*] **—dul'ly** *adv.* **—dull'ness, dul'ness** *n.*

FROM *AMERICAN HERITAGE*,
COLLEGE EDITION

**dull** (dŭl) *adj.* **duller, dullest. 1.** Lacking mental agility; slow to learn; stupid. **2.** Lacking responsiveness or alertness; insensitive. **3.** Dispirited; depressed. **4.** Not brisk or rapid; sluggish. **5.** Not sharp or keen; blunt. **6.** Not intensely or keenly felt: *a dull ache.* **7.** Arousing no interest or curiosity; unexciting; boring. **8.** Not bright or vivid; dim: *a dull brown.* **9.** Cloudy; gloomy. **10.** Muffled; indistinct. —See Synonyms at **stupid.** —*v.* **dulled, dulling, dulls.** —*tr.* **1.** To make less sharp; to blunt. **2.** To make less bright or distinct. **3.** To make (the senses, for example) less keen or receptive. —*intr.* To become dull. [Middle English *dul, dulle,* from Middle Low German *dul.* See **dheu-**[1] in Appendix.*] —**dul'ly** *adv.* —**dull'ness, dul'ness** *n.*
***Synonyms:*** *dull, blunt, obtuse.* These adjectives are compared as they apply to the absence of sharpness. In general usage only *dull* and *blunt* describe absence of physical sharpness. *Dull* implies loss of sharpness through use; *blunt* more often refers to what is thick-edged by design. Figuratively, *dull* implies lack of intelligence or slowness of perception, while *blunt* refers to unrefined manner. *Obtuse* implies marked insensitivity to what is directed to the intellect or emotions.

Most dictionaries list definitions in one of two ways—by frequency of use (beginning with the definition most commonly used) or in a chronological order (moving from the earliest meaning to the latest). Both methods are logical, and neither method predominates. The *Oxford American Dictionary, Random House,* and *World Book* use the order of frequency. *Webster's New World* and *Webster's Collegiate* use the chronological order. The *American Heritage* arranges its definitions "analytically," in patterns that tie together related meanings.

dict

## ❑ EXERCISE 6

Look up the definitions of the following underlined words. Among the definitions given, choose the one that best fits the context of the sentence in which the word appears.

1. The so-called Stockholm syndrome is the tendency for hostages to feel a close relationship with their captors as time passes.
2. It's hard to circumvent the rigid requirements of the agency.
3. Her sanguine disposition makes her the perfect choice for a mediator.
4. The players emerged from the crucible of the contest with a feeling of accomplishment.
5. In the walls of the old church, layers of bricks were sandwiched together.
6. They have forged a close relationship with their neighbors.
7. He is trying to shuffle out of the commitment to work the night shift.
8. The police were trying to extract information about the appearance of the terrorist.
9. As fast as they could, they shucked off their wet clothes.
10. The sculptor was trying to skewer a piece of wood to his creation.

## Etymology

Most dictionaries trace the stages in a word's history from its earliest known use. The history, or etymology, usually appears in brackets, with abbreviations to indicate the language or languages of origin. This information tells much about the development of the English language: the evolution of certain words directly from Old English, the Early French influence, the tremendous impact of Latin and Greek, and the productive borrowing from a multitude of other languages. *Webster's Collegiate* now adds to the historical information by giving a date in most entries for a word's "earliest recorded use in English."

Searching through a dictionary for the origin of words is like an archeological search, digging beneath the surface reality to discover the past. It reveals the numerous languages that have contributed to the vocabulary of English. Of these, only the most influential are introduced here, along with a brief description of their effects on English.

OLD ENGLISH (OE)

FROM *AMERICAN HERITAGE*

**love** [ME < OE *lufu*.]

In the middle of the fifth century A.D., tribes from northern Germany invaded England, at that time a Roman province. The Anglo-Saxon invaders were really a conglomerate of tribes that spoke very similar Germanic dialects. The language that developed from the time of this invasion until about 1066 is called Old English or Anglo-Saxon. From this source come our structural signals like pronouns, prepositions, conjunctions, and articles as well as many of our everyday words, such as *eat, drink, know, friend, home, beer, man, arm, blood, water, sun,* and *earth.* In fact, of the 100 most frequently used words in Modern English, all come from Old English. Of the second 100 most frequently used words, 83 come from Old English.



OLD NORSE (ON)

FROM *RANDOM HOUSE*

**ug·ly** [ME *ugly. uglike* < ON *ugglig(r)* fearful. dreadful = *ugg(r)* fear + *-ligr* -LY]

Hundreds of Old Norse words were absorbed into the English vocabulary after the arrival of the Vikings in A.D. 787. Most of these words, along with those from Old English, make up our everyday vocabulary. From Old Norse came words such as the pronouns *they, them, their;* the nouns *bag, ball, skin;* the verbs *get, hit, happen;* the adjectives *flat, low, tight.*

OLD FRENCH (OF OR O FR.)

FROM *WEBSTER'S NEW WORLD*

**in·fant** (in′fənt) *n.* [ME. *infaunt* < OFr. *enfant* < L. *infans* (gen. *infantis*), child < *adj.*, not yet speaking < *in-*, not + *fans*, prp. of *fari*, to speak: see FAME]

In 1066, a dramatic event occurred that eventually changed our language: England was conquered by the Normans. These conquerers, who had earlier migrated to France from Scandinavia, spoke a dialect of Old French. (Some dictionaries label this dialect "Norman French.") Old English was replaced as the official language, not only in government but also in the church and in the schools. But even though it became subordinate, English did not die out; it was preserved by the native speakers, who clung persistently to their language.

MIDDLE ENGLISH (ME)

FROM *WEBSTER'S COLLEGIATE*

[1]**gag** \'gag\ *vb* **gagged**; **gag·ging** [ME *gaggen* to strangle, of imit. origin]

In the twelfth century, English emerged from its subordinate status, but in a somewhat altered form. This language, called Middle English, blended the Germanic influences of Old English with the French influences of Norman French. Middle English was spoken until roughly 1500, when it evolved into what is called Modern English.

LATIN (L OR LAT.)

dict

FROM *SHORTER OXFORD ENGLISH DICTIONARY*

**Conflict** (kǫ·nflikt), *sb.* ME. [– L. *conflictus*, f. *conflict-*, pa. ppl. stem of *confligere*, f. *com* CON- + *fligere* strike.]

The influence of Latin has been pervasive. Before the Anglo-Saxon invasion, the Germanic tongues had been influenced by the language of the Romans. After the invasion, Old English was influenced by the classical Roman writers, by the Roman church, and by Roman merchants. Even Norman French had been derived from Latin. And Modern English has been so influenced that now about half of our words can be traced to a Latin origin. To show this widespread impact, many dictionary etymologies make such distinctions as Old Latin (OL), Vulgar Latin (VL), Medieval Latin (ML), Late Latin (LL), and New Latin (NL).

FRENCH (FR)

FROM *WEBSTER'S COLLEGIATE*

**rou·tine** \rü-'tēn\ *n* [F, fr. MF, fr. *route* traveled way]

Long after the Norman invasion, French continues to lend words to English. While the French have sought to keep their language free of English contamination, the English-speaking peoples have not reciprocated. Instead, they have been borrowing French words for centuries, most heavily in the Middle Ages and the Renaissance.

GREEK (GK)

FROM *RANDOM HOUSE*

**bi·ol·o·gy** [< G *Biologie*]

Because the Romans borrowed many Greek words, Greek has indirectly influenced English through Latin. But the clearest influence is probably on our scholarly and scientific words that have been deliberately derived from Greek.

## ❑ EXERCISE 7

What is the etymology of each of these words?

1. boycott
2. aisle
3. ballet
4. chauvinism
5. playwright
6. subtract
7. bravado
8. gospel
9. coyote
10. hamburger
11. book
12. explore
13. religion
14. solar
15. tantalize

### Synonyms

Many dictionaries include synonyms with some entries. Especially useful are entries with brief paragraphs that not only list synonyms but also discuss their similarities and differences in meaning. Suppose, for example, that you wanted a word similar to *confirm* but with an emphasis on validity. Looking up *confirm* in *Funk & Wagnall's New Standard College Dictionary* would lead to the paragraph about synonyms. And here is listed a word with just the sense you were looking for—*substantiate.*

FROM *FUNK & WAGNALL'S*

**Syn.:** corroborate, establish, fix, prove, ratify, sanction, settle, strengthen, substantiate, sustain, uphold. [*Confirm* (L. *con*, together, and *firmus*, firm) is to add firmness or give stability to. Both *confirm* and *corroborate* presuppose something already existing to which the confirmation or corroboration is added.] Testimony is *corroborated* by concurrent testimony or by circumstances; *confirmed* by *established* facts. That which is thoroughly *proved* is said to be *established;* so is that which is official and has adequate power behind it; as, the *established* government; the *established* church. The continents are *fixed.* A treaty is *ratified;* an appointment *confirmed.* An act is *sanctioned* by any person or authority that passes upon it approvingly. A statement is *substantiated;* a report *confirmed;* a controversy *settled;* the decision of a lower court *sustained* by a higher. Just government should be *upheld.* The beneficent results of Christianity *confirm* our faith in it as a divine revelation.

## ❑ EXERCISE 8

For each of the following words, find a synonym with the particular implied meaning that is indicated.

1. banish (implying banishment from one's own country)
2. scold (implying strong anger or hatred)
3. shorten (implying something incomplete)
4. little (implying extreme smallness)
5. smell (implying a pleasant odor)
6. fierce (implying uncivilized ferocity)
7. tough (implying determination)
8. clumsy (implying lack of ability)
9. puzzle (implying "to confuse")
10. attempt (implying great effort)

### Illustrations of Words in Context

The unabridged dictionaries frequently quote from varied sources to illustrate a word's use in context, sometimes over a long time span. Context is very useful for totally unfamiliar words and words that appear only in restricted patterns, like transitive verbs and adjectives. The smaller dictionaries cannot provide such extensive coverage and therefore either do not use illustrative examples or abridge their use. *Webster's Collegiate,* for example, illustrates the usage of some entries with familiar phrases, as in this entry for *multilayered.*

dict

FROM *WEBSTER'S COLLEGIATE*

**mul·ti·lay·ered** \-ˈlā-ərd, -ˈle(-ə)rd\ *or* **mul·ti·lay·er** \-ˈlā-ər, -ˈle(-ə)r\ *adj* (1931) **:** **having or involving several distinct layers, strata, or levels**

Other entries, such as this one for the verb *damnify,* include quotations.

FROM *WEBSTER'S COLLEGIATE*

**dam·ni·fy** \ˈdam-nə-ˌfī\ *vt* **-fied; -fy·ing** [MF *damnifier,* fr. OF, fr. LL *damnificare,* fr. L *damnificus* injurious, fr. *damnum* damage] (1512) **:** to cause loss or damage to ⟨intimidation — the freedom to ~ another person with impunity —Henry Hazlitt⟩

## ❑ EXERCISE 9

Look up the following words in a dictionary. Quote the phrases or sentences that illustrate the typical contexts for the words. If your dictionary does not include a particular context, check in other dictionaries, especially unabridged ones, in your library.

1. sensuous
2. rampant
3. indigenous
4. expansive
5. routine
6. obviate
7. insinuate
8. rough-and-tumble
9. worm's-eye
10. expiate

## Usage

The term *usage* refers to current, correct, and appropriate use of words and phrases. The usage labels and notes in dictionaries help writers choose expressions that will be acceptable to their readers.

The methods for indicating usage vary. Some dictionaries use context labels—that is, labels that tell in what contexts words are appropriate: *informal* or *colloquial* indicates that a word is used in conversational rather than formal speech or writing; *slang* indicates that a word is used even more informally.

Sometimes usage labels note that a word or a certain meaning is common to a particular group (*British, Canadian, Southwest, New England*) or to some particular discipline (*music, chemistry, botany, law*). Terms like *archaic, obsolete,* and *old use* indicate that the word or a certain meaning is no longer current. The *Oxford American Dictionary* labels certain words *contemptuous* to indicate that a word "implies contempt."

Some dictionaries go beyond mere labels and include usage notes. Notes in the *Oxford American* usually run a sentence or two. For example, the entry for *and* mentions that "Careful writers do not use and/or," and the entry for *consensus* notes, "It is incorrect to say or write *consensus of opinion.*" The *American Heritage* consults a usage panel of over 150 "outstanding writers, speakers, and thinkers." This dictionary's usage notes often fill a paragraph that includes references to the opinions of the panel members. For example, the note that follows the definition of *medium* comments on the acceptability of using the plural form *media* as a singular noun.

dict

FROM *AMERICAN HERITAGE*

***Usage:* *Media* (means of mass communication) is often used as a singular noun: *Television is an unpredictable media.* This is unacceptable in writing to 90 per cent of the Usage Panel, and in speech to 88 per cent. The use of *medias* as a plural form is condemned even more severely.**

In addition to comments about appropriateness, many dictionaries warn readers not to confuse words like *continual* and *continuous, presumptive* and *presumptuous,* or *allusion* and *illusion.* All dictionaries that warn against word confusion do not cite the same pairs, however.

Thus, checking several dictionaries may be necessary to locate a usage note to solve a writing problem. Probably a better solution is to check the usage glossary in a handbook such as this one, where there is likely to be a thorough list of usage notes.

## ❑ EXERCISE 10

What usage, if any, is specified in a good desk or college dictionary for the following?

1. ain't
2. booze
3. prioritize
4. dollarwise
5. imply, infer
6. shall, will
7. irregardless
8. nerd
9. cayuse
10. croft

## Specialized Dictionaries

Sometimes, it may be more efficient to use a specialized dictionary, one that restricts coverage to such areas as etymology, synonyms, usage, idioms, and slang. Specialized dictionaries provide more complete coverage of these areas than do general works.

dict

### Etymology

Klein, Ernest. *A Comprehensive Etymological Dictionary of the English Language,* 1971.

Morris, William, and Mary Morris. *Morris Dictionary of Word and Phrase Origins,* 1977.

Onions, Charles T., et al. *The Oxford Dictionary of English Etymology,* 1966.

Partridge, Eric. *Origins: A Short Etymological Dictionary of Modern English,* 1966.

Shipley, Joseph T. *Dictionary of Word Origins,* 1979.

### Synonyms

*The New Roget's Thesaurus in Dictionary Form,* 1978.

*Roget's International Thesaurus,* 1977.

*Roget's II: The New Thesaurus,* 1980.

*Webster's Collegiate Thesaurus,* 1976.

*Webster's New World Thesaurus,* 1983.

### Usage

Bernstein, Theodore M. *The Careful Writer: A Modern Guide to English Usage,* 1965.

Bryant, Margaret M. *Current American Usage: How Americans Say It and Write It,* 1962.

Copperud, Roy A. *American Usage and Style: The Consensus,* 1980.

Evans, Bergen, and Cornelia Evans. *A Dictionary of Contemporary American Usage,* 1965.

Follett, Wilson. *Modern American Usage: A Guide,* 1966.

Fowler, H. W. *A Dictionary of Modern English Usage,* 1983.

### Idioms

Freeman, William. *A Concise Dictionary of English Idioms,* 1976.

Whitford, Harold C., and Robert J. Dixson. *Handbook of American Idioms and Idiomatic Usage,* 1973.

SLANG

Partridge, Eric, ed. *A Dictionary of Slang and Unconventional English,* 1970.

Wentworth, Harold, and Stuart Flexner. *Dictionary of American Slang,* 1975.

## ❑ EXERCISE 11

Check your library's collection of specialized dictionaries. Use an appropriate dictionary or several dictionaries to answer each of the following questions.

1. What is the etymology of the word *jazz?*
2. What is a synonym for *taciturn?*
3. Is the usage of *data* as a singular form (as in "the data is clear") considered acceptable in edited English?
4. What does the idiom *pull one's leg* mean?
5. Why is *spud* a slang expression for *potato?*

## Vocabulary Development



The best way to increase vocabulary is to read widely and to keep a dictionary close by. With the dictionary beyond reach, you may be tempted to skip unfamiliar words or to guess at meanings. Of course, sometimes you can figure out the meaning of unfamiliar words from their contexts. For example, assume that you do not know the meaning of *dissonant* and you read this sentence: "She suggested we name our parrot some dissonant name like 'Glumdalclitch.'" Obviously, the sentence contains a clue that indicates that *dissonant* means "inharmonious." Sentences, however, do not always provide clues. If you do not already know the meaning of *euphonious,* you cannot figure it out in this context: "His euphonious poetry had little meaning." When you have no clue, your best resource is a dictionary that explains that *euphonious* means "sweet sounding."

All dictionaries provide definitions. They also provide other aids to understanding meaning—the part of speech of the word, the etymology, and illustrations of the word in context. In addition, the dictionary breaks many words into their parts. If you look in a dictionary for *dissonant* or *euphonious,* you find within their etymology that *dis-* means "apart" and *son* means "sound" and that *eu-* means "good" and *phon* means "voice."

A breakdown of words into parts helps to build vocabulary because a part of one word may appear as a part of another. Thus, it is possible to use the meaning of one part as a clue to the meaning of a number of different words. For example, the *eu-* in *euphonious* also appears in *euphemism, euphoria, euthanasia,* and *eurythmic* and thus provides the clue that all these words have something to do with being "good." Likewise, the *son* in *dissonant* appears in *sonata, assonance,* and *sonic* and indicates the underlying meaning of "sound."

Some words can be broken down into prefixes, roots, and suffixes. A prefix is a syllable like *dis-* or *eu-* that attaches to the beginning of a word. A root provides the base meaning, as does *son* or *phon.* A suffix is a syllable or sound that attaches to the end of a word; the endings *-ant* and *-ous* are suffixes. These three possible components can affect a word's meaning in some way. A root contains a word's primary meaning. A prefix modifies the meaning of a root. A suffix can also modify meaning, but more often it changes a word from one class to another, for example, from a noun to an adjective or from a verb to a noun. The *-ant* and the *-ous* on the ends of *dissonant* and *euphonious* change the nouns *dissonance* and *euphony* to adjectives. Additionally, suffixes can change words to plural forms *(-s),* show possession *(-'s),* change the forms of verbs *(-s, -ed, -en, -ing),* and indicate the comparison of adjectives and adverbs *(-er, -est).*

Prefixes and suffixes must be attached, or "bound," to a root; they cannot appear alone as words. However, many roots can appear alone, or "free." For example, the roots in *dissonant* and *euphonious* stand alone in the words *sound* and *phone.*

**VOC**

Knowledge of common prefixes, roots, and suffixes is important for building a good vocabulary. Thus, as you look up words in the dictionary, pay close attention to their makeup. You also may have occasion to look up prefixes, roots, or suffixes. They sometimes appear in dictionaries in the same alphabetical list as words.

The following lists show how a prefix, root, or suffix can provide a clue to the meaning of several words. Although the list is extremely brief, it does show the value in searching not only for the meaning of a whole word but also for the meanings of its parts.

| Prefixes | | |
|---|---|---|
| *a-, an-* | without | *anarchy*—without rule<br>*atheism*—without god<br>*amorphous*—without shape |
| *ad-* | to, toward | *adduct*—draw toward<br>*adhere*—stick to<br>*advent*—a coming toward |
| *ante-* | before | *antecedent*—going before<br>*antediluvian*—before the flood<br>*antebellum*—before the war |
| *com-, con-* | together | *confluent*—flowing together<br>*congregate*—gather together<br>*commingle*—blend together |

| | | |
|---|---|---|
| *de-* | down | *descend*—go down<br>*degrade*—downgrade<br>*depress*—press down |
| *hyper-* | over | *hyperactive*—overactive<br>*hypertension*—overly tense<br>*hypercritical*—overly critical |
| *in-*, *im-* | not | *indecent*—not decent<br>*insignificant*—not significant<br>*imbalanced*—not balanced |

ROOTS

| | | |
|---|---|---|
| *carn* | flesh | *incarnate*—in the flesh<br>*carnal*—of the flesh<br>*carnivore*—flesh eater |
| *dem* | people | *democracy*—government by the people<br>*epidemic*—spreading among the people<br>*demography*—statistical analysis of people |
| *flux* | flow | *influx*—a flowing in<br>*confluence*—a flowing together<br>*fluid*—flowing |
| *graph* | write | *graphite*—writing material<br>*calligraphy*—beautiful writing<br>*monograph*—a writing on one subject |
| *path* | disease | *pathological*—caused by disease<br>*psychopath*—a mentally diseased person<br>*pathogenic*—causing disease |
| *phil* | love | *philharmonic*—loving harmony<br>*Anglophile*—a lover of England<br>*philosophy*—a love of wisdom |

SUFFIXES

| | | |
|---|---|---|
| *-ion* | changes verbs to nouns | *action, creation, translation* |
| *-ment* | changes verbs to nouns | *movement, government, adornment* |

| | | |
|---|---|---|
| *-en* | changes words to verbs | *harden, darken, strengthen* |
| *-ize* | changes words to verbs | *legalize, fraternize, theorize* |
| *-y* | changes nouns to adjectives | *mighty, tasty, rainy* |
| *-ous* | changes nouns to adjectives | *spacious, hazardous, poisonous* |
| *-ness* | changes adjectives to nouns | *laziness, happiness, darkness* |
| *-ly* | changes adjectives to adverbs | *cheaply, frequently, firmly* |

## ❑ EXERCISE 12

Use a dictionary to determine the meaning of the underlined words in the following sentences. Identify any prefix, root, or suffix that provides a clue to the meaning of each underlined word and the words in brackets. Remember that the prefixes, roots, and suffixes may be listed in the etymology section or listed as separate items.

VOC

1. He could never overcome being maladroit at crucial moments. [malediction, malevolence, malicious]
2. Patrons avoided the clerk with the dyspeptic temperament. [dysgenic, dystrophy, dysfunctional]
3. The manual says to emulsify the substance. [pacify, falsify, mystify]
4. That paragraph is superfluous. [supercharge, superlative, superscript]
5. Faulkner believed that honor was a verity of the "human heart." [veritable, verisimilitude, veracious]
6. The humidity has made everyone lethargic. [synchronic, diagnostic, formulaic]
7. I see no way to solve our dilemma. [dichromatic, digraph, dimorphism]
8. The text contradicts what I have in my lecture notes. [contraindicate, contravene, contraband]
9. Before Copernicus, most people believed in a geocentric universe. [geochronology, geometric, apogee]
10. The main character's emotions were very circumscribed. [circumvent, circumlocution, circumstellar]

# Glossary of Usage

This glossary provides a brief guide for commonly confused words and phrases, such as *illusion, delusion; ensure, insure; differ from, differ with.* In addition, the glossary serves as a guide for usage, that is, the acceptable use of words and phrases. Usage is sometimes determined by clarity and logic but other times merely by the preferences of influential writers and language experts. Thus, usage is subject to controversy and to change. The advice here is based on information found in current dictionaries and usage guides. However, you should bear in mind that some readers—your instructor, for example—may occasionally have other preferences.



## A, An

Use *a* before words with an initial consonant sound; use *an* before words with an initial vowel sound. Remember that the sound, not the letter, controls your choice: *a thought, an idea; a heel, an honor; a unicorn, an uncle; a "k," an "s."*

## Accept, Except

*Accept* is a verb that generally means "to receive something or someone willingly" or "to believe": *We accept your terms. Jefferson accepted the ideas of deism. Except* is usually a preposition meaning "with the exclusion of" or a conjunction (often coupled with *that*) meaning "if it were not for the fact that": *The walls of every room except the kitchen were decorated with silk screens. He is fairly well qualified for the position except that he has no experience in public relations.*

### Adverse, Averse

*Adverse* usually describes some position or thing that is hostile or antagonistic: *adverse criticism, adverse reaction, adverse publicity, adverse report. Adverse* can also refer to something unfavorable or harmful: *The pioneers struggled against the adverse conditions of the Rocky Mountain winter. Antibiotics kill infection but can have an adverse effect on the digestive system.*

*Averse* is part of the idiom *averse to,* which describes someone who dislikes or opposes something: *The Mormons are averse to any kind of artificial stimulant. The editorial board, averse to all Democratic candidates, used the magazine as a Republican forum.*

### Advice, Advise

*Advice* is a noun, with the *c* pronounced as an /s/ sound: *Your advice is welcome. Advise* is a verb, with the *s* pronounced as a /z/ sound: *We advise beginning students to take BASIC.*

### Affect, Effect

*Affect* is usually a verb that means "to influence" or "to bring about a change": *The weather often affects our emotions.* Sometimes *affect* is a verb meaning "to pretend": *Although he was actually from Wisconsin, Gibbs affected a British accent.* The use of *affect* as a noun is confined to psychology, where it refers to a feeling or an emotion as opposed to a thought or action: *He denied feeling guilty, but his affect was revealed in his blushing and stammering.*

usage

*Effect* is usually a noun that means "a result": *The prolonged cold spell had a devastating effect on the citrus crop.* As a noun, *effect* is also used in idioms like *take effect* and *come into effect: The drug should take effect within two hours. When will the new regulations come into effect?* But *effect* occasionally is used as a verb meaning "to bring about": *Her efforts effected a change.*

### Aggravate, Irritate

In formal English, the verb *aggravate* means "to make worse," "to make more troublesome or more serious": *Unusually heavy traffic aggravated the deterioration of the bridge pilings. The star's frequent lateness aggravated the tension among the cast members. Irritate* means "to annoy," "to exasperate," "to provoke": *Khrushchev's behavior at the U.N. irritated the Western delegates.*

Informally, some people use *aggravate* for *irritate: The dog's constant barking aggravated the neighbors.* This usage, however, is not acceptable to many readers and should be avoided in formal writing.

### Agree to, Agree with, Agree on or about

Used with *to, agree* means "to give consent": *The board agreed to hear the evidence on Friday.*

*Agree with* usually indicates accord: *He agreed with the philosophy of the transcendentalists. Agree with* can also refer to health or constitution: *Mexican food doesn't agree with many people. The desert air agrees with me.*

With *on* or *about, agree* indicates a coming to terms: *We agreed on a meeting in May. The judges could not agree about the criteria for evaluating the contestants.*

### All, All of

Before noun phrases, especially in written English, *all* is appropriate: *All the circuits were busy. In all the excitement, I forgot where I parked the car.* However, *all of* is also acceptable: *All of the circuits . . . In all of the excitement . . .*

Before pronouns or proper nouns, *all of* is required: *All of us were embarrassed. In all of Europe, the plague raged.*

In the subject position, *all* takes a singular verb when the meaning is "everything": *All is forgiven. All* takes a plural verb when referring to individuals in a group: *All were refunded their money.*

### All Ready, Already

*All ready* is pronounced with a distinct pause between the two words and means "everything or everyone in a state of readiness": *The floral arrangements were all ready for delivery. The swimmers were all ready to begin the competition.*

The single word *already* means "previously," "by this or that time," "before this or that time": *By the time dinner was served, some of the guests had already left. By January, local hotels are already booked for the summer.*

### All Right

*All right* should always be written as two words, not run together as *alright.*

### All That

Do not use *all that* in formal writing to imply comparison: *The movie was not all that bad.* Instead, write something like *The movie was better than we had expected.*

### All Together, Altogether

The two-word phrase *all together* means "all at one time," "all in one place," "collectively": *They were standing all together against the menace. The students were housed all together in one run-down barracks.*

The adverb *altogether* means "completely," "in all," or "on the whole": *These statistics are not altogether accurate. The meal cost fifty dollars altogether. Altogether, I wish I had never met the man.*

### Allusion, Delusion, Illusion

The noun *allusion* comes from the verb *allude,* which means "to make an indirect reference to something or someone." Thus, *allusion* means "an indirect reference" or "a hint": *Although she was never specific, she made a vague allusion to something sinister in his past.*

Deriving from the verb *delude,* which means "to mislead deliberately and harmfully," *delusion* means "a deception": *Her innocence was a delusion she cultivated cunningly.*

The noun *illusion* has no corresponding verb form. It means "a false perception of reality": *Alan Ladd's stature was an illusion; he usually stood on a box to kiss his leading lady.*

### Almost, Most

In very informal prose, some people use *most* as an adverb to mean "almost." In formal prose, *almost* is required: *We go to San Francisco almost* [not *most*] *every year. Almost* [not *most*] *all the cement has dried.*

### A Lot (of), Lots (of)

These expressions are informal substitutes for such words as *much, many, frequently: You're in a lot of trouble. We went to the movies a lot that summer. He uses lots of Tabasco in his chili. I miss you lots.*



Do not write *a lot* as one word *(alot).*

### Among, Between

Many guides dictate the use of *between* only with two items or persons and *among* with more than two: *Rivalry between the two teams was intense. Rivalry among the three teams was intense.*

Nevertheless, the *Oxford English Dictionary,* the most scholarly of word collections in English, states, "In all senses *between* has been, from its earliest appearance, extended to more than two. . . . It is still the only word available to express the relation of a thing to many surrounding things severally and individually; *among* expresses a relation to them collectively and vaguely: we should not say 'the space lying *among* three points,' or 'a treaty *among* three powers,' or 'the choice lies *among* the three candidates in the select list,' or 'to insert a needle among the closed petals of a flower.'"

*Between* is also used with more than two when it refers to intervals occurring regularly: *Between dances, the boys stood around sweating and the girls combed their hair. I cannot stop eating between meals.* Certainly *among dances* and *among meals* would make very little sense.

*Among* is more properly used to suggest a relationship of someone or something to a surrounding group: *She lived among the natives for almost ten years. There is honor among thieves.*

### Amount, Number

*Amount* should be used with nouns that name something that cannot be counted (or made plural), such as *noise, information, linen, mud: Judging from the amount of noise inside, we expected the movie to be outrageous.*

Number should be used with nouns that name things that can be counted (or made plural), such as *shrieks, statistics, handkerchiefs, rocks: Judging from the number of shrieks inside, we expected the movie to be outrageous.*

### And Etc.

*Etc.* is an abbreviation for the Latin phrase *et cetera,* which means "and other (things)." Therefore, the expression *and etc.* is redundant. See also **Et Al., Etc.**

### And/Or

Writers sometimes use *and/or* to indicate three options: *Merit is rewarded by promotion and/or salary increase* means that merit is rewarded (1) by promotion or (2) by salary increase or (3) by both. Some readers, however, object to the *and/or* device outside of legal, business, or technical writing. To be on the safe side, you can write out the options.



### Ante-, Anti-/Ant-

*Ante* is Latin for "before" or "in front of." It serves as a prefix in English in such forms as *antebellum* ("before the Civil War") and *antechamber* ("a small room in front of, or entry to, a larger room"). *Anti/ant* comes from Greek, meaning "against" or "opposite," and serves as prefix in such forms as *antibiotic* ("against bacteria") and antacid ("opposing acid"). A hyphen after *anti-* can clarify reading when the root word begins with a capital letter *(anti-Truman)* or an *i (anti-intellectualism).*

### Anxious, Eager

In conversation, *anxious* and *eager* are often used interchangeably: *I am eager to move into my new apartment. I am anxious to move into my new apartment.* Nevertheless, in formal situations, most usage experts recommend *anxious* to convey apprehension and *eager* to convey impatient desire: *The pilot was anxious about the high winds. The Senator was anxious to avoid scandal. An eager understudy waited in the wings. The fans were eager for victory.*

### Any More, Anymore

The two-word adjective *any more* means "some more" or "additional": *Are any more tests necessary to confirm the presence of radiation? The department has not hired any more clerks since 1984.*

The single-word adverb *anymore* means "presently" or "from now on": *The deer aren't seen in the marshes anymore. Will the shop carry imported cheeses anymore?*

### Any One, Anyone

The two-word phrase *any one* refers to any person, place, thing, idea, and so on. It is followed by *of* when it precedes a noun or pronoun: *Any one of the desks will serve our purposes. Any one of you is qualified to serve. Any one* may occur without *of* if its referent has been previously stated: *Four options are available. Choose any one.*

The single word *anyone* means "anybody"; it is never followed by *of* and does not precede nouns and pronouns: *Anyone with drive and a high-energy level can succeed.*

### Anyplace, Anywhere

*Anyplace* is usually restricted to informal situations; *anywhere* is acceptable in both formal and informal English.

### Any Way, Anyway, Anyways



The two-word phrase *any way* refers to any course or any direction: *They were trapped any way they turned. Anyway* means "nevertheless" or "regardless of circumstances": *The plot is weak, but the film succeeds anyway. Anyways* is a nonstandard variant of *anyway* and should be avoided.

### As, Like

In informal situations, speakers often substitute *like* for the subordinate conjunctions *as, as if, as though* to introduce dependent clauses: *Unfortunately, he dances like he sings. It looks like it's going to rain.* But most usage experts agree that in formal situations *like* should not introduce dependent clauses; the *as* conjunctions are more appropriate: *In a democracy, the government acts as the people dictate. The speaker clutched her throat as if she were gasping for air.*

### As to

*As to* occurs frequently in published prose, particularly in journalism: *The weather service kept residents posted as to the position of the hurricane. The mayor and city council members refused to make any comment as to whether the project would require higher taxes. We consulted an efficiency expert as to how to proceed.* In all cases, *about* may be substituted and probably sounds better.

### Averse, Adverse (See Adverse, Averse.)

### Awful, Awfully

*Awful* is an adjective meaning "fearsome," "awesome," or "great"; *awfully* is the adverb form of *awful: The dragon's awful roar shook the knight's confidence. The dragon roared awfully, shaking the knight's confidence.*

Informally, some speakers use *awful* and *awfully* as intensifiers equivalent to *very: The children were awful [awfully] tired.* Such use, however, should be avoided in formal writing or speaking.

### A While, Awhile

The two-word phrase *a while,* consisting of an article and a noun, functions as the object of a preposition: *After a while in the city, I began to long for the quiet nights of the country. They stopped for a while in a roadside park.* The single word *awhile,* an adverb, does not occur after a preposition: *The fire will smoke only awhile.*

### Bad, Badly

*Bad* is properly an adjective and thus should modify nouns and pronouns: *We always have bad weather this time of year. This headache is a particularly bad one. Badly* is properly an adverb of manner and should modify verbs and verbals: *She performed the piece badly. The editor soon tired of reading badly written poems.*

Confusion between the two words often occurs after a linking verb in a subject complement position, typically after the verb *feel,* in a sentence such as *I feel badly about not calling my parents.* In this sentence, the position after *feel* is a subject complement position and should be filled with an adjective modifying *I,* not an adverb modifying *feel.* Thus, the correct usage is *I feel bad about not writing my parents often enough.*

Sports announcers frequently use *bad* for *badly* in such expressions as *He's playing bad today* and *He just threw the ball bad.* Standard usage is *playing badly* and *threw the ball badly.*

### Beside, Besides

The preposition *beside* means "at the side of" *(she was seated beside the guest speaker)* or "compared with" *(my game looked shabby beside his expertise)* or "having nothing to do with" *(in this case, your opinion is beside the point).*

*Besides* can function as a preposition meaning "other than" *(Jamison had no ambition besides doing a good job)* or as a transitional expression meaning "moreover" *(the restaurant was too expensive; besides, the food was only mediocre).*

Be careful not to substitute *beside* for *besides: Besides* [not *beside*] *being lazy, the new secretary could not type.*

**Between, Among (See Among, Between.)**

**Between You and I, Between You and Me**
Because *between* is a preposition, it requires an objective case pronoun. Thus *between you and I* (or *he, she, they*) is incorrect. Use *between you and me* (or *him, her, them*).

**Bring, Take**
In standard English, both *bring* and *take* mean "to convey." However, *bring* suggests movement toward the speaker or focal point, whereas *take* suggests movement away from the speaker or focal point: *The teacher asked the students to bring a newspaper article to class. The governor took three antique chairs from the mansion when he left office.*

In some dialects, speakers use *bring* to mean "convey away from," as when one speaker says to another in the same location, *I'll bring you to work this morning.* This substitution, however, is not acceptable in formal English.

**Bunch**
Conversationally, *bunch* is frequently used to mean a group: *A bunch of guys went to the ball game.* In formal English *bunch* should refer only to things growing together in a cluster—like *a bunch of grapes.*



**Burst, Bust**
The standard verb *burst, burst, burst* usually means "to explode" or "to fly apart suddenly." In formal English, the verb *bust, busted, busted* is inappropriate for these meanings: *The tank burst* [not *busted*] *suddenly.*

**But However, But Yet**
In informal situations, speakers sometimes combine *but* with contrastive adverbs—possibly for emphasis: *He was practicing medicine, but yet he had never been to medical school.* Such combinations are not acceptable in formal English. Write, *By 1800, the French were satisfied with wounding an opponent, but* [not *but however*] *American dueling practice still demanded death.*

**But That, But What**
Informally, writers sometimes introduce dependent clauses with *but that* and *but what* (particularly after a negative and the word *doubt*): *No one doubted but that* [or *what*] *Miss Marple would perservere.* In formal English, the proper connector is *that: No one doubted that Miss Marple would perservere.*

### Can, May

*Can* indicates ability *(we can meet the deadline if we work the whole weekend)* or power *(a dean can overrule a department head)*. *May* indicates permission *(you may invite three guests)*. Generally, in formal writing, *can* should not replace *may*. In negative contractions, however, most usage experts accept *can't* for permission, since *mayn't* seems stilted and archaic: *You can't* [not *mayn't*] *be excused from the graduation exercises except in dire emergencies*. Also, many experts accept *cannot* for permission in negatives: *May I have this dance? No, you cannot.*

### Can't Help But

*Can't help but,* a rather common idiom, is appropriate only in informal situations: *I can't help but wish I had kept my old Volkswagen bug.* The idiom can be deleted with no change of meaning.

### Capital, Capitol

*Capital* usually means "head," "very serious," "principal": *capital city, capital error.* It also refers to crimes involving the death sentence: *capital offense, capital punishment.* And in finance, *capital* refers to money or property, particularly that used for investment: *capital for the venture, capital gain, capital goods. Capitol* refers to the building in which a legislature meets.

### Censor, Censure

The verb *censor* means "to examine material for immoral or harmful content" or "to ban material" for those reasons: *Some state school boards appoint committees to censor textbooks.* The verb *censure* means "to criticize, blame, or rebuke": *Admiral Stanley was censured for unnecessarily endangering the lives of his men.*

usage

### Center Around

Most usage experts prefer *revolve around* to *center around: The controversy revolves* [not *centers*] *around misappropriation of funds.* This notion rests on the argument that one thing cannot logically "center around" something else; thus *centers* is more properly followed by *on* or *in: The controversy centers on* [or *in*] *misappropriation of funds.* Nevertheless, language does not follow the logic of mathematics, and *center around* is widely used by many respectable writers.

### Climatic, Climactic

Confusion of *climatic* and *climactic* is not a matter of usage but rather a matter of meaning. The adjective *climatic* refers to climate, to weather: *Fluctuations in the earth's orbit probably affect climatic conditions.* The adjective *climactic* refers to climax, to a turning point or high point: *My childhood was so uneventful that the climactic moment occurred when I was chosen a bus-patrol boy.*

### Complected, Complexioned

*Complected* is a regional variation of *complexioned.* In formal situations, use *complexioned: She was so fair complexioned* [not *complected*] *that she used a number forty-four sunscreen.*

### Complement, Compliment

*Complement* derives from *complete;* thus the verb *complement* usually means "something that completes or perfects": *The oriental garden complemented the architecture of the house.* The verb *compliment* means "to praise or congratulate": *She complimented the photographer on his ability to capture mood.*

### Comprise, Compose

Strictly, the whole *comprises* the parts; the parts *compose* the whole: *The bureau comprises five departments. Five departments compose the bureau.* The passive expression *is comprised of* is often used to mean "is composed of": *The bureau is comprised of five departments.* Even though *Webster's Collegiate* points out that this usage has been in existence since the eighteenth century, some readers still find it objectionable. To be safe, you should probably avoid *is comprised of* altogether and use instead *is composed of* or *is made up of.*

usage

### Conscience, Conscious

The noun *conscience* means "moral sensibility," "recognition of right and wrong": *How could you in good conscience use my money to pay your debts?* The adjective *conscious* means "aware" or "deliberate": *She was suddenly conscious of a shadowy figure ahead. I am certainly not guilty of a conscious insult.*

### Consensus

*Consensus* comes from Latin *con ("together")* and *sentire ("to think"* or *"to feel").* Thus, *consensus of opinion* is considered by many to be redundant. In any case, the phrase has become a cliché and should be avoided. *Consensus* is sufficient.

### Continual, Continuous

Careful writers distinguish between the two adjectives *continual* and *continuous.* Strictly speaking, *continual* indicates recurring actions, repeated regularly and frequently; *continuous* indicates something unceasing, occurring without interruption: *Continual irrigation of crops is dangerously lowering the water table. The continuous motion of the sea lulled me to sleep.*

Theodore Bernstein offers a mnemonic device for remembering the difference: "Continuous ends in *o u s,* which stands for *o*ne *u*ninterrupted *s*equence."

### Convince, Persuade

Most people do not distinguish between *convince* and *persuade;* however, careful writers associate *convince* with belief, and *persuade* with action: *He convinced me of his sincerity. The recruiting officer persuaded her to enlist.* One difference between the two words is that *persuade,* but not *convince,* is best followed with an infinitive: *They persuaded me* [not *convinced me*] *to get back on the horse.*

### Could have, Could of

*Could of* is a misrepresentation of the way *could have* sounds in running speech. Write *I could have* [not *could of*] *left.*

### Credible, Creditable, Credulous

*Credible* means "believable," "plausible": *Her account of the day's events was too amusing to be credible. Creditable* usually means "deserving commendation": *Only one of the divers gave a creditable performance. Credulous* means "believing too readily," "gullible": *Lisa was too credulous to be a probation officer.* See also **Incredible, Incredulous.**

### Data

*Data* is the plural of the Latin noun *datum,* which means "fact." Rarely do writers use the singular *datum;* instead they use a more familiar word, such as *fact, result, statistic.* But *data* is very commonly used, traditionally with a plural verb: *The data show that most voters in this area vote for the candidate rather than the party. The data are in question; therefore, we cannot accept the conclusions of the study.*

Increasingly, however, in technical writing, *data* is considered a noncountable noun like *information* and is used with a singular verb: *Our data proves that the oyster beds beyond 2 miles should not be harvested. The data is inconclusive.* Outside of technical writing, the safe route is to use a plural verb with *data.*



### Device, Devise

Confusion between these two words is usually a matter of spelling. *Device,* the noun, is pronounced /dee viyce/ and means "something constructed for a specific purpose": *We need a device for holding the jack in place. Devise,* the verb, is pronounced /dee viyze/ and means "to construct something for a specific purpose": *She devised a scheme for undermining her partner's credibility.*

### Differ from, Differ with

The phrases are closely related, but *differ from* usually means "to be dissimilar," and *differ with* means "to disagree": *The two dialects differ from each other mainly in the pronunciation of vowels. Most experts differed with Jones's hypothesis.*

### Different from, Different than

Although some usage experts insist that *different* be followed by *from,* not by *than,* the rule is oversimplified. Because *from* is a preposition, *different from* should always have a noun or pronoun object—either stated or implied: *Moseley's batting stance is different from Griffin's [batting stance]. Different than* is preferable when a clause (usually an elliptical clause) follows: *James worked on a different assignment than we did.* To use *different from* in this example, you would have to insert an object for *from: James worked on a different assignment from the one we did.*

### Discreet, Discrete

*Discreet* means "cautious," "unobtrusive," "tactful": *The Secret Service made discreet inquiries into Mark's background. Discrete* means "separate," "distinct": *The language institute and the university were two discrete entities.* To help avoid confusion, you can remember that the noun forms of the two adjectives are different: *discreet, discretion; discrete, discreteness.*

usage

### Disinterested, Uninterested

Correct usage of *disinterested* and *uninterested* has long been disputed. Apparently, the word *disinterested* originally meant "not interested" but later took on the additional meanings of "free from self-interest" and "altruistic." *Uninterested* originally meant "impartial" but later came to mean "not interested." The best solution to the current problem of usage is to follow conservative guides. Use *disinterested* to mean "impartial," "uninfluenced by thoughts of personal gain" and *uninterested* to mean "not interested": *Some couples have a disinterested party to negotiate prenuptial financial agreements. Acting uninterested in class is likely to irritate the instructor.*

### Due to

*Due to* introduces adjective phrases and either immediately follows a noun or appears as a subject complement: *Many cases of depression due to chemical deficiencies go undetected. Many cases of depression are due to chemical deficiencies.* Because many people object to the substitution of *due to* for *because of* in adverbials, you are probably wise to avoid a construction such as *Due to advanced technology, contemporary ball players cannot realistically be compared to those of the past.* Write instead, *Because of advanced technology . . . .*

## Due to the Fact That

*Due to the fact that* is an unnecessarily wordy bureaucratic phrase; *because* is the better choice.

## Each and Every

*Each and every* is one of the favorite clichés of politicians and hucksters. Use simply *each* or *every* but not both.

## Eager, Anxious (See Anxious, Eager.)

## Effect (See Affect, Effect.)

## Emigrate, Immigrate

*Emigrate* means "to leave a country"; *immigrate* means "to enter." One *emigrates* from a place, but *immigrates* to it.

## Ensure, Insure

*Ensure* means "to guarantee" or "to make safe": *Organic gardening will ensure that produce is safe to eat. Safety goggles will ensure the worker against eye injury. Insure* means "to provide insurance against loss, damage, injury, etc.": *Our company will insure your home against loss due to flood, fire, and nuclear attacks.*

## Enthused

*Enthused* has not been fully accepted, although it is often substituted for *enthusiastic.* Avoid *enthused* in formal prose: *Everyone on the staff was enthusiastic* [not *enthused*] *about the new personal shopper service.*



## Et Al., Etc.

*Et al.* is the abbreviation for the Latin *et alii* or *et aliae,* meaning "and other people." This abbreviation is used in some documentation systems for citing books with more than two authors: *Yanella, D., et al.*

*Etc.* is the abbreviation for *et cetera,* meaning "and other things." *Etc.* is common in business memos and some technical documents but not in formal or literary writing. To punctuate *etc.,* put a comma before it when more than one item precedes but not when only one item precedes: *Use only the title and the last name—Ms. Jones, Mr. Jones, Dr. Jones, etc. Dress out completely with pads etc.* See also **And Etc.**

## Every Day, Everyday

The two-word phrase *every day* means "each day": *Mrs. Sommes went to the gym every day.* The single word *everyday* means "common" or "used on ordinary days." *He came to the dinner party in everyday work clothes.*

**Every One, Everyone**

The two-word phrase *every one* refers to every person, place, thing, idea, and so on. It is followed by *of* when it precedes a noun or pronoun: *Every one of the candidates has an image problem. Every one of these ancient civilizations had vanished by 500 B.C. Every one* can occur without *of* if its referent has been previously stated: *Four proposals were submitted, and every one called for a budget of over $500,000.*

The single word *everyone* means "everybody"; it is never followed by *of* and does not precede nouns and pronouns: *Everyone in the audience stood and cheered Ms. Gordon for over fifteen minutes.*

**Except, Accept (See Accept, Except.)**

**Except for the Fact That**

Shorten this long, bureaucratic phrase to *except that.*

**Explicit, Implicit**

*Explicit* means "not implied or suggested but stated outright": *The job description was so explicit that it even prescribed height and weight requirements. Implicit* means just the opposite, "implied or suggested, not stated outright": *Implicit in the advertisement was the notion that waxing floors is a joyful experience.*

**Farther, Further**

usage

*Farther* usually refers to distance; *further* usually means "in addition" or "additionally": *The mountains are farther away than they appear. Regular exercise promotes weight loss, and further, increases the energy level.* Also, as a verb, *further* means "to help to progress": *Derrick would use any means available to further his career in Hollywood.*

**Fewer, Less**

*Fewer* is used with nouns that can be counted and made plural: *fewer files, fewer paintings, fewer letters. Less* is used with nouns that cannot be counted or made plural: *less software, less art, less mail.*

**Further, Farther (See Farther, Further.)**

**Good, Well**

In formal English, *good* is always an adjective, appearing either before a noun or after a linking verb like *be, seem, look, feel, sound, smell, taste: The good food lifted our flagging spirits. The newly mowed grass smelled good. That hat looks good on you.*

*Well* functions as an adverb when it refers to the manner in which an action is performed: *She spoke German well. He hits the ball well but his concentration is not good. Well* functions as an adjective only when it refers to health. *Don't you feel well? Get well soon.*

### Had Better

*Had better* means "ought to." In running speech, the *had* sometimes disappears but should never be omitted in writing, except in dialogue. Write *The cabinet had better* [not *better*] *be more responsive to foreign affairs and less to partisan politics.*

### Had Ought To

*Had ought to* is nonstandard; instead, use *ought to: We ought to* [not *had ought to*] *send a housewarming gift.*

### Half

You may write *a half* or *half a,* but most usage guides do not approve *a half a: The distance of the cabin from the lake was only a half mile* [or *only half a mile;* not *only a half a mile*].

### Hanged, Hung

In every sense but one, the correct forms of the verb *hang* are *hang, hung, hung.* However, in the sense of execution, the verb is *hang, hanged, hanged: The picture was hung. The traitor was hanged.*

### Hardly

usage

Because *hardly* has a negative meaning ("insufficiency"), it should not be used with another negative—particularly, with *can't* or *couldn't.* Instead of *can't hardly* or *couldn't hardly,* write *can hardly* or *could hardly.* Also, when *hardly* means "barely," a completing clause begins with *when,* not *than: Hardly had the class started when* [not *than*] *the alarm sounded.*

### Healthy, Healthful

*Healthy* describes people, animals, plants, and economies in a state of good health. *Healthful* describes such things as climate and food that contribute to good health. Increasingly, writers use *healthy* for both senses, but a distinction between the terms often adds clarity.

### Hisself

Never use *hisself,* a nonstandard variation of *himself.*

### Historic, Historical

*Historic* narrowly means "making history"; *historical* means "relating to history." *Uncle Tom's Cabin* is a "historic" novel, which affected history. *Gone with the Wind* is a "historical" novel, which uses history as the setting.

### Hopefully

*Hopefully* is a generally accepted adverb meaning "full of hope": *We watched hopefully for a change in the weather.* Many people, however, object to its use as a sentence modifier meaning "it is hoped": *Hopefully, the weather will change.* Logically this second use of *hopefully* makes as much sense as *fortunately, happily, regrettably,* or *certainly,* and according to *Webster's Ninth New Collegiate Dictionary,* has been in well-established use since 1932. But as the *American Heritage Dictionary* wisely points out, "This usage is by now such a bugbear to traditionalists that it is best avoided on grounds of civility, if not logic."

### If, Whether

In some sentences, *if* and *whether* are equally acceptable and clear: *I do not know if* [or *whether*] *the plan is feasible.* But in some sentences *if* is ambiguous, expressing either an alternative or a condition: *Tell me if they are late.* An alternative is more clearly expressed with *whether: Tell me whether they are late.* A condition is more clearly expressed when the *if* clause is moved to the front of the sentence: *If they are late, tell me.*

### Illusion, Allusion, Delusion (See Allusion, Delusion, Illusion.)

### Immigrate, Emigrate (See Emigrate, Immigrate.)

### Implicit, Explicit (See Explicit, Implicit.)

usage

### Imply, Infer

*Imply* means "to suggest"; *infer* means "to arrive at a conclusion." Words and actions can imply meaning. From them, readers, listeners, and observers can infer meaning. *The toss of her head implied a defensive attitude. From the toss of her head, he inferred a defensive attitude.*

### In, Into

*Into* rather than *in* more clearly shows movement from outside to inside: *The fumes seeped into the room.*

### Incredible, Incredulous

*Incredible* describes something that is hard to believe: *The circus act was incredible. Incredulous* describes someone who is skeptical: *She was incredulous despite their assurances.*

### Infer, Imply (See Imply, Infer.)

### In Regards to

To mean "in reference to," write *in regard to, with regard to, regarding,* or *as regards*—never *in regards to.*

**Insure, Ensure (See Ensure, Insure.)**

**Into, In to**
*Into,* written as one word, is a preposition: *into the water, into the room, into the matter.* Sometimes *in* is a part of a phrasal verb and is followed by the word *to.* Then, *in* and *to* are not joined: *She went in to check the temperature. Turn your papers in to me.*

**Irregardless, Regardless**
Never write *irregardless* to mean *regardless: I am going regardless* [not *irregardless*] *of the weather.*

**Irritate, Aggravate (See Aggravate, Irritate.)**

**Is When, Is Where**
*When* refers to time, and *where* refers to place. The words are misleading in contexts that do not have these meanings. For example, do not write *A hologram is when people use a laser to create a three-dimensional photograph.* Instead write *A hologram is a three-dimensional photograph produced by a laser.* Also, do not write *A quarterback sneak is where the quarterback, with the ball, plunges into the line.* Instead write *A quarterback sneak is a play in which the quarterback, with the ball, plunges into the line.*



**It's, Its**
The apostrophe in *it's* shows that the word is a contraction meaning "it is" or "it has." *Its,* like the other possessive personal pronouns that end in *s (hers, his, yours, ours, theirs),* contains no apostrophe. The form *its'* does not exist.

**Kind of, Sort of**
The expressions *kind of* and *sort of* to mean "somewhat" or "rather" are informal. Avoid them in formal writing: *The work was somewhat* [not *kind of*] *tedious.*

**Kind of (a), Type of (a), Sort of (a)**
The *a* should not appear in expressions such as *this kind of a book, this sort of a plan, this type of a day.*

**Later, Latter**
*Later* (pronounced /layt r/) refers to time; *latter* (pronounced /lat r/) means "the second of two."

**Lay, Lie**
The forms of these two verbs are

| | *To Lay (To Put or Place)* | *To Lie (To Rest or Recline)* |
|---|---|---|
| ***Present*** | lay | lie |
| ***Past*** | laid | lay |
| ***Participles*** | laid, lying | lain, lying |

When *lay* (present tense of *lay*) means "put" or "place," it has an object: *Lay the cards on the table.* When *lay* (past tense of *lie*) means "reclined," it has no object and either has or could have the word *down* after it: *The dog lay [down] in the mud.* Write *The valuable diamond lies* [not *lays*] *in a case unprotected. He lay* [not *laid*] *in bed all day. I was lying* [not *laying*] *on the beach.* When there is no object and when the meaning is "recline," the proper verb is *lie (lay, lain, lying).*

**Lend, Loan**
Some people prefer the verb *lend (lent, lent)* and scorn the verb *loan (loaned, loaned)* even though *loan* has a long history, especially in America. The verb *loan* is common in financial contexts: *The bank loaned the money.*

usage

**Less, Fewer (See Fewer, Less.)**

**Lie, Lay (See Lay, Lie.)**

**Like, As (See As, Like.)**

**Lose, Loose**
*Lose* is pronounced /looz/ and means "misplace" or "get rid of." *Loose* is pronounced /loos/ and means "not tight." *If you lose your receipts, you can't be reimbursed. To hide his weight gain, he wore only loose-fitting clothes.*

**May, Can (See Can, May.)**

**May Be, Maybe**
The verb *may be* is two words. The adverb *maybe* (meaning "perhaps") is one word. *We may be late. Maybe we are late.*

**Might Have, Might of**
*Might of* is a misinterpretation of the way *might have* sounds in running speech. *I might have* [not *might of*] *picked the winning numbers.*

**Moral, Morale**
*Moral* (meaning "ethical" or "ethical lesson") is pronounced with the stress on the first syllable /mor' al/: *The moral of the fable is "haste makes waste." Morale* (meaning "spirit") is pronounced with the stress on the second syllable /mo ral'/: *The defeat destroyed the team's morale.*

**Most, Almost (See Almost, Most.)**

**Must Have, Must of**
*Must of* is a misinterpretation of the way *must have* sounds in running speech. *They must have* [not *must of*] *left the play during the third act.*

**Myself, Me or I**
Confusion about whether to use *me* or *I* in compound constructions probably leads to the incorrect use of *myself: The staff and myself thank you. Myself* must refer to a previous *I* or *me* in the same sentence: *I saw the incident myself. I wrote myself a note. They told me to answer the letter myself.*

**Noplace, Nowhere**
Use *nowhere,* not *noplace,* in formal prose.

**Number, Amount (See Amount, Number.)**

**Of**
In formal writing

- Do not use *of* after words such as *large* and *good: That is too large* [not *too large of*] *a meal.*
- Do not use *of* after *off: The cat jumped off* [not *off of*] *the ledge.*
- Do not omit *of* after *type: What type of* [not *type*] *car did you buy?*

usage

**O.K.**
*O.K.,* also spelled *OK* and *okay,* is informal. In formal writing use instead an expression such as *acceptable, satisfactory,* or *correct.*

**Oral, Verbal**
The distinction between *oral* and *verbal* can be useful, even though the two meanings are very close. Whereas *verbal* refers to either spoken or written words, *oral* refers specifically to spoken words.

**Orient, Orientate**
As verbs, both *orient* and *orientate* can mean "to get properly adjusted or aligned." In American English, *orient* is more common: *Orient yourself to the map before you start through the unfamiliar area.*

### People, Persons

*Persons* implies a small and specific group: *The elevator will hold only six persons. People* is more versatile and can refer to any group.

### Percent, Per Cent, Percentage

When you do not specify an amount, *percentage* is preferred in formal writing: *A large percentage* [not *percent*] *of the text was destroyed.* When you do specify an amount, use *percent* or *per cent: Employees get a 20 percent discount.*

### Persuade, Convince (See Convince, Persuade.)

### Playwrite, Playwright

Even though a playwright writes plays, he or she is not called a "playwrite." The correct term is *playwright. Wright* (as in *wheelwright* and *shipwright*) means "one who makes or constructs something" and has no relation to *write.*

### Plenty

In writing, avoid *plenty* as an intensifier. Instead, use words such as *very* and *quite: Legal action was quite* [not *plenty*] *appropriate.*

### Plus

In formal writing, do not use *plus* to mean *and: They couldn't find summer jobs, and* [not *plus*] *they owed the school for tuition.*

usage

### Practicable, Practical

*Practicable* means that something is possible; *practical* means that something is sensible: *A new bridge is practicable but not practical because of the cost.*

### Precede, Proceed

The root *cede/ceed* means "go." The prefix *pre-* means "before," and the prefix *pro-* means "forward"; therefore, *precede* means "go before," and *proceed* means "go forward."

### Principal, Principle

Because *principal* and *principle* sound alike, they are frequently confused. *Principle* is an abstract noun meaning a "truth," "law," "rule," "code": *He advocates the principle of separation of church and state. Principal* can be both a noun and an adjective. As a noun it generally means "chief official," "main participant"; and as an adjective it means "most important," "chief": *The principal of the school insisted on a dress code. The principal role in the drama is that of the son.*

**Proceed, Precede (See Precede, Proceed.)**

**Prosecute, Persecute**
*Prosecute* usually means "to start legal action." *Persecute* means "to treat oppressively." *The Allies prosecuted those who had persecuted the Jews.*

**Quote, Quotation**
The use of the verb *quote* for the noun *quotation* is informal. *The speaker began with a quotation* [not *quote*] *from Emerson.*

**Raise, Rise**
*Raise (raised, raised)* usually means "to lift" and always has an object: *They raised the Confederate ship from the muddy bottom of the Mississippi. Rise (rose, risen)* usually means "to go up" and has no object: *The sun rose before we could get good photographs of the eclipse.*

**Real, Really**
The use of *real* as an adverb to mean "very" is informal. Instead of *real angry,* write *really angry* or *very angry.*

**Rear, Raise**
One of the meanings of *rear* is "to nurture a child," although many people now use *raise* in this same sense. According to Theodore Bernstein, this meaning of *raise* is established. He comments: "At one time . . . the battle cry was, "You raise pigs, but you rear children." However, in this country at least . . . we raise both pigs and children, and some parents will testify that you can't always tell the difference."



**Reason Is Because, Reason Is That**
Instead of *reason is because,* write *reason is that: The reason for the lack of job openings is that* [not *because*] *people are retiring at the age of seventy, not sixty-five.*

**Regardless, Irregardless (See Irregardless, Regardless.)**

**Respectfully, Respectively**
*Respectfully* means "showing respect": *She respectfully responded to the request. Respectively* means "in a specific order": *The record and the tape cost $8.99 and $9.99, respectively.*

**Right**
*Right* as a modifier is vague; it can mean "somewhat" or "to a large degree": *right confusing, right ridiculous, right dumb.* Consequently, it should be avoided in writing.

### Same

*Same* is a substitute for *it* or *them* in legal documents but in no other writings: *After you have written the letter, submit it* [not *same*] *for approval.*

### Scarcely

In a negative construction, *scarcely* is nonstandard. Do not write *Without scarcely a notice, they moved.* Instead write *With scarcely a notice, they moved.* Do not write *I couldn't scarcely breathe.* Instead write *I could scarcely breathe.*

### Scarcely When, Scarcely Than

*Scarcely when* is preferred over *scarcely than: Scarcely had the announcement been written, when* [not *than*] *the reporters arrived.*

### Seldom, Seldom Ever

*Ever* is unnecessary in the phrase *seldom ever.* Do not write *We seldom ever attend movies.* Instead, write *We seldom attend movies. Ever* is acceptable in the phrase *seldom if ever: We seldom if ever attend movies.*

### Set, Sit

The verb *sit, sat, sat* does not have an object: *Sit in row H.* The verb *set, set, set,* meaning "to position or place," must have an object: *Set your glass on the coaster.* A few special meanings of *set,* however, require no object: *The sun sets. The hen sets on her nest.*



### Shall, Will

In the past, grammars dictated that *shall* be used with the subjects *I* and *we, will* with other subjects. These grammars also prescribed that for emphasis, promise, determination, or command, the pattern be reversed: *will* with *I* and *we, shall* with other subjects.

Attention to actual usage shows that even in formal prose, people have never used *shall* and *will* consistently in this fashion. Instead, *will* appears commonly with *I* and *we* and also with other subjects in emphatic statements: *I will visit China. They repeated that they will strike if their demands are not met. Shall* seldom appears except in a question with *I* or *we* as the subject: *Shall we reject the offer? Where shall I look?* Frequently, the question is an invitation: *Shall we have lunch? Shall we dance?* In other contexts, *shall* seems extremely formal—almost stuffy.

### Should, Would

Following the pattern of *shall* and *will,* many early grammars prescribed the use of *should* with the subjects *I* and *we, would* with all other subjects (see **Shall, Will**). The prescription, however, is seldom followed. *Should* is used with all subjects to indicate obligation or expectation: *The public should support the bill. He should be here shortly.* With all subjects *would* can indicate promise: *I swore that I would work out two hours every day.* Furthermore, with all subjects *would* can express a hypothetical situation: *If the schedule were more realistic, more people would fly the shuttle.* Finally, either *should* or *would* is acceptable in certain idioms expressing desire or preference: *I would [should] like to direct your attention to paragraph 3. We would [should] prefer to delay discussion until the next meeting. Would* is more common than *should* in American English.

### Should Have, Should of

*Should of* is a misinterpretation of the way *should have* sounds in running speech: *I should have written* [not *should of written*].

### Sit, Set (See Set, Sit.)

### Situation

Do not unnecessarily add the word *situation* to a sentence: *If you are in an accident* [not *accident situation*], *you may need legal advice. The questions were too vague to be used on tests* [not *in a testing situation*].

### Slow, Slowly

Both *slow* and *slowly* have long been used as adverbs but in special ways. *Slow* occurs only after the verb and usually in short commands: *Drive slow. Slow* also occurs frequently with the verb *run: The clock runs slow. The trains were running slow.* If the rhythm and sense are satisfied, *slowly* can occur either before or after the verb: *The cat slowly stalked the robin across the yard* or *The cat stalked the robin slowly across the yard.*

When the adverb follows a verb describing a process, either *slow* or *slowly* is acceptable, particularly with a compound adverb: *The boat drifted slow [slowly] and steady [steadily] toward the reef.*

Only *slowly* can occur as a sentence adverb. In such cases, it usually appears at the beginning of the structure: *Slowly, Earp rose to his feet, laid four aces on the table, and drew his gun.*

### So, So That

*So that* makes the sentence structure clearer and the tone more formal than *so: Keep a record of your blood pressure so that* [not *so*] *your doctor can make an accurate interpretation.*

### So, Very

In writing, do not use *so* to mean "very": *The film was very* [not *so*] *maudlin.*

### Some
In formal writing, do not use *some* to mean "somewhat": *The way we speak may differ somewhat* [not *some*] *in the locker room and at a cocktail party.*

### Someplace, Somewhere
*Someplace* is more informal than *somewhere.* In formal prose, write *Supposedly, there is a symbol somewhere* [not *someplace*] *in the poem.*

### Sometime, Sometimes
*Sometime* means "at some unspecified time": *I plan to read the complete works of Shakespeare sometime. Sometimes* means "now and then": *Stray radio signals sometimes open garage doors.*

### Sort of
*Sort of* is more informal than *somewhat* or *to some extent.* In formal prose, write *They are somewhat* [not *sort of*] *confused by the instructions.*

### Stationary, Stationery
*Stationary* means "fixed"; *stationery* means "writing paper." Remember that stationERy is made of papER.

### Such a
usage

In formal writing, do not use *such a* to mean "very": *It was a very* [not *such a*] *witty play. Such a* should be used only when it is followed with a *that* clause stating a result: *It was such a witty play that I would like to see it again.*

### Suppose to, Supposed to
Do not write *suppose to* for *supposed to.* Although the *d* sound often is not pronounced in running speech, it should always be written: *We were supposed to* [not *suppose to*] *attend the conference.*

### Sure
*Sure* as an adverb is more informal than *surely* or *certainly* and should be written only in friendly correspondence and dialogue. In formal prose, write *The book surely* [not *sure*] *is radical.*

### Sure to, Sure and
Use *sure to,* not *sure and,* in a construction like *Be sure to* [not *sure and*] *go.*

### Take, Bring (See Bring, Take.)

### Than, Then

*Than,* a conjunction, completes a comparison; *then* indicates time: *We then learned that the matter was more serious than we had thought.*

### That, Which

Although the distinction is not always observed, to be unquestionably correct, you should use *that* to introduce restrictive clauses (no commas) and *which* to introduce nonrestrictive clauses (commas): Flashman *is a book that makes a shameless cad entertaining.* Flashman, *which makes a shameless cad entertaining, is worth reading.*

### Their, There, They're

*Their,* which shows possession, appears only before a noun: *their work, their music, their beliefs. There* indicates location *(go there)* or introduces an inverted sentence *(there are three possible answers). They're* means *they are (they're late).*

### Theirselves, Themselves

Never write *theirselves* instead of *themselves: They declared themselves* [not *theirselves*] *bankrupt.*

### Them, Those

A phrase such as *them people* or *them pencils* is considered illiterate. Instead, always write *those people* or *those pencils.*

### Then, Than (See Than, Then.)



### This Here, That There

*This here* and *that there* are not Standard English. Omit the *here* and *there: This* [not *this here*] *attempt was unsuccessful. He did not hear that* [not *that there*] *warning.*

### This Kind of, These Kinds of

Use the singular *this* with *kind of* and the plural *these* with *kinds of: this kind of food, these kinds of food.*

### Thusly

An *-ly* added to *thus* is unnecessary; *thus* is already an adverb. *We will thus* [not *thusly*] *cancel plans.*

### Till, Until

*Till* and *until* are both correct and interchangeable. The spelling *'til* is incorrect.

### To, Too
*To* can be a preposition *(to them, to school)* or an infinitive marker *(to go, to win). Too* is an adverb meaning "excessively" *(too tired, too much)* or "also" *(we too left).*

### Toward, Towards
*Toward* and *towards* have the same meaning; however, the sound of *toward* is usually preferable: *The camera faced toward* [or *towards*] *the crowd.*

### Try to, Try and
Write *try to,* not *try and: You should try to* [not *try and*] *understand.*

### -type
The suffix *-type* can be used to create adjectives: *A-type personality, European-type clothes, a* Playboy*-type publication.* If you use an adjective with a *-type* suffix, be sure that the suffix creates the right meaning. *A Bogart hero* refers to one of the characters Humphrey Bogart made famous. *A Bogart-type hero* only resembles those characters. In some constructions the addition of *-type* is unnecessary: *compact car* (not *compact-type car*), *spy novel* (not *spy-type novel*), *suspension bridge* (not *suspension-type bridge*).

### Type, Type of
Do not omit the *of* after the noun *type: It is the type of* [not *type*] *computer they recommend.*

usage

### Uninterested, Disinterested (See Disinterested, Uninterested.)

### Unique
Some people object to phrases like *more unique, somewhat unique, almost unique,* or *very unique.* They argue that *unique* is absolute and thus cannot be compared, modified, or intensified. According to *Webster's Collegiate Dictionary, unique* is absolute when meaning "without like or equal"; but when meaning "distinctively characteristic" or "unusual," *unique* can properly appear in phrases such as *a very unique region* and *a somewhat unique school.*

### Until, Till (See Till, Until.)

### Up
Omit *up* in verb phrases where it adds no meaning, as in *join up, check up, end up, fold up, call up, divide up, lift up.*

**Use, Utilize**
The verb *use* means "to put to use." *Utilize* means "to find a special purpose for something." Although these verbs are sometimes thought of as synonyms, *utilize* actually has a narrower meaning than *use: They used the detergent for washing clothes. They utilized the detergent as an insecticide.*

**Use to, Used to**
Do not leave the *d* out of *used to: The family used to* [not *use to*] *believe in flying saucers.*

**Verbal, Oral (See Oral, Verbal.)**

**Wait for, Wait on**
Some people say *wait on* to mean "await." But the expression is not Standard English; write instead *wait for: He waited for me* [not *on me*] *under the clock at Holmes'.*

**Way, Ways**
Write *They have a long way* [not *ways*] *to drive.*

**Well, Good (See Good, Well.)**

**Whether, If (See If, Whether.)**

**Which, That (See That, Which.)**



**Which, Who**
Do not use *which* to introduce a relative clause modifying a person or people: *They reprimanded the doctor who* [not *which*] *prescribed the drug.* Do not use *who* with animals and things: *The plate pictured an eagle, which* [not *who*] *clutched an olive branch.*

**Who's, Whose**
Do not confuse *who's* and *whose. Who's,* which is somewhat informal, means *who is: Who's going? Whose* is the possessive form of *who: Whose responsibility is the statistical analysis?*

**Will, Shall (See Shall, Will.)**

**Would, Should (See Should, Would.)**

**Would Have**
In *if* clauses, use *had,* not *would have: If they had* [not *would have*] *checked the engine, the accident would not have occurred.*

### Would Have, Would of

*Would of* is a misinterpretation of the way *would have* sounds in running speech: *Except for the Vietnam War, in 1968 Lyndon Johnson would have* [not *would of*] *run for President.*

### Your, You're

*Your* is the possessive form of *you: your idea, your order, your assignment. You're,* which is somewhat informal, is a contraction of *you are: You're indecisive. You're trapped.*

# Glossary of Terms

This glossary provides a quick reference to terms—some useful and some essential for writers to know. Many definitions provide all the necessary information. Other definitions may require supplementary information from the text.

**Absolute Phrase**
An absolute phrase—usually a participial or infinitive phrase—modifies the whole sentence to which it is connected: *Speaking of problems, have you seen our new assignment? To be blunt, Jones has no sense of rhythm.* An absolute phrase that begins with a subject is sometimes called a nominative absolute: *The reservation confirmed, we called a cab. The climbers struggled up the mountain, their lungs aching.* (Section 5d)

terms

**Abstract Noun**
An abstract noun names something with no physical existence: *beauty, fury, dishonesty.*

**Acronym**
An acronym is a word formed from the initial letters or syllables of the words in a phrase: *awol* (absent without leave), *COBOL* (common business-oriented language), *CINCPAC* (Commander in Chief, Pacific), *Fiat* (Fabrica Italiana Automobili, Torino).

**Active Voice**
A verb is in the active voice when its subject acts or controls the action: *Harry bet on the winner. The jury convicted him.* See also **Passive Voice.** (Section 4e)

### Ad Hominem Attack
An argument that involves an attack on an individual's character rather than on ideas and positions is called an ad hominem attack.

### Adjective
An adjective is a word that describes, limits, or qualifies a noun or a noun equivalent: *a tart apple, a foolish remark, a successful opening.* (Section 3a)

### Adjective Clause
An adjective clause modifies a noun or pronoun. These clauses are introduced by relative pronouns (*who/whom/whose, which, that*) or relative adverbs (*when, where, why*): *The game, which will be televised, is a sellout. I returned to Pocatello, where I had spent my first ten years.* (Section 7c.2)

### Adverb
An adverb modifies an adjective (*fairly complex*), adverb (*very carefully*), verb (*moved backward*), or whole sentence (*certainly, we want to go*). (Section 3b)

### Adverb Clause
An adverb clause modifies a verb, adjective, adverb, or whole sentence. Adverb clauses are introduced by subordinate conjunctions (*when, until, because, since, if, unless, although,* etc.): *After they left Vermont, they moved to Quebec. He thought he was a woodsman, because he bought clothes at L.L. Bean.* (Section 7c.1)

### Adverbial Conjunction (See Conjunctive Adverb.)

terms

### Agreement
The term *agreement* refers to the correspondence of both verbs with subjects and pronouns with antecedents. A verb must agree in number with its subject, and a pronoun must agree in number with its antecedent (singular verb with singular subject, singular pronoun with singular antecedent; plural verb with plural subject, plural pronoun with plural antecedent): *The raccoon washes its food.* [*Raccoon, washes,* and *its* are all singular.] *Raccoons wash their food.* [*Raccoons, wash,* and *their* are all plural.] (Chapters 10 and 13)

### Alliteration
Alliteration is the repetition of the initial sounds of words to create a musical effect: "sunless sea," "the weary, way-worn wanderer," "the hunter home from the hill," "dusty death."

### Analogy
An analogy compares two dissimilar things to show that what is true of one is also true of the other. For example, language is analogous to a river; both have branches, and both constantly change. A false analogy distorts the points of similarity and arrives at an invalid conclusion.

### Analysis
In an analysis, a subject is broken into parts or segments in order to clarify the whole. (Section 35e)

### Antagonist
In a literary work the antagonist is the force that opposes the main character; the antagonist can be another character or characters, society, nature, or even some trait within the main character. (See also **Protagonist.**)

### Antecedent
An antecedent is the noun or noun phrase that a pronoun refers to: *In the 1960s Bob Dylan was at the height of his success.* [*Bob Dylan* is the antecedent of *his.*] *Mosquitoes filled the air; they ruined the entire picnic.* [*Mosquitoes* is the antecedent of *they.*]

### Antithesis
In rhetoric, an antithesis is an opposing idea—an idea contrary to the thesis. A writer may state the antithesis to an argument in order to attack it.

### Appositive
An appositive renames, restates, or explains the word or words it refers to: *She bought an expensive car, a BMW luxury model.* (Section 33a.6)

### Argument
Argument is one of the purposes of writing. In an argument, a writer tries to move readers to act or to agree. (Chapter 39)

### Article
An article is a word (*a, an, the*) that signals the presence of a noun.

### Audience
In rhetoric, the audience is the anticipated reader or readers of a composition. (Section 35b)

### Auxiliary Verb
An auxiliary verb combines with a main verb to form a verb phrase: *is burning, did stand, has been grown, could have watched.* (Section 4b)

### Balanced Sentence

A balanced sentence has a noticeable symmetry of structure and often vocabulary. This kind of sentence heightens comparison or contrast: *What is true about losing weight is not magic, and what is magic about losing weight is not true.* (Section 33b.4)

### Begging the Question

Begging the question is a logical fallacy in which a writer argues in a circle. The writer "begs" the audience to accept as true the very point at issue. (Pages 465–466)

### Bibliography

A bibliography is a list of sources on a particular subject. A bibliography most often appears at the end of a research paper as a record of the sources referred to in the text. Annotated bibliographies list and also describe writings relating to a subject.

### Blank Verse

Blank verse is poetry written in unrhymed iambic pentameter (a line pattern of five units, each composed of an unstressed and a stressed syllable). Milton's *Paradise Lost* is one example of blank verse.

### Brainstorming

In rhetoric, brainstorming involves jotting down anything that comes to mind in order to stimulate ideas. Brainstorming should be unstructured and spontaneous so that blocked ideas can come into consciousness. (Section 34c)



### Case

*Case* refers to the special forms of nouns and pronouns that indicate their function. Some pronouns have three cases.

Subjective (or nominative) case—used for subjects and subject complements: *I, we, he, she, they, who*

Objective case—used for objects: *me, us, him, her, them, whom*

Possessive (or genitive) case—used to show ownership, authorship, source, and description: *my/mine, our/ours, his, her/hers, their/theirs, whose*

Nouns and all other pronouns have two cases.

Common case—used for all functions except possession: *Linda, everyone, friends, actors*

Possessive (or genitive) case—used for the same functions as the possessive pronouns and formed by adding *'s* to singular forms and *'* to most plural forms: *Linda's, everyone's, friends', actors'*. (Chapter 14)

### Cause/Effect

Writers can structure a composition or a paragraph by explaining to readers the cause of a particular effect or the effect of a particular cause. (Pages 360 and 378)

### Characterization

*Characterization* refers to the way an author depicts characters. Characters may be "flat," not developed in any depth; or they may be "round," developed with lifelike complexity. Also, characters may be "static" (unchanged by experiences) or "developing" (changed by experiences).

### Chronological Order

The actions narrated in a composition are in chronological order when arranged according to the same time sequence in which they occurred, do occur, or should occur. (Page 382)

### Classical Topics

The classical topics, formulated by Greek rhetoricians and orators, reflect typical ways of thinking (definition, comparison, relationship, circumstance, and testimony). Writers can use these "topics" to find and develop a subject for a composition. (Section 34h)

### Classification

When a composition is structured according to classification, a general category is divided into smaller groups on the basis of some selected principle. (Pages 360 and 378)

### Clause

A clause is a grammatical construction with both a subject and predicate. Independent (main) clauses may stand by themselves as sentences: *My car had a flat.* Dependent (subordinate) clauses must be attached to independent clauses: *I was late <u>because my car had a flat.</u>* (Chapter 7)

### Cleft Sentence

A cleft sentence is a construction that emphasizes an element that follows a form of *be.* The construction occurs when an ordinary sentence with a subject-verb-object pattern is changed to one with this pattern: *it* plus a form of *be* plus the element to be emphasized plus a *who, which,* or *that* clause. The term *cleft* refers to the fact that the ordinary sentence is cleft, or cut, into parts. The ordinary sentence *The pitcher hit the home run* can be changed to these cleft sentences: *It was the pitcher who hit the home run. It was a home run that the pitcher hit.*

### Cliché
A cliché is an expression made stale and boring by overuse: *quick as a wink, last but not least, hour of need.* (Section 32c.1)

### Climactic Order
The parts of a composition may be arranged in climactic order, from the less important to the more important or from the small to the large.

### Climactic Sentence
The ideas in a climactic sentence move up a scale from less important to more important, from less intense to more intense, or from ordinary to extraordinary: *Once, in the early days before the buffalo herds had dwindled, Grinnel saw a Cheyenne Indian noiselessly ride his horse close to the side of a huge bull, and springing gracefully on his back, ride the beast for some distance, and then, with his knife, give it its death stroke.* (Section 33b.3)

### Coherence
*Coherence* literally means "the quality of sticking together." A composition whose parts fit together logically is said to have coherence. Coherence can be achieved by logical sequences, transitional devices, pronouns, connecting words, and repetitions. (Section 37c)

### Collective Noun
A collective noun refers to a group that forms a unit: *family, team, army, audience.* (Sections 10h and 13e)



### Comedy
Comedy is usually lighthearted entertainment. In drama, comedies end happily or at least with justice done.

### Comma Splice
A comma splice, a punctuation error, occurs when two independent clauses are connected, or spliced together, with only a comma: *Alcohol enhances confidence, at the same time, it impairs judgment.* Two independent clauses must be joined with a comma and a coordinating conjunction or with a semicolon: *Alcohol enhances confidence, but at the same time, it impairs judgment. Alcohol enhances confidence; at the same time, it impairs judgment.* (Chapter 9)

### Comparative Conjunction
A comparative conjunction is a subordinate conjunction with two parts: *as . . . as, so . . . that, such . . . that,* a comparative modifier . . . *than,* a superlative modifier . . . *that.* These conjunctions express comparisons: *He*

*laughed so loud that we got embarrassed. The train was more comfortable than we had expected. She was the hardest teacher that I ever had.* (Section 6b.4)

### Comparative Degree

The form of an adjective and adverb used to compare two items is called the "comparative degree." An *-er* ending and the words *more* or *less* usually indicate the comparative degree: *May was wetter than June. Cod is more plentiful than flounder. This paper is less expensive.* See also **Superlative Degree.** (Section 3c)

### Comparison/Contrast

In rhetoric, a comparison/contrast structure examines the similarities and differences between people, ideas, and things. (Pages 356–357 and 388–389)

### Complement

In a clause, a complement "completes" the meaning of the predicate. A complement may be

- The object of a transitive verb: *They ate pizza.*
- The indirect object of a transitive verb: *He told me a lie.*
- The object complement of a transitive verb: *They called the storm Frederic.*
- The subject complement following *be* or a linking verb: *The book is a challenge. The water felt hot.*

### Complex Sentence

A complex sentence contains one independent clause (ind.) and at least one dependent clause (dep.): *The bus filled* [ind.] *until even the aisle was jammed with people* [dep.]. *When the bell rang* [dep.], *the students raced from the room* [ind.]. (Section 7e.3)

### Compound-Complex Sentence

A compound-complex sentence contains two or more independent clauses (ind.) and at least one dependent clause (dep.): *In New England earthworms are called nightwalkers* [ind.]; *in the Midwest, where they are best known as bait* [dep.], *they are called fishing worms* [ind.]. (Section 7e.4)

### Compound Sentence

A compound sentence contains two or more independent clauses (ind.): *English has a phonetic alphabet* [ind.]; *Chinese has a pictographic system* [ind.]. (Section 7e.2)

## Computer Terms

Understanding computer terms can simplify computer-aided writing (CAW).

Backup command—a command to a computer to create a second copy of a file or a disk, usually on a floppy disk. For security, backups should be created for important material

Block command—a command to a computer to mark off a specific section of the material on the screen so that the section can be moved to another place or deleted

Bug—an error, defect, or problem in software or hardware

Copy command—a command to copy files from one disk to another

Database—a collection of information stored in a computer's memory. A *database* can be entered, sorted, searched, displayed, changed, and printed.

Filename—information is stored in a computer under a *filename.* This name, usually eight characters, goes into a directory and can be called up so that its content can be edited or printed.

Floppy disk—a magnetized plastic disk, inserted into a computer's disk drive, that stores the information typed on the keyboard

Fonts—various type styles and sizes available on some printers

Format command—a command to structure new floppy disks so that they can store data. The formatting process divides concentric tracts on the disk into sectors for data storage and retrieval.

Hard disk—a device, permanently installed in most computers, that can store more information than a removable floppy disk

Headers—short titles printed automatically at the top of each page

Justified margin—a straight right margin of a typed document made by automatically adjusting the letters and spaces across a line. This margin can be turned on or off.



Menu—a list that appears on the screen so that a user can choose a program or a command

Merge command—a command to copy material from one file into another or to print combined files

RAM—an acronym for "random access memory," referring to the storage space in a computer. The storage is temporary unless the information is saved on a hard or floppy disk.

Save command—a command to make a permanent copy of material on a floppy or hard disk. If not saved, material will be lost when the computer is turned off.

Scroll command—a command to move the text of a file up or down on a computer screen

Search and Replace command—a command to a computer to find a particular word, expression, or character on a page or in an entire document and to substitute another expression throughout—for example, to substitute *cannot* for *can't* throughout

Sort command—a command to shift data into an alphabetical or numerical arrangement

Windows—computer screen devices that display two or more documents or two or more parts of the same document at once. Users can then easily compare and edit the information.

Word wrap—the way a computer program automatically carries a word to the next line when the word will not fit inside the right margin

### Concrete Noun

A concrete noun names a material object that can be seen, touched, heard, tasted, or smelled: *rock, hamburger, wallet.*

### Conflict

In literature, a conflict involves a clash of forces. The usual plot pits the main character against an opposing force—another character or characters, society, nature, or some personal trait.

### Conjugation

A conjugation is a list of all the forms of a particular verb—its tenses (present, past, future, present perfect, past perfect, and future perfect), its voices (active and passive), its moods (indicative, imperative, and subjunctive), its persons (first, second, and third), and its numbers (singular and plural).

#### Conjugation of *Choose, Chose, Chosen*

INDICATIVE MOOD



PRESENT TENSE

ACTIVE VOICE: I/You/We/They choose.
He/She/It chooses.

PASSIVE VOICE: I am chosen.
He/She/It is chosen.
You/We/They are chosen.

PAST TENSE

ACTIVE VOICE: I/You/He/She/It/We/They chose.

PASSIVE VOICE: I/He/She/It was chosen.
You/We/They were chosen.

FUTURE TENSE

ACTIVE VOICE: I/You/He/She/It/We/They will choose.

PASSIVE VOICE: I/You/He/She/It/We/They will be chosen.

PRESENT PERFECT TENSE

ACTIVE VOICE: I/You/We/They have chosen.
He/She/It has chosen.

PASSIVE VOICE: I/You/We/They have been chosen.
He/She/It has been chosen.

PAST PERFECT TENSE

ACTIVE VOICE: I/You/He/She/It/We/They had chosen.

PASSIVE VOICE: I/You/He/She/It/We/They had been chosen.

FUTURE PERFECT TENSE

ACTIVE VOICE: I/You/He/She/It/We/They will have chosen.

PASSIVE VOICE: I/You/He/She/It/We/They will have been chosen.

SUBJUNCTIVE MOOD

PRESENT TENSE

ACTIVE VOICE: I/You/He/She/It/We/They choose.

PASSIVE VOICE: I/You/He/She/It/We/They be chosen.

PAST TENSE

ACTIVE VOICE: (same as indicative mood)

PASSIVE VOICE: I/You/He/She/It/We/They were chosen.



PRESENT PERFECT TENSE

ACTIVE VOICE: I/You/He/She/It/We/They have chosen.

PASSIVE VOICE: I/You/He/She/It/We/They have been chosen.

PAST PERFECT TENSE

ACTIVE AND PASSIVE VOICE: **(same as indicative mood)**

IMPERATIVE MOOD

PRESENT TENSE

ACTIVE VOICE: Choose.

PASSIVE VOICE: Be chosen.

**See also Progressive Forms.**

### Conjunction

A conjunction is a grammatical connector that links sentence elements—words, phrases, or clauses. See also **Coordinating Conjunction, Correlative Conjunction,** and **Subordinating Conjunction.** (Section 6b)

### Conjunctive Adverb (Adverbial Conjunction)

A conjunctive adverb serves as a transitional expression to link ideas: *however, therefore, thus, in addition, on the other hand,* and so on. See also the chart of transitional expressions, page 412.

### Connotation

*Connotation* refers to the feelings and memories evoked by a word. See also **Denotation.** (Section 32b.1)

### Controlling Idea

The controlling idea, or thesis, of a composition is central to the meaning to be conveyed. Everything included should contribute to the development of this idea. (Section 35d)

### Coordinating Conjunction

Coordinating conjunctions (*and, but, or, nor, for, so, yet*) connect grammatically equal structures—words, phrases, clauses. (Section 6b.1)

### Coordination

Coordination is the process of combining two or more grammatically equal structures—for example, two or more nouns, verbs, predicates, prepositional phrases, dependent clauses, or independent clauses. For techniques that use coordination, see Sections 33a.1–33a.2.



### Correlative Conjunction

A correlative conjunction is a coordinating conjunction that consists of a pair of words or phrases: *both . . . and, not . . . but, not only . . . but also, either . . . or, neither . . . nor.* (Section 6b.2)

### Count Noun

A count noun names something that can be counted. Thus, count nouns have plural forms. *Desk* and *bracelet* are count nouns with the plural forms *desks* and *bracelets. Furniture* and *jewelry* with no plural forms are not count nouns. See also **Mass Noun** and **Noncount Noun.**

### Couplet

A couplet is two lines of poetry ending with the same rhyme as in

> For sweetest things turn sourest by their deeds:
> Lilies that fester smell far worse than weeds.

### Critical Review

A critical review helps readers understand and evaluate some form of scholarship, art, or entertainment. (Chapter 43)

### Critical Thinking

Critical thinking is a systematic analysis of material for the purpose of judging its accuracy, relevance, and logic. (Chapter 39)

### Cumulative Sentence

A cumulative sentence begins with an independent clause and then piles up—or accumulates—structures at the end in order to create a dramatic effect: *Last night I had very discomforting dreams—full of evil creatures, plunges down precipices, and prolonged re-creations of embarrassing moments from my past.* (Section 33b.2)

### Dangling Modifier

A modifier with nothing nearby to modify is called "dangling." A dangling modifier is usually a verbal or an elliptical clause that appears at the beginning of a sentence: *Despising the habit, a resolution was made to quit smoking tomorrow.* The word modified should appear close to the modifier and should be the agent of the action expressed by the verb or verbal in the modifier: *Despising the habit, she resolved to quit smoking tomorrow.* (Section 16a)

### Deduction

Deduction is a method of logical reasoning whereby a conclusion follows accepted premises. In a classic example, the two premises "All men are mortal" and "Socrates is a man" are joined to produce the conclusion "Therefore, Socrates is mortal." A conclusion that does not follow logically is called a *non sequitur.*

terms

### Definition

The definition of a word can be a synonym or a formal explanation that puts the word in a general class and then differentiates it from other members of that class. In rhetoric, definition can be extended to a paragraph or a whole composition. A writer can explore the meaning of a word by a variety of methods: description, classification, comparison, illustration. (Pages 359 and 376)

### Demonstratives

The demonstrative pronouns are *this* and *that,* along with their corresponding plurals, *these* and *those.* These demonstratives fill a noun position or precede a noun and function as a determiner: *this pen, that tape, these marks, those noises.* (Section 2b)

**Denotation**
The denotation of a word is its literal and explicit meaning independent of any emotional association. See also **Connotation.** (Section 32b.1)

**Dependent Clause**
A dependent clause (also called a subordinate clause) has a subject and predicate but must be tied to an independent clause as a modifier or noun element: *When I noticed the menu's eight dollar hamburger, I quickly left. They insisted that I stay for the weekend.* (Section 7c)

**Description**
In description, a writer uses concrete details to create a representation of what something is or appears to be. (Page 355)

**Determiner**
A determiner is a word like *a, the, our, this,* or *Susan's* that signals the presence of a noun. (Section 6c)

**Direct Address**
Words in direct address (set off from the rest of the sentence with commas) name whoever or whatever is being spoken to: *This time, Ed, I'll pay. Get in the car, old dog.* (Section 21g)

**Direct Object**
A direct object is a word, phrase, or clause that receives or is affected by the verb's action: *Jessica likes historical romances. He said that he felt dizzy.*

**Direct Quotation**
A direct quotation, enclosed in quotation marks, duplicates the exact words of a speaker or writer: *"The first rule for taxi drivers," Mr. Geno said, "is to be sure the passenger is in the car."* The Times *of London called it "the latest American humbug."* See also **Indirect Quotation.** (Section 27a)

terms

**Double Negative**
*No, not, nothing, hardly, scarcely, and barely* are considered negatives in English. Use only one of these words to create a negative statement: *I have no cash. They have hardly begun.* A double negative is redundant and incorrect: *I don't have no cash. They haven't hardly begun.*

**Elliptical Construction**
In an elliptical construction, a word or several words are omitted, but their sense is clearly understood: *The bus takes an hour; a taxi, only thirty minutes.* [*Takes* is omitted in the second clause.] (Section 7d)

**Emphatic Pronoun**
An emphatic pronoun (also called an intensive pronoun) ends with *-self* or *-selves* and emphasizes a noun or another pronoun: *The Constitution itself says so. We were reprimanded by the conductor himself.* See also **Reflexive Pronoun.** (Section 2a)

**Enumeration**
Enumeration is a structural pattern for a paragraph or an entire composition. Details are listed to support the central idea. (Page 356)

**Equivocation**
In logic, *equivocation* refers to the use of an expression to mean more than one thing in a single context.

**Escape Literature**
The purpose of escape literature is to entertain, not to provide insights into human existence. See also **Interpretive Literature.**

**Essay**
An essay is a short nonfiction composition written from a personal point of view.

**Etymology**
The etymology of a word is its origin and development.

**Euphemism**
A euphemism, an expression such as *revenue enhancers* for *taxes* or *passed away* for *died,* is used for evading or glorifying reality. (Section 32c.2)

terms

**Evidence**
Evidence is the material used to support an opinion. Effective kinds of evidence are facts, details, and expert testimony. (Section 39d)

**Expletive**
An expletive is a meaningless word (*there* or *it*) that fills out a sentence's structure and allows its subject to be delayed: *There is a fly in the room. It is hard to translate the story.* (Section 6d)

**Exposition**
The purpose of exposition is to explain by supplying information. The main techniques used in exposition are description, narration, enumeration, comparison/contrast, classification, illustration, definition, analysis, and cause/effect.

### Fallacy

A fallacy in logic is any kind of faulty reasoning—primarily making an error in the reasoning process. (Section 39e)

### Figures of Speech

Figures of speech communicate through comparisons and associations. Common figures of speech are the metaphor, simile, personification, and hyperbole. (Section 33d)

### Finite Verb

A finite verb serves as the main verb of a clause or sentence. Unlike nonfinite verbs (infinitives, participles, and gerunds), finite verbs do not serve as modifiers and nominals.

### Fragment

A fragment is an incomplete sentence punctuated as if it were a complete sentence: *When the team lost eighty-two games.* A fragment can be corrected by incorporation into another sentence: *When the team lost eighty-two games, no one was playing well.* A fragment can also be rewritten as a complete sentence: *The team lost eighty-two games.* (Chapter 8)

### Freewriting

Freewriting, writing down whatever thoughts occur, is a technique for stimulating ideas and generating material for a composition. (Section 34e)

### Function Word

Function words (prepositions, conjunctions, determiners, or expletives) create structure. (Chapter 6)



### Fused Sentence

A fused sentence (sometimes called a run-on sentence) contains two independent clauses not separated by a conjunction or proper punctuation: *The students take regular classes however, all the subjects are taught in French.* The clauses must be separated: *The students take regular classes; however, all the subjects are taught in French.* For other ways of correcting fused sentences, see Chapter 9.

### Gender

In English, *gender* refers to the sex represented by third-person singular pronouns: masculine *(he, him, his),* feminine *(she, her, hers),* and neuter *(it, its).* A few nouns reflect gender: masculine *(actor)* and feminine *(actress).*

### General-Particular Order

In general-particular order, an entire composition or a paragraph begins with a general statement and moves to explain or develop that statement with particular details. (Page 383)

### General/Specific Words

General words refer broadly to categories: *food, book, person.* Specific words refer more narrowly to a member or members of a category: *burrito, telephone directories, Joe.* (Section 32b.2)

### Genitive Case

*Genitive case* is a term for possessive case or for an *of* phrase showing possession: *the coach's rule, the rule of the coach.* See also **Possessive Case.**

### Genre

*Genre* refers to a category of literature such as fiction, poetry, and drama.

### Gerund

A gerund is a verb form (the present participle, or *-ing* form) functioning in a sentence as a noun. A gerund phrase is a gerund plus another element—an object, subject, or modifier: *Writing well can be important in getting a good job.* [*Writing* is a gerund subject; *getting* is a gerund object of preposition. *Writing well* and *getting a good job* are both gerund phrases.] (Section 5c)

### Gobbledygook



Gobbledygook (also called bureaucratic language, double-talk, officialese, and doublespeak) is the abstract and confusing language used by officials who think simple, direct prose will not impress readers. (Section 32d.1)

### Hasty Generalization

A hasty generalization is a logical fallacy that involves jumping to a conclusion on the basis of too little evidence. (Page 461)

### Helping Verb

*Helping verb* is a name sometimes given to an auxiliary verb. See also **Auxiliary Verb.**

### Hyperbole

A hyperbole is a figure of speech that uses exaggeration rather than a literal statement to make a point: *We must have walked a thousand miles on this shopping trip.* (Section 33d)

### Idiom

An idiom is an expression peculiar to a language or dialect. The meaning of idiomatic speech is not always clear from the meaning of each word: *put up with his foolishness, carry on about the problem, make off with the loot.*

### Illustration

In a paragraph or a composition developed by illustration, an idea is supported with one or more examples. (Page 376)

### Image

An image is a vivid description that appeals to the sense of sight, sound, smell, taste, or touch.

### Imperative Mood

Verbs in the imperative mood are those used to give commands. *You* is always the understood subject: *Look out! Answer the roll. Delete the conjunction.* (Section 4f.2)

### Indefinite Pronoun

An indefinite pronoun (*anyone, everybody, each, either, both,* etc.) does not require an antecedent and need not refer to a specific person or thing. (Section 2e)

### Independent Clause

An independent clause, sometimes called a main clause, is a structure with a subject and predicate. It need not be connected to any other structure: *We drove to Atlantic City.* (Section 7b)

### Indicative Mood

Verbs in the indicative mood make statements and ask questions: *I saw the movie. Was the movie good?* (Section 4f.1)

### Indirect Object

An indirect object, usually a noun or pronoun, appears between a transitive verb and a direct object. The indirect object may be converted to a prepositional phrase with *to, for,* or *of* and moved after the direct object: *They gave the school an award. [They gave an award to the school.]*

### Indirect Quotation

In an indirect quotation, the exact words of a source are paraphrased. No quotation marks surround an indirect quotation: *Soren explained that he was curious about their everyday life.* See also **Direct Quotation.** (Section 27a)

### Induction

Induction is a method of logical reasoning whereby a conclusion follows the study of a representative group. For example, if every tap water sample contains chlorine, one can conclude that the source of the water also contains chlorine.

### Infinitive

An infinitive is a verbal made of *to* plus a verb: *to live, to listen, to appear.* An infinitive may function as a noun or as a modifier; it may appear alone or as part of an infinitive phrase: *To finish was his dream.* [*To finish* is an infinitive noun subject.] *She had the determination to finish the assignment.* [*To finish the assignment* is an infinitive phrase used as a modifier.] Though *to* is called the "sign" of the infinitive, it may be omitted after a few verbs like *let, make,* and *hear.* (Section 5a)

### Inflection

An inflection is a change in the form of a word that signals a change in meaning or in grammatical relation to another word. The parts of speech, or word classes, that have inflection are nouns *(bird, birds, bird's, birds'),* verbs *(go, goes, went, gone, going),* pronouns *(it, its),* adjectives *(tall, taller, tallest),* and adverbs *(badly, worse, worst).*

### Intensifier

An intensifier is a modifier that adds emphasis: *very ill, extremely successful, really hopeful.* See also **Qualifier.**

### Intensive Pronoun (See Emphatic Pronoun.)

terms

### Interjection

An interjection is an expression of emotion or exclamation (such as *oh, well,* or *wow*) structurally unconnected to a sentence: *Well! it's about time. Oh, I forgot the key.* (Sections 21g and 25g)

### Interpretive Literature

The purpose of interpretive literature is to comment on human existence in a meaningful way. See also **Escape Literature.**

### Interrogative Pronoun

An interrogative pronoun (*who, whom, whose, which,* or *what*) introduces a question that asks for information. *Whose, which,* and *what* can function as a pronoun or as a determiner: *Whose is this? Which job is available?* (Section 2d)

### Intransitive Verb

An intransitive verb expresses action but has no object: *The substance vanished. The package arrived quickly.*

**Irregular Verb**

The past tense and past participial forms of irregular verbs do not follow the predictable pattern of adding *-d* or *-ed*. Following is a list of most of the irregular verbs in English and their principal parts.

| *Base* | *Past* | *Past Participle* |
|---|---|---|
| arise | arose | arisen |
| awake | awoke | awakened, awoken |
| be | was | been |
| bear | bore | borne |
| beat | beat | beaten |
| become | became | become |
| befall | befell | befallen |
| begin | began | begun |
| behold | beheld | beheld |
| bend | bent | bent |
| bet | bet, betted | bet, betted |
| bid* | bade, bid | bidden, bid |
| bind | bound | bound |
| bite | bit | bitten, bit |
| bleed | bled | bled |
| blow | blew | blown |
| break | broke | broken |
| breed | bred | bred |
| bring | brought | brought |
| build | built | built |
| burn | burnt, burned | burnt, burned |
| burst | burst | burst |
| buy | bought | bought |
| cast | cast | cast |
| catch | caught | caught |
| choose | chose | chosen |
| cling | clung | clung |
| clothe | clothed, clad | clothed, clad |
| come | came | come |
| cost | cost | cost |
| creep | crept | crept |
| crow | crowed, crew | crowed |
| cut | cut | cut |
| deal | dealt | dealt |
| dig | dug | dug |
| dive | dived, dove | dived |
| do | did | done |
| draw | drew | drawn |
| drink | drank | drunk |

*When the verb refers to offering a price, *bid* is appropriate for both the past and past participle. Otherwise, either *bade* or *bid* is appropriate for the past; either *bidden* or *bid* is appropriate for the past participle.

| *Base* | *Past* | *Past Participle* |
|---|---|---|
| drive | drove | driven |
| eat | ate | eaten |
| fall | fell | fallen |
| feed | fed | fed |
| feel | felt | felt |
| fight | fought | fought |
| find | found | found |
| flee | fled | fled |
| fling | flung | flung |
| fly | flew | flown |
| forbid | forbade, forbad | forbidden |
| forecast | forecast, forecasted | forecast, forecasted |
| forget | forgot | forgotten |
| forgive | forgave | forgiven |
| freeze | froze | frozen |
| get | got | got, gotten |
| give | gave | given |
| go | went | gone |
| grind | ground | ground |
| grow | grew | grown |
| hang | hung, hanged* | hung, hanged* |
| have | had | had |
| hear | heard | heard |
| hide | hid | hidden |
| hit | hit | hit |
| hold | held | held |
| hurt | hurt | hurt |
| inlay | inlaid | inlaid |
| keep | kept | kept |
| kneel | knelt | knelt |
| knit | knitted, knit | knitted, knit |
| know | knew | known |
| lay | laid | laid |
| lead | led | led |
| leap | leaped, leapt | leaped, leapt |
| learn | learned, learnt | learn, learnt |
| leave | left | left |
| lend | lent | lent |
| let | let | let |
| lie | lay | lain |
| light | lit, lighted | lit, lighted |
| lose | lost | lost |
| make | made | made |
| mean | meant | meant |

*When the verb refers to execution, *hanged* is preferred for both past and past participle. Otherwise, *hung* is preferred.

| Base | Past | Past Participle |
|---|---|---|
| meet | met | met |
| melt | melted | melted, molten |
| mistake | mistook | mistaken |
| mow | mowed | mowed, mown |
| pay | paid | paid |
| prove | proved | proved, proven |
| put | put | put |
| quit | quit | quit |
| read | read | read |
| rid | rid, ridded | rid, ridded |
| ride | rode | ridden |
| ring | rang | rung |
| rise | rose | risen |
| run | ran | run |
| saw | sawed | sawed |
| say | said | said |
| see | saw | seen |
| seek | sought | sought |
| sell | sold | sold |
| send | sent | sent |
| set | set | set |
| sew | sewed | sewn, sewed |
| shake | shook | shaken |
| shave | shaved | shaved, shaven |
| shear | sheared | sheared, shorn |
| shed | shed | shed |
| shine | shone | shone |
| shoe | shod | shod |
| shoot | shot | shot |
| show | showed | shown, showed |
| shrink | shrank, shrunk | shrunk, shrunken |
| shut | shut | shut |
| sing | sang | sung |
| sink | sank | sunk, sunken |
| sit | sat | sat |
| slay | slew | slain |
| sleep | slept | slept |
| slide | slid | slid |
| sling | slung | slung |
| slink | slunk | slunk |
| slit | slit | slit |
| sow | sowed | sown, sowed |
| speak | spoke | spoken |
| speed | sped, speeded | sped, speeded |
| spell | spelled, spelt | spelled, spelt |
| spend | spent | spent |

| *Base* | *Past* | *Past Participle* |
|---|---|---|
| spill | spilled, spilt | spilled, spilt |
| spin | spun | spun |
| spit | spat | spat |
| split | split | split |
| spread | spread | spread |
| spring | sprang | sprung |
| stand | stood | stood |
| steal | stole | stolen |
| stick | stuck | stuck |
| sting | stung | stung |
| stink | stank, stunk | stunk |
| stride | strode | stridden |
| strike | struck | struck, stricken |
| string | strung | strung |
| strive | strove | striven |
| swear | swore | sworn |
| sweep | swept | swept |
| swell | swelled | swollen, swelled |
| swim | swam | swum |
| swing | swung | swung |
| take | took | taken |
| teach | taught | taught |
| tear | tore | torn |
| tell | told | told |
| think | thought | thought |
| throw | threw | thrown |
| thrust | thrust | thrust |
| understand | understood | understood |
| upset | upset | upset |
| wake | woke, waked | woken, waked |
| wear | wore | worn |
| weave | wove | woven |
| weep | wept | wept |
| win | won | won |
| wind | wound | wound |
| withdraw | withdrew | withdrawn |
| withhold | withheld | withheld |
| withstand | withstood | withstood |
| wring | wrung | wrung |
| write | wrote | written |



**Jargon**
Jargon is the specialized vocabulary of a group such as lawyers, sociologists, and linguists. Jargon should be avoided when it obscures meaning or overburdens style. (Section 32d.1)

**Journalistic Questions**
The journalistic questions, which can generate ideas about a subject, are *who? what? when? where? why?* and *how?*

**Linking Verb**
A linking verb requires a subject complement to complete its meaning. An adjective complement modifies and a noun complement renames the subject of the clause. Common linking verbs are *be, become, seem, look, feel: The discussion was painful. The supplies grew scarce.*

**Loose Sentence**
A loose sentence begins with the main idea and then adds modifiers: *Computer chess programs allow stronger play because new methods of searching have improved the evaluation of positions and moves.* See also **Periodic Sentence.**

**Lyric**
A lyric is a relatively short musical poem expressing a personal emotion such as sorrow, love, or admiration.

**Main Clause (See Independent Clause.)**

**Mass Noun**
A mass noun, also called a noncount noun, names something that cannot be counted. Thus, mass nouns have no plural form. In their normal senses, *clothing, money, water, garbage,* and *equipment* are examples of mass nouns. See also **Count Noun.**

terms

**Metaphor**
A metaphor is a figure of speech that conveys information in a nonliteral way by stating or implying that two things are similar: *The book is a passport into exotic, untrodden lands.* (Section 33d)

**Metonomy**
Metonomy is a figure of speech in which an associated word is substituted for the intended meaning. Instead of *the president,* the writer substitutes *the White House: The White House supports the tax bill.*

**Misplaced Modifier**
A misplaced modifier seems to relate to the wrong element in a sentence: *The delivery service brought the package to the house in a van.* [seems to modify *house*] Modifiers should be positioned so that they clearly modify the intended word: *In a van, the delivery service brought the package to the house.* [clearly modifies *brought*] (Section 16b)

### Mixed Metaphor

Sometimes several metaphors are strung together to form a mixed metaphor, an expression that begins with one overused metaphor and shifts into another or several: *We were out on a limb; but since we knew we were playing with fire and had all our eggs in one basket, we continued the struggle.*

### Modal Auxiliary

A verb auxiliary that cannot undergo conjugation is called a modal auxiliary: *can, could, shall, should, will, would, may, might,* and *must.* Modals express such ideas as ability, advisability, necessity, and possibility.

### Modifier

A modifier is a word, phrase, or clause that describes, limits, or qualifies some other word, phrase, or clause. Adjectives and adverbs (and words functioning as such) are modifiers: *The tribe had no written language. Without warning, the horse stumbled. I got a unicycle, which I could never learn to ride.*

### Mood

The mood of a verb is shown by form and meaning. The indicative mood expresses a fact or a question: *I attended. Was the problem solved?* The imperative mood expresses a command: *Buy bonds. Get help.* The subjunctive mood expresses desire or possibility: *I wish I were there.* See also **Indicative Mood, Imperative Mood,** and **Subjunctive Mood.** (Section 4f)

### Narration

Narration tells a story, recounts events, or outlines the stages of a process. (Page 356)



### Nominalization

A nominalization is an expression of action in noun form: *contribution, development, failure, inclusion.* Unnecessary nominalizations can sometimes be changed to more forceful verb equivalents: *contribute, develop, fail, include.* (Section 33c.1)

### Nominative Absolute (See Absolute Phrase.)

### Nominative Case (See Case.)

### Noncount Noun

A noncount noun, also called a *mass noun,* names something that cannot be counted. Thus, noncount nouns have no plural form. In their normal senses, *water, sand, furniture,* and *wealth* are examples of noncount nouns. See also **Count Noun.**

**Nonfinite Verb (See Finite Verb.)**

**Nonrestrictive Element**
A nonrestrictive element does not restrict or limit the word or phrase it modifies. Commas should surround a nonrestrictive element to indicate its loose connection with a sentence: *I heard someone called a "dork," which can't refer to anything complimentary. The research has led to the CD GUIDE, a successful software product.* (Section 21c)

**Non Sequitur**
A non sequitur is a logical fallacy in which the conclusion does not follow from the evidence: *If one pill is good, then two must be twice as good.* (Pages 466–467)

**Noun**
A noun names things in the physical and nonphysical worlds: *Jim, sister, novel, field, generosity, grief,* and so on. (Chapter 1)

**Noun Clause**
A noun clause is a dependent clause that functions in the same ways that all nouns do—as subjects, objects, and complements: *What you should do is quit. I know that* cheval *means "horse." The winner will be whoever spends the most money.* (Section 7c.3)

**Number**
*Number* refers to the form of a noun, pronoun, or verb that shows singularity (one) or plurality (more than one): singular—*car, it, sings;* plural—*cars, they, sing.* (Section 1b)

terms

**Object (See Direct Object, Indirect Object,** and **Object of Preposition.)**

**Object Complement**
An object complement, either an adjective or a noun, completes a clause's structure by modifying or renaming the direct object: *The drought made water scarce. She named her dog Josh.*

**Objective Case (See Case.)**

**Object of Preposition**
An object of a preposition, usually a noun, noun phrase, or pronoun, combines with a preposition to form a prepositional phrase: *at school, after washing the car, in front of them.* (Section 6a)

## Paradox
A paradox is the linking of seemingly contradictory ideas or feelings to express a truth: *arming for peace, spending money to make money, listening to silence.*

## Paragraph
A paragraph in a composition is a unit of thought or information set off by an indentation of the first line. Most paragraphs develop a topic sentence, stated or implied. (Chapter 36)

## Paragraph Block
A paragraph block is a group of paragraphs that together develop a single thought or unit of information. (Page 373)

## Parallelism
In grammar, *parallelism* refers to the use of the same grammatical structure for items in a compound structure, a series, a list, or an outline. (Chapter 20)

## Paraphrase
A paraphrase is a rewording of a passage without changing its meaning. (Section 40h.2)

## Parenthetical Element
A parenthetical element in a sentence is set off with commas, dashes, or parentheses to show its loose, interruptive, or nonessential nature: *A robot, at least to most people, is a manlike creature. The production—how can I put it politely?—lacks interest. In the story, Zeus had a child by Pluto (not to be confused with the god of the underworld).* (Sections 21f.1, 24d, 24e)

terms

## Participle
A participle is a verb form used as an adjective. Participles have two basic forms—the present participle (*-ing* verb form) and past participle (the form that follows *have* in a verb phrase). A participial phrase is a participle plus another element—an object, subject, or modifier: *Remembering, Eugene started over. Meat cut very thin is called scallopini.* [*Remembering* and *cut* are both participles modifying the subjects of both sentences. *Cut very thin* is a participial phrase.] See also **Absolute Phrase.** (Section 5b and 5d)

## Particular-General Order
In particular-general order, an entire composition or a paragraph begins with specifics and moves to a general statement—the topic sentence or thesis. (Page 383)

### Part of Speech

*Part of speech* refers to the grammatical classification of a word based on its form, function, or meaning. Traditionally, a word is classified as a noun, verb, adjective, adverb, pronoun, preposition, conjunction, or interjection.

### Passive Voice

A verb is in the passive voice when its subject receives the action. The verb consists of a form of *be* plus a past participle: *The purse was stolen. Your account has been credited.* See also **Active Voice.** (Section 4e)

### Past Participle

The past participle is the form of a verb that normally follows *have.* The past participle of regular verbs adds *-d* or *-ed* to the base form: *called, increased, pitched, assumed.* Irregular verbs do not have predictable past participles. The forms for the past participles of irregular verbs can be found in dictionaries and in appropriate lists. See also **Irregular Verb.**

### Perfect Tenses

The perfect tenses are formed by combining *has/have/had* or a modal and *have* with the past participle: *has escaped, had rebuilt, will have withdrawn, could have read.* (Sections 4c and 4d)

### Periodic Sentence

In a periodic sentence the main idea is postponed until the end: *Just at the height of his power when he could have become an American monarch, Washington went home to farm.* See also **Loose Sentence.** (Section 33b.1)

### Person

For pronouns, the term *person* refers to the form that indicates whether a reference is to the speaker or spokesperson (first person: *I, we*), to the person(s) spoken to (second person: *you*), or to the person(s) or thing(s) spoken about (third person: *he, she, it, they*). All other pronouns and nouns are in the third person. For verbs, the term refers to the form that goes with each of the three persons.

### Persona

*Persona,* a term that first meant "mask worn by an actor," refers to the voice an author uses to address the audience. The voice should sound natural whether it is or not.

### Personal Pronoun

A personal pronoun refers to a specific person or people (*I, you, she, they,* etc.) or to a specific thing or things (*it, them,* etc.). For a complete list of the personal pronouns, see Section 2a.

### Personification
Personification is a figure of speech in which something nonhuman is given a human characteristic: *The printer ate the paper. The unplugged TV stared blankly.* (Section 33d)

### Phrase
A phrase is a group of related words that together have a single function (as a noun, verb, or modifier). Unlike a clause, a phrase has no subject and finite verb: *a heavy eater, has been applied, in a rural town, tending to be jealous, to close the letter, the meal over.*

### Plot
*Plot* refers to the sequence of events that occurs in a work of literature.

### Point of View
*Point of view* refers to the way the narrator relates the action of a work of literature. The point of view may be omniscient (the narrator knows everything), limited omniscient (the narrator knows the thoughts of one character), first person (the narrator speaks as *I*), or objective (the narrator describes only what is seen and heard).

### Positive Degree
*Positive degree* refers to the simple, uncompared form of adjectives and adverbs: *crazy, evenly, complex, quick, angrily.* See also **Comparative Degree and Superlative Degree.** (Section 3c)

### Possessive Case
The possessive case is the form of a noun or pronoun that indicates ownership (*Sue's job, their vacation*), authorship (*Poe's story, her essay*), source (*paper's headline, teacher's assignment*), measurement (*a mile's distance*), and description (*a child's bike*). See also **Case.** (Chapter 14)



### Post Hoc Fallacy
In a post hoc fallacy, one reasons that whatever immediately preceded an outcome also caused it. For example, if a landing on the moon preceded bad weather, one cannot assume correctly that the landing caused the problem. (Page 464)

### Predicate
The predicate joins with the subject to form a clause. A predicate consists of at least one finite verb and may also include modifiers and completing words: *The dress was cut low in the front and lower in the back. He sent his grandmother a poinsettia for Christmas.*

**Predicate Adjective**
A predicate adjective, also called a subject complement, follows *be, seem, appear, become, grow, remain, taste, look, smell, sound,* or *feel* and modifies the subject: *The topic was boring. He remained angry.*

**Predicate Noun**
A predicate noun or nominative, also called a subject complement, follows *be, become, remain, seem,* and *appear* and names or refers to the subject: *The topic was euthanasia. He remained an enemy.*

**Prefix**
A prefix is a syllable that attaches to the beginning of a root to add or alter meaning: *pre-* in *preview* means "before"; *de-* in *devalue* means "reduce"; *mal-* in *malfunction* means "badly."

**Preposition**
A preposition is a function word like *in, to, from, by,* and *through* that connects its object to the rest of the sentence. The preposition plus its object is called a prepositional phrase: *Over the past year, the school in our neighborhood has deteriorated to the point of needing extensive repairs.* (Section 6a)

**Present Participle**
The present participle is the form of a verb that ends in *-ing: surviving, making, breathing, lying.* See also **Participle, Gerund,** and **Progressive Forms.**

**Principal Parts**
The principal parts of verbs are the base form (*see, step*), the past form (*saw, stepped*), and the past participle form (*seen, stepped*). (Section 4a)

**Process Analysis**
A process analysis is a composition that traces, usually in chronological order, the steps of an event or an operation.

**Progressive Forms**
The progressive forms of a verb indicate actions in progress. These forms appear in all six tenses and are made with a form of *be* plus the present participle (*-ing* form): *is looking, was looking, will be looking, has been looking, had been looking, will have been looking.* (Section 4d)

**Pronoun**
Pronouns are words that appear in the same positions as nouns. A pronoun usually substitutes for a previously stated noun or noun phrase, called its antecedent: *The language was easy to learn because it had many words similar to Latin. Pigs were used in the research; they were fed large amounts of sugar.* See also **Personal Pronoun, Interrogative Pronoun, Relative Pronoun, Demonstrative Pronoun, Indefinite Pronoun, Reciprocal Pronoun, Reflexive Pronoun,** and **Intensive Pronoun.** (Chapter 2)

**Proper Noun and Adjective**
Proper nouns and adjectives are specific names that begin with a capital letter: *Churchill, Xerox, Crimean War, Natchez Trace, Florida vacation, Easter service, October weather.* (Section 31b)

**Protagonist**
In literary works, the protagonist is the main character. See also **Antagonist.**

**Purpose**
Purpose is the writer's intention—to entertain, to explain, to argue, to move the audience to action. (Section 35a)

**Qualifier**
A qualifier is an adverb that serves to intensify or restrict an adjective or adverb: *very tired, highly motivated, somewhat bitter, rather large.*

**Quatrain**
A quatrain is a poetic unit of four lines. Coleridge's *Rime of the Ancient Mariner* is made up of quatrains.

terms

**Quotation (See Direct Quotation** and **Indirect Quotation.)**

**Reciprocal Pronoun**
The reciprocal pronouns, *each other* and *one another,* are only used as objects: *The two always give each other help. The noise was so loud we could not hear one another.* (Section 2e)

**Red Herring**
A red herring is a logical fallacy in which a writer diverts the reader from the issue by switching to another, vaguely related subject. (Page 459)

**Reflexive Pronoun**
A reflexive pronoun, ending in *-self* or *-selves,* is always an object that refers to, "reflects," the subject of the clause: *I wrote myself a note. They couldn't imagine themselves as losers.* See also **Emphatic Pronoun.** (Section 2a)

**Regular Verb**
A regular verb adds *-d* or *-ed* to the base to form the past tense and the past participle: *use, used, used; warn, warned, warned.*

**Relative Pronoun**
A relative pronoun (*who, whom, whose, whoever, which, whichever, what, whatever,* and *that*) introduces a dependent clause: *No one was injured by the tank that exploded. You can't trust whoever looks honest.* (Section 2c)

**Restrictive Element**
A restrictive element restricts, limits, or identifies the word or phrase it modifies. A restrictive element is not set off by commas: *The coach created an offense that used a variety of sets.* See also **Nonrestrictive Element.** (Section 21c)

**Rhetoric**
Rhetoric is the effective use of language.

**Root**
The root of a word provides its base, or primary, meaning. For example, the root of *telegraphy* is *graph,* which means "write"; the root of *amorphous* is *morph,* which means "shape."

**Run-on Sentence (See Fused Sentence.)**

**Satire**
Through satire, an author ridicules a subject and exposes weaknesses and vices.

**Sentence**
A sentence is an independent statement, question, or command beginning with a capital letter and ending with some terminal punctuation. Except for exclamations like "Oh!" and idioms like "The more, the merrier," sentences contain a subject and predicate, usually with modifiers and complements: *A man wearing sweaty, seedy clothes pushed his way in. Why did he enter a race that he was sure to lose?*

**Sentence Fragment (See Fragment.)**

**Sentence Modifier**
A sentence modifier is an adverbial that has an independent or parenthetical meaning. Sentence modifiers, sometimes called absolutes, relate to whole sentences rather than to particular words or phrases: *Obviously, she would like a job. Without a doubt, I will be there. She is fasting, although I don't know why.*

### Setting
The setting of a work of literature is the time and place in which the story occurs.

### Shift
A shift is an unnecessary change from one kind of construction to another. Shifts can occur in tense, voice, number, person, and structure. (Chapter 17)

### Simile
A simile is a figure of speech in which two dissimilar things are said to be alike. The words *like* or *as* distinguish a simile from a metaphor: *problems sprouting like weeds, the moon round like a Concord grape, a plot as complicated as an acrostic puzzle.* (Section 33d)

### Simple Sentence
A simple sentence has one independent clause (main clause) and no dependent clause (subordinate clause): *The smell of the food reminded me of my childhood.* (Section 7e.1)

### Slang
Slang is a kind of informal language that develops when people invent new expressions or change the meaning of existing expressions to create an individual and unique way of speaking: *pinkie* for *little finger, whirlybird* for *helicopter, cop out* for *refusal to commit oneself, yak* for *chat.* (Section 32a)



### Sonnet
A sonnet is a poem of 14 lines. The Italian, or Petrarchan sonnet, has an octave (8 lines) rhyming *abba abba* and a sestet (6 lines) usually rhyming *cde cde.* The Elizabethan, or Shakespearean sonnet, has three quatrains (4 lines each) rhyming *abab cdcd efef* and a couplet (2 lines) rhyming *gg.*

### Spatial Order
In descriptions with a spatial order, details are arranged so that readers can follow the eye's path.

### Split Infinitive
A split infinitive has a modifier between the *to* and the base form of the verb: *to slowly stroll, to desperately yell, to at the last second fall.* In most split infinitives, the modifier should be moved: *to stroll slowly, to yell desperately, to fall at the last second.* (Section 18d)

### Squinting Modifier
A squinting modifier appears between two words, both of which it might modify: *The woman he called reluctantly made an appointment.* [*Reluctantly* could modify *called* or *made.*] Squinting modifiers must be repositioned: *The woman he called made an appointment reluctantly.* (Section 16b.4)

### Straw Man
In an argument, a straw man is an opponent whose position is distorted or invented to make it easier to attack. (Page 459)

### Subject
The subject joins with the predicate to form a clause. A subject consists of a noun (or a noun substitute) plus any modifiers. A simple subject is the subject minus its modifiers. *The interior of the car lit up.* [The subject is *the interior of the car;* the simple subject is *interior.*]

### Subject Complement
A subject complement follows *be* or another linking verb and renames or modifies the subject of the clause: *He was a scrawny kid.* [*Kid* renames *he* and can be called a predicate noun or nominative.] *The conversation became serious.* [*Serious* modifies *conversation* and can be called a predicate adjective.] See also **Linking Verb.**

### Subjective Case (See Case.)

### Subjunctive Mood
The subjunctive mood primarily indicates that something is not a fact or that something should happen: *If I were qualified, I would apply for the job. The doctor insisted that Jack get a second opinion.* Unlike the indicative mood (*I was qualified* and *he gets*), the subjunctive mood has only one form for each tense and person. (Section 4f.3)

### Subordinate Clause (See Dependent Clause.)

### Subordinating Conjunction
A subordinating conjunction introduces a dependent clause and expresses relationships such as cause, contrast, condition, manner, place, and time. Common subordinating conjunctions are *because, although, if, as if,* and *when.* (Section 6b.3) For a more complete list, see 7c.1. See also **Adverb Clause.**

**Subordination**
Through subordination, writers show that one idea is dependent on another. Subordination can be achieved through dependent clauses, verbals, and appositives. For techniques that use subordination, see 33a.3–33a.6. See also **Adverb Clause, Adjective Clause, Noun Clause, Infinitive, Participle, Gerund,** and **Appositive.**

**Suffix**
A suffix is a syllable or sound that attaches to the end of a word to alter the word's meaning, to change the word from one class to another, or to change the word's form. The suffix *-itis* ("inflamed") added to the root *appendix* creates the word *appendicitis.* The suffix *-ly* changes the adjective *sad* to the adverb *sadly.* The suffix *-ed* changes the present tense verb *call* to the past tense *called.*

**Superlative Degree**
The form of an adjective and adverb used to make a comparison among three or more items is called the *superlative degree.* An *-est* ending and the words *most* and *least* indicate the superlative degree: *This is the largest hotel in the city. The video you selected is the one most frequently purchased. This brand of yogurt is the least fattening of all.* See also **Comparative Degree.** (Section 3c)

**Symbol**
A symbol is an image that stands for an idea or a complex of ideas. A vulture might symbolize death; spring might symbolize a new beginning; a closed door might symbolize lost opportunity.



**Synonym**
A synonym is a word with approximately the same meaning as another—for example, *accord* is a synonym for *agreement; stagnation* for *inaction; derision* for *ridicule.*

**Syntax**
*Syntax* refers to the arrangement of words to form structures—phrases, clauses, and sentences.

**Tag Question**
A tag question appears at the end of a statement and asks for verification. It is composed of an auxiliary verb and a pronoun: *The car has been repaired, hasn't it? You read the book, didn't you?* (Section 21g)

### Tense
Tense is the feature of verbs that indicates a meaning related to time. English is said to have three simple tenses (present, past, and future) and three perfect tenses (present perfect, past perfect, and future perfect). (Section 4c)

### Theme
A theme is the central idea of a work, primarily a work of literature. (Page 586)

### Thesis
The thesis is the central, or controlling, idea of a nonliterary composition. The content of the composition should support and develop the thesis. (Section 35d)

### Topic Sentence
The topic sentence of a paragraph is the main idea developed. If a paragraph has no stated topic sentence, one should be clearly implied. (Section 36a.1)

### Tragedy
Tragedy does not end happily. In the plot of a dramatic tragedy, the main character suffers a "fall," the loss of something dear, as the result of events and human weakness.

### Tragic flaw
In drama, a tragic flaw is the human weakness that combines with circumstances to ruin the main character.

### Transitional Expression
A transitional expression indicates the relationship between ideas: for example, *however* indicates contrast; *as a result* indicates cause/effect; *furthermore* indicates addition. Sometimes called conjunctive adverbs or conjuncts, transitional words and phrases serve to link independent clause to independent clause, sentence to sentence, and paragraph to paragraph. For a more complete list, see p. 412.



### Transitive Verb
A transitive verb expresses action and requires an object: *She wrote the letter. Mr. Williams speaks Japanese fluently.*

### Verb
A verb is a word that indicates action (*swim*), occurrence (*happen*), or existence (*be*). (Chapter 4)

### Verbal
A verbal is one of three verb forms functioning in a sentence as a noun or a modifier: infinitive (*to write*), present participle (*writing*), past participle (*written*). A verbal alone never functions in a clause as a finite verb. A verbal with a subject, object, complement, or modifier is called a verbal phrase. See also **Infinitive, Participle,** and **Gerund.** (Chapter 5)

### Verb Phrase
A verb phrase is a verb made up of more than one word: *is calling, will consider, have been reading.*

### Voice
The voice of a verb indicates whether the subject acts (active voice) or receives the action (passive voice). See also **Active Voice** and **Passive Voice.** (Section 4e)

## Permissions and Acknowledgments

**Pages 370–372:** From "Mostly About Nicklaus," copyright © 1983. Originally in *The New Yorker* by Herbert Warren Wind.

**Page 374:** From *Benjamin Franklin's Experiment,* Harvard University Press. Copyright © 1941 by the President and Fellows of Harvard College; © 1969 by I. Bernard Cohen.

**Pages 375–376:** From "Rolling Into The Eighties," *Esquire,* © 1983 by Sara Davidson. Reprinted by permission.

**Page 379:** From "Notes from a Native Daughter," in *Slouching Towards Bethlehem,* by Joan Didion. Copyright © 1965, 1968 by Joan Didion. Reprinted by permission of Farrar, Straus and Giroux, Inc.

**Page 380:** From "Facing the Public," by Will Manley. Reprinted by permission from the October 1984 issue of *Wilson Library Bulletin.*

**Page 380:** From "Nostalgia for the Dark Ages," copyright © 1984 by Cullen Murphy. Reprinted by permission from the May 1984 issue of *The Atlantic Monthly.*

**Pages 380–381:** From "Sight, Sound and the Fury," by Marshall McLuhan. Copyright © Commonweal Foundation. New York, New York.

**Page 381:** From "A Flash of Light," by Alan Lightman. Reprinted from *Science 84.* Reprinted by permission.

**Pages 381–382:** From "Rum + Vodka + Irish = Fight," in *The Red Smith Reader* by Red Smith. Copyright held by Random House, Inc. New York, New York.

**Page 385:** From "Million-Year Histories," by Edward O. Wilson, *Wilderness 48* (Summer 1984), p. 12.

**Page 387:** From "Aspertame: Some Bitter with the Sweet," by William F. Allman. *Science 84,* Vol. 6 (July/August 1984), p. 14. Reprinted by permission.

**Page 387:** From "Dried and True: The Lowdown on Lightweight Foods," by Lois Snedden. Reprinted from *Sierra,* Vol. 69, July/August 1984. Copyright © 1984 by Lois Snedden. Reprinted by permission.

**Pages 388–389:** From "The Not-So-Clean Business of Making Chips," by Joseph LaDou. Reprinted by permission from *Technology Review,* copyright 1984.

**Page 391:** From "Coping with Uncertainty in *The Duchess of Malfi,*" by Phoebe S. Spinard, *Explorations in Renaissance Culture,* 6 (1980), p. 47. Reprinted by permission.

**Page 391:** From *Ever Since Darwin: Reflections in Natural History,* by Stephen Jay Gould, by permission of W.W. Norton & Company, Inc. Copyright © 1977 by Stephen Jay Gould.

**Page 392:** From "Wasteland," by Marya Mannes, from *More in Anger,* published by Lippincott, 1958. Copyright © 1958, 1986. Reprinted by permission.

**Page 392:** From "Tiara 3600 Pursuit," by Richard Thiel, *Boating,* 85 (January 1985), p. 75. Reprinted by permission.

**Page 395:** From "Uses, Abuses, and Attitudes," by Barbara Tufty, *American Forests 90* (August 1984), p. 28. Reprinted by permission.

**Page 396:** From "Shakespeare," from *American Preservation.* Copyright by Patricia Leigh Brown. Little Rock, AR.

**Pages 396–397:** From "Are Women Human?" by Dorothy Sayers, which appeared in *Unpopular Opinions* by Gollancz Publishers. Reprinted by permission of David Higham Associates Limited. London.

**Page 397:** From "The Science of Making Wine," by A. Dismoor Webb,

*American Scientist* 72 (July/August 1984), p. 367. Reprinted by permission.

**Page 398:** From *Journal of College Student Personnel.* Article titled "Alcoholism Among College Students," by D. Beck and T.A. Seay. Reprinted by permission.

**Pages 398–399:** From "Why Don't We Complain?" by William F. Buckley, Jr. Copyright © 1960 by *Esquire.* Renewed. Reprinted by permission of the Wallace Literary Agency, Inc.

**Page 495:** From *Readers' Guide to Periodical Literature*, Vol. 43, March 1983–February, 1984. Copyright © 1983, 1984 by The H.W. Wilson Company. Material reproduced by permission of the publisher.

**Pages 510–511:** From "Business in Space," copyright © 1985 by David Osborne. Reprinted from the May 1985 issue of *The Atlantic Monthly.*

**Pages 511–512:** From *Asimov's Guide to Science*, by Isaac Asimov. Copyright © 1960, 1965, 1972 by Basic Books, Inc. Reprinted by permission of Basic Books, a division of HarperCollins Publishers.

**Pages 567–568:** From *The Road to Xanadu,* by John Livingston Lowes. Copyright 1927 by John Livingston Lowes. Copyright © renewed 1955 by John Wilbur Lowes. Reprinted by permission of Houghton Mifflin Company. All rights reserved.

perm/ ack

**Page 568:** From "Coleridge's Somerset: A Byway to Xanadu," by Wylie Sypher, *The Philological Quarterly,* Vol. 18, October 1939. Copyright © 1939 by the University of Iowa. Reprinted by permission.

**Page 568:** From *The Starlit Dome,* by G. Wilson Knight. Oxford University Press, London, copyright 1941. Reprinted by permission.

**Page 569:** From "The Theme of Love and Guilt in Coleridge's Three Major Poems," by Douglas Angus. *Journal of English and Germanic Philology,* University of Illinois Press. Copyright © 1960 by The Board of Trustees of the University of Illinois. Reprinted by permission.

**Page 570:** From "The Meaning of *Kubla Khan,*" by George Watson. *Review of English Literature,* University of Calgary Press. Reprinted by permission of *Ariel: A Review of International English Literature.*

**Page 570:** From *Visions of Xanadu,* by Marshall Suther. Published by Columbia University Press, New York, 1965. Reprinted by permission.

**Pages 603–604:** Reviews reprinted from *Choice* magazine, copyright of the American Library Association.

**Page 654:** Dictionary entry for "aggravate" reprinted by permission. From *Webster's Ninth New Collegiate Dictionary,* © 1991 by Merriam-Webster, Inc., publisher of the Merriam-Webster® Dictionaries.

**Page 655:** Dictionary entry for "harass" reprinted by permission from Webster's *New World Dictionary of the English Language*—third college edition. Copyright © 1988 and used by permission of the publisher, New World Dictionaries, a division of Simon and Schuster, New York, New York.

**Page 655:** Dictionary entry for "harass" reprinted by permission. From *Webster's Ninth New Collegiate Dictionary.* © 1991 by Merriam-Webster Inc., publisher of the Merriam-Webster® Dictionaries.

**Page 655:** Dictionary entry for "harass" reprinted by permission from *Oxford American Dictionary,* Oxford University Press.

**Page 655:** Dictionary entry for "harass" reprinted by permission from *The Random House Dictionary of the English Language*—second edition, unabridged. Copyright © 1987 by Random House, Inc.

**Page 656:** Dictionary entry for "often" reprinted by permission from *The Random House Dictionary of the English Language,* unabridged edition, copyright © 1983 by Random House, Inc.

**Page 657:** Dictionary entry for "abrade" reprinted by permission from *The American Heritage Dictionary of the English Language.* Copyright © 1981 by Houghton Mifflin Company.

**Page 657:** Dictionary entry for "dull" reprinted by permission from *The American Heritage Dictionary of the English Language,* paperback edition. Copyright © 1982 by Houghton Mifflin Company.

**Page 658:** Dictionary entry for "dull" reprinted by permission from *The American Heritage Dictionary of the English Language.* Copyright © 1981 by Houghton Mifflin Company.

**Page 659:** Dictionary entry for "love" reprinted by permission from *The American Heritage Dictionary of the English Language.* Copyright © 1981 by Houghton Mifflin Company.

**Page 659:** Dictionary entry for "ugly" reprinted by permission from *The Random House Dictionary of the English Languge,* second edition, unabridged. Copyright © 1987 by Random House, Inc.

**Page 659:** Dictionary entry for "infant" reprinted by permission from *Webster's New World Dictionary,* third college edition. Copyright © 1988. Used by permission of the publisher, New World Dictionaries, a division of Simon and Schuster, New York, New York.

**Page 660:** Dictionary entry for "gag" reprinted by permission from *Webster's Ninth New Collegiate Dictionary.* © 1991, by Merriam-Webster Inc., publisher of the Merriam-Webster® Dictionaries.

**Page 660:** Dictionary entry for "conflict" reprinted by permission from the *Shorter Oxford English Dictionary.* Copyright © 1973 by Oxford University Press. Reprinted by permission of Oxford University Press.

**Page 660:** Dictionary entry for "routine" reprinted by permission from *Webster's Ninth New Collegiate Dictionary.* © 1991 by Merriam-Webster Inc., publisher of the Merriam-Webster® Dictionaries.

**Page 661:** Dictionary entry for "biology" reprinted from *The Random House Dictionary of the English Language,* second edition, unabridged. Copyright © 1987 by Random House, Inc.

**Page 661:** Dictionary entry for "substantiate" reprinted from *Funk & Wagnall's Standard College Dictionary.* Copyright © 1977 by Harper and Row, Publishers, Inc. Reprinted by permission of HarperCollins Publishers.

**Page 662:** Dictionary entry for "multilayered" reprinted by permission from *Webster's Ninth New Collegiate Dictionary.* © 1991 by Merriam-Webster Inc., publishers of the Merriam-Webster® Dictionaries.

**Page 662:** Dictionary entry for "damnify" reprinted by permission from *Webster's Ninth New Collegiate Dictionary.* © 1991 by Merriam-Webster Inc., publisher of the Merriam-Webster® Dictionaries.

**Page 663:** Dictionary entry for "media" adapted and reprinted by permission from *The American Heritage Dictionary of the English Language.* Copyright © 1981 by Houghton Mifflin Company.

# Index

Numbers in **boldface** refer to sections. All other numbers refer to pages. The letter *G* refers to a page in the Glossary of Usage, and the letters *GT* refer to a page in the Glossary of Terms.



index

index

index

index

index

# Guide to the Plan of the Book

# Guide to the Plan of the Book

# Guide to the Plan of the Book